1845	First state teachers' associations organized in New York and Rhode Island
1852	First compulsory law for school attendance passed by the state of Massachusetts
1854	First Negro university (Lincoln University) chartered as Ashmun Institute and opened in 1857
1855	First kindergarten in the United States organized at Watertown, Wisconsin
1857	National Teachers Association formed, later becoming the National Education Association
1862	Morrill Act, creating federally supported land-grant colleges, signed by President Lincoln
1867	National Department of Education created by Congress, later becoming the United States Office of Education
1867	First large philanthropic educational foundation in the United States established by George Peabody
1873	First permanent public kindergarten established as part of the St. Louis public school system
1874	Taxation for secondary schools upheld by the Michigan Supreme Court in the Kalamazoo case
1876	First graduate work begun at Johns Hopkins University
1893	Committee of Ten report published—first of a series of significant NEA recommendations on curriculums
1895	American Association of School Administrators organized
1898	National Congress of Mothers (now National Congress of Parents and Teachers) organized

1900	Association of American Universities organized
1902	First public junior college organized at Joliet, Illinois
1905	A scale to measure educational achievement designed by E. L. Thorndike
1909	First White House Conference on Children and Youth held
1910	First public junior high schools opened in Berkeley, California, and Columbus, Ohio
1912	Federal Children's Bureau established
1916	American Federation of Teachers organized as affiliate of the American Federation of Labor
1917	Federal assistance for vocational education provided through Smith-Hughes Act
1917	American Association of Teachers Colleges organized, later merged in the American Association of Colleges for Teacher Education
1918	Compulsory education made effective legally in all states
1918	"Seven Cardinal Principles of Secondary Education" enunciated
1918	Progressive Education Association formed as an outgrowth of the progressive movement in American education
1919	Institute of International Education established in New York, accenting educational exchanges
1920	American Education Week initiated by presidential proclamation

This calendar of Historical Highlights of American Education is continued on the inside of the back cover.

*American
Education*

FOUNDATIONS IN EDUCATION

*The late Harold A. Benjamin was Consulting Editor of
the Foundations of Education Series from its
inception in 1935 until January 1969.*

McGRAW-HILL SERIES IN EDUCATION

ARNO A. BELLACK   Teachers College, Columbia University
Consulting Editor, Supervision, Curriculum, and Methods in Education
PHILIP M. CLARK   Ohio State University
Consulting Editor, Psychology and Human Development in Education
WALTER F. JOHNSON   Michigan State University
Consulting Editor, Guidance, Counseling, and Student Personnel in Education

Seventh Edition

American Education

Chris A. De Young
Dean Emeritus
Illinois State University

Richard Wynn
Professor of Education and Chairman
Department of Educational Administration
University of Pittsburgh

McGraw-Hill Book Company

New York	Kuala Lumpur	Panama
St. Louis	London	Rio de Janeiro
San Francisco	Mexico	Singapore
Düsseldorf	Montreal	Sydney
Johannesburg	New Delhi	Toronto

Credits for Photographs

Page 2   *San Francisco Examiner*
Page 14   Top: United Press International
Page 14   Below: University of Pittsburgh, Bud Harris, photographer
Page 37   United Press International
Page 43   United Nations
Page 50   National Education Association
Page 62   *American Education*, Paul Conklin, PIX, Inc., photographer
Page 70   Top: Board of Education, City of New York
Page 70   Below: Bell of Pennsylvania, Guild Photographers
Page 82   University of Pittsburgh
Page 88   National Catholic Education Association, Carl Balcerak, photographer
Page 92   State of Michigan Department of Education
Page 106   Executone, Inc.
Page 110   Miami-Dade Junior College
Page 116   Office of the Superintendent of Schools, Montgomery County, Pennsylvania
Page 120   Pittsburgh Public Schools, Vinard Studios, Lou Malkin, photographer
Page 134   University of Pittsburgh
Page 146   *Pittsburgh Post-Gazette*, Charles Stuebgen, photographer
Page 155   Children's Television Workshop
Page 157   Illinois State University, Nelson Smith, photographer
Page 162   Head Start, Office of Economic Opportunity
Page 166   State University of New York
Page 181   Left: National Education Association
Page 181   Right: Daverman Associates, Architects and Engineers
Page 186   Mamaroneck Public Schools, New York
Page 200   Top: Interlochen Music Camp and Arts Academy, Michigan
Page 200   Below: McGraw-Hill Book Company
Page 202   University of Pittsburgh, Bud Harris, photographer
Page 203   Howard County, Maryland, Public Schools and Johannes and Murray and Associates
Page 204   Bell of Pennsylvania, Guild Photographers
Page 210   Pittsburgh Public Schools, Vinard Studios, Lou Malkin, photographer
Page 216   Grand Rapids Press
Page 224   Michigan State University

Page 238   Office of Economic Opportunity
Page 246   Bell of Pennsylvania, Guild Photographers
Page 252   Newman-Schmidt Studios, Inc.
Page 257   *Pittsburgh Post-Gazette*, Morris Berman, photographer
Page 266   University of Pittsburgh, Bud Harris, photographer
Page 269   University of Pittsburgh, Herbert K. Barnett, photographer
Page 275   Pittsburgh Public Schools, Vinard Studios, Lou Malkin, photographer
Page 288   University of Pittsburgh, Bud Harris, photographer
Page 294   University of Pittsburgh, Harry Mooney, photographer
Page 317   University of Pittsburgh, Leonard Schugar, photographer
Page 319   Pittsburgh Public Schools, Vinard Studios, Lou Malkin, photographer
Page 322   University of Pittsburgh
Page 324   Pittsburgh Public Schools, Vinard Studios, Lou Malkin, photographer
Page 336   American Library Association and Sedgefield Elementary School Library, Charlotte, North Carolina
Page 337   University of Pittsburgh, Bud Harris, photographer
Page 342   Penn Hills School District, Pennsylvania
Page 345   American Library Association and Casis Elementary School Library, Austin, Texas
Page 350   Denoyer-Geppert, Dome City Photographers, Inc.
Page 368   Hewlett-Packard Corporation
Page 372   Board of Education, City of New York
Page 375   Board of Education, City of New York
Page 376   Mamaroneck Public Schools, New York
Page 390   The Pennsylvania State University Still Photography Service
Page 414   Human Resources School, Albertson, New York
Page 418   Patapsco Middle School, Howard County Schools, Clarksville, Maryland
Page 422   Addressograph Multigraph Corporation, The Griswold Eshleman Company
Page 429   Left: National Education Association
Page 429   Right: From *Teach Me!*, National Education Association
Page 452   Michigan State University
Page 463   Ford Foundation, Carleton Sarver, photographer
Page 476   Council on Student Travel
Page 478   Arabian American Oil Company

American Education

Copyright © 1955, 1960, 1964, 1968, 1972 by McGraw-Hill, Inc. All rights reserved. Copyright 1942, 1950 by McGraw-Hill, Inc. All rights reserved. Printed in the United States of America. No part of this publication may be reproduced, stored in a retrieval system, or transmitted, in any form or by any means, electronic, mechanical, photocopying, recording, or otherwise, without the prior written permission of the publisher.

Library of Congress Catalog Card Number 75-39293

07-016687-0

34567890 VHVH 79876543

This book was set in Folio by York Graphic Services, Inc., and printed and bound by Von Hoffman Press, Inc. The designer was Marsha Cohen; the drawings were done by York Graphic Services, Inc. The editors were Samuel B. Bossard and Susan Gamer. John F. Harte supervised production.

Contents

Preface

Perhaps the surest way to understand a people—their aspirations, problems, and values—is to study their educational system. This book is addressed to all who would seek deeper understanding of American education—undergraduate and graduate students, teachers, supervisors, administrators, school board members, other educational personnel, and laymen.

This seventh edition is the culmination of more than thirty years of intensive evaluation of the book in colleges and universities throughout the nation and around the world. The editions have undergone extensive revisions based upon the authors' own experience in several decades of teaching and administrative experience at all levels of education, the considered judgments of countless other professors who have participated in nationwide surveys of the book's utility conducted by the McGraw-Hill Book Company, and the critical evaluations of expert reviewers who have given valuable suggestions for its improvement. The list of people who have helped to improve this book over the third of a century of its existence is far too long for reproduction here. Nevertheless, we are deeply indebted to them.

This edition, like all the previous ones, is a thorough revision of the book. The pace of change in educational thought and practice is so rapid that it could not be otherwise. The historical, philosophical, social, and psychological foundations of each chapter have been strengthened and brought up to date. Contemporary developments in educational programs and practices have been added. More attention has been given to the future of educational development because of the more compelling necessity for looking ahead in a world so beleaguered by fateful problems and perplexing choices. The literary style has been enriched to challenge the more advanced maturity of today's college students.

Figures, graphs, charts, and tables have been revised to include up-to-date information. New photographs have been added, to illustrate the modern educational scene. The book has been redesigned to capitalize upon the latest artistry and technology of book production; and this has improved its aesthetic quality. The bibliographies and lists of suggested activities at the end of each chapter have been carefully revised to facilitate the reader's review of the content of the book. The reader should be aware of the revised glossary at the end of the book, which defines educational terms that may not be familiar to him. The very extensive index—probably the largest in any single volume book on education—facilitates the precise location of hundreds of concepts and developments throughout the book.

If this new edition enriches the reader's understanding of American education and helps him to contribute to the improvement of the human condition through education, our labors will have been well expended.

Chris A. De Young
Richard Wynn

Chris A. De Young

Chris A. De Young died shortly after we wrote this Preface. He died as he lived, in service to his fellow man. He entered his Father's house at the end of a meeting of Volunteers in Probation, a national organization of citizens which he headed, dedicated to the rehabilitation of first offenders in crime. Like Abou Ben Adhem, Chris is written as one who loves his fellow men. His love affair with all mankind and his magnificent heart shaped his career in education and his other good work.

He started his teaching career in India over fifty years ago as a teacher and principal of an elementary and secondary school. He served later in other countries abroad, including Cambodia, where he was knighted for his service in establishing a new college. He was a delegate to the first meeting of the World Confederation of Organizations of the Teaching Profession and was Secretary of the International Council on Education for Teaching, which he helped to organize. His educational service in the United States included assignments as teacher, superintendent of schools, professor and undergraduate and graduate dean at Illinois State University, and visiting professor at many universities.

When he retired from salaried service, he devoted his life generously to a host of public services: the development of a new community college, a new home for the aged, hospital nursing education, art museums, church work, urban planning, and the rehabilitation of juvenile delinquents. He answered many calls as a lay minister to various religious groups and as an inspiring speaker for many educational and civic associations.

Chris created in 1942 the first edition of this textbook, guided it through its first three editions, and coauthored it with me through its next four editions. His death, while this seventh edition was in press, followed the completion of his full share of labor in the revision of this book by which he deepened the understanding and quickened the faith in education of hundreds of thousands of readers around the world. He undertook the authorship of this book with rare diligence, scholarship, and literary style.

Chris had a penetrating insight into life, both mortal and spiritual; a genuine compassion for all mankind; a compelling sense of human rights; an engaging humor; a contagious smile; and a superb ability to communicate with hundreds of thousands of readers, students, and others for whom he wrote, taught, counseled, lectured, and preached. Through his labors Chris endures triumphantly far beyond his mortal years. His good work confers upon him an immortality as great as man dare reach in this terrestial life. As the minister noted at his graveside, "What we trust unto the dust is but the earthly garb he wore; what we love, lives on above and will live for evermore."

Richard Wynn

To
Mary De Young
Joanne Lindsay Wynn

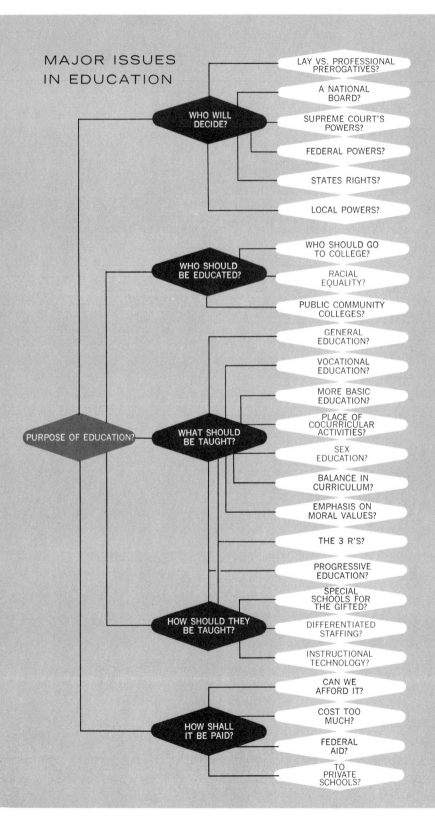

MAJOR ISSUES
IN EDUCATION

PURPOSE OF EDUCATION?

WHO WILL DECIDE?
- LAY VS. PROFESSIONAL PREROGATIVES?
- A NATIONAL BOARD?
- SUPREME COURT'S POWERS?
- FEDERAL POWERS?
- STATES RIGHTS?
- LOCAL POWERS?

WHO SHOULD BE EDUCATED?
- WHO SHOULD GO TO COLLEGE?
- RACIAL EQUALITY?
- PUBLIC COMMUNITY COLLEGES?

WHAT SHOULD BE TAUGHT?
- GENERAL EDUCATION?
- VOCATIONAL EDUCATION?
- MORE BASIC EDUCATION?
- PLACE OF COCURRICULAR ACTIVITIES?
- SEX EDUCATION?
- BALANCE IN CURRICULUM?
- EMPHASIS ON MORAL VALUES?

HOW SHOULD THEY BE TAUGHT?
- THE 3 R'S?
- PROGRESSIVE EDUCATION?
- SPECIAL SCHOOLS FOR THE GIFTED?
- DIFFERENTIATED STAFFING?
- INSTRUCTIONAL TECHNOLOGY?

HOW SHALL IT BE PAID?
- CAN WE AFFORD IT?
- COST TOO MUCH?
- FEDERAL AID?
- TO PRIVATE SCHOOLS?

Part One
Interpretation of Education

Few of man's endeavors are more important, more difficult, or more controversial than his efforts to educate. It is through this controversy that issues are raised, evidence is examined, values are appraised, alternatives are considered, and progress is made.

We think it both appropriate and instructive to open Part One, Chapter 1 with consideration of the major issues which our educational enterprise encompasses. These issues are organized under the five major topics with which this volume deals: (1) organization and administration of education, (2) areas of education, (3) personnel in education, (4) provisions for educational materials and environment, and (5) American education in today's world. The subheadings in each of these divisions correspond with the sequence of titles of each of the sixteen chapters which follow Chapter 1.

We hope that the reader's encounter with these issues will stimulate him to examine more deeply the historical and philosophical foundations, objectives, programs, practices, and trends of each issue as treated in the following chapters. Chapter 1 will also help the reader acquire an overview of the significant components of the broad topic to which this volume is addressed—American education. This chapter can also be used collaterally with the other related chapters and as a review of some of the current issues in American education.

Chapter 1   Issues in American Education

ORIENTATION

We think it instructive to begin our discussion of American education with an examination of some of the more fateful issues buffeting our schools. The learned man is distinguished most surely by the controversies he contemplates. Milton pointed out, "There is no learned man but will confess he hath much profited by reading controversies; his senses awakened, his judgment sharpened, and the truth which he holds more firmly established." If this chapter helps awaken the reader's senses, sharpen his judgment, and establish more firmly his sense of truth, its purpose will have been accomplished.

Criticism of education has become almost a national pastime. Few, if any, institutions of American life are subject to as careful scrutiny and intensive criticism as the schools. It may be helpful to consider some of the phenomena that characterize man's criticism of his schools, the general nature of the more central issues, and some characteristics of the critics.

Criticism of Education

Responsible Criticism Is Imperative to the Improvement of Education. Criticism is the lifeblood of free societies and the best antidote for dogmatism and complacency. Macaulay, the great English historian, observed, "Men are never so likely to settle a question rightly, as when they discuss it freely." Criticism is so essential to our democratic society that its preservation is guaranteed by the First Amendment to the Constitution. Alfred North Whitehead noted, "The clash of doctrines is not a disaster, it is an opportunity." A constructive critic of education is no more an enemy of schools than

These striking San Francisco teachers illustrate the controversy which arises over issues in education.

a music critic is an enemy of music, even though his criticism may seem unwise in the minds of some. But one who seeks only to destroy a worthwhile institution is indulging in subversion, not criticism. Edmund Burke asked: "Is it in destroying and pulling down that skill is displayed? The shallowest understanding, the rudest hand is more than equal to the task." Some critics are disposed to rage against what they do not want with no clear vision of what they wish to build. U.S. Commissioner of Education Sidney Marland has warned that "we have reached that point in time when further nonconstructive criticism of our educational system is no longer in any sense, or for any purpose, useful."

Criticism, if honest and responsible, causes open-minded people to reexamine assumptions, reconsider goals, gather and evaluate evidence, consider alternatives, and view problems anew. Through these processes of rational inquiry, educational policies and practices are reassessed and often improved.

Much of the Criticism of Education Is Justified. There are students who cannot read, curriculums that are irrelevant to the needs of students, teachers who cannot teach, and schools that are poorly administered. There is a great gap between what is and what could be in our schools. Reasonable people easily disagree over the dimension of this gap. They also disagree over what should be. Like most of man's other public institutions, schools have been slow to respond to social change, for reasons noted later. Many schools have neither formulated their goals nor measured their progress very carefully. Many educators have not listened well to the protests of students or the aspirations of parents. A few have squandered their resources and abused their public trust. It is imperative that their quality and their responsiveness to the great demands of the times be reexamined.

3

The Schools Are the Target of Intense Public Interest. It is precisely because schools serve the public's most vital legacy, the children, that they become the center of urgent public interest. Quite understandably, people can get more aroused over the well-being of their children than almost any other concern. Education has become so pervasive and its power so crucial to the human condition that its policies and the manner in which its policies are formulated must be reexamined and revised.

The American Association of School Administrators has pointed out in its publication *Imperatives in Education*, "The schools have become a stage upon which ills that trouble groups of people are called to public attention."

Moreover, education is very expensive. It represents by far the largest local expenditure in many communities. The price is high, and it is increasing. The public is not inclined to pay the freight willingly unless it has an opportunity to examine the needs and resources carefully. On the other hand, most people are eager to provide the best that they can afford for their children when the need is made clear.

The Schools Are a Convenient Scapegoat. When the Soviet Union preceded the United States in placing a satellite in outer space, many people were sure the fault lay largely with our schools. We looked to our educational system as the cause of our embarrassment and the salvation of our pride. (Curiously, when our own space effort later surpassed the Soviets', no one insisted that our schools take the credit.)

The schools have been called upon to arrest drug abuse, reduce highway fatalities, combat venereal disease, overcome racial injustice, reduce unemployment, entertain the public with sports extravaganzas, produce wise consumers, conduct charitable drives, and perform a host of other tasks. Almost any problem in society is viewed almost immediately as "an educational problem," and people turn to the schools expecting instant success. Thus the schools become both the scapegoat for the ills of society and the source of hope for their cure. Just as the schools are only a part of the cause of these complex problems, so they can be only a part of the cure. As one popular magazine noted, television stations of one city carried, in one week, 7,887 acts of violence. One episode of a western series garnished Christmas night with thirteen homicides. Between the ages of 5 and 14, children who are average viewers witness the annihilation of 12,000 human beings. Schools are expected to make good the shortcomings of the rest of society.

In some ways, schools are the victims of their own success. In the late 1960s there was great concern over the one student in four who dropped out of school before completing high school, and a drive was undertaken to eliminate school dropouts. Thus American schools strove to accomplish what no other society had ever attempted—to provide full elementary and secondary education for all children regardless of their desire or talent or family circumstances. The public response was not gratitude for the near accomplishment of this unequaled miracle, but a plethora of books proclaiming that children were dying from the joylessness of classrooms. In many colleges, doors were thrown open to virtually all who wanted to attend, as well as to many who didn't want to, regardless of their academic abilities. When some failed to succeed, it was the colleges and not the students who stood accused. Few would contest Henry Steele Commager's conclusion that no other nation ever expected as much of its schools as the United States, and to our minds, no one should disagree with his conclusion that no other nation has been as well served by its schools. But many of the critics do disagree. As James Huneker noted, "a critic is a man who expects miracles."

The Critics Are Often Gifted in Hyperbole. Consider the titles of some recent books and articles written by the critics of education: *Murder in the Classroom, Our Children Are Dying, They Die So Young, Death at an Early Age, Requiem for Urban Schools, American Education: A National Failure.* If our schools were a failure, how successful were our churches, our homes, our mass media, our labor unions, our industries, our government? If, as James Russell Lowell believed, a wise skepticism is the first attribute of a good critic, why was their skepticism not manifested in the titles of their works or the rhetoric of their arguments? Some accused the schools of "the annihilation of the human spirit," "the processing of juveniles for the military-industrial complex," and "the deliberate frustration of real learning." Sometimes the hyperbole was tempered with the gratuitous confession that there were occasional exceptions to such conspiracies in a few schools.

This almost endemic exaggeration of the

shortcomings of schools, which characterizes the writings of so many of the popular critics, is mentioned here, not to disparage the legitimacy of well-reasoned criticism, but to protest journalistic overkill.

Everyone Thinks He Is an Expert on Educational Matters. Most people would not think of criticizing a surgeon's handling of an operation or a lawyer's conduct of a case. Indeed, few would even dare criticize a repairman's approach to an inoperative television set. Yet most people have no hesitancy in advising a teacher about reading instruction or telling the superintendent what is wrong with textbooks. The butcher, the baker, and the submarine maker can quickly identify the villain in education and prescribe surprisingly simple and unequivocal remedies. Since everyone has gone through school, everyone tends to regard himself as a qualified expert on education.

Much of the Criticism of Schools Is Quixotic and Contradictory. If educators are slow to respond to demands for educational reform, it may be because they well remember the short life of yesterday's panaceas. A few examples will illustrate the point. In 1949, that generally highly regarded critic of the educational scene, James Conant, sounded this strange caution: "My chief worry comes from a fear that we may educate more doctors, lawyers, engineers, scientists, college professors than our economy can support."[1] Less than a decade later, Conant was scurrying around the country in an attempt to discover why schools were not turning out more graduates in these fields. The tough high school curriculum which he prescribed in the late 1950s was a nearly perfect target for everything that the romantic critics despised in education a decade later. The Ford Foundation, in a burst of characteristic enthusiasm, hailed its multimillion-dollar experiment, educational television broadcast from airplanes hovering over the Midwest, as a wondrous revolution in education. A few years later, the ill-fated experiment was quietly grounded in what was probably the most expensive single failure in the history of educational experimentation. We object, not because it was attempted, but because it was hailed as a revolutionary success almost before it took off. In medicine, years of careful research are required

[1]James B. Conant, *Education in a Divided World*, Harvard University Press, Cambridge, Mass., 1949, p. 198.

before a new drug is offered to the public, but in education it is only necessary that it be "innovative," a "breakthrough," or "revolutionary." The evidence of value can be appraised later or ignored.

And so it goes. The examples are legion. Many of the critics are indeed quixotic and as fleeting as the reforms they invoke. They became strangely silent in the 1970s when their reforms of yesteryear were so obviously out of phase with the temper of the new romantic critics. Perhaps we should not be surprised that seasoned educators have gained some circumspection in viewing the panaceas invoked by the Johnny-come-latelies on the educational scene. The educators have been there before. They have seen the clamor rise and then wane for foreign language in the elementary schools, life adjustment education, Esperanto, phonics, teaching machines, conservation education, team teaching, language laboratories, homogeneous grouping, and all the other wonders of yesteryear. Small wonder that they don't leap on each passing bandwagon. The critics can indulge in the luxury of inviting "innovation," but the school authorities must tackle the larger task of "improvement." Innovation, like change, may be either good or bad. But the school administrator must ask: For what purpose? To accomplish what objectives? On the basis of what evidence? At what costs? With what benefits? With what unanticipated consequences?

Another important phenomenon in this kaleidoscope of school reform is worth noting. The pronouncements of the critics are very often in sharp disagreement with the expectations of the local citizens who pay the bill and supply the clientele. For example, many critics—among them Holt, Silberman, Kozol, Dennison, Goodman, Friedenberg—are calling for a relaxation of the regimen of the school and the granting of more freedom to the learners in the open schools which they advocate, a reform which we also endorse in principle and within reason. But a Gallup poll of public opinion in 1970 revealed that the most important problem in schools, in the minds of the general public, was not lack of freedom, but its opposite—discipline. When asked whether school discipline was too strict, not strict enough, or just about right, 53 percent of the public responded that discipline in schools was not strict enough. Only 2 percent felt it was too strict.

Many school reformers undertake their crusades with the allegation that schools are already demonstrable failures and that the public has lost confidence in them. Again this view is not held by the majority of parents, according to the Gallup poll. Only one-third of the parents of public school students think that "the school curriculum . . . needs to be changed to meet today's needs." It is true that slightly more than half of the high school juniors and seniors believe that the curriculum does need to be changed. But the prudent school administrator and school board must reckon more with the opinions of parents than with the unexamined charges of failure brandished by the critics.

The Nature of the Issues

Fundamentally, there are six classic issues in education: What are the purposes of education? Who shall be educated? What shall be taught? How shall it be taught? How shall it be paid for? Who will decide? These issues have been debated in one form or another since the early days of the republic, and such debates will probably continue. Although different controversies erupt from time to time, many of them are ramifications of these basic issues. Figure 1-1 shows the major problems of schools as revealed by a recent Gallup poll. Table 1-1 shows the major educational issues as revealed by a poll of public school superintendents.

The Nature of the Critics

Critics range all the way from competent, sober, thoughtful, constructive persons who are sincerely interested in improving schools to carping, incompetent, irrational, and sometimes vicious propagandists. Among the latter group are some who wish to destroy or, at best, severely circumscribe public education. It is important for the educator to be able to tell the constructive critics from the destructive ones, because the former should be treated with encouragement and respect which the latter do not merit.

Fortunately, the two types can frequently be distinguished by their behavior. The constructive critic asks questions, tries to understand positions contrary to his own, seeks improvement through study and fact finding, works through the superintendent and board of education, uses rational and objective language, and freely identifies any organization for school improvement with which he may be affiliated. The destructive critic often prefers to attack people rather than issues, uses hateful language, ignores legal authorities such as the superintendent and board of education and goes directly to the public with printed material, issues dogmatic statements rather than questions, claims to have all the facts already at hand, makes blanket accusations, and traces all faults to communist or "establishment" conspiracies, holds inflexible positions, seeks action through threats and disruptions, and often refuses to identify the organizations for which he is spokesman. Most of them have no difficulty explaining what they oppose but have great difficulty explaining what they are for. Such critics should be revealed for what they are—subversive influences

TABLE 1-1 SUPERINTENDENTS' RANKING OF ISSUES AND CHALLENGES FACING THE SUPERINTENDENCY

Rank	Type of educational issue or challenge
1	Financing schools to meet increasing current expenditures and capital outlay
2	Demands for new ways of teaching or operating the educational program
3	Greater visibility of the superintendent
4	Changes in values and behavior norms
5	School staff relations; strikes, sanctions, or other forms of militancy among teachers
6	Growing federal involvement in education
7	Reorganization of small districts into larger units of administration
8	Assessment of educational outcomes
9	Caliber of persons assigned to or removed from local school boards
10	Caliber of responsibilities assigned to or removed from local school boards
11	Social and cultural issues such as race relations, integration, or segregation
12	Rapidly increasing student enrollments
13	Changing priorities in curriculum, such as black studies courses or sex education, and eliminating others
14	Use of drugs in schools
15	Increasing attacks on the superintendent
16	Growing pressure for public support of non-public schools
17	Student activism, such as underground newspapers and student strikes
18	Decentralization of large districts into smaller units of administration

SOURCE: Adapted from American Association of School Administrators, *The American School Superintendent*, American Association of School Administrators, Washington, D.C., 1971, p. 58.

themselves because they destroy public confidence in schools and because they use the tactics of totalitarianism, which are inimical to a free society. In general, the more destructive critics have apparently not had very much impact upon public opinion. Studies through the years reveal that the vast majority of teachers believe that there has been relatively minor impact locally by the destructive critics of schools.

We turn now to specific issues; in the following sections, these are organized around the rest of the chapters of this book.

ORGANIZATION AND ADMINISTRATION OF EDUCATION (PART 2)

Education is said to be an interest of the federal government, a legal function of the states, and a responsibility of the local school districts. It has also been said that the federal government has the money, the states have the legal powers, and the local districts have the problems. Many contro-

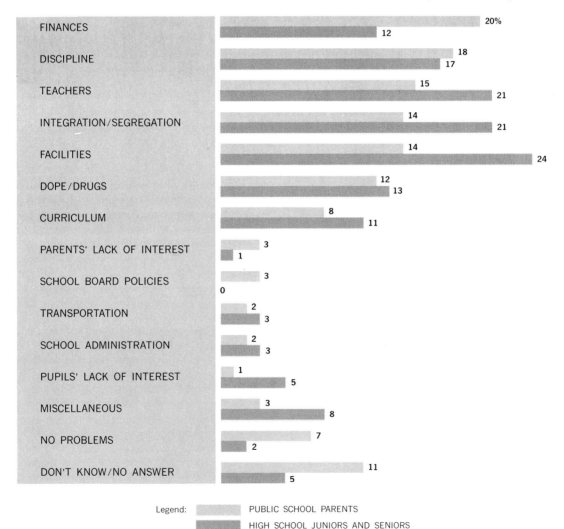

FINANCES — 20%, 12
DISCIPLINE — 18, 17
TEACHERS — 15, 21
INTEGRATION/SEGREGATION — 14, 21
FACILITIES — 14, 24
DOPE/DRUGS — 12, 13
CURRICULUM — 8, 11
PARENTS' LACK OF INTEREST — 3, 1
SCHOOL BOARD POLICIES — 3, 0
TRANSPORTATION — 2, 3
SCHOOL ADMINISTRATION — 2, 3
PUPILS' LACK OF INTEREST — 1, 5
MISCELLANEOUS — 3, 8
NO PROBLEMS — 7, 2
DON'T KNOW/NO ANSWER — 11, 5

Legend: PUBLIC SCHOOL PARENTS
HIGH SCHOOL JUNIORS AND SENIORS

FIGURE 1-1 *Opinion poll on major problems facing local schools. Public school parents' and high school juniors' and seniors' answers to the question "What do you think are the biggest problems with which the public schools in this community must deal?" showed relatively minor differences. These responses are not very compatible with the criticisms expressed by popular writers. (Adapted from the Second Annual Gallup Poll on "How the Nation Views the Public Schools," Phi Delta Kappan, vol. 52, October, 1970.)*

versies arise over the collision of powers and interests in education by the various levels of government—federal, state, intermediate, and local. Obviously decisions regarding the determination of educational policies, the planning of educational programs, and the allocation of resources by these levels of government have very important consequences upon the educational opportunities of students. It is no wonder that the controversies which arise are often spirited and acrimonious.

National Program (Chapter 2)

Although the United States Constitution clearly delegates legal responsibility for education generally to the states, there are many national interests—development of manpower, racial integration, international educational exchanges, among many others—which transcend state boundaries. These and other interests have prompted the intervention of the federal government in the educational enterprise, sometimes in collision with state and local interests in education. Sometimes the intervention is imposed by the federal courts—the bans on Bible reading and racial discrimination are examples—when educational practices contravene the protections of the Constitution. Sometimes the intervention is manifested by congressional action in legislation granting funds for various educational programs, such as the Drug Abuse Education Act and the Higher Education Act. Sometimes agencies of the federal government, such as the U.S. Office of Education, intervene in the formulation of school policies, such as guidelines for the desegregation of schools.

What Should Be the Function of the Federal Government in Education? Without any doubt, the federal government's participation in the educational enterprise has had many salubrious effects upon our civilization beginning with the very founding of our republic. As described in Chapter 2, federal support of education has helped to provide the educated manpower needed to support the miraculous rise in our productive capacity and to make higher education available to literally millions of persons who would not otherwise have had access to it because of economic disadvantage; has stimulated research and development in curriculum and teaching; has helped countless destitute people rise above their poverty through better educational opportunity; and

has provided buildings and educational materials that were sorely needed. The list is by no means complete.

With full recognition of these accomplishments, we are still falling far short of realizing the federal government's full potential for educational improvement. There are many reasons for this and, at the risk of oversimplification, we shall call attention to only a few of the more important ones. First, as a nation we have never faced very realistically the question of what we expect our educational system to accomplish. We have frequently imposed upon the schools, often through federal grants, responsibility for achieving certain national objectives which were clearly not uniquely educational goals. A good example is the National Defense Education Act, which sought to strengthen our defense posture through education, thereby corrupting the purposes of education and unbalancing the curriculum.

The nation seems to regard the schools as the prime agency for relieving social injustice, arresting pollution of the environment, curbing drug abuse, reducing crime and delinquency, improving mental health, eliminating unemployment, elevating our moral standards, and solving virtually any other social, economic, or political problem. Consequently, schools are lured into adopting programs financed by federal funds and designed to ameliorate these important problems. Although better schooling can often help, the ultimate solution lies very often in forces over which the school has little influence. Without definition of the national purpose in education, there can be no definition of national policy. As Wynn noted elsewhere: "A well-defined national policy on education is long overdue. Spasmodic, crisis-oriented federal legislation, with its often unanticipated and sometimes unfortunate dislocations of federal-state-local relations, must be supplanted by a coherent, rational, long-range plan for the general improvement of the nation's schools."[2]

The lack of a well-defined national policy on education can be explained but not excused by a number of factors. Changes in the White House, rapid turnover of U.S. Commissioners of Education, intrusion of partisan political considerations, the fragmentation of special educational interest groups lobbying in Washington, schizophrenic Congresses which enact significant educational legislation and

[2] Richard Wynn, "Centralizing Tendencies in Education," in American Association of School Administrators, *Federal Policy and the Public Schools*, Washington, D.C., 1967, p. 16.

then refuse to appropriate sufficient funds to implement the legislation—these and other circumstances all contribute to federal programs that are too often ill-conceived, hastily implemented, and at cross purposes with state and local aspirations. Moreover, responsibility for decision making on education is badly fragmented among many federal agencies of government: the U.S. Office of Education, the Bureau of the Budget, the President, the various education committees in both houses, and the Congress itself. A former U.S. Commissioner of Education complained of the "inordinate influence of politics on educational decision making."

The consequences of this quixotic, crisis-oriented approach to federal participation in the educational enterprise are readily discernible. As President Nixon noted: "This system of carving up federal aid to education into a series of distinct programs may have adverse educational effects. Federal 'pieces' do not add up to the whole of education and they may distract the attention of educators away from the big picture and into a constant scramble for special-purpose grants." Crisis funding tends to be sporadic, starts too quickly to permit adequate recruitment of personnel to operate the programs, and terminates too soon to permit accomplishment. A proliferation of federal guidelines, however well intended, are frequently restrictive and agonizing to state and local authorities. Frequently the obtaining of federal funds has been an exercise in proposal writing rather than in educational planning. The objectives of the funded programs are often poorly related to those educational purposes, valid or otherwise, held by state and local educational authorities. Their special-purpose character permits state and local officials to view them as a conglomeration of projects rather than as fundamental parts of a coherent total educational program. Some of the federal appropriations have not been prudently managed. For example, six civil rights groups examined the use of $75 million appropriated by the Congress to assist desegregation in the South. They concluded that the consequences were a "fraud upon the Congress." They reported discovery of funds going to several programs which were "racist in conception and which were leading to the resegregation of schools."[3] Much of the work in compensatory education funded by the federal government has failed to yield

[3]"Fiasco in Integration Spending?" *The Nation's Schools*, vol. 87, pp. 20–21, 92, January, 1971.

any demonstrable results—sometimes because the money was spread too thin and sometimes because it was spent without adequate planning or for unproductive purposes.

These misfortunes could be reduced through the efforts of a national body charged with the responsibility of developing a comprehensive national policy on education and by a Congress and a President dedicated to the enactment and administration of federal programs consonant with that policy. Many commissions have reached this conclusion and formulated recommendations for the development and implementation of a national policy in education. Several extralegal groups have formulated statements which could serve as the basis for such national policy in education. At the time of this writing, their work has remained virtually ignored.

What Changes Are Needed to Strengthen Federal Participation in Education? The national interests in education are fragmented by the division of administrative responsibility over federal activities in education among the several departments of the executive branch of government, as discussed in Chapter 2. This division of authority adds to the confusion and ambivalence of federal policies and practices in education. Many have argued that more of these federal programs should be consolidated in the U.S. Office of Education and that the Office should be strengthened.

The National Academy of Education, among others, has recommended that education be separated from the conglomerate department in which it is now located and raised to full, independent department status as the Department of Education, with the Commissioner holding Cabinet rank. It further recommended that a National Board of Education be established to formulate national educational policy. Similar proposals over the years have been unheeded.

Should Categorical Aid to Education Be Replaced by General-Purpose Aid or by Revenue Sharing with the States? Categorical aid has the advantage of directing fiscal support from the federal government directly at points of greatest need—education of slum children, development of educational technology, improved instruction, drug education, vocational education, environmental studies, and others. It has prompted educational innovation and development that might have proceeded much more slowly under other circumstances. Moreover, categorical aid has permitted the improvement of education of students in both public and private schools, which would have been much more difficult to achieve under proposals of general federal aid. Categorical aid, although not ideal, was politically feasible at a time when congressional support of general nationwide federal aid to education was not.

The concept of federal support for education without federal control has appealed strongly to most Americans. But the increased funds have brought profound changes in the historic roles of federal, state, and local government of education. This special-purpose aid—which provides massive largess for special sectors of the educational enterprise—is in itself a form of federal control over the development of education. It leaves it up to the federal government to decide which activities in education are to be emphasized, often at the expense of the unrewarded sectors.

This is not to say that federal financial support has been nefarious or ineffective, but it does suggest an increase in federal control of educational policy making. The solution to this invasion of state and local decision-making prerogatives appears to lie in the provision by the federal government of general aid for education. General aid would permit state and local educational authorities to use the money for whatever needs are most urgent; to study, plan, and evaluate expenditures in terms of local priorities; and to build greater stability and coherence in overall school finance than is possible with short-term special allocations.

In 1972 two bills were proposed by the President to remedy most of the dysfunctions described here. The Educational Assistance Bill was designed to give states almost total control of educational programs supported by federal funds by transferring funds directly to them after their plans were submitted to the federal educational agency. The Educational Assistance Bill was designed to replace existing programs with flexible block grants for use directly by the states in five major areas. Others have proposed that even more simplified arrangements be made to turn over to the various states, under some type of equalization fund, their fair share of federal money for education to be spent as they see fit. This proposal is commonly spoken of as "revenue sharing." It is designed to make available to the states and local communities—most of which are in dire financial difficulties—the much more abundant tax yields of the federal government without the federal controls which exist in categorical aid. However it is done, it is imperative that the federal share of spending for education be substantially increased if our educational needs are to be met. This problem is discussed in more depth later in this chapter and in Chapter 16.

What Is the Proper Distribution of Control over Education among the Various Levels of Government? Much controversy has been generated over the distribution of power over the educational enterprise among the federal, state, intermediate, and local levels of government. Attempts by the federal government to withhold federal funds from school systems allegedly discriminating against persons of minority groups have prompted impassioned speeches on states' rights. The examples are legion. Campbell and Sroufe believe that we have within the Constitution an adequate framework for a viable local-state-national partnership in education, which they speak of as "national federalism." They advance these elements of the partnership:

1. **A sharing among local, state, and national agencies is necessary in educational government.**
2. **If we are to have an effective partnership among local, state, and national agencies, each of the partners must be strong.**
3. **The several states should exercise their plenary power in education creatively.**
4. **As far as possible, the operation of schools should be delegated to local school districts.**
5. **The federal government should address itself to national needs in education and should provide financial assistance to the states and localities to meet these needs.**[4]

R. L. Johns speaks of the concept of "creative federalism":

The concept of creative federalism is based on the assumption that the power to deal with educational problems is not a fixed quantity but that it is expanding very rapidly. The increase in the power of one level of government to deal with a particular educational problem does not reduce the power of another level of government to deal with the problem. . . . The increase in the educational power of the federal government to deal with social and economic deprivation actually increased the power of the state and local school districts to deal with the

[4]Roald F. Campbell and Gerald R. Sroufe, "Toward a Rationale for Federal-State-Local Relations in Education," *Phi Delta Kappan*, vol. 47, pp. 6–7, September, 1965.

same problem . . . It is a concept of partnership in which the federal, state, and local school districts operate as equals, each assuming the responsibility to perform the educational functions that can be most appropriately dealt with at that level.[5]

State Systems (Chapter 3)

As noted earlier, education is a legal function of the state. The organization and operation of state government in education are described at length in Chapter 3. In brief, the state legislature enacts broad educational policies through statutes. A state board of education enacts more specific policies, formulates plans, and generally oversees the administration of the state system of education. A state superintendent or commissioner of education, with the help of a professional staff in the state department of education, administers the state's functions in education.

School issues are frequently contested bitterly in state politics. Here are some examples. Referenda proposing changes in state constitutions to permit the distribution of public funds to private schools have been bitterly contested in New York, Nebraska, and Michigan in recent years. Statutes authorizing collective bargaining by teachers have precipitated spirited debate in many state legislatures. Educational issues are also debated with vigor in states where the state superintendent of education is elected by the people. In California, for example, a hot campaign for the office in 1970 matched the incumbent Max Rafferty, a conservative, against his deputy superintendent, Wilson Riles, a Negro liberal. Rafferty advocated a "return to the good old days," a crusade against "arch-progressives," a revival of emphasis on the three R's, and more law and order in the schools. Riles won the election and became the first Negro to serve as chief state school officer in California. We turn our attention now to some of the major issues which relate to state educational agencies.

What Reforms Are Needed in State Educational Agencies? Authorities are generally agreed that the state level of governance of education is especially crucial and usually weak. First, the state is both the major source of school revenues and the prime legal authority over schools. Second, the state educa-

[5]R. L. Johns, "State Organization and Responsibilities for Education," in Edgar L. Morphet and Charles O. Ryan (eds.), *Designing Education for the Future*, no. 2, Citation Press, New York, 1967, p. 263.

tional authority occupies a strategic linkage between the federal and the local levels of educational effort. When state educational leadership is weak, local districts are limited in the progress they can make, and the federal government is tempted to intervene in the struggle to help schools meet the crucial problems of the times. R. L. Johns, a noted authority on school administration, insists that "the evidence is clear that the importance of the role of states in education in the future will be determined by how effectively the states discharge their educational responsibilities and not by any outworn legal theory of 'states rights.'"[6] If federal control of education is to be avoided, state educational agencies must be improved and their leadership strengthened so that federal incursions designed to ameliorate educational neglect may be rendered unnecessary.

How well are state educational agencies presently discharging their functions? Two major categories of functions of the state are commonly recognized. The *regulatory functions*—enforcement of minimum standards, allocation of state funds, and certification of teachers, for example—are discharged reasonably well by most state educational agencies. The *research, planning, development*, and *leadership functions* are not presently well fulfilled in the majority of states. Most states have quite inadequate master plans for the development of their educational systems. Many states have no overall coordinating or advisory body that is responsible for statewide planning for the improvement of all levels of education. It is at the state level that educational leadership is most sorely needed and, unfortunately, quite often lacking.

Many factors contribute to the states' incapacities in educational leadership. State educational agencies are often limited by the quality of the state boards of education. Membership on these boards is too often considered a political reward for the party faithful rather than one of the most important civic responsibilities to be discharged by the finest educational statesmen available. As Johns points out, the quality of the entire state department of education is constrained by the quality of the state board: "No state department of education can become distinguished unless some of the state's ablest citizens are willing to serve on its board."

The position of the state superintendent of

[6]Johns, *op. cit.*, p. 247.

education is also very crucial. The National Academy of Education recommends that the state superintendent be appointed by the state board and be responsible to the board so that he may be freed from untoward political pressures. In some states the tradition of political patronage fills the state departments with the party regulars rather than with the best professional talent available. Most state departments of education are too small to discharge much more than the regulatory function. In most states the majority of state education department personnel are recruited from rural and suburban communities and often lack understanding of the problems of urban schools. This brief diagnosis of the causes of inadequacy in state educational agencies suggests the cures.

The Elementary and Secondary Education Act has provided funds for the strengthening of state departments, and there is some indication that progress is being made in this direction. The establishment of the Compact for Education, discussed at length in Chapter 3, offers some hope that this confederation of state educational leaders may help states strengthen their systems of education through more adequate planning and policy making.

As the National Academy of Education points out, most governors and state legislatures need more adequate staff services to help them carry out their responsibilities in formulating school legislation more effectively.

Are State Governments Preempting Too Much Control over Education from the Local District? Recently there has been a distinct trend toward increasing power over education at the state level of government. Since the state clearly has plenary legal power over education, the question is more a matter of sound policy than of law. Some state legislatures enact laws which prescribe certain curriculum content; some states have created state textbook authorities which approve or select textbooks for use in all the schools of the state; some governors have insisted upon firing certain teachers in public institutions because they held unpopular beliefs; some states have mandated the reorganization of school districts; some exercise very close control over budgets, tax rates, and debt limits in local school districts. Some state constitutions are hopelessly outdated in their provisions regarding education.

The question posed above is impossible to

answer in the abstract. One must first ask: What decisions can be made more effectively and wisely at the state level than at the local level? What decisions are of such importance to the state that local determination cannot be tolerated? Should the state mandate only general educational goals, or specific goals as well? How much uniformity in educational policy and practice is desirable across the state? Are states justified in assuming a degree of control over local schools commensurate with the proportion of revenue for education which the states supply? For example, if the major portion of school revenue comes from state funds, are the states justified in limiting the levels of salaries which local boards of education negotiate with teachers, as some states have done? Figure 3-4 shows the percentage of revenue for public elementary and secondary schools that comes from each of the states (see page 105).

Should the States Assume Full Responsibility for the Financing of Education? Several authorities on school finance as well as a few governors have advocated that states increase their share of financial support of schools to relieve local communities almost entirely of the need for local school revenues. The Advisory Commission on Intergovernmental Relations, in testimony before the Senate Committee on Equal Educational Opportunity, supported this proposal with the following arguments:

State financing would represent a giant step toward equalization of educational opportunity.

State assumption for the responsibility for school financing is necessary in order to fix political accountability for educational finance where it belongs—at the doorstep of the governor and state legislature.

State financing would give greater impetus to the measurement of student achievement and a full disclosure of results.

State financing of schools is necessary because the combined expenditure demands of education and local government are placing too great a burden on the property-tax base in general and on our low-income householders in particular.

State financing would produce less social segregation and a more orderly development of metropolitan areas.

County and Intermediate Units (Chapter 4)

What Shall Be the Role and Nature of the Intermediate Unit? Three-fourths of the states have intermediate units—intermediate in the sense that they function between the local and state levels. In most of these states, the intermediate district is coterminous with the county. Yet it is clear that the county is not always the logical boundary for intermediate districts. In sparsely populated areas, several counties should be combined to form an intermediate unit large enough to function effectively. In more populous areas, the county should be subdivided into several intermediate units. Yet, because of the long tradition of the county in American government, it is often most difficult to alter its structure in relation to school organization.

The county unit began as an arm of state government, a downward extension of state control. Yet it is apparent that the proper role of this unit lies in leadership and service rather than control. A number of states have transformed their county administrative units, which formerly served largely regulatory functions, into regional service agencies that offer cooperative services to the constituent local school districts that would be too small to provide these services for themselves. In some states the old county office has become an ambiguous office with little real function remaining. This office is discussed in more detail in Chapter 4.

Local Districts (Chapter 5)

Much of the responsibility for the operation of schools in this country rests with the 18,000 local school districts. This decentralization of control of schools is uncommon, as most other countries maintain highly centralized educational systems. In our decentralized system, the local board of education, which is elected by the people except in many large cities, establishes educational policy, plans the development of the school system, and through the administrative staff, generally oversees the operation of the schools, as described at greater length in Chapter 5. Here, in the local governance of schools, is one of the few last bastions of participatory democracy in public affairs. Some are already proclaiming that its days are numbered and insisting that local school districts are obsolete. Some believe that their powers should be absorbed by state and federal government, while others insist upon the opposite—that their powers be delegated to community groups within the district.

In any event, it is at the local level that some of the most spirited educational debate fills local school auditoriums with citizens concerned about the tax rate, sex education in the schools, drug abuse by students, the militancy of teachers, Com-

munist doctrine in the textbooks, profanity in the students' underground newspaper, the salary of the football coach, the fate of the three R's, prayers and Bible reading in the schools, racial balance, and countless other issues. Here in microcosm is enacted the drama of a free society seeking to improve the human condition through the education of young citizens.

Should Provision for School District Reorganization Be Permissive or Mandatory? A great many school districts are too small in terms of both population and wealth to offer an educational program that is adequate at a cost that is reasonable. This results in both marginal educational opportunity for some children and an exorbitant cost to the taxpayer. Authorities differ in their judgment of what constitutes a sufficiently large school district. There is some evidence to suggest that, except in very sparsely settled areas, the minimum size of a school district should be 50,000 total population. If this goal were attained, it would mean that the present 17,000 school districts would be reduced to somewhere between 2,000 and 3,000. This indicates the magnitude of the school district reorganization which remains to be accomplished. Although the state has the legal power to reorganize districts at its pleasure, many states are hesitant to exercise this power arbitrarily, feeling that this is an unwarranted invasion of local control and initiative. Yet progress is often painfully slow under permissive arrangements. Meanwhile, a generation of students may suffer from the handicap of an inadequate program. Stated simply, the choice is between speed through mandatory legislation and dilatory action with the preservation of local initiative.

What Is the Progress and Promise toward Eliminating Racial Segregation in Schools? The United States Supreme Court in 1954, in the historic *Brown v. Board of Education* case, ruled, "In the field of public education, the doctrine of 'separate but equal' has no place. Separate facilities are inherently unequal." The court also held that racial discrimination in public education was unconstitutional and that schools must strive to end racial discrimination "with all deliberate speed." Too many recalcitrant officials interpreted the latter phrase to mean "as slowly as possible." The decision did not bring immediate redress to racial injustice in education but did precipitate a long bitter struggle that was fought in the courts, in the legislative chambers, and sometimes in the streets. In the decade and a half which followed the decision, Southern states engaged in ingenious legislation, delay, and outright resistance to the decision. Many districts adopted the "freedom of choice" policy by which students were presumably free to enroll in any school of their choice in the district. But many black students were harassed in their attempts to enter predominantly white schools. Sometimes minor changes were made in school-attendance areas to permit a few blacks to attend white schools while maintaining in effect the old dual school system. These and other efforts created traces of desegregation, or "tokenism," but failed to measure up to the spirit of the Court's decision.

Meanwhile in urban centers of the country where *de jure* segregation (deliberate discrimination by race in assigning students to schools) had not been practiced, *de facto* segregation (circumstantial separation of students by race because of segregated housing patterns) was exacerbated. As *de jure* segregation receded, *de facto* segregation began to emerge in the South and to accelerate rapidly in the North, where it had long existed. In many urban areas, parents who balked at sending their children to desegregated schools moved from the cities to the suburbs, and their vacated homes were occupied increasingly by blacks. Thus it became more and more difficult—in some cities impossible—to achieve racial balance in schools when the population was predominantly black. More and more parents enrolled their children in private schools. In several large urban areas, there are more white children attending private schools than there are in the entire public school system. Fifteen years after the Court's decision, seven out of eight black first-graders and two-thirds of the black high school seniors in the United States were still attending predominantly Negro schools. White students were even more segregated than black students. For the nation as a whole, until 1969, desegregation had progressed at the rate of only 1 percent a year. In many communities segregation had actually increased, in some instances dramatically.

In 1969 a federal court finally ruled that the time for "deliberate speed" had ended and that dual school systems must be dismantled immediately. In 1971 the United States Supreme Court upheld the constitutionality of busing as a means of reducing racial segregation in public schools. Except for the

Angry whites overturned school buses in Lamar, South Carolina, in protest over the forced integration of schools.

Confrontations between whites and blacks arose over racial issues in schools in many parts of the country.

Deep South and some large cities throughout the country, desegregation progressed rather rapidly and smoothly, thanks usually to the determination of school authorities, the support of most parents, and the friendliness of children of all races. A Gallup poll in 1970 revealed that only two parents in five across the nation disapproved of immediate desegregation of schools. Among black parents, 85 percent approved of desegregation, and the percentage has not declined, notwithstanding the strident demands by some black militants for separate schools controlled by blacks. By the early 1970s only a few dual school systems could still be found in a few states in the Deep South, although individual schools within desegregated districts were often segregated as were many classrooms within biracial schools. In communities with predominantly black populations both in the Deep South and in some Northern cities, many white families fled to the suburbs or sent their children to private schools. Private schools, or segregation academies, sprung up throughout the South and in some Northern communities. Some Southern school districts practically gave away public school buildings to the academies, declared new textbooks and school furniture "surplus" and gave them too, and permitted the private school students to use public school buses. Many used retired teachers and uncertified teachers. Some occupied abandoned stores or church basements or any other available building. Virtually none of them were accredited. Ironically, the segregation academies offered their white students an education that was "separate but inferior" to that which they would have received in the public schools. Nevertheless, by the early 1970s, more than half a million white students were attending the segregation academies and the number was rising.[7] In these localities, the public schools became predominantly black and the private schools predominantly white and a dual resegregated system was, in effect, recreated. The flight of white students from biracial schools appears to become nearly a mass exodus when black-student enrollment reaches approximately 40 percent. Some flee because they are racists; some because they prefer schools with similar social, economic, or cultural group identity; some because they fear the greater unrest which appears in biracial student bodies; some because they object to having their children bused past schools in their neighborhood to more distant schools in strange and often hostile climates.

Can Decentralization and Community Control Correct the Failures of Urban School Systems? In the closing days of its 1969 session, the New York

State Legislature was held captive in a grueling ten-day debate that continued through the last day without a break. The debate involved considerations of racism, ethnocentrism, unionism, bureaucracy, partisan politics, and poverty. At issue was a bill, eventually enacted, which dictated the division of the New York City school system, the nation's largest, into thirty semiautonomous districts, each with a locally elected board of education.[8] Similar demands for decentralization and community control of schools have been advanced in virtually all the cities, and many have responded.

What are the reasons for this stratagem of reform? As was noted earlier, it is widely believed that schools have failed to meet the needs of people in the inner cities, especially people of low income and blacks. Originally it was hoped that the integration of urban school systems, compensatory education, and more effective school programs would correct the educational disadvantage of inner-city youths. In balance, these reforms have not really solved the problems in any fundamental manner. Although most liberals have not abandoned school desegregation as the ultimate long-range goal, it is nevertheless clear that no proposal will eliminate racial imbalance in most big-city schools, particularly those in which the majority of students are black. Even in metropolitan school districts that are predominantly white, racial balance is often elusive because of segregated housing patterns. The objective of some parents from minority races is therefore toward control over the schools their children attend, rather than districtwide desegregation. Some members of minority groups, particularly militant blacks, are not sure that integration of schools, even if feasible, would be desirable if schools were still committed to perpetuating middle-class, white culture. Some opportunists see black control of black schools as less a struggle for educational reform than a struggle for political power. Some regard the doctrine of black power as the only realistic way blacks can achieve high-quality education relevant to them and the only way they can eventually "connect" or integrate with the white society in a position of parity rather than of disadvantage. Christopher Jencks, a Harvard educator, recommends that public support be given to help

[7] For further description of the segregation academies, see Reese Cleghorn, "The Old South Tries Again," *Saturday Review*, vol. 53, pp. 76-77, 88-90, May 16, 1970.

[8] For further descriptions of the controversy over this legislation, see Richard K. Scher, "Decentralization and the New York State Legislature," *Urban Review*, vol. 4, pp. 13-19, September, 1969.

black nationalists create their own private schools after the fashion of Catholic parochial schools.[9]

Apart from the racial issues, highly centralized urban school systems, we are told, manifest the dysfunctions usually associated with bureaucratic organizations: unresponsiveness to needed reforms, unnecessary constraint of behavior and opportunity, inflexibility and inability to adapt to variations in educational need among different neighborhoods of the city, lack of accountability of school authorities to the wishes of the people, discrimination against minorities, and a generally closed system. Others reject this view. A plethora of widely read books have described these circumstances, including Kaufman's *Up the Down Staircase*, Kozol's *Death at an Early Age*, Silberman's *Crisis in the Classroom*, Hentoff's *Our Children Are Dying*, Herndon's *The Way It Spozed to Be*, and Haskins' *Diary of a Harlem School Teacher*.

Ghetto citizens, we are told, are asking for only the same educational rights that nonurban citizens have always enjoyed: the right to participate in making decisions about their children's education, the right to help set educational priorities, and the right to help develop programs and evaluate them. These are the rights that suburban parents enjoy, largely because they live in smaller school districts less encumbered by bureaucracy. However, unlike suburban systems, some citizens of the urban ghetto have demanded the right to select principals, to approve teachers for tenure or transfer, or in other ways to interfere with the professional prerogatives typically reserved for administrators and boards.

Some people despair of ever integrating society if blacks insist upon separatism in the schools. Some argue that the decentralization of control will perpetuate balkanization of society. City boards of education and administrative authorities often view decentralization as invasion of their powers and point to the ward politics, corruption, and inefficiency which resulted generations ago when city schools were highly decentralized. Some fear that lay persons will replace professionals in decision making, that valuable wisdom and experience will be unheeded, and children's education will be weakened. The counterargument is that schools in the inner city are now failing their students anyway and that changes are worth trying.

Perhaps the most formidable collision of powers is found between "teacher power" and "black power." Teachers have gained victories at the bargaining table with a single city board of education, victories that include increased control over assignment, transfer, tenure, salaries, and other working conditions as well as a greater role in educational decision making generally. When community control of local schools is granted and semiautonomous boards of education are created, the organized teachers see the despair of trying to negotiate with many boards rather than one, as well as the invasion of their professional rights by lay persons. In a sense, the conflict is between professional rights and laymen's rights in decision making in education. This struggle, although not new on the educational scene, is often intensified in the inner city because of greater militancy by both teachers and minority groups in the urban areas. Indeed, the type of conflict in the Ocean Hill–Brownsville district in New York City, in which the United Federation of Teachers and black citizens collided over the transfer of teachers out of the schools, and which precipitated a lengthy strike, may become endemic in many cities.[10] We believe that this type of conflict between organized teachers' groups and organized minority groups will become more commonplace. If the result is a stronger alliance of parents and teachers in improving educational opportunity for more city children, it should be applauded. On the other hand, it would be alarming if the self-interests of teachers preempted considerations of student welfare.

In understanding the problem, it is essential to distinguish between decentralization and community control, which may or may not be related. Decentralization is understood to mean that important decision-making prerogatives and management authority are delegated to local schools or clusters of schools rather than residing in the board of education and central administrative offices. If delegation is made to the administrative officers and faculties of the schools, no factor of community control is introduced. If authority is delegated to lay citizens in large measure, then community control results. Thus it is possible in large cities to have decentralization of administrative control without community control, but the converse is not possible. Much difficulty arises over what kinds of decisions might better be made by laymen and what kinds by professionals. This delineation of prerogatives must be

[9]Christopher Jencks, "Private Schools for Black Children," *New York Times Magazine*, pp. 30, 132-136, Nov. 3, 1968.

[10]For further discussion of this controversy, see Martin Mayer, *The Teachers Strike—New York, 1968*, New York: Harper and Row, Publishers, Incorporated, 1969.

made carefully. In any case, few enlightened educators would disagree with the idea that in most school systems citizens should have far greater opportunity than they now have to advise authorities on school matters. Reasonable people will continue to disagree, however, as they always have, over how much actual control should be delegated to lay persons.

Some opponents of decentralization fear that it will result in several dozen bureaucracies rather than one. In some cases local community control has resulted without much increase in the involvement of parents. Some insist that decentralization and community control will simply transfer to the local boards the bankruptcy of funds and expertise which formerly rested in the central office. Some urban school authorities believe that decentralization and community control will raise citizens' expectations but will eventually fail unless the more compelling problems of poverty, which appears to be the primary cause of learning difficulties for ghetto children, are relieved.

It is hoped that some form of increased participation of ghetto citizens in public education will give to parents a better grasp on the destiny of their children, and to teachers a more wholesome understanding with the community and possibly new allies in the quest for the improvement of education, and to children a school system that is more responsive to their needs and more positive in its expectations of them.[11] John Dewey posed the challenge well: "What the best and wisest parent desires for his own child, that must the community want for all its children. Any other ideal is narrow and unlovely; acted upon, it will destroy democracy."

Will the Reorganization of Cities and Surrounding Municipalities into Metropolitan Units of Government Improve Urban Education? It is increasingly advocated that city governments be merged with governments of surrounding suburbs to create a single metropolitan authority for the governance of schools as well as other functions of public administration. Among other advantages,

[11] For further discussion of the issues of decentralization and community control, see Eli Ginzberg, "The Reform of Urban Schools: Illusion or Reality?" *Phi Delta Kappan,* vol. 52, pp. 176–179, November, 1970; Delbert K. Clear, "Decentralization: Issues and Comments," *Clearing House,* vol. 44, pp. 259–267, January, 1970; Arthur E. Salz, "Formula for Inevitable Conflict: Local Control vs. Professionalism," *Phi Delta Kappan,* vol. 50, pp. 332–334, February, 1969; Warner Bloomberg and John Kincaid, "Parent Participation: Practical Policy or Another Panacea?" *Urban Review,* vol. 2, pp. 5–11, June, 1968.

this would broaden the tax base and equalize the fiscal advantage and disadvantage now incumbent upon the suburbs and the inner city, respectively. It would also permit, through busing, a better racial balance in the schools than is possible when the city schools are largely black and the surrounding suburban schools largely white. Obviously many residents of the suburbs would not see these as advantages. Political power is deeply entrenched in the metropolitan municipalities, and major changes toward metropolitanism are likely to be vigorously resisted. Many observers, like Robert Bendiner in his *Politics of Schools,* would regard metropolitan organization of schools as in the general best interests of society but very difficult to accomplish because of the political and social realities of our times.

How Much Integration of the Schools Is Possible and Desirable? The terms "desegregation" and "integration" hold different meanings for many people. Desegregation may be achieved by eliminating dual public school systems for whites and blacks and by not barring access to any school on the basis of race. This, as we have seen, may or may not bring about the kind of integration in which whites and blacks in substantial numbers attend the same classes. The courts have struck down the legal defenses of segregation but have not accomplished integration across the country. Integration is an elusive and difficult accomplishment. Many crucial questions are involved. How much mixing of white and black students is necessary to achieve integration? Must there be a racial balance in every school in the district, or can predominantly black schools be permitted in predominantly black neighborhoods? Is massive two-way busing of both black and white students within a district required to overcome *de facto* segregation resulting from segregated housing patterns? These and other issues have been contested widely and sometimes bitterly, with school authorities caught in the middle. Figure 1-2 shows various plans for reducing segregation in schools.

Some school districts have been required by the courts not only to end racial discrimination in school admissions but to bus white students from white neighborhoods to schools in black neighborhoods and black students in the other direction in order to achieve a balanced racial mix in all schools. As we have already noted, the Supreme Court has upheld the constitutionality of busing for this purpose. In some school districts this requires enormous fleets of buses and encounters resistance

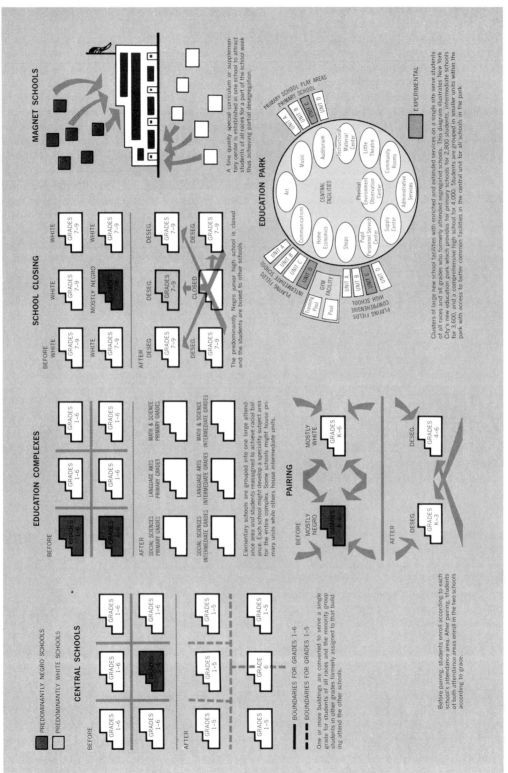

FIGURE 1-2 *Various plans for achieving school desegregation. (Adapted from U.S. Commission on Civil Rights, Schools Can Be Desegregated, The Commission, Washington, D.C., 1967, pp. 4-10.)*

from both black and white parents. A Gallup poll revealed that parents oppose forced busing of students by an 8 to 1 margin. Ninety percent of the school superintendents oppose widespread busing of students, perhaps because they feel that the enormous cost of this operation could be spent with better results on the educational program. They may also view with alarm the accelerated exodus of white persons from the districts, which often follows this tactic. Many have become discouraged over the prospects of trying to stabilize the schools racially. John Letson, superintendent of schools in Atlanta, concluded, "We're beyond the point of being concerned about race. From now on we're going to be concerned with the quality of education for all children."

On the other hand, a fair degree of racial balance has been achieved in many school districts across the country, particularly in districts without major concentrations of black students. With the help of citizens' groups, both black and white, many school boards and administrators have moved forth courageously and wisely with plans for school integration. Sacramento and Berkeley, California; Evanston, Illinois; Rochester and White Plains, New York; Hartford, Connecticut; and Seattle, Washington, are especially noteworthy for the statesmanship of their superintendents and boards of education in working toward the integration of their schools. Massachusetts became the first state to enact legislation implementing the principle of desegregation in a statute which threatened the withholding of state financial aid to any district which contained a school whose enrollment was more than 50 percent nonwhite. Other states established various commissions to monitor the progress of schools and to spur on the laggards.

Nevertheless, the actual integration of all schools across the land on any significant scale is enormously difficult and appears to create about as many problems as it purports to solve. Forced integration arouses intense political considerations serious enough to become major issues in national elections. Stephen K. Bailey, an authority on the politics of school organization, concluded sadly that "compulsory desegregation has proved as tactically bankrupt as it continues to be morally and constitutionally correct." As the Kerner Commission concluded, the schools in general appear to be traveling the same road as the rest of society, toward two nations divisible by race, separate and unequal, rather than toward one nation indivisible.

When whites reject and isolate blacks in the

school system, it is quite understandable that blacks would want to control what they are left with. Some of the more disenchanted blacks have abandoned integration of schools and society as a goal in the present times. Malcolm X, for example, declared that "desegregation as a concept is irrelevant. Every time we desegregate with the white man, we lose. Equality is what we're after." And so the black-power advocates have abandoned the fight for integration and argue instead for black control of schools in black communities. Some people speak of this as separatism and disparage it, while others regard it as no different from the whites' advocacy of "freedom of choice." However, as noted earlier, the vast majority of black persons have not abandoned the ideal of integration. Roy Wilkins, executive director of the NAACP, for example, rejects black separatism in school organization:

The separatism called for by a highly vocal minority of Negro-Americans will harm the multiracial, pluralistic society America is seeking to perfect. It is certain to isolate black population, to the joy of the white segregationist. With its unconcealed aspects of racial hatred, violence, especially its predilection for paramilitary strutting and boasts, it could foreshadow a tragedy in human relations comparable in concept, if smaller in scope, to the hateful Hitler dictatorship.[12]

The authors agree with Wilkins, as do the majority of the American people both black and white. There is no future in separatism, even on the strategy of withdrawing temporarily to gain strength in the struggle for integration. We believe that, in balance, the prospects for integration of our schools throughout most of the country are still more hopeful than discouraging, although progress is slower than we would like. All the evidence suggests that the people, both black and white, who are most favorably disposed toward the integration of society and most effective in their race relations are those who have had experience in interracial groups. Separatism will not increase the number of future adults who have had this interracial experience; integration will. The American people cannot isolate themselves from the injustices which they have imposed upon members of minority groups. The distinguished educator Ernest Melby has prophesied that "the Negro is going to save American civilization because

[12] Roy Wilkins in "Black Leaders Speak Out on Black Education," *Today's Education*, vol. 58, p. 32, October, 1969.

he is going to force you and me to face up to our heritage."

In this discussion, we have dealt largely with the political and organizational aspects of school integration. Later in this chapter and in Chapter 11, we speak at greater length of the educational aspects of the school integration problems and challenges.

What Is the Future of Catholic Schools? Several recent studies of the Roman Catholic school system in this country have focused attention on the problems that these schools face. A report by the National Catholic Education Association, *What Is Happening to Catholic Education?*, concluded that it is improbable that the Catholic Church in this country will ever be able to accomplish its ideal of "every Catholic child in a Catholic school." As noted in Chapter 5, Catholic schools have had difficulty keeping up with rising costs. Although Catholic school enrollments increased by 80 percent between 1960 and 1968, they have been declining in the early 1970s. Two studies, *The Education of American Catholics* and *Catholic Schools in Action*, report that a high proportion of Catholic schools operate with classes larger than would be tolerated in most public schools and that their lay teachers are underpaid and generally less well prepared than public school teachers. In some communities, parochial schools have become unwitting handmaidens in school resegregation. In New York City, black students constitute half of the public school enrollment but only 6 percent of the private school enrollment. In Philadelphia, Negro enrollment is 59 percent in the public schools and 10 percent in the parochial schools. This condition is circumstantial and not the result of any deliberate attempt by parochial schools to hinder school integration.

According to the studies cited above, the academic achievement of parochial school students exceeds the national norms, which may be explained in part by the practice of selective admissions in many Catholic schools. *Catholic Schools in Action* revealed no evidence that Catholic schools were "divisive." In another study of pupils' social standards, skills, and conduct, reported in his book *The Parochial School*, Fichter found that public and parochial school students are practically identical in their standards of conduct and that children in both

schools accept and demonstrate in about the same proportions traits of honesty, obedience, gratitude, self-control, and kindliness. On the other hand, the book reported that public school students consistently show themselves more socially alert than parochial school students and that a larger proportion of public school graduates increase their interest in religious issues after graduation.

These considerations have prompted several writers to consider whether the religious benefits derived from parochial schools are worth the high cost of maintaining them. *Catholic Schools in Action* concludes that maintaining parochial schools is not necessary for the survival of American Catholicism.

Father McCluskey, one of the authors of *What Is Happening to Catholic Education?*, believes that Catholic education will have to make serious choices. He believes that in some instances the Catholic Church should close down many second-rate four-year colleges and utilize its resources for more and better parochial high schools and junior colleges, and that, in other instances, shared-time arrangements should be worked out with public schools. The Confraternity of Christian Doctrine, which has charge of the religious education of Catholics attending public schools, is building, instead of parochial schools, special schools near public schools to handle only religious instruction on a released-time basis for Catholic students in the public schools. Some Catholic educators believe that this arrangement permits the best opportunity for the Roman Catholic Church to use its limited resources to advantage.

The United States Supreme Court in 1971 ruled that public funds could not be used for general operating expenses of private schools. This decision prompted the closing of many church-related schools and the merger of others. Some Catholic schools in the more affluent parishes continue as before, while others have curtailed their programs to include only part-time instruction in religious education.

AREAS OF EDUCATION (PART 3)

Our free public education system began with elementary schools. Secondary schools became a part of free public education much later, after considerable struggle. Colleges and universities—some public and some private but few free—began to become more open to all students in the second half of the present century. The last two sectors at the ends of the lifelong continuum of learning, pre-elementary education and adult education—perhaps the most important parts of all—are still fragmentary and underdeveloped. They are certainly not yet free and open to all. We shall consider the issues involved in these areas of education which, in the ultimate, constitute an unbroken continuum of education throughout life.

Pre-elementary Education (Chapter 6)

Although kindergartens have been fairly numerous for years, prekindergarten education, until recently, has been available only to those who could afford the tuition of private nursery schools. As noted in Chapter 6, the nation's concern for underprivileged children has led to the recognition of the importance of the nursery school. The programs commonly known as Head Start seek to enrich the backgrounds of slum children and give them a "head start" when they reach the elementary school.

Are Early-childhood Education Programs Effective? It is difficult to answer this question categorically. One national study of Head Start programs concluded that these compensatory education programs had little effect on the academic progress of the children. Others discounted the study, maintaining that it was narrow and ill-conceived. Evidence from other sources suggested that federally funded programs for poor children had beneficial impact on their self-image, quickened their readiness for schooling, and strengthened their sense of security. Certainly these programs have done much to alert school authorities to the educational disadvantages of children from low-income families, quickened our research into and understanding of early-childhood education, and called attention to the very great importance of early-childhood education for all children. Seasoned experts in early-childhood education emphasize that the "crash" nature of the federally funded programs resulted in their being thrown together hastily and in their being frequently staffed by people, often parents, who knew little about teaching methods appropriate for young children. Certainly more careful planning, greater continuity of early-childhood programs from age 3 through age 9, and better research will help to make these programs more productive. The evidence is strong that the potential impact of early-childhood education is great even though it may not now be realized very

well through existing programs. One essential reform involves the formulation of more explicit objectives for this early-childhood education.

What Should Be the Nature of Pre-elementary Education Programs? Early-childhood school programs vary widely, and considerable disagreement arises over the virtues of various types of programs. Most such pre-elementary programs conducted by the public schools have been low-pressure, permissive programs that emphasize the child's socialization and emotional development. They tend to be rather unstructured, and they deliberately postpone formal instruction until kindergarten or first grade in the belief that children are not ready for formal instruction in reading and other subjects until they have acquired a mental age of six. These programs are disputed by some authorities who believe that reading readiness can be developed much earlier and that students' intellectual growth can be seriously stunted by delaying formal instruction. Advocates of this view prefer childhood education programs, such as the Montessorian method, which are highly structured approaches to self-instruction in which the child is free to progress at his own rate through a programmed sequence of cognitive tasks. The Montessorian method, which has recently enjoyed rising popularity in this country,[13] is described more fully in Chapter 6.

The Bereiter-Engelmann approach to early-childhood education, also described in Chapter 6, is an even more controversial departure from traditional early-childhood education. In this program, young children are drilled vigorously in cognitive tasks which would be confronted by much older children in more conventional schooling. Some educators have sounded strong warnings against this trend, cautioning that children can be harmed emotionally by discouragement resulting from tackling tasks for which they are not ready. Even though young children can acquire certain skills early, it is probable that they could manage the same skills with less effort and frustration later and that teaching could be more efficient if undertaken somewhat later. The problem revolves around the need to protect unready children from precocious learning while maintaining a school organization flexible

[13] For further discussion of the Montessorian method, see Kathy Ahlfeld, "The Montessori Revival: How Far Will It Go?" *Nation's Schools*, vol. 85, pp. 75–80, January, 1970.

enough to permit others, who are ready, to proceed.[14]

Should Pre-elementary Education Be Available for All Children? By the early 1970s, pre-elementary education was available to the children of well-to-do families who could afford the tuition of private nursery schools and to the children of low-income families who attended Head Start programs. Children of middle-income families were largely excluded. Some argued that there was no evidence that the favored children needed early education and that they profited very little from it. Rice believes that pre-elementary education for all children is both unnecessary and impractical. He feels that public schools lack the funds, the teachers, and the experience necessary for a universal program of nursery school education. He believes also that the school must not try to take the place of the home for most young children, but should rather seek to educate people better for parenthood.[15]

Several professional organizations have advanced trenchant argument for the extension of free, universal public education downward to all 4- and 5-year-olds.[16] Many authorities, as described in Chapter 6, would advocate the extension of education to even lower age groups. In balance, this would appear to be a sound development if it were properly conceived and if the overall welfare of children were carefully protected from unreasonable pressure. There is compelling evidence that the earliest experiences of childhood can have profound and irreversible effect upon intellectual growth throughout life. As shown in Chapter 6, one's achievement in life depends greatly upon his educative experiences prior to age 6, the point at which public education still begins for most children. We believe that the implications of this important discovery challenge the old doctrine that the public has no responsibility for the education of children below the age of 6 unless they are from homes of poverty. We regard the area of early-childhood education as the last great frontier of educational development which, if properly conceived and developed, can have profound benefit upon our entire educational system.

Elementary Education (Chapter 7)

How Can Reading Ability Be Improved? Reading is regarded as the prime means by which most learning is acquired and the means by which man acquires competence as a productive worker and a citizen. Yet, in the early 1970s, there were 3 million illiterate adults. Half of the unemployed youth were functionally illiterate and therefore virtually unemployable. Most juvenile offenders are greatly retarded in reading. Former U.S. Commissioner of Education James E. Allen, Jr., insisted that this failure was a matter of grave import and urged that improvement in reading instruction become the major educational objective for the 1970s. He urged that the right to read should become a reality for all, that no child should leave school without acquiring the skill and the desire to read to the full limit of his capacity. The National Reading Center and the National Reading Council were established in 1970 to marshal educational resources for this task.

For many years authorities have disagreed over the best method of teaching reading. Some have advocated the word-recognition, or "look-say," method. Others insist that reading should be learned through phonetic analysis of words. Others prefer newer approaches, such as the Initial Teaching Alphabet. These and other methods are described in Chapter 14. The best approach is probably through a combination of several methods. However this may be, the 1970s will probably witness substantial improvement in this central task of instruction.

Should Elementary Schools Be Ungraded? There has been a trend recently away from the graded school organization, particularly at the primary levels. The disadvantages of graded organization are fairly apparent: the unrealistic assumption that all students should master the same material in the same period of time and that all students will repeat either all or none of the material, depending on whether or not they are promoted. Neither retardation nor acceleration within the graded organization

[14] Maya Pines' book, *Revolution in Learning: The Years from Birth to Six*, Harper & Row, Publishers, Incorporated, New York, 1968, presents a well-written description of the wide variety of pre-elementary school programs, with a fair analysis of their advantages and limitations.

[15] Arthur H. Rice, "Let's Not Force Preschool Programs on Everybody," *Nation's Schools*, vol. 78, pp. 10, 12, September, 1966.

[16] Educational Policies Commission, *Universal Opportunity for Early Childhood Education*, National Education Association, Washington, D.C., 1966.

has satisfactorily accommodated individual differences.

Nongraded or ungraded schools are those in which traditional grade lines have been eliminated for a sequence of several years and in which pupils are permitted to move in a multitracked program at their own best pace. The nongraded school, or "continuous-progress plan," as it is sometimes called, is described more fully in Chapter 7.

Secondary Education (Chapter 8)

Although many of the issues and trends in the elementary field apply also to secondary education, the latter has certain unique problems. Some issues in secondary education also arise in higher education.

For many decades this nation has sought to provide secondary education for all American youth. As noted in Chapter 8, the proportion of high school youth has risen steadily until today, when nine out of ten young people of high school age are enrolled.

What Should Be the Nature of Secondary Education? It is argued by some that by opening secondary education to all, we have debased the quality of our high schools and thereby disadvantaged the abler students. Some of the fundamentalist reformers, such as Max Rafferty, James Conant, Arthur Bestor, and Hyman Rickover, have urged the creation of rigid and rigorous high school curriculums, the enforcement of high academic standards, and the rerouting of less able students into nonacademic or vocational education. But this elitist view of secondary education is incompatible with the egalitarianism of the civil rights movement. The reforms which they advocate are antithetical to both the youth culture and the more humanistic educational climate advocated by the romantic critics of education, such as Charles Silberman, Paul Goodman, John Holt, and George Dennison. These reformers advocate that secondary education become much less structured, that students be given more opportunity to write their own educational prescriptions, and that the school environment be humanized. Some critics have given up on the public high school. As noted later in this chapter and in Chapter 16, some people are advocating that vouchers be given to parents to permit them to send their children to private schools if they wish, thereby stimulating competition and variety and making all secondary schools better accountable to the public's expectations. As described in Chapter 8, a variety

of unorthodox secondary schools are appearing—schools without walls, street academies, and others, many of them variations of the Summerhill model.

One critic, Paul Goodman, has even advocated the abandonment of high schools. He reasons that schools alienate, corrupt, and exploit youth. He believes that most school disorders are like prison riots in that most of the students, like prisoners, don't want to be where they are. He believes that most students would learn more through incidental learning in community activities. Although we share some of Goodman's discomfort about secondary education (this is discussed at length in Chapter 8), we consider the comprehensive high school to be both essential and salvageable. We share John Gardner's superb conception of the comprehensive high school:

The comprehensive high school is a peculiarly American phenomenon. It is called comprehensive because it offers, under one administration and under one roof (or series of roofs), secondary education for almost all the high school age children of one town or neighborhood. It is responsible for educating the boy who will be an atomic scientist and the girl who will marry at eighteen; the prospective captain of a ship and the future captain of industry. It is responsible for educating the bright and the not so bright children with different vocational and professional ambitions and with various motivations. It is responsible, in sum, for providing good and appropriate education, both academic and vocational, for all young people within a democratic environment which the American people believe serves the principles they cherish.[17]

Clearly there need be no forced choice between quality and quantity of secondary education. Our society has the ability and the obligation to educate everyone up to the level of his ability without sacrificing excellence in education.

How Serious Is the Disadvantage of the Small High School? The primary problem in improving secondary education in many states is the elimination of the small high school through school-district reorganization. Less than one-fourth of the nation's public high schools are large enough to provide the breadth of curriculum, size and quality of staff, and scope of facilities adequate for a modern secondary education. However, those which are large enough

[17] John W. Gardner, "Foreword," in James B. Conant, *The American High School Today*, McGraw-Hill Book Company, New York, 1959.

enroll over two-thirds of all high school students in the country. Obviously the three-fourths of the high schools which are too small, even though they serve less than one-third of the total youth in secondary school, nevertheless present a real obstacle to the improvement of high school education. Although further progress in district reorganization will continue to reduce the number of these schools somewhat, many of them are destined to remain for the foreseeable future. In sparsely settled and mountainous regions of the country, it is difficult to consolidate the schools. There are hundreds of isolated villages which must continue to operate small high schools and somehow improve them.

Higher Education (Chapter 9)

As higher education moves toward greater democratization, it faces many of the same problems that confronted secondary education in its similar move in the past. Should all who wish to attend college be permitted to do so regardless of academic or financial means? Will opening the doors of college to all debase the quality of higher education? What adjustments will be necessary to accommodate students with inferior educational backgrounds? Will the presence of many students of marginal ability intensify student protest and disruption? How will we meet the costs of this rapid expansion of higher education? What are the fundamental purposes of higher education? These and other questions trigger spirited debate wherever college officials, students, and legislators congregate. We turn our attention to some of them here.

Should Higher Education Be for Everybody? Figure 1-3 shows the steady rise in the percentage of youths attending college. Nevertheless several injustices remain. Children of high-income families are five times as likely to enter college as are children of low-income families. Although the number of black college students is increasing, by 1972 only 7 percent of college student bodies were black as compared with 12 percent of blacks among the college-age group. Clearly race, family income, geographical location, and additional factors other than academic ability are constraining the educational opportunity of our young people. "Open admission" has become a battle cry among the social reformers, while others see it as a plot to destroy the quality

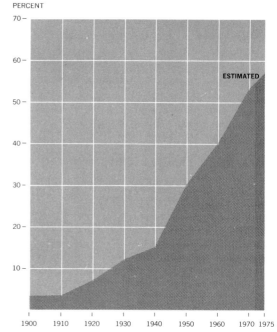

FIGURE 1-3 *College enrollments as a percentage of population 18 to 21 years of age.*

of higher education. Some put the question more adroitly: Could higher education be both universal and excellent?

The Carnegie Commission on Higher Education recommended in its report in 1970 that by 1976—the nation's two-hundredth anniversary—all financial barriers should be removed from college gates. It called for "open access" to public systems of higher education, but not necessarily to each institution, for any high school graduate regardless of his academic record. The report carefully distinguished between universal higher education for all students, which it opposed, and open access to most public institutions for those who wished to attend, which it favored. Some viewed this as the last great step in removing racial and economic injustice. The late Whitney Young, Jr., as head of the NAACP, called for a "firm national higher education policy based on college admissions for any high school graduate who desires it, with full scholarships available to low-income students, and ultimately a policy of free higher education for all."

The concept of open admission to higher education is not new. Many state universities, particularly in the Midwest, have been open to any high school graduate in the past, although most of the less able students soon dropped out or flunked out in the "revolving door" stream, as it was called. California for more than two decades has promised college admission for all high school graduates to the state's vast network of university centers, state colleges, and two-year community colleges. In 1970 the giant City University of New York became the first municipal institution to open its doors to all high school graduates. Since tuition is free at this university, both academic and economic barriers were absent. Meanwhile Governor Rockefeller had proposed open admission on a statewide basis to all high school graduates for the university system of the State of New York. In New York, resources were provided to help the severely underprepared to fill the gaps of their previous education so that they could succeed in college and not get caught in the "revolving door"—in one year and out the next. In many other states community colleges are helping to make higher education more available to all high school graduates.

Not everyone applauded this move toward open admission in higher education. Some felt that throwing open the doors meant that academic standards would have to be lowered and that better students would be driven away to institutions which did not practice open admission. Some called attention to the high number of students already in college who did not want to be there and who were involuntary students only because of parental pressure or a desire to evade work or military service. These opponents contended that the presence of these marginal students rejected the accepted norms and purposes of the colleges, created anti-intellectual pressures, and in some cases threatened the disintegration of colleges.

We believe that open admissions will affect our system of higher education profoundly. We believe that there is no essential contradiction between the expansion of opportunity in higher education to all who wish to attend and the maintenance of excellence in our institutions as long as certain cautions are exercised. These include the exclusion of some institutions of extraordinary excellence from the open admissions policy, counseling programs to help students choose institutions whose programs and admissions policies are most compatible with their needs, very substantial modification of curriculums and instructional methodology appropriate for students of modest academic ability, delay of admission to college for youths who need work or service in the community to acquire the maturity necessary

for success in college, and the expansion of community colleges and technical schools to meet the needs of students who cannot succeed in four-year colleges. All this of course requires far better financing of our system of higher education.

How Should Colleges Respond to Student Unrest?
In the early 1960s professors complained of a generation of college students who were apathetic about social issues, more interested in panty raids than in women's liberation, more interested in finding economic security and social acceptance than in rectifying social injustice. But suddenly and without warning there appeared a new generation of college students in the mid-1960s who rejected the traditional isolation of the campus and the disengagement of the university from the troubled world, and who accepted, even demanded, for itself a measure of responsibility for the university and the world—for life as well as for education. Many people saw the student revolt as the distress of a generation of youth with adult indifference to humanity. Others saw it as the revolt of an uncivilized minority of students who didn't belong in college in the first place. However that may be, we shall discuss the causes and the morality of student activism at length later in this chapter and in Chapter 11. Here we shall confine the discussion to the responses which colleges and universities may make that may help to ameliorate the legitimate causes of student unrest.

Bruno Bettelheim believes that much of the student discontent arises from an extravagantly protracted adolescence. If so, this would suggest that the educational continuum should be shortened, perhaps to three years (as is common abroad), permitting students to complete undergraduate studies at an earlier age. Year-round academic schedules in high school and college would then make sense. On the other hand, some insist that student unrest is a product of adolescent immaturity. If this is the cause, it would suggest that young people might well engage in some kind of employment, work-study program, or community service, such as the Peace Corps, for a year or more before entering college.

Henry Steele Commager, the noted historian, cautions against the proliferation of courses in college resulting from misguided student demands. This development, if not curbed in the smaller colleges, can bankrupt them academically. Commager believes that most colleges attempt to teach too many courses, many of which could be eliminated through the use of independent study or mini-courses. Commager also warns against capitulating to the students' demand for "relevance" as undergraduates commonly understand the term.

Almost the whole of our society and economy—and, alas, much of our educational enterprise—is engaged in a kind of conspiracy to persuade the young that nothing is really relevant unless it happened yesterday, and unless it can be reported in the newspaper and filmed by television. . . . It is not the business of the university to be relevant. . . . What the college can do . . . is to provide a place, a time, an atmosphere in which the young can find out what is relevant to them.[18]

There is a general feeling that the traditional survey courses, or general culture courses, are in serious need of revision if students are to be rescued from boredom. Some reformers even suggest the complete abandonment of required courses to permit students the freedom to elect courses of their choice. Although this stratagem has much to recommend it in terms of pleasing the students, it practically abandons hope of providing all students with a broad, general education. This issue poses familiar questions of balance in the curriculum and of the appropriate mix of general and professional or vocational education. It is pertinent to note that most of the discontent has been manifested among students majoring in the humanities and the social sciences, while students preparing for professions are not commonly discontented with their education. Whether the former are restive because their career goals are less secure or because the social studies and humanities attract students with keener social awareness and sensitivity has not been established. These dilemmas relative to the curriculum in higher education are pursued at greater length in Chapters 9 and 14.

Perhaps the greatest college reforms resulting from student discontent are to be found in the management of student affairs. Almost overnight, most colleges have abandoned the old concept of *in loco parentis* and have given students heretofore unheard-of freedom with respect to curfew hours, coeducational dormitories, visiting hours in fraternity houses and dormitories, and other social affairs.

Substantial student autonomy in nonacademic affairs is now commonplace, often to the consternation of old alumni and parents who never expected to find contraceptive clinics or crash pads in Old Main. Although this relaxation of parietal rules is new to this country, it is quite old abroad. Many colleges are now doing a far better job of listening to students through rap sessions, encounter groups, counselors, and ombudsmen. Very often this intensified communication helps to relieve incipient discontent through response to legitimate student complaints before they prompt unruly protest. It also helps students understand the reasons behind administrative actions. In academic affairs too the voice of students is receiving more attention. The appropriate role of students in university governance is commonly contested. Some students press for student participation in the general government of the university. Although university administration should seek the counsel of student representation, particularly on matters relating to student affairs, it is unwise to regard the university as a political democracy. As the distinguished philosopher Sidney Hook points out, the democratic process and the educative process are too frequently confused.

The university is not a political community. Its business is not government but primarily the discovery, publication, and teaching of the truth. Its authority is based not on numbers or the rule of the majority but on knowledge. Although it can be organized in a spirit of democracy, it cannot be organized on the principle of one man, one vote. . . . The responsibility for decision cannot be shared equally without equating inexperience with experience, ignorance with expertise, childishness with maturity. The assumption of a political democracy is that there are no experts in wisdom, that each citizen's vote is as good as any other's.[19]

This view, although most common among university administrators, is not shared by all educators. Harold Taylor, former president of Sarah Lawrence College, for example, would urge that students be given substantial opportunity to participate in the making of university policy as an essential part of the educative process. Some schools—Antioch College, for example—function on this principle.[20] This issue is discussed at greater length in Chapter 11.

---

[18] Henry Steele Commager, "Has the Small College a Future?" *Saturday Review*, vol. 53, p. 88, Feb. 21, 1970.

[19] Sidney Hook, "The War against the Democratic Process," *Atlantic*, vol. 223, p. 47, February, 1969.

[20] For an interesting exchange of views on the role of students in university affairs, see Harold Taylor, "The Student Revolution," and Sidney Hook, "The Architecture of Chaos," *Phi Delta Kappan*, vol. 51, pp. 62–67, October, 1969.

It is important that colleges and universities, as an essential part of the educative process, help students acquire a sense of good citizenship in their protest, a sense of citizenship that has been lost among many of the campus radicals. Students must learn to realize that violence is usually unproductive of the reforms sought. As a *New York Times* editorial noted, "Every worthy objective which the mass of student rebels favor . . . has been harmed rather than helped by student unrest." Protests that deprive others of their freedoms are incompatible with the nature and high purpose of educational institutions. There is no such thing as virtuous violence, because violence begets violence and the good that was sought becomes indistinguishable from the evil to be destroyed. As the ancient Stoic philosophers concluded, "Violence is the last refuge of the incompetents."

Students must be helped to realize that, as William Pitt phrased it, "where law ends, Tyranny begins." Although order is possible without justice, justice is impossible without order. Civil disobedience is justifiable, as Gandhi and Martin Luther King demonstrated, to change unjust laws but never to abolish the rule of law. President Nixon has warned that "in a free society, the rights of none are secure unless the rights of all are respected." Students are often understandably impatient with the imperfections of democratic society and are sometimes tempted to abandon its hallowed values for a more direct and powerful assault on the injustices which still persist. However, as Winston Churchill observed, "Democracy is the worst system of government—except for all the others."

After having helped students refine their sense of citizenship, universities, frail institutions at best, must deal forthrightly with protesters who invade the freedom of others and who invoke undemocratic means for achieving their ends. Many mistakes were made in the early days of student confrontations by some university administrators who capitulated to unreasonable demands. Fortunately most university administrators have come to realize that violent student action must be repressed with the least possible force necessary. With full recognition of this necessity, we nevertheless agree with the position of the American Association of University Professors that student discontent can only be made worse by vengeful reprisals, excessive punishment, repressive legislation, and punitive reduction of public financing that penalizes all students alike. Most students are now learning that violence is self-defeating and are dissenting more peacefully.

What Should Be the Purposes of Higher Education? As stated in Chapter 9, the three traditional purposes of colleges and universities have been instruction, research, and service. The first two are universal; the third is uniquely American. The first two purposes are commonly accepted, although questions remain concerning relative emphasis and implementation of them.

College students frequently complain that professors publish while their students perish. Professors sometimes comment, perhaps not entirely facetiously, that universities would be great places if it were not for the students. Do research and service divert limited talent, energy, and money from the primary function of teaching? Is teaching indeed the primary function? Is it superseded by the need to generate new knowledge? Could the dissemination of knowledge be discharged more effectively through the mass media of instruction and computer-assisted instructional programs, freeing the scholar-professor to inquire rather than to lecture? Should professors be rewarded by promotion and salary for their teaching or their scholarly research? Obviously these are questions of priority which have been neither well defined nor resolved.

The anguish of this kind of questioning is felt when underclassmen are instructed by graduate students while the professor assigned to the course is in his laboratory or in Washington seeking a grant, when an assistant professor who has concentrated on his teaching rather than his publication fails to get promoted, or when a professor's fund of knowledge is exhausted by his failure to keep up his scholarly work.

Perhaps the greatest controversy rages over the place of the service function in the university. This function is largely absent from most universities abroad. The public-service function probably had its greatest impetus in this country in the land-grant colleges. With their strong emphasis upon the improvement of agriculture and the mechanical arts, they set a contagious precedent of important but not necessarily scholarly public service. Most universities today find themselves engaged in a wide array of nonscholarly public services, such as preparing teacher aides, providing recreational courses for adults in schools of general studies, improving grain production in Afghanistan, conducting school surveys, helping to select superintendents of schools, developing more effective weapons of war—the list goes on and on. Although these may be important enterprises, they are not necessarily the most prudent tasks for institutions of higher learning with limited resources. They may distract students and faculty from more vital tasks more uniquely germane to the university. As Jacques Barzun complains in his book *The American University: How It Runs, Where It Is Going*, the American university has become "a service station to every conceivable interest and agency in society—an institution which has forsaken its true role and wandered far afield from 'the idea of a university.'" Robert Hutchins, former president of the University of Chicago and president of the Center for the Study of Democratic Institutions, notes that "in no other country in the world is the university the cannibal that it is in the United States." He points out that whatever the society wants, the university will do, provided it gets the money to pay for it. Maybe we lose something in the process; maybe we lose the university. Hutchins believes that the greatest service the university can render, the one the nation needs most, the one which cannot be rendered by a service station, the one which only the university can provide, is intellectual leadership. While the university should be fashioning the mind of the age, the demands of the age are instead fashioning the mind, according to Hutchins.

How Will the Rising Costs of Higher Education Be Met? Many colleges, both public and private, are in a state of severe financial crisis. Part of the problem derives from their inefficient use of human and physical resources, which are idle during long vacation periods. Inefficient instructional methods are common. Even when allowance is made for the business management reforms that could be effected, the problem of rising costs remains.

Although tuition has quadrupled in the last quarter-century, it still produces only one-fifth of the revenue of most institutions. The tuition burden has become especially heavy at private colleges. How can able youth of modest financial means keep up with these skyrocketing fees? Will more and more choose public institutions where the tuition is lower? If so, what does this portend for the future of the private colleges? Will an increasing share of the cost be borne by public funds? Some people oppose increased public subsidies, contending that those who go to college should pay the costs, that it is unfair to tax everyone for the privilege of the

few. Yet this nation has done just that for elementary and secondary school education. Everyone is taxed to help support the public schools, whether or not his children attend. Apparently the nation has reached a point where higher education is as important and universal as secondary school education was a generation or so ago. If educated manpower is our scarcest and most productive resource, should it not be subsidized by public money? Many believe that it must and that government subsidy will continue to be increased at both the federal and state levels.

Adult and Continuing Education (Chapter 10)

Can Adult Education Help Man Reach His Full Potential? The charts reproduced in Figure 1-4 reveal results yielded by a decade of research based upon observations of human physical and intellectual behavior.[21] The upper lines reveal man's potential of physical and mental growth; the lower lines reveal his more usual performance. The difference between the "success" curves and the "failure" curves represents a tremendous loss to society in productivity and human happiness. Joseph Still, who reported the data illustrated in these charts, asks:

Why do so many fail to achieve their physical and mental potentials? It seems pretty clear that it is not because of poor heredity but because they fail to discover that they are able, if they choose, to make more of their lives. How to prevent these failures constitutes one of the great unsolved questions facing our society today. As a starter, everyone should say: "If I want respect as a human being I have the obligation to respect and care for and develop my body and mind." This is the basic philosophy for successful living—and for a successful society.[22]

Clement Martin, in his book *How to Live to Be 100*, argues with cogency that man's "natural" life expectancy would be 100 to 125 years, rather than his present 70 years, if he cared for himself as we now know he should. Dr. Martin believes that the secrets to increased life expectancy lie in (1) improved physical fitness through better diet, exercise, recreation, rest, and medical care and (2) improved mental activity. He notes that ". . . in studying peo-

[21] Joseph W. Still, "Man's Potential and His Performance," *New York Times Magazine*, p. 37, Nov. 24, 1957. © 1957 by the New York Times Company. Reprinted by permission.
[22] *Ibid.*

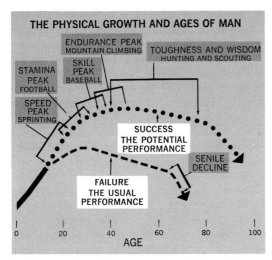
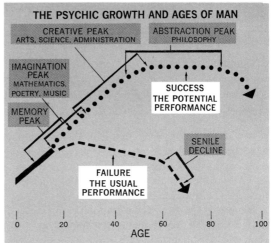

FIGURE 1-4 Man: his potential and his performance. The upper lines indicate the physical and psychological potentials of normal people, with peak periods for various activities; the lower lines indicate how most people fail to measure up. (© 1957 by The New York Times Company. Reprinted by permission.)

ple who are ninety and more—successful agers—one common possession among them stands out. These individuals from various nations and all walks of life share a common mental outlook; an ability to apply, in life, the best thoughts of the ages."[23]

Certainly adult education alone cannot bring man closer to his goal of a longer and healthier life. Health and safety education, medical care, proper diet, recreation, and many other factors are essential. But adult education does offer opportunity for more adults to "apply, in life, the best thoughts of the ages." Although an increasing number of adults are participating in some type of organized adult and continuing education, more than two-thirds of them are not. Imaginative, appealing, and inexpensive programs of adult education could help to keep alive a positive mental outlook, quicken adults' sense of purpose and meaning in life, and sustain the intellectual capital that permits one to live up to his full mental potential.

Clearly our present programs of adult and continuing education described in Chapter 10 fail to reach enough of our people. Although we take pride in our nation's low illiteracy rate, we cannot be complacent as long as 3 million American adults cannot read or write. Only a small fraction of these illiterate adults are going to school. We need to disabuse ourselves of the myth that schools are for children and youth, that one "completes" his educa-

tion upon graduation. We must come to view citizens of all ages as learners and put our educational system at their service. The cost in dollars, although large, will be small in comparison with the cost in human productivity lost, as shown in the difference between the "success" curves and the "failure" curves in Figure 1-4.

How Shall Adult and Continuing Education Be Financed, When Funds Are Insufficient for the Preceding Phases of Learning? Studies reveal that public adult education does not cost much (approximately 2 percent of the day-school expenditures), since it is largely on a part-time basis. In most cases regular taxes, plus small fees, furnish most of the receipts. But as adult education grows in scope, in enriched services, and in numbers involved, much more money will be needed. Support for adult education will have to come from public and private funds. The main source for the former obviously is taxes. There are many sources for the latter: personal fees, private donations, parochial funds, and contributions from industry and labor.

PERSONNEL IN EDUCATION (PART 4)

We turn now to a consideration of the issues that are endemic to the people of the educational enterprise—the students, the teachers, and the many other professional and nonprofessional school employees.

[23]Clement G. Martin, *How to Live to Be 100*, Frederick Fell, Inc., New York, 1963, p. 179.

Students (Chapter 11)

Students are the clientele of American education. They are what schools are all about. They come in all ages now that we regard education as a continuum starting with birth and lasting until senility or death. They come in a wide range of individual differences in intelligence, motivation, behavior, values, aspirations, and social class background. This characteristic of individual differences poses difficult problems for a system of mass education. In the United States, students constitute a far higher percentage of the total population than in any other country. This too poses some problems that are unique to our educational system, since our system does not reject in such large numbers those who do not do well in school. In Chapter 11 we discuss at length the mental, physical, social, and emotional growth of students and the major types of exceptional students. In a broader sense, concern for students is so ubiquitous to education that they are treated throughout all chapters of the book. We direct our attention now to some of the issues in education most directly related to the students.

What Are the Causes and Cures of Student Unrest? Student discontent with schools is probably as old as schools themselves. Its causes, its manifestations, and its intensity vary with time and circumstances. But during the past decade student unrest in our schools reached an intensity and a violence that prompted extraordinary concern. Beginning on the University of California's Berkeley campus in 1964, "the movement," as students speak of it, spread quickly to other colleges large and small throughout the country and indeed around the world. By the late 1960s, students in some high schools too were in revolt against the established order. Sit-ins, teach-ins, strikes, boycotts, and demonstrations became more common than house parties or panty raids on many campuses. By the early 1970s, student protest had become violent in some campuses, and burning buildings rather than pep-rally bonfires illuminated the evening skies. At many schools and colleges police and national guardsmen were called to restore order, and at Kent State University, Jackson State University, and other universities and high schools, lives were lost in tragic and senseless brutality. The wide coverage of these events by the news media and the plethora

of articles and books on the subject sometimes confused the fact that most college and high school campuses remained free from disorderly protest.

In 1970 the President's Commission on Campus Unrest issued its report, which distinguished between orderly and disorderly protest. It defined orderly protest as "peaceful manifestation of dissent, such as holding meetings, picketing, vigils, demonstrations and marches—all of which are protected by the First Amendment." It identified three categories of disorderly protest: (1) disruptive—interferences with the normal activities of a school, (2) violent—infliction of physical injuries to people or willful destruction of property, and (3) terroristic—deliberate use of violence in a systematic way to create an atmosphere of fear to obtain revolutionary change. The Commission condemned disorderly protest and violent action whether by students or police and insisted that violent or terroristic actions are criminal. The Commission called for a national cease-fire. It insisted that crimes committed by one do not justify crimes by another and pointed out that schools are particularly vulnerable to violence. It insisted that no progress is possible where violence prevails and that no nation can tolerate violence without resorting to repression.

The Commission felt that student protests arose from three major concerns: war, racial injustice, and the schools themselves. A great majority of students and many elders opposed the war in Southeast Asia and felt that all the policies and practices which supported it were equally immoral—ROTC, the draft, recruitment for defense industries, among others. Blacks and others of minority races were demanding that the pledges of the Declaration of Independence and the Emancipation Proclamation be fulfilled with full dignity and equality to all. High school and college students were also protesting the impersonality of their schools, the irrelevance of their studies, harsh discipline, restrictive control of student affairs, and bureaucratic institutions which imposed juvenile rather than adult behavior upon their members.

The Commission held that behind the crisis of violence was a crisis of understanding between the students and their elders. Elders were disturbed by youth's life-styles, disorderly protest, impatience with the slow procedures of democracy, intolerance of others, arrogance, and lack of appreciation of the benefits provided for them through adults' sacrifices. Students, on the other hand, saw their elders as trapped by materialism and competition and as prisoners of outdated social forms. They saw the military establishment as draining resources from the urgent needs of social and racial reform. The Commission called for a reconciliation between the two generations, a renewal of our compassion for each other and our tolerance of diverse thought. It pointed out that most youths are striving toward the ultimate values and dreams of their elders and their forefathers.

The Commission recommended that student extremists, perpetrators of violence, be removed swiftly from school and prosecuted; that citizens of all ages strive to prevent violence, to create understanding, to reduce bitterness, and to establish respect for the processes of law and the tolerance of dissent. It urged the President to offer reconciling leadership to unite the nation, and governors and other state and local officials to do the same; it urged that no one play irresponsible politics with the theme of "campus unrest"; it urged that schools and students not be punished for student disruption by reduction of public funding (indeed, financial support for education should be increased, especially for students of minority races). It further urged that schools prepare themselves more adequately to respond to disruption, to clarify limits of permissible conduct and the penalties for infractions, and to respond more sensibly to reasonable student demands; that universities remain politically neutral and free from both outside interference and internal intimidation. It concluded that faculty members who participate in disruptive conduct have no place in the university community. It also urged students to present their ideas in more reasonable and persuasive manner; to become more understanding of those who differ with their views; to help protect the right of speakers to be heard; to remember that language that offends seldom persuades; and to respect the imperative of majority rule in a democratic society. The Commission insisted that we who seek to change America must build on the accomplishments and freedoms already won, a considerable inheritance which we must not squander or destroy.[24]

Despite the statesmanship of the Commission's findings and the elegance of its language, many national political figures continued to exploit student unrest for political purposes and exacerbated the crisis of understanding. Although most educators and students seemed to view the Commission's

[24]This summary has been paraphrased from the "Call to the American People," *Report of the President's Commission on Campus Unrest*, 1970.

statement as reasonable, student unrest continued. Some reduction in violence, however, became evident in the early 1970s.

To some extent American schools have been the victims of their own success. Having exhorted students for years to acquire some sense of social justice, some commitment to ideals other than self, some agnosticism with respect to dogma, the educational system should hardly be startled that they now mean to do exactly that even before they graduate. If the country insists that equal educational opportunity be available to all, it should not be surprised by the inadequacies of the old educational programs and practices that were originally designed to serve only those unwilling to drop out. No other educational system has ever before attempted to serve all students, and clearly many schools and colleges are not yet prepared for the task. Although the goal is salubrious, it is not yet certain how schools can serve those students who choose not to learn.

And so the debate about student activism continues. Indeed, it must always continue, since both students and their elders seek the golden mean between freedom and responsibility, just as free men have always done. Educators and citizens disagree over the nature of the problem and the proper response to it.

Edmund Muskie urges greater student participation in decision making in education:

If a university is to encourage its students to be active and participating members of society after graduation, that university should make it possible for students to contribute to the enrichment of campus life before graduation. Universities have traditionally been the fountainhead of ideas of social progress in our nation. It would be wasteful now not to give this generation of college students an opportunity to participate meaningfully in giving new relevance to our universities. I view as reasonable student demands for participation in the major decisions of the university which affect so directly the lives of the students. The idea of giving students a greater voice in the development of relevant and selected courses and curriculums makes sense.

Ross Toole, professor of history at the University of Montana, advocates the opposite view:

Since when have children ruled this country? By virtue of what right, by what accomplishments, should thousands of teenagers, wet behind the ears and utterly without the benefit of having lived long enough to have either judgment or wisdom, become the sages of our time? . . . I have watched this new generation and concluded that most of them are fine. A minority is not— and the trouble is that this minority threatens to tyrannize the majority and take over. I dislike that minority. . . . I have yet to talk to an 'activist' who has read Crane Brinton's The Anatomy of Revolution *or who is familiar with the works of Jefferson, Washington, Paine, Adams or even Marx or Engels. And I have yet to talk to a student militant who has read about racism elsewhere and/or who understands, even primitively, the long and wondrous struggle of the NAACP and the genius of Martin Luther King—whose name they invariably take in vain. . . . I assert that we are in trouble with this younger generation not because we have failed our country, not because of affluence or stupidity, not because we are antediluvian, not because we are middle-class materialists—but simply because we have failed to keep that generation in its place.*[25]

Meanwhile adults often lost sight of the fact that young people themselves differed sharply on both the means and the ends of social reform. Tom Hayden, a founder of Students for a Democratic Society, for example, declared that "first we will make the revolution, and then we will find out what for." Roger Crossland, former student chairman of the Columbia University Conservative Union, on the other hand, feels that "extralegal action, such as occupying buildings, not only jeopardizes the reforms he [the conservative student] wishes to initiate, but those aspects of society he wishes to preserve." SDS, a national organization of student rebels oriented toward socialism, is striving hard to mobilize high school students to revolt. The Weatherman group of revolutionaries is a curious mixture of Maoists, Marxists, anarchists, and nihilists who are clearly committed to violent destruction of society. Other groups of the radical left include the Progressive Labor Party of the Youth Socialist Alliance, the Youth International Party, and the Third World Liberation Front. The combined membership of all of these organizations amounts to less than 5 percent of the student population.

On the conservative side, Young Americans for Freedom is the major right-wing student group, with an estimated membership of 51,000 members in 1969. The National Student Association, discussed in Chapter 9, is the largest organization of college students and is much less politically energized than the other student groups mentioned here.

[25] K. Ross Toole, "Sick of Young Generation Nonsense," *Pittsburgh Post-Gazette*, p. 35, June 18, 1970.

While views differ widely on the wholesomeness of student rebellion, perhaps most of us would agree with Oliver Wendell Holmes' admonition that "it is required of a man that he should share the passion and action of his time at peril of being judged not to have lived." A passion for social justice by today's youth may be precisely the antidote so needed to ameliorate the great problems plaguing the world.

What Are the Educational Consequences of Racial Segregation in the Schools? Earlier in this chapter we spoke of the political and legal aspects of school desegregation. What are the effects of racial segregation on the student? Is there any evidence that black and white children fare better in integrated schools? Figure 1-5 shows that the gap in school achievement between whites and blacks increases with schooling, although the gap in years of schooling is being reduced, as revealed in Figure 1-5.

Some argue that the solution to minority students' educational disadvantage lies outside the school and that any changes in school organization, control, curriculum, and pedagogy will have little consequence until the more fundamental problems of poverty, poor housing, poor diet, poor health, low

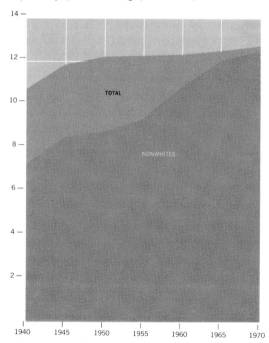

FIGURE 1-5   Years of schooling completed by the total population and the nonwhite population. (U.S. Bureau of the Census.)

educational aspirations, high mobility, and other handicaps are overcome. Others are not persuaded by this view. They insist that a generation of ghetto children cannot wait until the complex social, political, and economic problems are solved; that slum children are simply more dependent upon the schools than are middle-class children; and that schools must undertake innovations to overcome school failures which they regard as unavoidable and as more the fault of the school than the child.

One of the most ambitious studies of the effects of segregation upon success in school by students from minority groups was commissioned by the U.S. Office of Education and reported in the volume *Equality of Educational Opportunity*, commonly referred to as the "Coleman Report" after the Johns Hopkins professor who wrote it. This study yielded several important conclusions.

Minority groups do suffer from very great inequality in their schooling. For example, at the beginning of the twelfth grade, students from minority groups are three to five grade levels below whites in reading comprehension and four to six grade levels below whites in mathematics.

The physical and economic resources going into the school have very little relation to the achievement of the various ethnic groups, and there is really very little difference in these resources between schools whose enrollments are predominantly white and those whose enrollments are predominantly nonwhite.

The factor that showed the clearest relation to a child's achievement was his home environment—the educational and economic resources provided within his home.

Students do better when they attend schools where their fellow students come from family backgrounds strong in educational motivation and resources. This good effect results from social class background rather than race and applies to all students but is especially great for students from educationally deprived backgrounds.

Evidently children from the more favored environment influence the less favored with their interests, motivation, higher levels of achievement, and approach to learning. Then too, these schools seem to expect students to learn, and community influence is brought to bear when their education falters. The report implied—without saying specifically—that integration was a better bet than compensatory education in improving the lot of ghetto students.[26]

Another study, sponsored by the U.S. Commission on Civil Rights, reported in the volume *Racial*

Isolation in the Schools, revealed that racial isolation in schools was damaging to both white and black students. Like the Coleman report, it revealed that homogeneity of social class, rather than race, was the vital factor. It found that both white and black students who had been to school with each other were more disposed to form friendships with students of other races and to prefer interracial schools. People who had attended desegregated schools were much more likely to prefer desegregated schools for their own children. Persons who had never attended interracial schools were more inclined to do all that they could to keep their own children from attending interracial schools.

Although the evidence regarding the comparative advantage of desegregated schools over segregated schools is not as conclusive as one might like, the advantage of the former is nevertheless assumed by most educators.

As was noted earlier in this chapter, integration is not presently feasible in many communities, for one reason or another. Consequently many attempts have been made to improve the quality of education in slum schools, often through the allocation of more intensive resources—such as teachers, counselors, and instructional materials. This is commonly spoken of as "compensatory education." So far the record of this compensatory education is not very impressive. The National Advisory Council on the Education of Disadvantaged Children concluded that most of the compensatory education programs funded by federal subsidies were ill-planned, fragmentary, and shackled by low, vague values.[27] Most authorities and citizens are agreed that neither compensatory education nor racial mixing is adequate alone. James Coleman believes that integration is not the only means, nor even necessarily the most efficient means, for increasing the achievement of lower-class students. Whatever the benefits of integration, a more intensive improvement of the child's social environment than school integration alone can possibly provide is necessary if the handicaps of a poor family background are to be relieved.

Within the school, several needed reforms seem evident. The subject matter and the methods and materials of instruction must be made more

[26] For a summary of the Coleman Report, see Christopher Jencks, "A Reappraisal of the Most Controversial Educational Document of Our Time," *New York Times Magazine*, pp. 12-13, 34-38, 42-44, Aug. 10, 1969.

[27] For a review of the failings of compensatory education, see Joseph T. Durham, "Compensatory Education: Who Needs It?" *Clearing House*, vol. 44, pp. 18-22, September, 1969.

compatible with the interests, needs, and learning styles of the children of poverty. More emphasis must be given to the affective development of students from impoverished families. The traditional middle-class ethos of the schools must be modified to accommodate the values and life-styles of children from low-income homes. Adequate numbers of faculty members must be drawn from the minority races in both segregated and desegregated schools. Teacher-education programs should emphasize methods of teaching that are effective with slum children. Intensive programs for teachers are needed, both during their initial training and after they begin teaching, to help them overcome various misconceptions about children from minority groups and to remove the unfavorable bias which some teachers have toward these children, primarily the notion that they are less capable of learning than other children. Teachers should become persuaded that ghetto children can and must learn, for there is reason to believe that many students do only as well as teachers expect them to do. Other reforms are noted in Chapters 11 and 14 of this book. The authors share the view held by Roy Wilkins, executive director of NAACP, that the struggle for school integration must be sustained whatever the difficulties but that fundamental improvement must also take place both in integrated schools and in the schools that remain segregated. Wilkins believes that "the error is in believing that there is a choice to be made between correcting segregation and raising educational standards. The danger is to substitute one for the other."

Clearly the ultimate solution lies not only in rearranging school-district attendance areas but also, through education, in raising man's understanding of and concern for his fellow citizen regardless of color; in insisting that all men be granted the equal opportunities guaranteed by our Constitution; and in realizing that the educational impoverishment of any group of citizens weakens the nation's economic and moral strength. Hopefully, through interracial interaction and appropriate relations within our schools, we can bring up a new generation of young Americans liberated from the racial prejudice that plagues much of the present adult generation.

What Is the Proper Role of Testing in the School?
For many years intelligence was regarded as a stable quality established by heredity. Since a student's native intelligence presumably established most of his capacity for learning, intelligence testing was practiced in practically all schools in this country. However, a number of studies, summarized in Chapter 11, generated a different belief: that intelligence is influenced to a considerable degree by the student's environment before adolescence, especially during the years of early childhood. Since children of minority races are commonly the victims of poverty and poor environment, compensatory education programs such as Head Start have become a strategic part of the war on poverty as a means of reducing the educational disadvantage of slum children before they enter the elementary school and as a stratagem for reducing their lack of privilege in school and society. Some argued that intelligence tests were culturally biased and therefore revealed a spuriously low measure of intelligence for certain persons. One controversial experiment demonstrated that when students chosen at random were reported to their teachers as having superior intelligence, these children showed significantly greater gains in achievement than did the other children who had not been singled out. Presumably the change in the teachers' expectations regarding the intellectual performance of these allegedly brilliant students had led to a self-fulfilling prophecy: an actual change in their intellectual performance, although they were in general not brighter than the others. It was therefore argued that intelligence tests set the academic destiny of children in school and in life far beyond what was warranted, particularly if intelligence is modifiable by changes in the environment. Demands were made that intelligence testing be discontinued, and some school districts abandoned the practice.

The issue was intensified with the appearance in 1969 of an article by Prof. Arthur Jensen of the University of California, one of the nation's leading educational psychologists.[28] Jensen contended that intelligence was largely a function of heredity and that changes in environment would affect intelligence in only a few unusual cases. He argued further that blacks were about 15 points lower than whites in the standard distribution of IQ throughout the population, although he conceded that "the full range of human talents is represented in all the major races of man." He argued further that no

[28] Arthur R. Jensen, "How Much Can We Boost IQ and Scholastic Achievement?" *Harvard Educational Review*, vol. 39, pp. 1–123, Winter, 1969.

amount of compensatory education could improve intelligence because it was a matter of nature rather than nurture.

Bruno Bettelheim and Benjamin Bloom, also noted educational psychologists, argued on the contrary that environment does have an impact upon children's IQs. The National Academy of Sciences also disagreed with Jensen, stating that "there is no scientific basis for the statement that there are or are not substantial heredity differences in intelligence between Negro and white populations." The controversy continued to raise disagreement on whether intelligence is immutable after birth, whether blacks have generally as much intelligence as whites, and whether intervention in the improvement of environment of young children offers hope for the betterment of their learning. The preponderance of current educational thought would appear to sustain positive responses to each of these issues. It is to be hoped that additional research will help in time to reduce the disagreement of these issues.[29]

Although education without measurement would be inconceivable, many educators have become alarmed over the undiscriminating use of all tests. A booklet, *Testing Testing Testing*, called attention to the limitations of tests and warned against blind faith in them, the great expenditure of time and money involved, duplication in their use, and the possible dangers involved in their unwise use.

What Are the Causes of Rising Emotional Disturbance in Youth, and How Can They Be Reduced? As noted in Chapter 11, the number of mentally ill persons is alarmingly high and is rising. The causes of emotional disturbance can frequently be traced to early childhood, and the symptoms often appear then. There is substantial evidence that the mental health of our young people, like their physical health, is in serious condition. Many elementary school children have ulcers, and more and more pediatricians are prescribing tranquilizers for them. The incidence of suicides among children and youths is increasing. The growth of drug addiction, a problem discussed at length in Chapter 11, is often symptomatic of inadequate emotional adjustment.

There are those who believe that much of this emotional disturbance can be traced to increased

[29] For further discussion of these issues, see Lee Edson, "Jensenism, n., The Theory That IQ Is Largely Determined by Genes," *New York Times Magazine*, pp. 10–11, 40–41, 43–47, Aug. 23, 1969.

school pressures upon children and youth. Others insist that maintaining high levels of expectation for students is not in itself detrimental to mental health, as long as the work expected is within the mental capacity of the student. They contend that high expectations can have a salubrious effect on the mental health of children by enhancing their self-realization, self-understanding, and healthy expectation of their potentialities and limitations, as well as those of others. Certainly many children, like adults, achieve more when under pressure.

Rather than decrying or defending academic pressure in general, it is reasonable to analyze the nature of the pressure and its application. Wrong pressures, or pressures wrongly applied, can change stress to distress and debilitate the student. Wrong pressures include attempting to motivate students by tough grading for the sake of toughness, using extrinsic rewards and punishments rather than intrinsic ones, expecting students of limited ability to achieve arbitrarily set standards beyond their reach, and telling already diligent students that they can do better if they will work harder. Teachers should be conscious of both the debilitating and the wholesome consequences of pressure and should analyze their own teaching practices and classroom environment to be sure that their students' mental health is threatened as little as possible. The school may be the only place where children from distressed homes find real serenity, affection, and encouragement.

How Can the Number of School Dropouts Be Reduced? The nation has become increasingly concerned over school dropouts and has looked to its schools for appropriate remedial action. We have learned that it costs far more to provide welfare benefits for the unemployed, rehabilitation of the delinquent, and treatment of the mentally ill than to finance school programs that can reduce the number of these social and economic misfits. In the long run, poor education is far too expensive.

Dropout rates are particularly high in urban school systems; frequently as many as one student in four leaves high school before graduation. Dropout rates are much higher among nonwhite students than white.

What do we know about dropouts? Contrary to popular belief, lack of mental ability is not a significant characteristic of students who leave school. The most important factors are cultural and socioeconomic differences. Most of the fathers and mothers of dropouts were also dropouts who place little value on education and offer little encouragement to stay in school. Dropouts tend to be withdrawn from the social life of the school. Very often their attendance record is poor, and they have unsatisfactory but not necessarily misbehaving relations with teachers and other students. The symptoms of their disenchantment with school can often be detected—and remedied—even at the elementary level. When asked why they quit school, they give these reasons, in this order of frequency: lack of interest, lack of success, marriage and pregnancy, and economic factors.

It is clear that schools can do a better job of retaining potential dropouts. For example, many school systems expel girls who become pregnant—a real anachronism in a society that otherwise promises equal educational opportunity for all.

For many potential dropouts, the cure lies in the rehabilitation of the school curriculum to meet the particular needs of disadvantaged children. More and better vocational programs of the work-study variety permit them not only to acquire vocational skills but also to earn money that may relieve their financial distress. School systems should also establish adult education programs that give dropouts a second chance to complete their education, should they have a change of heart in later years. All teachers should be alerted to call to the counselor's attention students who indicate any intention of quitting school. Counselors should be alerted unerringly to provide counseling sessions for them and their parents. The exact nature of the potential dropout's dismay should be determined and relieved if possible.

Teachers (Chapter 12)

Like the students, the nation's teachers have become increasingly restless and self-assertive. Better prepared, better organized, more aware of their professional prerogatives, and invigorated by the success of confrontation tactics by other groups, teachers have become far more aggressive in their quest for the improvement of their profession, which is being consummated rapidly. However, this drive for the improvement of teaching conditions is encumbered by many problems, which we now consider.

What Should Be the Role of Teachers in Policy Development? A great many boards of education have developed school policies unilaterally and have denied the counsel of their professional employees even on matters directly related to their work. In some cases the policies have been administered capriciously. Teachers, particularly in large districts, have been made to feel rather anonymous when school administration became bureaucratic and depersonalized. Through their two national organizations, the National Education Association and the American Federation of Teachers—both engaged in a spirited rivalry—teachers across the country were rapidly winning the right to bargain collectively with boards of education. More than half the states had enacted laws by 1972 either mandating or permitting local school boards to engage in collective bargaining with their faculties. The National Education Association had proposed a federal law governing collective bargaining for teachers across the nation.

Many boards of education have accepted various forms of collective negotiations in states where they are not required by law to do so. These boards have viewed collective negotiations as another evolutionary step in the democratization of personnel administration. In many districts, more informal negotiations—without written agreements, formalized procedures, or provisions for appeals in case of impasse—have been the mode for years. These boards regard this procedure as a civilized way of reaching important decisions and as a means whereby the knowledge and experience of the professional staff may be released to improve personnel policies and practices. These boards have recognized that the participation of teachers in policy making strengthens the commitment of teachers to make the policies work.

What are the consequences of this new drive by teachers for greater participation in development of personnel policy? Although the returns are not yet all in, several tentative observations can be made. In most cases, better communication has resulted between the teachers and the board of education on matters of mutual interest. In many situations, personnel policies and practices have improved. Many boards of education have found money for higher salaries for teachers, money which would otherwise not have been made available. As a result of better salaries and improved working conditions, morale has been strengthened, turnover reduced, and the supply of teachers greatly increased. Teachers have become less servile, and boards of education have become more civilized in their treatment of teachers. In other situations, a spirit of continuing conflict has been generated, and severe cleavages between boards of education and teachers have developed. A few teachers' associations and boards of education, too, have been corrupted by power and have failed to assume the responsibilities concomitant with their prerogatives.

Not everyone is agreed that collective negotiations have been in the best interests of society. Edward Shils, a University of Pennsylvania professor and author and consultant in industrial and educational negotiations, feels that these negotiations may be destroying education. He accuses teachers of acting selfishly and not considering the best interests of their students. The same view is commonly held by many parents, particularly persons in low-income communities. One parent, while noting that the teachers were rejoicing over having won a "real voice in school decisions," asked if the teachers were now willing to shoulder their share of responsibility for the "massive academic deterioration found in our schools." He asked: "Where is the voice of the community during the one-sided negotiations? Who protects the vital interests and concerns of parents and students?" Like many others, he was asking that teachers' accountability for the performance of their work be increased.

Collective bargaining is accompanied by a host of related issues. How will the official bargaining group for teachers be determined? Who will be included in it? What matters can be included in the negotiations? How will impasses be resolved? How will grievances be decided? Will teachers be permitted to strike? If so, under what conditions? These and other problems of bargaining have engaged teachers, school boards, and legislators in spirited and sometimes acrimonious discussion.[30]

If there is one lesson to be learned from school systems long engaged in collective negotiations, it is that negotiations can be either constructive or damaging to the school system. Like that of any form of human interaction, success or failure of collective negotiations depends upon the level of civilization of those who enter into it. The question is not whether teachers, superintendents, and boards of education will learn to live with collective negotiations, but whether we will move quickly and wisely enough to take advantage of them for the ultimate benefit of children.

[30] For further study of these issues, see Patrick W. Carlton and Harold I. Goodwin (eds.), *The Collective Dilemma: Negotiations in Education*, Charles A. Jones Publishing Company, Worthington, Ohio, 1969.

Should Teachers Be Permitted to Strike? Few issues in education will trigger a dispute more quickly than the question of whether teachers should be permitted to strike should they fail to win a satisfactory agreement at the bargaining table. David Selden, president of the American Federation of Teachers, is unequivocal:

What American schools need most is more teacher strikes. . . . What is so terrible about a strike by teachers? The traditional answer is, "Think of the children!" Yet it is often more harmful to the children for teachers not to strike than it would be to close down the schools for a while. . . . It is better for a child to lose a few days or weeks of schooling now than to go through life handicapped by years of inferior education. . . . Where the right and willingness to strike exists, most disputes will be settled without an actual walkout.

U.S. Commissioner of Education Sidney P. Marland, Jr., holds an opposite view:

Would the present phenomena of student rebellion, defiance of authority, hostility, vandalism, obscenity, and other forms of unacceptable social behavior in many of our schools have occurred if large numbers of teachers had not, themselves, first broken the laws, defied the courts, and coerced students to support strikes by absenting themselves from school illegally? . . . No sound evidence has been offered by teacher organizations to demonstrate that improved circumstances for teachers have brought improved learning for children. Certainly, public funds have been diverted to teacher benefits as against other school needs.

The courts have consistently held that strikes by public employees are illegal unless permitted by the statutes of the states, as they are in a few states. These decisions are based on the opinion that public

High school students in Sharon, Pennsylvania, protest the closing of their schools over a strike by teachers.

services, such as teaching, are for the benefit of the public and not for the benefit of any group and that every government employee is enjoined not to interrupt these essential governmental services. Nevertheless teacher strikes continue throughout the country, in violation of the law in most states. We think that these warnings by the National Commission on the Causes and Prevention of Violence are germane:

Is each group to be free to disregard due process and to violate laws considered objectionable? If personal or group selectivity of laws to be obeyed is to be the yardstick, we shall face nationwide disobedience of many laws and thus anarchy. . . . Every time a court order is disobeyed, each time an injunction is violated, each occasion on which a court decision is flouted, the effectiveness of our judicial system is eroded. How much erosion can it tolerate?

Without access to the strike or other forms of work stoppages, teachers are of course disadvantaged in their negotiations with employers. But, on the other hand, any form of work stoppage is deleterious to the education of children and to the public welfare. The dilemma is the familiar one of how society can protect at the same time the interests of both children and teachers and, should this be impossible, how the better choice can be made.

Can the Organizational Rivalry between the AFT and NEA Be Relieved? At the time of this writing, the two large national teachers' organizations are engaged in vigorous competition nationally and locally for the allegiance of the nation's teachers. To a degree, this rivalry has been beneficial to both organizations. However, we believe that the point of diminishing returns has been reached. Valuable time and effort are being dissipated in the struggle, which is often bitter and hostile, to gain ascendancy rather than to improve the profession and education. No other learned profession in this country is encumbered by two rival organizations. Overtures toward merger of the two organizations have been made by the AFT. The merger of the organizations poses some difficult obstacles. The much greater size and fiscal affluence of the NEA and its greater success in membership competition makes merger less attractive to that organization. The AFT's insistence upon continued affiliation with the AFL-CIO is anathema to the NEA which insists upon independence. Meanwhile students and society are the victims of the sometimes unwholesome competition between the two organizations which, according to some, must eventually merge.

What Is the Necessity for Academic Freedom? Academic freedom is fundamentally a protection of *freedom of learning* rather than a privilege of the teacher. The student cannot be free to learn unless the teacher is free to teach. Academic freedom is essentially the protection of rational inquiry, which is fundamental to the democratic process. In principle, most people would probably support the academic freedom of teachers. But in practice, many people would impose severe restrictions. The history of these restrictions would fill a volume. At one time or another, teachers have been chastised for teaching about evolution, the Reformation, the United Nations, *The Merchant of Venice*, the germ theory of disease, communism, the New Deal, sex education, Russia, the Whiskey Rebellion, and scores of other topics. More recently, academic freedom has been constrained at times by the capitulation of schools to the demands of students and minority groups who have insisted upon the application of sometimes spurious considerations in the development of the curriculum and the selection and promotion of personnel.

The process of free rational inquiry into controversy has always been regarded as the foundation of our liberties. Many teachers' associations and boards of education have attempted to establish reasonable policies regarding the treatment of controversial issues in the classroom and the protection of the teacher's academic freedom.

How Can School Faculties Be Integrated? We spoke earlier of the difficult problems involved in desegregating student bodies, particularly in urban school districts. When difficulties are encountered in desegregating pupils, attention is naturally turned to the possibility of desegregating teachers. Negro teachers tend to teach in the schools of the Negro neighborhoods in which they live, just as white teachers are attracted to schools in white neighborhoods. To change this pattern, it is necessary to assign white teachers to Negro schools in areas where they will not live, and Negro teachers to schools in white neighborhoods where they often cannot live. Teachers of both races are reluctant to undertake the additional commuting required. Most white teachers prefer to teach in predominantly white schools, and many Negro teachers prefer to teach Negro students. Teachers' organizations in several large cities have threatened to strike if teachers are involuntarily assigned to schools not of their preference.

The pressures are intensified by guidelines for teacher integration issued by the U.S. Office of Education under the authorization of the Civil Rights Act. The federal government is committed to providing more and better teachers for slum schools and to fostering integration. Yet each of these goals appears to be inimical to the other. Thus civil rights groups and organizations are on a collision course, and well-intentioned boards of education are often caught in the middle.

In the South, and occasionally in the North too, the desegregation of schools has imposed injustice upon Negro teachers and administrators. When formerly black and white schools are merged, it is usually the white principal, white coach, and white teacher who are favored for appointment in the integrated school. Thousands of black faculty members have been dismissed, demoted, or assigned to positions for which they are not qualified. This discrimination is, of course, both unjust and tragic, a legacy of the imperfection of man which it is hoped will one day recede. It is small wonder that many black teachers have lost faith in the profession.

Other Personnel in Education (Chapter 13)

A complete discussion of the issues inherent in the work of the growing array of specialists in education would fill a volume. As schools have added administrators, supervisors, learning programmers, teacher aides, and a host of other paraprofessionals, described in Chapter 13, role conflicts have been intensified. As the task of the school becomes increasingly complex, the staff sometimes staggers under the burden of new and unfamiliar responsibilities. Here we give our attention to a few of the more persistent problems involved in the administration of this new array of school personnel.

Are New Patterns of Selecting and Deploying Personnel Necessary? In Chapter 13 we describe differentiated staffing, a new way of assigning variable tasks and responsibilities to teachers on the basis of their individual talents and preparation. This scheme is designed to promote more effective utilization of professional capabilities, better accommo-

dation to individual differences, and differentiation of salary on the basis of the quality of each teacher's input. Other types of more flexible deployment of teachers and other specialists are being tried, all of which have advantages as well as problems. The problems include disturbance of the traditional power structure within the school, introduction of new distinctions in salaries, dilution of accountability for results throughout a group of professionals with shared responsibilities, more role conflict, and the introduction of more subprofessional personnel. Such disturbances have precipitated opposition to the schemes by teachers, supervisors, and administrators, as well as organized teacher groups. Sometimes the proposals are disparaged almost before they have been evaluated. David Selden, president of the AFT, for example, has declared that differentiated staffing is "merely a device to introduce merit rating in disguise." As Charles Frankel observed, "Most people's recognition of the need for reform grows in direct proportion to the distance of the proposed reform from their own territory."

Questions also arise with respect to the selection of teachers, administrators, and other specialists. Selection policies based upon examinations or civil service specifications are commonly criticized on the grounds that they discriminate against minority groups. These critics urge that certification and selection requirements be liberalized to permit the hiring of professionals from minority groups in the same ratio that they exist in the community. Others argue that the relaxation of quality controls in the selection of professionals, particularly those in leadership capacity, can only weaken the schools and open the gates to political favoritism.

These illustrate a few of the many problems involved with reform in the selection and utilization of school personnel. Most reforms are opposed by certain sectors of the organized teaching profession usually because they disturb the power structure that the organization has already adjusted to. However, many individual teachers do not necessarily share the objections. The innovations are often sustained by the community in its search for better ways of serving children. The dilemmas fall into the familiar pattern of uncertainty between the security of old and familiar practices and the anxiety generated by new ways. They arise over the contest between the new versus the old, the innovative versus the orthodox, and change versus stability.

Are Positions in School Administration Becoming Uninhabitable? Throughout this book we speak of the pressures which surround positions of educational leadership in our schools and colleges. School administration has always been a troubled profession because the school administrator is often caught in the crossfire generated by controversy in the schools. Regardless of his action or his position in any controversy, he is sure to attract the wrath of some segment in the community. He is often held responsible for forces over which he has little control. We are fond of making him personally the scapegoat for whatever is wrong in school or society. Some radicals appear intent only upon making his office uninhabitable as a means of destroying the organization.

In many cities, the superintendent of schools can hardly endure the position for more than a few years. Many college presidents are retiring earlier. It is often hard to find replacements who are willing to tackle nearly impossible tasks and suffer the abuse which their positions attract. Some people have reasoned that the fault lies in the shortage of outstanding leadership talent among educators and urge that school administrators be drawn from fields other than education. Reforms in the preparation of school administrators are often called for. Again the organized profession tends to resist these proposals and the controversy goes on.

EDUCATIONAL MATERIALS AND ENVIRONMENT (PART 5)

Quite understandably, much of the controversy in education focuses upon what should be taught in the curriculum. These dilemmas are as old as schools themselves and have been debated since the beginning of educational thought. With the advancement of instructional technology, new debates have been stimulated over the proper place of educational television, computer-assisted instruction, and various other modes of teaching. All these issues arouse disagreement over how much should be spent for education, where the money should come from, and how it should be distributed to schools. We consider now some of the more compelling issues related to the educational environment.

Curriculum (Chapter 14)

Much of the controversy over what should be included in the curriculum arises from different views of the *purposes* of education. Should sex education, driver education, black studies, and environmental education be included in the curriculum? How much emphasis should be given to vocational education? life adjustment education? general education? These are but a few of the issues relative to the curriculum. Fundamental to all these questions is the question of the *purpose* of education. Unfortunately, much discussion of educational issues is preoccupied with empirical matters apart from the larger questions of values and purpose in education. Conant, for example, dodges the question of purpose in education by taking the absurd position that he is willing to think of education as "what goes on in schools and colleges."[31] Small wonder that when Conant tried his hand at reforming the secondary school curriculum, he never got beyond simple prescriptions of four years of English, four years of mathematics, three years of science, and so on. He never faced the question: English for what? He never said whether the four years of English should include grammar or composition or creative writing or literature. If one is willing to define education as "what goes on in school," then one could define the English curriculum as "what goes on in English classes" and never mind about its content. Curriculum building by course counting is exceedingly naïve and practically meaningless.

We insist that the most compelling question in education in our time, as it was in Spencer's time, is: Education for what purpose? Charles Silberman, author of *Crisis in the Classroom*, shares this concern and points out that much of the fault of our schools is attributable to their lack of well-defined purpose.

What Is the Purpose of Education in a Free Society? The question of purpose is fundamental to consideration of so many issues in education that we shall devote several pages to it. We shall tackle this central question by drawing attention to the major educational philosophies of our time, which do attempt, each in its own way, to resolve the question of purpose.

[31]James B. Conant, *The American High School Today*, McGraw-Hill Book Company, New York, 1959, chap. 3.

William O'Neill, a professor of social and philosophical foundations of education at the University of Southern California, has stated the point of view of *existentialism:*

The aim of existentialist education is not simply to help the individual cope *with his existence. Its primary purpose is to help him to* experience his existence *by confronting it with a sense of defined purpose. For the existentialist, the proper outcome of education is a certain sort of attitude toward life. . . . The educated man is characterized not only by what he* knows *but also, and perhaps even more, by what he is* capable of knowing and experiencing. *In a basic sense, then, the hallmark of an existentialist education is not knowledge as such but rather "educability."*

The existentialist advocates "education for choice" because he has a keen awareness that the most basic educational problem pertains to the criteria for selecting appropriate knowledge and not with the techniques for disseminating knowledge as such. The existentialist is concerned above all with "the habit of growth." He focuses on values precisely because he recognizes that values are directive and, therefore, determinative of most subsequent knowledge.[32]

Existentialists believe that it is far more important for the student to be capable of making rational moral choices for himself than to accept indoctrination in making the "right" choice as established by the dictates of society. Existentialists believe that morality cannot be taught didactically, but must be caught by self-discovery through discussion and living. The existentialist would certainly share our position that the questions of value and purpose in education are fundamental and that consideration of content or method in education is inappropriate until the prior question of purpose has been dealt with. The existentialist view of education has enjoyed wide currency among the more activist youth culture, as well as many of the new romantic critics of education, such as John Holt.

Opponents of existentialism believe that schools should indoctrinate students with commonly accepted moral values rather than encourage nonconformity through self-determination of values; that society cannot tolerate such a high degree of self-interest and self-determination without severe damage to common interests; that existentialism can lead to chaos or anarchy rather than to social solidarity; and that excessive attention to values

[32] William F. O'Neill, "Existentialism and Education for Moral Choice," *Phi Delta Kappan*, vol. 46, p. 49, October, 1964.

distracts from the acquisition of essential knowledge.

Stratemeyer, Forkner, McKim, and Passow have stated the case for *life-adjustment education* in these terms:

To provide an education that will function effectively in the lives of all children and youth, the school must relate what has meaning for the learner and the basic values of society. This requires a curriculum in which the problems and interests of everyday living which have meaning for children and youth are the starting point. From these immediate concerns, new insights are developed and dealt with in such a way as to provide sound bases for future action. This happens when present concerns or situations of everyday living are seen in the light of continuing life situations—keeping well, understanding self and others, making a living, adjusting to the natural environment, dealing with social and political structures and forces, developing a sustaining philosophy or set of values. These are the situations that recur in the life of every individual in many different ways as he grows from infancy to maturity.[33]

The supporters of life-adjustment education maintain that it helps to prepare all American youth for more useful and satisfying lives as citizens and homemakers; that it has been a powerful force in retaining a large number of students who would have dropped out of school otherwise; and that it is born of the problem of universal education and is most fundamental if schools are to serve all youth, even those of modest abilities and aspirations. Life-adjustment education has been the philosophical basis of a number of antipoverty educational programs, such as the National Youth Corps.

This type of education has been severely criticized. It is charged that this education is not academically respectable; that it attracts able learners who ought to be pursuing more rigorous courses; that it represents expensive fads and frills that schools could well do without; and that it has transformed the school from an educational institution to a gigantic recreational gymnasium and welfare service agency.

Harold W. Stoke, formerly the president of Queens College, expresses the view that *national survival* is the main goal of education:

[33] Florence B. Stratemeyer, Hamden L. Forkner, Margaret McKim, and A. Harry Passow, *Developing a Curriculum for Modern Living*, Teachers College Press, Columbia University, New York, 1957, chap. 5.

The new nationalism assumes that under conditions of life today all of the activities of our national life must be so conducted to contribute to the strength of the nation, and to this principle education is no exception. It has begun to dawn upon us that education is an instrument of power on which national survival itself depends, and this indisputable fact has imposed upon education and upon educators a new obligation superior to any other; namely, to keep the nation strong. There would be little education, at least of any kind we now think desirable, unless there is national survival; and if national survival depends upon education, it is easy to conclude that education must be consciously enlisted to serve the national needs. The swift developments of recent years begin to make such a direct relationship between education and national necessity appear not only natural and acceptable but inevitable.[34]

This point of view is widely held by patriotic organizations. It served as justification for the passage of the National Defense Education Act. Its opponents insist that education for national security corrupts the values of man and misdirects his education.

The concept of education as a means to *personal psychological development* has been expressed by Prof. Arthur Jersild of Teachers College, Columbia University:

Education should help children and adults to know themselves and to develop healthy attitudes of self-acceptance. . . . The crucial test in the search for meaning in education is the personal implication of what we learn and teach. . . . We must make an effort to conduct education in depth, to move towards something that is personally significant beyond the façade of facts, subject matter, logic, and reason behind which human motives and a person's real struggles and strivings are often concealed. . . . To encourage the process of self-discovery we must raise the question of personal significance in connection with everything we seek to learn and everything that is taught from the nursery school to postgraduate years. What does it mean? What difference does it make? What is there in the lessons we teach, the exercises we assign, the books we read, the experiences we enter into, and in all of our undertakings, that can help us to find ourselves, and through us help others in their search?[35]

This philosophic view is compatible with the educational reforms advocated by Paul Goodman. Summerhill exemplifies the type of school which tends to fulfill this expectation of education. Education for personal psychological development is also compatible with the expectation of youths in the so-called "turned-on" generation who demand "relevance" in education, usually understood to mean relevance to self-understanding and deeper understanding of interpersonal relations. This drive helps to explain the great interest of many youths in introspective "mind-expanding" experiences with hallucinatory drugs, encounter groups, sensitivity training, communal living, Eastern mysticism, and astrology. Opponents of this view claim that it substitutes passion for reason, feelings for thought, means for ends, and relevance for significance.

In Chapter 14, where the movement of curriculum reform is dealt with at length, we call attention to the collision between those who advocate the *essentialist* point of view in education and the more humanistic reformers. We associate the Council for Basic Education and James Conant, Max Rafferty, and James Koerner with the essentialist or basic education philosophy of education. The rationale for essentialism in education is illustrated by Clifton Fadiman's statement:

The primary job of the school is the efficient transmission and continual reappraisal of what we call tradition. Tradition is the mechanism by which all past men teach future men. . . . Basic education concerns itself with those matters which, once learned, enable the student to learn all the other matters, whether trivial or complex, that cannot properly be the subjects of elementary and secondary schooling. In other words, both logic and experience suggest that certain subjects have generative power and others do not have generative power. . . . It has, up to our time, been the general experience of men that certain subjects and not others possess this generative power. Among these subjects are those which deal with language, whether or not one's own; forms, figures, and numbers; the laws of nature; the past; and the shape and behavior of our common home, the earth. Apparently these master or generative subjects endow one with the ability to learn the minor or self-terminating subjects. They also endow one, of course, with the ability to learn the higher, more complex developments of the master subjects themselves.[36]

The advocates of basic education, or essentialism, insist that the fundamentals must be empha-

[34] Harold W. Stoke, "National Necessity and Educational Policy," *Current Issues in Higher Education,* National Education Association, Washington, D.C., 1959, p. 13.

[35] Arthur T. Jersild, *When Teachers Face Themselves,* Teachers College Press, Columbia University, New York, 1956, pp. 5, 80, 88, 136.

[36] Clifton Fadiman, in James D. Koerner (ed.), *The Case for Basic Education,* Little, Brown and Company, Boston, 1959, pp. 5–6.

sized and that real intellectual discipline can be acquired in no other way; that far greater mastery of subject matter is necessary for an educated citizenry; that it is best suited for the education of gifted students, who should be our primary concern; that knowledge for knowledge's sake is perfectly defensible; and that it stimulates competition in meeting rigorous standards of achievement.

The most common criticisms of basic education include contentions that it is more interested in what is taught than in what is learned; that it fails to bridge the gap between learning and living; that it is based upon the training-of-the-mind concept of learning, long since discredited by modern psychology; that it represents a return to sterile emphasis upon drill and memorization, tried earlier and rejected; and that it fails to take into account individual differences. Perhaps the most devastating criticism of basic education is that it cannot possibly serve the needs of a system of mass education. A curriculum that is strictly academic cannot serve students who are not college-bound. No society has ever attempted to educate an entire population in a curriculum based largely upon the humanities.

Supernaturalism is a philosophy of education which emphasizes moral and ethical development based upon revealed truth. This is the philosophy of education which is usually invoked to justify the existence of church-affiliated schools. Pope Pius XI enunciated the Roman Catholic position with respect to the ends of education:

The true Christian, product of Christian education, is a supernatural man who thinks, judges and acts constantly and consistently in accordance with right reason illumined by the supernatural light of the example and teaching of Christ. The proper and immediate end of Christian education is to cooperate with Divine grace in forming the true and perfect Christian, that is, to form Christ Himself in those regenerated by Baptism. For the true Christian must live a supernatural life in Christ, and display it in all his actions.

For precisely this reason, Christian education takes in the whole aggregate of human life, physical and spiritual, intellectual and moral, individual, domestic and social, not with a view of reducing it in any way, but in order to elevate, regulate it and perfect it, in accordance with the example and teaching of Christ.[37]

Some of the proponents of religious education insist that the salvation of mankind lies in strong

[37] Pope Pius XI, "Encyclical on the Christian Education of Youth," in *Five Great Encyclicals*, Paulist Press, New York, 1939, pp. 64–65.

Some critics insist that the fine arts and social studies have been neglected in American schools.

intellectual commitment to the common virtues; that knowledge unattuned to morality is of little value; that moral growth is the essence of all learning; that secular education is necessarily unmoral; that religious instruction must permeate and illuminate all other aspects of teaching; and that ultimate truth is found in the Scriptures or church doctrine rather than through individual discovery.

The critics of church-oriented education claim that although the public schools should inculcate commonly accepted moral and spiritual values, they should not attempt to teach sectarian doctrines; that the concept of revealed or supernatural truth is too doctrinaire, failing to illuminate many fateful issues in light of changing times and circumstances; that it discourages independent thought and self-realization; that it fragments the educational enterprise; and that religious instruction is the responsibility of the church rather than the school.

John Dewey, the classical exponent of the experimentalist or *progressive* point of view, reasoned:

The school is primarily a social institution. Education being a social process, the school is simply that form of community life in which all those agencies are concentrated that will be most effective in bringing the child to share in the inherited resources of the race, and to use his own powers for social ends. Education, therefore, is a process of living and not a preparation for future living. The school must represent present life. . . . The true center of correlation on the school subjects is not science, nor literature, nor history, nor geography, but the child's own social activities. . . . There is therefore no succession of studies in the ideal school curriculum. If education is life, all life has, from the outset, a scientific aspect, an aspect of art and culture, and an aspect of communication. It can not therefore be true that the proper studies for one grade are mere reading and writ-

ing, and that at a later grade, reading or literature, or science, may be introduced. The progress is not in a succession of studies, but in the development of new attitudes towards, and new interests in, experience. Education must be conceived as a continuing reconstruction of experience; that the process and the goal of education are one and the same thing.[38]

The proponents of progressive education claim that it has made learning meaningful by relating it to life; that achievement should be assessed in terms of personal capacities; that schools must be concerned with the total development of the learner; that self-discipline is more important than discipline imposed externally; that it has made learning more interesting; and that better results have been achieved. Many of the contemporary educational reformers have rediscovered progressive education. Charles Silberman, for example, contends that "the best of American progressive education is still vital and profoundly relevant to our contemporary needs." Many of the reforms proposed in *Crisis in the Classroom* are compatible with the philosophy of progressive education.

The critics of progressive education charge that the curriculum has been diluted with a lot of intellectually barren activity; that it has failed to train the mind; that it has removed competition as an incentive; that it has abandoned rigid standards of achievement; that subject matter has been lost; that the fundamentals have not been properly taught; and that discipline has been neglected.

The reconstructionist's view of education is illustrated in this statement by Theodore Brameld, professor of educational philosophy at Boston University:

While repudiating nothing of the constructive achievements of progressivism, while recognizing also the importance both of essential knowledge and clear rational analysis, this philosophy commits itself, first of all, to the renascence of modern culture. It is infused with profound conviction that we are in the midst of a revolutionary period out of which should emerge nothing less than the control of the industrial system, of public services, and of cultural and natural resources by and for the common people who, throughout the ages, have struggled for a life of security, decency, and peace for themselves and their children.

Education sufficiently dedicated to this purpose no longer remains, to be sure, on the fence of intellectual

[38] John Dewey, "My Pedagogic Creed," *School Journal,* vol. 54, pp. 77-78, Jan. 16, 1897.

"impartiality." But it is an education which, for that very reason, is inspired with enthusiasm for research, for diffusion of knowledge, for humanly realized beauty, goodness, and truth—an education which, through the schools of America and all other democracies, could at last demonstrate its capacity to play no longer a minor but a major role in the reconstruction of civilization.[39]

This view of education is compatible with that of many of the youth who call for a major reconstruction of society but clearly not with those who seek only to destroy it.

What is the ultimate purpose of education? To assure our national survival? To teach the "generative" subjects? To help the student live a "supernatural life in Christ"? To enable him to discover for himself his own morality? To help him meet the everyday problems of life? To help him understand and accept himself? To reconstruct civilization? The tempting answer for many is that all these constitute the purpose of education. Indeed, many schools have adopted an eclectic philosophy of education that includes some commitment to many of these ends. Unfortunately, the answer is not that simple. Quarrels over the relative emphasis to be given each invariably remain. Some of the ends of education stated above are in harmony with one another—education for personal psychological development, for example, is not in conflict with progressive education. Others are in such sharp disagreement that they can hardly coexist in the same educational system—the concept of education as the pursuit of truth revealed supernaturally, for example, is incompatible with the existentialist's view that the goal of education is self-discovered truth and values. Until the most fundamental of all educational issues, namely, what the purpose of education is, has been settled to the satisfaction of all—if indeed it ever can or should be—other controversies must remain. In a pluralistic, open society such as ours, there is opportunity for diverse points of view and open debate of the values of each. Indeed, this cleavage of views and diversity of practice constitute the viable force of a free and dynamic society.[40]

[39] Theodore Brameld, *Education for an Emerging Age,* Harper & Row, Publishers, Incorporated, New York, 1961, pp. 26-27.

[40] For an excellent discussion of various philosophies of education and the values which guide curriculum decisions, see Harry S. Broudy, *Building a Philosophy of Education,* 2d ed., Prentice-Hall, Inc., Englewood Cliffs, N.J., 1961.

Is Too Much Emphasis Placed upon Innovation in the Curriculum? Many modern educational reformers have built almost a holy crusade around the word "innovation." The word "innovation" is synonymous with the word "change," and change can be for the worse as well as for the better. The early progressive educators also supported widespread change in educational organization and method, but with a very important difference. They spoke of change in terms of growth, development, and improvement. The real progressives, such as Dewey, were careful to establish a philosophical basis for change, a conceptual design, and a careful means for evaluating the change in terms of specific goals. The word "improvement"—unlike "innovation"—implies the responsibility for demonstrating the superiority of the change over the practice which it displaces. Compulsive innovators are adept at ignoring research evidence. Their evaluation, if indeed there is any, of the innovation often occurs after much advertising of the alleged advantages of the practice in the popular press. They tend to view progress in education as an accumulation of innovations, which are advocated much too often in the hope a new educational practice that is dramatically titled, well-financed, and highly publicized will do some good in some ill-defined way. This compulsion for innovation has in part been generated by special-purpose federal grants for education which emphasize innovation. There is always the danger that these innovations, if untested, may become the new orthodoxies. In medicine, extravagant and premature claims for cures are not tolerated. Improvement in education may go as slowly as the search for a cure for cancer, but this is the better means toward real improvement. It is to be hoped that the new research and development centers and educational laboratories will place greater emphasis upon the evaluation of new educational practices and will stress improvement rather than innovation.

How Shall Controversial Matters Be Dealt with in the Schools? School auditoriums have been packed with citizens and college presidents' offices with students aroused over something that is taught, or not taught, in the schools and colleges. The list includes such diverse matters as evolution, communism, ROTC, religion, and fluoridation of water. At the time of this writing, sex education and black studies are two cases in point and we will consider them briefly.

The case for sex education is founded on the need to reduce divorce, teen-age pregnancy, and venereal disease; to reduce fears, myths, and misconceptions; to help prepare children for more wholesome family life and for adjustment to a sex-saturated culture. Advocates insist that it is necessary because few parents are able to do the job. A Gallup poll revealed that 71 percent of people queried favor sex education in the schools, as do many educational, medical, and religious groups.

Much of the opposition to sex education is stimulated by certain fundamentalist religious groups, such as the Christian Crusade, and super-patriotic political groups, such as the John Birch Society, who regard sex education as "part of a gigantic conspiracy (Communist) to bring America down from within." They equate sex education with advocacy of free love, loose morals, and homosexuality. The real questions, in the minds of many, are: What constitutes good sex education, and where does it belong in the curriculum? These questions are discussed in Chapter 14.

Mary Calderone, physician and executive director of the Sex Information and Education Council of the United States (SIECUS), insists that "one does not decide whether or not one will have a program of sex education. Sex education is going on at every instant of the child's life." The more fundamental question, she believes, is: "How can we counteract the negative aspects of what boys and girls are already getting from their culture?"

The demand for black studies in schools and colleges—Negro history, culture, economics, political science—has been the center of intensive and often bitter debate. Black studies are deemed important in offering both black and white students a more balanced perception of the role of black Americans and the injustices they have suffered, to improve racial relations, to improve the self-concept of blacks, and to produce an intelligentsia of black persons to occupy leadership roles in society. However, none of these goals can be fully realized if the black studies are conducted in an environment of separatism on the campus. Black persons cannot assume leadership positions, nor help themselves or whites in a pluralistic society if they insist upon isolation in school. Although we regret the unequal treatment given to black people in our school curriculums and the damage this has done to their sense of dignity and self-respect, we believe that the only satisfactory solution is to correct these fundamental injustices throughout the school curriculum rather than to create separate curriculums or separate studies or separate schools. However, these stratagems may be necessary over the short term until racial balance is achieved in our educational programs and organizations. Bayard Rustin, executive director of the A. Phillip Randolph Institute and black civil rights leader, takes a similar position:

I am very much opposed to separation under any circumstances and I'm also opposed to black studies. I believe it is a grievous mistake that there has not been the study of Negro culture history, but I'm opposed to it as black studies, because I believe there should be the integration of Negro contributions into the American historical forces, into the economic forces, and into other forces.

Roy Wilkins, executive director of the NAACP, although not opposed to black studies, is opposed to separatism in academic life, which he believes to be self-defeating. On the other hand, many black militants do favor separatism in academic life out of their concern that attempts at integration of either the curriculum or the school society will lead to racial discrimination against blacks by the larger population of whites.

We have spoken of these two issues because they illustrate, in our judgment, the anti-intellectualism that threatens a free society's access to controversial issues in the classroom. The opponents of sex education advocate avoidance of the problem by eliminating it from the curriculum. Meanwhile miseducation in sex continues in the mass media, and society pays the price in the wretched lives of the miseducated. The alternative to trusting our schools with instruction in a sensitive area such as sex is to trust instead the miseducative forces in society—because the controversial issues cannot be hidden from our young. In the case of black studies, the dilemma is different. The issue is not so much whether they will be included in the curriculum as whether they will be available to all, presented in balance, and advanced for scholarly purposes rather than for political or racial purposes. We believe that virtually all constraints on free access to knowledge are opposed to the best interests of a free society.[41]

[41] For an excellent statement on the importance of integrating black studies and black students fully into the

How Much Emphasis Should Be Placed upon Cocurricular Activities, Particularly Athletics? This is an issue apparently of more concern to the professional educator than to the lay public. Most citizens seem to enjoy the spectacle of interscholastic athletics, elaborate bands, fancy yearbooks, professional-looking school newspapers, and many other manifestations of cocurricular activities. Local newspapers cover in detail the performance of the high school football team, while important curriculum changes may go virtually unnoticed in the press. Class schedules are often interrupted for cocurricular functions. Expensive stadiums and other equipment are provided, even though they may be used less than a dozen times a year. Such uneconomical use of any other expensive school facilities would surely bring the most vigorous protests. Extra pay scales must be established to take care of the coach or band director, often to the consternation of other teachers working on important but less spectacular enterprises. Time and money are spent to help a few students excel at rugged team sports, in which few can participate in later life. Professionalism, particularly at the college level, often creeps in, and students learn to wink at practices that could not be condoned elsewhere in the educational program.

Certainly it must be granted that competitive athletics have a long and noble heritage in the American educational tradition. There is much to be said for the character-building value of sport. Surely school plays, newspapers, and yearbooks have some contribution to make to the development of American youth. The question becomes one of their *relative* importance and balance.

Educational Materiel and Technology (Chapter 15)

What Is the Future of Educational Technology? The term "educational technology" requires some definition. It refers to the application of systematic thought or science to the solution of problems. Only a witch doctor or a mystic could be opposed to that. However, in common parlance, technology is often understood to mean machines. It is foolish to fear machines, but it is prudent to be apprehensive about

school, see W. Arthur Lewis, "Black Studies: A Black Professor's View," *The Wall Street Journal*, p. 18, May 15, 1969.

the uses man may make of some machines. We describe in Chapter 15 the technological devices that are being applied to the educative process. Here we shall consider the advantages and limitations of only two of the more important technological developments in education—programmed instruction and educational television. The former is an example of an instructional system, the "software"; the latter is an example of a communications system, the medium or "hardware."

What are the advantages and limitations of programmed instruction? Although it is still too early to answer this question with any finality, certain tentative conclusions can be drawn on the basis of present evidence. Programmed instruction is quite adaptable to independent study. Students may use programmed material to gain mastery of courses not offered in small high schools or to make up work missed through absence. It helps students and adults to study independently at home. It relieves teachers from much of the drudgery of presenting routine information, correcting tests and homework, tutoring, and reviewing, thus freeing them for more creative aspects of teaching. It yields valuable understanding of how children learn by forcing attention upon the dynamic aspects of human understanding. This gives us insight into how courses and curriculums should be organized for most efficient mastery by students and will undoubtedly improve the organization of textbooks and other instructional media.

If the instruction is programmed well, it does permit the student to move through the material at a pace compatible with his learning capability. Although advocates of programmed learning speak effusively of its ability to accommodate individual differences and often create fancy euphemisms for its nomenclature, most programs presently in use accommodate individual differences only with respect to the pace of learning. True, some programs are branched and do permit some variation along alternate routes of remedial instruction depending upon the nature of an individual student's difficulty with an item. Few, however, are programmed to handle much variability in students' interests, needs, or individual learning styles. Some of the enthusiasts have compared programmed instruction with some form of variation on what can be called the "tutorial method" of teaching. However, as Harry Broudy has pointed out so trenchantly, the two methods are exact opposites. Programmed instruction offers a canned and predigested dialogue of imposed re-

sponse; any good tutorial method, on the other hand, offers genuine, open, inquiring dialogue.[42] This difference is apparently recognized in one of the more notable programs, called "individually *prescribed* instruction." Thus programmed instruction is, so far, individualized only with respect to the learner's pace of learning. It is certainly not *personalized*. We do not deny that programmed learning is capable of becoming far more accommodative of total individual differences, particularly when it is linked with the computer's marvelous capacity for sorting out and presenting material uniquely responsive to individual differences among students. The software for such an almost infinite combination of learning styles, interests, and needs has not yet been developed and will be enormously expensive. However, with the advent of mass-produced computer-assisted instructional systems, the unit costs will undoubtedly be reduced and may eventually come within the financial reach of many larger school systems. Although computer-assisted instruction may never actually reduce per-pupil instructional costs, it may raise the classroom output to a level where it would still be a bargain, particularly if the number of teachers needed could be reduced.

Certainly some kinds of learning—problem solving, discrimination, and convergent thinking—can be managed efficiently through programmed instruction. However, it is appropriate to ask for more evidence that programmed instruction can manage appreciative learning or attitude formation as effectively as the live teacher. Many fear that overuse of programmed instruction may dehumanize the school, the last bastion of close, interpersonal relations in an otherwise automated culture. Students who want to be treated as human beings will find little comfort in the teaching machine or the television screen.

Educational television, as noted earlier, is a communications system only. Although a marvelous invention, it has no magic beyond one-way audiovisual communication. To assert that the medium is the message is a canard. One cannot generalize about the educational advantages of this piece of hardware until he has seen the software. If the software turns out to be "Sesame Street," it is one matter. If the software is "Gunsmoke," it is a differ-

[42] Harry S. Broudy, "Socrates and the Teaching Machine," *Phi Delta Kappan*, vol. 44, p. 347, March, 1963.

ent matter. One can speak no more intelligently about television in the abstract as curriculum than one can speak of cereal boxes as nourishment. Yet many of its proponents and its detractors continue to do so. One can speak only of its potential advantages and limitations as a mode of communication, which is all that it is. Television does have the obvious capabilities of bringing worldwide—even universe-wide—contemporary events into the classroom live, of bringing superb or terrible teachers into the view of large numbers of students, and of making each seat a front-row seat for viewing experiments, demonstrations, or murders along with other events. Unlike programmed instruction, conventional televised instruction lacks the capacity to accommodate the individual differences of learners. Conventional television does require that the pace of instruction be set at the rate of learning of the average viewer and forces the television teacher to depend largely upon the lecture method of teaching, with its well-known limitations.

Frederick Raubinger, New Jersey's former commissioner of education, also put it bluntly:

The master teacher in the classroom is not a master teacher on TV. She can't be. She's teaching in a vacuum, using the outdated lecture method with no lively questions from boys and girls to stimulate discussion and to arouse interests. I have never seen a really good lesson on TV. Without considering its enormous cost, in my opinion televised instruction on the grade school level direct and day-to-day is not good education.

It is difficult to see the advantages of educational television over the movie projector in the classroom except for the former's ability to provide instantaneous coverage of current events—which is already available through commercial channels. The motion picture, although a valuable aid to instruction, has not revolutionized teaching in its decades of existence, even though it has the added advantages of color, superior technical quality, a much larger screen, and the fact that it can be stopped and repeated in sections or as a whole.

Clearly, television offers the school a useful instructional aid. Like the motion picture or tape recorder, it has a unique and valuable contribution to make to the improvement of learning. But the evidence produced from experience with it so far does not warrant the unrestrained praise of its most ardent exponents. Schramm, director of the Institute for Communications Research at Stanford, believes that educational television has in many ways been a disappointment, although it can be exciting and effective. The Carnegie Corporation, in another study, concluded that its disappointing results can be attributed largely to the fact that television, like radio and moving pictures, has never been truly integrated into the educational process.

Perhaps one decade is a relatively short period within which to measure the extent and effectiveness of this innovation. A willingness to experiment further, an objective open-mindedness, and a patient delay in judgment until more experience is gained would seem to be in order.

The challenge of technology in education, as in all man's enterprises, is how man can capitalize upon the wonders of the machine without being enslaved by it. Broudy has phrased the challenge in these terms.

We have no real choice but to try to outwit the machine age: to seek therein the potentialities for human values that it undeniably has. One might hope that we in the educational profession could take the lead in finding a new integration to unify the differentiations that mass production technology entails. We shall not do so, however, if we merely ape the industrialist and the business man and in the name of efficiency, fractionate further the totality of value that constitutes the life syndrome. Because we are moving closer and closer to the mechanics and methods of the market place, let us not adopt its outlook on life itself. If we come to prize only what it prizes and reward only as it rewards then all the real promise of the machine will come to nothing.[43]

Perhaps the question of most interest to the reader is whether or not the live teacher may eventually be replaced by the machine. Some are sure that the machine will replace the teacher, or at least most teachers. Others are sure that it cannot replace the teacher. The answer probably lies somewhere in between. We believe that machines can indeed perform certain limited functions better and perhaps more economically than the live teacher. On the other hand, the computer can never substantially replace the teacher in terms of our concept of education as an essentially human encounter between the learner and the teacher as an exemplar of knowledge, tastes, values, and feelings. We repudiate both man systems and machine systems but look with favor upon man-machine systems. We rather like this admonition by B. F. Skinner, the inventor

[43] H. S. Broudy, "Teaching Machines: Threats and Promises," *Educational Theory*, vol. 12, p. 156, July, 1962.

of the first teaching machine: "Any teacher who can be replaced by a machine, should be." Clearly, teachers will be threatened by machines when the benefits which they can deliver are no longer commensurate with their costs as compared to the costs of machines.[44]

Educational Finance (Chapter 16)

The total cost of public elementary and secondary schools has more than doubled during the past ten years. Experts in school finance estimate that it will double again in the next ten years despite a plateau in enrollments. In Chapter 16 we discuss the reasons for the increase in costs, the sources of school funds, the nature of school expenditures, and the major aspects of school business management. We turn our attention now to some of the more compelling issues which are prompted by the schools' almost insatiable demand for more money. Most of these issues, along with others, are examined at length in the report of the President's Commission on School Finance, published in 1972.

Does Money Make a Difference in the Quality of Education? Perhaps the most basic question to raise with respect to school finance is whether or not the amount of money spent has any effect upon the quality of education. Some persons speculate that it is possible to increase the quality of education without raising the cost. Many schools could certainly operate more efficiently and, as noted in Chapter 16, cost-benefit analysis, when applied to education, will increasingly force schools to function more efficiently.

Much as we might like to think otherwise, high-quality education and low expenditures just do not coexist. There are no bargains in education. Fortunately, there is considerable research to illuminate this issue. Studies of this problem have been conducted all over the country for more than half a century. Although the cost-quality relationship is not a simple one, a relationship does exist. Norton, who has reviewed the research evidence carefully, concludes that higher-quality education is generally provided in school systems which spend larger amounts per pupil, and lower-quality education in

[44]For further discussion of the advantages and limitations of technology applied to instruction, see American Association of School Administrators, *Instructional Technology and the School Administrator*, Washington, D.C., 1970.

school systems spending smaller amounts per pupil.[45] This conclusion is supported by most of the factual studies of the cost-quality relationship, although the Coleman Report failed to reveal any relationship between the achievement of black and white students of a given family background and the level of school expenditures. Nevertheless, the preponderance of evidence suggests that money spent is the most important single determinant of quality of education, although it is certainly not the only factor.

Can We Afford to Educate Everybody Well? In Chapter 16 we take the position that the cost of education should not be viewed as a burden to society but rather as an investment in our most precious resource—people. The President's Commission on Higher Education has emphasized clearly the investment nature of the costs of education:

Education is an investment, not a cost. It is an investment in free men. It is an investment in social welfare, in better living standards, in better health, in less crime. It is an investment in higher production, increased income, and greater efficiency in agriculture, industry, and government. It is an investment in a bulwark against garbled information, half-truths, and untruths; against ignorance and intolerance. It is an investment in human talent, human relations, democracy, and peace.

We know that unemployment is highest among the undereducated. It is estimated that the unskilled boy will cost his country, on the average, about $1,000 per year for the rest of his life in welfare and/or penal costs, far more than it would cost to educate him through high school. The salary lost by the typical adult male breadwinner in just one year of unemployment is only slightly more than it would cost to provide twelve years of education for him. The cost of public welfare exceeds the cost of public education in most of our cities. We can skimp on expenditures for education but we will spend the money we save—and more—on supporting the people who do not have the education they need to support themselves.

Adequate education permits man to participate more fully in the good life; to find personal meaning and purpose in his existence; to develop a sense

[45]John K. Norton, *Dimensions in School Finance*, National Education Association, Washington, D.C., 1966, pp. 38–39.

This dreary school building illustrates the impoverishment of schools in many poor neighborhoods.

of dignity and worth through his greater contribution to the world of work; to participate more wisely in the body politic; to quicken his self-respect as a more competent head of his family; and to deepen his aesthetic sensibility. It is no longer appropriate to ask whether we can afford to educate our citizens as they should be educated. We can no longer afford poor education: it is too expensive.

What Reforms Are Needed in the Financing of Education? Study of the financing of education is a complicated and difficult undertaking to which many persons have turned their attention. There is considerable disagreement concerning many specific reforms that are needed in school finance, and the issues are complex. At the risk of oversimplifying the issues and their solutions, an attempt is made in the following paragraphs to summarize the major reforms that are needed. Space does not

permit an elaboration of the arguments pro and con. For these, the reader is referred to the bibliography at the end of Chapter 16.

Figure 1-6 reveals a serious problem in school finance. Although the federal government collects 74 percent of the taxes, it provides only 7 percent of the school revenue. Local school districts, which pay more than half of the costs of education, collect less than one tax dollar in five. The federal government's progressive income tax is particularly responsive to the nation's growth in both productivity and public-service needs. State and local government taxes, on the other hand, are based usually upon regressive property, sales, and excise taxes which strain the taxpayers' tolerance. It is small wonder that many local school districts are impoverished and that communities are increasingly voting down higher local school tax rates. The noted economist Walter Heller has expressed this warning:

Washington must find a way to put a generous share of the huge federal fiscal dividend (the automatic increase in tax revenue associated with economic growth) at the disposal of the states and cities. If it fails to do so, federalism will suffer, services will suffer, and the state-local taxpayer will suffer. . . . Whether our concern is for justice and efficiency in taxation, or for better balance in our federalism, or, most important, for a more rational system of financing our aching social needs, there is no escape from the logic of putting the power of the federal income tax at the disposal of beleaguered state and local governments.[46]

Virtually every agency that has studied school finance has recommended substantial increase in the federal participation in the financial support of schools. Some authorities believe that approximately one-third of the total cost should be borne by the federal government.

There is good reason to favor the abandonment of the federal government's fragmented subsidy of education through a miscellany of special-purpose grants, or "categorical aid" as it is called, which are administered by many agencies of the government, in favor of general-purpose aid for education through block grants administered through one agency, the U.S. Office of Education. It has been proposed further that it is even more desirable that much of the federal share of the costs of education and other public services be made available directly to the states through revenue sharing by returning

[46]Walter W. Heller, "Should the Government Share Its Tax Take?" *Saturday Review*, vol. 52, p. 27, March 22, 1969.

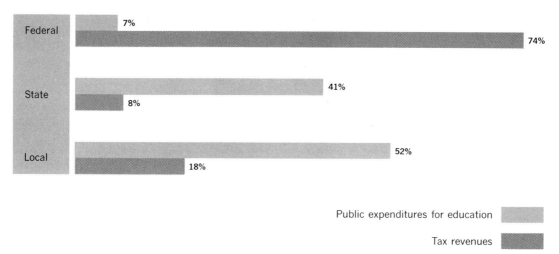

FIGURE 1-6 *Comparison of percentages of total tax revenues and public expenditures for elementary and secondary schools by federal, state, and local governments.*

to the states directly their share of federal tax revenues, to be administered directly by the states as they see fit. Certain categorical grants might remain for special educational needs.

Each state should have one or more broad-base taxes, such as the sales tax or income tax, and loopholes and exemptions in the collection of these taxes should be eliminated. However, state revenue for schools should come from the state's general fund rather than from earmarked taxes. State aid to school districts should be distributed with consideration of the local district's financial effort and need. State aid for education should be designed to guarantee a minimum foundational level for each pupil in the state and should place as few restraints as possible on maximum local financial effort. State-imposed limitations on local taxing powers should be liberalized. State financial support should be mainly in the form of general-purpose aid rather than special-purpose grants, although several kinds of categorical aid may be necessary. State financial programs should be monitored carefully to be sure that they do not discriminate against urban school systems, as many now unfortunately do.

The National Educational Finance Project, an ambitious study of school finance undertaken by a panel of distinguished citizens appointed by the President, recommended in 1971 much heavier funding of education. To relieve the inequitable and overburdened property tax, it recommended a slash in local revenue from 52 percent to 10 to 15 percent and a boost in the federal share from 7 to 30 percent.

These and other revenue reforms have been endorsed by a number of authorities on school finance.[47] State supreme courts in California and Michigan ruled that the local property tax as a principal source of school revenue is unconstitutional because it sustains unequal educational opportunity. Several states—New Mexico, North Carolina, Delaware, Louisiana, Alaska, and Hawaii—are nearing full state funding of schools. Many educators fear that increased state and federal funding will result in the erosion of local control. However local control is a questionable privilege if schools are impoverished.

Regardless of the percentage of educational revenue provided by the state, dilemmas will continue with regard to the basis of its distribution to local districts. Chapter 16 describes the evolution of state aid formulas now commonly based upon the foundation-program approach, in which each district is guaranteed sufficient funds to provide a minimum dollar value of education per child. However, under most of these formulas, wealthier districts remain free to provide more expensive education. Fiscal reform in education is a constant struggle between two goals: nearly equal educational opportunity for all and the best education that a particular family can afford. Both are salutary, but the two are antithetical. Wealthy districts and states tend to oppose

---

[47] For further discussion of this proposal, see Theodore J. Miller, "The Case for Fiscal Reform Now," *School Management*, vol. 13, pp. 50-54, 60-63, November, 1969; and Bryce Baggett, "Full State Funding," *Compact*, vol. 4, pp. 58-59, October, 1970.

formulas which distribute a greater proportion of state aid to poor districts, while poor districts insist that a child's education should not be constrained by low levels of financial ability. Inequalities of three to one in dollar costs per student are not unusual in some regions of the country. Thus the quality of education in many districts is a direct function of the wealth of the district and inversely proportional to the needs of the district.[48] This circumstance stimulates the migration of the more affluent families to the wealthier districts and exacerbates the inequality.

Charles Benson, an authority on school finance, in 1967 began to expose the injustice of state foundation program formulas based upon local school districts' wealth. He recommended that state aid be based upon a percentage of the local school district's budget with higher percentages going to poor districts, rather than the other way around. This would reward local effort rather than local wealth. It would remove poverty as a factor in determining educational opportunity. Maine and Wisconsin have adopted this "power equalizing" approach to state funding of schools.[49]

At the local level, public understanding of the importance of high-quality education and its relation to community well-being should be strengthened. As long as the property tax is the main source of local school revenue, essential reforms in the administration of this tax should be consummated. Property tax assessments should be uniform and equalized to reduce the inequities to taxpayers. Exemptions to the property tax should be examined carefully and reduced as much as possible. Public school revenues and expenditures should be subject to strict prudential controls through careful accounting and auditing. The school budget should be regarded as the prime vehicle for the projection of the district's educational and financial plans and should be subject to careful public scrutiny and discussion.

[48]Some states have been sued by poor districts for discriminating against them in the distribution of state funds. See August W. Steinhilber, "The Judicial Assault on State School Aid Laws: Problems and Prognosis," *Phi Delta Kappan*, vol. 51, pp. 151-153, November, 1969.

[49]For more extensive discussion of this proposal, see John E. Coons, William H. McClure III, and Stephen D. Sugarman, *Private Wealth and Public Education*, The Belknap Press, Harvard University Press, Cambridge, Mass., 1970.

Is Performance Contracting in the Best Interests of Education? Various prototypes of performance contracting are under way in several communities including Camden, New Jersey; Philadelphia; and Texarkana, Texas. In this arrangement, private firms contract with the district to provide instructional and sometimes other services, with remuneration based on a sliding scale in relation to the degree of success in the instruction as measured by students' performance. This arrangement is regarded as an alternative to the alleged failure of the public schools to provide satisfactory education, particularly in ghetto schools. At the time of this writing, the development is still experimental and too new to permit any conclusions regarding its success. In some schools, as in Mesa, Arizona, the performance contract is executed with the teachers, who receive bonuses on the basis of the success of their instruction. The AFT is opposed to performance contracting, regarding it as "an invasion of the responsibility of teachers." The NEA appears to be unopposed to performance contracting with teachers. The Council of Chief State School Officers recommends an open mind with respect to this development. Federal legislation has been proposed to permit performance contracting on a much broader scale in ghetto schools.

Should Public Funds Be Available for Private Schools? The First Amendment to the United States Constitution specifies that "Congress shall make no law respecting an establishment of religion, or prohibiting the free exercise thereof. . . . " This provision is commonly spoken of as a "wall of separation between church and state" and is interpreted by some to mean that public funds should not be made available for the support of religious activities, including church-supported schools. Many state constitutions also provide that public moneys may not be used for the support of sectarian or denominational schools. Nevertheless, a number of states have enacted laws permitting the expenditure of public funds for transportation, textbooks, health services, and other services in private schools. Federal funds were also available to schools for some of these purposes. These statutes have usually been upheld by the courts on the basis of the "child-benefit" theory, which contends that such moneys benefit the child but do not constitute direct support of the school he attends.

A few states had enacted laws providing public funds for part of the salaries of teachers in nonpublic schools. Three of these statutes—Rhode Island, Connecticut, and Pennsylvania—were appealed to the U.S. Supreme Court, which in 1971 held that they violated both the First Amendment and the Fourteenth Amendment (which guarantees "due process"). In the Supreme Court's opinion, these laws involved "excessive entanglement between Government and religion." The Court ruled that "we cannot ignore the dangers that a teacher under religious control and discipline poses to the separation of the religious from the purely secular aspects of pre-college education" and called attention also to the danger of the government's imposing "regulation and surveillance" to ensure that private schools receiving public funds were not teaching religion. It commented also on the "divisive political potential" which could arise in lobbying for public funds. This landmark decision wiped out similar laws in four other states.

In another case, the Supreme Court upheld the constitutionality of the Federal Higher Education Facilities Act of 1963, which authorized federal funds for the construction of academic buildings for private colleges, including those which were church-related. In this case the Court ruled: "Since religious indoctrination is not a substantial purpose or activity of these church-related colleges and universities, there is less likelihood than in primary or secondary schools that religion will permeate the area of secular education."

Bills were then introduced in some states to provide vouchers to parents whose children attended private schools. Their sponsors hoped that this type of indirect aid to private schools would not violate the Constitution. Various other kinds of indirect aid were also proposed, and the litigation continued to explore the line between the "child-benefit theory" and the "excessive entanglement doctrine." The Chief Justice stated that "complete candor compels acknowledgement that one can only dimly perceive the line of demarcation in this extraordinarily sensitive area of constitutional law."

The advocates of public aid for private schools contend that these schools render a public service and should not be denied public support. They insist that parents should not be impeded in their constitutional right to send their children to private schools. If parents must pay taxes for the support of public schools, in addition to fees for the support of the private schools, they are, according to the argument, subject to "double taxation" and are discriminated against. They regard the withholding of

public moneys from private schools as a form of discrimination.

The Supreme Court's decision has had profound impact upon the operation of private schools. Some have been forced to close from lack of funds. Many have curtailed their programs drastically, and enrollment has declined, particularly in parochial schools. These students have been diverted to public schools which were not prepared to handle them in many communities. An increasing number of parents of parochial school students were unconvinced of the necessity of church-related schools which were often not representative of the larger society. Although many church-related schools continue to thrive, the overall future of private elementary and secondary schools remains uncertain at the time of this writing.

On the other hand, many people contend that public funds should not be given to private schools, over which the public has no control. They contend that the constitutional right of citizens to send their children to private schools does not oblige the government to help pay the costs, any more than the guarantee of the right to bear arms obliges the government to subsidize the citizen's purchase of guns. They believe that private school attendance is a voluntary choice and that the contention of discrimination is therefore not relevant. Many persons believe that public financial support of private education will spawn a proliferation of private schools by many religious, political, and other special-interest groups. In some communities this is already occurring.

Thus the debate continues on the difficult issue of how our pluralistic society can assure that universal education is universally available to all with the least invasion of the constitutional rights of any. According to a recent Gallup poll, public opinion is sharply divided on the issue of whether public taxes should be used to support church-affiliated schools: 48 percent of the respondents favored public support of religious schools, 44 percent opposed it, and 8 percent were undecided. Further judicial definition of the boundaries of the First Amendment with respect to education is clearly needed.

Should Vouchers Be Used to Permit More Alternatives to Public Schools? The "voucher plan" is another stratagem for providing funds for private schools, either church-affiliated or independent.

Several persons—notably Christopher Jencks, Milton Friedman, James Coleman, Kenneth Clark, Paul Goodman, and Theodore Sizer—have advocated that parents be given vouchers, roughly equal to the per-pupil costs of public schools (except for poor children who might get more) which could be applied to students' education in any schools of their choice, public or private. The plan is advanced on the assumption that public schools are unsuccessful, particularly with poor children, because they are unresponsive to the needs of these children. Presumably this occurs because public schools are monopolies. Through the use of vouchers, students would be given a choice. This would create a variety of competitive schools, stimulating improvement in public schools, making all schools more accountable for results, and driving bad schools out of business in an open market for education.

Virtually all professional organizations in education are strongly opposed to the voucher plan. They argue that many people would use their vouchers to help children escape from racially integrated schools and that vouchers would encourage hucksterism, promote inefficiency through the proliferation and duplication of school facilities in the same community, increase school transportation costs, exacerbate the inequities which exist in educational opportunity, and eventually destroy the public school system. The National Congress of Parents and Teachers is opposed to the voucher plan. A recent Gallup poll revealed that adults are about evenly divided on the matter, while high school juniors and seniors favor the voucher plan by a margin of more than two to one.

Edgar Fuller, former executive secretary of the Council of Chief State School Officers, contends:

Should private schools be tax-financed, the elementary and secondary public schools would be left to educate children from denominations too small to operate their own schools, the unchurched, the culturally deprived, and the rejects and problem students from the private schools which can choose their own pupils. Tax funds would be combined with private funds to finance schools segregated on the basis of religion, social status, wealth, and special interests, and would seriously affect the public schools as an effective educational agency as would the segregation by race. . . . Most serious would be the religious, social, political, and economic divisiveness that would follow.[50]

[50]Edgar Fuller, "Government Financing of Public and Private Education," *Phi Delta Kappan*, vol. 47, p. 371, March, 1966.

Thus the issue persists: Can we provide more equal and effective opportunity for all by strengthening the public school system or by supporting a variety of alternative schools? The argument is spirited and the evidence needed to settle it is not yet available.[51]

How Can Schools Be Made More Accountable for Their Performance? Several of the proposals discussed here are supported by the argument that public schools must be held more accountable for their results. Costs increase while the effectiveness of schools declines in the opinions of many. Largely monopolistic, the public schools are relatively free from competition in their survival. The power of the teaching profession, it is argued, has increased at the expense of the public's control. Under these circumstances, it is argued, means must be found to make the schools more answerable and more responsive to the public which they serve. A recent Gallup poll revealed that parents, by a margin of three to one, would favor a "system that would hold teachers and administrators more accountable for the progress of students." The great attention devoted by governors, legislators, and school boards to this concern for accountability in our schools can be overlooked by educators only at their own peril. The question is not really whether schools should be answerable for their product, but rather what kind of accountability should prevail. Barro has identified the sticky operational questions involved:

To what extent should each participant in the educational process—teacher, principal, and administrator—be held responsible for results?

To whom should they be responsible?

How are "results" to be defined and measured?

How will each participant's contribution be measured?

What will be the consequences for professional educators of being held responsible.[52]

Barro has also classified neatly the various schemes for ensuring accountability:

[51]For further argument on both sides of this issue, see: Peter A. Janssen, "Education Vouchers," *American Education*, vol. 6, pp. 9-11. December, 1970; Christopher Jencks, "Giving Parents Money for Schooling," *Phi Delta Kappan*, vol. 52, pp. 49-52, September, 1970; Stephen Arons, "The Joker in Private School Aid," *Saturday Review*, vol. 54, pp. 45-47, 56, Jan. 16, 1971.

[52]Stephen M. Barro, "An Approach to Developing Accountability Measures for the Public Schools," *Phi Delta Kappan*, vol. 52, p. 196, December, 1970.

Improved output-oriented management methods—emphasis is on accountability for effective use of resources through systems analysis to determine how well goals are achieved in relation to input; cost-benefit models are commonly used.

Institutionalization of external evaluations or educational audits—emphasis is upon use of outside auditing agencies to insure objectivity in comparing results with normative data from other schools.

Performance incentives for school personnel—emphasis is on monetary rewards (or reprisals) for educators based upon the effectiveness of their instruction.

Performance contracting—emphasis is upon monetary rewards for outside agencies based upon the quality of their performance of contracted services.

Decentralization and community control—emphasis is upon the decentralization of authority and the shifting of authority from professionals to citizens in the school neighborhoods.

Alternative educational systems—emphasis is upon stimulation of competition among several schools through the use of educational vouchers by parents who are free to choose among them.[53]

All the possibilities above depend upon two common elements for success: systematic evaluation of performance and communication of the results of the evaluation. The element of competition is also inherent in all the schemes in one form or another. Obviously, combinations of several of the schemes, which are not mutually exclusive, can be established. Additional proposals will also be advanced. Thus it is not assumed that any one of the above stratagems represents the only way to achieve accountability.

What are the arguments surrounding attempts to achieve accountability? The opponents commonly complain that the connotation of the proposals is negative, that they constitute retribution against teachers and schools and imply that they must either shape up or suffer the consequences. For someone to be held accountable, his performance must be measured, and opponents call attention to the great difficulty of measuring instructional performance. Teachers fear that the performance tests would be based upon academic progress that is quantifiable (largely cognitive development) as opposed to progress that is more difficult to quantify (affective development). Teachers also insist that it is unrealistic to hold teachers accountable for results without giving them greater control of all the variables—allocation of resources, determination of the curriculum, development of school policies, and self-

[53]*Ibid.*, pp. 197–198.

governance of the profession. Teachers also feel that they may be held responsible for children's failure to progress in cases where such failure is due to factors other than their teaching ability and is therefore beyond their control.

Teachers' organizations insist that any failures attributed to the schools are the result of inadequate funding of schools rather than the inadequacies of accountability systems which they believe are already existent. Many persons also believe that the systems approach to educational development is still too rudimentary to be successful. Most of the opposition to accountability systems arises from teachers' organizations.[54] However, the United Federation of Teachers, the largest local of the AFT, agreed to develop jointly with the New York City Board of Education a plan for achieving professional accountability in the schools.

The proponents of accountability systems base their arguments on four major contentions:

Educators would be forced to contemplate and specify their educational goals more precisely.
Methods of evaluating educational progress would become more refined and reliable.
Information regarding educational progress would be reported more effectively to the public.
The public would have more alternatives to choose from.

Sidney P. Marland, U.S. Commissioner of Education, supports the quest for accountability:

We must invent new ways of accounting for our effectiveness. And if we cannot account for our effectiveness, we should get out of the way. This applies particularly for school leaders at all levels. . . . The child no longer fails if his equal opportunity goes unfulfilled. The school, we are told, has failed, the teacher has failed, the superintendent has failed, the board of education has failed. This new overriding expectation cannot be turned back. Nor do I believe we as a profession would want it turned back.

Although we recognize the practical problems involved in most efforts to relate teachers' salaries to performance, we believe that the principle is defensible and that teachers should not assume a priori positions opposing it, as they have often done. Rather, they should join hands in an effort to overcome the practical problems, by means of carefully

[54]For a statement of the AFT's position on accountability, see Donald A. Collins and others: "Judgment Day in the Schools: Trial by Accountability," *American Teacher*, vol. 3, pp. 11–21, November, 1970.

controlled experimental situations. We believe that teachers can capitalize upon the growing demand for accountability in the profession to the advantage of both themselves and society: the demand for accountability can help to close the present credibility gap between militant teachers on one side and disappointed parents and exasperated taxpayers on the other. Clearly, however, our experience with the various proposals for increasing accountability is still too rudimentary to justify confident evaluations. We should be open-minded and willing to experiment with all reasonable possibilities, carefully monitoring results. Various prototypes of all the schemes are currently under development and their number is likely to increase.[55]

AMERICAN EDUCATION IN TODAY'S WORLD (PART 6, CHAPTER 17)

The need for better international understanding is axiomatic. International education is viewed increasingly as man's "last hope of survival," the only way to eradicate the scourges of war, hunger, poverty, disease, ethnocentrism, ignorance, and pollution. International education is essential to improving the human condition, especially in the less favored countries, and to enriching the culture of all countries. International education is defined broadly to include a wide variety of endeavors: the study of other cultures, the study of international forces and problems, and comparative education. These goals are sought through various international agencies such as UNESCO; the exchange of teachers, students, and materials such as the Fulbright Act provided; and direct assistance to other countries through programs such as the Peace Corps. These programs and their objectives are described in Chapter 17. Let us consider some of the issues inherent in present-day international education.

What Are the Purposes and Policies of American Education in World Affairs? The young nations, many of which are underdeveloped, view education as the key which will unlock their natural resources,

[55]For further discussion of the rationale of various accountability systems, see Myron Lieberman and others, "An Overview of Accountability," *Phi Delta Kappan*, vol. 52, pp. 194–239, December, 1970.

raise their economic productivity, and ensure their political stability. More and more they turn to this country for educational know-how. From this perspective our educational assistance abroad might be viewed as a form of foreign aid, a means of lifting underdeveloped countries to a higher standard of living through the power of knowledge.

At the same time, this country finds itself in the midst of a worldwide political and ideological struggle with the Communist-bloc nations. The ascendancy of either communism or democracy may ultimately depend upon which wins the hearts and minds of people in the uncommitted countries. From this perspective, education might be viewed as an instrument of national and international policy, a means of extending and strengthening democracy at home and abroad, as discussed in Chapter 17.

The choice between education as foreign aid and education as foreign policy poses a perplexing dilemma. In the first case, the education which we export might be free of ulterior purpose and national bias, pure knowledge made available to any nation that needs it for whatever intrinsic use it can make of it. In the latter case, our educational effort might be concentrated upon those countries which are truly uncommitted or fairly favorably oriented toward Western civilization. And this education might be designed deliberately to encourage the commitment of our friends abroad toward democratic values and objectives. That is, American education abroad could be designed to contain the spread of communism and counter its propaganda.

Another choice, the most pervasive and persuasive of all, is the extension of man's knowledge of his fellow man around the world as a means of improving international relations and sustaining cooperation among nations in assaulting the problems which threaten mankind. Our national position with respect to all these choices is not clear. Some of our educational efforts abroad fall under the jurisdiction of the United States Information Agency, others under the Department of State, others under the U.S. Office of Education, and others under the Peace Corps, indicating that the government views some as propaganda, some as foreign policy, some as education, and some as aid. In the private domain, universities, churches, industry, foundations, and other agencies assume varied undertakings. Governmental divisions and private agencies sometimes find themselves competing and refusing to cooperate in educational missions abroad. This division of purpose, responsibility, and activity is to some degree perhaps appropriate for a free and pluralistic society. Nevertheless it does result in duplication of effort, ambivalence of purpose, and rivalry for power.

Where do we turn for guidance in this new educational effort abroad? Actually we have no well-considered principles and strategies with which to direct our enterprise in international education. We operate without adequate definition of the expectations which we hold, without a clear concept of the role which education should properly play, and without a strategy by which we can best deploy our limited resources. Much more critical thought and research must be directed toward these issues before our efforts can become fully effective.

However we may decide these matters, one conclusion is evident; as Charles Frankel, former Assistant Secretary of State for Educational and Cultural Affairs, has pointed out:

Education is emerging progressively as the indispensible ingredient in the complex and painful process to which we have given the bland name of "economic and social development." The development of the poorer countries, we now know, is not in the main a material process, even though it has its material conditions and material rewards. Development is a psychological process, a moral transformation. If this transformation is to take place in a reasonably peaceful way, education must be our main hope.

We are being asked by many of the nations of the world to help establish modern educational systems. Most of these nations have turned not to the classical education models which some of them inherited from their former colonial powers, and not to the Soviet model, which Russia is eager to export, but rather to the United States' system. The newly emerging nations appear to find in the American system the blend of pragmatism and classicism that offers for them the best hope for rolling back ignorance, increasing production, reducing class cleavages, strengthening citizenship, ameliorating disease and poverty, and leading people closer to the good life. Although progress is being made in this undertaking, our efforts fall far short of the need. It is to be hoped that our nation, itself the cradle of free education for all, will quicken man's march for free, universal education around the globe through our efforts at home and abroad.

Are National and International Emphases in Education Incompatible? As is noted in Chapter 17, many countries, both the old and the young, are

fiercely nationalistic, often chauvinistic. They regard the loyalty of their people as a fixed-sum commodity and feel that increased emphasis on international interests and responsibilities will necessarily reduce their students' loyalty to their own nation. Many United States citizens have protested educational exchanges with the fear that our students will accept foreign ideologies abroad or that foreign nationals will bring unacceptable doctrines to our land. They see in this exchange a possible weakening in our resolve to champion the interests of our nation in the world scene. Other countries, notably China and some other totalitarian governments, are using education deliberately as a vehicle for indoctrination in chauvinism and hatred of other countries. The historian Arnold Toynbee, for example, sees fanatical nationalism as only a stage in the evolution of man. He states, "You don't want to get rid of your loyalty and affection for your own nation; but you need to give them also to a larger community."[56]

Nonetheless, the national interest is sometimes in conflict with the international interest in education. Young developing countries, particularly newly independent ones, are understandably proud and, in their determination to become rapidly self-sufficient, are often reluctant to recognize their need and to accept help. After years of colonial status, they are understandably wary of inroads which other countries may make upon their freedom while attempting to improve their schools.

This ethnocentrism is not peculiar to young nations. When the "reverse Peace Corps," which would bring people from new nations to work in the poverty areas of the United States, was proposed, a Congressman bellowed, "What the ---- do you think we are, an underdeveloped country?" National pride is not a monopoly of young nations. Some United States school systems have been forbidden by their boards to teach about the United Nations and other international organizations, lest the students' patriotism be weakened. And some people, particularly radical students and professors, see international studies as neo-imperialism.

When domestic and international education needs compete for scarce funds in the United States, as elsewhere, the former are likely to fare much better. The International Education Act, a bril-

[56]"Paul Hanna Interviews Arnold Toynbee," *Phi Delta Kappan*, vol. 49, p. 173, December, 1967.

liant plan for strengthening international understanding, has never been adequately funded by the Congress. Over the protests of the U.S. National Commission for UNESCO, the Congress with but one dissenting vote cut drastically the appropriations for the State Department's Bureau of Educational and Cultural Affairs. Many other examples of the low priority of international education could be cited.

There are no easy answers to the questions involving domestic and international considerations. However, as the educator Nevitt Sanford has pointed out, "In the shrinking world of today, there is no room for tribalism, and the person who regards himself as categorically different from peoples of other national, ethnic, or social groups is living in the past and is a threat to civic and world peace."[57] It is to be hoped that the compelling problems of mankind in an ever-shrinking world will quicken man's realization that his destiny is ultimately far more international than national.

THE ULTIMATE ISSUE

A number of the more fateful contemporary issues in American education have been discussed in this chapter. We hope that the chapters which follow will quicken the reader's commitment to the profession which bears so much of the responsibility for improving the human condition and will deepen the reader's understanding of the background of these issues. Although the issues may divide us, this common conviction should unite us: when those in dispute try to learn from each other, the profit is greater for all. As W. H. Ferry, vice-president of the Center for the Study of Democratic Institutions, has pointed out:

The trouble today is not indifference and lack of attention. There is no vacuum around education, but a wide firmament of clashing sounds and voices. It is hard to think of a subject which is at once so unanimously approved and so divisive of opinion. No institution breathes more of the common aspiration while producing more muddle. Yet we are all committed to it because education is, from any point of view, man's best enter-

prise. It is the fundamental premise of a democratic society and, in these dangerous days, perhaps the only final hope of survival.[58]

The high level of public interest in education is one of the most heartening and wholesome aspects of the current educational scene. Educators are challenged to nurture this interest and direct it toward constructive ends. But educators must also help society realize that most of the shortcomings attributed to schools are really the deeper failures of society itself. If there is a crisis in education, it is in reality a crisis in American values. As Henry S. Commager, one of our great historians, has pointed out, "Schools reflect the society they serve. Many of the failures we ascribe to contemporary education are in fact failures of our society as a whole. . . . To reform our schools is first to reform ourselves." The deeper cultural roots of the crisis in society are emphasized here, not to reduce the sense of responsibility which schools should assume in ameliorating that total crisis, but rather to emphasize the importance of a broad assault on the crisis of our time by all agencies of society, including schools. That so much attention is being given to schools in the midst of this crisis is an indication of *where* our people hope to find the thrust toward solution of these fateful problems. The issues in education will not be settled until the conflicts in American society are resolved. It is the destiny of the teacher, then, to share in this noble and exciting adventure. We urge the reader to engage in this adventure boldly and help shape the educational enterprise so that it may in truth become "man's best enterprise" and the "final hope of survival."

Suggested Activities

1. Explain your views on the causes and cures of student unrest in schools and colleges.
2. Prepare an essay on the topic "Race and Education."
3. Consider the various proposals advanced to strengthen the accountability of schools. Select those which you consider most promising and explain the reasons for your choice.

---

[57] Nevitt Sanford, "Aims of College Education," in Charles W. Hovice, (ed.), *Campus Values: Some Considerations for Collegians*, Charles Scribner's Sons, New York, 1968, p. 14.

[58] W. H. Ferry, "The Muddle in Education," *Center Dairy: 15*, Center for the Study of Democratic Institutions, Santa Barbara, Calif., 1966, p. 16.

4. Prepare an essay on the theme "The Proper Distribution of Control of Education among Federal, State, and Local Governments."

5. Prepare an essay on the topic "Problems and Reforms in Urban Education."

6. Prepare a statement of your views on the advantages and limitations of educational technology.

7. Select a popular magazine and make a list of the educational issues on which it has published articles during the past year. Then analyze these in comparison with your own list of critical issues in education.

8. Review the philosophical statements on curriculum in this chapter, decide which viewpoint you prefer, and prepare an essay defending it.

9. List a few issues in education which you consider most critical and conduct an opinion poll with respect to them.

10. Prepare a statement of your position with respect to independent versus labor-affiliated teachers' organizations.

11. Prepare a description of the ideal school of the future—its organization, purposes, curriculum, environment, faculty, community relations, etc.—and describe the ideal role of the teacher within it.

12. Interview several superintendents of schools to discover what they perceive to be the most critical issues in education and what solutions they recommend.

Bibliography

Bendiner, Robert: *The Politics of Schools: A Crisis in Self-Government*, Harper & Row, Publishers, Incorporated, New York, 1969. An account of political problems school boards and administrators face in dealing with teachers' militancy, discontent of minorities, and underfinancing.

Brameld, Theodore: *The Climactic Decades: Mandate to Education*, Frederick A. Praeger, Inc., New York, 1970. Explanation of reconstructionist views of education in contemporary milieu by one of its most articulate spokesmen.

Bruner, Jerome S.: *The Relevance of Education*, W. W. Norton and Company, Inc., New York, 1971. Essays dealing with historical and philosophical approaches to school reform and educational issues.

Crary, Ryland W., and Louis A. Petrone: *Foundations of Modern Education*, Alfred A. Knopf, Inc., New York, 1971.

Examination of current issues in education in relation to fundamental questions of educational philosophy.

Dropkin, Stan, Harold Full, and Ernest Schwarcz (eds.): *Contemporary American Education: An Anthology of Issues, Problems, Challenges*, 2d ed., The Macmillan Company, New York, 1970. An anthology of current concerns and problems of schools in transition.

Ehlers, Henry (ed.): *Crucial Issues in Education*, 4th ed., Holt, Rinehart and Winston, Inc., New York, 1969. Anthology of some of the most controversial issues in contemporary American education.

Glasser, William: *Schools without Failure*, Harper & Row, Publishers, Incorporated, New York, 1969. Discussion of the causes of failure in schools and the cures as prescribed in a program of increased involvement.

Goodlad, John I., M. Frances Klein, and Associates: *Behind the Classroom Door*, Charles A. Jones Publishing Company, Worthington, Ohio, 1971. Case material from observations in many schools illuminates the issues in educational change.

Gross, Ronald, and Beatrice Gross (eds.): *Radical School Reform*, Simon & Schuster, Inc., New York, 1969. Collection of writings from the more radical educational reformers.

Hook, Sidney: *Academic Freedom and Academic Anarchy*, Cowles Book Company, New York, 1970. Considerations of the impact of student disruption upon the academic freedom of schools.

Illich, Ivan: *Deschooling Society*, Harper and Row, Publishers, Incorporated, New York, 1971. Contends that the school's monopoly must be broken if our free society is to come to grips with reform.

Kroll, Arthur M. (ed.): *Issues in American Education*, Oxford University Press, New York, 1970. Collection of statements by leading scholars on issues in education.

National Education Association: *Schools for the 70s and Beyond*, Washington, D.C., 1971. Discussion guide covering the major dilemmas in education with suggested guides for redirection.

National Education Association, Research Division: *The Teacher's Day in Court*, National Education Association, Washington, D.C., 1972. Summaries of court decisions on various issues related to teachers.

Postman, Neil, and Charles Weingartner: *Teaching as a Subversive Activity*, Delacorte Press, Dell Publishing Co., Inc., New York, 1969. A critical discussion of repression and boredom in American schools.

Rafferty, Max: *Max Rafferty on Education*, The Devin-Adair Company, Inc., New York, 1968. Free-swinging, wide-ranging criticism of schools from a conservative, essentialist reformer.

Repo, Satu (ed.): *This Book Is about Schools*, Pantheon Books, Inc., New York, 1971. A collection of articles of unorthodox views of education.

Silberman, Charles: *Crisis in the Classroom*, Random House, Inc., New York, 1970. Widely read discussion of the depressing school environment with recommendations for reform of education.

TYPICAL ADMINISTRATIVE ORGANIZATION
IN EDUCATION

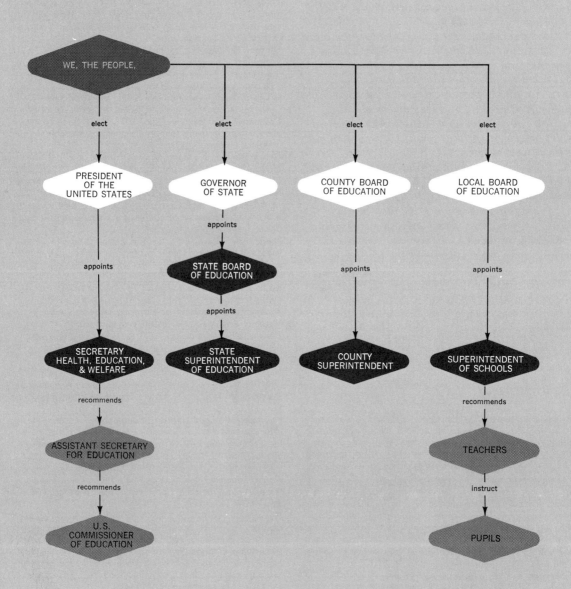

Part Two

Organization and Administration of Education

In Part 1 attention was focused upon the larger controversies in American education. Part 2 undertakes an examination of the organization and administration of education through the hierarchy of governmental units—federal, state, county and intermediate, and local—which are portrayed graphically on the opposite page. The broadest and highest unit in the hierarchy of educational organization is of course the federal. Although the United States Constitution does not mention education or schools, the federal government has both a direct and an indirect interest in education. It is a fact that the national government has become a very active partner in education. The chief educational agency of the United States is the Office of Education with its Commissioner of Education in the Department of Health, Education, and Welfare, a Cabinet-level department. In 1965 a new position was established, namely, Assistant Secretary for Education in the Department of Health, Education, and Welfare, which enhanced the importance of education in the nation. The U. S. Office of Education has expanded its staff markedly to meet and coordinate educational needs and demands. The national programs interrelate with the state, county, and local systems (see the chart on the opposite page) (Chapter 2).

The adoption of the Tenth Amendment to the Constitution of the United States in 1791 made education primarily a state function. Although the state may delegate some of its authority to the intermediate and local districts, each state board of education, acting through its state commissioner of education, serves as the chief centralizing agent for public education within each of the fifty states. In 1966 the Compact for Education—an interstate political and educational partnership—was organized officially as the Education Commission of the States (Chapter 3).

Recent years have witnessed a marked trend toward larger administrative units in education. Some school units are as large as a township or a county. These may be intermediate units between the state and local districts (Chapter 4).

American public education has its local application in the school district, which is usually administered by an elected board of education and an appointed superintendent of schools. The local school district is a striking example of grass-roots democracy. Laymen are important leaders in education in both public and private institutions. School administration in a dynamic democracy calls for a high order of educational statesmanship. Administration should be the servant of education (Chapter 5).

Chapter 2 National Program of Education

ORIENTATION

"The whole people," according to John Adams, "must take upon themselves the education of the whole people and must be willing to bear the expense of it." This was radical doctrine in Adams' time because there was not then any precedent in any other nation for this ambitious aspiration of educating all the people. The development of our universal, free, compulsory educational system is one of the most significant chronicles in our history. It accounts for much of the remarkable growth and prosperity of our country.

Despite the firm commitment of our founding fathers to universal education, there is no reference to education in the United States Constitution. This was not an oversight. Many of the colonists had come to the New World to escape the tyranny of autocratic central governments abroad, and they were not about to risk having the control of something as important as education in the hands of the federal government. Even today this fear of control of education by Washington remains quite strong.

Although the Constitution left control of education to the states, the federal government has nevertheless participated in the support and development of education throughout our history under the authorization of the clause of the Constitution that deals with the promotion of the general welfare. Indeed, federal support for education antedates the Constitution itself through the grants of land for schools authorized by the Continental Congress in 1785. From that time forward, as revealed by the historical calendar in this chapter, federal participation has significantly shaped the destiny of our educational system.

These Indian children represent one of the educationally disadvantaged minority groups.

An important distinction must be made between the terms "national" and "federal," which are often confused in common lexicon. Throughout this discussion, we shall use the term "federal" when speaking of the role of the federal government in education and the word "national" to describe the total educational enterprise in the country—federal, state, and local public and private school and nonschool agencies.

In this chapter we shall consider the philosophical and historical foundations of the national program of education, describe the federal educational agencies and their activities, and speculate on the future of the national system of education. Most of the issues germane to the national program of education are discussed in Chapter 1.

PHILOSOPHICAL FOUNDATIONS

The system of free, universal schools is one of the unique and significant characteristics of our society. It is unique because free public education for all is a bold and visionary ideal without precedent in the history of mankind. It is significant because the story of our national strength and prosperity is, in large measure, the story of our schools. Truly the development of our educational system is one of the noblest and most distinguishing expressions of American civilization.

Americans have always had great faith in the power of education, although they do not always express confidence in their schools. Alexis de Tocqueville, the brilliant French scholar who visited the young republic shortly after its founding, observed that "the universal and sincere faith that they profess here in the efficaciousness of education seems to me to be one of the most remarkable features of America." How well has this faith been justified?

Education and Democracy

The founders of our republic regarded education as the key to liberty. They looked upon the spread of knowledge as the fundamental safeguard of the freedom, equality, and self-government which had been won through the struggle for independence. Jefferson warned that "if a nation expects to be ignorant and free . . . it expects what never was and never will be." Universal suffrage cannot endure without universal education. Ignorant men will not long remain free. According to James Russell Lowell, "It was in making education not only common to all, but in some sense compulsory on all, that the destiny of the free republics of America was practically settled."

The public schools, through their great contribution to public knowledge and understanding, have strengthened and perpetuated the ideals of American democracy. Our schools have helped our people to make democracy work. We have carved a nation across a continent. We have established justice and domestic tranquility and have secured the blessings of liberty. We have held our nation together through all manner of crises, including a civil war. We have met successfully the challenge of domestic and foreign tyrants.

But the battle for freedom must be won anew with each generation. The false promises of communism and the threat of foreign ideologies to our national security press new and unprecedented demands upon American democracy. At home, a small but hardy band of domestic revolutionaries and anarchists, many of them students, disdain the democratic process, allegedly because it has been imperfect in realizing the great ideals of the nation. They offer no alternative to the democratic process, only a cry for its destruction.

We must give more forthright attention to helping students and other citizens acquire a sense of morality in dissent. Are we helping them distinguish between civil disobedience and lawlessness? Are we helping them determine when civil disobedience is moral or immoral? Are we helping them understand the inseparable relationship between the means and the ends of responsible citizenship? Are we helping them acquire forbearance when they are in disagreement with government with the same grace that they accept the rights and protections of government? If indoctrination is ever appropriate

in citizenship education, indoctrination into the essence of democracy, the willingness to accept the will of the majority is necessary. Without this acceptance there can be no representative government and no protection of any citizen. Surely minority rights must also be protected, but within the parameters of orderly, rational, responsible, and disciplined means for the refinement of society.

The school is viewed by the students as the establishment. It is that part of the establishment which is most immediate and important to them. It should stand as an object lesson to students and to all of society in how the establishment demonstrates the best of the democratic heritage. It should be man's best laboratory for the discovery and practice of responsible citizenship. This is a difficult assignment which challenges all the patience, enlightenment, and good pedagogy we can muster. But the stakes are high, including perhaps our very survival as a free society.

Education and Equal Opportunity

America was settled by the greatest migration in the history of mankind—a migration of poor and oppressed people, discontented with the tyranny and inequality of opportunity abroad. Immigrants came to our shores with vastly different languages, religions, cultures, political faiths, racial and national backgrounds, and social and economic status. To the public school fell the task of making 30 million new American citizens. No other nation ever assimilated such a heterogeneous population as rapidly and as completely. These people came to America in search of a classless society where there would be equal opportunity. Throughout our history, visitors from other lands have been struck by the general equality of conditions achieved by our people.

The United States, more than any other major nation, makes educational opportunity available to its citizens. For example, more than twice as many children from blue-collar families reach the final year of secondary school in the United States than in England. No other major nation retains 75 percent of its young people through high school, as does this country. Neither does any other nation provide higher education for as large a percentage of its youth as does the United States.

Free public education has unlocked the door of opportunity for millions. Great scientists, statesmen, athletes, artists, teachers, businessmen, physicians, lawyers, and men in other fields have risen in America despite diversity of race, religion, national origin, or social or economic position of family. In perhaps no other country is it possible for people of modest origin to rise so far and so fast. In no other country have the common people achieved such a large measure of political power, social status, and economic prosperity. The success of America is the story of faith in the common man.

But the ultimate in social equality has not yet been achieved. Although our schools helped the nation assimilate 30 million immigrants, we have not yet assimilated very well an equal number of native American racial and ethnic minority groups. Although class distinctions are less extant in our nation than in most others, serious discrimination and inequality of opportunity still exist. The children of migrant workers, Negroes, Mexican-Americans, Puerto Ricans, and American Indians have been disadvantaged by lack of respect and equal treatment, by schools which have not accommodated their needs very well, and by their own subcultures, which do not prepare them well for life in an industrialized society. More than half of the American Indians of school age do not graduate from high school. The dropout rate is twice as high for black students as for whites. Undereducated, dropouts become the victims of unemployment and poverty. Hubert Humphrey has warned:

Education is the keystone in the arch of democracy. Ignorance breeds only slavery. Enlightenment liberates the human mind and spirit. As a free people—as a democratic people—we must accept the moral obligation of providing the means whereby every American— regardless of race, color, age, religion, income, or educational achievement—has an equal opportunity for education and training limited only by his own capability and initiative.

Although progress is being made, sustained in part by the Civil Rights Act, the Economic Opportunity Act, and other federal programs, much more progress remains to be accomplished before our people can in fact become "one nation, under God, indivisible, with liberty and justice for all."

Education and Economic Well-being

Despite the many pockets of poverty, the march of American invention and production has indeed been the envy of the world. Although it contains only one-seventeenth of the world's population, the United States produces nearly half of the world's

goods and consumes nearly one-third of its goods and services. The real income of approximately 220 million Americans exceeds the real income of the nearly 700 million people in Europe and Russia and far surpasses the total income of about $1\frac{3}{4}$ billion inhabitants of Asia. The average American worker has completed twelve years of schooling—an average higher than that attained in any other nation— and is the most productive worker in the world. Widespread vocational education has contributed substantially to this record. Engineering and technical schools have provided thousands of persons with the technical knowledge needed to lead in the advance of discovery and invention. Agricultural colleges have helped develop a farming industry that feeds not only our people but also millions of people around the world. Although many other factors have contributed to our miracle of production, universal public education has been a preeminent force. Chester Barnard, former president of the New Jersey Bell Telephone Company, observed that "the basic process by which the productive capacity of society is maintained or increased is by education."

Nevertheless, our economic position is not without blemish. Although America finds the means for much of its material needs, there is often a dangerous lag in financial support for certain nonmaterial needs, notably education, public health, and social services. Relations between labor and management are often characterized by distrust and cleavage. If the intellectual level of advertising in America is any criterion, there is reason to believe that the American is not always a wise consumer. Many products, such as automobiles, are designed deliberately for early obsolescence rather than for long, efficient use. Worse yet, we have polluted the atmosphere and waters, spread debris over the countryside, permitted much housing to decay, slaughtered people on the highways, expended huge sums on military and space hardware, and often squandered material and human resources. More and more, Americans look to the schools for relief from these problems of an industrialized economy. Maurice Mitchell, president of Encyclopaedia Britannica, has said that "the American economy was built around the railroads in the last half of the 19th century, around the automobile in the first two-thirds of this century, and it will be built around education in the balance of the century."

Education and Individual Excellence

American democracy has always cherished the dignity and worth of the individual. Respect for the individual has been proclaimed in the Declaration of Independence and the Constitution. This doctrine has been invoked to resist special privilege and to sustain the social, economic, political, and civil rights of the people. Both democracy and the educational system are committed to the full development of the individual citizen. Perhaps no other nation guards the rights of the individual as zealously as the United States. No other educational system makes as diligent an effort to adapt learning experiences to the needs, interests, and capacities of the individual learner.

However, much progress remains to be made. American schools still fail to provide educational opportunity rich and extensive enough to enable each individual to reach his maximum level of self-realization. The precious talents of many people remain undiscovered and undeveloped, resulting in costly loss of manpower.

Kenneth Clark, an eminent psychologist and expert on the education of ghetto youth, admonishes:

A nation which presents itself to the world as the guardian of democracy and the protector of human values throughout the world cannot itself make a mockery of these significant ethical principles by dooming one-tenth of its own population to a lifetime of inhuman futility because of remediable educational deficiencies in its public schools.[1]

HISTORICAL DEVELOPMENT OF FEDERAL ACTIVITIES

The historical calendar in this chapter lists significant events in the evolution of federal interest in education. The events involving the federal government directly in the advancement of education are described below.

Basic Federal Legislation

Despite the fact that education is not mentioned in the United States Constitution, indirect justifi-

[1] Kenneth Clark, "Ghetto Education: New Directions," in Ronald Gross and Beatrice Gross (eds.), *Radical School Reform*, Simon and Schuster, New York, 1969, p. 121.

cation for a national program of instruction may be found in several of its provisions, the "general welfare" clause, and the Preamble.

That the central government is not to control education is evident from the Tenth Amendment to the Constitution, which by implication definitely leaves the subject of education to the individual states: "The powers not delegated to the United States by the Constitution, nor prohibited by it to the states, are reserved to the states respectively, or to the people." The implied prohibition against the establishment of a centralized system markedly influenced the direction and scope of federal participation in education.

Land Grants for Schools

During the first century of its existence, the federal government's support of education was manifested largely by grants of land to the states for the development of schools and colleges. The Continental Congress adopted in 1785 an ordinance, reaffirmed two years later, which ended with the significant words, "There shall be reserved the lot number sixteen of every township for the maintenance of public schools within the said township." Thus the economic foundation was laid for a future land and school policy in the Northwest. This provision, granting federal lands for school use, was the first enactment of federal support for education, antedating the ratification of the Constitution itself.

In the year 1787 the famous Northwest Ordinance stated that the following important principle should be applied to states to be carved from the territory: "Religion, morality, and knowledge being necessary to good government and the happiness of mankind, schools and the means of education shall be forever encouraged."

With the admission of the seventeenth state, Ohio, to the Union in 1803, the federal government actually inaugurated the epoch-making practice of giving the 1-mile-square section of each township for general educational purposes. With certain exceptions and variations, this practice was continued with each new state admitted. The total of these land grants is estimated at 90 million acres, or almost 150,000 square miles. The extent of this area is larger than the combined territory of Ohio, Indiana, and Illinois. The funds derived from the sale and lease of these original school lands form the major part of permanent school funds of several states. Although some of the funds were poorly managed, these gifts of the federal government to education have been extremely significant.

The first Morrill Act of 1862 provided 6 million acres of federal lands to the states for the support of colleges for instruction in "agriculture and the mechanic arts, without excluding other scientific and classical studies and including military tactics." This act established sixty-eight land-grant colleges, some of the best institutions of higher education in the nation. The act was conceived by a Vermont blacksmith's son, Senator Justin Morrill, who wanted to provide for other poor youth the low-cost college education he never had. The land-grant colleges did help to democratize higher education and throw open the doors of opportunity to youth, particularly in the fields of agriculture, engineering, and home economics. The original act was supplemented by other grants in the second Morrill Act of 1890, the Nelson Amendment, and the Bankhead-Jones Act of 1935. The second Morrill Act prohibited discrimination by race in institutions receiving funds.

Vocational Education and Manpower Development

One of the most pervasive interests of the federal government in education over the past hundred years has been the development of our greatest national resource, educated manpower. This interest has been especially quickened during periods of national emergency—such as wars and depressions, when shortages of trained manpower threaten the security or prosperity of the nation. The thrust of much of this effort by the federal government is in the form of money grants to schools and colleges for vocational and professional education and, in some instances, direct grants to students. This federal support of manpower development has had a salubrious effect upon our national productivity and prosperity and explains in great part the miraculous growth of the American economy in the twentieth century.

Agricultural Education. After the passage of the Morrill Act during the Civil War, there was little new support of education by the federal government for the next half-century until World War I, except for the Hatch Act of 1887 which did provide small annual sums to state agricultural colleges to stimulate the development of agricultural science. Many years later, in 1914, the Congress passed the Smith-Lever Act, or Agricultural Extension Act, to stimulate

farmers and their wives to make better use of the emerging new sciences of agriculture and home economics. Through the use of agricultural agents, conferences, classes, and demonstrations, the agricultural industry was greatly strengthened. The miracle of American agricultural production which followed these acts is well known.

Vocational Education. The early twentieth century brought a call for increased emphasis on vocational education from a number of agencies including the National Association of Manufacturers, the National Metal Trades Association, the National Education Association, the American Federation of Teachers, and the Commission on National Aid to Vocational Education. In 1917 President Wilson signed the Smith-Hughes Act, which provided annual federal funds for distribution to the states for vocational education in the public schools of less than college grade. The act required that federal funds be matched on a dollar-for-dollar basis by state funds and also stipulated greater provisions for federal control than had been common in most federal aid provisions in the first half of the present century. The act supported the training and employment of teachers and supervisors of agriculture, home economics, and trade and industrial subjects, and also research in vocational education. The Smith-Hughes Act marked the first massive federal money grants for education.

The scope of federal interest in vocational education was broadened in 1937 by the George-Deen Act, which provided "for the further development of vocational education in the several states and territories" and more than doubled the amount of money previously available for vocational education.

The George-Barden Act of 1945 increased the federal funds available for vocational education. Amendments made such funds available for counseling, training vocational counselors, and conducting allied activities, including research in guidance and placement. Other amendments extended the benefits of vocational education to the Virgin Islands, Puerto Rico, Guam, and American Samoa. The National Defense Education Act of 1958 amended the George-Barden Act, granting for the first time a new type of vocational education, namely, area vocational schools or centers.

The Vocational Education Acts of 1963 and 1968 opened a new era in federal governmental support.

Historical Calendar

The Development of Federal Relations to Education

1785	Land appropriated by Continental Congress in Northwest Territory to endow a common school system	1933	Emergency educational grants initiated during the Depression
1787	Objective that "schools and the means of education shall be forever encouraged" reconfirmed in the Northwest Ordinance	1939	U.S. Office of Education transferred to the Federal Security Agency
1791	Education reserved to the states by the passage of the Tenth Amendment to the Constitution	1940	Aid authorized to schools in federally impacted areas by Lanham Act
1800	First federal appropriation for books (nucleus of Congressional Library)	1944	GI Bill for veterans' education passed by Congress and expanded in subsequent years
1802	First federal institution of higher education established as the United States Military Academy at West Point	1944	Distribution of federal surplus property authorized by Congress for education, health, and civil defense
1802	Public lands given to Ohio for public schools	1950	Federal loans for college housing included in Housing Act
1818	First money for education granted to the states by the federal government	1953	U.S. Office of Education made part of Department of Health, Education, and Welfare, with Cabinet Secretary
1862	Land-grant colleges established by the first Morrill Act, supplemented later	1954	Segregation in public schools ruled unconstitutional by U.S. Supreme Court
1865	Freedmen's Bureau created to foster education in several Southern states	1958	National Defense Education Act enacted to strengthen education in science, mathematics, and languages
1867	National Department of Education created in Washington, D.C.	1962	Retraining of nation's labor force accelerated by passage of Manpower Development and Training Act
1917	Federal assistance for vocational education provided by Smith-Hughes Act	1962	Program of federal grants to match state appropriations for educational television transmission facilities approved
1920	Federal-state cooperation in vocational rehabilitation initiated through Smith-Bankhead Act		

1962	Use by schools of a prayer approved by the New York State Board of Regents ruled unconstitutional by U.S. Supreme Court	1965	National Foundation on the Arts and Humanities authorized by Congress
1963	Bible reading in public schools declared unconstitutional by U.S. Supreme Court	1966	Initial funds authorized by Congress for the National Teacher Corps, approved in 1965, enabling teachers to serve in poverty-stricken areas
1963	Funds for new programs in vocational education and college construction provided by Congress	1967	International Education Act of 1966 implemented by Congress by voting initial grant of funds
1963	Higher Education Facilities Act passed, providing loans and grants for construction of classrooms, libraries, and laboratories	1967	Education Professions Development Act enacted to improve quality of teachers and meet educational manpower needs
1964	Civil Rights Bill passed by Congress, containing a provision for the withdrawal of federal support from any community or school district in which discrimination is practiced	1969	Immediate end to racial segregation in schools demanded by U.S. Supreme Court
1964	Economic Opportunity Act (war on poverty) passed by Congress, with several provisions affecting education, such as Job Corps, work training programs, Volunteers in Service to America, and literacy education	1970	Office of Students and Youth established in U.S. Office of Education
		1970	White House Conference on Children convened
1964	Federal Interagency Committee on Education appointed, headed by United States Commissioner of Education	1971	White House Conference on Youth convened
		1971	Busing of students as a means of integration upheld by U.S. Supreme Court
1965	New post of Assistant Secretary for Education created in Department of Health, Education, and Welfare	1971	Attempts by several states to give direct financial aid to church-related schools ruled unconstitutional by U.S. Supreme Court.
1965	Elementary and Secondary Education Act approved by Congress, authorizing benefits to pupils in elementary and secondary schools, including some services to private school pupils	1972	Reforms in the federal government's participation in the educational enterprise recommended by President's Commission on School Finance
1965	Higher Education Act of 1965 approved, providing for the first time for scholarships for needy college students, plus funds for institutions	1972	Various amendments to earlier acts in elementary, secondary, and higher education enacted

These students in a New York City technical high school pursue vocational education, which has long been supported by grants from the federal government.

The first of these vocational acts in 1963 authorized appropriations increasing annually to a maximum of $225 million in 1967, and the later act extended authorization even beyond a quarter billion annually. These acts strengthened existing programs of vocational education in the secondary schools and broadened their scope to reach youth who had completed high school or dropped out of school or were sufficiently handicapped academically or socially to profit from regular vocational education programs. New emphasis was placed upon work-study programs with part-time employment of young people to supplement their classroom vocational training. Provisions were made for the construction of area vocational centers and for such ancillary services as teacher education, supervision, evaluation, and demonstration of promising practices in vocational education, as well as for the development of new instructional materials and state leadership in these fields. Many of the constraints imposed upon the schools by earlier legislation were reduced by these acts. Money was also provided for colleges and other nonprofit agencies and state boards of education to stimulate leadership in the development of vocational education. This important legislation with subsequent renewals and revisions is producing many changes in traditional programs and is quickening the vitality of vocational education in a period when new technologies are creating an insatiable demand for educated manpower in new occupations.

Vocational Rehabilitation. The line between vocational education and vocational rehabilitation is hard to draw. Several federal bills have been enacted which are targeted specifically upon the occupational rehabilitation of persons who are handicapped in one way or another. The Vocational Rehabilitation Act of 1920 appropriated money to the states for the training of handicapped persons so that they could, whenever possible, become self-supporting.

The Manpower Training and Development Act, passed in 1962, attacked the problem of retraining the hard core of unemployed persons, both the unskilled and those whose skills needed updating. The legislation permits the federal government to contract with vocational education departments of the state and with private industries to organize and conduct the training necessary to bring unemployed persons into the mainstream of productive life. More than a million persons, half of them school dropouts, have benefited from the provisions of this act since its inception. More than four-fifths of those who completed the program are now employed. The act has been liberalized and the funding increased in years subsequent to its enactment.

Some of the provisions of the GI Bill, discussed later, also were directed toward the rehabilitation of veterans of military service who, through injury in the defense of their country, would otherwise have found gainful employment difficult. Other acts mentioned later also contained provisions directed toward vocational rehabilitation of youth and adults.

Vocational rehabilitation for disadvantaged youth is one of many special school programs subsidized by the federal government.

Manpower for Defense. From the days of the earliest settlements through the modern age of nuclear energy and space travel, man has been interested in defense. In 1802, soon after the founding of the young republic, the United States Military Academy was established at West Point, New York, to train officers for the Army. The United States Naval Academy was established in Annapolis, Maryland, in 1845; the Coast Guard Academy in New London, Connecticut, in 1876; the Merchant Marine Academy in Kings Point, New York, in 1938; and the Air Force Academy in Colorado Springs, Colorado, in 1955. These institutions of higher education are administered under the auspices of the Department of Defense. The entrance requirements and academic standards of the service academies are high, and their graduates have won distinction not only in military service but also in civilian pursuits. The several branches of the services cooperate in the operation of the Reserve Officers Training Corps (ROTC) installations on the campuses of many of the nation's colleges and universities.

The educational programs of the armed forces extend from the first grade through the university level. The United States Armed Forces Institute at times enrolls thousands of students pursuing both military and general education. Thousands of soldiers have learned to read and write and have acquired other basic educational skills in the army. Thousands of other servicemen have acquired their high school diplomas or equivalency certificates after study in the armed forces and successful completion of the General Education Development Tests. It has been said that in every working day of the year, 10 to 15 percent of the personnel in the United States armed forces can be found in classrooms. During periods of national emergency, the educational establishment of the military is often the largest educational enterprise in the nation.

The National Defense Education Act (NDEA) of 1958 is related to defense in nomenclature, in the propulsion of its initial passage, and at least in part in its program. The act was largely a response to the Soviet Union's precedence in the exploration of outer space and to our national near-hysteria over the quality of an educational system that was presumably responsible for such embarrassment. However, other concerns, such as the knowledge explosion, technological and scientific revolution, rapid population growth, urbanization of our culture, school dropouts, and delinquency helped to assure its passage. Since its enactment the National De-

fense Education Act has provided approximately $4 billion to improve teaching in fields deemed crucial to space exploration and the national defense.

Under the provisions of the act, $1\frac{1}{2}$ million students annually have borrowed over $1 billion from the NDEA Student Loan Program, and thousands of graduate students have been awarded graduate fellowships. Preference has been given to students preparing for college teaching.

Instruction has been strengthened by more than $500 million in NDEA funds, granted on a matching basis for new laboratories and other equipment for the teaching of mathematics, physical sciences, and modern languages in the public elementary and secondary schools.

Subsequent extensions of the act have broadened its scope to include the teaching of English, reading, history, civics, geography, economics, and industrial arts and to educate teachers of disadvantaged youth, school library personnel, and educational media specialists. Over $500 million in loans has been made available to private schools for the same purposes. Thousands of new electronic language laboratories have been established, and more than 90 percent of the public school districts of the nation have received funds for science equipment. With NDEA funds, state education departments have increased sixfold the number of their specialists in science, mathematics, and foreign languages. Under the program for language development, elementary and secondary school teachers have gone back to summer school at nearly three hundred language institutes to become familiar with new methods and materials. In addition to these institutes, nearly a hundred language and area centers have been developed in colleges and universities for the study of both the languages and cultures of other countries. Research in language instruction has also been supported by NDEA funds.

A major objective of the National Defense Education Act has been the improvement and extension of guidance, counseling, and testing programs. The number of full-time guidance personnel employed by the public schools has more than doubled as a direct consequence of the act. Thousands of specialists have attended over a hundred guidance and counseling institutes established on college and university campuses to deepen their competency in counseling, guidance, and testing.

With the support of NDEA funds, area technical-training programs have been established to train youths and adults as skilled technicians in fields essential to the national defense, such as electronics, instrumentation, industrial chemistry, engineering, tool design, aviation, and industrial planning. The result has been a substantial increase in the nation's pool of highly trained manpower. It is estimated that by 1972 approximately 140,000 teachers and other educational personnel will have attended nearly 3,000 institutes for advanced study to improve their professional qualifications. Several million dollars have been allotted for hundreds of research projects in the use of new educational media in all fields of instruction—media such as radio, television, films, recordings, and programmed instruction.

This Act, smuggled into legislation originally as an instrument of national defense, has had a very powerful impact upon the strength of general education at all levels.

Education of Veterans. In 1944 Congress enacted, without a dissenting vote, the historic GI Bill of Rights, which included educational benefits for the military men and women who served in World War II. In 1952 the educational benefits and others were extended by legislation to include veterans of the Korean conflict who served between 1950 and 1955. In 1966, during the war in Vietnam, Congress passed the significant permanent GI Bill. This includes educational and other benefits not only for the veterans of the war in Vietnam but also for all who have served since the old GI Bill expired on January 31, 1955. The terms of the 1966 act apply to every veteran of the Army, Navy, Marine Corps, Air Force, and Coast Guard—male or female—who was on active duty for six months or more and has an honorable discharge. The provisions were further liberalized in 1967 and again in 1970 when additions were included to promote the education of disadvantaged veterans by providing funds for remedial courses, tutoring grants, equal-opportunity programs, open admission policies in the institutions of higher education enrolling the veterans. These provisions were enacted to increase the percentage of veterans benefiting from the bill, a percentage which had slipped from 50 percent after World War II to 27 percent in 1970.

The impact of the GI Bill and its supplementary extensions has been tremendous. Nearly 10 million veterans of military service have extended their education in countless occupations and professions, thereby raising tremendously the nation's supply of educated manpower and strengthening both its economic prosperity and its national security. The original $16-billion cost of educational provisions of the GI Bills has been repaid to the nation, and the return still increases yearly. Even more important has been the reduction of socioeconomic stratification of our people. Robert Hutchins, president of the Center for the Study of Democratic Institutions, wrote,

The GI Bill of Rights is a historic enactment because it makes it possible for the veteran to go to college even if his parents have no money. It thus removes, for a large class of our citizens, the greatest, the most unjust, and the most unwise limitation on higher education.

Education of Teachers. As part of its interest in manpower development, the federal government has assisted the preparation of persons for various professions. This discussion is limited to federal assistance in the preparation of educators. During the last decade and a half, various acts have supported the education of teachers of the deaf, the partially sighted, and other physically handicapped students as well as mentally retarded and emotionally disturbed students. The Civil Rights Act of 1964 provided funds to help teachers deal more effectively with problems resulting from the desegregation of schools. Other legislation provided for the education of teachers of adults, preschool children, and non-English-speaking students. The National Science Foundation and the National Foundation on the Arts and Humanities assisted teacher-education programs in these fields. Many provisions have been made by the federal government to support the international and intercultural components of teacher education. These provisions are described in Chapter 17. Many of the other federal acts discussed in this chapter contain provision for the preparation and in-service development of teachers related to the thrust of the various statutes because it is increasingly recognized that new educational programs have little chance of success until teachers are prepared to deal with them.

One of the boldest and most encouraging attacks upon the education of poor children is the Teacher Corps, which was established originally in the Higher Education Act of 1965. Title V of this act founded the National Teacher Corps, instituted a program of graduate fellowships to prepare elementary and secondary school teachers, and provided grants and contracts to improve teacher-education programs. The Teacher Corps is an effort to improve education at its weakest point, slum schools. It brings together dedicated teachers committed to use education to defeat poverty in the ghettos of the cities as well as in dilapidated rural areas. In a typical Teacher Corps program, teams of five undergraduate or graduate student interns and a master teacher from a local school system work together in a school in a poverty area. The student interns work part-time in the schools while continuing their professional study during the evenings, weekends, and summers. At the end of two years they earn their college degree and teacher certification along with two years of on-the-job experience. The success of the Teacher Corps is manifested in part by the fact that 86 percent of those who complete the program remain in teaching, most of them in schools in poverty areas, and by the fact that school administrators try to recruit these trainees for permanent teaching posts in numbers that exceed the supply. Every Teacher Corps program is a local program, planned and administered jointly by a school system and nearby university and with the counsel of various community groups. More and more characteristics of Teacher Corps programs are being incorporated into the regular training programs of teachers.

The Education Professions Development Act (EPDA) of 1967 was enacted as a series of amendments to the Higher Education Act and the National Defense Education Act mentioned earlier. EPDA brings together under one jurisdiction virtually all the federally supported programs for the development of professional persons in education and expands the nation's grasp of the manpower problems in education. The Education Professions Development Act embraces five major purposes:

1. To obtain accurate information on education's manpower needs
2. To provide high-quality preparation and retraining opportunities
3. To attract more qualified persons into teaching
4. To encourage persons who can "stimulate creativity in the arts and other skills" to accept short-term or long-term assignments
5. To make preparation programs more responsive to the needs of schools and colleges

EPDA represents a transition away from former piecemeal programs of teacher education by emphasizing the education of the child, particularly

disadvantaged or handicapped children, rather than the training of the teacher as an end in itself; by focusing on areas of most severe manpower shortages in education, namely, early-childhood education, vocational-technical education, special education, and student personnel services; by shifting from short-term, college-based programs of teacher education to long-term projects built upon the cooperation of colleges and local school systems; and by encouraging change in the total preparation programs of teachers to make them more responsive to the elimination of racial, financial, physical, and mental disadvantage.

EPDA provides six major components operationally. The Teacher Corps, discussed earlier, continues to recruit new persons into teaching who are committed to serving children from low-income families. The Trainers of Teacher Trainers, or Triple T Program, is essentially a university-based program intent upon bringing together the academic and education departments of universities to work with local school systems in the improvement of people responsible for the preparation of teachers, in both the universities and the local school systems. The Career Opportunities Program is a major effort to attract into teaching more persons from low-income families for positions in poverty-area schools. The States Grants Program seeks to prepare persons in specializations of critical shortage in education through intensive preparation conducted largely by local school districts. The School Personnel Utilization Program is an experimental attempt to perfect a variety of models for more effective utilization of educators in schools as, for example, in differentiated staffing patterns. The act also includes $3.5 million to train school personnel in attacking the tragic problem of drug abuse. The administration of EPDA is centered in a new Bureau of Educational Personnel Development in the U.S. Office of Education.

Some persons regard EPDA as the most significant federal legislation in the field of education in the 1960s. Certainly its impact is impressive on the basis of sheer numbers. In EPDA's first two years of existence it reached three times as many trainees as did NDEA in its first decade. Clearly this concentrated effort of the federal government helped to end the period of personnel shortages in education while raising materially the quality of persons in educational endeavor.

School Construction and Facilities

During the Great Depression of the 1930s the federal government assisted in the construction of various educational facilities through the Public Works Administration and the Works Progress Administration. The Lanham Act of 1940 provided federal funds for schools in localities where school enrollments were swelled by students of families attracted by defense installations. The act was extended in 1950 to provide aid for school construction. The College Housing Program, begun in 1951, provided long-term, low-interest loans to colleges for certain facilities such as dormitories and cafeterias. The Higher Education Act of 1963 has provided as much as $400 million annually for construction of facilities in colleges and universities and public community colleges and technical institutes. In 1965 the Appalachian Regional Development Act provided funds for the construction of vocational-education facilities in the Appalachian area. Several of the acts supporting vocational education mentioned earlier also contained provisions for subsidies for construction of vocational-education facilities. The Library Services and Construction Act of 1956, which provided funds for books and bookmobiles to improve library service for rural Americans, was expanded in 1964 to include funds for both services and construction assistance to libraries in both urban and rural communities. The National Defense Education Act in the first decade of its existence provided $40 million for the use of various educational media including television, motion pictures, radio, and computers. The Educational Television Broadcasting Facilities Act of 1962 with subsequent additions supported both operating and construction costs and brought educational television within reach of more than two-thirds of the nation's students and a total viewing audience of more than 150 million people. Subventions are available under the act to public school systems, colleges and universities, state educational-television agencies, and to nonprofit foundations engaged in educational telecasting.

Education of the Impoverished and the Handicapped

Vocational Rehabilitation. The Vocational Rehabilitation Act of 1920 was probably the first instance of the federal government's attempt to focus financial assistance directly upon the needs of handicapped persons. It helped physically handicapped persons become rehabilitated vocationally so that they might be economically self-supporting. Indeed, all the federal government's efforts in vocational rehabilitation mentioned earlier in this chapter could be recalled here as examples of federal concern for the impoverished and the handicapped.

Direct Aid to Indigent Families and Children. Beginning mainly with the Great Depression of the 1930s, the federal government has sought to reduce inequality in educational opportunity by making special funds available for the education of disadvantaged children and youth so that their station in life might not reduce too severely their social or economic mobility. During the Depression, the National Youth Administration provided stipends to permit needy youth to remain in school while the Civilian Conservation Corps and other acts provided modest wages to permit out-of-school youth to engage in productive work and learning. The Social Security Act, enacted originally in 1935 and broadened substantially through many later revisions, has provided through its welfare provisions financial assistance to poor families. In hundreds of thousands of homes across the nation this welfare has made it possible for youths to stay in school rather than drop out to search for employment—employment often so menial for undereducated youth that they are locked in hardship for life. As mentioned earlier, the National Defense Education Act has provided as much as $180 million annually for low-cost loans for college students, and the Higher Education Act has provided as much as $300 million annually for part-time employment and insured loans and "equal opportunity grants" for students from low-income families. The Economic Opportunity Act of 1964 helped to support college work-study programs to permit needy youth to earn some of the money needed to remain in college.

Education of the Poor. The greatest impetus in helping poor people educationally came with the enactment of the "war-on-poverty" legislation, or the Economic Opportunity Act (EOA), in 1964, which also contained many provisions not directly related to education. The purpose of the Economic Opportunity Act was "to eliminate the paradox of poverty and pools of long-term joblessness in the midst of plenty in the nation by opening to everyone opportunity for education and training, the opportunity to work, and the opportunity to live in decency and dignity."

In addition to its direct aid to students, mentioned above, this act established certain new educational programs designed to help relieve the tragic cycle of poverty, undereducation, unemployment, and disenchantment with the American promise of prosperity and the pursuit of happiness for all. These provisions included Head Start, Follow Through, VISTA, Teacher Corps, and the Adult Literacy Program. Head Start, which provided pre-elementary experience for children from low-income families, is described more fully in Chapter 6. The provisions of this act were later subsumed under the Handicapped Children's Early Education Assistance Act. Follow Through programs, initiated a few years later, were designed to reinforce and extend into the early elementary years the special programs that were begun in Head Start. The Volunteers in Service to America (VISTA) program established a sort of domestic Peace Corps in which volunteers worked with the poor people in the eroded hills of Appalachia, the dilapidated slums of the city ghettos, the modest sun-baked hogans of the Indians, and the shanties of migrant families to help break the dreary legacy of poverty. The Adult Literacy Program of EOA was later subsumed in the Adult Education Act of 1966 to provide basic education for adults who had dropped out of school. Several of these volunteer programs, such as VISTA and Teacher Corps, have been merged into a new federal agency called "Action."

One of the most controversial provisions of EOA was the Job Corps. This enterprise, like some of the other provisions of EOA, was administered by the Office of Economic Opportunity rather than the U.S. Office of Education. Prompted by the earlier prototype of the Civilian Conservation Corps, Job Corps sought to salvage youths who had dropped out of school and languished unemployed in slum communities; it placed them in camps across the country to give them the vocational and general education that would permit them to assume a constructive role in society. However, the costs of the program were high and the results were questionable, prompting the transfer of this program from the Office of Economic Opportunity into the Department of Labor's other manpower-training projects in an attempt to make the enterprise more efficient and productive. Thus many of the bold and imaginative efforts initiated under EOA have survived in modified form but integrated into other enterprises supported by the federal government.

Beginning in 1935 surplus foods purchased by the federal government to bolster farm prices were distributed to schools for lunches for students. This federally supported school lunch program was expanded in 1943 and 1946. In 1971 schools throughout the nation were required to serve free lunches to all children from low-income families through a revision of the National School Lunch Act, which formerly contained permissive rather than mandatory language. Presently about 8 million children are getting free or cut-rate lunches at an annual cost of $730 million, which is shared by the states and the federal government.

As mentioned earlier, the Educational Professions Development Act provides funds for drug education to help prevent drug addiction and to rescue the alarming number of youths who are becoming the tragic victims of the misuse of drugs and narcotics.

Another formidable assault on poverty through education was mounted in the passage of the Elementary and Secondary Education Act of 1965 and its later amendments. This act is discussed more fully later in this chapter, but attention will be directed here to the provisions of the act concerned with education of the impoverished. Title I of the act, which provides the largest program of federal aid specifically to elementary and secondary education, is called specifically Education of Disadvantaged Children. Since 1967 it has provided more than $1 billion annually to local districts to meet the educational deficiencies of the poor through such stratagems as remedial reading programs and special counseling programs. Funds are distributed to school districts on the basis of the number of children from low-income families enrolled in the schools. Additional special grants are given to both urban and rural districts which have an unusually high concentration of children from poor families. For children of migratory farm workers, $45 million annually was authorized in the 1969 amendment to the act. Another $27 million annually was authorized to improve the education of delinquent and neglected children in special state or local schools. Other moneys are made available for bonuses to supplement the salaries of teachers assigned to schools with high concentrations of educationally deprived children and to encourage programs designed to reduce school dropouts. The act also provides funds for the education of Indian children and other children whose native language is not English. These provisions of ESEA have been sharply debated in the Congress and elsewhere on the allegation that much of the money is wasted and diverted from poor people because of shoddy local accounting for the funds, lax supervision of expenditures by some states, and the misuse of the funds in some cases to replace rather than supplement local school revenues. This issue and others related to federal financial support of education are discussed more fully in Chapter 1.

Education of Physically, Mentally, and Emotionally Handicapped Children. The federal government has enacted a number of laws which provide financial support for the education of children who are mentally retarded, hard of hearing, or deaf; whose speech is impaired; who are visually handicapped, emotionally disturbed, or crippled; or whose health is otherwise impaired and who therefore require special attention in school. These young people constitute approximately one-tenth of the school population, although not all of them are receiving special education by any means.

A number of piecemeal attacks on the special education of these children have now been coalesced under Education of the Handicapped, Title VI of the Elementary and Secondary Education Act. Annual appropriations of more than $400 million were authorized for 1972 for the initiation, expansion, and improvement of projects and programs for the education of handicapped pre-elementary, elementary, and secondary school students; for regional resource centers for the education of deaf and blind children; for the preparation of teachers of the handicapped; for research on the education of the handicapped and development of instructional media; and for establishment of research and demonstration centers for students with special learning disabilities. The federal government's interest in these programs is now centered in the Bureau of Education for the Handicapped of the Office of Education. Chapter 11 provides a more extensive discussion of the problems of handicapped students and the nature of school programs designed to reduce those problems. It is hoped that this formidable assault on the education of the handicapped

will hasten the time when more victims of disease, birth defects, and accidents can find dignified and productive places in society.

Era of National Federalism in Education

The period since the Elementary and Secondary Education Act may be recorded by historians as the era of national federalism in education. This was an era in which the federal government increased substantially its expenditures for schooling, as shown in Figure 2-1. It was also an era in which the federal government, as one commentator put it, plunged "smack into the middle of the total educational enterprise—public and private" instead of playing the role of "passive and distant financial patron." Heretofore, federal aid had been piecemeal, limited to a few very specific targets. Although massive federal support for education had been sought ever since the Great Depression, three great issues had stood in the way: religion, race, and the principle of local control. The public school establishment had generally opposed federal grants for private schools, and the Catholic school establishment op-

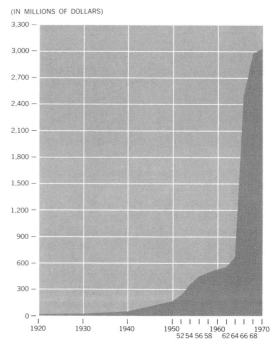

FIGURE 2-1   *Federal expenditures for elementary and secondary schools, 1920–1970. (U.S. Office of Education,* Digest of Educational Statistics.)

posed any aid which did not include its schools. Many Southern legislators feared that federal aid would be used to force the integration of schools. Others held that increased federal support would threaten local control of education.

But several forces converged in the 1960s and 1970s to prompt more generous financial support for education. The civil rights movement called attention dramatically to the tragedy of racial discrimination and poverty and their impact upon social and economic inequality among people. Advancing technology quickened the need of the economy for better-educated manpower. Domestic and international tensions continued to press for better-educated citizens. Schools were seen as man's best hope for improving the human condition.

These and other forces assured the passage of the Elementary and Secondary Education Act in 1965. President Lyndon B. Johnson, who had been a teacher, wished his administration to be remembered for its encouragement of education, and he adroitly handled the design and promotion of the bill. This remarkable bill is singled out for discussion here because it was perhaps so prototypic of the emerging new national federalism in education. First the bill required local schools to write their own plans for the use of the funds. This emphasis on local thinking, planning, and judgment was in sharp contrast with most earlier federal aid to education. It permitted the funds to serve a variety of uniquely local needs, whether it be the establishment of nongraded elementary school organization in Cleveland or classes in English for Navajo-speaking children in Kayenta, Arizona. Second, ESEA represented a high in federal financial support for education at that time, providing for the first time more than $1 billion under a single enactment. Although ESEA did not provide funds for the general support of education, it was an omnibus bill that was far more comprehensive in its impact on education than any previous legislation. It was also the first bill for federal aid to education which made substantial sums available to private elementary and secondary schools.

The bill consisted of seven sections or titles. Title I, the largest fund by far, was addressed to the development of children from low-income families. The provisions of this section were discussed earlier in this chapter. Title II supported three types of educational materials: school library resources, textbooks, and other instructional materials. Title III

supported various supplementary educational centers, sometimes called Projects to Advance Creativity in Education (PACE); and Title IV provided for research and related activities in education. Title V was addressed to the education of the handicapped. Title VI provided funds for bilingual education for students whose native language was not English. Title VII supported programs designed to prevent school dropouts. Clearly ESEA reached a far greater number of young citizens more profoundly than any other federal financial support of education at that time. Truly it marked a watershed in the flow of federal funds for education and ushered in a new era in federal participation in the support of our schools.

During the 1960s and 1970s more and more educationally oriented programs of the federal government were transferred to the jurisdiction of the U.S. Office of Education in the Department of Health, Education, and Welfare, although many other branches of the federal government still maintain important educational programs which are described later in this chapter.

U.S. OFFICE OF EDUCATION

Evolution of Office

The great educational reformer Henry Barnard went to Washington in 1838 in search of facts about the nation's schools. When he found none, he undertook the task of establishing a federal educational agency. Over the next thirty years he was joined in this effort by many educators and organizations which recognized the need for a federal office of education in Washington. The dire aftermath of the Civil War helped to quicken this interest. In 1866 a proposal for a federal bureau of education was presented to Congress by James A. Garfield. The Department of Education Bill was finally approved on March 2, 1867. It marked a milestone in the development of federal interest in American education. Two years later, owing primarily to opposition by some of the states, the department was made an Office of Education in the Department of the Interior. The title, changed in 1870 to Bureau of Education, was restored in 1929, and the agency is now officially the U.S. Office of Education.

On July 1, 1939, in connection with the general

governmental reorganization plans, the U.S. Office of Education was transferred from the Department of the Interior to the Federal Security Agency. In 1953 the Office became a part of the newly created Department of Health, Education, and Welfare, with a secretary in the President's Cabinet. This marked an important milestone in the history of federal education.

In 1964 President Johnson appointed the Federal Interagency Committee on Education, headed by the United States Commissioner of Education, to strengthen and coordinate federal policies and the various programs in education. Within the Department of Health, Education, and Welfare there was created in 1965 the new post of Assistant Secretary for Education, thus enhancing the role of education in the Department and in the nation.

The Office of Education, which commemorated its centennial in 1967, will undoubtedly witness many more changes. Eventually it may become a separate department of education with a secretary in the President's Cabinet.

Functions of the Office of Education

The three main functions of the Office of Education are (1) research, (2) administration of federal educational grants, and (3) educational services to local, state, national, and international agencies.

Research. The Office conducts numerous research projects of great variety. As the chief bookkeeper for the nation's educational institutions, it collects, interprets, and disseminates a mass of statistical data through its Educational Research Information Center. Its regional laboratories are helping to disseminate and apply research findings in education and psychology.

Administration of Federal Funds for Education. One of the major functions of the Office of Education is the administration of various grants for education and related activities. The personnel of the Office of Education has been expanded greatly during the past decade to manage this responsibility which grew so rapidly in the 1960s and 1970s.

Educational Services. In addition to the dissemination of research findings and the distribution of federal funds for education, the U.S. Office of Edu-

cation renders a variety of services to local, county, state, national, and international agencies. It conducts surveys and renders consultative help to local and state school systems. It conducts an extensive publications service through the Superintendent of Documents, Government Printing Office, Washington, D.C. These publications include research monographs, periodicals, newsletters, pamphlets, and reports. The best known of its periodicals is *American Education*. The Office calls conferences on various educational problems and presents exhibits. It cooperates with the State Department in international teacher exchanges and with the Agency for International Development in the technical training of foreign educators in America and the recruitment of American education specialists for service abroad. It serves as a clearinghouse for the assistance of foreign students entering American colleges and universities. The Office also provides an information center and library on all aspects of American education. In 1970 the Office of Education established a youth advisory panel to give students a larger voice in shaping federal educational policies that affect school and college life.

Its officials help to prepare, promote, and put into practice congressional legislation dealing with education. For example, it prepares guidelines for the desegregation of school districts to enforce the Civil Rights Bill of 1964, which contains a provision for the withdrawal of federal fiscal support from any community or school district in which discrimination is practiced.

United States Commissioner of Education

History of Commissionership. It was indeed fitting that Henry Barnard was selected as the first United States Commissioner of Education. The first principal of the New Britain Normal School, the first state superintendent of schools for Rhode Island, a former state superintendent for Connecticut, and the most vigorous crusader for a federal education agency, he brought to this new national office a rich experience in public education.

List of Commissioners. Many distinguished educators have held the office of United States Commissioner of Education, a title that has not changed. Their names and their years in office are indicated in the table at the top of the opposite page.

Commissioner	Years in office
Henry Barnard	1867-1870
John Eaton	1870-1886
N. H. R. Dawson	1886-1889
William T. Harris	1889-1906
Elmer E. Brown	1906-1911
Philander P. Claxton	1911-1921
John J. Tigert	1921-1928
William J. Cooper	1929-1933
George F. Zook	1933-1934
John W. Studebaker	1934-1949
Earl J. McGrath	1949-1953
Lee M. Thurston	1953-1953
Samuel M. Brownell	1953-1956
Lawrence G. Derthick	1956-1961
Sterling M. McMurrin	1961-1962
Francis Keppel	1962-1965
Harold Howe II	1966-1969
James E. Allen, Jr.	1969-1970
Sidney P. Marland, Jr.	1970-

Terms of Office. The Commissioner, appointed with the consent of the Senate by the President of the United States, upon the recommendation of the Secretary of Health, Education, and Welfare and its Assistant Secretary of Education, serves an indefinite term. Sometimes a change in presidents is followed by the appointment of a new commissioner. The terms have ranged from seventeen years, for W. T. Harris, to less than three months.

Commissioner's Role. The United States Commissioner of Education performs many duties and conducts a wide variety of activities. As chairman of the recently created Federal Interagency Committee on Education, he serves as coordinator of more than forty federal programs bearing on education, but administered by agencies other than the U.S. Office of Education.

As Commissioner, he is head of the Office of Education and performs the major duties already mentioned as belonging to that Office. Many other responsibilities have accumulated during the years. Among these may be listed special tasks assigned by the President of the United States, duties imposed by congressional enactments, and a growing list of other federal activities in education.

A government-published report entitled *A Federal Agency for the Future* explains the role of the Commissioner and the Office of Education thus:

It is the American conviction that the destiny of the Nation is secure only in the hands of the people. This critical fact of American life has great significance for the future of the U.S. Office of Education. Most importantly, it means that the federal educational agency must never isolate itself from the public. Indeed, it must do all in its power both to hear the voice of the people and to speak to the people on matters of education. It must, in a current phrase, be an Office of Education, not an Office of Educators.

OTHER FEDERAL ACTIVITIES IN EDUCATION

Education in Special Federal Jurisdictions

The national government assists in promoting education in the special school district of Washington, D.C., the federal reservations, and outlying areas, such as the Virgin Islands, Puerto Rico, the Panama Canal Zone, American Samoa, Guam, Wake Island, and the trust territories in the Pacific.

Education of Special Groups

During the 1960s Americans became more deeply aware of the serious economic, social, and educational disadvantages suffered by the nation's ethnic and racial minority groups, which together constitute approximately one-fifth of our people. Although our nation has prided itself on being a melting pot, on treating all men equally, and on giving equal opportunity for the pursuit of happiness, the reality of life in America has not matched this ideal. Many people of racial and ethnic minorities have found social and economic mobility, but they have had to overcome prejudice and unequal treatment to do so. Many more have not succeeded, and live in poverty outside the mainstream of American affluence. Small wonder that the epithet "racist" comes easily to their lips and that they see in education the best means of escape from economic and social disadvantage.

As President Nixon warned:

No man can be fully free while his neighbor is not. To go forward at all is to go forward together. This means black and white together, as one nation, not two. The laws have caught up with our conscience. What remains is to give life to what is in the law: to insure at last that as all are born equal in dignity before God, all are born equal in dignity before man.

Fortunately the nation is beginning to respond, although sometimes feebly and always belatedly, to the injustices which have occurred. In the following discussion we call attention briefly to some of these efforts with respect to the three largest racial and ethnic minority groups which are the principal victims of unfair treatment: the American Indians, Spanish-speaking immigrants, and Negroes.

American Indians. Concern for the education of Indians appeared early in the colonial period of our history. Dartmouth College, among others, was established for the education of "youth of Indian tribes and also of English youth and others." As the colonies emerged into the young republic, which eventually spread its domain across the continent, the government concluded some four hundred treaties with sovereign Indian tribes, usually promising education as one form of federal service in exchange for Indian lands.

Two great Indian nations, the Choctaw and Cherokee Republics, operated their own school systems with marvelous success, providing a higher rate of literacy in English among their people than prevailed among whites in the same regions. But elsewhere most of the relatively few Indians who were educated in the nineteenth century attended schools run much less effectively by the federal government or by religious denominations. Eventually the private schools for Indians were taken over by the federal government, with disastrous results. Indian children were removed long distances from their homes, sometimes forcibly, to attend schools in converted old Army forts, where their native languages, religions, and cultures were suppressed in a drive to "civilize the natives." This tragic circumstance was mitigated by two forces: the schools were too few to reach most Indian children, and many who were enrolled ran away to return to the reservations.

The impoverishment of educational and economic policies relating to Indian affairs continued as late as the 1920s, constituting one of the most sordid chapters in our history. By 1934, the Indian Reorganization Act under the New Deal administration initiated many reforms in the treatment of Indians. These included the construction of many schools for Indians on their reservations, although control of these schools still rested with the white man, who was still intent on "Americanizing" the Indians. As

recently as the 1950s, most of the Indians who were educated attended day schools and boarding schools administered by the Bureau of Indian Affairs, most predominantly in Alaska, Arizona, New Mexico, North Dakota, and South Dakota and in smaller numbers in other states.

Today the majority of elementary schools for Indians are located on reservations, while most of the secondary schools for Indians are boarding schools which are off the reservations. Today only a third of the Indians attend Bureau of Indian Affairs schools; the remainder attend public schools on or near the reservations. Enrollment of Indians in school is increasing rapidly, stimulated by the Indians' recent commitment to universal education beyond the elementary level as well as by the increase in the Indian population, which is growing faster than the general population. For example, a generation ago, only one Navajo child in four was in school; today 90 percent of the Navajo children are in school. For other tribes, the picture is less bright. Dropout rates are still too high and the turnover of teachers in Indian schools is excessive. Many of the entering students have no background in English. The goals of education for the Indians are not well defined. With few exceptions, the schools are not well adapted to Indian culture, and the climate of the traditional American classroom is not very compatible with the learning style of the Indians. However, Indian children, while materially impoverished, are not culturally deprived and do not suffer the psychological deprivation associated with the broken families of the urban poor. Indian family life is traditionally strong and supportive.

One report of a study of Indian education characterized it as "benevolent paternalism" masquerading as "community development" and concluded that the education of Indians has been largely a failure.[2]

One might surmise that Indians are embittered by this legacy of neglect and mistreatment at the hands of the white man. As President Nixon reminded the Congress, "The first Americans—the Indians—are the most deprived and the most isolated minority group in the nation. On virtually every scale of measure—employment, income, education, and health—the condition of the Indian people ranks at

[2] Report of a study of the education of Indians prepared under a grant by the Carnegie Corporation to the National Indian Youth Council and summarized in "Give It Back to the Indians," *Carnegie Quarterly*, vol. 17, pp. 1-5, Spring, 1969.

the bottom." With few exceptions the Indian has strangely remained unswervingly loyal to the United States. The first real Indian Commissioner of the Bureau of Indian Affairs, Robert Bennett, pointed out that "no Indian youth has been known to burn a draft card or trample the flag. If Indian blood is ever spilled on the streets, it will be shed in defending this country, not defaming it."

Several recent analyses of Indian education have yielded a number of proposed reforms including: the establishment of a National Indian Board on Indian Education; Indian control of local schools serving Indians; better funding of Indian schools; development of curriculum materials that better reflect the history, culture, and values of these noble people; the preparation of more Indian teachers for service in their schools; more support for college rather than vocational education for Indian high school graduates; and the strengthening of public schools serving the reservations.

Several exemplary Indian schools are beginning to emerge. The Institute of American Indian Arts in Santa Fe is doing a remarkable job of transforming the brightest and some of the most rebellious young Indians into outstanding leaders by helping them find self-direction and self-respect through a "return to Indianness" and escape from dependence on white culture. Another exciting departure is the experimental school at Rough Rock, Arizona, which is controlled by an all-Navajo school board and where the curriculum is bicultural and the instruction is bilingual. The first new Indian college, the Navajo Community College at Many Farms, Arizona, appears to be the prototype for other Indian community colleges which will appear increasingly. It is to be hoped that the nation will someday finally redress the shameful racism which has demeaned and impoverished the first Americans and reward these noble people for their fierce loyalty to this country, their pride in their culture, and their hope for the future.

Spanish-Speaking Immigrants. The 1970 census revealed that 5 percent of the United States population consists of persons of Latin-American origin, a total of about ten million citizens. Approximately six million are Mexican-Americans, two million are of Puerto Rican origin, one million are of Cuban origin, and the remaining one million come from other Spanish-speaking countries. The Mexican-Americans reside in largest numbers in the South-

western states, the Puerto Ricans in the New England and Middle Atlantic states, and the Cubans in Florida and the New York metropolitan area.

Some of the Latins are migrant crop workers whose squalid residences shift with the harvests, but most are city dwellers who live in "barrios." With large families and limited education, they suffer severely from unemployment and poverty. The children of the migrant families are further handicapped educationally by frequent transfers among schools, and many of them do not speak English well upon entry into school. Too many schools have discouraged their use of Spanish in the classroom and have failed to help them acquire a sense of dignity and self-confidence. According to a report by the U.S. Civil Rights Commission, many of the Mexican-Americans attend schools predominantly isolated from American children and youth. Nearly two-thirds of them are reading below grade level and more than half of the Mexican-Americans drop out of school before completing high school.

The federal government has attempted belatedly to improve the education of these Latin Americans. The Elementary and Secondary Education Act provided funds to local school districts for support of special education programs for children of minority groups. The Bilingual Education Act of 1968 provided funds for school districts to establish bilingual programs in English and Spanish for these long-neglected Americans. The act also supported programs designed to strengthen pride and knowledge of their ancestral culture. The Migration and Refugee Assistance Act established a loan fund to aid Cuban refugee college students. Federal funds are also available for programs for pre-elementary school and for adult education programs for Spanish-speaking Americans. It is hoped that these programs will help persons of these minority groups to acquire a sense of personal identification and self-respect and will open the doors of equal employment opportunities for them.

American Negroes. American Negroes constitute more than 11 percent of the population of the nation and reside in virtually all parts of the nation but more predominantly in the Southeastern states and in large cities. Long-time victims of discrimination and disadvantage in employment, housing, and education, black Americans are understandably insistent in their demand for more equal opportunity. Their

Compensatory education programs, many of them supported by federal funds, help disadvantaged young children develop readiness for formal schooling.

deep faith in the power of education forces much of their attention upon the schools.

The history of their disadvantage is long and sordid. General public support for the education of blacks began in New Jersey in 1777, where public funds were made available for the support of schools for blacks. Other Northern states and a few cities in the South provided funds for a few schools for Negroes. But these were the exceptions rather than the rule. More typical was the experience of Reverend David Alexander Payne, the great minister of the African Methodist Episcopal Church and the first Negro president of Wilberforce University. At the age of 18, the Reverend Mr. Payne opened a school for free Negroes in Charleston. In 1835 the state of South Carolina, alarmed by this enterprise, forbade any person to operate a school for Negroes. The few schools for Negroes that did remain in the South were forced to operate underground. Many whites risked fines and imprisonment by secretly teaching eager blacks. Prior to the War between the States there were only two Negro institutions of higher education: Lincoln University in Philadelphia and Wilberforce University in Ohio. Wilberforce was later presided over by William Scarborough, an ex-slave who became an eminent scholar largely through his own efforts.

The big drive for education of Negroes came after the War between the States. Nearly 200,000 black soldiers received a modicum of education during their service in the war. After the war, the Freedmen's Bureau, supported by federal funds, helped to establish over four thousand schools for blacks in the South. Various missionary societies joined in the effort. Many schools for blacks grew out of the determined efforts of a remarkable band of hardy ex-slaves who saw in education the prime hope for the rise of their people. The little-known but nevertheless admirable work of the great Negro educators of the late nineteenth and early twentieth centuries in establishing schools and colleges for Negroes is discussed in detail in Chapter 9. The stories of the rise of great Negro colleges, such as Bethune College, Tuskegee Institute, Fisk University, Howard University, Morehouse College, Wilberforce University, and the Normal and Theological Institution of Kentucky, parallel in many respects the biographies of their distinguished Negro presidents, Mary McLeod Bethune, Booker T. Washington, Charles S. Johnson, Mordecai Johnson, Benjamin Mays, William Scarborough, and William Simmons, respectively. Federal lands were appropriated to Tuskegee Institute, and Howard University, located in the nation's capital, is one of the few private universities which receives annual appropriations from the federal government for operating purposes.

Although the Fourteenth Amendment to the Constitution prohibited states from denying equal protection of the laws because of race, color, or previous conditions of servitude, this noble pronouncement was a far cry from the reality of life for the blacks. The provision was contravened by the practice of the Southern states and several Northern communities of providing separate and usually unequal schools for the blacks. Booker T. Washington, along with other blacks and many whites, made spirited pleas for better educational opportunity for blacks. Charles T. Walker, a Negro pastor from New York City, made an impassioned appeal before the 1903 convention of the National Education Association for the educational needs of Negroes, arguing that good schooling for Negroes could become a vital force in the economic regeneration of the South. These pleas went unheeded for half a century, resulting in the greatest anachronism in our history as a nation.

The decade spanned by the Supreme Court decisions on school desegregation in 1954 and the Civil Rights Act of 1964 was the period during which the legal foundations of racism in America were destroyed. The historic decision of 1954 held that segregation by race in the schools violates the United States Constitution and ruled that such practices must be discontinued with "deliberate speed." But for many years school districts found ways of abrogating the spirit of the decision. Segregation continued in the South as a matter of deliberate policy and in many school districts in the North either by policy or as an artifact of segregated patterns of housing within school-attendance areas. Armed with mandates specified in the Civil Rights Act, the Office of Education formulated guidelines for the desegregation of schools. These guidelines, considered controversial by many, nevertheless gave deliberately segregated districts the impetus for integrating their schools.

The Civil Rights Act required the Commissioner of Education to conduct a survey "concerning the lack of availability of equal opportunities" by reason of race, religion, or national origin. The survey, the second largest social science research project in the nation's history (Project Talent was the largest), became known as the Coleman Report, after its director, James S. Coleman of Johns Hopkins University. The major findings of the Coleman Report were discussed in Chapter 1.

Chapter 1 also deals with some of the controversies over school desegregation which continue to rage. Some persons of both races argue for segregated schools in which black people would have more control over schools with predominantly black enrollments. The vast majority of Americans—black and white—would prefer to see Dr. Martin Luther King's great dream realized, as he described it in his address at the March on Washington in 1963:

I have a dream that one day . . . little black boys and black girls will be able to join hands with little white boys and white girls and walk together as sisters and brothers. . . . This will be the day when all of God's children will be able to sing with new meaning "My country 'tis of thee, sweet land of liberty, of thee I sing. Land where my fathers died, land of the Pilgrims' pride, from every mountainside, let freedom ring."

Meanwhile several statutes targeted federal funds toward the improvement of ghetto schools. In 1970 the Office of Education established a post to serve as "advocate for Black Americans," similar in function to other offices serving Mexican-Americans and Indian-Americans. These and other forces were evidently helpful to some degree. As

Charles Wesley points out, in 1960 whites averaged 12.3 years in school compared with 10.7 for blacks, but by 1970 the gap was reduced to 12.6 years for whites and 12.2 for blacks. But the inequality of opportunity was by no means redressed in full. By 1970 the percentage of high school graduates was 78 for whites and only 60 for blacks, and the percentage of white college graduates outran the percentage of blacks 20 to 8. Nonetheless, Wesley concludes that "equality is in the making."[3] This problem of equalizing educational opportunity for Black Americans is so important and so pervasive that various facets of it are dealt with throughout this book, particularly in Chapters 1, 6 to 9, 11, and 14.

Educational Programs Sponsored by Other Federal Agencies

More than half of the total expenditures of the federal government for education are administered by agencies other than the Office of Education. The full account of these far-flung enterprises would fill chapters. Several are selected here for brief treatment for illustrative purposes.

In 1950 Congress created the National Science Foundation "to develop and encourage the pursuit of a national policy for the promotion of basic research and education in the sciences." Its chief functions are to support basic research, education, and training in the physical sciences and to disseminate scientific information. Its specific goals are focused on the following basic areas: (1) supplementing the learning of teachers of science, mathematics, and engineering; (2) improving subject matter in these areas; (3) identifying and motivating high-caliber students for these fields; and (4) granting funds for further education of graduate students and advanced scholars in these areas.

These goals are implemented, for example, by: (1) establishing institute programs for elementary school teachers and giving undergraduate and graduate fellowships to secondary school and college teachers; (2) providing new textbooks, new equipment, new facilities, and "traveling science libraries" for elementary and secondary school pupils; (3) awarding scholarships to undergraduates;

[3] Charles H. Wesley, "The Nation's Two Societies," *Negro History Bulletin*, vol. 33, p. 113, May, 1970.

and (4) instituting postdoctoral programs for scientists with Ph.D. or equivalent degrees. The major overall object is to stimulate scientific research.

The National Foundation on the Arts and Humanities, created in 1965, maintains a similar but less ambitious program for those fields.

The National Aeronautics and Space Administration performs several educational services to deepen our understanding of the educational, social, economic, and political implications of man's peaceful exploration of space and, in cooperation with universities, sponsors research and training programs essential to the understanding of the universe.

The new U.S. Postal Service, in conjunction with the Department of Labor and the Office of Economic Opportunity, opened in 1970 a number of "street academies" in six large cities to offer high school dropouts part-time postal jobs and a second chance at getting an education. The U.S. Postal Service also has extensive educational programs in the nation's inner cities which provide basic education for many lower-grade civil servants from ghetto neighborhoods.

The massive educational undertakings of the Department of Defense have already been noted. These include the service academies, the ubiquitous schools on military installations, and schools for dependents of military service personnel almost wherever servicemen are stationed around the world.

In Chapter 17 we describe the educational enterprise in the international realm conducted by the Peace Corps, the U.S. Information Agency, the Agency for International Development in the Department of State, and other federal agencies.

The education of inmates in federal correctional institutions is administered by the Department of Justice. The Neighborhood Youth Corps is a responsibility of the Department of Labor. The Department of Housing and Urban Affairs administers various educational activities related to its mission. The Veterans' Administration has domain over the educational benefits provided by the GI Bill. Many other illustrations of educational activities administered by the various departments of the government could be cited.

In addition, various independent federal establishments furnish educational services, including the Library of Congress and its Copyright Office, the Government Printing Office, the Pan American Union, the Smithsonian Institution, the National Museum, the National Gallery of Art, the National Academy of Sciences, the Commission of Fine Arts, the Atomic Energy Commission, and the National Science Foundation. Much educational research is conducted in the nation's capital and sponsored by Congress. It was to coordinate and strengthen the numerous and varied federal educational activities that President Johnson appointed in 1964 the Federal Interagency Committee on Education, headed by the United States Commissioner of Education.

Presidential Commissions

Over the last half-century, United States presidents have appointed nearly fifty special commissions, committees, and conferences to study various aspects of American education and to advise the chief executives accordingly. The reports of these groups have yielded some of the most statesmanlike views of the nation's educational needs and the resources required to meet them. Some of the more important of these commissions, committees, and conferences and their major recommendations are reviewed briefly below.

In the midst of the Depression, President Franklin D. Roosevelt appointed an Advisory Committee on Education, which recommended general-purpose federal aid for education. In 1947 President Harry S Truman appointed the President's Commission on Higher Education, which recommended that education through the thirteenth and fourteenth years be established at public expense and that general-purpose federal aid and a national scholarship program be established to support this upward extension of public education. President Dwight D. Eisenhower appointed a Committee on Education beyond the High School, which also advised a general extension of higher education with increased federal support.

The President's Commission on National Goals, which in 1960 studied all aspects of national life crucial to the nation's well-being, set forth a number of recommendations pertinent to education:

Segregation of students should be eliminated.

Two-year community colleges should be established within reach of nearly all high school graduates.

The comprehensive high school should be extended and strengthened.

The number of school districts should be reduced by 75 percent through mandatory reorganization.

At the request of President Kennedy, a panel of consultants examined and recommended changes in the federal government's vocational education programs. The findings of this panel of experts were reflected in the Vocational Education Act of 1963—"a milestone in the history of vocational education."

A presidential Commission on Instructional Technology studied the potential of technology for the improvement of learning and recommended the establishment of the National Institute for Instructional Technology, which was supported by President Nixon along with his proposal of the National Institute of Education. President Nixon also supported the creation of the National Foundation for Higher Education. In 1972 the President's Commission on School Finance recommended various improvements in the generation and allocation of school revenues and the business management of the nation's educational enterprise.

President Nixon in 1970 appointed thirty-eight distinguished Americans to the National Reading Council to advise the Office of Education and direct the work of a new National Reading Center. This undertaking, in the words of its chairman, Walter Starley, was "to build a widespread public determination that in this decade we can and will secure the 'Right To Read' . . . [through] a new partnership of public and private interest."

The White House Conferences on Education, held approximately every ten years, have crystallized citizens' expectations of educational enterprise and have resulted in many excellent recommendations for strengthening schools, including massive increase in the federal financial effort. The 1970–1971 White House Conferences focused their attention on the problems and needs of children, youth, and adults.

United States Supreme Court Decisions

The United States Supreme Court, other federal courts in the judiciary system, and the United States Attorney General have had profound impact upon education. The Supreme Court has rendered more than sixty decisions bearing upon controversy in education, decisions which have helped to shape educational policy fatefully across the nation. This high tribunal does not legislate educational policy directly. Indeed it has never challenged the principle that education is a state function. It does not adjudicate educational policies established by state and local authorities unless such policies contravene provisions of the United States Constitution.

Most of the Supreme Court's decisions about education have invoked considerations of the effect of the First Amendment on the relation of church and state, the Fifth Amendment on due process of law, and the Fourteenth Amendment on the rights of citizens to equal protection under the law. Other decisions have hinged upon considerations of state or federal powers or functions with respect to education. Several of the more fateful decisions of the Supreme Court germane to education are summarized here.

The first important decision upheld the charter of Dartmouth College in 1819 and enhanced the security and early growth of private colleges. Similar protection was given to private elementary and secondary schools in 1925 when the high tribunal ruled that an Oregon statute which inhibited private schools by compelling students to attend public schools violated the Fourteenth Amendment.

Many of the cases litigated before the Supreme Court involve considerations of the relation between state and church. In 1930 the Court ruled that a Louisiana statute which provided free textbooks to students attending church-related schools did not violate the Constitution. In 1947 it ruled similarly in a case in which New Jersey law provided transportation at public expense to children attending church-related schools. These cases helped to establish the "child-benefit theory," which dictates that subsidies for privileges granted to the child cannot be regarded as establishment of religion by the government. However, in 1971 the Court ruled unconstitutional the statutes in Rhode Island and Pennsylvania which allocated public subsidies for teachers' salaries in private schools. The Court held that this kind of public support encouraged "excessive entanglement" between state and church interests. These issues are discussed at length in Chapter 1.

Religious instruction in the schools was held unconstitutional by the Court in 1948 in a case arising in Champaign, Illinois. However, in a case arising in New York State the Supreme Court held in 1952 that religious instruction on released time from school was not unconstitutional if it was held off school grounds and with no compulsion upon the

THE UNITED STATES SUPREME COURT SPEAKS

On the right to attend private schools

The fundamental theory of liberty upon which all governments in this Union repose excludes any general power of the State to standardize its children by forcing them to accept instruction from public teachers only. (1923)

On students' objection to saluting the flag

It is now commonplace that censorship or suppression of expression of opinion is tolerated by our Constitution only when the expression presents a clear and present danger . . . [There is no] allegation that remaining passive during a flag salute ritual creates a clear and present danger . . . The compulsory flag salute . . . left it open to public authorities to compel him to utter what is not on his mind. (1943)

On students' civil rights in school

Educating the young for citizenship is reason for scrupulous protections of Constitutional freedoms of the individual, if we are not to strangle the free mind at its source and teach youth to discount important principles of our government as mere platitudes. (1943)

On public funds for private schools

No tax in any amount, large or small, can be levied to support any religious activities or institutions, whatever they may be called, or whatever form they may adopt to teach or practice religion . . . In the words of Jefferson, the clause against establishment of religion by law was intended to erect "a wall of separation between church and state" . . . That wall must be kept high and impregnable. We could not approve the slightest breach. (1947)

On religious instruction in public schools

The nonsectarian or secular public school was the means of reconciling freedom in general with religious freedom . . . Designed to serve as perhaps the most powerful agency for promoting cohesion among a heterogeneous democratic people, the public school must keep scrupulously free from entanglement in the strife of sects. (1948)

On segregation by race in schools

To separate them [students] from others of similar age and qualifications solely because of their race generates a feeling of inferiority as to their status in the community that may effect their hearts and minds in a way unlikely ever to be undone. . . . We conclude that in the field of public education the doctrine of "separate but equal" has no place. Separate educational facilities are inherently unequal. (1954)

On the states' right to prescribe school prayers

The First Amendment was added to the Constitution to stand as a guarantee that neither the power nor the prestige of the Federal Government would be used to control, support or influence the kinds of prayer the American people can say . . . Its first and most immediate purpose rested on the belief that a union of government and religion tends to destroy government and to degrade religion. (1962)

On providing textbooks free to parochial school students

The law merely makes available to all children the benefit of a general program to lend school books free of charge . . . The financial benefit is to the parents and children, not to the schools. (1968)

On the right of students to wear anti-war symbols

In our system, undifferentiated fear or apprehension of disturbance is not enough to overcome the right to freedom of expression. Any departure from absolute regimentation may cause trouble. . . . But our Constitution says that we must take this risk. (1968)

On "deliberate speed" in school desegregation

The obligation of every school district is to terminate dual school systems at once and to operate now and hereafter only unitary schools . . . Continued operation of segregated schools under a standard of allowing "all deliberate speed" for desegregation is no longer constitutionally permissible. (1969)

On the constitutionality of busing to end segregation

All things being equal, with no history of discrimination, it might well be desirable to assign pupils to schools nearest their homes . . . [But] desegregation plans cannot be limited to the walk-in school. (1971)

On the use of public funds for salaries of teachers in private schools

We cannot ignore the dangers that a teacher under religious control and discipline poses to the separation of the religious from the purely secular aspects of pre-college education. (1971)

student to attend. In 1962 the Court ruled that the recommendation by the New York Board of Regents of a prayer for use in the schools was an abrogation of the Constitution. Similarly, a year later, the Court held that state statutes requiring the reading of the Bible or the recitation of the Lord's Prayer contravened the Constitution. In a case in 1943 the Court ruled that students could not be compelled to salute the flag in school when such activity violated their religious beliefs.

A number of cases have dealt with the civil liberties of students and teachers. A Nebraska law which prohibited the teaching of German in public or private schools was held unconstitutional by the Supreme Court in 1919 on the grounds that it violated the liberty of parents to have their children educated as they see fit. The Court held in 1969 that schools could not prohibit students from wearing armbands or engaging in nondisruptive protest, that students have the same constitutional guarantees of freedom of speech and expression that are granted to all persons. In 1952 the Court declared that a loyalty oath for teachers, which was prescribed by law in Oklahoma, was an unconstitutional violation of freedom of thought, speech, and action as guaranteed by the First and Fourteenth Amendments. But in the same year, the Supreme Court upheld the Feinberg Law in New York, in which members of organizations deemed to be subversive were disqualified as teachers. In this instance, the Court held that the right to protect society from subversive doctrine took precedence over the freedom of expression of teachers.

The Supreme Court has reviewed many cases dealing with discrimination by race in the public schools. In 1896 the Court ruled that the segregation of students by race in schools was not in violation of the Constitution so long as the separate facilities were equal. In 1954 the Court reversed this position in the famed *Brown v. Board of Education* case, which precipitated great controversy and affected educational policy and practice most profoundly. In this litigation, the Court maintained that separate school systems were inherently unequal and deprived black children of rights guaranteed them under the Fourteenth Amendment. The Court later ruled that segregation by race in schools must be terminated "with all deliberate speed." But many states and local school districts found adroit stratagems for violating the spirit and sometimes the letter of the 1954 decision, and litigation over the many implications of the decision was contested bitterly

in the courts thereafter. Its patience exhausted, the Supreme Court ruled in 1969—fifteen years later—that the deadline for deliberate speed has been exhausted and ordered an immediate end to delay in desegregation of schools. In 1971 the Supreme Court upheld the constitutionality of busing of students to reduce segregation.

Educational practices and social outlook will continue to change. The tempo of civil disobedience is quickening, particularly among students, calling various civil liberties into question. Difficult decisions will need to be drawn between the right of students to protest and the right of educational institutions to protect themselves from destruction. These and other issues are dealt with at greater length in Chapter 1. Certainly the Supreme Court will speak to these and other issues and thereby help shape educational policy.

PRIVATE PROGRAMS

The national program of education in the United States is not a federal system. All the educational agencies of this country—federal, state, county, and local; governmental and nongovernmental; public, private, and parochial—constitute the national program of education. The educational activities of the federal government are only a part of the national program. Public, meaning tax-supported, education, though very important, is only a portion of the national effort in education. Private education, including parochial schools, colleges, and seminaries, was, is, and will be an important component of our national program of education.

The earliest schools and colleges were parochial. Educational advance in the early years was due primarily to the support of church and synagogue, just as overseas today much financial and scholarly impetus is given to education by missionary funds and zeal. Many children do not go to public schools, and it is not compulsory for them to do so. In the parochial field, the Roman Catholic Church maintains the largest number of secondary schools; the Seventh-day Adventist Church is second in number. The private, independent schools which are nonparochial are also often trailblazers because of their greater freedom. These schools are described at length in later chapters.

In the field of higher education, many colleges

These children attending a Roman Catholic school represent a sizable proportion of students who receive their education through private schools.

and universities are nonpublic; that is, they are private or parochial.

Numerous nongovernmental professional organizations wield much power in education. The largest professional organization is the National Education Association, formed in 1857. The largest parochial professional group is the National Catholic Education Association, organized in 1904. Professional organizations such as the American Council on Education and the national and regional accrediting associations affect secondary and higher education more than the federal government per se does.

As indicated in Chapter 14, the various private foundations have had a great impact on the national program of education in the United States. Very

influential, financially and innovationally, are the money grants given for education by numerous nongovernmental foundations, such as Carnegie, Ford, Duke, Mott, Rockefeller, Kellogg, and countless others. For example, in 1965, with the fiscal and moral support of the Carnegie Corporation, the National Academy of Education was established. The Academy, which will be limited eventually to fifty of the nation's most outstanding scholars, seeks "to promote scholarly inquiry and discussion of the ends and means of education in the United States and abroad."

The National Assessment for Educational Progress is an important enterprise financed in part by the Carnegie Corporation, the Fund for the Advancement of Education, and the Office of Education. This program functions under the aegis of the Education Commission of the States and under the direction of the Committee on Assessing Progress of Education (CAPE). This first massive effort to measure the output of our educational enterprise gives the nation very useful bench marks of progress and helps schools allocate resources and select programs and practices of instruction more effectively.

Various other national testing programs have also had great indirect impact upon our schools. The College Entrance Examination Board, begun in 1901, is supported by the resources of the Educational Testing Service, the Carnegie Foundation for the Advancement of Teaching, and the American Council on Education. In 1959, another testing agency, the American College Testing Program, was established. These national testing programs, used by many colleges and universities to help determine which applicants should be admitted to college, have shaped instruction in secondary schools because the results of the tests are viewed as a measure of the effectiveness of the high schools.

Private corporations producing educational materials—textbooks, reference works, tests, and audiovisual materials of instruction—have also influenced the development of instruction in our schools. Within the last decade a score or more of large industrial corporations have purchased publishing houses to link the hardware of the former with the software of the latter, both in design and distribution. In some cases the federal government has contracted with these firms to stimulate the research and development necessary for the new technology of instruction. Since the market for these products is immense, the financial thrust behind this enterprise is massive. If a few of these giant firms should dominate the field, the possibility of monopoly or near monopoly in the production of educational materials poses the possibility of standardization of instructional materials which could have great impact for better or worse.

The Council for Basic Education is one of many national, private, nonprofit groups which attempt through study and discussion to shape the future of educational practices and policies in the direction of their interests. The council presses for more rigorous academic standards and more concentrated attention upon the academic subjects in the curriculum.

Many illustrations in the remaining chapters depict governmental and nongovernmental educational activities which are *national* in scope and significance, but which are not *federal* in the strict sense of the word.

Diversity in support, purposes, program, and organization is indeed a vital characteristic of the American national program in education, as it should be in a dynamic democracy. Although diversified almost to the point of confusion to the layman, education in the United States is a dynamic organism united against ignorance, intolerance, and poverty.

FUTURE

One of the persistent problems confronting American education has been the search for the best blend of local, state, and national participation in the total educational enterprise. President Kennedy put the problem in proper perspective:

The control and operation of education in America must remain the responsibility of state and local governments and private institutions. This tradition assures our educational system of the freedom, the diversity and the vitality necessary to serve our free society fully. But the Congress has long recognized the responsibility of the Nation as a whole—that additional resources, meaningful encouragement and vigorous leadership must be added to the total effort by the Federal Government if we are to meet the task before us. For education in this country is the right, the necessity, and the responsibility of all. Its advancement is essential to national objectives and dependent on the greater financial resources available at the national level.

Without doubt the role of the federal government in education will continue to increase. Federal

subsidies for education will expand both in magnitude and influence. The concept of national federalism is indeed evolving in the United States. It will continue to be a system that maintains the vigor and vitality of our long tradition of local and state control in combination with the broader interests and greater resources of the federal government.

Principles and Proposals for Improvement of the National System

Basic Policies and Proposals. Four basic policies and principles have been suggested by various authorities to guide the future developments of the federal program in education as a service of primary importance:

1. **The federal government, within properly defined limits and without federal control, should continue to exercise educational functions demanded by changing national needs.**
2. **The federal government should limit its action in the states to two broad functions: financial assistance, when and where needed, and leadership of a stimulating but noncoercive character.**
3. **The decentralized pattern of public educational organization developed in the United States, involving basic control and administration of education by the states and localities, is sound democratic policy and should be continued and improved.**
4. **The heterogeneous pattern of administration needs to be better coordinated so that education receives from each political unit—federal, state, county, intermediate unit, and local district—the maximum contribution that it can and should make in a dynamic democracy.**

Specific Proposals. Suggestions by various groups and individuals for improving the national system of education in the United States include:

1. **Creating a national commission or board to articulate national educational policy**
2. **Establishing a separate department of education, with a secretary for education in the President's Cabinet**
3. **Coordinating many federal-state programs through a national council on public education, composed of the several state superintendents, under the chairmanship of a secretary or commissioner of education**
4. **Developing a national curriculum comprising a common set of values and contributing a common fund of knowledge by a nongovernmental national association of scholars**
5. **Continuing current categorical federal grants to education but giving more to general-purpose education**

6. Redistributing or returning to the states some of the federal taxes to be used by the states to enhance education
7. Consolidating educational agencies and aid programs at the national level to achieve greater coordination and efficiency of effort

In its quest for the best, the nation will ever seek improvement in education. The role of the federal government in this thrust for improvement will continue to be the focus of sharp debate. The issues which prompt this debate are discussed in Chapter 1.

SUMMARY

The advance of American civilization is largely the story of the improvement of American education. Education is regarded as the vehicle for the preservation of democracy, the improvement of society, the economic well-being of our people, and the strengthening of morality.

Unlike most countries, this nation has no national system of education but rather fifty state school systems influenced variously by the executive, legislative, and judicial branches of the federal government under the provisions of the "general welfare" clause and the amendments to the Constitution.

Federal support for education has historically been directed toward several major purposes: development of manpower, defense of the nation, provision of school facilities and services, rehabilitation of handicapped and disadvantaged persons, and eradication of poverty. The federal government has granted funds for education at all academic levels: pre-elementary, elementary, secondary, higher, and adult. It has provided this aid to both public and private schools and colleges.

The U.S. Office of Education, a part of the Department of Health, Education, and Welfare, conducts and stimulates research, administers some of the federal grants for education, and provides certain direct services for local, state, national, and international educational agencies. The Office is administered by the United States Commissioner of Education. This Office has recently undergone a major reorganization and is in need of increased financial support and a clearer definition of its role and function. Education in the nation was enhanced in 1965 by the creation of a new post, Assistant Secretary for Education in the Department of Health, Education, and Welfare.

Many other agencies of the executive branch of the government conduct major educational undertakings, including the National Science Foundation, the National Foundation on Arts and Humanities, the Veterans Administration, the Peace Corps, the Agency for International Development, and the Library of Congress.

The national government maintains schools in the District of Columbia, in the territories and outlying possessions of the United States, and on federal reservations. Through the United Nations, UNESCO, and its own overseas programs, the United States government contributes to the improvement of education in other lands. The Departments of Defense, Justice, and the Interior, as well as the governmental agencies, operate certain special-purpose schools. Various presidential commissions and the White House Conferences on Education have made important recommendations regarding the role of the federal government in improving education.

The federal court system has rendered many important decisions which have had powerful impact on educational policy and practice. These courts usually intervene in educational practices only when constitutional guarantees are abrogated, usually the provisions of the First, Fifth, and Fourteenth Amendments. The most significant decisions of the Supreme Court have dealt with the allocation of public funds to private education; school prayers, Bible reading, and religious instruction in the public schools; civil liberties of students, teachers, and parents; and discrimination by race in the schools.

In addition to the federal government, many private organizations influence education at the national level: private school systems, philanthropic foundations, professional organizations of educators, various testing programs, and private corporations engaged in the production of educational materials.

It is widely believed that the federal government should continue to exercise certain educational functions without controlling state or local systems of education and that these functions should include primarily financial support, leadership, and stimulation. Several proposals have been advanced for improving national provisions for education. A national system of education is gradually evolving in the United States, from Florida to Alaska and from Maine to Hawaii. As the federal government becomes more involved in education at home and in a shrinking world, its role as an active partner in our national program of education will inevitably grow.

Suggested Activities

1. Meet with the spokesmen of minority groups in your community and report on the educational needs and reforms which they consider most compelling.

2. Visit a local school system to observe the kinds of programs that have been made possible through federal aid and report your observations and conclusions.

3. Investigate special programs for the preparation of educators which might be of interest to you in planning your own career, such as the National Teacher Corps and the provisions of the Education Professions Development Act.

4. Review the Coleman Report and derive from it the major changes in educational organization and practice which would seem to have the most promise for improving educational opportunity for black Americans.

5. Give the pros and cons of federal aid to education and state your own conclusions.

6. Review all the Supreme Court decisions dealing with a topic of interest to you, such as civil liberties of students and teachers, church and state relations in education, or racial discrimination in the schools, and summarize the Court's pronouncements.

7. Study the literature dealing with categorical versus general federal support for education, listing the advantages and disadvantages of each, and state your own convictions.

8. Study the arguments pro and con on federal support for private educational enterprise and express your own position on the matter.

9. Describe the nationwide educational program of some nongovernmental, private organizations, such as the Ford Foundation.

10. Prepare an anthology of the most important statements on education made by the early leaders of our nation, such as Washington, Adams, Jefferson, Madison, Monroe, and Franklin.

Bibliography

Campbell, Roald, Luvern L. Cunningham, Roderick F. McPhee, and Raphael O. Nystrand: *The Organization and Control of American Schools*, 2d ed, Charles E. Merrill Publishing Company, Columbus, Ohio, 1970, chapter 2. Discussion of the function of the federal government in education and its relationship with other levels of government.

Carnegie Commission on Higher Education: *Quality and Equality: New Levels of Federal Responsibility for Higher Education*, New York, 1969. Report of the "Kerr Commission" recommending changes in the federal government's support of higher education.

Fellman, David (ed.): *The Supreme Court and Education*, Teachers College Press, Columbia University, New York, 1969. Review of twenty-two of the significant opinions of the Supreme Court on education—minority and majority opinions, with notes on the constitutional and educational issues at stake.

Fuller, Edgar, and Jim B. Pearson: *Education in the States: Nationwide Development since 1900*, National Education Association, Washington, D.C., 1969, chap. 11. Treatment of historical development of federal aid programs with considerations of their consequences as well as treatment of trends, prospects, and issues arising therefrom.

Knezevich, Stephen J.: *Administration of Public Education*, 2d ed., Harper & Row, Publishers, Incorporated, New York, 1969, chaps. 9, 10. Discussion of the role of the federal government, private schools, professional organizations, and informal agencies in the development of national programs of education.

Koerner, James D.: *Who Controls American Education?* Beacon Press, Boston, 1968. Statement focusing primarily on the issue of establishing a proper role for the layman in the control of education in relation with the many other groups influencing American education.

Shaw, Russell, and Richard J. Hurley (eds.): *Trends and Issues in Catholic Education*, Citation Press, New York, 1970. Articles and papers by leading Catholic educators on timely topics and forces shaping the future of Catholic schools.

U.S. Office of Education: *Fact Book: Office of Education Programs*, 1972. Statements of the purposes, appropriations, and other information relevant to every current federal educational program administered through the Office of Education in this annual publication.

U.S. Office of Education: *Progress of Public Education in the United States of America*, 1968. Excellent statistics on education and descriptions of federal programs to improve education, as prepared for UNESCO International Conference on Education.

U.S. Office of Education: *The Unfinished Journey: Issues in American Education*, The John Day Company, Inc., New York, 1968. A collection of twelve original essays by outstanding Americans commemorating the centennial of the Office of Education and looking at the future of the national system of education.

Chapter 3   State Systems
of Education

Orientation

Foundations

State boards

State superintendents and
    commissioners

State departments

State programs

Regionalism and the states

Summary

ORIENTATION

"The powers not delegated to the United States by the Constitution, nor prohibited by it to the States, are reserved to the States respectively, or to the people."

This Tenth Amendment to the Constitution of the United States, a part of what is popularly known as the "Bill of Rights," was proposed and sent to the states by the first session of the First Congress. It became effective December 15, 1791. By implication this amendment leaves education as a field reserved for the states.

A coalition, formed in 1966, that seeks to implement education as a state function and to coordinate and to stimulate educational planning among the states and territories is the Education Commission of the States. The germ idea for this organization was presented by James Conant in his book *Shaping Educational Policy.* The preliminary discussion led to the adoption of the "Compact for Education" by representatives from various states. Today nearly all states and territories are contributing members of the Education Commission of the States, either by state legislation or by executive orders of the governors. Its official periodical is *Compact.* A separate division supervises the National Assessment for Educational Progress.

The Commission has established these four major purposes:

1. **To establish and maintain close cooperation and understanding among executive, legislative, professional education, and lay leadership on a nationwide basis at the state and local levels**

2. **To provide a forum for the discussion, development, crystallization, and recommendation of public policy alternatives in the field of education**
3. **To provide a clearinghouse of information on matters relating to educational problems and how they are being met in different parts of the nation**
4. **To facilitate the improvement of state and local educational systems so that all of them will be able to meet adequate and desirable goals**

The Commission is viewed by one of its prime movers, Terry Sanford, former Governor of North Carolina, as a means of marshaling the political forces of the states, primarily the governors, to come to grips more effectively with the educational needs of the states and the nation. The Commission is not seen as a policy-making body, but rather as a forum through which policy makers at all levels of government may arrive at better decisions on educational matters. The agendas of the organization are broad and varied, including such items as pre-elementary education, teacher education, certification of teachers, urban schools, school finance, and private education. The Education Commission of the States is also viewed as a means for forging better national policy and more effective federal participation in school development.

Not all the Commission's observers view it optimistically. It is too early to make confident judgments about the contribution of this new organization. The returns are not yet in.

FOUNDATIONS

Historical

Evolution of State Control and Leadership. The Education Commission of the States and the countless regional developments between states

Dr. John Porter, the first Negro state superintendent of education, visits with junior high school students in Lansing, Michigan.

raise such historical questions as: How did the states accumulate such strength in education? What were the foundations and some of the specific historical events that helped put so much power in the hands of the states? As indicated briefly in the material that follows, state authority in education has developed because of bold basic beliefs, accumulated traditions, favorable legislation, pertinent court decisions, and powerful pioneers in state leadership.

The early colonists hewed the logs to build first their cabins, then their churches, and then their schools. The records of colonial legislatures, town meetings, and county courts contain frequent mention of education. As early as 1642, the Massachusetts General Court enacted a law requiring parents to provide education for the children and levying fines for those who failed to do so. This was the first instance of colonial public authority requiring compulsory education for children. The laws expressed the political aspiration that children be educated properly for the sake of the commonwealth. Apparently recognizing that this law could not be enforced unless there were schools for children to attend, the Massachusetts General Court five years later passed the famous act of 1647, requiring the towns to provide schools. This act established the principle that colonial government had the authority to control education. It was a principle of profound importance, for it set the precedent in this new society that later permitted the states to promote education as a public and civil enterprise. The Massachusetts example was followed in other New England colonies. As Butts and Cremin note, there were four important principles in this pattern of development in New England: (1) the state could require children to be educated; (2) the state could require towns to establish schools; (3) the civil government could supervise and control schools by direct management of public officials; and (4) public funds could be used for the support of public schools.[1]

Many of the schools of colonial America were essentially private in terms of both control and support, and many of the colonies lagged behind Massachusetts and other New England colonies in establishing civil authority over schools. Never-

[1]Freeman Butts and Lawrence A. Cremin, *A History of Education in American Culture*, Holt, Rinehart and Winston, Inc., New York, 1953, p. 103.

theless, when the federal Constitution was drafted in 1787, the tradition of local and state control of schools was so well accepted that there was little disposition to make education a responsibility of the new federal government. Thus the Constitution makes no mention of education. As indicated earlier, the Tenth Amendment delegates to the states those powers, including control of education, which are neither reserved to the federal government nor denied to the states.

The first 100 years following 1779 mark the era of the development of the great state school systems. This development was not easily achieved, because there were many who felt that education was properly a matter of local concern. Others felt that education should be left to the private domain. But under the vigorous leadership of Horace Mann, the first secretary of the Massachusetts State Board of Education; Henry Barnard, chairman of the State Board of Education in Connecticut; Calvin Wiley, the state superintendent of schools in North Carolina; and Samuel Lewis, the state superintendent of schools in Ohio, the struggle for state control of public education was gradually won. Thus the young republic forged what Horace Mann regarded as America's most revolutionary and significant contribution to civilization—its state-controlled public school systems. Our fifty state systems of education have grown in importance since these early days and even greater importance is portended for them in the years ahead.

Education Primarily a State Function. Thus education has become a legal function of the states, and fifty different state school systems have emerged. Although states delegate much of the operational responsibility for schools to local school districts, all states make constitutional or statutory provision for the organization and coordination of educational effort in the state.

Of course, the federal government may "promote the general welfare" and may contract with the states. It may, indeed, establish and support schools or offer contributions in aid of education; but its legal status seems to be that of an outside party contracting with the state, for it may not levy on state property for the support of such schools, nor may it attempt to guide the state-approved administrative machinery. The federal government has, however, enforced certain stipulations regarding the use of the land which it gave to the states. It has exercised indirect control over various aspects of education through the granting of funds and has established conditions for the use of these funds. The Elementary and Secondary Education Act of 1965 provides a significant illustration of the federal government's interest in strengthening state leadership in educational development. Under the provisions of this act, Congress each year appropriates several million dollars to be used for the improvement of the basic administration of state education agencies, for experimental projects and research in education carried on under state auspices, and for the strengthening of state departments of education.

Since education is a responsibility of the various states, its control is said to be decentralized. Obviously, the absence of a strong centralizing agency does not promote uniformity among the states, and certainly not within the states. Although the power to enact laws may be centered in the state government, the administration of such laws may be decentralized in that they are enforced by scores of county and local superintendents and boards of education. Dissimilarity, a striking characteristic of the state school systems, naturally produces marked inequalities.

Most states have general constitutional provisions for the establishing of schools. The Constitution of Hawaii, which has a strong centralized state system, stipulates that:

The State shall provide for the establishment, support and control of a statewide system of public schools free from sectarian control, a state university, public libraries and such other educational institutions as may be deemed desirable, including physical facilities therefor. There shall be no segregation in public educational institutions because of race, religion or ancestry; nor shall public funds be appropriated for the support or benefit of any sectarian or private educational institution.

Consequently, the real locus of legal power over schools resides at the state level of government. Collectively, the state systems form the firm foundation for free education in America.

Relation of Education to State Government. It is difficult to generalize about the fifty state school systems because they vary so much in their organization and operation. Figure 3-1 portrays a model of a state system of organization for education, which is fairly typical for many states. The reader, in considering Figure 3-1, should be reminded that the figure does not represent accurately the situation in some states.

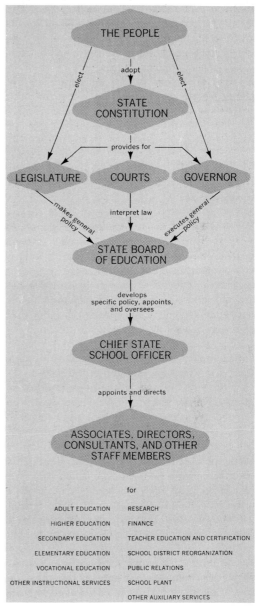

FIGURE 3-1 *Organization of a typical state system of education.*

As indicated in Figure 3-1, the legislature, which represents the people, enacts broad educational policy through statutes. The legislature is the most important and influential agency for educational policy making in the state. It establishes the general organization for education, determines the scope of education, establishes the means for the financial support for schools, appropriates money for state aid to education, charters institutions of higher learning, and approves or denies plans to extend or alter the educational system in any major way. In a few of the states, the legislature may also appoint the members of the state board of education. As the Supreme Court of Indiana observed,

The authority over schools and school affairs . . . is a central power, residing in the legislature of the state. It is for the law-making power to determine whether the authority shall be exercised by a state board of education, or distributed to county, township, or city organizations throughout the state.

Thus the legislature is regarded as the ultimate source of authority over public education within the state. In recent years there has been a distinct trend in most states toward a sharp increase in legislative power over education through the enactment of more and more specific prescriptions for the educational program and the management of schools. This issue is discussed more fully in Chapter 1.

The governor, who is elected by the people, has important powers over education. He has authority over the administration of the state budget, which finances the work of the department of education as well as that of the other agencies of government. He exercises influence over legislation. A few governors serve as ex officio members of state boards and commissions which develop educational policies and programs. In a few states the governor appoints the chief state school officer, and in the majority of states he appoints the members of the state board of education. Aside from his formal powers, the governor exercises considerable influence through his leadership of the body politic.

Role of Courts. The state judiciary also exercises considerable influence over educational practice and policy. Courts are frequently called upon to protect the legal rights of individuals and organizations, to clarify the legal prerogatives of schools, and to interpret the law. The proper safeguard against unwise educational policy is at the polls. However, relief from illegal or unconstitutional educational practice is properly sought through the courts. It is commonly accepted in America that the law is what the courts say it is. Thus judicial decisions have the effect of law until the law in controversy is

changed by the legislature. Many important decisions by courts have altered the course of public education. Some of these decisions include affirmation of the right to establish high schools at public expense, the right of teachers to act in the place of parents in their relations with pupils, and the protection of the teacher against dismissal without cause. Many state court decisions affecting education go on to higher tribunals, including the U.S. Supreme Court. Some of its decisions affecting education within the states are mentioned in Chapter 2. (See page 107.)

Role of State Education. From his long experience as New York's distinguished commissioner of education, James E. Allen, former U.S. Commissioner of Education, concluded that the state administrative agency should hold local school districts more rigorously to increased minimum educational requirements because schools are no longer purely local in character and the states can no longer afford to tolerate lagging districts. Stimulation is a better method for improving schools than compulsion, but compulsion is sometimes necessary. The National Council of Chief State School Officers recommends that each state

Coordinate all education within its borders
Determine the extent and quality of the foundation program
Establish minimum standards
Prepare a plan of financial support
Develop, evaluate, and adapt plans
Cooperate in a system of uniform records and reports
Provide consultative services
Administer programs made available by the federal government
Promote equality of educational opportunity for all
Utilize local, state, and national resources
Help plan, produce, and approve educational materials

In order that the state program may function, the work must be structured properly.

State Organization and Administration. No state has undertaken to administer and supervise public education entirely through constitutional provisions or legislative action; instead, each one has delegated at least some of these responsibilities to state or institutional boards. Although a state board of education is general, the powers and duties of these boards differ markedly. One central agency or several boards may be in charge of public schools and other educational institutions, as explained later.

The usual pattern consists of (1) the state board of education, which is the policy-making body; (2) the state superintendent of public instruction, who is the chief executive of the board; and (3) the state department of education with its staff members, who carry out the policies of the board of education under the immediate direction of the superintendent. Together, these three forces are responsible for developing a state program of education. The relationships of these bodies are illustrated in Figure 3-1.

STATE BOARDS

In order to develop a broad program of education, the state had to create an agency through which it could act. Just as a local community has a board of education to determine policies to be carried out by its chief executive officer, as discussed in Chapter 5, so too the state has a central body to plan for education.

Evolution of State Boards of Education

The earliest foundation for a state school board was the Board of Regents for New York, organized in 1784. Other boards were started later in various states for special purposes. Not until Massachusetts established its State Board of Education in 1837 were many powers and duties assigned to any of them.

This board was empowered to appoint a secretary and to fix a reasonable salary, not to exceed $1,000 a year. Although he did not seek the office, Horace Mann was appointed the first secretary. From the perspective of nearly a century and a half, it is easy to see that the pioneering efforts of the inspired and indefatigable Horace Mann as secretary of the State Board of Education in Massachusetts rightfully earned him the title "father of public school education." Other leaders, such as Henry Barnard, DeWitt Clinton, Thaddeus Stevens, Caleb Mills, and John Swett, also helped to develop American public education through their harmonious and productive relationships with state agencies.

Every commonwealth in the United States has one or more state boards, dealing with special aspects of education. For example, the federal government required some type of state board before it would grant aid for vocational education. Some

states have special boards which deal with a limited area of education, such as a selected phase of higher education, the state-supported community colleges.

The state board with some control and supervision of elementary and secondary school systems is organized in all the commonwealths except Wisconsin. Some of these states have had such a board for years, whereas a few are of very recent origin.

Just as the county and local school systems need a board of education, the state as a whole should maintain such a group. This board, as the chief educational authority, helps to develop policies and programs for the state department of education. Some of these state boards are vigorous and effective; others are timorous and are dominated by the governor, the legislature, and lobbies for special-interest groups.

Selection of State Boards of Education

The major modes of determining membership on the state boards of education are by ex officio status, election, and appointment. The trend over the past fifty years has been away from ex officio boards. As shown in Figure 3-2, board members are elected by the people in a minority of the states. In a majority of the states, the governor appoints members to the state board of education. Election is recommended by the National Council of Chief State School Officers. In four states, the majority of the members of the state board are ex officio, and in one state, the members are appointed by the state superintendent. Appointment by the governor is the method of selection in most frequent use and most often recommended.

Qualifications of State Board Members

The question of professional qualifications of board members is a controversial one. There are those who insist that the board be composed entirely of laymen. A few states require that some of the members be educators. Most states omit any specific reference to professional qualifications as a prerequisite for board membership.

A qualifying clause in a few states where members are appointed is that "different parts of the state shall be represented." In Wyoming "not more than four members of such board shall be from one political party." That state adds the important general qualifications, which should be applied everywhere, that the members "shall be appointed solely because of their character and fitness. All members of the board shall be persons of mature years, known for integrity, culture, public spirit, business ability, and interest in public education." The National Council of Chief State School Officers recommends that "the non-partisan lay state board be composed of 7 to 12 able citizens, broadly representative of the general public and unselfishly interested in public education." The legal qualifications for members of the state board of education take on significance only as public-spirited citizens demand the best. The size of state boards ranges from three to twenty-three members; the median size is nine. Their terms of office range from two to thirteen years, with six-year terms being most common.

The composition of the state boards of education is gradually being changed. Statistically, the average age of state board members is being lowered. More women and more members of minority groups are being elected or selected.

Duties of State Boards

A state may have many boards for specific purposes. In most instances, however, the major educational responsibilities are assigned to one central agency, which is usually the general state board of education. Originally its chief task was the distribution of state "literary" funds and kindred duties. Today this board is invested with greatly enlarged powers, including the general oversight of the entire state public school system. Like the school board in the local district, it is usually the policy-forming body, determining state educational policies within the statutory framework provided by the legislature. Its major task in some states is the appointment of a state superintendent, who serves as the chief executive officer of the board. Like city boards, it also makes appointments recommended by the

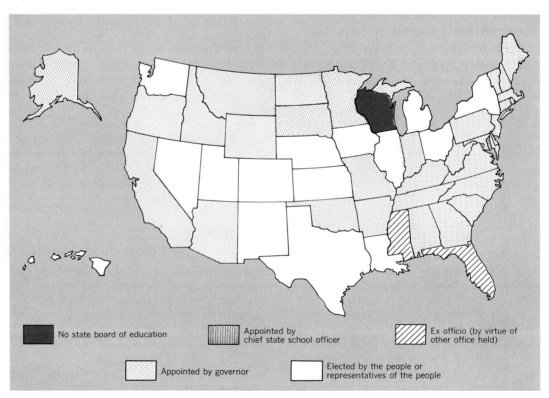

FIGURE 3-2 Methods of selecting members of state boards of education.

superintendent and approves budgets prepared by him. Relevantly, Frank W. Lutz in "The Politics of Education" writes: "Perhaps because education is a function of the separate states, there has been a greater interest in the state politics of education than in the local politics of education."[2]

Other State Education Boards

Many commonwealths assign to bodies other than the state board of education various aspects of the educational program. Among the several hundred special-purpose state educational boards or commissions are:

The curriculum commission, which recommends programs of studies

The textbook commission, which selects textbooks to be used in schools throughout the state

The board of trustees or regents, which manages the state university

The community college board, which presides over the affairs of the state community colleges

The board or boards of control, which have charge of one or more institutions of higher learning

The board for vocational rehabilitation, which collaborates with the federal board in reestablishing in industry persons injured or otherwise handicapped

The board for vocational education, which works with the federal government especially in promoting Smith-Hughes activities

The board of examiners, which prepares and conducts examinations for teachers seeking to be certified

The retirement or pension board, which collects the receipts and controls the distributions for teachers' pensions

The board of charities and corrections, which takes charge of, and provides for, the proper training of feebleminded, deaf, blind, crippled, and otherwise handicapped persons

The dormitory authority, which approves the construction of living and dining facilities on college campuses

In recent years one notes a tendency toward reducing the number of ancillary state boards and centralizing the control of educational affairs in the hands of a single state board of education, which has general supervision of all the schools. This may be supplemented by another board, which has charge of the institutions of higher learning in the state. One also detects a trend toward making the state superintendent the coordinator of all educational activities in the commonwealth.

[2] Frank W. Lutz, "The Politics of Education" in *The School Administrator*, American Association of School Administrators, Washington, D.C., August, 1970, p. 8.

STATE SUPERINTENDENTS AND COMMISSIONERS

In several instances the president or secretary of the state board of education is the chief educational executive of the state. The evolution of this central office often antedated that of the state board of education.

Evolution of State Superintendency

Historically and professionally, instruction preceded administration. In the earliest schools there were only pupils and teachers—no administrators. Then the profession of educational administration slowly evolved. The establishment of city superintendencies was preceded by the creation of a chief state official for education. New York in 1812 was the first to have a state school officer. The first commonwealth continuous office was established in Michigan in 1829. The Massachusetts State Board of Education, in engaging Horace Mann as its energetic secretary in 1837, exerted much favorable influence. Even before the Civil War, each employed a chief school officer, designated by various titles. In 1913 Delaware reestablished the office after abandoning it for a quarter of a century. Since then all states have had the office continuously.

The most common designation is "state superintendent of public instruction." The term "commissioner of education" is also widely used, especially in the Eastern states. A title in harmony with the concept of public *education* rather than mere *schooling* is that used by Louisiana, namely, "state superintendent of public education." In line with the trend toward cooperation among educational agencies—public, private, and parochial—the term "state superintendent (commissioner) of education" seems the best. The name, however, is not so significant as the manner in which the official is selected and his qualifications for the all-important task of providing strong educational leadership in the state.

Selection of Chief Educational Officer

Three methods of selection of the chief state school official are popular election, appointment by the governor, and appointment by the state board of education, as shown in Figure 3-3.

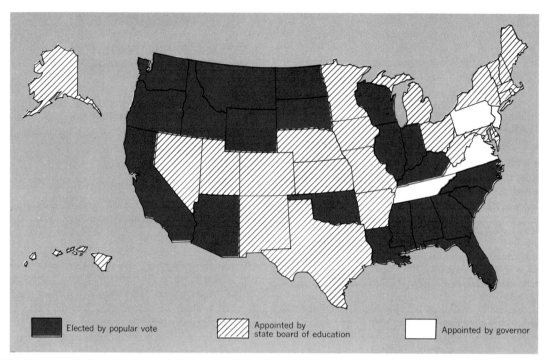

FIGURE 3-3 *Methods of selecting chief state school officers. Illinois changes to appointment in 1975.*

It is unfortunate that in two-fifths of the states the chief school officer is elected by popular vote. In a recent caucus, one political party selected its candidate for state superintendent on the basis of geography, since the political leaders wanted their candidates for the various offices to be distributed throughout the state. Many state superintendents have had to spend much time in office, particularly during the latter part of the term, building political fences for reelection. These superintendents are likely to have to think more about the next election than about the next generation. Fortunately, there is a sharp trend away from the election of chief state school officers. In five states the chief state school officer is appointed by the governor. The preponderance of opinion is against this practice also.

As revealed by Figure 3-3, the chief state school officer is appointed by the state board of education in about half the states. The number of states utilizing this practice is increasing rapidly. This is the method recommended by the National Academy of Education and generally favored by experts in education. It is considered desirable that the candidate for this important office be chosen by the small group of competent people most directly concerned with the position and directly related to the work

of the state superintendent, namely, the state board of education.

Through the two processes of appointment by the state board and election by the people, two Negroes were made state superintendents for the first instance in 1970, when John W. Porter was appointed state educational administrator in Michigan and Wilson C. Riles was elected in California to head the nation's largest state school system.

Qualifications and Term of Office

Qualifications. An example from the school laws of Maryland indicates the general tenor of the requirements for the state superintendent: "He shall be an experienced and competent educator; a graduate of a standard college, have not less than two years of specific academic and professional graduate preparation in a standard university, and not less than seven years' experience in teaching and administration." Most legal definitions of qualifications are general, and rightly so; however, they should be specific enough to provide a pattern by which the electors, or the group or person selecting the superintendent, may be guided in the quest for the most competent person. Usually a master's degree is the minimum and a doctorate the optimum academic preparation.

Term of Office, Tenure, and Salary. The median legal term of office for the superintendent or commissioner is between three and four years. Tenure is longer when he is appointed by the state board than when he is elected or appointed gubernatorially. Sound educational administration suggests that the term of office be many years, subject to the best judgment of the state board, in order to ensure continuity in policy and staff personnel. Furthermore, the salary must be commensurate with the importance and labors of the office. Some cities pay their local superintendents more than the state gives its chief educational official. Naturally this does not draw the best talent into the state office. The National Academy of Education suggests that "the median income of college presidents in the area should be the minimum standard of remuneration."

Duties of State Superintendents

Most of the duties of state superintendents and their staffs fall into a few major categories:

Leadership
Drawing public attention to the state's educational needs and encouraging public action

Trusteeship
Reporting to the public on educational accomplishments; compiling data on school enrollments, expenditures, school construction, measures of academic progress, and so forth

Advisory
Giving counsel to local boards of education and administrators; interpreting school law to administrative officials; offering testimony on proposed legislation and regulations to state legislatures and other governmental bodies

Planning
Preparing required state plans for federally financed programs, such as vocational education, and planning intrastate programs

Experimenting
Innovating and implementing various pilot projects

Judicial
Resolving controversies within local school systems; hearing appeals in much the same manner as an appellate court

Ministerial
Regulating public and private elementary schools, secondary schools, colleges, and universities; distributing state and some federal moneys; certifying teachers; approving school buildings; managing such diverse enterprises as museums, libraries, historical sites; and even,

in some states, approving motion pictures and licensing barbers and beauticians
Coordinating
Attending meetings of various state boards and coalescing the various educational efforts of the state
Appointive
Filling vacancies in the state department of education, in county superintendencies, and in other positions
Evaluating
Participating in state and national assessment programs

Superintendent's Relationships with Others

State superintendents confer with officials from other states, integrate the disparate efforts of the numerous educational workers within the state, and cooperate with subordinates.

Nationwide Relationships. No state can exist by itself economically, nor can any do so educationally. The state superintendent therefore seeks to learn from other departments of education and to pool his interests and achievements with others. To this end he affiliates himself with other state superintendents and commissioners in their national organization, the National Council of Chief State School Officers. Occasionally he and other officials may be called by the United States Commissioner of Education into conference on nationwide problems. The state superintendent's work is connected with the U.S. Office of Education, to which he sends statistics and other data and from which he receives rapidly increasing amounts of federal grants for a wide variety of educational programs. Most superintendents have contacts with the Education Commission of the States mentioned earlier.

Statewide Relationships. The state superintendent also has important working relationships within the state he serves. First of all comes his relationship to the state board of education. Usually the superintendent serves as secretary or president, or at least as an ex officio member. He may also belong to other state boards which have numerous educational and semieducational duties. Here, serving as a coordinator, he tries to integrate the work of all the boards. He comes into close contact with many other state officials in the health, highway, safety, buildings, legal, and other departments, and with the officers of the state education association.

County and Local Relationships. Naturally the state superintendent, in the hierarchical form of organization, can demand that certain duties be fulfilled by subordinates. In a sense the county superintendent of schools is a member of the state department, representing it in dealings with the local boards of his county. Many state commissioners call an annual conference of all county superintendents and local school directors to promote better relationships and to improve the schools. Naturally the state superintendent will have to depend largely on his headquarters staff to represent him in many of these vital relationships.

STATE DEPARTMENTS

Evolution of State Departments

In the days when Gideon Hawley was the state superintendent of schools in New York and Horace Mann the secretary of the State Board of Education in Massachusetts, each was the only member of the state department of education. But as the concept of the state's function in education broadened, no single official, even in a small commonwealth, could handle all the work; gradually there was an increase in staff personnel. As late as 1890, however, the median number of staff members was only two. After 1917 came a rapid growth in department personnel resulting from four major causes: the new duties devolving upon the department as a result of the passage of the Smith-Hughes vocational-education law; the startling revelations from physical, mental, and literacy tests administered during World War I; the growing appreciation of the need for a strong state program of education to meet present-day needs; and the task of administering the greatly expanded programs in education supported by federal funds, many of which are administered through state departments of education. Today every state provides its chief school officer with an organization and staff, usually known as the "state department of education."

Organization of State Departments

At the head of the state department is the state superintendent or commissioner of education. Next in line are the assistant or associate superintendents or commissioners, other assistants, supervisors, and staff members.

Figure 3-1 shows the organization of a typical state system of education, the divisions of the state department, and the relationships between the state department, superintendent, state board, governor, legislature, and courts.

The department of education is usually located in the state capital and housed in the capitol building. With the increasing complexity of their work and the numerous additions to their staff, most departments are cramped in small quarters designed many years ago. In large states a separate building houses the state superintendent, his assistants, and other members of the staff. New York State was the first to have a state superintendent of schools—Gideon Hawley—and was also the first to erect a building for education. "Central schoolhouses," such as those in Sacramento, Harrisburg, and Albany, are needed in many states to house the chief educational agency.

Personnel of State Departments

The personnel of the department should be employed by the state board of education upon nomination by the chief state school officer. All appointments should be made on the basis of merit and fitness for the work. The state department should be adequately staffed to provide all needed services.

The Advisory Council on State Departments of Education recommends that the U.S. Commissioner of Education appropriate part of federal training funds "to help meet the manpower needs of state departments." State department staffs, now totaling more than 33,000, are increasing in order to meet old and new demands.

Functions of Departments

The many specific functions of state departments of education are commonly classified into four general categories:

1 Regulatory
These embrace the so-called "police powers" of the state—developing minimum standards, rules, and regulations; observing and inspecting practices to identify cases of noncompliance; and instigating, where necessary, procedures to enforce compliance.

2 Operational

These include enterprises actually administered by the state, such as the operation of schools for the blind, the licensing of teachers, and the maintenance of state educational television networks, among others.

3 Financial

These include program budgeting, educational and fiscal auditing; authorizing funds for state and federal-state approved projects; plus recommending appropriate sources of revenue for education in the state and in local units of administration.

4 Leadership

These include the determination of educational purposes and goals for the state; planning, research, and development activities; coordination of the various educational programs of the state; evaluation of the state system of education; and public relations activities.

There has been a trend in recent years in the more effective state departments to place greater emphasis upon the leadership functions.

STATE PROGRAMS

Chapters 4 and 5 emphasize the important role played by the educational subdivisions within the state. However, in a hierarchical form of organization, authority flows from the head or source. Upon the individual state, therefore, rests the grave responsibility of developing a program of education for all its people. Supreme Court decisions reinforce constitutional and legislative provisions for establishing state programs of education.

Each commonwealth is faced with the direct responsibility of organizing and promoting a functional statewide system of public education which should extend from kindergarten through college and adult life. In the development of this program, certain principles or procedures ought to be adopted as a tentative guide. In line with these principles, under the direction of the state department, all the people and agencies of the state participate in developing the plans.

Elements in Statewide Programs

Many basic ingredients make up a state program of education. A few of these are presented here with illustrative material.

Effective State Educational Policy Making. State school systems can be no better than the policies that govern their operation. As pointed out earlier,

general educational policies should be enacted by the legislature, and more specific and comprehensive policies should be established by the state board of education. In some states, the legislatures cannot resist dealing with specific educational policies, often to the detriment of the schools. The legislators have neither the time nor the knowledge needed for detailed policy making. They are often subject to the pressures of special-interest groups that lobby for preferential treatment. This can result in policies that are not in the best interests of the total society. Moreover, when detailed educational policy exists in statute form, it is too difficult and time-consuming to amend it to satisfy changing circumstances. Yet many state legislatures are jealous of the legitimate prerogatives of state boards of education and chief state school officers, with the result that these officers are often figureheads with little or no opportunity to exercise their important functions.

Chief state school officers and state boards of education should be relatively free from partisan political influences and beholden only to the educational imperatives of the commonwealth. Only a few states, most notably New York, have established sound and effective relationships among the governor, legislature, state board of education, chief state educational officer, state department of education, and other groups interested in the educational system.

Careful Development of Educational Goals for the State. The central question in most matters of educational policy making is: Education for what? Until educational purposes and priorities are set, much of the debate over programs, policies, and procedures is meaningless. Yet many states have neglected this essential consideration of purpose. There are, happily, a growing number of exceptions to this neglect. For example, the Pennsylvania State Board of Education was directed by the state legislature to develop procedures and standards for the measurement of educational quality in the schools of the commonwealth. The board took the sound position that evaluation of schools could not be undertaken confidently until the purposes of education had been made explicit. Thus steps were taken to involve a large number of educators and laymen in Pennsylvania in the development of a statement of educational purposes as a basis for the evaluation. From this effort there emerged a superb statement of the goals of education and the "inputs."

Machinery for Harmonizing the Various Educational Interest Groups. In every state there are many groups vitally interested in schools. There are associations of teachers, school board members, administrators, parents, taxpayers, and many others. Frequently there is disagreement among these groups, and often within a particular group, on educational policies. County superintendents have been known to oppose policy favored by local superintendents. Teachers' associations and administrators' associations are sometimes in disagreement. This internecine conflict within the education profession itself permits legislators to "divide and conquer," playing off one lobby against another and thereby stalemating policy making that could improve education.

In some states these groups have developed extralegal coalitions to harmonize their interests as much as possible. For example, the New York Educational Conference Board is a coalition of the New York associations of teachers, principals, superintendents, PTAs, and citizens' committees for the public schools. It serves as a forum in which the various groups attempt to resolve their differences privately among themselves, reaching compromises when necessary, so that a united front can be presented in support of agreed-upon policy or legislation. After agreement is reached, the Educational Conference Board becomes a powerful energizer of policy formulation and political action. Similar examples of coalitions of educational groups for political action in other states could be cited, such as the New Jersey Princeton Group, the Illinois School Problems Commission, and the Utah Cooperating Agencies for the Public Schools. Since these groups exist in most of the states that have made the greatest progress in education, many observers believe that they play a vital role in state educational policy development. In any case, there should be machinery for integrating the many diverse interests in education so that all may have a voice in educational policy making and have an opportunity to reach the greatest possible accord on important issues.

Adequate Educational Research and Development. Goal setting and program development have been handicapped in many states by the paucity of data relevant to the problem at hand. Necessary information is often lacking, without which good decisions are seldom reached. Although most state departments have had for years a director of research, this office has traditionally been preoccupied with the gathering of the most rudimentary kind of data on enrollment, attendance, and costs. Sophisticated studies of important and complex problems—such as what practices are most successful in reducing dropouts or what kind of vocational education is needed for out-of-school youth—were often neglected. An example of a salubrious piece of research undertaken by a state department is the study made of the dynamics of instructional changes in the schools of New York with recommendations for better educational organization to accelerate educational innovation in that state.

The social dislocations of the 1960s and 1970s have quickened the urgency of such problems as crime, unemployment, and race relations. The increase of federal funds under the Elementary and Secondary Education Act for the strengthening of state departments of education has enabled most states to expand their research and fact-finding facilities. Most states have installed automatic data processing equipment and computers, which multiply the research capacity of the departments, thereby increasing their yield. Many states have undertaken comprehensive surveys of their school systems as a basis for evaluating existing programs and pointing directions for the future. These surveys, if well done, play an important role in the long-range planning of educational development in the state.

High-quality Professional Leadership. Just as the individual school can hardly rise above the quality of its professional leadership, so a state educational agency is heavily dependent upon the excellence of its executive talent. This leadership is manifest in the governorship and the legislature as well as in the state board of education, the state department of education, and the chief state school officer. Where the state board of education is appointive, seats on the board may be regarded as rewards granted under political patronage rather than as positions of great trust for the finest lay leaders available. The same is often true of the office of the chief state school official. Where this condition prevails, it is not surprising that these officials tend to behave in a manner dictated by the fortunes of politics rather than the imperatives of education. In some states the department of education is thought of as part of the spoils system, and political rather than educational considerations determine the appointments, as well as the behavior of the appointees in office. In many states the salaries of the positions in the state department lag dangerously behind those paid in local school systems. Many authorities believe that the state departments of education are the most important but also the weakest link in our educational enterprise. Frequently the prerogatives of the legislature, state board, and state superintendent are confused and acrimony results. On the other hand, some states, such as Maryland, New Jersey, and New York, among others, have been quite distinguished by real leadership.

A Sound Program of State Financial Support for Local School Systems. A problem basic to the development of a stable, statewide program of education is that of financial support, considered in detail

in Chapter 16. An appraisal of state-aid systems reveals that not a single state has attained a desirable status with respect to the financing of public education. Nowhere, however, is the entire burden of school support left to the local school districts; the relative amount of the total cost borne by the state treasury varies from less than 6 to over 90 percent. Delaware adopted in 1921 the policy of paying for the entire state-approved cost of all public schools. Figure 3-4 shows the percentage of revenue for public elementary and secondary schools received from state governments. Hawaii furnishes nearly all the support for public schools from the state treasury.

A marked trend in the financing of education in recent years has been the establishment of a fund for equalizing the educational opportunities and burden within the state. These funds, discussed in Chapter 16, are based on the important principle of collecting the school money where the money is and distributing it where the pupils are. The es-

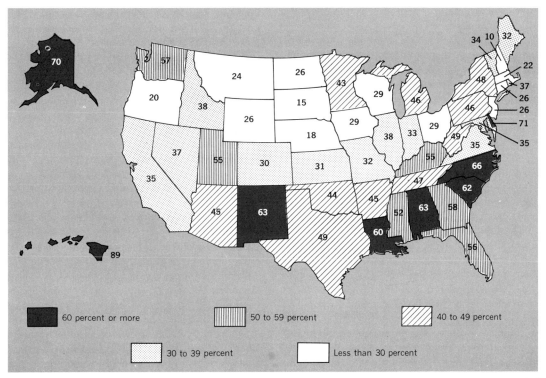

FIGURE 3-4　*Percentage of revenue for public elementary and secondary schools from state governments. A few states, particularly Hawaii, Delaware, and Alaska, have moved fairly close to full state funding of public education.* (*National Education Association, Research Division,* Estimates of School Statistics, 1970-71. *Copyright by the National Education Association.*)

Most states provide special funds for the education of handicapped children, such as this homebound boy, who receives instruction by school-to-home telephone service.

tablishing of an equalization fund which is scientifically sound and administratively feasible demands a searching survey of the educational needs, a careful estimate of the costs, and an accurate analysis of the ability of the state to support education and other activities.

A Comprehensive Program of Higher Education. Other state educational boards previously mentioned are those that control the state universities and colleges or the state system of higher education. California has a most extensive system of decentralized control, with the campuses of the University of California governed by the Board of Regents, the state colleges by the Board of Trustees, and the community colleges by a Board of Governors. The largest centralized system of higher education in the United States is the State University of New York. The state, with its Full Opportunity Program, enrolls more than 300,000 students.

The Education Commission of the States, discussed at the beginning of this chapter, is active in promoting nationwide cooperation in higher education. In 1970 the first issue of *Higher Education in the States* appeared, published by the Commission in consultation with the State Higher Education Executive Officers Association. It furnishes staff for the Council of State Higher Education Agencies, founded in 1970. Since a large share of the educational budgets of the various states goes to higher education, the fifty commonwealths are increasingly concerned with this critical area in American education.

Well-coordinated Working Relations with the Federal Government and with Local Districts. With the rapid growth of federal participation in the financial support of education, the state educational agency has become an increasingly important intermediary between the federal government and the local operating school systems. Working relations exist between the state and federal levels of government that were unheard of a few years ago.

One by-product of federal-state cooperation is reported by the Advisory Council on State Departments of Education, which found "marked progress by state education agencies in strengthening their leadership roles, largely attributable to federal funds granted under Title V of the Elementary and Secondary Education Act." In 1970 the U.S. Office of Education started sending teams of program specialists to several state departments to review their management of federal assistance programs for elementary and secondary education. The team approach to analysis of state administration of federal programs is designed to assess and help improve state capabilities in management functions.

The relationship between state and local school administrators is also becoming more difficult and complex. Many examples of strained relations at all levels of government are evident, as is natural perhaps with the growing interdependence at all levels. It is clear that the future demands even greater coordination of local-state-federal relations in education and the best leadership that can be mustered.

The Massachusetts Business Task Force for School Management has recommended that the state department establish a separate office to promote coordination among school districts within the state.

Several surveys have recommended that units within the state departments of education have the "explicit responsibility of promoting change and innovation." All states are being challenged to make constructive changes, especially in curriculums and methodology of teaching and learning. In connection with the new Environmental Protection Act, Illinois' Governor Richard B. Ogilvie said: "Individual concern and individual action are the ultimate keys that will prevent this *affluent* society from becoming an *effluent* society—one drowning in its own trash and waste." State educational agencies in the United States are being programmed to help fight pollution through education.

New machinery may be needed to implement certain aspects of a total statewide program. For

THE STATE COURTS SPEAK*

On the right to extend free education through the high school

Throughout the territory a system of most liberal education should be supported at the public expense for the benefit of the whole people. (Michigan, 1874)

On relationship of state and local powers over education

The authority over the schools and school affairs . . . is a central power, residing in the legislature of the state. (Indiana, 1890)

On the requirement of compulsory school attendance

A parent, therefore, is not at liberty to exercise a choice in that regard, but, where not exempt for some lawful reason, must send his child to the school where instruction is provided suitable to his attainments as the school authorities may determine. (Indiana, 1925)

On courts' review of local boards' actions

In the absence of fraud, abuse or discretion, arbitrariness or unreasonableness, . . . this court will not interfer . . . [with the board's] authority nor substitute its judgment for that of . . . [the] board upon matters delegated to it to decide in conducting the affairs of the school. (Ohio, 1951)

On de facto segregation

Where such [residential] segregation exists it is not enough for a school board to refrain from affirmative discriminatory conduct . . . The right to an equal opportunity for education and the harmful consequences of segregation require that school boards take steps, insofar as reasonably feasible, to alleviate racial imbalance in schools regardless of its cause. (California, 1963)

On free transportation of students to private schools

Bringing children together in buses on their way to the temple of learning can only hasten the eventual attainment of the true brotherhood of man. (Pennsylvania, 1967)

On teachers' right to strike (unless specifically authorized by law)

The notion that some higher right justifies concerted defiance of the law can have no role in the courtroom. . . . There is no right to "compel" government to change its ways by blocking the administration of the law until it yields. (New Jersey, 1968)

On violation of injunctions against teacher strikes

[To] permit the breakdown of governmental functions, would sanction the control of a governmental function for private gain; and further, to allow such action is the same as saying that government employees may deny the authority of government through its duly elected representatives. To permit this is to take the first step toward anarchy. (Florida, 1968)

On schools' authority to regulate student grooming

Some undefined fear or apprehension of disturbance if they did not require the boys . . . to keep their hair cut . . . is not enough to overcome the constitutional right of the plaintiff. (Alabama, 1969)

On teachers' rights to protest

It is imperative that the courts carefully differentiate in treatment those who are violent and heedless of the rights of others as they assert their cause and those whose concerns are no less burning but who seek to express themselves through peaceful, orderly means. In order to discourage persons from engaging in the former activity, the courts must take pains to assure that the channels of peaceful communication remain open and that peaceful activity is fully protected. (California, 1969)

On a teacher's liability for injury to students under his supervision

California law had imposed on school authorities a duty to "supervise at all times the conduct of the children on the school grounds and to enforce these rules and regulations necessary for their protection." The standard of care required of an officer or employee of a public school is that which a person of ordinary prudence, charged with this duty, would exercise under similar circumstances. (California, 1970)

On school finance systems based on local property tax

Dependence on local property taxes is the root of the constitutional defect . . . Affluent districts can have their cake and eat it too. They can provide a high-quality education for their children while paying lower taxes. Poor districts, by contrast, have no cake at all. (California, 1971)

* Courts vary in their interpretations of state constitutions and statutes, which themselves vary. Therefore, these pronouncements would not necessarily apply equally in all jurisdictions.

example, a special organism for planning for education and manpower has been urged: "Each state should establish a State Comprehensive Manpower Development Council. . . . The Council would review all state plans relating to manpower administration and develop a total state plan which would become both a short-term and long-term guide to manpower development."[3]

These, then, are a few of the potential new elements of statewide programs of education. The situation is one of flux and development, understandably fraught with controversy and even hostility at times. The issues involved are often subject to controversy, even among people of high purpose and dedication. Some of these issues are discussed in more detail in Chapter 1.

REGIONALISM AND THE STATES

Regional Educational Laboratories

One of the developments in the 1960s in interstate cooperation in education was manifested in the Regional Educational Laboratories and several related agencies financed by the U.S. Office of Education. These centers brought together the public and private school systems, colleges and universities, and other educational agencies of neighboring states that can be considered geographical regions, with fairly common demographic characteristics and educational problems. These centers are expected to channel the demonstration and dissemination of the fruits of research into the lifeblood of schools and colleges. The great gap between the production of educational research and the implementation of the research findings is well known among educators. It is hoped that the regional educational laboratories will help to reduce this gap between know-how and practice in education.

The financial support of these laboratories is quite substantial, and they will certainly have an increasing impact on educational programs.

Other Regional Associations

Many other examples of interstate cooperative associations could be cited. For example, the Southern

[3]Grant Venn, *Man, Education, and Manpower,* American Association of School Administrators, Washington, D.C., 1970, pp. 254-255.

Regional Educational Board is a voluntary coalition of educational agencies in sixteen Southern states interested in common problems and programs in that region, and the New England Board of Higher Education, with representation from the six New England states, seeks to coordinate programs in higher education and to profit from the sharing of resources and facilities. Numerous regional programs have evolved because the individual states have basic authority in education. Among them are the numerous accrediting agencies, such as North Central, New England, and Southern associations. Regionalism is further discussed in Chapter 4.

SUMMARY

The Tenth Amendment of the federal Constitution delegates the function of education to the states. Although local districts assume much of the operational responsibility for schools, education is a legal function of the fifty states. The incidence of interstate cooperation in educational development is also increasing rapidly. The most significant recent examples of this development are the new Education Commission of the States and the regional research and development laboratories established with federal funds. Many other examples of regional enterprise in educational development are evident. Both the increased federal participation in educational development and the regional enterprises have introduced cleavages among educational authorities that will continue and perhaps intensify for years to come. The nation is in great need of more clarification of authority over education and better cooperation between educational bodies at the local, state, and national levels of government.

In general, the state constitution sets the general legal framework for education; state courts maintain the constitutionality and legality of educational practice; the legislature enacts broad educational policy; the state board of education establishes specific policy and regulations; and the state department, under the leadership of the state superintendent or commissioner, administers the state program of education.

In a few states the state board members hold ex officio status, and in some they are elected by the people, but in most they are appointed by the governor. The chief state school officer serves as executive officer of the board and as the leader of the department of education. In many states the chief state school officer is elected by the people. In more states he is appointed by the board of education, which is regarded as preferred practice. The major functions of the department of education are classified as regulatory, operational, and leadership. These departments vary widely in their size, scope, function, and influence. There has been a trend toward an increase in authority over education at the state level.

The sharply increasing activity of the federal government in educational development has extended and complicated federal-state-local relations and has changed the power structure of educational decision making.

Suggested Activities

1. Discuss the purposes and programs of the Education Commission of the States.

2. Prepare a report on the purposes, constituent agencies, and work of the regional research and development laboratory serving your area.

3. Discuss the implications for state support for education in the Tenth Amendment to the United States Constitution.

4. Prepare an interesting biography of Horace Mann, the first secretary of the Massachusetts State Board of Education. Similar reports may be made about Henry Barnard, Thaddeus Stevens, Caleb Mills, John Swett, and John D. Pierce.

5. Investigate and report on some important state court cases that have affected educational practice in your state.

6. Draw an organization diagram of your state, showing the educational boards and the relationships that exist between them.

7. Find out the following in regard to your state superintendent of education: term of office, qualifications, salary, and duties.

8. Examine the last annual report of your state superintendent of public instruction.

9. Discuss the desirability of state adoption of textbooks for all schools.

10. Define what is meant by a foundation or minimum education program for a state.

11. Review the historical development of education in your state or in the one where you plan to teach.

Bibliography

Advisory Council on State Departments of Education: *The State of State Departments of Education,* 6th annual report, 1971. One of the annual reports issued through the U.S. Office of Education, dealing with the fifty state departments.

Bendiner, Robert: *The Politics of Schools: A Crisis in Self-Government,* Harper & Row, Publishers, Incorporated, New York, 1969, chap. 11. A journalistic account of the state's role and problems in the government of education.

Campbell, Roald F., and others: *The Organization and Control of American Schools,* 2d ed., Charles E. Merrill Publishing Co., Columbus, Ohio, 1970, chap. 3. Conceptualization, organization, operation, and future of state governmental relations with education.

Frey, Sherman H., and Keith R. Getschman (eds.): *School Administration: Selected Readings,* Thomas Y. Crowell Company, New York, 1968, chap. 10. State boards, state departments, state superintendents, and their relationships with other agencies of state government.

Fuller, Edgar, and Jim B. Pearson (eds.): *Education in the States: Nationwide Development Since 1900,* National Education Association, Washington, D.C., 1969, chap. 2. Discussion of state departments of education by a state superintendent, a deputy superintendent, and a former secretary of the Council of Chief State School Officers.

Goldhammer, Keith, and others: *Issues and Problems in Contemporary Educational Administration,* Center for the Advanced Study of Educational Administration, Eugene, Ore., 1967. Role of state departments of education as viewed by school superintendents.

Hack, Walter G., and others: *Educational Administration: Selected Readings,* 2d ed., Allyn and Bacon, Inc., Boston, 1971, chap. 10. Discussion of state and federal government relationships in education.

Kirst, Michael W. (ed.): *The Politics of Education at the Local, State and Federal Levels,* McCutchan Publishing Corporation, Berkeley, Calif., 1970, part 2. Discussion of the politics of education at the state level.

Knezevich, Stephen J.: *Administration of Public Education,* 2d ed., Harper & Row, Publishers, Incorporated, New York, 1969, chap. 8. Discussion of state legislatures, boards of education, and departments of education.

Meranto, Philip: *School Politics in the Metropolis,* Charles E. Merrill Publishing Co., Columbus, Ohio, 1970, chap. 5. Analysis of the politics of school administration and financing at the state level.

Miller, Van: *The Public Administration of American School Systems,* The Macmillan Company, New York, 1965, chap. 5. State governance of education through state departments, state boards, and other educational authorities and organizations at the state level.

Morphet, Edgar L., and Charles O. Ryan (eds.): *Planning Education for the Future,* No. 3, Citation Press, New York, 1967, chaps. 11, 12, 13. A look at the future of state planning and leadership in public education.

Chapter 4   County and Intermediate Educational Units

ORIENTATION

James B. Conant has aptly described the pattern of educational organization in the United States as a "Noah's Ark." The variegated pattern is revealed in part in Figure 4-1, which shows the prevailing types of school organization. The four prevailing types are: (1) state, (2) town or township, (3) other local district, and (4) county, which is also sometimes a local administrative unit. The organizational pattern of the state is discussed in Chapter 3; of local bodies, in Chapter 5; of the county and intermediate units, in this chapter.

The role and development of county educational "establishments" and the more recent evolution of intermediate units are briefly traced here under *Foundations*, and then they are treated separately in some detail, along with the current thrust of area schools and colleges and the present and potential power of partnerships and reciprocity in regionalism within and between counties.

FOUNDATIONS

Role of Counties in the United States. County government has a long history in the United States. Its origin goes back to the county system in England—a political and geographical organization which the early settlers brought to America with them. Hence counties were established early in all the thirteen colonies. As the colonies became states and as new states were created, county government spread all over the United States. One criterion for determining the size of many counties in the "horse and buggy

This Hall of Science on the Miami-Dade Junior College campus is part of Florida's junior college system which is organized by counties.

age" was that a citizen should be able to drive his horse and buggy to the county seat, transact necessary business, and return in one day. Unfortunately, most county boundaries have changed little in this car and jet age of transportation.

Except for a number of independent cities, such as Baltimore, Maryland, and the three states of Alaska, Connecticut, and Rhode Island, nearly every square foot of land in the United States is in a county. Several of the large cities are coextensive with the counties, as, for example, Denver, Colorado. In contradistinction, New York City contains five counties. San Bernardino, California, is the largest county, with more than 20,000 square miles. According to the 1970 census Los Angeles County in California has the largest population, with almost seven million people. The 1970 census also revealed that the smallest is Loving County in Texas, with a population of only 150.

The number of counties in a state varies markedly. Delaware has only 3, while Texas has 254; the average is 50. The number of counties in the United States varies from time to time, due to additions and subtractions. In Louisiana, the county type of government is called a "parish"—a holdover from the French and Spanish traditions. New Jersey, with twenty-one counties, is the only state to preserve the governance title of "freeholders," dating back to the history of England.

The more than three thousand counties in the United States have historically been strong and important units of government. The current aims of the National Association of Counties are to provide national leadership in solving the problems of county governments and to help them shape their future destinies as coequal partners in the family of governments. As North Carolina's former Governor Terry Sanford, active in the Education Commission of the States, put it, "Some things can be done more efficiently from the county court house, some from the state house, and some from Washington."

Evolution of County Educational Organization. One of the major types of school districts to be discussed later is the county system. The history of the county's participation in educational work also harks back to the early days of our nationhood. The county became the actual, complete unit of educational administration in only a few states, mostly in the South, where they now have "strong" county systems. Most commonwealths did establish county boards of education and a county superintendent of schools, but often with "weak" administration.

Some county districts, however, are relatively new. For example, Nevada's seventeen county districts have been in existence only since 1955. Furthermore, categories overlap. An illustrative state is Utah, which has forty county districts. some of which have more than one school district in a county.

The county, as previously mentioned, has been an important educational unit. School organization in America developed first at the local level. But as state systems of education began to emerge, the need for an intermediate unit between the state and the local level became apparent. The county educational office then had its beginnings as an arm of the state. At first this office performed all the administrative services because the local school districts under its jurisdiction did not have administrators. Consequently, the county superintendent recruited, certified, and recommended teachers for employment. Once they were employed, he supervised their work, assisted them in instructional methods, and conducted in-service institutes. Later as states began to collect more school information and otherwise increase reporting activities, the amount of clerical and statistical work increased. Then other duties were added. Today many county superintendents are becoming directly involved in, or being chosen as the chief official of, intermediate educational units.

Evolution of Intermediate Units. Dissatisfaction with many of the traditional county school units and the numerous local school districts led to a second type of organization, first within counties and then also between counties.

Among the many leaders in developing the intermediate units, discussed in detail later in this chapter, have been: the former commissioner of education for New York State F. P. Graves, Prof. Julian E. Butterworth, Prof. Russell T. Gregg, and former county superintendent Robert M. Isenberg, now associate secretary of the American Association of School Administrators.

Evolution of Area and Regional Coordination. The National Commission on School District Reorganization, sponsored by the Department of Rural Education of the National Education Association, was one of the forces that helped stimulate reorganization of schools through such historic publications as *Your School District* (1948). Leadership in the reorganization of districts and the development of larger area and regional planning has come from many persons, including Profs. E. P. Cubberly, Paul R. Mort, John Guy Fowlkes, and Frank W. Cyr. The educational plight of rural youth resulting from inadequate school-district organization and other factors has become the focus of intensive research.[1]

One of the professional educators who was a leader in promoting area technical institutes and county community colleges was Prof. Leonard V. Koos. The concept of regionalism in education has been furthered by many factors, including the establishment by the U.S. Office of Education of several regional, interdisciplinary, university-based Educational Research Laboratories and Centers and a number of Regional Laboratories. The Elementary and Secondary Educational Act helped to stimulate changes in organizational patterns through professional personnel and the power of the purse.

This terse historical overview of the three major developments within and between counties is now followed by a look at the present and future tense of the three major educational patterns: (1) county organization, (2) intermediate units, and (3) area and regional coordination.

COUNTY EDUCATIONAL ORGANIZATION

County Units

The county as an entity is the common geographical and political denominator in the United States. The three thousand counties, as smaller

---

[1] Everett D. Edington, "Disadvantaged Rural Youth," *Review of Educational Research*, vol. 40, pp. 69–85, February, 1970.

subdivisions, are creatures of the state. Counties usually have an amorphous organization, lacking definite form. The county generally has no responsible head comparable to a mayor, although a few counties have an areawide manager. In most states the county is the only unit of rural administration. In fact, most counties have been largely rural in character. The movement for reform in county government, including educational reorganization, has progressed very slowly. In California and Michigan, among other states, some counties are effecting changes through "county home-rule charters."

Although the county is the unit for some of the school administrative functions in most states, it is the actual operating unit for all schools in Florida, West Virginia, and Nevada, which contain only county school units. Utah, Virginia, Kentucky, Tennessee, Georgia, Alabama, North Carolina, South Carolina, Mississippi, Maryland, and Louisiana, with its "parishes," are also in the fourteen-state group generally organized on the county unit, except for a city or a few larger cities in each state which are separately organized as city districts. (See Figure 4-1.)

In all the above states, with the exceptions noted, the schools are under elected or appointed

county boards of education. School revenue is gathered largely through county taxes. Schools are administered by the county superintendent of schools, who is appointed by the county board in some states and elected by popular vote in others. In county units of organization, the county superintendent's functions are similar to those of a local superintendent. Where the county is the local or basic educational unit, the county superintendent directly administers elementary and secondary schools. No intermediate unit exists.

In contrast to the fourteen states previously mentioned as having "strong" county units, most states have so-called "weak" county organization for education. In these states the county's educational officer does not directly administer the independent school systems in the county. The county board of education coordinates and stimulates but does not control education. In most states this type of county unit is controlled by a county board of education, elected by the people or by the local boards of education within the county. The unit is administered by a county superintendent who is elected by the people in most states and appointed

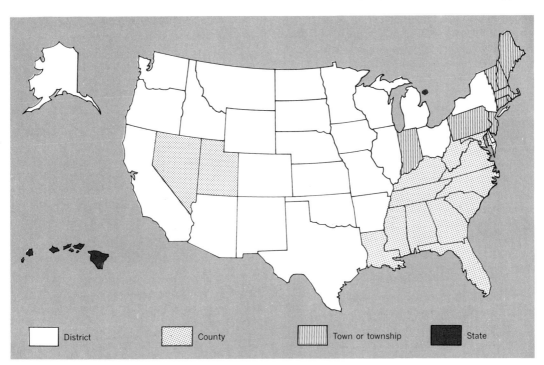

FIGURE 4-1 Prevailing types of school-district organization by states.

by the board in others. This position is now regarded as a professional position. However, short terms of office, low salaries, inadequate finances, and the rigors of campaigning for the job—conditions that prevail in many states—detract from the attractiveness and the effectiveness of the position. The county superintendent serves as the executive or advisory officer for small towns, townships, or districts within the county that are too small to employ a full-time administrator.

Intermediate Units

There is a growing tendency toward regarding the intermediate unit as an entity not necessarily coterminous with the county. Counties are being combined in a number of states into substantially larger intermediate-unit areas. Consequently, the terms "county unit" and "intermediate unit" are not necessarily synonymous, although the county is the intermediate unit in most states. The situation will not remain so in years to come. The National Commission on School District Reorganization has defined the intermediate unit as "an area comprising the territory of two or more basic administrative units and having a board, or officer, or both responsible for performing stipulated services for the basic administrative units or for supervising their fiscal, administrative, or educational functions."

Robert Isenberg, formerly executive secretary of the Department of Rural Education of the National Education Association, describes the emerging intermediate unit as "a regional service agency" and illustrates this concept with a few specific service programs: special education, instructional materials, data processing, curriculum leadership, and additional services, such as vocational and technical education, instruction for children and youth in institutional centers, cooperative purchasing, training programs for school bus drivers, custodians, and school lunch personnel, and consultant help to districts in the development of federal project proposals and grant requests.[2]

What Are the Desirable Components of an Intermediate Unit? A study of the intermediate unit in

[2] Adapted from Robert M. Isenberg, "Intermediate Units and Small High Schools," *Bulletin of the National Association of Secondary-school Principals*, vol. 50, pp. 1–10, February, 1966.

Wisconsin established the following criteria with respect to satisfactory intermediate units.

The major functions of the intermediate unit should be to provide high-quality educational leadership and services to local school districts, to perform liaison and reporting functions between the state and local districts, and to offer specialized instructional programs which the districts cannot provide.

There should be a minimum enrollment of 10,000 pupils in the area included in the intermediate unit except under unusual conditions of topography or sparsity of population. [Some authorities suggest 50,000 to 100,000 pupils.]

The boundaries of the intermediate unit should have no required relationship with the boundaries of the county, but should include a logical combination of local school districts.

Each intermediate unit should be under the direct control of an elected board of education which appoints the intermediate superintendent and determines his salary and tenure.

The intermediate board of education should be fiscally independent, with its own taxing power and supplementary state aid.

The intermediate superintendent should be of outstanding competence.

The legal functions of the unit should be clearly defined.

The basic orientation of the unit should be to provide assistance to local districts. It should also have responsibilities to the state department of education.

The intermediate unit should be sufficiently flexible to adapt to changing educational conditions and needs, and there should be legal provisions for its reorganization which are similar to the provisions for the reorganization of local districts.[3]

Currently there are twenty-four states that have some intermediate structure.

What is actually happening today, according to Robert Isenberg, is a reorganization of the intermediate school districts—from a county to a multicounty base of operation, from an arm of the state to a regional service agency.

Area Schools and Colleges

Two fast-growing educational institutions within and between counties are (1) the area vocational-technical schools and (2) the county or community colleges.

[3] Russell T. Gregg, "The Intermediate Unit of School Administration," *Administrator's Notebook*, vol. 8, p. 4, October, 1959.

Area Vocational-Technical Schools. The Vocational Education Act of 1963, which, as previously indicated, has had a great impact on the national program in vocational and technical education, has stimulated the growth of many county and/or area schools. Under this act, federal grants are given for construction of vocational-technical facilities in an amount up to 50 percent of the costs. The funds, allocated to states, are used to "improve, maintain, and extend" the facilities of existing vocational schools or to build new area vocational-technical schools in other geographic areas, such as a county or group of counties.

The term "area" describes schools which provide training for workers in the industries of a defined geographic area. The four types of area vocational-technical schools that are federally aided are:

1. *Specialized high school used exclusively or almost so to provide full-time vocational education in preparation for full-time work in industry*
2. *A department of a high school used exclusively or principally to provide training in at least five different occupational fields to those available for full-time study prior to entering the labor market*
3. *A technical or vocational school providing vocational education predominantly to persons who have completed or left school and who are able to study on a full-time basis before going to work*
4. *A department or division of a junior college, community college, or university providing vocational education in at least five different occupational fields, under the supervision of the State board, and leading to immediate employment but not toward a baccalaureate degree*[4]

Since the passage of the Vocational Education Act of 1963, more than a thousand of these vocational-technical schools have been federally aided, and thousands of boys and girls, as well as adults, have been occupationally helped.

A good example of one of these schools is the De Kalb Area Technical School in Georgia, established jointly by the De Kalb County Board of Education and the State Department of Education of Georgia. This school offers courses in twenty occupational fields and covers the chief vocational interests of a six-county area.

County and/or Community Colleges. As discussed in Chapter 9, the fastest-growing segment of American education is the junior or two-year community

[4]Michael Russo, "Area Vocational Schools," *American Education*, vol. 2, p. 15, July, 1966.

college. Especially active in this area of higher education are the counties, either individually or as consortiums of counties in regional colleges.

There are many variations in organization of these community colleges. They are operated as part of local school districts in the states of Washington and Virginia; as separate districts in Pennsylvania, Missouri, and Colorado; as state institutions in Georgia, Louisiana, and Maine; and as part of the state's higher education system in New York and California.

Most of them confine their curriculums to the thirteenth and fourteenth years (first and second year of college). Many, as in the state of Michigan, also provide vocational-technical education for the cooperating secondary schools in the area.

Other Area and Regional Developments. A distinct trend is toward the growth of the intermediate unit as a *regional* agency. In Nebraska, for example, legislation has set up "educational service units," made up of two or more counties. Each service unit has a "board of educational services" with the power to levy taxes on property within the unit. Many other states, including Iowa, Washington, Oregon, and Wisconsin, have passed laws to reorganize or restructure their intermediate educational units.

There have been numerous examples of city-county school mergers, including Greenville and Greenville County, South Carolina, in 1951, and Albuquerque and Bernalillo County, New Mexico, also in 1951. The city of Nashville and the county of Davidson merger in Tennessee in 1964, on the other hand, is a new type of comprehensive, all-services unification. The merger covers all aspects of government—fire and police protection, water, sewer, assessments, and other services including education. This total community concept is in line with the current accent on "environmentalism," and the curricular concept that education is broader than schooling, and hence needs the rich resources of the total community.

Helpful initial steps toward functional regionalism have been the development of numerous Councils of Government (COGs) which are voluntary organizations of counties and municipalities attacking areawide problems, including education. The National Service to Regional Councils, an organization based in Washington, D.C., was formed by the National Association of Counties and the National League of Cities to assist in the regional development of councils of local governments.

IN-COUNTY AND INTERCOUNTY PROGRAMS

The following are a few of the countless creative programs in education conducted by county systems, intermediate units, and regional consortiums:

Jefferson County, the largest school system in Kentucky, initiated in 1971 a year-round school program, replacing its two-semester, 176-day school calendar with four 60-day quarters.

Dade County, Florida—the seventh largest school system in the United States—has special bilingual instruction for the thousands of Cuban refugees who have come there.

Instructional television via closed circuit, stimulated by the Ford Foundation's pioneering project, has become a regular part of the school program in Washington County (Hagerstown), Maryland.

The schools in San Diego County, California, have through their intermediate unit joined to data-process their payrolls and student accounting.

A two-county Metropolitan Youth Education Center, established through agreement by the Denver City (Denver County) and Jefferson County, Colorado, schools, accents flexibility and adaptability for potential and actual dropouts.

The Jefferson Committee for Better Schools, a citizens' organization, has worked for better educational organization in the Jefferson, Louisiana, parish—a political subdivision analogous to the county.

Clark County, Nevada, in planning and constructing its new Southern Nevada Vocational-Technical Center at Las Vegas, used a systems approach to school design, utilizing some of the components developed in the California School Construction Systems Development Project.

School districts in areas such as Monroe County purchase from the New York State Board of Cooperative Educational Services many high-cost special services, such as vocational and occupational training, classes for the handicapped, library services, audiovisual programs, and data processing.

Nearly all counties and intermediate units participate in programs financed in part by congressional legislation, such as the Elementary and Secondary Education Act and its amendments. In Indiana one of the projects reached through agreement was the initiation of a four-county consortium for mobile guidance services in the Bedford

This school science fair, sponsored by the Montgomery (Pennsylvania) County schools office, is one of many educational enterprises sponsored by county educational units.

area. The Weber County school district in Utah established the Exemplary Center for Team Teaching.

Parochial schools used the multicounty approach in establishing a pioneering board of education consisting of four clergymen and six laymen to help determine policy for almost one hundred Catholic schools in southern Michigan (Lansing diocese).

More than three hundred Roman Catholic schools are linked in the eight-county archdiocese of Detroit (Michigan).

Many of these examples of current programs involving county intermediate and regional areas indicate some of the trends for the future.

FUTURE

In the years ahead the federal government will become a more active partner for progress in the schools of the counties, both directly through federal funds earmarked for the states to reorganize their administrative districts and indirectly through grants for various activities related to education. For example, in the Action program the Volunteers in Service to America will continue to work with many families migrating to all areas.

An apocalyptic view also sees the individual states developing a major concern and responsibility for renovating and enriching education in all the three thousand counties of the nation. With the states supplying an increasing percentage of the budget for public elementary and secondary education, the "power of the purse" will help accelerate innovations in structure and in instruction.

The future is focused on functional changes in the organization of counties. Reorganization, discussed in detail in the next chapter, is inevitable: "Most students of government agree that two-thirds of the counties could be abolished by rearranging boundaries and combining facilities. Thousands of officials could be taken off the payrolls. Local government would be more efficient and there would be a subsequent savings in tax money."[5] This obviously applies also to many small county educational units.

Replacing a large part of what was a stable, land-based rural population in the counties are mobile millions. The mobility of Americans is such that those living in many county rural areas today feed their problems and special characteristics into urban

[5] Reprinted from the book *U.S. Politics—Inside and Out*, Copyright 1970 by U.S. News and World Report, Inc., Washington, D.C., p. 100.

and suburban populations. Cushman warns that:

Urban administrators of education will find it to their own best interest to support greatly increased educational financing and the reorganization of local and intermediate district structures. Let us not continue to expect local departments to put out ghetto fires when their fuel is continuously brought in from the country and is fanned by country winds.[6]

The future presages greater interest and activity in county educational activities and administrative offices by minority groups, including migrants, mountain whites, Indians, Mexican Americans, Negroes, and other educationally disadvantaged groups. As an illustration, Alonzo Harvey was named in 1969 by the Macon County Board of Education as superintendent of the county schools—the first Negro to hold such a position in the state of Alabama.

Tomorrow intermediate units will serve urban areas and larger school systems (with the exception of the very largest cities) as much as they serve school districts in rural areas. Their potential for rural areas is great, but the greatest development of intermediate service programs up to this time has been in metropolitan areas.

County educational leaders will continue to provide leadership in two very significant programs: vocational education and county colleges. The rapid increase in county and area vocational-technical institutes will bring more motivation and practicality in the education of many youth. With the marked increase in county and community colleges many more youth will benefit from two years of additional education.

One of the techniques that holds great promise for the future of counties is collaboration in data processing and resultant program planning. Before the end of the 1970s many or all of the governmental units within a county, including schools, will initiate a program of participation in one central data-processing center. The possibilities of data processing and programming are further discussed in Chapter 15.

Great educational changes may take place in the reorganization of intermediate units in the future. It is clear that the county-regional form of educational governance will be an area of great progress

[6] M. L. Cushman, "Rural Schools Need Help Too," *The School Administrator*, p. 12, March, 1970.

in the 1970s. Hence there follows a brief discussion of its possibilities.

Regionalism—a Developing Imperative. In addition to the further development and enrichment of intermediate service units, the greatest potential on the educational horizons of counties is regionalism. In regional groupings are "embryonic building blocks that can form a foundation for an imposing structure," and "a framework of policy cutting across the entire spectrum of state educational concerns" for at least three reasons:

One, is that high-cost special services are a useful foundation for regional administration and cost-sharing; two, that county broad-based taxes and county government can be linked with school government in a way that would fertilize such other activities as planning; and three, that through a regional board the state can apply itself to the problems of urban education more effectively than by attempting to deal with each local unit. It is not difficult to imagine large new areas for state-regional cooperation.

If effective local government of any kind is, as we often declare, the seedbed of democracy, then it is at the roots that we should develop the capacity to comprehend problems and work at their solution, and it is to this end that state policy should be directed. . . . We can make a great many problems easier to deal with, for the great potential of regionalism is that it can enhance the capacity of local citizens and their elected officials to deal with them themselves.[7]

Another development in area education is the organization of numerous regional associations of parochial schools. Two examples from the state of Michigan are the Area Catholic Board of Education in Jackson and the United Christian Schools of the Christian Reformed Church in the Grand Rapids area.

SUMMARY

As indicated in the map at the beginning of this chapter, the four major types of school organization in the United States are: (1) state, (2) county, (3) township and town, and (4) local.

The county is still the common geographical and political unit in many states. Historically it has been an important political unit of government. Educationally, too, it has been, often still is, and in some

[7]Jerome Zukosky, "Governing the Schools," *National Civic Review,* vol. 59, pp. 140, 147, March, 1970.

states will continue to be an important pattern of governance. Its board of education and its county superintendent of schools are generally elected by the people of the county, although increasingly the county superintendent is appointed by the board. Jointly the board and the superintendent direct the policies and administer the program where there is a "strong" form of county control and the county is the educational unit. In states with a "weak" form of county educational governance, the board and administrator supervise programs in many rural and other small schools and also coordinate work in the county.

Numerous counties have reorganized or reoriented their programs as intermediate units between the state and the local units. These intermediate districts specialize primarily in educational services. They are currently undergoing metamorphoses, changing in size, services, programs, and personnel.

The 1960s witnessed the birth of numerous county vocational-technical schools and institutes and also hundreds of county community colleges, which often incorporate adjacent areas from neighboring counties. Many counties have their own junior college board of education, administrator, and staff.

The greatest potential involving counties is some form of regionalism within the state system of education. The county is often too small an educational unit. Many counties voluntarily or officially cooperate with one another to extend services to larger areas than the long-established political unit controlled from the county courthouse. These regional units, groupings, and associations are embryonic building blocks for constructing and furnishing more and better services to larger areas in the entire state. Some regional pacts transcend state boundaries.

Parochial and private schools are regionalizing their services and control. Innovative practices in organization, administration, and instruction, such as publicly supported auxiliary services for nonpublic schools, are crossing public, private, and parochial borders, geographically, politically, and financially. Enhanced pupil power can be the "output" from the programming of interdependent "input" by professional personnel working in enlarged educational areas.

While there is much coordination and cooperation between the fifty states, regionalism within each state is being designed for mutual reinforcement and educational interdependence. Regionalism within each state is becoming an added, intermediate level of public educational governance, services, or both, in the following hierarchical arrangement: (1) federal, (2) state, (3) regional, (4) county, and (5) local.

Suggested Activities

1. Describe the current educational organization in a county or intermediate district with which you are familiar.

2. Review the history of this county or intermediate district to ascertain what and how changes have taken place in educational organization, administration, and programs.

3. Visit the office of a county superintendent of schools or an intermediate district superintendent and interview him about education in the county.

4. What is meant by "intermediate unit"?

5. Examine in the school laws of your state the legal relationships between the local and county school officials and between the county and state school officials.

6. Draw a map showing the location of public schools in a specific county or intermediate district.

7. Investigate the movement toward regionalism in your state, such as combinations of educational services by counties, townships, or local school districts.

8. Describe area vocational-technical schools and the financing thereof.

9. Evaluate the significance of the rapidly growing county community college movement.

10. Discuss the following statement made by a longtime student of educational administration Dr. Calvin Greider: "As society changes in needs and forms, the disappearance of the once important office of county superintendent of schools is inevitable."

Bibliography

Campbell, Roald, and others: *The Organization and Control of American Schools*, 2d ed., Charles E. Merrill Publishing Co., Columbus, Ohio, 1971, chap. 5. Historical account of the intermediate unit, its current problems, its future, and socioeconomic factors affecting it.

Isenberg, Robert: "The Intermediate Unit," in Sherman H. Frey and Keith R. Getschman (eds.), *School Administration: Selected Readings*, Thomas Y. Crowell Company, New York, 1968, chap. 11. A description of the services which intermediate units offer to local districts.

Knezevich, Stephen J.: *Administration of Public Education*, 2d ed., Harper & Row, Publishers, Incorporated, New York, 1969, chap. 7. Explanation of the development, modification, organization, and function of the intermediate school unit.

U.S. News and World Report: *U.S. Politics—Inside and Out*, Washington, D.C., 1970, chap. 7. Pertinent information about county governments and the political situations.

Chapter 5　Local Districts and Educational Agencies

ORIENTATION

One of the most distinguishing characteristics of American education has been the high degree of control over schools exercised by local authorities. Although education is a legal function of the state, much of the operational responsibility for schools is delegated to the local school district. This responsibility is vested in a board of education, which is usually elected by the people, and in professional school administrators, who are usually appointed by the boards. Thus the history of public education in this country is largely the story of the local school system.

Now this local control of education is sorely troubled. Many local districts are still too small to provide adequate school enrollments and to muster resources sufficient for a good educational program. Many large, urban school districts face almost insurmountable problems—decentralization, inadequate tax bases, *de facto* racial segregation, overcrowded buildings, exodus of teachers to the suburbs, and impoverished and apathetic homes. Even the more affluent suburban districts are often troubled by rapid population growth, unstable and amorphous community structure, and high population mobility.

Substantial stresses have been imposed upon all levels of government—federal, state, and local—and upon all functions of government, including education. Some of the most severe and fateful of these stresses have been placed upon the local administration of schools. As local school authorities become less able to deal with problems of morality, race relations, poverty, unemployment, national de-fense needs, teachers' welfare, and many others, society turns more and more to the state and federal levels of government for solutions to vexing problems. This has resulted in a dilution of local authority over education—a development viewed by some as necessary and hopeful and by others as tragic and perhaps even dangerous. However this may be, the local educational authority will, for the present at least, continue to play a significant role in forging the destiny of our society through education. Currently boards of public education affect the schooling of 85 percent of the more than fifty-three million students in public elementary and secondary schools. (Figure 5-1).

FOUNDATIONS

The little villages of the colonies were the first school-unit prototypes in America, preceding by many years county, state, or national units of school organization. The local school district had its beginning in a quaint law, known as the "Old Deluder Satan Law," enacted by the Massachusetts Bay Colony in 1647, nearly 150 years prior to the founding of the republic. This statute required every town of fifty families or more to appoint one of its people to teach reading and writing, since "one chief point of that old deluder, Satan, [is] to keep men from knowledge of the Scriptures."

Colonial America was largely rural. Wide-open spaces separated the little villages that dotted the land. Transportation and communication were difficult. It was quite natural for schools to be organized around local communities, since state and national government had not yet emerged. The founders of America, who had struggled for independence from oppressive centralized government, were not disposed to let the important function of education rest with the central government after it was established.

Large numbers of citizens are often attracted to local school board meetings, where much of the drama and controversy in society is enacted in microcosm.

121

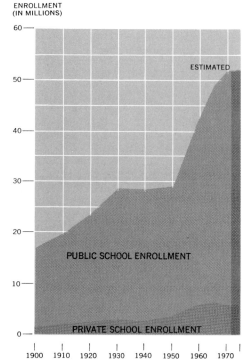

ENROLLMENT
(IN MILLIONS)

ESTIMATED

PUBLIC SCHOOL ENROLLMENT

PRIVATE SCHOOL ENROLLMENT

1900 1910 1920 1930 1940 1950 1960 1970

FIGURE 5-1 Enrollment in public and private elementary and secondary schools. (U.S. Office of Education, Projections of Educational Statistics.)

These and other circumstances established firmly the traditon of strong local control of education in America. Because of America's great faith in education, the schools have been kept close to the people. This has also helped to keep the people close to the schools.

Local School Districts

The United States has approximately 100,000 independent units of government, each with the power to spend money and to perform services for the citizenry. These units range in size from the federal government, with millions of employees, down to the smallest type of school district, with one teacher. About seventeen thousand of these legal units are school districts of various types and sizes. About one thousand operate no schools of their own, sending their students to other districts.

In the broad sense, the local school district is the smallest administrative unit. Local school districts are administered by a superintendent of schools under the direction of the board of education, which is commonly elected by the people. Districts too small to employ an executive are administered by the board of education.

Legal Status of Local School Districts

The Tenth Amendment to the Constitution definitely implies that education is a function of the states and not of the federal government. Usually the states delegate the major responsibilities for school operation to the local educational subdivision, which may be as small as a rural school district of 5 square miles in Illinois or as large as a county unit of 17,000 square miles in Nevada. Legally, then, subject to the laws passed by the state legislature, the control of the school system resides in the board of education elected by the people in the district, as indicated on the chart at the beginning of Part 2. The board is both a local and a state instrument.

According to school laws, the board of education is the legal authority representing the state. It is an artificial body created by a general or specific law to maintain a system of public education in a certain territory. A state attorney general says, "A school board is a body politic and corporate. It is purely a creature of the state. Its power may be enlarged, diminished, modified, or revoked by the legislature." Although there are limitations, the board has broad legal powers, such as the right to buy and sell property, erect buildings, and enter into contracts. It is a quasi corporation, subject to numerous laws.

TYPES OF LOCAL SCHOOLS

Attendance and Administrative Units

The state legislature creates or makes possible the establishment of school districts of various types. At the outset it is desirable to distinguish between units for attendance and those for the administration of education. An attendance unit, usually established by the local board, is defined as the area served by a single school building, such as a Horace Mann school in a city system. An administrative unit, usually the legal school district, embraces all the area under a single system of control and may include one, two, or over a hundred attendance areas.

Types of School Units

State Districts. Even though both are state systems, the contrast between the Alaskan and the Hawaiian school organization is striking. Alaska School District One, the largest in the country, contains all the schools of the forty-ninth state except those of twenty-seven cities and villages. This enormous district, which spans four time zones and includes about 586,000 square miles, is almost one hundred times as large as Hawaii, and yet it is only one-third the size of Hawaii in terms of population. In the twenty-seven cities and villages of Alaska where schools are operated autonomously, control of education is vested in the local municipal governments—city councils and borough assemblies—since no local boards of education exist in Alaska. Hawaii, with only one school district, is the state district in its purest form. In all the other states, a larger measure of responsibility for the operation of schools is delegated to many local units.

County Units. As is shown in Figure 4-1, the county is the basic unit for educational administration in fourteen states. These units, discussed in detail in Chapter 4, often serve as intermediate districts, rendering many services to the school children of the county. In some states counties are becoming parts of larger educational entities known as regional service areas.

Town and Township Units. The educational systems of the New England states, Pennsylvania, New Jersey, and Indiana are organized on a town and township basis.

In most states, the original survey divided the county into towns and townships, which became the basis for school organization. Under the township system, many cities, incorporated villages, and towns and some consolidated schools are set apart as independent school districts. In some states, such as Illinois, high schools are organized on a township basis, but smaller districts within the township operate their own elementary schools.

The New England town, which usually comprises a cohesive combination of urban and rural territory, is a natural geographic center and a much more logical school unit than the townships of most states, which took their form from early surveys,

Indian trails, or cow paths. In many instances, town school districts exist within township units. Town and township units are controlled by popularly elected local boards of education and administered by superintendents or supervising principals appointed by the board. In town and township districts, much of the school revenue is derived from local taxes. Many town and township districts are too small to operate efficient school programs and in recent years have to some extent been combined into larger units.

District Units. In most Western states and in Michigan, Delaware, Ohio, and New York, the district is the local school unit. The majority of these districts are smaller than the other types of units described previously. Some still exist even though they operate no schools at all, sending their students to other school systems. In most instances, these districts were established by early surveys and have little relationship to natural community boundaries or to logical school organization. This type of organization is generally considered least efficient.

Districts are controlled by elected boards of education. Larger districts are administered by superintendents or supervising principals appointed by the board. However, many districts are too small to justify the employment of an administrator.

Included in the above-mentioned four categories of public school districts are three designated primarily by their locale or milieu: (1) rural, (2) suburban, and (3) city public elementary and secondary schools.

Rural Education

Decline in Rural Population. Among the many intercounty and intracounty changes affecting American education is the altered composition of the populace. The increase in and dispersion of the population in the United States are blurring or blotting out the traditional distinction between rural and city life. As a result, rural education, which once dominated the American landscape with its thousands of one-room schoolhouses, is steadily losing ground. Teacher-education institutions, which once had special curriculums for rural teachers, have long since dropped this classification.

The 1970 census found that 75 percent of the 204 million people in the United States lived in urban or urbanized areas. It also showed that people continue to leave the farm or, if they remain there, seek jobs in industries that are increasingly moving to countrysides. The farm population, long associated with rural education, dropped from 15 million in 1960 to 10 million in 1970. Farmers and their families make up 5 percent of the population.

Changes in Rural Prestige and Political Power. With the decline in population has come a legislated loss in prestige and voting power for rural areas. The representation in state legislatures and on county, intermediate, and township boards of education, along with other political subdivisions, has been ordered changed in many states. Court decisions and legislation are giving less representation to rural or sparsely populated areas in important ruling boards in numerous counties. More equitable apportionment is desirable, but certainly rural residents should have appropriate representation on a board of education in a county where even a minority of the students come from nonurban areas.

Rural School Districts. The smallest district, the one-teacher school, is sometimes one-pupil and one-room as well. The one-teacher schools of America are disappearing rapidly in favor of more modern and consolidated schools. Some of the rural elementary schools have two or more teachers, and most rural high schools have at least three teachers. Not all rural schools are small.

In spite of progress in the reorganization of school districts, many small systems remain, although they enroll a very small fraction of the nation's students. These small schools, almost without exception, are unable to provide instruction of reasonable breadth and quality at reasonable cost. They typically offer narrow curriculums, send a relatively small proportion of their graduates to college, have difficulty hiring and keeping good teachers, and are unable to provide necessary supporting facilities and personnel such as guidance and health services. In a report entitled "Disadvantaged Rural Youth," Edington states:

There are a number of major cultures represented by disadvantaged rural youth. Some of the most distinctive and well known include the rural Negro, the mountain whites, the American Indian and the rural Mexican Americans. Students with the greatest cultural differences to overcome are American Indians.[1]

As this research points out, "rurality does impose certain conditions which exacerbate educational problems."

Although many rural schools have been consolidated into large systems that are modern and efficient, it is inevitable that sparsity of population and topographical conditions in some areas of the country will force the continued existence of many small districts and small schools.

Next to rural schools, the most plenteous district is the village school, which typically employs several teachers and may have more than one building. Larger towns offer their own high school programs; smaller ones usually send their secondary school students to nearby high schools on a tuition basis. Like rural schools, small-town schools are usually too small to offer a modern educational program at reasonable cost, and many have been consolidated with the districts of the surrounding rural areas or other nearby communities.

Rural Educational Renaissance. Despite the traditional limitations of small schools, a rural renaissance is taking place in many areas of the nation that are isolated permanently by mountains, valleys, rivers, and impassable roads. To bring better educational facilities, programs, personnel, and services to these continuously isolated small schools, many rural, in-county and multicounty, and state and interstate projects have been launched. Some regional educational programs are described briefly below.

Various meaningful programs for small schools are being developed with the aid of federally financed, interdisciplinary, university-based educational research laboratories and centers, and the regional educational laboratories, also supported by the U.S. Office of Education. In "Hitching Up the Small School Districts," Frank L. Heesacker states: "More than 70 distinct categories of shared service programs are now operating, and many children in rural and small schools are receiving a richer education because of them."[2]

For example, the Western States Small School Project launched a "rural renaissance with funds

[1] Everett D. Edington, "Disadvantaged Rural Youth," *Review of Educational Research*, vol. 40, pp. 69–85, February, 1970.
[2] Frank L. Heesacker, "Hitching Up the Small School Districts," *American Education*, vol. 6, p. 21, April, 1970.

from the Kettering and Rockefeller Foundations, by a cooperative program to help small schools exchange ideas and materials." The schools, which once had limited facilities and programs, now have flexible scheduling, multiple classes, programmed self-instruction devices, and modern texts, films, television, and other teaching and learning aids.

The rural renaissance is not confined to students of school age. For example, the University of Wisconsin has established a basic education program for adults in four counties.

The Department of Rural Education of the National Education Association has lent vital leadership and has sponsored numerous publications and reliable research for the improvement of the educational opportunities of rural citizens.

Rural people, too, are experiencing "the revolution of rising expectations," especially in and through education. Ovid F. Parody of the U.S. Office of Education has expressed this hope in regard to area projects, financed in part by the Elementary and Secondary Education Act: "Perhaps some of the big ideas from this rural renaissance will serve to spread a nationwide rebirth of education."

Suburban Education

Growth of Suburbs. The 1970 census revealed that the nation's suburbs have become the largest sector of the population. For the first time in American history, the population of the suburbs exceeds that of the central cities and the rest of the country. Between the 1960 and the 1970 decennial enumerations the central cities gained about 1 percent in population while the suburban population increased by more than 25 percent.

What significance does this marked increase have for suburban living and education? The United States Civil Rights Commission has been concerned about suburban jurisdictions that remain all or largely white and are adjacent to cities with heavy concentrations of blacks. Theodore Hesburgh, chairman of the Commission and president of Notre Dame University, has called attention to "the apparently hopeless" encirclement of black central cities by impenetrable coils of indifferent or hostile white suburbs.

A recent significant demographic statistic is that the exodus of Negroes and other minority groups from cities to suburbs is increasing rapidly. The departure of many blacks from the congested cen-

tral cities to suburban towns and adjacent areas is bringing more Negroes into the suburban schools, although the proportion is still small. In some areas black children are bused to predominantly white schools in the suburbs or environs. The number of teachers from minority groups is increasing in many suburban school districts.

Suburban School Districts. One of the most interesting frontiers of American education has been the suburban school districts. Some of the best educational systems in the country are to be found in affluent suburbs such as Bronxville, Scarsdale, Newton, Lower Merion, Shaker Heights, Grosse Point, Evanston, Webster Grove, Winnetka, Anaheim, Palo Alto, and Pasadena. Much of the real impetus for educational innovation and improvement springs from the well-financed suburban school districts, which are able to employ a sufficient number of teachers and administrators of quality to staff outstanding programs. The highest teacher salary schedules and the highest expenditures per pupil are typically found in suburban school districts.

However, the educational scene in the suburbs is not entirely rosy. Many suburban areas consist almost entirely of mushrooming low-cost housing developments which are long on children to be educated and short on industries to furnish a tax base. School enrollments often outrun the construction of new buildings. Classes spill over into church basements and firehouses. Double sessions are not uncommon. These amorphous "bedroom communities," made up of highly mobile families whose breadwinners commute to the nearby city, often lack cohesion and stability. School and municipal governments designed to serve rural and village settings are overwhelmed by the suburban growth. Natural community lines frequently do not exist and, if they do, often are not congruent with school-district boundaries. Reorganization of these districts is complicated by outmoded legislation, lack of common identity, competition for the annexation of rich areas, and reluctance to join with less favored communities.

Suburban development will continue to pose complex problems. The difficulty of keeping schools attuned to this rapidly growing segment of American society is likely to increase in many areas before it decreases. It is predicted that the Atlantic seacoast from Boston to Washington, for example, will before long become one continuous complex of contiguous urban and suburban congestion, posing new problems in the realms of housing, transportation, water supply, and sanitation, as well as in education.

Urban Education

Decline of the Cities. As stated by New York's Mayor John V. Lindsay in his book *The City,*[3] a large city is governable, but it has many problems. Many cities are in a state of decline, numerically and qualitatively. The 1970 census revealed that the population in many central cities declined sharply in the past decade. For example, thirteen of the twenty-five largest cities lost population between the decennial census enumerations. Nationally, as previously mentioned, city populations increased only 1.2 percent over the ten-year period.

Yet, over sixty-two million people live in cities, and their schools and their education are extremely important. Furthermore, the number of children of school age has increased substantially in cities with large black populations because black families tend to be larger than the national average. As James Conant stated more than a decade ago: "Social dynamite is building up in our large cities in the form of unemployed out-of-school youth, especially in Negro slums."[4] Furthermore, racial troubles in schools often are a reflection of tensions existing in the surrounding adult community. The McCone Report on the riots in Watts, California, asked the significant question about relative values: "Of what shall it avail our nation if we can place a man on the moon but cannot cure the sickness in our cities?"

Urban Renewal and Model Cities. Recent years have witnessed greatly increased activity on the part of the federal government and the city authorities in renewing the dying core of many cities and in building model metropolitan areas. Slum clearance, once considered a big-city concern, is being promoted in cities of all sizes across the country. Over a thousand cities have federally supported urban-renewal projects under way. But the costs of urban

renewal are colossal—in the billions of dollars. The Model Cities program is usually concerned with recreation, health, and education, involving cooperation with the local school administrators who are seeking to accent "human renewal through education."

City School Districts. Before World War II, many city schools were the aristocrats of American education. But the past quarter-century has brought a tragic decline in the quality of education in most of the nation's large cities. Several forces have contributed to this decline.

The urban milieu has changed drastically. Millions of middle-class families have moved to the suburbs, to be replaced in the central city by Southern Negroes, Appalachian whites, Mexican-Americans, Puerto Ricans, and Indians from reservations. The influx of nonwhite people has engendered severe racial problems. Because they are poor and are discriminated against in housing, many of them must live in ghettos and attend schools that are as segregated as their neighborhoods.

Many of these former rural families have difficulty adjusting to urban life and to a culture that is almost alien to them. Very often they and their families must live in blighted and overcrowded housing. Often the children and parents are not home at the same time, and in many cases parents are separated. All around their ghetto they see poverty, unemployment, crime, disease, alcoholism, and drug addiction. Small wonder that these children are easily disenchanted with school and drop out as soon as they can. They have little opportunity for gainful employment in an age of automation, in which there is little need for uneducated labor. Undereducated, they are unable to compete occupationally, and their segregation by economic class persists despite any gain made in racial desegregation. The only escape for the victim of this self-perpetuating cycle of underprivilege is through education. As Hubert Humphrey has warned:

Education is the keystone in the arch of democracy. Ignorance breeds only slavery. Enlightenment liberates the human mind and spirit. As a free people—as a democratic people—we must accept the moral obligation of providing the means whereby every American—regardless of race, color, age, religion, income, or educational achievement—has an equal opportunity for education and training limited only by his own capability and initiative.

[3]John V. Lindsay, *The City,* W. W. Norton & Company, Inc., New York, 1970.

[4]James B. Conant, *Slums and Suburbs,* McGraw-Hill Book Company, New York, 1961, p. 146.

Urban schools are hampered further by economic strictures. Formulas of state aid to school systems, designed years ago, before the era of urban crisis, now discriminate badly against city districts in many states. The underrepresentation of city interests in state legislatures dominated by rural influence militated against the correction of the city's disadvantageous position in relation to state aid to schools. The problem is complicated further by blurred lines of responsibility among city school boards, municipal officers, and state education agencies. City schools are often hamstrung by municipal control of school finances, state control of the city's tax rates and debt limits, and political control of the board of education and even of professional staff appointments.

The bureaucratic nature of many urban school organizations handicaps schools by establishing a climate of inflexibility, depersonalization, conformity, close supervision, evasion of responsibility, and inertia. Under these conditions teachers develop feelings of frustration, servility, and even despair.

Without doubt this is the most serious blight on our entire educational scene, but the picture is not hopeless. It must not be assumed from this discussion that all urban schools are poor. All metropolitan communities include some very adequate schools. Many cities are taking imaginative steps to alleviate the problem. The Elementary and Secondary Education Act has provided millions of dollars specifically earmarked for the improvement of education in slum schools. Federally aided urban-renewal projects, under way in most cities, offer some hope for an educational and cultural renaissance along with physical rehabilitation of our cities. Several states have revised their state-aid formulas and have not only discontinued financial discrimination against urban areas but also provided additional sums for what has become known as "compensatory education," that is, programs designed to compensate for the cultural disadvantages that slum children bring to school.

The NEA, through its Special Project for Urban Services, has stepped up its assistance to professional associations of teachers in metropolitan areas. The fifteen largest cities have joined in an association, subsidized by Ford Foundation grants, called the Research Council of the Great Cities Program for School Improvement, whose mission is described by its name. In a few cities, organizations such as the Public Education Association in New York have

been stimulating people to understand urban school problems and rally public pressure for improvement. Chicago, Atlanta, New York, Miami, and other cities have worked toward the decentralization of administrative authority over schools, trying to break up the colossal bureaucracies of central offices and to return to neighborhoods some measure of control.

Colleges and universities have lent their know-how and leadership in attempts at physical and cultural renewal of urban areas, particularly those surrounding their campuses. Several universities have mounted major programs for the recruitment and special preparation of teachers for the hard work of teaching in slum areas. The University Council for Educational Administration, a confederation of fifty major universities, has undertaken a cooperative program to prepare administrators better for the difficult tasks of city school administration.

These are some of the significant attempts that have been made to alleviate the vexing problems of urban education. But the problems of large metropolitan areas are complex and enormous, and the hour is late. Nothing short of our most vigorous effort can arrest the deterioration of our large cities and their schools. Truly, this is the nation's gravest educational challenge.

Nonpublic Education

Among the many types of local schools are the nonpublic pre-elementary, elementary, and secondary institutions, here classified for discussion purposes as (1) independent and (2) parochial schools connected with churches or synagogues.

Independent Schools. Many independent or private schools have a long and noble tradition. Independent schools are supported by tuition and endowment; they do not offer instruction in the tenets of a particular religion and do not ordinarily restrict admission to students of a particular faith. Independent schools usually charge rather high tuition, and some of them are exceptionally fine schools, with small classes, select teachers, excellent facilities, and carefully screened students. Very often these schools, unhampered by the strictures of public education, pioneer in the development of progressive teaching methods and curriculums. Not all independent schools are good.

Some private schools have joined in consortiums as Independent School Councils to merge some of their business and academic efforts in order to reduce costs and increase efficiency. Most of the long-standing, high-quality schools are members of the National Association of Independent Schools.

A few states have provided fiscal assistance by awarding stipends to parents who choose to send their children to private schools. The U.S. Internal Revenue Service, which once granted tax-exempt status to such schools, has ruled against continuing their favored tax status if they practice segregation.

Many Southern communities have opened private schools, which are sometimes church-related and usually have tuition high enough to make them unavailable to Negroes. This, of course, is a stratagem that appeals to families who prefer not to have their children attend integrated schools. The same development is occurring in several Northern cities, particularly New York, Philadelphia, and Washington. The authors view this development with dismay, fearing that influential people will resist, or at least withdraw their support from, public school improvement. There may be the danger in many Southern communities and some Northern cities that public schools will become "pauper schools," as they were in some communities in an earlier period of our history.

Often the financing of these white segregated schools is inadequate, with money coming primarily from tuition, donations, and limited endowments. The buildings may be abandoned factories or stores or some other structures not originally planned for educational purposes. Many of the faculty members are recruited from the ranks of retired teachers, recent college graduates or dropouts, housewives, and paraprofessionals. The less affluent white pupils thus attend inferior schools and receive substandard instruction, because of educational erosion in facilities, faculties, and funds. However, it must not be assumed that all private schools are havens for children seeking escape from integrated public schools. Conversely, projects such as "A Better Chance/Independent Schools Talent Search," based in Boston, seek out, counsel, and place students of minority groups in better secondary schools.

Parochial Schools. The vast majority of private elementary and secondary schools are church-related. By far the greatest share of these are affiliated with the Roman Catholic Church. These parochial schools, as they are commonly called, enroll nearly six million elementary and secondary school students (less than half of the Catholic children and youth in the country) in 10,000 elementary schools and 2,500 secondary schools. Like other church-related schools, these parochial schools were established to provide instruction in church doctrine, a function that is unconstitutional for public schools. As James Michael Lee states in *Catholic Education in the Western World:*

In most Catholic schools . . . attendance at certain religious exercises is a part of the religious instruction program of the school. Elementary schools normally require students to attend Mass one weekday and also go to Confession. . . . Some secondary schools retain compulsory Mass or Confession during weekdays.[5]

Studies of the entire Catholic school complex reveal that many Catholic schools are extremely overcrowded, are operated on a much lower per-pupil cost than the typical public school, and employ teachers who have less academic preparation than public school teachers. One of the studies revealed that students in Catholic schools are superior to public school students both in academic achievement and in ability but that this advantage can be attributed largely to the Catholic schools' selective admission of students. Indolent and undisciplined students are frequently refused admission or, if already admitted, are transferred to the public schools.

Many of the teachers in local Catholic schools are priests, seminarian brothers, and nuns; but the proportion of lay teachers is increasing. Teachers in these schools are banded together in numerous religious educational organizations, such as the National Catholic Education Association and the Catholic Lay Teachers groups. An influential agency is the Division of Elementary and Secondary Education of the United States Catholic Conference. Comparable in organizational purposes to the public schools' National Congress of Parents and Teachers is the National Home and School Association. Many Catholic schools have their own councils or school boards at the diocesan, area, and parish levels. Many members of these control or advisory boards of education are laymen.

These denominational schools represent a small

[5]James Michael Lee (ed.), *Catholic Education in the Western World*, University of Notre Dame Press, Notre Dame, Ind., 1967. pp. 294, 295.

but important minority in education today. These schools, too, have as a major objective spiritual development, with religion "integrated in all elements of the curriculum." The boards of education of these precollege schools employ qualified teachers who are generally members of the particular denomination running the school. Each institution usually has its own local board of education. Some of the denominations have area and/or national organizations, as, for example, the National Union of Christian Schools (Christian Reformed Church). With the increase in church and denominational mergers, with the development of broad-gauged ecumenicity among Protestants and other faiths, and with the rising costs of financing both public and nonpublic schools, many of these small denominational schools face the practical problems of enrichment and even survival.

One of the studies reported that, contrary to popular belief, there is no evidence that Catholic schools are divisive or vehicles of prejudice. The study of Greeley and Rossi[6] pondered the question of whether the continuation of this large Catholic school system is desirable; it concluded that Catholic schools are not necessary for the survival of American Catholicism. However, the writers reported that they did not expect this massive school system to be terminated. To continue with their present standards and proportion of total enrollments, these private schools will require a tremendous increase in income. This problem has prompted vigorous efforts by the Roman Catholic Church to secure increased indirect financial support in such areas as transportation, textbooks, and student services. Adherents of the doctrine of strict separation of church and state oppose such policy. This issue is discussed in Chapter 1.

The states of Pennsylvania and Rhode Island provided aid for part of the salaries of teachers in parochial schools. The U.S. Supreme Court declared these acts unconstitutional in 1971. This decision shattered hopes for public support of private schools in Pennsylvania and Rhode Island as well as in many other states where similar aid was being considered. Because of the financial pinch, many Catholic elementary and secondary schools have closed temporarily or permanently. The result is that many public school districts, already heavily in debt, will go deeper into deficit spending. Many Hebrew

[6] Andrew M. Greeley and Peter H. Rossi, *The Education of American Catholics*, Aldine Publishing Company, Chicago, 1966.

and Protestant day schools are also experiencing financial and recruiting problems.

Of the three major religious faiths in the United States—Catholic, Protestant, and Jewish—the last represents about six million people (about 3 percent of the national population), including one million children. The Jews have long cherished education. The first Hebrew day schools in this nation were established in the seventeenth century. Today Hebrew- or Yiddish-language day schools are supplemented by afternoon and Sabbath schools that teach primarily religion. The American Association for Jewish Education is supported by several major organizations, representing all branches of Judaism: Orthodox, Conservative, and American Reform. Torah Umesorah is the National Society for Hebrew Day Schools. With the cooperation of the National Hebrew Culture Council, Hebrew language courses are offered in some public schools.

Reciprocity and ecumenicity are major aspects of interfaith education in American communities, along with group identity, as each nonpublic and public school has its own board of education and administrators.

Other Types of Districts and Schools

Special Charter School Districts. Some schools, usually city schools, have a special charter granted directly to the local district by the state. Although the majority of these districts were established in the early history of the state's educational development, some of them operate under a special charter of special laws because of the size of the district. The multiplication of specially chartered districts is likely to complicate school administration within the state; hence there is a trend toward bringing all school districts under the general school laws.

Laboratory Schools. Many laboratory or experimental schools on the elementary and secondary levels are in reality public in that they are practice or training schools for state institutions that prepare teachers. Generally no tuition is required, and the pupils are admitted as they would be to a public school, although the limitation of facilities and the experimental nature of the work may restrict the enrollment. The American Association of Colleges for Teacher Education has been active in improving the laboratory schools. Numerous laboratory schools are affiliated with, or are part of, nonstate or independent institutions. Experimental schools have stimulated profound changes in educational practice throughout the United States and abroad. Many laboratory schools affiliated with teacher-education institutions have been discontinued or their functions have been modified, as more and more student teaching and interning are done in affiliated public and private schools.

BOARDS OF EDUCATION

Evolution and Nature

Nearly every school district in the United States is governed by a group of laymen called the "selectmen," "board of education," "school board," "board of trustees," "school committee," "township board of education," or "county board of education." These board members are the direct representatives of the people in the school district.

Development of School Boards. Historically the board of education developed in the following manner. At first the planning was done by all the interested persons in the community. Then developed the practice of appointing temporary committees. Then these temporary committees were replaced by permanent committees. There gradually developed the pattern of selecting boards of education, accountable to the people, who were given the responsibility for organizing and administering free schools. The autonomous school district, organized separately under an elected board of education, is essentially an American institution.

Electorate and School Boards. Basically control of public education resides in the people. "We, the people," elect representatives who, as a board of education, take the place of the unwieldy larger group, the electorate. Citizens should maintain active interest in their schools. This interest should be manifested in voting at school elections, visiting schools, attending board meetings, and participating in parent-teacher associations. Good schools tend to be found in the communities where there is a high level of public understanding of, and interest in, education.

In recent years, there has been evidence of a substantial renaissance of public interest in, and concern for, education. This interest has been intensified by persistent social problems such as discrimination against minority groups, poverty, and student unrest. Newspapers, magazines, radio, and television are focusing attention upon educational issues and problems to an extraordinary degree. Citizens' advisory committees on education at local, state, and national levels have multiplied from a handful at the close of World War II to many thousands. There are now over ten million members of parent-teacher associations, making this the largest type of organization in American society.

Never before in the nation's history has American education enjoyed such unprecedented public interest and criticism. Wise boards of education are seeking to capitalize on this surge of public interest for the improvement of education.

Size, Tenure, and Selection of Boards of Education. There has been no uniformity in the number of persons on a board of education or in their term of office. The trend in recent years has been toward boards composed of not more than nine elected members. There should be enough members to represent the different points of view in the community.

Methods of nominating board members vary greatly. They may be nominated by petition, primary election, individual announcements, citizens' committees, mass meetings, or school-district meetings. The members are usually elected, although they may be appointed by the mayor and council, by county commissioners, by city managers, or by self-perpetuating boards.

Terms of office for school board members vary from one year to several. Authorities in educational administration recommend the election of board members at large rather than by wards, on a nonpartisan basis, and for fairly long, overlapping terms.

Early studies of the social composition of city boards of education revealed a heavy preponderance of business and professional men to the exclusion of men and women from the middle and lower socioeconomic levels of society. In recent years, the composition of boards appears to be shifting to include more members of minority groups and more skilled and semiskilled workers. Collectively, the members of the board of education should reflect a variety of vocational experiences, economic levels, educational interests, and leadership abilities so as to represent the community broadly. School board members should be chosen from among the best men and women obtainable in the community and given adequate orientation and preservice training in boardmanship.

Qualifications of Board Members. The magnitude of education, as expressed by its annual expenditure of more than $50 billion, emphasizes the need for a very careful selection of board members. Among the qualifications usually specified by law are that the candidate be over twenty-one years of age, a legal voter, and a resident in the school district. Besides these legal stipulations, however, a member of a board of education should possess many other desirable qualities: an interest in schools, the willingness to subordinate self-interest, an open-minded and creative outlook, courage in facing criticism, willingness to give time to the office, skill in working with people, the respect of the community, a forward-looking attitude, a reasonably good education, friendliness and cooperativeness, an understanding of the community, and the ability to discuss school affairs. Of greatest benefit is intelligent cooperation among the members of the board and among the board, teachers, and community.

Unfortunately board members do not always promote the best welfare of the school. Hardened politicians, not content with the devastation inflicted on city governments, realize that the schools, employing many people and handling millions of dollars, are tempting objects for despoilation. The school system should be made an uninteresting and unattractive field to political spoilsmen. By and large, however, the schools are governed honestly, largely because the majority of board members take their responsibilities and duties seriously.

Functions and Powers of Boards of Education. The board of education is primarily a policy-forming and appraisal-making group. The board is generally granted broad powers by the state and is invested with much discretionary power in the details of its work. The chief responsibilities of the board of education include:

1. **The development and improvement of the educational program**
2. **The selection of the chief administrative officer and the provision of the professional and nonprofessional staff**
3. **The provision of funds and facilities**
4. **The maintenance of good relations between the school and the community**

Board Organization and Procedure. Most boards of education are organized with a president, who presides at the meetings, and a secretary or clerk, who may serve as the treasurer. Business is conducted usually in regular open meetings held in the school once a month, in addition to special meetings held as the need for them arises. In cities and larger districts many school boards, instead of holding all their meetings in the central administrative building, move their official sessions to various school buildings in the district. Some boards distribute bulletins after each session. The Richmond, California, district distributes a special edition in Spanish.

Much planning is transacted through committees. Among the typical standing committees are finance, buildings and grounds, school management, personnel, and public relations. In recent years, however, the tendency is away from standing committees. If the whole board meets as a committee, each member will be more thoroughly informed on all school affairs and will be able to render more intelligent service. As a general rule there should be no standing committees, since too frequently committee action predetermines board action. If there are committees, certainly the superintendent of schools should serve on all of them as an ex officio member in order to integrate the policies and actions of the board.

Relationships of Boards of Education

The board of education plays a unique role in American life. Its work impinges on so many areas of public interest that it becomes interdependent with many groups. As the elected representatives of the people, the board members must be able to keep in contact with their constituents or at least to gauge their pulse. The importance of such connections is manifested in the increasing prevalence of committees on public relations, community relations, and human relations. Many boards encourage laymen, teachers, and students to attend their sessions, except when personnel matters make a closed session desirable.

Among the vital relationships maintained by the local school board with other organizations and officials are those with the city government; with other school boards; in area, state, and national affiliations; and with the superintendent of schools, whose work is treated in the last part of this chapter. Many school boards work closely with citizens' committees.

Fiscal Independence and Dependence. The tendency has been to divide school districts into two categories on the basis of their fiscal relationship to the city government:

1. *Fiscally independent* **School districts in which the board of education generally has authority to raise and expend funds without the consent of the municipal government are financially independent.**
2. *Fiscally dependent* **Conversely, school districts which are a department of some civil agency, such as a city, and hence must depend on it for budget approval and revision are said to be fiscally dependent.**

Authorities in political science usually favor the dependent boards, whereas educational writers in the main agree that the school district should be fiscally independent. Cooperation between the two civic agencies—city council and board of education—is increasing. In many communities an appointee from the municipal council meets regularly with the board of education and vice versa. Reciprocally these appointees serve in listening and advisory capacities.

School Board Organizations. A significant development is the banding together of school boards in the common cause of education. In many states the board members have joined formal organizations, by counties, by groups of counties, or by the entire state. The state associations are linked in the National School Boards Association—a group that is emerging as a potent force in American public education. In 1967 this association took over the publication of the *American School Board Journal,* the nation's oldest educational journal. It has established the Educational Policies Service for "leadership methodology." A recent publication of the association entitled *New Dimensions in School Board Leadership* contains many suggestions for board members trying to cope with the "crises of authority."[7] The volume suggests the restudying of traditional board roles and urges board members to "learn how to manage change and not just react to it." Many board members have profited by attending the annual conventions of county, state, and national school boards' associations. These associations render many other valuable services to local boards and their administrators.

ADMINISTRATION

The Evolution of School Administration

As the one-room school was displaced by multiroom schools, it became necessary to have someone in charge. Frequently, one of the teachers was designated head teacher, or principal teacher, with certain authority over other teachers. However, as the school grew still larger and its operation more complicated, the principal teacher became the full-time principal in many schools. In others a full-time building administrator, or principal, had to be appointed. Thus the principalship emerged in America long before the superintendency.

As villages grew into cities, several school buildings were established within a school district, and the need arose for systemwide administration and supervision of schools. At first this task was undertaken by a school committee of laymen. But the supervision of schools by committees proved quite unfeasible, and the committees were supplanted in time by a single school superintendent. In early times, he was a layman, usually paid less than the principals, and responsible only for the business affairs of the district. The first school superintendents were appointed in Buffalo and Louisville in 1837. The importance of the superintendency became increasingly apparent, and the responsibilities of the office were gradually expanded. As the office became more responsible, the qualifications became more professional.

As school systems grew larger and administration more complicated, administrative staffs were increased by the addition of assistant superintendents, instructional supervisors, and other specialists. Positions such as business manager, curriculum director, personnel manager, director of buildings and grounds, and others became quite common in city districts. After the beginning of the twentieth century the study of educational administration and supervision was introduced into the curriculums of graduate schools of education. Certification requirements for administrative positions were established by the states. School administration was well on its way toward professionalization.

[7]Seminar Staff, *New Dimensions in School Board Leadership*, National Association of School Boards, Evanston, Ill., 1970.

Functions of School Administration

The functions of administration can be classified into four general areas: administration of the educational program, administration of finance and facilities, personnel administration, and administration of school-community relations. The following outline illustrates some of the responsibilities included in these major functions:

Administration of the educational program
Scheduling of the school program

Planning and supervising school activities

Supervising the work of teachers

Evaluating the school program

Supervising the processes of curriculum revision

Administration of finance and facilities
Budgeting, expending, and accounting for school funds

Requisitioning and controlling the use of school supplies

Supervising the use of school buildings and facilities

Planning new school buildings

Supervising the maintenance and repair of school facilities

Personnel administration
Recruiting, selecting, and assigning personnel

Helping teachers to grow professionally

Serving as liaison leader in relationships between board and staff

Administering salaries, sick leaves, teachers' records, etc.

Promoting, dismissing, and retiring personnel

Enumerating, admitting, and placing students

Supervising behavior of students

Supervising the guidance, records, and attendance of students

Administration of school-community relations
Reporting educational progress and needs to the public

Meeting with community groups interested in education

Planning parent workshops, open houses, study groups, etc.

Participating in community life

The administration of the education program is regarded as the central and most important function of administration. School buildings, records, faculties, budgets, and all the rest of the school environment have meaning and importance only to the extent that they contribute to the quality of instruction and learning.

Qualifications of School Administrators

School administration has become a complex and exacting profession that demands a high order of competence and statesmanship. In general, the

competencies or skills required for the school administrator can be classified into three categories: conceptual (ideas), human relations (people), and materiel (things).

He should visualize himself as the energizer of all the educative forces in the community. Indeed, there is some disposition to title him the superintendent of *education* rather than the superintendent of schools. Moreover, the ablest school administrator sees his community ultimately in national and international terms, rather than in terms of neighborhood or city limits.

The school administrator should have a broad background in general education and a wide understanding of the society which education serves. He must also have a rich professional education from which he derives his understanding of teaching, curriculum, guidance, supervision, finance, public relations, research, and many other fields of specialized knowledge in education. Most states now require at least a year of graduate study for certification in school administration. Approximately one-third of the states have increased certification requirements for administrators to include two years of graduate study. The American Association of School Administrators requires applicants for membership to have two years of graduate study. The number of school administrators with doctorates is gradually increasing.

The school administrator gains much of his competency through experience—experience both as a teacher and as an administrator. Most states require a minimum of three years of teaching experience for certification in administration. In addition, the school administrator gains valuable experience in his professional associations. Most superintendents belong to the American Association of School Administrators. The association established in 1969 the National Academy of School Executives as a quasi-autonomous nonprofit institution dedicated to the in-service development of school administrators. The association issues many helpful books and periodicals, such as the *School Administrator* and *Hot Line*, the latter dealing with federal interest in education.

The school administrator must be a person of high character. He should possess a rich philosophy of education and of life, anchored in the enduring values of Judeo-Christian morality. His conduct should be attuned to the golden rule if he is to set an exemplary moral tone for the system. His behavior should demonstrate high professional ethics, and he should be fair and honest in his relations with people. He should be able to subordinate personal interests and self-aggrandizement to the best interests of public education. The school administrator should be aware of the great social consequences of his position.

The distinguished school administrator is a person of broad vision who sees the full potential of education in its march toward the improvement of mankind throughout the world. His concept of the job must not be limited by the walls of his school or the boundaries of his school district.

The able school administrator is a person of sound personality, well-balanced emotionally and socially. He should be friendly and personable, self-confident and modest, adaptable and creative. He should have a deep understanding and acceptance of self.

The qualifications of school administrators have been discussed at some length because of the crucial importance of educational leadership in our society. The quality of the school system, like that of any other organization, is to a large extent measured by the shadow of the man who leads it. Educational administration represents a high order of social responsibility, surpassed in importance by few, if any, other professional callings.

Recruitment of Administrators

Heretofore school administrators have been recruited primarily from the ranks of those with training and experience in the educational field. However, the U.S. Office of Education in 1971 launched a five-year project designed to attract and train successful administrators from outside education to become school superintendents. The program provides two years of on-site, in-depth training and experience for competent leaders selected from such fields as law, business, government, public and private service, civil rights, and finance. The experiences are designed to prepare them to serve in the enlarging area of school superintendence. Conversely, the project offers training to prepare interested school administrators for leadership positions in other fields. The chief source of recruitment for school superintendents will continue to come from the field of education itself. Assistant superintendents, on the other hand, may come from various fields.

ORGANIZATION

Some of Its Characteristics

School organization may be described as a means of clarifying and distributing tasks, responsibilities, and authority among individuals and groups in an orderly manner consistent with the purposes of the enterprise. The internal structure of school systems varies widely according to the size and nature of the enterprise. Small school systems have small, simple organizations. Larger districts have much larger and more complex structures. Moreover, there are substantial differences of opinion regarding the form of effective organization. Studies reveal an appalling lack, in most districts, of sufficient administrative and supervisory personnel to discharge the ever-increasing responsibilites of school administration and supervision.

Figure 5-2 illustrates the organization proposed for a large Maryland system by a survey team. This chart illustrates several important principles and promising trends in school organization and administration.

The many dilemmas in school administration make the superintendency a troubled profession.

Unit Control. The organization provides for unit control, which means that there should be one responsible head, namely, the superintendent, who reports directly to the board of education. Opposed to this are a number of school systems that operate under dual or multiple control, in which a business manager and perhaps others are coordinate with the superintendent. Unit control also implies that each subordinate will be directly responsible to only one superior rather than to a number of bosses.

Democratic Organization and Administration. Good organization provides for wide participation in educational planning and decision making. Figure 5-2 indicates the machinery for democratic school administration—lay advisory committees, teachers' councils, curriculum committees, PTA councils, and student councils. If schools are to prepare young persons for intelligent and effective citizenship in a democracy, opportunity must be provided for the observation and practice of democracy at work within the school. Moreover, it is increasingly apparent that wiser decisions are usually reached when many minds tackle the problem. Perhaps no aspect of school administration has received as much attention in recent years as the importance of democratizing the administration of schools. Administration is no longer thought of as synonymous with a *position* but rather as a cooperative *process*, engaging at times the best talents of all the people in the organization.

New Role for Administrators. The role of the administrator and supervisor is increasingly regarded as one of stimulation, assistance, coordination, mediation, appraisal, and help, rather than one of inspection and command. In former years when teachers were poorly trained and when the administrator or supervisor was expected to be more expert than all others in all aspects of schoolwork, administrators and supervisors operated largely through inspection and command. They exercised power *over* people rather than power *through* and *with* people. Classrooms were inspected, and teachers were instructed or commanded with respect to their duties. However, as teachers acquired better education, higher professional stature, and increased power through collective bargaining, and as newer and better concepts of the leadership role emerged, the processes of administration and supervision also changed.

Today the educational leader is regarded as the

stimulator, coordinator, or helper of teachers. Titles such as "director" and "supervisor" are giving way to "coordinator," "consultant," and "helping teacher." Note in Figure 5-2 that many specialists work as staff officers (helpers) rather than as line officers (commanders). This trend, while not yet universal, promises better and more effective working relationships between supervisors and teachers. The older, more monolithic organizations had top-heavy staffs of experts in line positions who tried to influence change through their status rather than through solid help and service. More and more ideas and changes are being initiated at the bottom rather than at the top of the organizational hierarchy. This newer trend is consistent with learnings yielded by the study of group dynamics.

Greater Freedom for Schools, Students, and Teachers. Good organization provides a maximum of freedom and initiative to teachers, students, and schools, consistent with efficient operation and prudential control. In simpler words, school organization is being decentralized. Organization charts are becoming flatter rather than taller. The number of levels in the administrative hierarchy between the teacher and the superintendent is being reduced, with the result that greater autonomy is being given to individual teachers and buildings within the system. Teachers are being given more room to be different, experimental, creative, and adaptive.

Homogeneous Assignments. Homogeneous assignments are becoming more common. Note in Figure 5-2 that administrative positions are assigned to particular *functions*, such as program, plant and business, research, adult education, and others, rather than to educational *levels*, such as elementary and high school. An effort is made to center ultimate responsibility for discrete functions in one person so that accountability is not divided and so that the same function is not administered piecemeal by a number of persons with narrow and conflicting responsibilites.

Written Policy Statements. Although it is not apparent from Figure 5-2, there is a distinct and desirable trend in school organization toward written policy statements and job descriptions. These are commonly made available through handbooks and local school codes so that they may be known to

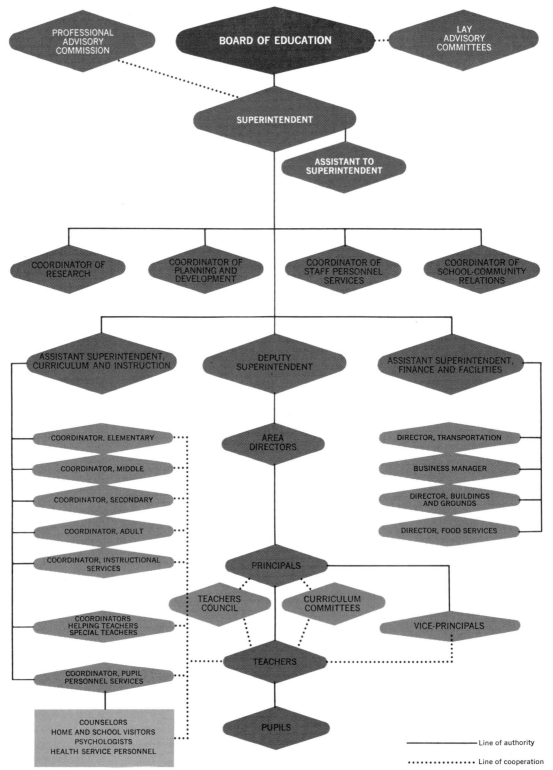

PROFESSIONAL ADVISORY COMMISSION

BOARD OF EDUCATION

LAY ADVISORY COMMITTEES

SUPERINTENDENT

ASSISTANT TO SUPERINTENDENT

COORDINATOR OF RESEARCH

COORDINATOR OF PLANNING AND DEVELOPMENT

COORDINATOR OF STAFF PERSONNEL SERVICES

COORDINATOR OF SCHOOL-COMMUNITY RELATIONS

ASSISTANT SUPERINTENDENT, CURRICULUM AND INSTRUCTION

DEPUTY SUPERINTENDENT

ASSISTANT SUPERINTENDENT, FINANCE AND FACILITIES

COORDINATOR, ELEMENTARY

AREA DIRECTORS

DIRECTOR, TRANSPORTATION

COORDINATOR, MIDDLE

BUSINESS MANAGER

COORDINATOR, SECONDARY

DIRECTOR, BUILDINGS AND GROUNDS

COORDINATOR, ADULT

DIRECTOR, FOOD SERVICES

COORDINATOR, INSTRUCTIONAL SERVICES

PRINCIPALS

TEACHERS COUNCIL

CURRICULUM COMMITTEES

VICE-PRINCIPALS

COORDINATORS HELPING TEACHERS SPECIAL TEACHERS

COORDINATOR, PUPIL PERSONNEL SERVICES

TEACHERS

COUNSELORS HOME AND SCHOOL VISITORS PSYCHOLOGISTS HEALTH SERVICE PERSONNEL

PUPILS

———— Line of authority

·············· Line of cooperation

136

all. When the ground rules are established in writing and when they are determined before, rather than during, controversy, there is less opportunity for misunderstanding, conflict, and arbitrary action among the people involved.

REORGANIZATION

Organization is often subject to reorganization. The four major types of structural changes in district organization and philosophy are (1) redistricting, (2) decentralization, (3) desegregation and (4) community education.

Redistricting

The reorganization—or consolidation or redistricting, as it is sometimes called—of school districts involves the rearrangement of school-district boundaries in order to construct larger, more efficient local units or to consolidate resources so as to provide special services, such as area vocational-technical schools and community colleges.

At the close of World War II there were about 103,000 school districts in the United States. Through reorganization this number has been reduced to about eighteen thousand. The number of districts too small to operate their own schools has been reduced by more than two-thirds since the war. The number of one-teacher schools has been reduced by more than 95 percent since 1930, as indicated in Figure 5-3. This progress has been phenomenal. Nevertheless, there is room for much more improvement. There are still nine hundred small districts—mostly in the Great Plains states—which do not operate any schools, but pay neighboring districts to educate their children. Approximately four thousand one-teacher schools remain. More than one-fourth of the schools in the nation enroll fewer than ninety pupils. Approximately half of the districts operate no high schools. A great many districts are still too small to provide even the most basic educational opportunity for children. Eventually, the total number of school districts should be reduced to approximately five thousand, and the number of intermediate districts to five hundred. The number of operating districts in each state is shown in Figure 5-4.

FIGURE 5-2 Administrative organization of a large school system.

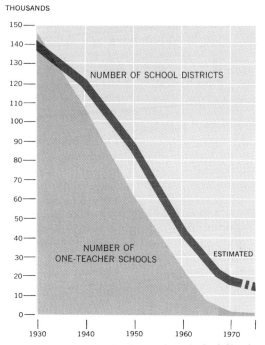

FIGURE 5-3 Decline in the number of school districts and one-teacher schools. (U.S. Office of Education, Digest of Educational Statistics; and National Education Association, Rankings of the States, copyrighted by the National Education Association, 1971.)

Advantages of Reorganization. The reorganization of school districts into larger administrative units usually results in a number of advantages. The larger enrollment makes feasible the extension and enrichment of the educational program through the addition of new curriculums such as vocational and business education, new courses, advanced study in other courses, and remedial instruction. In consolidation, the curriculums of the reorganized schools usually tend to be combinations of the best from each district.

The wider area enlarges the educational clientele. Larger districts are better able to provide their own high schools, junior colleges, and adult education programs. The employment of additional specialized personnel—such as librarians, counselors, administrators, supervisors, and health personnel—becomes feasible. More specialized school facilities—such as laboratories, shops, health rooms, libraries, gymnasiums, and auditoriums—can be provided. The proportion of high school graduates in reorganized districts attending college is strikingly larger than the proportion in smaller districts. Larger districts also permit the more efficient use of personnel and facilities. For example, more teachers teach in their fields of specialization. The pattern of services enlarges with the increase in the size of the districts. Thus the reorganization of local school units results in a richer instructional program and supporting services as well as greater equalization of educational opportunity and financial burden. Poorer rural sections do not have the fiscal resources for high-quality educational programs.

A commission of the American Association of School Administrators studying school organization concluded that ". . . the real trouble is outmoded school district organization—school district organization that is now called upon to provide services, to perform functions, and to operate programs that were scarcely dreamed of when it was established."

Disadvantages of Reorganization. Although the advantages of reorganization generally far outweigh the disadvantages, the consolidation of school units may give rise to new problems. The close relationship of the schools to the people may be weakened as the locus of authority becomes further removed from the local community. The reorganization of districts is frequently inhibited by the persistence of the American tradition of home rule. Attempts to enlarge district boundaries are often viewed as threats to the homogeneity and autonomy of the community. Total school costs inevitably rise, although greater educational opportunity is provided at modest increases in costs per pupil.

Fleets of school buses are needed to transport pupils to the consolidated schools. These buses involve some hazards for the students and driver. The lengthened day, caused by long bus rides, induces extra fatigue, especially for young children. The possibilities for parent-teacher conferences and for parental participation in the educational program decrease as the size of the district increases.

The Criteria for an Adequate School District. In general, it can be said that an adequate school district should satisfy three basic criteria. First, it should be large enough to be able to provide adequate basic educational opportunity at reasonable cost. Esti-

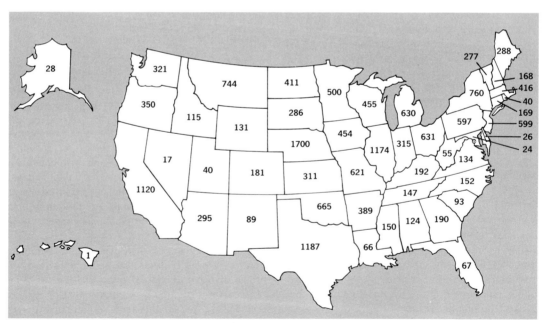

FIGURE 5-4   Number of operating administrative units, by states. By comparing the number of school districts in a state with its population and area, one may assess the state's progress toward reorganization. Least progress appears to have been made in the central states. (National Education Association, Research Division, Estimates of School Statistics, 1970-71. Copyrighted by the National Education Association, 1971.)

mates of adequate size vary. The National Academy of Education recommends the following: "The number of school districts in the United States should be drastically reduced, and normally no school district should contain fewer than 5,000 nor more than 150,000 pupils. . . . We probably need no more than 5,000 such districts."[8] If a district implemented recommendations and instituted a sixteen-year program, extending downward to include the nursery school and kingergarten and upward to embrace the two-year junior college, then obviously the minimum numerical requirement for student enrollment should be raised, probably to the optimum figures just cited.

Second, a school district should be large enough to include sufficient wealth. Although small districts are not necessarily poor, nor large districts wealthy, the per-pupil wealth tends to increase as the size of the district increases. Again, there is no universal agreement on what level of wealth is adequate. One common rule of thumb suggests that there should be about $40,000 of true valuation per child of school age. A reasonable tax would yield from this base sufficient money for a fairly adequate program. Obviously, the amount of state aid would influence this consideration.

Third, a school district should include a natural geographic area. Ideally, a school-district boundary should include people who are held together by common economic, social, and cultural ties and interests. School districts should encompass rather than bisect natural communities.

Methods of Reorganization. The reorganization of school districts is usually accomplished (1) through legislative decree, (2) through local initiative, or (3) permissively, through planned programs.

Some states have accelerated reform by passing "K-12 laws," which require that every square mile of a state be covered by a school-district organization offering thirteen years of schooling, from kindergarten to the twelfth grade. Some states, such as Nevada, have abolished all local school districts and have reorganized them into county units by legislative decree. Several states have abolished the office of county superintendent. Some state legislatures have decreed that all districts beneath a certain size must be reorganized into larger units.

Most states have attempted to accomplish re-

[8]Committee on Educational Policy, *Policy Making for American Public Schools*, National Academy of Education, Washington, D.C., March, 1969, p. 7.

organization through laws prescribing the procedures by which local citizens or officials might reorganize local districts on their own initiative. This may be done through merger, annexation, or transfer of territory. In this procedure, proposals for reorganization are initiated locally or by the county board and are sometimes presented to the voters on referendum, which usually requires the approval of the state.

Many state legislatures are reluctant to compel reorganization but disinclined to endure the slow progress that is made under local initiative. Thus an increasing number of state legislatures are enacting laws that will stimulate reorganization where needed but also retain some permissive features. Such plans often provide for the development of a statewide plan for reorganization based upon studies of local needs and conditions. In many states, encouragement is generated through state-aid programs that provide financial advantages to reorganized districts.

A combination of three procedures which is used increasingly involves passage of general legislation by the state's highest lawmaking body, adoption of a framework of a master plan by the state board of education, and consideration of locally recommended reorganization plans by the state superintendent of education.

Transportation of Students. In a consideration of consolidation and the state minimum program of education for all children, one cannot ignore the important factor of the availability of education. The democratic principle of equal educational opportunity demands the daily transportation of students to school. Some states have dormitories for secondary school students. At present some rural youths are denied high school education because they cannot reach the school.

The transporting of students is not a new educational undertaking. Beginning in a Massachusetts district in 1840, it continued without legal authorization until 1869, when Massachusetts passed the nation's first permissive transportation law for the conveyance of pupils to and from public schools. By 1920 pupils were being carried to and from school in all the states, with or without specific legal sanction. Today the provision of transportation facilities for schoolchildren is generally mandatory under certain conditions. It is estimated that nearly 40 percent of all students ride to and from school each day in more than 200,000 vehicles, including buses, station wagons, and other cars, at an annual estimated cost of well over $1 billion.

The transportation of students is more than a local problem. Many state treasuries provide financial assistance in defraying the cost of travel for both public and parochial school students as a means of equalizing educational opportunity and burden. Several state departments lend technical assistance in the mapping of school bus routes. Because of the close relationship between the transportation of students and the consolidation of districts, each state should make continuous analyses of both matters.

Transportation of students is one of the means used to obtain some measure of integration. This volatile issue is further discussed in Chapter 1.

Decentralization and Community Control

The term "decentralization" is often used interchangeably with "community control," but there is a real difference, as is connoted by the following definitions, prepared by the Educational Research Service of the National Education Association:

"Decentralization" is a managerial technique whereby a central authority delegates functional responsibility and some decision making to officials of sub-units of the local school system, each of which administers schools in a particular geographic area. Although "community control" implies some form of administrative decentralization of decision making and responsibilities, it has another meaning. Community control denotes decision making and responsibility regarding the expenditure of money by an elected group representative of the community served by the school or group of schools.[9]

The movement to decentralize large school systems started in New York City in the late 1960s. It is spreading to many other cities, especially the large ones. Mario D. Fantini, who directed the Ford Foundation's 1967 study, which recommended decentralization of the New York City schools, listed three major concepts of the New York City decentralization movement which are being discussed and acted on elsewhere:

1) decentralization itself, which in theory brings the school boards and administration closer to the people by

breaking large school systems down into smaller sub-systems;
2) participation by students, parents, and the community in general in making decisions about what is taught and how it is to be taught, and
3) giving the community more control of the schools by actually allowing members of the local community to occupy policy-making and administrative positions.[10]

In 1970 the New York City school system was divided into thirty-one local school districts, each having its own elected school board and appointed area superintendent of schools, with the chief administrator in the city being designated as "chancellor." The thirty-one districts administer the elementary and junior high schools, but the city board retains the crucial powers of channeling funds, employing personnel, and selecting textbooks. The city board administers the high schools.

The Detroit public schools are divided into seven districts. Many local school systems are decentralizing in various degrees to create smaller and more viable units of administration which are more responsive to the groups they serve.

Desegregation or Integration of Schools

Another form of reorganization taking place within the individual public school, the district, or both, is that of desegregation or integration of students and staff. This movement is discussed in detail in Chapter 1 and is presented here briefly as one type of internal reorganization taking place across the nation. Local school districts are faced with the continuing problems of racial relations and of equality of educational opportunity for minority groups. Dual school systems, established by tradition or by law, have prevailed in the South for many years, and also in many large Northern cities. In its historic Brown decision in 1954, the U.S. Supreme Court stated that "separate but equal" schools were unconstitutional and that schools should proceed with desegregation "with all deliberate speed."

Districts have desegregated in various degrees. Some schools have reached rather complete integration, with the racial balance in schools approximating the racial composition of the community. Some schools use the principle of "gradualism"— gradually approaching complete integration. Some districts have token integration, and some have none. Many schools are eliminating segregation of staff.

[9]"Decentralization and Community Involvement in Local School Systems," *NEA Research Bulletin*, vol. 48, p. 3, March, 1970.

[10]"Decentralization Grows," *Phi Delta Kappan*, vol. 51, p. 10, June, 1970.

Naturally schools cannot achieve total integration alone. There must be changes in the way people live and in their attitudes toward one another. There is a large complex of problems involving housing, job discrimination, and poverty levels of living. Federal, state, and local funds are being channeled into Model Cities programs, low-cost housing, retraining of low-income workers or the unemployed, and guaranteed annual income programs. Federal funds have recently been made available to meet the extra burdens of schools in the process of desegregation and to improve education in schools where *de facto* segregation exists. There is no quick or easy answer to this complex and emotionally charged problem.

Community Education

Since education is broader than schooling, the local school district, irrespective of its legal control or size, becomes the core of the community's total educational program. The modern local school is a community-centered institution in an education-oriented community. Its doors swing in and out. Furthermore, lines that traditionally separated formal and informal education are being erased, and fresh new community approaches are being made in the perennial quest for more and better education.

Many community resources—personal and material—have rich educational overtones. Many community organizations can enrich education. The whole community has rich resources on all educational levels. Many of the programs for early-childhood education are communitywide projects. Head Start, for example, involves parents and other community workers. Many elementary school buildings are neighborhood centers. Secondary school courses in sociology give academic credit for useful volunteer services with people and organizations in the community. The local community colleges are catalysts for constructive change in the surrounding areas, as indicated in the research study *The Community Dimension of the Community College*. The land-grant colleges and universities, which have long extended themselves into the rural areas with their extension departments, are also serving urban and metropolitan areas and being served by them.

As indicated in Chapter 13, many schools employ community agents to work with families and community agencies within the total school district to improve educational experiences for young people. The Community Development Soci-

ety for the advancement of the profession of community workers was organized in 1969. Its periodical is devoted to the improvement of knowledge and practice in purposive community change. Community education, in its broad aspects, has the great potential not only of environmental improvement but also of *human* renewal. The practical and nationwide locus for accelerating constructive changes in education is the local school and its community.

FUTURE

New Cities Challenge Educational Planners

One of the important future developments involving local educational authorities will be the creation of new towns and cities. The bipartisan National Committee on Urban Growth Policy has recommended that 100 cities of 100,000 population and ten larger cities of over one million population be built by the year 2000 "to keep the troubled cities from growing to unbelievable dimensions" and to care for the increase in population. The New Communities Program in the Department of Housing and Urban Development (HUD) has projected the need for 300 new communities by the year 2000 when at least 100 million more people will live in the United States. In cooperation with the newly established National Council on Environmental Quality, the U.S. Office of Education, and other governmental and non-governmental agencies, HUD may launch many new communities, which obviously must provide appropriate local educational facilities and programs.

In 1968 Congress passed initial legislation to spur the development of new cities. The plans include building twenty-six million more homes in the 1970s. The first community to receive federal funds under a program to stimulate the development of new cities was Jonathan, a suburb southwest of Minneapolis. The plan calls for a city of 50,000 persons in twenty years. The 5,000-acre layout includes school sites, churches, and other community features, such as recreation.

The first successful new town in the United States in recent years is Columbia, Maryland, on a 15,000-acre site between Baltimore and Washington, D.C. Educators helped to plan this "sociological breakthrough."

Other Local School District Trends

Boards of education will change in membership to include more official representatives from the minority groups, more women, and more younger voters. School administrators will continue to be recruited primarily from the professional ranks of educators, but their preparation will change:

In the decades ahead administrators will be required to make many complex decisions which they are not now being prepared to make wisely. The problems faced by the educational manager are changing rapidly. Tomorrow's educational manager will have to be able to handle a variety of responsibilities, many of them outside the walls of the school or college or state department. He will need a background in education certainly; but he will also need training and experience in the behavioral and social sciences, in finance, in management, and in the development of human resources.[11]

The future will bring more joint accountability for professional development with the teacher-education institutions, as the local schools become "cooperative clinical teaching centers" or "educational professional development centers."

George Shuster, special assistant to the president of Notre Dame University, has suggested a gradual cutback of Catholic primary schools, upgrading and expansion of Catholic high schools, plus a major effort to develop first-rate universities.

Neil G. McLuskey, in *Catholic Education Faces the Future*, states that there should be more widespread cooperation between parochial schools and public school systems. More public schools are sharing auxiliary services with parochial schools. In some cities many facilities are shared. The future planning of an entire city's educational plan may well embrace the close juxtaposition of sites for both public and private schools, so that playgrounds and some other facilities can be shared on an alternate or a regular basis.

Parochial education at all levels is moving outward away from isolation. There is some movement toward building a new type of church school devoted exclusively to the religious education of students who attend public schools, as in most Jewish educational programs. The future may also witness much more development of church-related pre-elementary education.

[11]Sidney G. Tickton, *To Improve Learning: An Evaluation of Instructional Technology*, R. R. Bowker Company, New York, 1970, p. 54.

Consolidation of small schools into larger districts will probably continue except in remote, inaccessible areas. Conversely, the decentralization of large city districts into smaller community units will continue to bring the schools closer to the people. Decentralization and community control, both very complex concepts and difficult processes, will increase in this decade. Comprehensive planning, based upon wide participation, will delineate rights and responsibilities for all groups concerned.

Financing and overall policy-making functions will remain with the central board of education and its administrators. As to decentralization and community control, the special committee of the Council of Big City Boards of Education recommended as one guideline that periodic review of arrangements involving local people be made so that the process may remain dynamic and self-renewing.

SUMMARY

Most of the responsibility for the operation of schools resides with the local school district. However, school districts are regarded legally as creations of the state. This delegation of operational control has resulted in a wide variety of educational quality and practice and given rise to a tradition of local control of education, one of the most unique characteristics of American education.

Serving the cities, suburban communities, and rural areas of America are numerous types of local districts: (1) state, (2) county, (3) town and township, and (4) community. There are also junior college or community college districts and intermediate school districts.

The nonpublic schools are usually local institutions too. They are basically of two types: (1) independent schools, such as private academies, and (2) religious schools. Most of the religious schools are Roman Catholic.

At the top of the organizational pattern for the public schools is a local board of education. Except in some city districts, local boards of education are elected by the people. The major functions of the board of education include the development and improvement of the educational program, the selection of the chief administrator and the professional and nonprofessional staff, the provision of funds and facilities, and the maintenance of good relations between the school and the community. School board members should be chosen from among the most able, interested, and forward-looking citizens in the community. These boards of education should be fiscally independent from municipal government and free from political influence and control.

The superintendent of schools is the executive officer of the board and is appointed by the board. The superintendent, principals, and other administrative officers are responsible for the administration of the educational program, personnel, funds and facilities, and school-community relations. These administrative positions call for persons with vision and ability. Many states are strengthening the requirements for these positions.

The internal organization of school systems is undergoing several significant changes in the direction of larger, better-prepared central staffs; more democratization through the use of lay committees, teachers' councils, and other cooperative efforts; and more orderly assignment of functions through written rules and regulations.

Reorganization of school districts is the mood and mode of the times. The reorganization movement has four major dimensions: (1) consolidation of small schools into larger districts, (2) decentralization of large city districts into smaller units, (3) desegregation and integration of minority groups, and (4) community education, which seeks to make the school a community-centered educational institution in an education-centered community.

The future is laden with many changes in local school districts, including participation in the building of new cities and in urban and human renewal.

Suggested Activities

1. Discuss the legal status of a local public school district.

2. Visit a small school district and a large one. What are your conclusions?

3. Attend a meeting of a city board of education and report on the nature of the problems and solutions for educational organization in a large city system.

4. How can and do community colleges, city colleges, and municipal universities aid the local school district and vice versa?

5. Visit a private school in your area. Prepare a report comparing it with a public school you are familiar with, citing strengths and weaknesses of both.

6. Discuss the role of the local board of education and the superintendent of schools in negotiations with the employees.

7. Interview a superintendent of a local school and evaluate his numerous activities.

8. Should school superintendents be recruited from such fields as business and law?

Bibliography

American Association of School Administrators: *Profiles of the Administrative Team*, Washington, D.C., The Association, 1971. A description of the administrative functions of a local school district.

Bendiner, Robert: *The Politics of Schools: A Crisis in Self-government*, Harper & Row, Publishers, Incorporated, New York, 1969. An analysis of the politics of local governance of education as it responds to the social, economic, and educational issues of the times.

Brown, William E., and Andrew M. Greeley: *Can Catholic Schools Survive?* Sheed and Ward, Inc. New York, 1970. A discussion of the problems facing Catholic schools and the reforms which are necessary for their survival.

Campbell, Alan K. (ed.): *The States and the Urban Crisis*, Prentice-Hall, Inc., Englewood Cliffs, N.J., 1970. Papers presented by eight authorities to the American Assembly on the role of states in the urban crisis, including education.

Fantini, Mario D., and Milton A. Young: *Designing Education for Tomorrow's Cities*, Holt, Rinehart and Winston, Inc., New York, 1970. A model projecting a modern school system for a hypothetical community.

Iannaccone, Laurence, and Frank W. Lutz: *Politics, Power and Policy: The Governing of Local School Districts*, Charles E. Merrill Books, Inc., Columbus, Ohio, 1970. A case description of the politics and government of a local school district.

Johns, R. L.: "State Organization and Responsibilities for Education," in Edgar L. Morphet and Charles O. Ryan (eds.), *Designing Education for the Future*, No. 2, Citation Press, New York, 1967, chap. 14. An expert's forecast of the future organization and operation of state educational agencies.

Kirst, Michael W.: *The Politics of Education at the Local, State and Federal Levels*, McCutchan Publishing Corporation, Berkeley, Calif., 1970, pt. 1. Political influence in local education policy, especially in large cities and suburbs.

Morine, Harold, and Greta Morine: *A Primer for the Inner City Schools*, McGraw-Hill Book Company, New York, 1970. Helpful volume for those planning to teach or already teaching in the inner city.

National Public Relations Association: *The School Board Meeting*, Washington, D.C., 1970. Report of current practices in meetings of local boards of education.

MAJOR LEVELS	SOME TYPES OF INSTITUTIONS	CONSECUTIVE GRADES OR YEARS	SOME ALTERNATE INSTITUTIONS	
		ADDITIONAL YEARS		
	GRADUATE SCHOOLS	YEAR 7	POSTGRADUATE UNIVERSITY	
		YEAR 6		
HIGHER EDUCATION		YEAR 5		
	SENIOR COLLEGE	YEAR 4		
		YEAR 3		
		YEAR 2	UNDERGRADUATE COLLEGE	
	JUNIOR COLLEGE	YEAR 1		
		12TH GRADE		
	SENIOR HIGH SCHOOL	11TH GRADE	HIGH SCHOOL	
		10TH GRADE		
SECONDARY EDUCATION		9TH GRADE		
	JUNIOR HIGH SCHOOL	8TH GRADE		CONTINUING EDUCATION
		7TH GRADE	MIDDLE SCHOOL	
		6TH GRADE		
	INTERMEDIATE SCHOOL	5TH GRADE		
		4TH GRADE		
ELEMENTARY EDUCATION		3D GRADE	LOWER ELEMENTARY SCHOOL	
	PRIMARY SCHOOL	2 D GRADE		
		1ST GRADE		
		KINDERGARTEN		
	PREPRIMARY INSTITUTIONS	NURSERY SCHOOL		
PRE-ELEMENTARY EDUCATION		CHILDHOOD AND INFANCY POSTNATAL CARE	VOLUNTARY SCHOOLS	
	HOME	PRENATAL CARE		

Part Three
Areas of Education

Education is as pervasive as life itself, beginning at birth and ending at death. Part 3 is addressed to this lifelong continuum, which is portrayed graphically on the opposite page. The four major sequential levels of lifelong learning are (1) pre-elementary, (2) elementary, (3) secondary, and (4) higher education; related to these is (5) adult and continuing education.

The pre-elementary period includes prenatal and postnatal care as well as the early nurture and education of the child. The principal agencies for providing care and education at this early level are the home, the nursery school, and the kindergarten. This period reaches up to the elementary school age of approximately six years. Although enrollments are rising, less than half of the 4- and 5-year-olds attend school (Chapter 6).

Elementary education lays the firm foundation for all-round growth of the child by developing in him basic skills, attitudes, and knowledges. The elementary schools in the United States are the main instruments for equipping persons with a common, general education, and virtually all children of elementary school age are enrolled (Chapter 7).

Secondary education is broadened and lengthened to include all the curricular and cocurricular activities of the preadolescent, adolescent, and postadolescent youth. Theoretically it spans the period covering the junior high school or middle school and the senior high school. It adds to the general education of youth and often provides some degree of specialization. More than 90 percent of the youth of high school age are in school (Chapter 8).

Higher education includes both undergraduate and postgraduate study. College and university undergraduate life with its crowded activities may be a prelude to intensive postgraduate work, but more often it is the terminus of formal schooling. College enrollments are increasing (Chapter 9).

Education for out-of-school youth affords to an ever-increasing number of young Americans the opportunity for intellectual and social growth. Adult and continuing education, the final stage in lifelong learning, can yield satisfying fruits through a rich and varied program of activities (Chapter 10).

Chapter 6 Pre-elementary Education

ORIENTATION

Pre-elementary education is no longer all doll-houses and ring-around-the-rosy. It is rapidly becoming psychoneurobiochemeducation, massive environmental intervention, Sesame Street, and crib learning. These are all recent developments and are discussed in this chapter; in the previous edition of this book they were not even mentioned, for at that time they were nonexistent. They illustrate the exciting changes that are transforming early-childhood education. Samuel Kirk, an expert on special education, was once asked, "What is the most appropriate age to introduce children to a formal educational program outside of or in collaboration with the home?" Kirk answered, "During the mother's first month of pregnancy."

There is persuasive evidence that the mother's diet and general health during the period of pregnancy affect both the physiology and the intellectual capacity of the fetus. As described later in this chapter, the emotional and intellectual climate established in the early home life of the child can have profound impact upon his ability to succeed in school and in life. Indeed his relations with his parents and siblings in infancy may ordain his entire future. Clearly these circumstances underline the importance of both early-childhood education and parent education on child care and development. No wonder that observers are referring to the 1970s as the decade of one of the most remarkable developments in our educational history, the extension of education to reach the child even before his birth.

Elizabeth Koontz, the first Negro president of the National Education Association and head of the

U.S. Children's Bureau, stressed that: "America was made great because it offered educational opportunity to all men, free. And the demands of today tell us that we must extend that free education beyond the high school and before the first grade."[1]

It is ironic that the first years of life, the most important years in human growth and development, should be the last to be included in schooling. Clearly, pre-elementary education constitutes the last frontier in the development of our lifelong educational system. In the long run, it may be the most exciting.

We prefer to speak of this new frontier as "pre-elementary education" rather than "pre-school education." It precedes the elementary unit, but it does not precede schooling. It is schooling. Pre-elementary education covers the entire period from the child's birth to his entry into the elementary school, usually at the age of 6 or 7. We shall discuss it in terms of four components: foundations, home care and training, nursery school education, and kindergarten.

FOUNDATIONS

It is instructive to consider the historical and philosophical backgrounds of pre-elementary education. Let us consider first those persons who were pioneers in early-childhood education and the study of child development, both here and abroad; second, the historical roots of pre-elementary education; and finally, its contemporary development.

Pioneers

Many educators have contributed significantly to thought and practice in early-childhood education.

Pre-elementary education stimulates creative expression by young pupils.

[1] Elizabeth D. Koontz, "Once a Teacher, Always a Teacher," *NRTA Journal*, vol. 19, p. 30, November-December, 1968.

They perceived most clearly the compelling importance of the early years in the educative process and undertook the pioneering work upon which society can now build this last frontier of educational development.

Jean Oberlin, a French minister and educator, established an exemplary infant school in France in 1769 for children from impoverished homes. Oberlin, one of the less well-known pioneers of early-childhood education, was deeply moved by the miseries and oppression of poor children. Oberlin sought in his school to relieve these poor children of the great disadvantages they would otherwise encounter in elementary schools. In this effort, he became a sort of eighteenth-century precursor of what we commonly call "compensatory education" for children from low-income families.

Friedrich Froebel is generally regarded as the father of the kindergarten movement. Froebel was influenced by Pestalozzi, whose work is discussed in Chapter 17. Froebel felt that the educative process should be started when the child is 3 or 4 years of age. He established the first kindergarten ("garden for children") in Blankenburg, Germany, in 1837. Froebel saw the importance of play, not simply as amusement, but as the natural means by which the young child gathers information about his world and learns to adjust to it, a classic concept which still permeates modern kindergartens. Froebel, drawing upon the work of Rousseau, helped establish a new respect for the child, for his individuality and his self-expression. Froebel emphasized the importance of the child's own informal exploration of his environment and his participation in group activity as a natural means of social expression.

Other schools for young children were being established elsewhere, here and abroad. Susan Blow, an American teacher interested in Froebel's concepts of the kindergarten, attended a training school for kindergarten teachers in Germany. Upon her return to this country, Miss Blow opened the first continuous public school kindergarten in 1873 in St. Louis with the cooperation of her superintendent, William T. Harris. Although there were earlier, abortive attempts at establishing the kindergarten here, Miss Blow was the first to operate a kindergarten in a public school system in this country and make it work. St. Louis kindergartens became so successful that they attracted nationwide attention. Miss Blow soon opened a training school

for kindergarten teachers, who contributed to the success of the kindergarten movement across the country. As will be noted later, the Macmillan sisters, Rachel and Margaret, established in London the prototype school from which both the concept of the nursery school and its name were derived. Abigail Eliott, after studying with the Macmillan sisters, organized a training center for nursery school teachers in Boston.

G. Stanley Hall in 1883 undertook a memorable study of the "contents of children's minds upon entering school," which revealed that beginning pupils understand far less of the world about them than had been assumed. His study led to other, similar studies which provided a sounder basis for the development of learning experiences for early-childhood education. The writings and teachings of William James and John Dewey stressed the importance of the early-childhood years in the educational and social development of children and youth. Dewey's famed University Elementary School at the University of Chicago, established in 1896, admitted 4-year-olds into an educational program that was well articulated with the entire elementary school.

Maria Montessori was the first woman ever granted a medical degree from an Italian university. Early in life she became interested in the education of mentally defective children and developed methods and materials that permitted such children to perform as well on school tasks as normal children experiencing instruction. Later she concentrated her prodigious energies on the education of children of normal intelligence from the slum neighborhoods of Rome. Thereafter, by her own desire and by public demand, she was an educator and no longer a practicing physician. She established the propositions that very young children are capable of grasping rather sophisticated concepts and skills, that they like to learn under proper conditions, and that they learn most effectively through their senses.

Dr. Montessori felt that a "prepared environment" is necessary; that is, special teaching materials should be provided to stimulate pupils' senses—geometric forms, letters cut from sandpaper blocks, and other models. She discovered that young children often chose her teaching materials in preference to toys and dolls, a result of their natural desire to learn, and thereby create order and understanding out of the environmental confusion that surrounds them. Dr. Montessori believed that from birth to age 6, the child has an "absorbent mind" that "develops from within." She felt that "things are the best teacher" and that the child should be confronted with many sensory stimuli to quicken his urge for discovery. With these didactic materials carrying the burden of instruction, the teacher should remain in the background diagnosing the child's interests and level of understanding and manipulating the objects in his environment. She felt that children should be permitted to learn at their own pace. Her pedagogy enjoyed a quick but temporary success in the United States in the early 1900s but died out almost as quickly, although her methods were kept alive in some European schools.

Recently there has been a strong renewal of interest in Montessorian method in the United States among certain groups. Beginning with the Whitby School established in Greenwich, Connecticut, in 1958 by Nancy Rambusch, there has been a revival of the Montessorian method in the United States in more than six hundred schools across the nation. Some of these schools are nonprofit institutions organized and financed by parent groups; others are profit-making schools franchised by a national corporation. This revival has been stimulated by several forces: the articulate persuasiveness of Nancy Rambusch herself, the compatibility of the method with modern theories of early-childhood education, and the lure of an attractive market for early-childhood education by business ventures.

This new thrust has produced a new professional organization, the American Montessori Society, which has ideological differences with the Association Montessori Internationale. The latter accuses the former of "mongrelizing" Montessorian method through eclectic additions, such as the "new math," linguistics, and electronic training devices.

As noted in Chapter 1, other issues arise with respect to Montessorian method—questions about the impersonality inherent in the instruction, its permissive nature, and the fact that these schools accommodate children of well-to-do families who need it least. Although her concepts contain certain serious limitations and are opposed by some experts, Montessori has contributed valuable insights into the nature of the learning process and has demonstrated some effective methods of helping disadvantaged children learn.

Jean Piaget, a Swiss psychologist, also influenced early-childhood education to a great extent by studying the process of developing intelligence and by stimulating research. Although Piaget's work began nearly half a century ago, it has only recently

been put to use in American educational thought. Piaget found that intelligence emerges from a child's sensory experience with concrete objects that he can act upon, that language development is essential to increased powers of thinking, that repeated exposure to a thing or an idea in different contexts contributes to the clarity of comprehension, and that accelerated learning of abstract concepts without related direct experience may result in symbols without meaning. Much of contemporary thought, research, and experimentation about appropriate educational experiences for young children is being rooted in concepts of educational psychology and pedagogy advanced by Piaget and his Swiss colleagues, as well as many other psychologists.

For forty years, Dr. Arnold Gesell, formerly of the Yale University Clinic of Child Development, studied children and added much to our understanding of their intellectual, physical, emotional, and social growth. His classic books, *The First Five Years of Life: A Guide to the Study of the Preschool Child* and *Infant and Child in the Culture of Today: The Guidance of Development in Home and Nursery School*, were widely read and not only had a profound impact upon nursery school programs, but also contributed much to the education of a generation of parents on home and family life for young children. Gesell's studies have helped to bring increasing awareness to the importance of the first five years of life in the educative process.

Samuel Shepard, one of St. Louis' enterprising principals and later assistant superintendent of schools in that city, began in the Banneker school of St. Louis one of the first attempts to help young children from slum neighborhoods overcome the heavy disadvantage of cultural deprivation before their problems were further complicated by failure in school. Shepard, a Negro himself, perceived clearly that many Negro children were destined to unhappy and fruitless experience in school unless in their pre-elementary years they could be helped to acquire some self-respect, self-confidence, mastery of language, and satisfactory social relationships. Shepard also recognized the importance of capturing the attention of parents, overcoming their apathy, and inspiring their hope in the education of their children. His contagious enthusiasm stimulated many Negro parents to participate for the first time in school affairs and to support the schools.

The Development of Pre-elementary Education

1826	First nursery school in the United States established		1933	Nursery kindergartens started by Federal Emergency Relief Act
1855	First kindergarten in America founded in Watertown, Wisconsin		1936	Legislation implemented by Congress for maternal, child health, and child welfare services (Social Security Act)
1868	First training school for kindergarten teachers started in Boston		1962	Earmarked funds for day-care services made available to state welfare departments (Social Security Act)
1873	First permanent kindergarten established as part of the St. Louis public school system		1964	Economic Opportunity Act (war on poverty) passed by Congress, containing several provisions for compensatory schooling, including pre-elementary education for the disadvantaged
1884	Kindergarten Department added to the National Education Association		1965	Project Head Start, introduced originally as part of the summer program in the war on poverty, made a year-round part of preeducational programs
1892	International Kindergarten Union (now Association for Childhood Education) formed			
1897	National Congress of Mothers (now the National Congress of Parents and Teachers) organized		1966	Free public schooling for all children on reaching age 4 recommended by the Educational Policies Commission
1897	Association of Day Nurseries of New York City organized		1967	Head Start extended upward experimentally by Follow Through Project for disadvantaged pupils
1908	Child Study Association of America organized		1968	Handicapped Children's Early Education Assistance Act passed by Congress
1912	Federal Children's Bureau established		1969	Office of Child Development started in U.S. Office of Education
1913	Division of Kindergarten Education created in the U.S. Office of Education		1971	Inclusion in public school systems of pre-elementary programs for all children age 4 and beyond recommended by Education Commission of the States Task Force on Early Childhood Education
1919	First permanent nursery schools opened			
1921	Sheppard-Towner Maternity and Infant Act adopted by Congress			
1925	National Council of Parental Education formed		1972	Federal funds for day-care centers and child development authorized

The remarkable success of this program in St. Louis and of similar programs in other cities provided prototypes for the development of the later Head Start programs, discussed in this chapter.

Martin Deutsch, director of the Institute of Developmental Studies at New York University, is another who saw the importance of pre-elementary education as an instrument of social salvage, now spoken of more commonly as "compensatory education," in that it seeks to compensate for the barrenness in the lives of children from low-income families. Deutsch saw pre-elementary programs as something more than crash efforts mounted hastily and dramatically without a proper pedagogical rationale (as so many educational innovations are). He saw them as the first stage in a fundamental restructuring of the entire educational program through elementary and secondary levels as well. He helped educators understand that early compensatory education is of little benefit unless there is consistent follow-up. Deutsch helped make compensatory education the spark that could change the structure of the entire educational system to accommodate better the needs of all children, not only the culturally disadvantaged ones.

Benjamin Bloom in 1964 published a report of classic researches in learning under the title *Stability and Change in Human Characteristics*. This book documented what many educators had long suspected—that from conception to age 4, the individual develops 40 percent of his mature intelligence; from age 4 to age 8, another 30 percent; and after age 8, the remaining 30 percent[2] (Figure 6-1). More than three-fourths of a human being's total intellectual capacity is established by the time he reaches third grade. This finding underlined the importance of early-childhood education and helped educators understand why $1 spent to overcome learning disabilities early in life could accomplish more than $10 spent on remedial education in the upper elementary years and in high school. There is reason to believe that if children do not receive intellectual stimulation during those important early years, their capacity to learn may be severely stunted. For the children of poverty, this often means preordained failure in school and in life. Many writers—Myrtle Imhoff, James Hymes, Jerome Leavitt, Lillian Gore, Minnie Berson, Maya Pines, and Laura Zirbes, among others—have contributed to the literature of early-childhood education.

[2]Benjamin Bloom, *Stability and Change in Human Characteristics*, John Wiley & Sons, Inc., New York, 1964, p. 69.

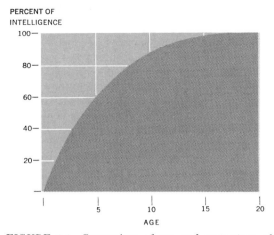

FIGURE 6-1 Comparison of age and percentage of mature intelligence achieved. (Adapted from Benjamin S. Bloom, Stability and Change in Human Characteristics, *John Wiley & Sons, Inc., New York, 1964, p. 136.)*

O. K. Moore, of the University of Pittsburgh, demonstrated that the years from 2 to 5 are the most creative and intellectually active period in life. He showed that children are capable of extraordinary feats of inductive reasoning if left to themselves in what Moore calls a "properly responsive environment." Moore uses such devices as the "talking typewriter," a typewriter with jumbo-size type that automatically pronounces the sounds of the letters which the child types. As a new letter pops up in the exhibitor, the child faces the exciting task of "try to find me." When he finds the key that prints the letter, the sound of the new letter is given, and the child thus learns phonics and touch-typing without much effort. If the typewriter is linked with a computer, the child can be led through a program that encourages him to discover for himself the spelling and sound of words, to create simple sentences, and to carry on a simple dialogue with the typewriter through the computer. Moore believes that the human mind is extraordinarily open between the ages of 2 and 5 and that, in arranging the child's education, we should not miss this critical period. Moore has developed new and creative means of helping children play an active role in discovering knowledge for themselves. Children like the adventure of self-discovery so well that they form positive attitudes toward school and learning.

McVicker Hunt, director of the Psychological Development Laboratory at the University of Illinois and former head of the National Laboratory on Early Childhood Education, has directed his attention to learning in the crib. Hunt believes that it is possible to speed infant development rapidly by enriching the baby's environment through recorders that produce interesting sounds and voices, mobiles that respond to the baby's reactions, and a variety of simple toys for the crib. This activity is combined with increased interaction between the infant and his parents. All of this transforms life in the crib from boredom to joy, entertainment, quickening of perception, development of simple motor skills, and an increased zest for life at the very outset of human experience. Hunt concludes from his experiments that the time to prevent cultural retardation is infancy and that programs that begin as late as age 4 are probably already remedial education. He contends that infants in a culturally deprived background could be elevated from the upper levels of mental retardation to successful college work through the enrichment of their environments in infancy.[3]

Other pioneers of early-childhood education will be mentioned in the following discussion of the historical development of pre-elementary education.

Early Parental Education

Many have drawn attention to the importance of preparing parents for the delightful but often arduous adventure of child rearing. Interest in parental education can be traced at least as far back as the chapter in Comenius' *Great Didactic* on the "school of infancy" or the "mother school," as the Germans translated the idea. Pestalozzi prepared a *Book for Mothers*, a manual on child rearing, and wrote *How Gertrude Teaches Her Children*, a case description of an experiment in teaching mothers "how to bring up their little ones."

One of the early records of parental education in this country arose from a conference for mothers called in 1894 by a kindergarten teacher in Chicago. Three years later the National Congress of Mothers was organized in Washington, D.C., by a group interested in little children, the home, the school, and the community. In 1900 a formal charter was

[3] For an account of Hunt's interesting work, see Patricia Pine, "Where Education Begins," *American Education*, vol. 4, pp. 15-19, October, 1968.

granted to this organization, which is now called the National Congress of Parents and Teachers. The parent-teacher associations are local, county, state, national, and international in scope. Their major objective is child welfare.

Dr. Benjamin Spock spent much of his career studying and describing young children. His popular book *The Common Sense Book of Baby and Child Care* has sold millions of copies around the world. In this and his later book *Dr. Spock Talks with Mothers*, this eminent student of early childhood combined his knowledge of pediatrics with rare insight into the social, emotional, and intellectual dimensions of growth in childhood. Although Spock's main contribution has been in the realm of parental education, his belief that growing and learning proceed more smoothly if permitted to occur in the child's own way and time has helped shape our concepts of pre-elementary education.

Early Nursery Education

The genesis of nursery education goes back to the beginning of families, and in some countries parents are still solely responsible for teaching their young children.

Plato was among the first to emphasize the importance of education in early childhood, incorporating a community school for very young children into his ideal republic. Comenius is generally credited with the establishment of the first nursery school, although it was not known as such. In England the Macmillan sisters, Margaret and Rachel, at the turn of the last century began experimenting with the education of young children in cooperation with hospitals, combining pedagogy with psychology and hospital experience in nursing under medical supervision. Hence the name "nursery school" and the beginning of its gradual spread through England, where early-childhood education is today more common than in the United States. The British style of "open education," which is defined in the Glossary and described in Chapters 7 and 14, has influenced pedagogy in American pre-elementary programs. It has tended to make many of them more flexible, more humane, and more child-centered.

The first nursery school in the United States was opened by Robert D. Owen in his famous model community at New Harmony, Indiana, in 1826. The Association of Day Nurseries of New York City was organized in 1897. In 1915, a group of faculty mothers at the University of Chicago opened two nursery schools; and in 1919, the first public nursery school in the United States was started.

One of the leaders in nursery school development during the 1920s was Patty Smith Hill, a professor at Teachers College, Columbia University, who invited Grace Owen, principal of a college in England for nursery school teachers, to lecture in this country. Demonstrations in nursery education were conducted at the Horace Mann School. In 1922 the Ruggles Street Nursery, now the Eliot-Pearson School, was established in Boston by Abigail Eliott; in the same year the now famous Merrill-Palmer School opened in Detroit with a nursery school and a laboratory in child development under the leadership of Edna White. About the same time, Lucy Gage went to George Peabody College to establish preparation programs for leaders in early-childhood education in the South. Most of these early nursery schools were affiliated with universities and established as laboratory schools for the preparation of childhood education leaders and for the systematic study of young children. Later a number of private nursery schools were opened. Occasionally public school systems provided nursery schools. The Great Depression of the 1930s prompted a federal program of financial support for nursery schools as a means of enriching the lives of young children from destitute families. World War II stimulated further growth of nursery schools, as an increasing number of mothers went to work in war industries, thereby creating a demand for daytime care and education of their children.

Strong impetus to the development of nursery schools was generated by the Economic Opportunity Act of 1965, with its subsequent extensions. This act provides funds for public schools and other community agencies for use in pre-elementary education programs for children of low-income families as an essential part of the war on poverty. These programs, commonly referred to as Head Start programs, reach half a million youngsters annually. The Elementary and Secondary Education Act also stimulated the development of pre-elementary education for children of poverty. By 1972 about 40 percent of the 3- to 5-year-olds were enrolled in preprimary education—a figure which has more than doubled over a five-year period. Head Start led in 1967 to the initiation of pilot programs in Follow Through—a project to reinforce and extend upward, into the kindergarten and lower elementary grades in public and private schools, the role of early education in the war on poverty.

Early Kindergartens

The first kindergarten in America was established by Mrs. Carl Schurz in her home in Watertown, Wisconsin, in 1855. Four years later, Elizabeth Peabody and her sister, Mrs. Horace Mann, established a kindergarten in a house in Boston. Elizabeth Peabody is often spoken of as the "apostle of the kindergarten in the United States."

The growth of the kindergarten may be divided roughly into five periods: (1) The pioneer stage, which had Boston as its center, stressed a few of the most important of Froebel's teachings. (2) The philanthropic era, which began in Florence, Massachusetts, valued the kindergarten largely as a reformatory of redemptive influences. (3) The strictly educational stage, which started in St. Louis, Missouri, accented scientific study of the principles underlying kindergarten education. (4) The fourth period, which started in Chicago and spread over the nation, is the child-development and parental-involvement era. Like the third stage, it is still extant. It aims at making the kindergarten a link between the home and the school and at strengthening the foundations of family life. (5) The current period is one of "massive intervention" in the child's environment, characterized by experimentation and increased federal participation. The Department of Elementary-Kindergarten-Nursery Education of the NEA, the Association for Childhood Education International, and the World Organization for the Education of Young Children are professional associations that have enrolled thousands of members and served educators of very young children through conferences, research, and publications.

With the impetus of this historical background, pre-elementary education promises at this late hour in our educational history to find its destiny as an essential part of a lifelong continuum of education that commences with birth or earlier and closes with death. We shall view the three sectors of pre-elementary education in detail: (1) home care and training, (2) nursery education, and (3) kindergarten.

HOME CARE AND TRAINING

The home is the child's first school. No teacher can afford to underestimate the power of the home, for it is a physical, mental, social, emotional, and spiritual center for the child.

Parental and Family-life Education

The child's first teachers are his parents; hence they should have definite knowledge of, and guidance in, their responsibilites and duties. Parental education is child- and parent-centered. With this dual and immediate objective of better and happier children and parents is coupled the ultimate aim of a better civilization. Parental information may be offered to young people long before they marry and have children, while they are still in high school, college, or continuation school. Usually, however, it is given to adults who are already parents, and it may embrace prenatal and postnatal care as well as child study.

Parental education includes such considerations as the role of mother and father and siblings in early-childhood development, conscious and unconscious motivations of parents in their relations with their children, family group dynamics, interaction between parent and child, parents' needs and expectations, and children's needs and expectations.

Some parent-teacher associations sponsor the project of enrolling expectant mothers in classes that meet with the school nurse or doctor. Many city, county, and state health departments distribute free literature on the care of mothers and babies. Uncle Sam's best seller is a publication of the Government Printing Office entitled *Infant Care*.

Among the organizations which today promote the study of children and family life are the National Council of Parent Education, the National Congress of Parents and Teachers, the Child Study Association of America, the American Association of University Women, and the American Home Economics Association. Many universities, as well as state departments of education, have received financial aid for child study from similar foundations.

Colleges and Family-life Education. Many colleges are performing significant services in the fields of preparental and postparental guidance. Vassar College, for example, in 1926 inaugurated an Institute of Euthenics—the improvement of the race through environment. The study of pre-elementary children has been advanced by numerous child institutes, such as the Department of Child Development and Family Relations at Cornell University, the Institute of Child Development and Welfare at the University of Minnesota, the Iowa Child Welfare Research Station at the University of Iowa, the Harvard Center for Research in Child Health and Development, and the Yale Clinic of Child Development. Universities commonly offer courses on child growth and development and parental education as part of their adult-education programs.

Local Schools and Parental and Family-life Education. Of the various formal agencies promoting parental education, the local school—public or independent—offers the greatest possibilities for development. These established institutions give instruction to future parents—both boys and girls—in home economics, conduct classes for adults who are expectant parents, hold baby clinics, provide guided observation in play groups, and organize family centers for consultation. They may become the nucleus of the parental education program in the community, with the cooperation of all agencies interested in child welfare, especially the home.

Churches and Community Agencies. Many churches have established programs of home- and family-life education, often with emphasis on the role of the home in establishing moral values in early childhood. The United Presbyterian Church of the United States maintains a national office of family-life education research. Other community agencies offer courses, clinics, lectures, and study groups addressed to early-childhood education.

Early-childhood Education in the Home

In the early life of the child, the home is preeminently the educational and social center: it is both a school, with the parents as teachers, and a social laboratory of human relationships. Consequently, the home should be a well-designed and appropriately furnished place for living and learning. In a world of change, the child should find the home a haven of hope, love, and security, a place made increasingly secure by local, state, and national efforts in child and maternal welfare.

It is easy to overlook the tremendous amount of learning that takes place before the child enters school, even before he goes to nursery school. He learns to walk, dress himself (after a fashion), and feed himself; he acquires a conversational command of the language and a pretty fair vocabulary (unless he comes from a culturally barren home). He learns to enjoy having stories read to him, to create simple stories himself, and to draw, play, and perhaps even read a little. Truly these are surprising accomplishments for such young minds.

After years of study and practice in elementary education, the famous educator John Goodlad observed that "what the child brings to school from his home and what he encounters from others seems to add as much to learning as what the school itself puts in."

The Preschool Project at Harvard's School of Education has provided deeper insight into the early years of the child's development. The project was undertaken to discover why some 3-year-olds were able to develop intellectual skills rapidly while others were not. To find the answer, the researchers looked at the first three years of the child's family life, and they found these years to be extremely important. In these early years the child has an insatiable curiosity, a grasp of language, and a zest for learning. If parents and siblings respond with fluent conversation and warm relations, the child's cognitive development is quickened.

If the home is unresponsive, the child can actually be trained in helplessness. These discoveries suggest that schools should undertake better programs of parental education to help the family in the education of preschoolers.

An experiment at the University of Illinois demonstrated that children whose mothers received such special training in wholesome family life gained as much as 7 points in IQ scores. Another experiment at Catholic University revealed an average rise of 17 points in IQs of 15-month-old Negro boys in Washington who were tutored for one hour weekly. In Pacoima, California, surprisingly good results have been obtained by having fifth- and sixth-graders tutor kindergarten children from a ghetto in suburban Los Angeles.

Perhaps the most dramatic demonstration of the power of institutionalized early-childhood education is manifested in the kibbutz day-care centers in Israel. Here trained teachers offer excellent education from earliest infancy, resulting in IQ gains as high as 30 points for some children.

The Central Cities Educational Development Center in Fort Worth is focusing attention on very young children in developing educational materials, teaching techniques, and teacher-training programs for teachers of 2- and 3-year-olds. The National Program on Early Childhood Education of the U.S. Office of Education is sponsoring studies of early-childhood education at the University of Florida, Yale University, the University of North Carolina, the

University of Arizona, the University of Oregon, the University of Chicago, Cornell University, George Peabody College for Teachers, and the Family Service Association of Nassau County, New York. These demonstrations and studies indicate strongly that more and more attention in the future will be devoted to family-life education and the development of infants.

Certainly the prevalence of television in many homes has extended the young child's perception of his world. Indeed, "Sesame Street," the popular television series for preschool children, may prove to become one of the most revolutionary breakthroughs in early-childhood education. This hour-long daily program aims to combine delightful entertainment with education to help prepare the nation's preschool children for formal education. It is estimated that half of America's twelve million 3- to 5-year-olds have seen the program, and it is telecast in more than twenty other countries. Other programs have also demonstrated the potential of television for mass education, and programs are increasingly addressing themselves to the preschool audience. "Sesame Street" is carefully planned and produced, and its presentation of fast action, sing-alongs, memory-catching jingles, animated color cartoons, celebrity guests, puppets, and friendly hosts is designed to help this tough audience recognize letters of the alphabet, develop simple number skills, discern geometric shapes, and sharpen reasoning skills. Even the spot commercials

The popular television series "Sesame Street" provides fascinating education for millions of tiny viewers in their own homes.

are designed to teach. In addition to these cognitive skills, the human warmth which permeates the program appears to give the tiny viewers a sense of security. "Sesame Street" was the precursor of a growing volume of educational television programs beamed into the homes of children.

National Educational Television, with a grant from the Office of Education, is producing other educational television programs aimed at 3- to 5-year-old preschool children, as well as programs for elementary school children.

Certainly the potential for both commercial and educational television is enormous, although much of the commercial fare is probably miseducative. Ninety-five percent of American families own television sets. The average preschooler has plenty of time to watch. Studies reveal that the average child will have chalked up approximately four thousand hours of television viewing before he enters school. Since approximately two-thirds of a child's intellectual development occurs before the age of 6, this period in his life is extraordinarily formative. Evaluation of the impact of "Sesame Street" on the educational achievement of its young viewers is extremely encouraging. The studies suggest that mass educational television is the most effective, inexpensive, and delightful way to help most children get a "head start" at home.

The ready availability of fine children's books, records, and toys helps the child advance his interests, knowledge, and talents. Unhappily, in some homes these stimuli are missing. In other homes, ambitious parents expect too much from precocious children, and the roots for later discord between parent and child, and for a poor self-concept on the child's part, are established.

A number of books[4] are available to help parents understand better this period of early childhood and the manner in which they can strengthen the development of their children.

Recently a number of Parent and Child Centers (PCCs) have been established with support from the federal government to tackle defects of body and mind that date back to infancy. Many of them are modeled after the prototype developed by Ira Gordon at the University of Florida. Neighborhood residents are trained to go into the homes to teach and play with babies and toddlers and to help parents, grandparents, and siblings create a model home for sound mental, physical, and social growth. These home-centered programs are especially vital in rural areas where travel to preschool centers might be impossible and in communities where space for child-care centers is unavailable.[5]

NURSERY EDUCATION

Scope of Nursery Education

The majority of adults have never attended either nursery school or kindergarten, since the full development of these institutions is of relatively recent date.

The day nursery and the nursery school are the most common forms of organized education for very young children. The day nursery is a social-welfare institution designed to give day care to the child of the working mother. As approximately half of the married women in this country are employed, the day nursery is an important educational agency. The federal government has supported day-care centers as a means of helping mothers on welfare find employment by relieving them of baby-sitting during the day. Day-care centers have been booming, a process which has been intensified by the demands of the women's liberation movement. The movement contends that mothers should not have to be withdrawn from employment any more than fathers should by the need to care for their children. The nursery school, which has characteristics of both a nursery and a school, in a sense is a downward extension of the kindergarten, enabling younger children to benefit from supervised educational and social experiences.

General Types. There are five basic types of nursery schools. Some city school systems operate nursery schools that are organized within the elementary school unit. This arrangement, similar to that of most kindergartens, is considered quite acceptable. A few school systems have organized nursery schools within an administrative unit of early-childhood education that includes nursery, kindergarten,

[4]See, for example, Vivian E. Todd and Helen Heffernan, *The Years before School: Guiding Preschool Children*, The Macmillan Company, New York, 1964, parts 1, 2; and D. Bruce Gardner, *Development in Early Childhood: The Preschool Years*, Harper & Row, Publishers, Incorporated, New York, 1964, parts 2, 4.

[5]See Alice U. Keliher, "Parent and Child Centers," *Childhood*, vol. 16, pp. 63–66, March-April, 1969, for a fuller description of the centers.

and primary levels. A few secondary schools have affiliated nursery schools, thereby providing high school homemaking and social studies classes with direct experiences with young children. A number of colleges and universities have established nursery schools to serve as laboratories for the training of nursery school teachers or for education in child care or family life, child development, and psychology. But more than half of the nursery schools in America are separate from other educational units. Most of these independent nursery schools are sponsored by private franchise, welfare agencies, foundations, churches, parents, or other private organizations or individuals.

Head Start Programs. As mentioned earlier, the Economic Opportunity Act of 1965 created a vast number of nursery-level programs commonly referred to as Head Start. When the first plans for Head Start were announced in 1965, some hailed this as the beginning of a revolution in which this important sector of education would at long last become a permanent and integral part of the regular educational system. By 1972 more than one million children were enrolled in federally supported pre-elementary programs. The Office of Child Development was created in the U.S. Office of Education to coordinate Head Start and other federally supported early-childhood education programs. Head Start was born of the nation's concern for helping young children from poor homes in the metropolitan ghettos, the Appalachian hills and valleys, the Indian reservations, the Eskimos' arctic wastes, the tropical territorial schools, and the migrant-worker camps escape the vicious cycle of poverty and despair by giving them a "head start" in school. Many middle-class families have a so-called hidden curriculum for their young children at home—travel, story reading, books, records, toys, discussions, and the ubiquitous television set—that does an effective job of preparing them for kindergarten. Impoverished families do not. Children from such homes may never have heard a complete sentence spoken, held a pencil in their hand, seen a museum or art exhibit, visited a physician or dentist, seen themselves in a mirror, or played with children other than their siblings; they may not even know their own names. Lacking an understanding of the language, an acceptable image of themselves, robust health, and intellectual curiosity, they are destined to failure in school even before they begin. Head Start was initiated to remedy this situation.

The activities of Head Start programs are fairly similar to those which have typically characterized good nursery schools. A typical day might include *free play*—digging in a sandbox or looking at picture books; *group activity*—singing or telling stories; *outdoor exercise*—playing with large blocks or climbing jungle gyms; *field trips*—excursions to the zoo or a boat ride; a *rest period;* and a *snack* or *meal.* Classes are usually small, limited to fifteen or twenty children. Emphasis upon intellectual achievement is increasing in many nursery schools, focusing largely upon reading and language development. Mothers and lay volunteers usually help the teachers. The involvement of parents in the program is deliberate as a plan for arousing their interest in the education of their children and as a means of improving slum parents' attitudes toward school and teaching them methods of child care. The programs tend to emphasize the personal. Children's names are displayed prominently on their desks and lockers to give them a sense of personal identity and importance. Dental and medical examinations are included to identify and attempt to correct physical disabilities that might impede learning and development.

How well are the Head Start programs succeeding? The evidence is somewhat mixed. Gains of 10 to 15 points in IQ scores are not uncommon. First-grade teachers commonly report that Head Start pupils make a much faster and better adjustment to first grade. An elementary school principal in a slum neighborhood reports that since Head Start, "School is a place that families have begun to trust for the first time." But there are problems

Good nursery schools emphasize the development of cognitive skills along with social development.

too. The shortage of qualified nursery school teachers has forced the use of many lay people with little or no preparation for teaching. Some Head Start programs try to deal with the children as they would first-graders—teaching the alphabet, regimenting them, and assigning them tasks for which they are not yet ready. When Head Start programs are poorly conceived or poorly handled—and many of them still are—they may help children to hate school sooner. Many of the programs are run by nonschool agencies that are long on good intentions but short on professional know-how. In many cases the objectives of Head Start programs are undefined or poorly defined. Frequently the programs are followed by primary units in the elementary school that fail to accommodate the unique needs, problems, and limitations of slum children. When this happens, the advantages gained from Head Start programs are soon lost.

A study conducted by the Westinghouse Learning Corporation concluded that preschool compensatory programs had very little effect upon children. Some argued that the study was technically faulty and the conclusions unreliable.

In balance, many gains from Head Start are evident. Head Start has acquainted us with the problems of educating children of poverty, stimulated research and creative practice in dealing with them, quickened parents' interest in pre-elementary education and in interacting with the schools, pushed our attention to human growth all the way back to the crib, and above all, helped hundreds of thousands of children from poor families gain enough academic development, confidence, and self-esteem to tackle later schooling with a better chance of success. Chapter 1 deals at greater length with the controversies surrounding pre-elementary education.

Private Nursery Schools

One of the most astonishing developments in early-childhood education in the last decade has been the remarkable rise of thousands of private nursery schools sponsored by private industry. They bear an array of both staid and quaint names—Universal Education, American Child Centers, L'Académie Montessori, Little Shavers, Mary Moppets Day Care Schools, Romper Room Enterprises, Institute of Contemporary Education, and Playcare Centers, among others. Day care centers

provided by industries for the children of their female employees, long popular in Europe, are becoming increasingly common in this country.

An increasing number of public employers are also now providing day-care centers for children of their employees. The U.S. Office of Education, for example, in 1971 opened a model day-care center for children of persons employed there, the first instance of the Office of Education operating an educational program for children on its premises. The Center is used as a workshop to demonstrate important concepts and practices in early-childhood education as part of the federal government's interest in encouraging and strengthening this movement through both public and private auspices.

Many nursery schools are designed primarily as day-care centers, providing play, recreation, and custody for children of working mothers; but many also strive to develop the children's intellect. Some day-care centers have little educational value and should not be misrepresented as educational institutions if they serve only a baby-sitting function. Some schools are very well staffed by professionally trained educators and are furnished abundantly with instructional materials. Others are less well organized, staffed, and equipped. Some accept children between the ages of 2 and 6; others limit their clientele to 4- and 5-year-olds. Some operate all day and year-round; others offer only half-day sessions during the regular school year. Most charge rather impressive tuition fees. Some, usually with public subsidies, are designed to serve children of low-income families or children whose mothers work.

Another type, the parent-cooperative nursery school, sponsored and administered as a nonprofit enterprise by parents, has grown up in the 1970s. Its expenses are met by tuition fees. Parents and teachers together develop policies and programs and some parents participate in the school as aides to teachers.

Enrollments. Although Head Start programs and other public and private nursery schools and day-care centers have grown a great deal over the past decade, prekindergarten programs still serve less than half of their potential population. The percentages of white and nonwhite students enrolled in prekindergarten programs are approximately equal. Prekindergarten programs are more available to children of low-income and high-income families than to children of middle-income families. Enrollments are substantially lower in nonmetropolitan areas of the country.

Aims of Nursery Education

A study of the primary goals of nursery schools administered by public school systems revealed the following objectives in decreasing order of frequency: growth in self-esteem, social development, emotional development, language development, growing independence, physical development, mental development, preparation for regular school years, awareness of needs and strengths, and awareness of physical needs.[6] Considerable controversy exists concerning the relative emphasis which should be placed upon cognitive development versus affective development of children. It appears that increasing emphasis is being placed upon the former in many schools.

Program and Procedures

Curriculum. The curriculum of the nursery school is broad in scope, for it is planned to meet all the needs of growing youngsters from 2 to 4 years of age.

Authorities agree that it is necessary to look upon the child as a learner from birth and to realize that the habits of learning are more important than the actual material learned. The learning activities are of two general kinds: those which are routine in nature—that is, occur at a specific time every day—and those in which the child is given a choice of activities which vary from day to day.

Organization. Nursery schools connected with public schools most commonly offer a one-year program in half-day sessions for 5-year-olds. A few public school nursery programs and many private nursery schools enroll children younger than 5, sometimes as young as 3 or even 2 years of age. The average size of classes in public nursery schools is about sixteen or seventeen. Public nursery schools are about evenly divided between those which accept all students and those which accept only disadvantaged students.

Nursery School Staff. The quality of the nursery school, like that of any school program, depends on the teacher. The effective nursery school teacher has a thorough background of preparation in child development, teaching method, parental education,

[6]National Educational Association, *Nursery School Education*, Research Report 1968-R6, Washington, D.C. 1968, p. 18.

children's literature, science, music, art, and social science. She is able to choose instructional material and equipment according to the needs of young children and to understand the importance of the physical environment in early-childhood education. Above all, she has the personal qualities important for all teachers and especially important for teachers of young children—warmth, friendliness, affection, honesty, respect for children and parents, and self-understanding. If she teaches the underprivileged, she must have the capacity to accept and respect youngsters who are not always well-scrubbed, well-mannered, and able to learn easily with conventional instruction.

Current Practices in Nursery School Education

The scope of the nursery school is being broadened. Now it is not merely a safe place to leave a child; rather, it is an educational center for all-round growth. Emphasis is placed upon emotional as well as mental, physical, and social adjustments.

The clientele is changing and enlarging. The nursery school is no longer either a luxury for a few favored children of well-to-do families or a pauper's home. The middle economic group is beginning to reap the benefit of preschool service. Children in new housing projects and in rural areas are being included. A marked trend is the provision of nursery school education for exceptional and underprivileged children. Many handicapped boys and girls profit even more from early training than normal youngsters.

More storefront academies, such as the East Harlem Block Schools in New York, are providing nursery and kindergarten education as well as tutoring services for older children. These schools in ghetto-area stores are usually private or semipublic and help to bring early-childhood education closer to the community.

More attention is being devoted to nursery school learning experiences. Among the main factors considered in determining a child's readiness for group experiences are his age and general maturity; his ability to give and take, to form attachments to other adults besides his mother, and to exchange affection and interests with his peers; and his desire to come to nursery school.

The experimental school for 4-year-olds at the University of Illinois Institute for Research for Exceptional Children illustrates a sharp departure from traditional early-childhood doctrine. In this school, which serves both black and white, both poor and middle-class children, the emphasis is upon rigorous development of cognitive skills and children are subject to considerable pressure to learn. Learning is dominated by the teacher, and the learning regimen is rigid and logical. This pedagogy, as well as a book[7] by the school's two innovative leaders, Carl Bereiter and Siegfried Engelmann, contrasts sharply with orthodox doctrine, which insists that early-childhood education should be relaxed, permissive, and child-centered.

Other than the federal funds mentioned earlier, few states provide funds for prekindergarten education. Most of the funding comes from local tax levies.

State departments of education are providing more guidance for, and supervision of, nursery schools, including higher standards of certification for teachers. The number of nursery school personnel is being enlarged, and better-qualified teachers are being hired. Some nursery schools have specialized workers such as recreation directors, dietitians, parental-education specialists, home counselors, and other social caseworkers. Welfare services, such as those performed by visiting housekeepers, are helping to improve conditions in the home. These traveling mothers render many services for children. The health program includes appropriate physical activities, proper food and rest, the regular services of a physician, and a daily inspection by a qualified person.

Future of Nursery Schools

Nursery schools—like elementary schools, academies, and colleges—were initially established under private auspices and were available at first only to the wealthy, who could afford to pay the tuition. Pauper schools, or special schools for children and youth with unusual disabilities, were first supported by philanthropy and were provided later at public expense. Eventually it became apparent that what was good for the rich and the poor and the disadvantaged was good also for all children.

Experience with Head Start, Follow Through,

[7] Carl Bereiter and Siegfried Engelmann, *Teaching Disadvantaged Children in Preschool*, Prentice-Hall, Inc., Englewood Cliffs, N.J., 1966.

and Parent-Child Centers aimed at the poor will certainly accelerate what has been called "massive intervention in the child's environment" to permit the child to thrive in school and in life. This development may indeed revolutionize education and provide unprecedented opportunity for upward mobility for all.

Sound educational theory would dictate that the present hodgepodge of pre-elementary education should be restructured. Nursery education—largely private—and kindergarten education—largely public—do not mesh very well. Indeed kindergarten itself is not articulated very well with elementary education in many school systems. Ideally early-childhood education should be organized as an integral part of the total public education system, permitting all 2- or 3-year-olds to progress smoothly and continuously through a three- or four-year unit which leads to the elementary unit.

In many countries, notably England, France, Sweden, Israel, and the Soviet Union, nursery schools are an integral part of the regular primary unit. Pre-elementary education should not be thought of as preparation for the first grade but as an important, clearly the *most* important, unit in the entire educational continuum. Neither should it be thought of as a conglomeration of programs administered by extraschool agencies. Our base of experience and research with such education is still too limited to permit crystallization of the programs into standard prototypes. Great flexibility and experimentation should be encouraged with diverse forms and practices. The organization of the schools should be relatively open, nongraded, flexibly scheduled, and enriched by television and other instructional technology. Collegial patterns of collaborative teaching with liberal use of teacher aides and parents help to maintain both easy relations between school and home and more one-to-one relations between child and adult during these tender years. The costs of such arrangements in additional personnel, space, and materials will plague many districts of limited means.

The sharp rise in the number of day-care centers operated by private industry will probably continue in response to the need for pre-elementary education for children in communities without public programs. In all probability, nursery schools will accommodate many more children of younger age as the importance of infancy in educational development is increasingly recognized. This recognition is being accelerated by the recommendations of many eminent persons and organizations. The Educational Policies Commission, the Committee for Economic Development, and the Education Commission of the States, as well as other organizations, have endorsed early-childhood education as a top-priority educational need.

However, the goal of universal early-childhood education will be difficult to attain because of the enormous costs involved. Although great diversity in programs will continue to exist because of the variety of purposes served, much of the present controversy over purposes will probably be reduced. After more research and experience, better development of technology and programming—as on "Sesame Street"—we will probably learn that the conflict between academic and personal-social objectives is unnecessary; both will be achieved in the same environment.

KINDERGARTEN

Scope of Kindergarten Education

Kindergarten education usually covers the period of schooling just before the child enters the first grade, whether he has had nursery school experience or not. The entrance age is generally set at approximately 4 or 5 years, although some junior kindergartens admit younger children.

The separate problems of the nursery school and the kindergarten are joined in the common responsibility of providing continuous, broadening, and deepening experiences for the child.

Early experience with Head Start programs revealed that gains of children in these programs were soon lost if the kindergarten and primary units which followed were not addressed to the same purposes and methods introduced in Head Start. The importance of compatibility and articulation between prekindergarten and kindergarten experiences was recognized by the introduction of Follow Through programs supported by the federal government through the provisions of the Economic Opportunity Act. These programs brought to the kindergarten and primary unit the same attention to individual differences; parental cooperation and involvement; and the child's social, psychological, physical, and mental problems which had characterized Head Start programs.

Types of Kindergartens. Kindergartens may also be classified by type according to general categories,

namely, research, teacher education, home economics, social service, behavior problems, cooperative, summer school, nursery school and kindergarten combined, private, federally supported, and public school kindergarten. The two most common forms of affiliation are with private organizations and the public school. According to methodology of teaching, kindergartens are sometimes Froebelian, Montessorian, conservative, or child-development-oriented. Whatever the label, the prevailing type of kindergarten is that which seeks to educate the whole child from 4 to 6 years of age by supplementing the home, the nursery school, and other educational agencies.

Enrollments. Although most kindergartens are found in systems of 2,500 enrollment and over, the increase in consolidated elementary schools is bringing the advantages of the kindergarten to many rural communities. It is estimated that kindergartens now serve approximately one-third of the potential kindergarten population. The percentages of white and black 5-year-olds attending kindergartens have been approximately equal in recent years. Because of increased recognition of the importance of kindergartens, enrollments have been increasing as more states and local districts undertake the provision of kindergarten education.

Aims of Kindergarten

For those who have not attended a nursery school, the kindergarten is an extension of home life; for others, it is a continuation of the work begun in the home and the nursery school. The general aim of the kindergarten, which is unhampered by requirements in subject matter and skills, is to give the child abundant opportunity for enriched experiences.

James Hymes, specialist in early-childhood education, has described the goals of kindergarten education:

We have kindergarten because fives are fully ready to learn, if we will but have the wisdom and the sensitivity to adjust the ways of teaching to fit them. . . .

We teach the kindergartner to live this year of his life with more joy, with more meaning, with more purpose, with more satisfaction. We have kindergartens so that the individual youngster can be more glad he is alive during this year of his life. So that he can function with more freedom and ease and zest—being true to himself, using his powers, being his best. The responsibility to

Kindergarten education stresses the development of wholesome interpersonal relations.

the individual is a moral imperative. The joy school brings to his life, the sense of fulfillment, is the prime standard by which to judge a program. This one basic goal sets the pace for the quality of the adult—child relationship, of child-to-child relationships, of space and materials and methods and content. If these do not add up to a tingling sense of vigorous living within the youngster, a fundamental point has been lost, no matter what other gains may seem to show up on any tests.

But schools—kindergartens—are not for the individual alone. Schools are society's insurance policy. We rely on them to ensure that our world will become an ever better place. As we seek to nurture the best quality of the child's living now, at this moment in his life, we must simultaneously seek to build those human qualities that make the child good for all of us to live with. . . .

The second major goal of kindergarten—from the standpoint of the rest of us, from the standpoint of society—is to have the child begin to breathe in the air of the best of human society, the healthiest form of human association that a teacher's finest dreams can devise.[8]

Program and Procedures

The kindergarten program is extremely flexible—it has no required subjects as such, but does have content. The key principle is learning by doing. In planning the curriculum, attention is given primarily to promoting physical, mental, social, and emotional growth.

Until recently, kindergarten did not provide certain formal training, such as instruction in actual reading, but it did provide experiences that helped prepare the child for the elementary grades. Such

[8]James Hymes, Jr., "The Goals of Kindergarten Education," in American Association of Elementary-Kindergarten-Nursery Educators, NEA, *Kindergarten Education*, Washington, D.C., 1968, pp. 12-13.

experiences include bringing the child into a school learning environment; enlarging his circle of friends through the addition of another adult—the teacher—and many peers; enriching his speaking vocabulary; training in speech through careful enunciation and pronunciation; creating interest in books through storytelling and looking at books; developing left-to-right eye movements through reading a story told in pictures; stimulating arithmetic concepts and simple skills through counting objects while seeing numbers and through seeing spatial relations, size, and order; and facilitating development in writing through drawing, cutting, and other forms of eye and hand coordination, including creative painting, rhythms, music, dramatic play, and science experience. The goals are implemented through a flexible schedule of activities. The kindergarten has traditionally been more concerned with the child's learning and development, including readiness for reading, than with his mastery of content. More and more, however, kindergartens have been introducing advanced content and seeking to impart some mastery of the fundamental skills, particularly reading and language development.

Other valuable experiences gained through kindergarten activity are those which strengthen social relationships, such as learning to care for possessions, developing respect for the property of others, gaining a concept of group property, taking turns and sharing, listening to the group, talking before the group, group planning, evaluating experiences, and using conventional greetings and requests. However, experimenting, problem solving, clarifying ideas, acquiring information about the environment, and participating in creative ideas are especially important.

Perhaps the most valuable gains from kindergarten experience derive from growth in self-understanding, self-realization, and self-esteem by the young learner.

Current Practices

Current kindergarten practices, supplementing those reported previously for nursery schools, are discussed here.

The general pressure through education for more intensive and earlier learning has resulted in the increasing introduction in some schools of reading and other fundamental skills at the kindergarten level.

Unfortunately, the size of the typical kindergarten is increasing as a result of a shortage of funds and an abundance of children. The typical public school kindergarten program runs one year and enrolls the student for half a day, five days per week. Except for reading and number work, the program is usually unstructured. Children are usually grouped heterogeneously and housed in an elementary school building.

A public-relations program for the kindergarten, including a brochure for parents, has been developed in many schools. The National School Public Relations Association has prepared a very helpful handbook for parents of pre-elementary children entitled *The First Big Step*. The National Education Association has produced a documentary film, *The Time of Their Lives*, to encourage public interest in the kindergarten.

A trend is to integrate the kindergarten as part of a continuous program in early-childhood education. The kindergarten is losing its status as an isolated part of the school system and is being incorporated as part of a primary unit embracing the nursery school and kindergarten, plus the lower two or three grades. There is more intervisitation between nursery school, kindergarten, and first-grade teachers.

More attention is being given to developmental tasks which are set by the maturing of the child, his creative self-motivation, and the demands of society.

Although the primary emphasis of the kindergarten is upon the basic skills, particularly reading and language development, many other subjects are introduced at a rudimentary level. Music, fine arts, and drama, for example, are usually emphasized because of their contribution to creative self-expression.

Many multisensory aids, such as phonograph records and films, help the child to understand the world of material things. They also assist the teacher in interpreting to parents and the public the role of the kindergarten. Radio and television are being used increasingly, especially in parental education.

As with the nursery school, more kindergartens are being established for exceptional children as well as for children from poor families. Greater attention is now given to psychiatric and psychological treatment of emotionally disturbed children.

Parochial and private school kindergartens continue to play an important role in early-childhood education and research.

Many state legislatures have considered early-

childhood education of sufficient importance to enact legislation providing specifically for the establishment and maintenance of kindergartens as a part of the public school system, but a third of the states still provide no state funds for the support of kindergartens. Very often minimum standards for facilities, class size, and certification of kindergarten teachers are inadequate.

Future of Kindergarten

The wide diversity of programs and practices in kindergarten education will continue. Experimentation and research will greatly improve and enrich the education of 5-year-olds. Newer instructional technology, such as television, will help to strengthen learning in the kindergarten. Emphasis upon programs for children from poor families will continue. Attention to cognitive development of all 5-year-olds will be increasingly emphasized.

The future presages a steady growth in the number of kindergartens and their enrollments. More state departments will add to their staff specialists in the supervision and guidance of local programs for early-childhood education. Permissive legislation will be replaced by the compulsory establishment of kindergartens on a voluntary attendance basis. In view of the fact that waves of retrenchment often cause public school authorities to abandon kindergartens, the interest of the young children must be safeguarded against such reverses through adequate legislation. The gradual acceptance of the kindergarten as a legitimate and permanent part of the public school system is inevitable. It will continue its vestibule function and open doors to wider horizons.

In the future, further expansion of pre-elementary education is certain. Whether this expansion will be manifested in the continued conglomeration of programs run by both public and private agencies, many of them poorly conceived and badly articulated, or whether we shall see pre-elementary education become largely an integral three- or four-year seamless unit incorporated in the public school system remains to be seen. We would prefer the latter but we expect the former. Certainly pre-elementary education, whatever its form, will reach downward to serve children at much earlier ages, even below 2 years of age. At this level the better programs will be well integrated with programs of parent education. Recent programs have demonstrated that massive intervention in the lives of young children to provide rich academic, medical, and social services can have a far more profound impact on human development than anything in later life. Some predict that this will prompt an inversion of our educational priorities in which the most money, ablest teachers, best facilities, and finest curriculums are made available to the youngest rather than the oldest students. This could indeed become a revolution in educational thought and practice. However, it will unfortunately be many years before worthwhile educational experiences become widely available at public expense to the vast majority of children.

Increased use will be made of the concept of environmental mediation through which the child's milieu during his early life is deliberately structured to offer him the most favorable climate for personal growth. By improving the young child's environment it is possible, according to the research of David Krech,[9] to increase the memory cells, the brain, and the cerebral hemispheres, thereby increasing the capacity to learn and raising the child's IQ. Another development, which Krech calls "psychoneuro-biochemeducation," involves the application of biochemistry to the stimulation of learning through the use of drugs to alleviate learning problems in early childhood. The promise of television in early-childhood education has already been mentioned. Many other exciting developments suggest that early-childhood learning will be remarkably improved in the decades ahead with profound positive impact upon the human condition generally.[10]

SUMMARY

Two major forces have prompted tremendous thrust in the development of pre-elementary education in the past decade: (1) new insights into the critical importance of early childhood in human development, and (2) rediscovery of the poor and the origin of their handicaps in early childhood. Pre-elementary education relates to the very important early years of child growth and development, covering the period from birth to entry into elementary education.

The pioneering work in pre-elementary education dates back to Froebel. Although there were a few prototypes of pre-elementary schools in early America, the movement did not really gain momentum until after World War I. It is rapidly becoming widely established.

Pre-elementary education begins with the preparation of parents for child rearing and with the care and training of the young child in the home. In many ways, these are the most important years in life because they include the period of most rapid growth. These are very formative years, and children are influenced greatly by the quality of their home life.

Day nurseries and nursery schools exist in many forms—sometimes operated privately, sometimes integrated with the public school program, sometimes associated with high schools or colleges as laboratories. However, most nursery schools are separate from other educational units and are operated by private agencies. Head Start programs have generated a strong thrust toward the development of pre-elementary programs and have demonstrated the powerful impact that such programs have upon the growth of young children, particularly those from low-income families.

Nursery schools were originated to care for children of working mothers. But today nursery school education seeks to bring organization, planning, and guidance to the growth and development of children during their formative years. These programs are very informal, providing for supervised play, storytelling and discussion, singing, dancing, and other similar activities. Nursery schools aim to smooth the young child's difficult transition from the family setting to the school environment. They provide an opportunity for children to adjust to larger groups before the more formidable tasks of kindergarten and first grade are encountered.

The kindergarten also exists in both the public and private domain. However, a larger proportion of kindergartens than nursery schools are affiliated with public school systems. Nevertheless, large numbers of young children, particularly those in small school systems, are still denied kindergarten experience. The kindergarten seeks to guide the mental, social, emotional, and physical development of the child. Thus his experience with people and with the world is broadened so that more effective learning can take place in later years.

[9] David Krech, "Psychoneurobiochemeducation," *Phi Delta Kappan*, vol. 50, pp. 370-373, March, 1969.

[10] For an interesting discussion of some of these developments, see Harold G. Shane, "The Renaissance of Early Childhood Education," *Phi Delta Kappan*, vol. 50, pp. 369, 412-413, March, 1969.

Suggested Activities

1. *Visit a private nursery school for children from well-to-do families and a Head Start program for children from low-income families and prepare a report comparing and contrasting the two programs.*
2. *Prepare a case study of a child under 6 years of age whom you know well.*
3. *Prepare a report describing the kind of home environment that is ideal for early-childhood development.*
4. *Visit a pre-elementary program for children from low-income families and prepare a report on the desirable qualities of teachers for such work.*
5. *Prepare a report, based on your reading, predicting the nature of pre-elementary education a decade or so hence.*
6. *Discuss the selection of books, toys, and games for pre-elementary children.*
7. *Prepare a critical analysis of the Montessorian method of teaching in nursery schools and kindergartens.*
8. *Outline an ideal program of professional preparation for teachers at the pre-elementary level.*
9. *Study Montessori's and Piaget's theories of early-childhood education and prepare a report comparing and contrasting them.*
10. *Read as much as you can about Head Start programs and prepare your own critical evaluation of them.*

Bibliography

Bereiter, Carl, and Siegfried Engelmann: *Teaching Disadvantaged Children in the Preschool*, Prentice-Hall, Inc., Englewood Cliffs, N.J., 1966. An explanation of theory and practice of unorthodox approach to early-childhood education, which emphasizes academic learning through direct verbal instruction.

Dowley, Edith M.: "Early Childhood Education," in Robert L. Ebel (ed.), *Encyclopedia of Educational Research*, 4th ed., The Macmillan Co. of Canada, Limited, Toronto, 1969,

pp. 316–330. A review of research related to early-childhood education.

Frost, Joe L. (ed.): *Early Childhood Education Rediscovered: Readings*, Holt, Rinehart and Winston, Inc., New York, 1969. Short essays and statements by scholars in the field of early-childhood education.

Hess, Robert D., and Roberta Meyer Bear (eds.): *Early Education: Current Theory, Research, and Action*, Aldine Publishing Company, Chicago, 1968. A collection of major statements about central issues in early education by leaders in the field.

Hymes, James L., Jr.: *Teaching the Child Under Six*, Charles E. Merrill Books, Inc., Columbus, Ohio, 1968. A practical treatment of teaching the preschool child, focusing on specific teaching problems.

Leeper, Sara Hammond, et al.: *Good Schools for Young Children*, 2d ed., The Macmillan Company, New York, 1968. An interdisciplinary description of the interrelationships of the cultural setting, knowledge about children, goals, and desirable practices.

Montessori, Maria: *The Absorbent Mind*, Holt, Rinehart and Winston, Inc., New York, 1969. A translation of 1949 lectures on early childhood—teaching theory and ideology.

National Education Association: *Kindergarten Education*, Washington, D.C., 1968. A discussion of the kindergarten child, goals of kindergartens, readiness for kindergarten, and typical programs.

National School Public Relations Association: *Preschool Breakthrough: What Works in Early Childhood Education*, National Education Association, Washington, D.C., 1970. A description of successful early-childhood education programs and an analysis of the controversies involved.

Pines, Maya: *Revolution in Learning: The Years from Birth to Six*, Harper & Row, Publishers, Incorporated, New York, 1967. Observations and unfavorable criticisms of preschool and early-childhood programs.

Pitcher, Evelyn Goodenough, et al.: *Helping Young Children Learn*, Charles E. Merrill Company, New York, 1966. Methods and procedures for enriching the environment to stimulate learning for the young child; a listing of sources for teaching materials.

Weber, Lillian: *The English Infant School and Informal Education*, Prentice-Hall, Inc., Englewood Cliffs, N.J., 1971. Descriptions of how English educators have reformulated educational practice through strengthening the human dimension of learning.

Wills, Clarice Dechent, and Lucille Lindberg: *Kindergarten for Today's Children*, Follett Publishing Company, Chicago, 1967. A treatment of the modern kindergarten program with important information about its growth here and abroad.

Chapter 7   Elementary Education

ORIENTATION

A story is told of Col. Francis Parker, a pioneering educator in elementary education, who came to Quincy, Massachusetts, as superintendent of schools. When asked by many of his teachers to explain his theory about the place of the individual pupil in education, Parker called a faculty meeting. When the teachers were assembled, Parker entered the room with a little elementary school pupil at his side, whom he seated at the front of the room. He then gave the shortest and most insightful address in the annals of education: "My fellow teachers, you ask me to tell you why we are making so many changes in our schools." Placing his hands on the pupil's shoulders he said, "Here is your answer." He then went out, leaving them to wonder and think.

A million teachers today are wondering and thinking about educational freedom for each of the thirty million pupils in the elementary schools of our nation. In 1928 Harold Rugg and Ann Schumaker wrote in their pioneering book *The Child-centered School:*

What is this new freedom based upon? Nothing less than the reorientation of the entire school around the child. These schools are child-centered institutions in contrast to teacher-centered and principal-centered schools of the conventional order. They believe that the ability to govern one's self grows only through the practice of self-government.[1]

The *National Elementary Principal,* in an editorial by Dorothy Neubauer, former editor, gave the following warning:

[1] Harold Rugg and Ann Schumaker, *The Child-centered School,* World Book Company, Yonkers, N.Y., 1928, p. 56.

Elementary education stresses the development of basic skills.

The school has a heartening potential for humanizing, and a frightening potential for dehumanizing. It is staffed with people who, by their behavior, determine in large measure whether the school will have a humanizing or a dehumanizing effect on children.[2]

In his national survey report, *Crisis in the Classroom,* and in syndicated excerpts such as "Murder in the Classroom," Charles E. Silberman points out the need for humanization:

If the United States is to become a truly just and humane society, the schools will have to do an incomparably better job than they are now doing of educating youngsters from minority-group and lower-class homes. . . . The failures of the urban and rural slum schools are in large part an exaggerated version of the failures of American schools as a whole—a failure in Comenius' phrase, to educate all men to full humanity. . . . The remedy for the defects of slum schools is the remedy for the defects of all schools: namely, to transform them into free, open, humane and joyous institutions.[3]

Many of the humanized schools incorporate ideas of Dewey, Kilpatrick, and Piaget, and adapt methods from Montessori and the British Infant School. The American Montessori Society and many other organizations are promoting a growing national movement of teachers and parents to forge the new philosophy and strategy that often result in the "humanized elementary school" or "the informal classroom." Grants have been made by the Ford Foundation to help American schools adapt for their own use those human and informal approaches of British primary schools that are applicable here.

The elementary schools have been and are the

[2] Dorothy Neubauer, Editorial, *National Elementary Principal,* vol. 49, pp. 2–3, May, 1970. Copyright 1970, National Association of Elementary School Principals, National Education Association. All rights reserved.
[3] Charles E. Silberman, *Crisis in the Classroom,* Random House, New York, 1970, pp. 54, 62.

experimental seed plots for many modern theories of learning and practices in teaching. For example, Individually Prescribed Instruction (IPI) was initially launched in elementary schools. There is much hope for reform in the elementary school. John Goodlad, a specialist in elementary education, sees a "humanistic curriculum" as one of the major developments of the 1970s. There is much stress today on behavioral objectives and outcomes. More alternatives are provided elementary teachers today, for, as Harold Rugg once stated, "In order to free the child it is necessary first to free the teacher."

In order to appreciate and evaluate some of the current trends in elementary education, it is necessary to look at the foundations and the historical evolution of continuing change.

FOUNDATIONS

Establishment of Public Elementary Education

Beginnings of Elementary Education. In colonial America elementary schools were organized much later than the universities. An exception occurred in New York State, where, under Dutch rule, a free, tax-supported elementary school was established in Fort Amsterdam in 1633. When New Netherlands became New York, the resultant change in policy retarded the development of public elementary education in New York State.

Colonial New England and especially Massachusetts took the first steps toward the permanent establishment of schools for the common people. Some time after the settling of Massachusetts, the law of 1642 was passed. It gave to town officials the "power to take account from time to time of their parents and masters and of their children, especially of their ability to read and understand the principles of religion and the capital laws of the country, and to impose fines on all those who refuse to render such accounts to them when required." This was followed by the "Old Deluder Act" of 1647, which required the various towns to establish and maintain schools and even imposed a fine of £5 for failure to do so. Numerous laws were passed in the colonies in regard to free education. But permissive rather than mandatory legislation was the usual type of school regulation. Thus the colonists permitted free public education in theory, but in practice supported few free schools.

Dame Schools. Elementary education in the eighteenth century was entrusted to reading and writing schools. These were followed by "dame schools," the first record of which dates from 1651, in New Haven, Connecticut. Usually a woman taught her own children and others from the neighborhood in her home between household tasks. These dame schools were primarily for little children; when older pupils came to school in the winter, a man teacher was usually employed. The dame schools were followed by primary schools, which became the nonsectarian forerunners of today's elementary schools.

Nonsectarian Schools. Public education struggled to become nonsectarian. Throughout the colonial period, elementary education had a strong religious tone. Moral and religious truths were emphasized constantly. The school was often made the servant of the church, and numerous religious denominations established their own schools. The pupils were usually taught reading, writing, arithmetic, singing of hymns, prayers, and catechism. Often parochial schools were granted aid from state funds. Gradually the pendulum swung from sectarianism to secularism. The first state to adopt a constitutional provision prohibiting sectarian instruction in public schools was New Hampshire in 1792. Today it is unconstitutional to read the Bible, conduct prescribed prayers, or give sectarian instruction in publicly supported schools.

Elementary Schools Free and Open to All. Elementary education in America encountered many obstacles, including the social beliefs and prejudices that the colonists carried with them from the old country. Prevailing ideas in England, Germany, France, and other countries influenced the New World. The concept of social classes or castes extant in England during the colonial period made education a matter of private rather than state support. Persons of wealth sent their children to privately supported schools or engaged tutors to teach them at home. For those unable to do this, pauper schools were established. But because of the stigma attached to being a pauper, these schools were often not patronized by them.

The struggle to make schools free to everyone and the financial responsibility of all was one of the most bitterly contested conflicts in our history.

The Development of Elementary Education

1633	*Elementary school established by the Dutch in New York*
1642	*Earliest colonial educational law passed in Massachusetts*
1647	*"Old Deluder Act" passed by Massachusetts, requiring towns to establish and maintain schools*
1651	*Existence of dame school recorded in New Haven*
1789	*Massachusetts school law enacted, requiring a school in every community*
1834	*Free elementary education first adopted by Pennsylvania*
1837	*Calvin E. Stowe's Report on Elementary Education in Europe published*
1837	*"Common-school revival" started by Horace Mann*
1852	*First compulsory law for part-time school attendance passed by Massachusetts*
1890	*First full-time compulsory school attendance law passed in Connecticut*
1893	*Six-six plan of school organization recommended by the Committee of Ten*
1895	*Report of NEA Committee of Fifteen on Elementary Education presented*
1896	*Experimental school established at the University of Chicago by John Dewey*
1918	*Compulsory education made effective in all states*
1948	*Basic policy for elementary education presented in Education for All American Children*
1953	*Report of Mid-century Committee on Outcomes in Elementary Education published by Russell Sage Foundation*
1965	*Elementary and Secondary Education Act passed by Congress, directed mostly toward students from low-income families*
1968	*Five years of college work required for a permanent elementary school teaching certificate in many states*
1968	*Follow Through Project expanded nationally and extended upward into the early elementary grades*
1969	*Grants made by Ford Foundation to help American schools adapt applicable aspects of British primary education*
1970	*Department of Elementary School Principals (founded in 1921) reorganized as National Association of Elementary School Principals*
1970	*Right to Read, a nationwide program with accent on elementary schools, launched by former U.S. Commissioner James E. Allen, Jr.*
1970	*Elementary and Secondary Education Act, largest of all federal grants to education, extended by Congress for three-year period*
1971	*Daily television reading series premiered by Children's Television Workshop as "The Electric Company"*
1972	*Fewer enrollments recorded in elementary schools, reflecting decline in birth rates since 1961*

The passions ran high. Opponents held that it was "heresy to partially confiscate one man's property to educate another man's child." Some objected to public schools because they were secular. Some opposed state control of education. Some thought it improper for the children of well-to-do families to attend the same school as children from ordinary homes. Others preferred distinctions based on religion, race, or sex. A few simply did not believe in education at all. Small wonder that opposition existed: at no time or place in history was there a precedent for the concept of free, universal education.

But the supporters of the public school movement were men of determination and vision. They argued that the well-being and vitality of the nation depended upon the knowledge of all men, that universal suffrage could not succeed without universal education, and that public wealth must be used to save underprivileged children from ignorance and poverty. Social reformers joined the cause, hoping that free education for all in the same schools would spare the new nation from the rigid class system typical of the Old World, from which many emigrants had sought escape in America. The crusade was won in Massachusetts in 1837 under the leadership of Horace Mann, who insisted that "the general intelligence which they [the public schools] are capable of diffusing, and which can be imparted by no other human instrumentality, is indispensable to the continuance of a republican government." In 1834, Pennsylvania, under the leadership of Thaddeus Stevens, adopted a state program of free schools. Other states followed this example—some of them not until the twentieth century—and eventually elementary education, and later secondary education, was transformed from a private luxury into a public necessity.

Elementary Education Compulsory. Making elementary education compulsory involved another struggle. A hundred years ago attendance was generally optional. The histories of the colonies reveal the gradual adoption of the principle of compulsory elementary education, but records are strangely silent about the degree of its enforcement. One may look to Massachusetts for the contribution of the law and to Connecticut for its administration and methods of enforcement. The first state compulsory school-attendance law was adopted in Massachusetts as late as 1852; this legislation for part-time compulsory attendance was followed in 1890 by Connecticut's full-time requirement. Compulsory schooling was bitterly opposed by many people who argued that it deprived the parents of their inalienable rights, that it was not necessary in order to secure attendance, that it was an uncalled-for assumption of powers by state governments, that it was inimical to the spirit of free democratic institutions, and that it was an obstacle in the employment of child labor.

The majority of states now demand that every normal child attend the elementary school for at least eight months annually between the ages of 7 and 16, or until he has completed the eighth grade. Several states have enacted laws raising the compulsory school age to 18.

Many Foreign Influences on Elementary Education. Compulsory education was one of several ideas that were undoubtedly borrowed from other lands, particularly Prussia. In Chapter 17, reference is made to the influence of educational pioneers from abroad. Among the overseas innovators who especially affected American elementary education in theory and practice were Johann Amos Comenius, Jean Jacques Rousseau, Johann Pestalozzi, and Johann Herbart.

For several years elementary education abroad was studied intensively for suggestions that could be adopted by, or adapted to, the American primary school. Victor Cousin's *Report on the State of Public Instruction in Prussia*, which appeared first in French and in about 1835 in English, was widely read in America. Calvin E. Stowe exercised a tremendous influence upon American education through his *Report on Elementary Education in Europe* (1837), which was studied by many state legislators. Later, Horace Mann published his famous *Seventh Annual Report* (see Chapter 3). Henry Barnard's *National Education in Europe* (1854) also left its imprint on American elementary education.

American Pioneers in Elementary Education

Although American education has been influenced from abroad, the American elementary school—indeed, our entire educational system—is distinctly American. It had no precedent anywhere in the world. Its singular character has been shaped largely by ideas, visions, aspirations, and values unique to America.

Among the American historical leaders who enhanced elementary education were Horace Mann, Henry Barnard, Colonel Francis Parker, John Dewey, and William Heard Kilpatrick.

Horace Mann (1796-1859). Known as the "father of the common schools," Horace Mann, during his twelve years as the secretary of the State Board of Education in Massachusetts, started the common-school revival. Armed with no legal authority, Mann, by dint of persuasion, helped to improve the housing of pupils and the professional preparation of teachers in Massachusetts. He lengthened the elementary school term and won an increased measure of popular and financial support for the schools and teachers. In his twelve annual reports, published at the end of each year of his secretaryship, and in his *Common School Journal,* which he started in 1838, Mann covered almost every aspect of education. Much of this material is up-to-date even today. Through his efforts the first normal school was established at Lexington, Massachusetts, in 1839. His indefatigability extended his influence beyond Massachusetts to the nation and, through his friend Sarmiento, to the public schools in Chile and Argentina.

Henry Barnard (1811-1900). Henry Barnard occupied a place similar to that of Horace Mann in Massachusetts by serving as state commissioner of education in Connecticut from 1838 to 1842 and in Rhode Island from 1843 to 1849. After having absorbed Pestalozzi's ideas in Europe, Barnard promoted these ideas in America. His book *Pestalozzi and Pestalozzianism* is one of the outstanding books in English on the subject. Barnard edited the *American Journal of Education,* which treated almost every aspect of education here and abroad. He established the first teachers institute in 1839 and improved the training of elementary teachers. As the first United States Commissioner of Education, Barnard helped to raise the status of education, particularly in elementary schools.

Colonel Francis Parker (1837-1902). Among the American educational pioneers who enriched the elementary curriculum was Francis Parker, who became the leader of the progressive movement.

He was elected superintendent of schools at Quincy, Massachusetts. There he became famous as a leader of the Quincy movement, which embodied some of Froebel's principles in making the school less artificial and conventional. Children were taken outdoors for lessons in science and geography, and teachers were given much freedom and expert supervision. His greatest work was done as principal of the Cook County Normal School at Chicago and later as principal of the Chicago Institute, afterward the School of Education of the University of Chicago. Parker was a lover of children, and he had the rare insight to see teaching problems from the standpoint of the child.

John Dewey (1859-1952). The leading American educational philosopher and molder of the policies of the elementary school was John Dewey. In 1896 Dewey established an experimental school at the University of Chicago where he tried out some of his educational plans. In 1904 he joined the faculty of Teachers College, Columbia University, where he taught and influenced thousands of teachers. His book *School and Society,* published in 1899, affected markedly the function of the school in society. Among his other publications, some of which have been translated into a dozen languages, were *Interest and Effort, Democracy and Education, How We Think, Quest for Certainty, Experience and Education,* and *Logic: The Theory of Inquiry.* It is said that the contributions made by most of his books are in inverse proportion to their size; the small ones, such as *School and Society,* had a greater influence than his huge volume, *Quest for Certainty.* He was known around the world.

The Gary public school system, which modified its program in 1941, and other systems which made innovations in elementary school organization, such as the Winnetka system, were inspired by John Dewey. His emphasis upon doing and living was basic in the elementary school program. The following quotation is a brief sample of his philosophy:

I believe that education, therefore, is a process of living and not a preparation for future living.

I believe that the school must represent life—life as real and vital to the child as that which he carries on in the home, in the neighborhood, or on the playground. . . .

I believe that as such simplified social life, the school life should grow gradually out of the home life; that it should take up and continue the activities with which the child is already familiar in the home. . . .

I believe finally, that education must be conceived as a continuing reconstruction of experience; that the process and goal of education are one and the same thing. . . .

I believe that education is the fundamental method of social progress and reform. . . .

I believe that every teacher should realize the dignity of his calling; that he is a social servant set apart for the maintenance of proper social order and the securing of the right social growth.[4]

Dewey's philosophy was not so simple that it can be summarized adequately by one quotation or in one chapter. In America, the John Dewey Society publishes a yearbook on various aspects of his pragmatic philosophy and of progressive education. Some of Dewey's ideas have been misinterpreted and misapplied. Nevertheless, the progressive idealism of John Dewey and his followers has had a very significant and constructive influence upon all learning levels, especially the elementary school.

William Heard Kilpatrick (1871–1965). As a professor of education for many years at Columbia University, and following his retirement in 1937, Kilpatrick indoctrinated thousands of elementary and secondary school teachers who flocked into his classes, attended his lectures, or read his books. Among his publications are *The Project Method, Foundations of Method,* and *Source Book of Philosophy.* Kilpatrick stimulated the emphasis upon life activities for children and defined learning as living.

Other Leaders. Numerous leaders, including traditionalists like William Chandler Bagley and psychologists like Edward L. Thorndike, have made substantial contributions to elementary education. Among the superintendents of schools who have instituted drastic reforms in elementary education are W. T. Harris, of St. Louis, who led the revolt against rigid gradations of pupils and inflexible promotions; Edward A. Sheldon, who started the Oswego movement for improving elementary curriculums and methods in Oswego, New York; and Carleton Washburne, formerly of Winnetka, Illinois, who introduced the so-called "Winnetka plan" for meeting individual differences in the elementary school.

Among contemporary leaders in elementary education are John Goodlad, director of the famous University Elementary School at UCLA and professor of education at that university. Goodlad's pioneering work with the nongraded organization in his school and his writing, teaching, and speaking on elementary school organization, curriculum, and method are widely respected. Professors Harold Shane of Indiana University, Robert Anderson of Harvard University, Henry Otto of the University of Texas, and Harold McNally of the University of Wisconsin in Milwaukee have also done much to shape current thought and practice in elementary education.

Present Status

Articulation with Pre-elementary Education. The modern elementary school is closely joined to pre-elementary work, particularly for children who enter the first grade with some school experience in the nursery school, kindergarten, or both. Although an increasing number of students have this orientation, the first school contact for many children comes in the first grade. Many children presently benefiting from Head Start programs lose much of the advantage gained there after a few years in primary grades that are traditional in organization and unresponsive to the particular needs of children from slum neighborhoods. Hence, the Follow Through Project, initiated experimentally in 1967, now extends services into early elementary education.

The experiences in the nursery school and kindergarten should be vitally related to the first year of the primary school, and vice versa. The so-called primary unit, an organization embracing kindergarten through grade 2 or 3, has provided a setting in which beginning elementary school experiences may be adjusted so as to remove or to reduce failure.

Scope of Elementary Education. Elementary education is difficult to define because of the extreme variety of practices in its organization, administration, and curriculums. In terms of children's ages, it is the educational institution for pupils from ap-

[4]John Dewey, "My Pedagogic Creed," *The School Journal,* vol. 54, pp. 77–80, Jan. 16, 1897.

proximately 6 to 12 or 14 years of age. In terms of grades, elementary education generally includes grades 1 to 6. In many smaller districts, however, it generally embraces grades 1 to 8, as indicated in Figure 7-1.

The common subdivisions of the elementary school are usually grouped as follows: primary, grades 1 to 3; intermediate, grades 4 to 6; and upper, grades 7 and 8. Naturally there is overlapping between divisions and organization units. The kindergarten may be included in the primary level, whereas the junior high school is usually considered a part of secondary education.

These three major areas should not be construed as disparate units, but rather as components of an organized whole, since child growth and development are continuous rather than periodic.

Some schools obliterate grade lines and organize the six or seven years as a unit, the latter embracing the kindergarten, as indicated in the last column of Figure 7-1.

As will be noted later, a number of school districts are organizing middle schools, or intermediate schools, as they are sometimes called. Middle schools may comprise grades 7 and 8; grades 6 to 8, or grades 5 to 8. In many cases the middle school is thought of as something "in the middle," between the elementary school and the secondary school and organizationally apart from both.

Elementary School Enrollments. A significant phenomenon in American education has been the

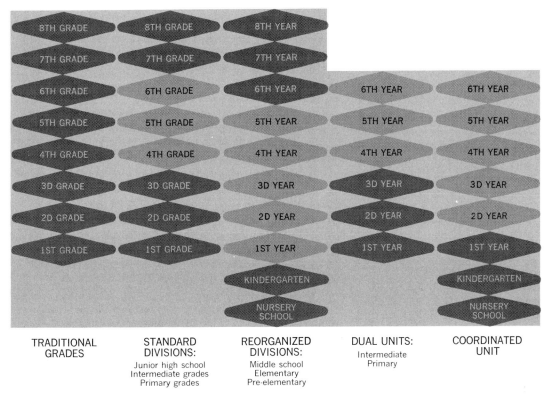

| TRADITIONAL GRADES | STANDARD DIVISIONS: Junior high school Intermediate grades Primary grades | REORGANIZED DIVISIONS: Middle school Elementary Pre-elementary | DUAL UNITS: Intermediate Primary | COORDINATED UNIT |

FIGURE 7-1 Scope and organization of elementary education. In the first column on the left, elementary education is shown to consist of eight compartments called grades, with rigid promotion practices. In the next pattern, the number of divisions is reduced to three—primary, intermediate, and upper grades—with greater articulation and flexibility. In the middle column, kindergarten and nursery school have been added and combined into a pre-elementary unit; the upper three years have been combined into a middle-school unit, which many communities no longer regard as elementary education. In the second column from the right, the seventh and eighth grades are assigned to secondary education, and the two remaining components become the upper and lower elementary school. In the pattern at right, there is one continuous six-year unit—perhaps ungraded—with kindergarten and perhaps nursery school added.

Immediate Objectives

Although the various parts of the entire American school system contribute markedly to the general objectives of education, each has its unique role to play in the drama of education. These special functions are the immediate objectives or directives.

Commitments of the Elementary School. An excellent publication by the Association for Supervision and Curriculum Development, entitled *The Elementary School We Need,* summarizes the major commitments of the modern elementary school:

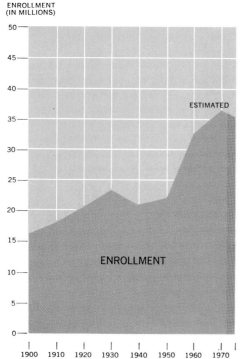

FIGURE 7-2 *Total combined enrollment in public and private elementary schools. (U.S. Office of Education,* Digest of Educational Statistics.)

marked increase during the 1950s and 1960s in the number of pupils enrolled in both public and private elementary schools, as shown in Figure 7-2. The number of births feeding our school system is approaching a fairly stable figure of four million per year. It is estimated that public and private elementary school enrollments (kindergarten to grade 8) in 1980 will equal those of 1970. At present about 99 percent of children of elementary school age are attending school. About one in seven is enrolled in a private or parochial school.

PURPOSES

Elementary education generally is concentrated upon developing in the child a command of the fundamental processes or tools of learning and a general understanding of the world he lives in. Although it accents the intellectual, it is broader than this, giving attention also to the development of desirable attitudes and systems of values.

1 Health and physical development of children. *Elementary schools seek not only to maintain but also to improve the health status of children. Through planned programs of physical education, health education, and safety education, as well as through physical examinations, elementary schools demonstrate a major concern for health and physical development. The willingness of elementary schools to adapt their programs to provide for the physical needs of children has made it possible for many pupils who have serious physical handicaps to enter the regular school program.*

2 Mental health and personality development of children. *The importance of helping children to achieve an adequate concept of self dominates the activities of many elementary schools. There is concern for providing opportunities for children to experience success and a sense of achievement in what they do. Efforts to provide a setting which minimizes tension for children characterize much of the teaching in the elementary school. Teachers are aware of the needs of children to be secure and to feel that they belong as worthy human beings.*

3 Development of understanding of the social and scientific worlds. *The importance of helping children to understand their environment has led to reorganization of content materials. There is a conscious effort in many elementary schools to bring the immediate world of children into a perspective that affords them a better understanding of the remote and abstract. Fundamental skills and knowledge are presented in a more functional setting in order that these concepts may lead to further learning and more effective living in the world of today.*

4 Development of the skills of effective participation in a democratic society. *The attention that many elementary schools direct to the early participation of children in group living has altered the content of instructional activities as well as the ways in which they are organized. In seeking to help children develop responsibility, self-direction, and effective communication with others, elementary schools provide a climate as well as varied opportunities for learning and practicing the responsibilities and the skills of living in a democratic society.*

5 Development of the values consistent with democratic living. *Closely related to the skills for participating in*

a democratic society are the values implied in maintaining such a society. Some of these values are honesty, respect for individual personality, personal and social responsibilities, freedom of thought and of speech, and the learning and use of methods of intelligence. Elementary schools seek to help children develop a sense of commitment to these values. Social issues and concerns are a part of these classroom experiences, and there is an emphasis on intrinsic motivation to help children aspire to worthy human roles.

6 *Creative activity. In seeking to stimulate creativity, many elementary schools strive to achieve a program that is less rigid and sterile than the programs of some schools in past decades. Creativity is perceived as an aspect of behavior that permeates all areas of the curriculum and is a characteristic of all children. Creative classrooms are stimulating and supportive places in which varied approaches are used to solve problems, to express ideas, and to communicate with others.*[5]

TYPES

It is impossible to group all elementary schools into mutually exclusive categories, for there is overlapping even within major types. Some schools defy classifications or labels. Among the major types are those classified according to (1) size, as one or two teachers, and location, as rural or urban; (2) sources of financial support, as public or private; (3) internal organization, as graded or ungraded; and (4) special purposes, as schools for atypical children—the crippled, for example. A description of these types follows.

Size and Location of Schools

The simplest form of elementary organization is the small school—the one-teacher or one-room school. Here all six, seven, or eight grades are seated in one room, and a teacher may have as many as thirty classes a day, depending upon the number of pupils, their placement in grades, the curriculum, and the flexibility of administration.

The medium-sized elementary schools are found in the villages and the small cities. Usually one teacher is assigned to each grade or class, and a principal serves as the head of the building or system.

The large schools are located in the larger population centers. Two or more teachers may be

[5]Adapted from George Manolakes, *The Elementary School We Need*, Association for Supervision and Curriculum Development, National Education Association, Washington, D.C., 1965, pp. 20–21. Copyright 1965, Association for Supervision and Curriculum Development.

assigned to a grade, or a departmental organization may be utilized. The median elementary school has an enrollment of slightly over five hundred. The size of the elementary school tends to increase with the size of the community.

One type of elementary institution based primarily on its location is the neighborhood school. It is intended to serve the children of the immediate small community. This elementary school, consisting often of only the lower primary grades, has helped to eliminate or reduce long-distance travel for younger children. Recently it has been brought into the political and judicial limelight because of issues in desegregation. The neighborhood school is not an effective means for promoting integration, and it is often invoked to avoid desegregation. *De facto* segregation—that caused by residence patterns—often leads to predominantly white schools in some suburbs, and a continuation of mostly black schools in certain ghetto areas. Related to the plans for desegregating neighborhood schools is the plan to bus or cross-bus pupils to secure better racial balance. Several neighborhood schools have parent councils and advisory committees to help solve problems and innovate constructive ideas. Unfortunately, the educational possibilities of neighborhood schools are often subordinated to emotionalism and racial conflicts. The issue of desegregation is further discussed in Chapter 1.

Sources of Support and Control

The elementary schools may also be grouped according to the main sources of their financial support or control, namely, public or nonpublic, the latter embracing both parochial and other private schools.

Public Elementary Schools. The elementary schools supported by public taxation are by far in the majority and enroll approximately 85 percent of all the pupils who attend the elementary grades. These form the backbone of American public education.

Nonpublic Elementary Schools. Five million (about 15 percent of all American elementary pupils) attend private elementary schools—both parochial and nonparochial. Many of these schools are closing because of fiscal problems. Private schools are discussed at greater length in Chapters 2, 5, and 7.

Internal Organization of Schools

There are two major dimensions of school organization—vertical and horizontal. Vertical organization relates to the movement of students in time through the levels of the educational system. Graded, multigraded, and nongraded classrooms are systems of vertical organization. Horizontal organization relates to the grouping of students at the same educational levels within class groups and their assignment to teachers. Team teaching, self-contained classrooms, departmentalized classrooms, and ability groupings are some of the systems of horizontal grouping.

Vertical Organization. The traditional pattern of vertical organization has been the graded school. Five-year-olds are accepted in kindergarten and under normal circumstances are moved along one grade each year. Teachers and textbooks are assigned by grades and are known as "third-grade teachers" or "fifth-grade geographies." A specific body of subject matter is assigned each grade level. Children who fail to meet the standards are sometimes retained for one or more years.

The graded school's major disadvantage is its unrealistic assumption that all children should cover the same material at the same rate. At the end of the year, the school is forced to decide whether a slow learner will repeat all or none of the same grade, even though his progress may have been satisfactory in part of the curriculum. Retardation often results in poorer performance during the pupil's second year in the grade, in his resignation to failure, and in problems of social and physical adjustment because he is older than the other children in his grade. More homogeneous classes do not result, and teachers are not freed from the inescapable task of providing for student differences, even though the graded school sometimes creates that illusion for unperceptive teachers.

Growing dissatisfaction with the graded school has led several school districts to modify or depart from graded organization. The best known of the earlier forerunners in this direction were the St. Louis, Pueblo, Dalton, Cambridge, and Winnetka plans, named after their cities of origin, which attempted in one way or another to permit students to progress through the school at their own rates.

Although all of them have been discontinued or greatly modified, they were the early prototypes of the present broad-scale attack on the lockstep nature of the graded school.

Some schools have adopted multigraded organizations in which grade designations are retained but two or more grades are combined in the same classroom. A child works at several grade levels simultaneously—perhaps studying fifth-grade reading, sixth-grade science, and fourth-grade arithmetic. Some schools provide for an exchange of pupils from different grades or classrooms for part of the school day so that they can study with other children at similar levels of achievement.

The most common contemporary departure in vertical organization is the nongraded, or ungraded, system, in which grade lines are eliminated completely. Nongraded schools have appeared with increasing frequency, largely since 1954. Many of the school systems with enrollments over 100,000 are using nongraded sequences in one or more of their schools. Nongraded plans exist most commonly at the lower age levels; that is, children between the kindergarten and fourth grade are grouped in the primary unit. However, some districts have developed an entire elementary school program, and in some cases even middle school programs, along the nongraded plan.

In most nongraded schools the same educational experiences are undertaken by all, but at different rates of speed. The units are subdivided to permit the children to move among the divisions, at intervals of a few weeks, to join others at their same level of achievement. Grouping is usually determined on the basis of reading achievement. Sometimes the same teacher stays with the group for three years. The nongraded school—or, as it is sometimes called, the "continuous-progress plan"—attempts to practice the philosophy that the school organization should adapt to the child rather than the child to the organization. It has brought corresponding changes in curriculum organization, reporting of pupil progress, teacher development, and other aspects of teaching practice.

Horizontal Organization. A basic problem in any system of horizontal grouping is class size. The median size of elementary classes, about 27 students, has remained fairly constant in recent years. The number tends to be smaller in the primary than in the middle and upper grades and smaller in small districts than in large ones. A poll of teachers' opinions conducted by the NEA revealed that most teachers regard an elementary class size of twenty to twenty-five as ideal. To reduce all elementary classes to this size would require the expenditure of billions of dollars for new classrooms and for teachers' salaries and other services. Many innovations have been undertaken in the direction of more flexibility in class size. The use of team teaching, differentiated staffing, and electronic and mechanical devices has resulted in classes of 100 or more, at times, and in much smaller groups, at other times, for different learning experiences.

The self-contained classroom and departmentalization are alternative horizontal organizations. In the self-contained unit, a single teacher meets with a single class for the entire school day and has complete and sole responsibility for its instruction. The departmentalized class is instructed by more than one teacher, often by a different teacher for each subject. Platoon organization is a pattern of partial departmentalization in which the students move, but not always with the same group, from teacher to teacher for different learning activities. Departmentalization is uncommon in the primary grades, somewhat more common in the middle grades, and quite common in the upper elementary school grades and in high school. Although departmentalization rose in popularity between 1900 and 1925, it later fell into disrepute in elementary schools and was gradually replaced by self-contained classes. The number of self-contained classrooms in elementary schools was reduced by more than half during the decade 1958–1968, indicating a clear trend toward departmentalization in elementary schools. However, in the vast majority of elementary classrooms, departmentalization is only partial—that is, one teacher retains a major share of identification with a particular class. Departmentalization is less common in smaller schools than in large ones, probably because it is less feasible when enrollments are small.

The self-contained classroom enables the teacher, who is with the students for the entire school day, to establish better understanding and rapport with them. It also facilitates integration of learning among the various subject fields. Departmentalization requires teacher specialization in a single subject or a few subjects. The growing use of differentiated staffing has, of course, increased the frequency of teacher specialization. Research

into the relative advantages of these arrangements has so far been inconclusive.

Another choice in horizontal organization lies between heterogeneous and homogeneous grouping. In heterogeneous classes students are grouped by age or grade without regard for ability or achievement. Schemes of homogeneous grouping, usually referred to as "ability grouping," seek to reduce the range of abilities in a classroom by sorting the pupils into classes on the basis of their intellectual capacity or their academic achievement. In one type of homogeneous grouping, sometimes referred to as a "multiple-track plan," the pupils are arranged according to ability. The curriculum is held constant for all groups, but the time to complete it varies according to the student's speed of achievement. Thus bright students might complete the elementary program in five years, while slower learners might take eight. Like departmentalization, ability grouping was once common in elementary schools, then waned in popularity, but has been revived since 1954 in a growing number of school systems.

Its advocates claim that it enables the schools to adapt the content and methods of instruction to students of different levels of ability. Teaching is supposedly simplified and improved when the range of ability in a single class is reduced. Brighter students, it is claimed, can learn more, progress more rapidly, or both, when instruction can be attuned to their superior ability. Homogeneous grouping has been criticized on the grounds that it is to some degree an illusion, since students grouped on the basis of ability may be quite different with respect to achievement, or vice versa. Moreover, students who are grouped according to their ability or achievement in reading may vary with respect to ability or achievement in other subjects. Several studies have shown that regardless of the basis of grouping, the reduction in the range of ability is too small to permit the teacher to ignore the individual differences which remain. It is also argued that such grouping encourages intellectual snobbery among the bright students and resignation to mediocrity among the less able. Research evidence, limited largely to comparisons of academic achievement, has failed so far to establish the superiority of one system over the other.

Another pattern of organization that has re-

Other Special Types of Organization

ceived wide attention recently is the "dual progress plan."[6] It is a semidepartmental scheme in which elementary school children are grouped according to ability for half the day to study the "cultural imperatives"—speech, vocabulary, spelling, grammar, reading, writing, literature, and social studies. The remainder of the day is spent in an ungraded vertical system studying the "cultural electives"—mathematics, science, art, music, and foreign languages. In essence it is an effort to combine the advantages of both departmentalized and self-contained classes, and of both graded and ungraded organization, with ability grouping.

Individually Prescribed Instruction and other types of programmed instruction, described in Chapter 14, will tend to reduce some of the traditional dilemmas in the grouping of students for instruction. Programmed instruction permits the prescription of instructional tasks individually tailored to the abilities and needs of each student, thus accommodating a wide range of individual differences in abilities in the heterogeneous classroom. Widespread use of individually prescribed instructional systems and differentiated staffing will eventually render obsolete the debate over homogeneous versus heterogeneous grouping when the former becomes unnecessary.

So far research has failed to demonstrate the superiority of one pattern of grouping over another, even though one type may have evident face validity.

Hence, the decision to organize schools in one manner or another must be made largely on the basis of the school's educational philosophy and purposes. No organizational pattern, however ingenious, is a panacea for poor teaching or a substitute for good teaching. Although a sound pattern of organization will facilitate more effective teaching, the essence of good teaching is still the skilled teacher in the classroom bringing the resources of the curriculum into harmony with the learner's needs and capabilities.[7]

Further discussion of the issues involved in various patterns of vertical and horizontal organization is presented in Chapter 1.

[6]George D. Stoddard, *The Dual Progress Plan*, Harper & Row, Publishers, Incorporated, New York, 1961.

[7]Willard S. Elsbree, Harold J. McNally, and Richard Wynn, *Elementary School Administration and Supervision*, 3d ed., American Book Company, New York, 1967, pp. 133–134.

Experimental Schools. Although all schools are in a sense experimental, some are especially designated as experimental or demonstration. These include the large number of elementary schools affiliated with various universities and colleges as the training ground for student or cadet teachers. Where practice teaching is done entirely off the campus in affiliated schools, the campus elementary school may become a purely laboratory or experimental school for research, exploration, and demonstration.

The elementary school is noted for its experimental procedures. Sometimes these follow a special plan of teaching or curriculum, such as the Gary plan, the Dalton plan, the McDade plan (Chicago), the Winnetka plan, the community school (Glencoe), and the San Angelo plan. Sometimes they are noted for the use of new instructional modes, such as individually prescribed instruction, PLAN, responsive environments, and computer-assisted instruction.

Many variations are found in the length of the school year. One is the all-year school, which offers the complete program throughout the entire calendar year. Some schools follow a modified form by offering a summer term after the regular year. As will be indicated later, the elementary school is the testing ground for many reforms that later creep up into the secondary schools and colleges.

Schools for Atypical Children. In the larger cities a marked trend is to separate by buildings particular types of students for special instruction. More frequently special rooms and teachers are set aside for the care of the nontypical pupils. One type of school is for gifted pupils, and another for slow learners; other schools are for the physically handicapped, such as the Spalding School for crippled children in Chicago, or for the socially atypical, such as the Montefiore School in the same city. Classes in these schools are usually smaller, grade lines are often obscured, and teachers have been given special preparation. Classes for handicapped children provide special facilities and materials, and the content and method of teaching are adapted to the particular needs of the students. Standards of achievement appropriate for their abilities are set for them.

PROGRAMS AND PROCEDURES

Educational Program

The programs of the elementary grades, as mentioned earlier, are usually grouped into (1) the primary grades, (2) the intermediate grades, and (3) the middle school.

Primary Grades. The first three grades are usually called "primary." Where the kindergarten is a basic part of the early schooling, the grouping may be kindergarten-primary. Some also add the nursery school.

The basic academic activity in the primary grades is reading. Publications such as Rudolf Flesch's *Why Johnny Can't Read* and the nationwide Right to Read Program for the 1970s have stimulated great interest in reading, especially in the elementary school. The major types of reading stressed in the primary grades are: (1) developmental, which is designed to initiate and improve reading skills, (2) functional, which is aimed at obtaining information, and (3) recreational, which is mainly for enjoyment and to develop tastes and appreciations. Obviously reading is not an isolated skill; social science, sciences, mathematics, and the creative arts all are integrated into the total process of reading, silent or oral. In certain areas reading is a bilingual activity. In many elementary schools the speaking and reading of a foreign language seeps down into the primary grades. Environmental education often has its genesis in the primary school. Many Head Start programs are being succeeded by the Follow Through activities in the primary grades. Follow Through, which serves several thousand disadvantaged children, reinforces the educational and other gains made by learners from Head Start or similar programs. Follow Through youngsters receive medical and social services as well as intensive instruction.

The young learner develops not only mentally, but also physically, socially, and emotionally. The primary school years, which fortunately for most pupils now follow a school experience before primary school, constitute a most interesting and significant division of education.

Intermediate Grades. These are usually the fourth, fifth, and sixth grades. The most important curricular activity is still reading, but the emphasis is on extensive and enriched reading, rather than its me-

chanics, and on the skillful use of the basic tools acquired in the primary grades. Subjects other than those taught in the primary grades are usually added in the fourth grade. The heavy load of new subjects results in an abrupt transition into the fourth grade and a high percentage of failure. In the more progressive schools no one subject or field of interest is the particular domain of any grade or year. A student, whatever his grade or age, is not withheld from learning materials useful to him at his particular stage of development.

Hence, several new curricular accents are being brought into the program during these crucial years of a youngster's life. Education on drug abuse, sex education, and consumer education are three of the newer areas in the intermediate grades. This is the age level when many boys and girls develop a lasting interest in science. History, which often begins as a subject in these grades, is more multiethnic. A San Francisco ethnic program includes a sixth-grade section on the history of civil rights and the protest movement. Many instructors use programmed instruction to help individualize the program. Greater creativity and freedom of learning are stressed. In some of these grades the students help to write their own textbooks and learning materials in such fields as environmental education. Some intermediate institutions, like many primary schools, do away with traditional report cards. As in many primary schools, the major emphases are on intellectual development and on development of desirable social skills, habits, and attitudes.

Middle School. In the 8-4 plan of organization that prevailed for many years, grades 7 and 8 were regarded as the "upper grades" of the elementary school. During the past quarter-century, many school systems moved from the eight-grade elementary school and four-grade high school to the 6-3-3 plan, which comprised six years of elementary education, three years of junior high school education, and three years of senior high school education. Although the 6-3-3 plan is still most common, a new pattern of organization is emerging in many forward-looking school systems. This plan includes five or six years of elementary education beyond the kindergarten, followed by a four-year or, more commonly, a three-year middle school. This middle school, or intermediate school, as it is frequently called, contains pupils who would ordinarily be enrolled in grades 5 to 8 or, more frequently, 6 to 8. The middle school is an attempt to overcome the weakness of the junior high school, which, as suggested by the name itself, is often only a *junior* imitation of the high school, rather than a distinctly unique institution in its own right that is adapted to the particular needs of preadolescents. Moreover, the age of puberty has dropped a year or so as children have begun to mature earlier. Ninth-graders today are more like high school students (adolescents) than like junior high school students (preadolescents). Sixth-graders today are frequently entering pubescence and are increasingly out of place in the elementary school. Advocates of the new middle school claim several additional advantages for it:

It permits a four-year sequence of courses in high school.
It avoids mixing 11- and 12-year-olds with adolescents.
It groups together children passing through the awkward age of pubescence.
It permits more gradual transition of students from the directed study in the elementary school to the more independent study in the high school.
It encourages more flexibility of curriculum and more enrichment of instruction than the traditional arrangement.
It permits teachers and administrators to specialize in developing educational programs uniquely designed for preadolescents.
It relieves temporary enrollment bulges at either the elementary or the secondary level.

Several school systems, such as those in New York, Philadelphia, Sarasota, El Paso, Saginaw, and Bridgewater, are developing four-year middle schools, but the more common pattern is toward three-year (in some cases two-year) middle schools. Obviously, present building facilities do not permit many districts to change grade-organization patterns overnight, nor would it be desirable for such sudden changes to take place. Consequently, changes of this sort develop slowly. More experience with and evaluation of the middle school (or intermediate school) organization are needed before its advantages and limitations can be seen clearly. However, many authorities believe that such schools offer far more promise than the junior high school as an institution for serving the educational needs of preadolescents. On the basis of child growth and development theory, middle schools appear to be sound in principle. Currently there are more than one

thousand of these middle schools. Their real destiny will be determined not by the magic of realignment of grades but by how well these new institutions can develop curriculums, instruction, and service uniquely adapted to the needs of pupils between childhood and adolescence.

Current Practices in Elementary Education

Some current practices in elementary education are here presented in abbreviated form.

Organization and Administration. The primary purpose of the pattern of an elementary school is to foster the maximum development of every child. Hence, the trend in organization is toward flexibility. A reduction in arbitrary divisions is effected through a reorganization of administrative units, as, for example, a unified six-year program in place of eight disparate grades. Grade classifications are made more flexible or are eliminated, especially in the primary area. Recent trends toward individually prescribed instruction, differentiated staffing, grouping by ability, and variable class size have already been noted. A reduction has been made in the number of grades, classes, and subjects. One-teacher schools, often epitomes of flexibility, are being reduced in number.

More schooling is being provided. The school day has been lengthened in some communities to provide time for enrichment activities. The school week has been lengthened in some cities, such as Madison, Wisconsin, to include informal activities on Saturdays. Many systems provide summertime recreational and educational programs in an elongated educational year. Rochester, Minnesota, has offered a full-time summer program for several decades. Some elementary schools operate a twelve-month program.

Buildings and Other Facilities. Each elementary school building should be designed as a unique unit, planned to meet the educational needs of the community, to suit as well as possible the particular climate and site, and to house the specific educational program and learning activities of the school at a cost commensurate with the people's ability to pay. The ideal enrollment for most elementary schools is probably between four hundred and eight hundred. The modern elementary school includes a large and well-equipped outdoor play area and parking facilities on a well-landscaped site of 10 to 12 acres. There should be special education rooms specifically planned to meet the needs of the handicapped—an adequate library and instructional-materials center with workrooms and storage facilities, plus many other special rooms and facilities.

Recent developments in land usage, including elementary school buildings, are educational parks. These parks are discussed further in Chapter 15.

More and more buildings for elementary schools are of the one-story type. They blend harmoniously with surrounding residential buildings and are homelike to the young children. Many are small neighborhood schools. Several are called "schools without walls."

School buildings and equipment have become more flexible and functional and are more creatively designed. In many elementary schools, a workroom is placed between two classrooms or is a part of the room, so that small groups can work on construction activities at any time during the day. Equipment with a high degree of flexibility is installed. Running water and toilet facilities are within or adjacent to classrooms, especially for small children. Each classroom is provided with its own outside exit. Libraries are used extensively for enrichment. The elementary school library is becoming a multimedia center with multifaceted services, and is spoken of as the "instructional-materials center." The modern elementary school is equipped to handle television, programmed instruction, and other electronic and mechanical teaching media. Carpeting, bright fabrics, and bright furniture have added to the comfort and homelike atmosphere of many new elementary schools.

Despite the fact that elementary school enroll-

ments are static or declining, many boards of education cannot provide permanent elementary school buildings, and hundreds of temporary or semipermanent structures have been erected. Many are portable schoolhouses. Overcrowding in elementary schools persists in spite of the thousands of new classrooms built since World War II. Several thousand elementary school students are still attending half-day sessions.

Another development in facilities is the use of trailers. For example, the Whisman School District of the San Francisco Bay area brings reading clinic facilities directly to pupils and teachers, with daily communication between clinic specialists and the classroom elementary teachers.

Curriculum and Teaching-Learning Procedures.
The pupil in the elementary school is introduced gradually to the curriculum. A well-graduated program of preprimary experiences facilitates the work of the first year. Reading readiness is emphasized.

The curriculum is becoming more flexible. Some schools set up time allotments for major fields of learning in terms of weekly percentage ranges; minimum and maximum ranges of time are allotted weekly to each major division. There is an increase in programmed learning, that is, self-instruction by means of organized material built into computer-assisted instructional systems and programmed books.

Curricular materials are being reorganized into different relationships and with different purposes. The correlation, or fusion, of related materials and activities into broad fields such as language arts and

These two elementary school classrooms illustrate the contrast between traditional education—dominated by the teacher, regimented, undifferentiated, and often crowded—and open education—less structured, more adaptable to individual differences, better equipped, usually less crowded, and with a more flexible use of space.

social studies helps to integrate learning. Many teachers organize materials as teaching-learning units.

Many curricular materials are being shifted in the light of studies on maturation. There is a downward extension of several fields—such as social science, mathematics, and science—into the lower grades. More work is expected of students. Perhaps the most significant trend has been the increased emphasis upon the humanization of the curriculum and greater relevance to the needs of students.

New and neglected areas are being emphasized. Instruction in science is being extended and enriched. The Educational Development Center at Newton, Massachusetts, has produced a widely used program, Elementary Science Study (ESS)—a series of units of learning which stress investigation, placing the student in the role of the experimenting scientist. In many elementary schools the study of and practice in ecology are integral parts of the science program. One of the many special mathematics projects is Special Elementary Education for the Disadvantaged (SEED), used in several schools in California and elsewhere. The project is designed to help teach abstract math to disadvantaged students. Elementary schools in Oakland, California, are using computer-assisted arithmetic teaching programs for the educationally disadvantaged. The newly developed system, Arithmetic Test Generation, is designed to give the teacher precise identification of a student's strengths and weaknesses in arithmetic.

Much more opportunity is given to elementary pupils to use more than one language in school. Bilingual programs extending through grade 6 have been developed by the Southwest Educational Development Laboratory (SEDL) for Spanish-speaking children. Appropriately, first-grade students in selected Alaskan schools study arithmetic, language arts, and social studies in two Eskimo dialects.

Grade school pupils manifest much interest in handicrafts, including pottery, metalwork, and woodworking. Language and the fine arts are used increasingly as a means of unleashing the creative efforts of pupils. Manuscript writing, rather than cursive writing, is used in the lower grades because of its similarity to the printed words. United States history and the values and ideals of representative government are stressed. More emphasis is placed on helping children to learn about other peoples of the world and to develop sympathetic attitudes and understandings toward them—cultural empathy.

Learning in the elementary school is a cooperative enterprise. The classroom work is actively and realistically coordinated with other service departments of the school. The guidance function is being strengthened. A greater effort is being made to identify potential school dropouts at the elementary school level and to alleviate their disenchantment with school and correct their educational disabilities before they reach the end of the compulsory school attendance age. The home is taken into partnership in many school experiences of the learner. Class mothers and teacher aides often assist in routine tasks. The elementary schools have extended their learning experiences into the community, especially through the "go-and-see" plan of education trips.

Television (both on closed-circuit and commercial channels), computer-assisted instruction, language laboratories, films, taped recordings, cassettes, and other audiovisual media are being used widely in elementary school instruction. Sometimes the educational television program is received in the classroom as part of the formal school program, and sometimes the student is asked to view certain programs of educational importance at home. In metropolitan New York, several hours of educational programs are telecast daily over a radius of 100 miles. These programs range from English lessons for children of Puerto Rican descent to science lessons for teachers.

Outdoor education, including school camping, soil conservation, reforestation, wildlife study, farming, historical research, recreation, and therapy for handicapped children, has been introduced in various areas of the country, particularly Illinois and Michigan.

Many improved practices are becoming statewide or regional in scope. For example, the elementary schools of North Dakota are becoming "informal classroom with tested educational innovations." Schools in several states are testing the bold experiments of Individually Guided Education and the Multiunit Elementary School, produced by the eminent Research and Development Center for Cognitive Learning, based at the University of Wisconsin. Specific learning tasks are used by pupils, and traditional textbooks, lockstep grades, and self-contained classrooms are discarded by teachers. Packaged materials have been developed to spread the program across the nation, with the aid of the National Center for Educational Research and Development, a part of the U.S. Office of Education. Methods such as the British-originated Initial Teaching Alphabet (ITA) for reading and spelling are imported. Methods and motivations are borrowed from private educational firms, as contract learning and performance contracting spread in public and private elementary schools. Many other curricular developments in elementary schools are discussed in Chapter 14.

Pupils and Teachers. Pupils receive much individual attention. Opportunities to enhance further individualization are available due to the current surplus of elementary teachers and the increase in educational technology. Pupil progress is evaluated carefully, especially in view of the current criticism of elementary education. Teachers, especially in the primary unit, are often assigned for a period of two or three years to the same group of pupils. Special attention is being given to enriched programs of instruction for gifted students. Provisions for handicapped children are being improved and expanded. The mobility of the population causes many changes in class rolls.

The modern elementary school should stress both cognitive and affective development and guidance. Several elementary schools have established child-guidance clinics. Cumulative records, including anecdotal reports, contribute to evaluation and guidance. Sociometric devices are more widely used.

In line with the modern accent on relevance in the curriculum, there is increased opportunity for pupils to do socially useful work. Student councils are used increasingly as a means of promoting democracy in the administration of elementary schools. A cooperative attack upon elementary school problems is made by pupils, teachers, school administrators, parents, and community leaders. As noted earlier, more extensive use is being made of team teaching, counseling, tutorial reading teams, and differentiated staffing.

Probably the most significant development in elementary education in the past two decades has been the remarkable rise in the level of preparation of elementary teachers. Since 1950, the proportion of elementary school teachers with four or more years of college-level preparation has increased from 50 to 98 percent, a truly remarkable rise when one considers the sharp increase in the demand for teachers and for workers in competing occupations during the same period. At no time in the past has

the professional preparation of the elementary school teacher been as good as it is at present.

The typical elementary school staff is being enlarged and improved. Many schools have added specialists. For example, a rather new position is instructional diagnostician, combining the functions of counseling, diagnosis, prescription, evaluation, and instruction. Child-development specialists are being added. More elementary schools are employing librarians who are developing into multimedia specialists.

Several "models" for education of elementary teachers have been developed. Broadly speaking these techniques, first developed in other fields, fall into three main categories: educational models, systems analysis, and learning systems.

FUTURE

The Center for Urban Education has developed a fourth- and fifth-grade social studies curriculum to help elementary pupils in poverty areas understand the ways they can improve their neighborhoods, their entire social environment, and their own future. For all—young and old—the future of elementary education is critically important.

On the horizon are the possibilities of even greater individualization of instruction, since elementary school enrollments are declining for the first time since World War II. It is estimated that the number of pupils will drop back to 35,500,000 in the mid-1970s.

With Head Start being succeeded by Follow Through for many pupils, elementary education will become better articulated with the pre-elementary education preceding it. The dynamics of the new middle school, in turn, will bring better articulation with the secondary education following it.

Curriculum builders will be devoting more attention to elementary school programs and teaching-learning procedures, since the main foundation for future learning is established in elementary school. The first of the three R's is still reading. Former U.S. Commissioner of Education James E. Allen set this future goal:

We should immediately set for ourselves the goal . . . that by the end of the 1970's . . . no one shall be leaving school without the skill and desire necessary to read to the full limits of his capability. . . . This goal cannot be easily attained. It will be far more difficult than landing on the moon.

Although some nursery schools and some kindergartens teach reading, these schools are not universal and hence the major responsibility for meeting this "right to read" goal in the decade of the 1970s will be placed on the shoulders of the elementary school teachers.

The traditional three Rs will be supplemented by many new academic accents. Career education will begin in the elementary school. Sex education and environmental studies will have their genesis in the early years. Youth volunteer services will enlist many pupils and teachers. Despite the reservations of some teachers and administrators, many elementary schools will present some type of programs concerning blacks and other minority groups. The curricular materials about blacks and other ethnic groups will be presented as separate courses, integrated social studies offerings, interdisciplinary materials, or all three.

Jerome Harris, writing in *Profiles of Significant Schools*, states: "Children should be introduced at an early age to the realities of wage earning, to ideas about working for a living. Exploration of the various aspects of commerce and industry could provide elementary school students with such an introduction."[8]

The graded elementary school will be replaced gradually by the ungraded school, which is far better adapted to the individual differences of students. Differentiated instruction and various individually prescribed instructional systems, with flexible groupings by subject, will become more common. Team teaching with flexible class size will become increasingly popular. However, the quality of elementary schools will still not depend on organizational arrangements but on the teachers' talent.

Programmed instruction, television, and other new instructional media will become increasingly common. Relatedly, the successful nationally televised show "Sesame Street," designed for children below primary school age, initiated in 1971 a new series designed for second-graders.

In sum, the dilemmas that will confront the elementary schools in the last quarter of the twentieth century will not be those of growth, which domi-

[8]Jerome Harris, *Profiles for Significant Schools*, Educational Facilities Laboratories, New York, 1970, p. 4.

nated recent decades, but those of enrichment and improvement of the educational experiences and services which are necessary for the basic education of children. The most pervasive change will be prompted by society's growing recognition of the importance of childhood education.

SUMMARY

The modern elementary school, although distinctly American in character, has been influenced by European traditions. Comenius, Rousseau, Pestalozzi, Herbart, Mann, Barnard, Parker, Dewey, Kilpatrick, and Goodlad have made particularly important contributions to the development of elementary education. Enrollments have nearly doubled in the past half-century, making elementary schooling virtually universal in America. Elementary school enrollments, however, are headed for declines in the 1970s. Many pupils from Catholic elementary schools are enrolling in public schools because of the fiscal problems of nonpublic schools as well as discontent with the cloistered nature of many nonpublic schools, a crisis of confidence in Catholic schools, and the belief that church-related schools may not be necessary.

Elementary schools provide basic learning for all children. They seek to stimulate mental, physical, social, emotional, aesthetic, and moral development, as well as understanding of the world and its people, communication skills, and quantitative relationships. The general goals of elementary schooling emerge from the broad values of American democracy.

There is much variety among elementary schools, in terms of programs, organization, philosophy, size, and control. There are public and private schools; large, medium-sized, and small schools; traditional and progressive schools; and schools organized by grades, subjects, student activities, and other factors.

Considerable contention exists about whether elementary education ought to be based upon the philosophy and methodology of the progressives or the essentialists. Elementary education in general is more progressive and experimental than other levels of education.

The elementary school is presently adopting a variety of new procedures largely in the direction of increased flexibility and democracy. Curriculums are being reorganized and extended to provide better integration of subject matter and enriched learning. Increased emphasis is being given to mathematics, science, environmental education, sex education, and languages. Greater effort is being made to adapt learning experiences to the individual abilities and needs of students. Grouping of children according to their ability and the elimination of grade classifications are growing trends in this direction. Increased attention is being given also to the needs of the gifted and handicapped children. The middle school is emerging as a hopefully better arrangement for meeting the needs of children in the upper elementary years.

Elementary school buildings have become more flexible and functional, as well as more creative, in design. Instructional materials are more plentiful, attractive, and effective. Television and other media of the new instructional technology are being used more widely and effectively. Standards of preparation and in-service development of teachers have been strengthened.

In this decade for the first time there is a surplus of elementary teachers. This added reserve resource of human talent can help to add new services and to reduce per-pupil loads if the needed resources can be found. For eight significant years of the pupil's life, elementary education will continue to be the most important time segment in his all-around development.

Suggested Activities

1. Discuss the major objectives of the elementary school.

2. Read Horace Mann's Tenth Annual Report *or* The Republic and the School: Horace Mann on the Education of Free Men, *and outline the arguments which Mann marshaled in support of the common school.*

3. Visit an ungraded primary unit and describe how it differs from the typical graded school.

4. Visit a middle school; explain its philosophy and program, and tell how well it meets the unique needs of preadolescent pupils.

5. Contrast the methods of teaching and discipline in a typical elementary school of fifty years ago with those in use today.

6. Visit a nonpublic elementary school and indicate its strengths and weaknesses.

7. Describe the Right to Read Program proposed by

former U.S. Commissioner of Education James E. Allen, Jr., and its effect on the elementary school.

8. Volunteer to teach reading on a one-to-one basis, tutoring a child from one of the minority groups.

9. Read John Dewey's My Pedagogic Creed *and report on its appropriateness or inappropriateness in relation to modern needs for elementary education.*

10. Interview an elementary school teacher about teaching in the elementary school.

Bibliography

Association for Supervision and Curriculum Development and National Association of Elementary School Principals: *The New Elementary School,* National Education Association, Washington, D.C., 1968. A description of new problems and developments in elementary education.

Goodlad, John I., M. Frances Klein, and Associates: *Behind the Classroom Door,* Charles A. Jones Publishing Company, Worthington, Ohio, 1970. A report on findings of visits to 150 classrooms, kindergarten through grade 3, in twenty-six school districts.

Holt, John: *How Children Fail,* Pitman Publishing Company, New York, 1964. Classic study of how children learn or fail to learn.

Kimbrough, Ralph B.: *Administering Elementary Schools,* The Macmillan Company, New York, 1968. Thorough treatment of all aspects of elementary school organization and operation.

National Education Association: *Elementary Education Today,* The Association, Washington, D.C., 1971. A collection of articles from NEA publications dealing with elementary education and its impact on children.

National Education Association: *Schools for the 70's and Beyond: A Call to Action,* The Association, Washington, D.C., 1971, Section 2. Prescriptions of the "humanistic school" of tomorrow, with numerous suggestions for elementary schools.

Palardy, J. Michael (ed.): *Elementary School Curriculum,* The Macmillan Company, Riverside, N.J., 1971. An anthology of trends and challenges presented in eight sections.

Rogers, Vincent R. (ed.): *Teaching in the British Primary School,* The Macmillan Company, New York, 1970. Thirteen chapters written by British educators, with the last chapter by an American educator, making comparisons between British and American programs.

Schuster, Albert, and Milton E. Ploghoft: *The Emerging Elementary Curriculum,* Charles E. Merrill Books, Inc., Columbus, Ohio, 1970. A child-centered approach which gives teaching methods equal emphasis with content.

Silberman, Charles E.: *Crisis in the Classroom,* Random House, Inc., New York, 1970. A report, financed by Carnegie Corporation, of a survey of American schools, with many examples from elementary grades.

Chapter 8   Secondary Education

ORIENTATION

Adolescence is a period of turbulence in human development, and the schools that serve adolescents are undergoing an unprecedented period of turbulence. More than two-thirds of the high schools in the nation have experienced some kind of student protest—sit-ins, boycotts, strikes, riots, or destruction. Unlovely as some of the protests may be, they are forcing a reexamination of the purposes, programs, and practices of high schools across the country. The charges being made against secondary schools are too insistent to be ignored.

Consider, for example, these statements from high school underground newspapers.

It is not with a feeling of joy that I daily journey to the hallowed halls of my high school.

Tick, tock. Tick, tock. It's never going to end. I'm going to die in here. I wonder if he'd give me a pass to the nurse. Or the bathroom. Anywhere.

I meant "Give me a chance to think about what's happening," but he interrupted and said, "Listen, buster, don't give me any of that give-me-a-chance business. . . ."

Substantial reward to anyone who can successfully sabotage the PA system.

In study hall you cannot study because of the insistent voice of a teacher telling everyone to be quiet.

One teacher, forcing his way into the lunch line, said to a boy with long hair, "I always let little girls go first."

How can you truly value your freedom if you've never been oppressed? Schools are excellent teachers of what liberty isn't.

Some educational critics applaud high schools' emphasis upon social development; others disparage it as an unnecessary frill.

There is a fence around the school. The gates are locked during school.

Ivanhoe, Silas Marner, Christmas Carol, Julius Caesar, Lady of the Lake: the names of these books are familiar to us. Why? Have these books ever been on the best seller list? Have we ever seen them being bought up feverishly at the newsstands? Are these books the ones that our friends are recommending?

These reflections on the repressiveness, boredom, and irrelevance of high schools are not restricted to students. Professor Allison Davis of the University of Chicago, after studying high school seniors and their fortunes in later life, concluded that there is little correlation between good grades in high school and success in life and no relationship between social activities in high school and anything in adult life. Even in the 1950s, Professor Davis was urging that schools start to deal with the reality of life. He concluded that "the nonsense in the textbook has nothing to do with the student's immediate environment. Students who sleep through class probably aren't stupid; they are just bored to tears." More recently the Coleman Report enunciated what is well known by most high school students, if not by their teachers and principals: "Students do better when they sense the school is relevant and responsive to them, that it is in some sense theirs, that, in short, they have power over it."

In this nation we take justifiable pride in providing secondary education to a far larger proportion of our youth than does any other nation in the world. Our task now is to make this experience more relevant, more viable, and more joyous.

In this chapter we shall examine the cultural and historical foundations of secondary education, the purposes which it is intended to serve, the types of secondary schools, and their organization, program, practices, and future.

FOUNDATIONS

Historical Development of Secondary Education

The history of secondary education in the United States is usually chronicled in four rather distinct periods, named after the institutions that were characteristic of them: (1) the era of the Latin grammar school, (2) the era of the tuition academy, (3) the era of the free public high school, and (4) the era of the vertically extended or reorganized secondary school. The significant events in the evolution of secondary education are listed in the historical calendar.

The Latin Grammar School. The first step toward organizing the Latin grammar school in America was taken by Bostonians on April 23, 1635, in a town meeting, where it was voted "that our brother, Philemon Pormont, shal be intreated to become scholemaster for the teaching and nourtering of children with us." Such efforts as this mark the beginnings of secondary education in the colonies, and by 1700 approximately forty grammar schools had been founded in New England. The schools of secondary education were not so common.

In the Middle and Southern colonies private tutors were engaged, and many young boys and girls were sent to Europe for schooling. The academy in the South, as in other parts of the United States, was called a product of the frontier period and the laissez-faire theory of government. It was usually private or denominational.

The main purpose of the Latin grammar school was to prepare pupils for college. The Latin grammar schools, especially the earlier ones, offered a limited curriculum. As indicated by its name, the school was primarily restricted to the study of classical languages and literature. It was very selective in character and sought to establish an aristocracy of educated intellectuals.

Admission to the Latin grammar schools was usually conditioned by the social and economic rank of the applicant. A sort of dual system, patterned on a European plan, prevailed in early American education. In this system an elementary education open to all was distinct from a secondary education closed to all but a chosen few.

Financial support for the Latin grammar school was provided in one or more of the following ways: tuition, donations, taxation, leases, legacies, lotteries, and land grants by civil authorities or private persons. Its control was at first considered the right and duty of the clergy, since most of the pupils pursued studies that fitted them for the ministry or professions. Gradually the Latin grammar schools, with their emphasis on theology, began to lose their popularity. Leadership in the community was no longer with the clergy but rather with the town and commercial executives. Out of the new economic and social conditions in America arose the next period of secondary education, namely, that of the tuition academy.

The Tuition Academy. Benjamin Franklin was primarily responsible for the establishment of the first academy. Franklin in his *Autobiography* describes the genesis of the academy and details many practical and progressive suggestions. According to Carl Van Doren, "In a day of rigid classical schools, Franklin took his stand with reformers like Milton and Locke and the most advanced contemporary Americans."[1] This academy, which later became the University of Pennsylvania, opened in a house in Philadelphia in 1751. The curriculum was broader than that of the Latin grammar school, although not so extensive as Franklin planned it should be. Since it aimed to prepare for life as well as for the ministry, its students included those not intending to go to college as well as the college-bound. The academies permitted young women to enter.

Although a large number of academies were founded between 1750 and 1800, the movement reached its peak in the decade 1840–1850, flourishing best in Massachusetts and New York.

The academy, supported in the main by tuition and donation, was semipublic in control. In its organization, administration, and program it was more democratic than the Latin grammar school. The person in charge was usually called the headmaster or principal. Several private academies still exist in the United States as military academies or special schools, but most of the older ones have either disappeared or been transformed into public high schools.

The Free Public High School. The third period in the history of the American secondary school covers the rise and growth of the free public high school.

[1] Carl Van Doren, *Benjamin Franklin*, The Viking Press, Inc., New York, 1938, p. 192.

The Development of Secondary Education

1635	First Latin grammar school founded in Boston	*1938*	Classic study of youth, Youth Tell Their Story, *published by American Youth Commission*
1751	Franklin Academy organized in Philadelphia	*1940*	Influential report, What the High School Ought to Teach, *published by Special Committee on the Secondary School Curriculum*
1821	First high school for boys organized in Boston		
1826	First high school for girls initiated in Boston	*1941*	Eight-year Study *by the Progressive Education Association published*
1856	First coeducational high school established in Chicago	*1944*	Report, Education for All American Youth, *published by Educational Policies Commission*
1874	Taxation for secondary schools upheld in the Kalamazoo case	*1960*	Massive study of high school students' talents and achievements launched in Project Talent
1884	Manual training high school started in Baltimore	*1960*	Conant's study Recommendations for Education in the Junior High School *published*
1893	Recommendations of the Committee of Ten published		
1904	G. Stanley Hall's classic, Adolescence, *published*	*1964*	Job Corps and work training programs for impoverished youth established by Economic Opportunity Act
1910	First public junior high schools opened	*1965*	Elementary and Secondary Education Act passed by Congress, authorizing educational benefits directed mostly toward pupils from low-income families
1918	Report of the Commission on Reorganization of Secondary Education published		
1933	Reports of the National Survey of Secondary Education presented	*1967*	Conant's findings reported in The American High School Today *updated in* The Comprehensive High School
1933	Cooperative Study of Secondary School Standards launched	*1971*	Urban Education Service Center established by National Association of Secondary School Principals to aid large-city high schools
1936	Reports—Issues of Secondary Education *and* Functions of Secondary Education—*published by Department of Secondary School Principals*	*1971*	Model secondary schools established to demonstrate pattern of secondary education for the future

It started with the establishment of the English Classical School in Boston in 1821. This school for boys, later called the English High School, was followed by a high school for girls in the same city in 1826. In 1827 Massachusetts passed a law requiring the larger towns "to supply free, tax-supported instruction" in such high school subjects as surveying, logic, Latin, and Greek. A distinguished educational historian, Adolphe E. Meyer, thus evaluates this precedent-making though short-lived law:

Despite its ignoble fate, the law was of deep and vital importance. It not only mandated the public maintenance of free secondary education; it also became the model on which other states patterned themselves when the desire seized them to stake their children to something more than the usual lower learning.[2]

During the next half-century various types of high schools were organized. Among these were the first coeducational high school, started in Chicago in 1856, and the first manual training school, founded in Baltimore in 1884. Many factors contributed to the steady development of these schools, particularly in the democratic West.

The Kalamazoo case decision of the Supreme Court of Michigan in 1874 became famous in school law because it lent legal sanction to the movement for the establishment of publicly supported high schools. Similar decisions followed in several other states, thus removing any question about the legality of having communities tax themselves for the support of public high schools. The Kalamazoo decision thus paved the way for a phenomenal growth in this new institution of democracy.

Needless to say, the coming of the high school proved momentous. From its shaggy and resented beginnings, it has become an institution as familiarly American as TV and the coffee break, and it doubtless is no less essential to the pursuit of a good and useful American life than the Bill of Rights. The high school gave coherence and unity to native public education. . . . Meanwhile, Europe, holding fast for the most part of its effete traditions, committed itself to a double educational system, with one set of schools for the "masses," and another, separated and unrelated, for their so-called "betters," whether intellectual or otherwise.[3]

[2]Adolphe E. Meyer, *An Educational History of the Western World*, McGraw-Hill Book Company, New York, 1965, p. 399.

[3]*Ibid.*, p. 400.

Comprehensive High Schools. The comprehensive high school is by far the most common model of American secondary education. It strives to meet the needs of practically all youth of secondary school age through its parallel curriculums—college preparatory, general, vocational, and commercial—all of which include some common courses in general education. Within each curriculum some flexibility is maintained through the use of electives. By bringing together under one "educational umbrella" students of varied backgrounds, interests, and abilities, it has, like the common school, played a vital role in the great melting pot of American society. It has harmonized the diversity of our youth and helped to build strong national unity. The comprehensive high school—a distinctly American product—is increasing in enrollments and significance. The Public Education Association of New York City has stated well the essential characteristics of comprehensive high schools.

1 Every comprehensive high school will have one student body with no pre-sorting into academic and vocational tracks.
2 The academic program will include the traditional academic requirement for college entrance and offer advanced courses to students who qualify.
3 The comprehensive high school will accept the responsibility for intensive efforts to improve the basic learning skills of the educationally deprived pupils.
4 The program of instruction and guidance for each student will be based on his achievement and his actual abilities and hopes.
5 Pupils will not have to begin to make vocational choices until the 11th year.
6 Every student, whatever his background and ambitions, will have the opportunity to explore a wide range of vocational possibilities.
7 In providing general education and training for a changing job market, the comprehensive high schools will maintain close cooperation with labor and employers.
8 The comprehensive high school will conduct an active program of art, music, drama, sports and a variety of clubs so that students will be included in some activity outside the classroom program.
9 The comprehensive high school will award one type of diploma only, with an accompanying record of the student's achievement.
10 The comprehensive high school will provide counseling services for all the students to help them make the most appropriate choices whether in jobs, in job training, or in continuing education.[4]

The widespread availability of the comprehensive high school has contributed greatly to the sharp rise

[4]Public Education Association, *High Schools for a Changing World*, New York, 1967, pp. 10-11.

MILLIONS

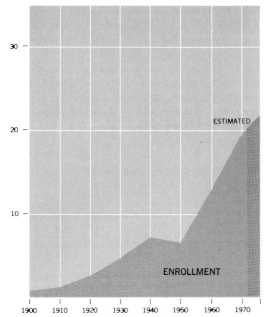

ESTIMATED

ENROLLMENT

1900 1910 1920 1930 1940 1950 1960 1970

FIGURE 8-1 Total enrollment in public and private secondary schools. (Source for 1900–1950: U.S. Office of Education, Digest of Educational Statistics; for 1950–1976: U.S. Office of Education, Projections of Educational Statistics to 1977–78.)

in secondary school enrollments shown in Figure 8-1.

Secondary Education for All. Many factors have contributed to quicken the realization of secondary education for all American youth, as portrayed in Figure 8-2. Young people are realizing that in an automated and cybernetic economy there is very little attractive employment for persons without a high school education. The choice of whether to complete high school or drop out and get a job is disappearing. The nation's increasing economic prosperity has reduced but not yet eliminated the number of adolescents who feel obliged to quit school to help support their families. State laws that raise the minimum age limit for beginning employment or lift the maximum compulsory school attendance age are factors in the great increase in secondary school enrollments. Secondary education reaches a larger proportion of youth in the United States than in any other country. More than 90 percent of the population between 14 and 17 years of age (approximately high school age) is enrolled in schools in the United States. The enrollments in

high school grades 9 to 12 show a greater percentage of increase than those in the elementary grades. Figure 8-1 reveals total secondary school enrollments from 1800 to 1976.

Secondary schools have increased their power to hold students until graduation, thus reducing the number of dropouts and "pushouts." The attrition rate has been and is being reduced to the point where now more than 80 percent of the public school ninth-graders go on to be graduated from high school. Furthermore, many dropouts and older persons are returning to high school or are completing work for their diplomas by means of night schools, correspondence schools, or other institutions offering established and approved secondary school courses, such as the United States Armed Forces Institute and penal and corrective institutions. Federally supported programs, such as those sponsored under the Economic Opportunity Act of 1964 and the Elementary and Secondary Education Act of 1965, are bringing into or retaining in high school thousands of youths who might not otherwise be there. Contemporary schools, such as the street

PERCENT OF
17 YEAR-OLDS

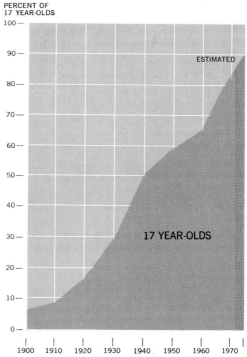

ESTIMATED

17 YEAR-OLDS

1900 1910 1920 1930 1940 1950 1960 1970

FIGURE 8-2 High school graduates as a percentage of 17-year-olds. (U.S. Bureau of the Census.)

academies, are helping to reclaim those students normally rejected by conventional high schools. These varied secondary school programs for adolescents and postadolescents have helped establish at 12.5 the median number of years of schooling completed by adults 25 years and older. Indeed a major trend in American education in the first three-fourths of the twentieth century has been the marked increase in the number of people and the proportion of the total population attaining at least secondary school education.

Nowhere in the world is so large a percentage of youth attending high school as in America. In most European countries, less than one-fifth of the population of high school age is in school. The attainment of high school education by virtually all American youth is one of the truly great phenomena of American democracy and one of the greatest sources of our strength.

Schools Without Walls. Perhaps the most unorthodox development in secondary education has been the creation of a number of "schools without walls" in several urban areas. Like the street academies described later, these schools have been created to fill the breach created by conventional high schools' failure to reach ghetto youth. The earliest of the "schools without walls" was the Parkway School in Philadelphia. It was followed by Metropolitan High School in Chicago and John Adams High School in Portland, Oregon. These schools are characterized by great informality and freedom.

The Parkway School functions not only without walls but also without marks, bells, authority figures, dropouts, attendance areas, and last names, and certainly without boredom. Its campus is the community and its classrooms are the public institutions and businesses bordering the Benjamin Franklin Parkway, from which the school derives its name. Its headquarters are in an abandoned office building. Students go there for the only required part of their program, the tutorial groups, which consist of fifteen students and two teachers meeting for two hours, four days a week. Here the students plan their outside activities, receive personal counseling and satisfy the only two subject requirements— mathematics and English. The tutorial also helps handle the extensive written evaluations of both students' and teachers' work, which take the place of marks.

The remainder of the students' time might be spent studying zoology at the zoo; art at various museums, commercial art studios, or libraries; welding at a machine shop; automotive mechanics at a garage; law enforcement at city hall; or an array of about a hundred pursuits almost as varied as life itself. These activities are chosen according to the interests of the students. Many students devote far more time to their work than would be required in the conventional school day. Although many of the students would be potential dropouts in conventional high schools, few drop out of Parkway. Except for the tutorials, attendance is voluntary; but interest is high because the emphasis upon community motivates students almost as if it were a religious force. Students are selected by lottery from long waiting lists, but teachers are carefully chosen because it takes a special breed of teacher for such a sharp departure from conventional pedagogy. Parkway offers a four-year, full-time program satisfying state requirements and gives a diploma. Although student-teacher ratios are kept small to sustain close interpersonal relations between faculty and students, the costs per student at Parkway are the same as at other Philadelphia high schools. The major difference is that capital costs are much less because the modest facilities are leased and no large expensive school plant is needed.

As was noted earlier, similar unorthodox high schools are being tried in other cities. Although they vary somewhat in operation, the basic educational concept of informality and freedom to follow individual interests is the same. How well are they working? In the minds of some, these unconventional programs are sheer chaos, incapable of sustaining any academic discipline. But in the mind of Mario Fantini of the Ford Foundation, the initial sponsor of the Parkway School, these schools point the way to a new design for the education of ghetto students, and perhaps other students as well, that will succeed where conventional schooling has failed. The answer may lie somewhere between these two extremes.

The Extended Secondary School. As indicated in Figure 8-3, some secondary schools are extended downward and upward. Some secondary institutions include students of junior high school age who are housed and programmed in the same building with those of senior high school age, thus producing a six-year secondary school. A few institutions include the lower division of higher education in the secondary school organization.

Two new public institutions have arisen to challenge any neat division of secondary education between elementary education and higher education; namely, the junior college and the middle or intermediate school. Whether the middle school is more closely associated with secondary education than elementary education or whether it is indeed indigenous to neither is still a moot question. In any case, we have chosen to deal with the middle school in the chapter on elementary education (Chapter 7). The same dilemma exists with respect to the junior college, which in some communities is organized as an extension of secondary education but is more commonly regarded as a sector of higher education. We have chosen to deal with the junior college in the chapter on higher education (Chapter 9). The junior high school, on the other hand, is traditionally regarded as a part of secondary education and is discussed in this chapter.

Leaders in Secondary Education

Three and one-half centuries of secondary education in America have produced many leaders in this field. Only a few can be mentioned here. One of the earliest was the versatile Benjamin Franklin (1706–1790), previously mentioned. G. Stanley Hall (1846–1924), through his monumental work *Adolescence*, published in 1904, helped to make secondary education more aware of the psychological needs of youth.

Another pioneer thinker in this field was Charles W. Eliot (1834–1926). Although he is best known for his long and effective service as president of Harvard University, his imprint upon secondary education is indelible. His efforts to raise the entrance requirements for Harvard were reflected in the improved standards in the high schools. His provisions for choice in entrance units allowed greater freedom in secondary curriculums. His work as chairman of the national Committee of Ten (1890) led eventually to the junior high school movement.

Another university president who directly influenced the secondary schools was William Rainey Harper (1856–1906). As chairman of a national committee, he recommended that the period of elementary education be reduced. His argument that the small, ineffective college should drop senior work and become a junior college earned for him the title "father of the junior college."

The University of Chicago added another leader in secondary education in the person of Leonard V. Koos, who was actively connected with the new

extended secondary school and the National Survey of Secondary Education. He has emphasized the role of the reorganized secondary school.

Another personality in secondary education was Thomas H. Briggs, former professor of secondary school administration at Teachers College, Columbia University. Through his contact with hundreds of secondary school principals and teachers in his college classes, through his numerous publications, and through his chairmanship of the Committee on Orientation of Secondary Education, he has had tremendous influence on secondary education in America and abroad.

James Bryant Conant, another former president of Harvard University, in 1959 completed his widely influential study of American secondary education. This study, originally reported in *The American High School Today* and followed in 1967 by its sequel, *The Comprehensive High School*, emphasized the importance of identifying the most able high school students and challenging them with advanced work, but without segregating them into special schools. He concluded that high school guidance programs should be strengthened to encourage wise selection of courses and vocations. It was Conant's finding that the most compelling problem confronting secondary education is the elimination through district reorganization of small high schools with their sharply limited programs. Conant helped to reinforce Americans' faith in the soundness of the comprehensive high school concept.

To this list one could add many other distinguished leaders in secondary education. The studies of Francis Spaulding, Ralph Tyler, Philip Jackson, Allison Davis, John Flanagan, and Robert Havighurst have deepened our understanding of adolescents. The teaching and writing of John Dewey, William Kilpatrick, Will French, Floyd Reeves, Paul Jacobson, and many others have influenced the professional practice of thousands of secondary school educators privileged to be instructed by them.

PURPOSES

The objectives or directives of secondary education have been numerous and varied. These objectives have been enunciated by various committees, commissions, and other study groups whose recommendations are summarized here.

Committee of Ten

The National Education Association appointed the Committee of Ten, whose controversial report was published in 1893. Although it stated that secondary schools did not exist primarily to prepare youth for college, it nevertheless proceeded to outline a curriculum satisfactory for college preparation which tended to standardize the academic offerings in high schools. It was the first major document to have widespread impact on secondary education in this country.

Commission on the Reorganization of Secondary Education

A well-known set of objectives of historical significance is that prepared in 1918 by the Commission on the Reorganization of Secondary Education, which advocated "such reorganization that secondary education may be defined as applying to all pupils of approximately twelve to eighteen years of age." Briefly stated, these seven objectives, usually called the Cardinal Principles of Education and applied to elementary as well as secondary education, are (1) health, (2) command of fundamental processes, (3) worthy home membership, (4) vocational efficiency, (5) civic participation, (6) worthy use of leisure time, and (7) ethical character.

American Youth Commission Studies

The American Council of Education appointed the American Youth Commission, a panel of distinguished educators, to study the relevance of secondary education to the needs of youth. Its first report, *Youth Tell Their Story*, published in 1938, made it clear that high schools were not meeting the needs of youths very well, particularly adolescents from disadvantaged educational, cultural, and economic backgrounds. Its second report, released two years later, *What the High Schools Ought to Teach*, urged greater emphasis upon the social sciences in high school, especially in behalf of improved interpersonal relations and better family life. It stressed independent reading skills and urged more humane and pleasant methods of teaching in high schools. These reports were timely and influential.

Progressive Education Association Study

In 1941 the Progressive Education Association published *Eight-year Study*, a report of the results of application of progressive education theory in selected experimental secondary schools. These schools built their curriculums around youth's experiences and interests rather than around subject-matter formats designed for college preparation. The progressives, building on the educational theory of John Dewey, were more interested in the reconstruction of students' everyday experiences than in formal presentation of subject matter. The study concluded that success in liberal arts colleges did not depend upon formal study of subjects, because the youths in the experimental schools generally performed better in college than did graduates of more traditional schools. Much of the doctrine of the progressive educators, although disparaged for two decades following the study, is being rediscovered and applied in contemporary schools.

Education for All American Youth

The Educational Policies Commission published, in 1944, *Education for All American Youth*, in which it formulated policies for secondary education. This was supplemented by *A Further Look*. Schools should be dedicated, said the commission, to the proposition that every youth in the United States—regardless of sex, economic status, geographic location, or race—should experience a broad and balanced education.

The commission added that it is the duty of a democratic society to provide opportunities for such education through its numerous schools. It is the obligation of every youth, as a citizen, to make full use of these opportunities; and it is the responsibility of parents to give encouragement and support to both youth and schools.

Life-adjustment Education

The Commission on Life Adjustment Education for Youth was created by the U.S. Office of Education in 1947. Its report, published four years later, stressed the importance of "practical education," especially for youths who did not plan to attend college. It identified the essential elements of secondary education: guidance and student personnel services; ethical and moral living; citizenship education; self-realization and use of leisure; health and safety; consumer education; tools of learning (numbers and language); work experience, occupational adjustment, and competencies. Like the Progressive Education Association doctrine before it, this report was attacked vigorously by basic educationists who preferred hard academic discipline. Ironically, the essential doctrines of life-adjustment education were rediscovered in the mid-1960s and found expression in such programs as the Job Corps, the street academies, and other contemporary educational styles.

American Association of School Administrators

In 1958 the AASA Yearbook Commission, in its study *The High School in a Changing World*, emphasized these dual goals for secondary education: the maximum development of (1) powers to enjoy a rich personal life and (2) abilities and desires to contribute as much as possible to humanity through good citizenship.

Project Talent

One of the most ambitious studies of American secondary education, Project Talent, was mounted in 1960 under the direction of John Flanagan of the University of Pittsburgh with support from a grant from the Office of Education. This study pursued five major goals: an inventory of human resources, a set of standards for educational and psychological measurement, a comprehensive counseling guide indicating the patterns of aptitude and ability which are predictive of success in various careers, a better understanding of how young people choose their lifework, and a deeper knowledge of the educational experiences which prepare students for their lifework. The study included a national sample of half a million secondary school students. Flanagan and his associates concluded from their study that the full potential of a large portion of the nation's young people is not being developed; that the number of young people who graduate from high school with vague and inadequate plans for the future should be reduced; and that the greatest reform necessary in secondary education was greater individualization of instruction to accommodate the great variation in knowledge, abilities, aptitudes, interests, and backgrounds of high school students. The study underscored the importance of assisting the non-college-bound student develop appropriate educa-

tional and occupational goals and of providing him with educational opportunities to facilitate his progress toward those goals. Project Talent provided insight through research into some of the reforms which were to be invoked by the popular critics of education in the late 1960s and 1970s.

National Education Association

The National Education Association's Project on the Instructional Program of the Public Schools brought together leading teachers, administrators, scholars in the academic disciplines, professors of education, and laymen. Their report, *Schools for the 60s*, published in 1963, enunciated these basic objectives of highest priority:

Learning how to learn, how to attack new problems, how to acquire new knowledge
Using rational processes
Building competence in basic skills
Developing intellectual and vocational competence
Exploring values in new experience
Understanding concepts and generalizations[5]

The NEA's Center for Instruction, in its publication *Schools for the 70s and Beyond: A Call for Action*, stressed the importance of humanizing schools for the purpose of helping young citizens develop deeper understanding of themselves and their fellow men.

Phi Delta Kappa Educational Foundation

In 1968 this national honorary fraternity in education established a committee to consider the objectives and responsibilities of schools. Although their statement, *An Educational Platform for the Public Schools*, did not deal with secondary schools exclusively, it did include the following objectives: critical and effective methods of thinking, curiosity and creativity, useful work habits and study skills, constructive social attitudes and relationships, a range of significant interests, appreciation of the fine arts (music, art, literature, and other aesthetic experiences), social sensitivity, personal-social adjustment, effective communication and expression, important

[5]National Education Association, Project on the Instructional Program of the Public Schools, *Schools for the 60s*, Washington, D.C., 1963, p. 9.

information and knowledge, physical and mental health, ethics, and a consistent philosophy of life. The committee recommended that secondary schools divest themselves of the overwhelming influence of higher education and orient their curriculums and practices toward objectives more attainable by the majority of youth.[6]

TYPES

To meet the varied purposes of secondary education and the diverse needs of secondary school pupils, many types of schools have been developed. The types of secondary institutions illustrated schematically in Figure 8-3 are discussed in the next section.

Four-year High Schools

General High School. During the heyday of the combination junior and senior high school the role

[6]George H. Reavis and Carter V. Good, *An Educational Platform for the Public Schools*, Phi Delta Kappa, Bloomington, Ind., 1968, p. 11.

of the traditional or general four-year high school declined. However, in many instances the four-year organization was never changed to the junior-senior combination. For example, in some states, such as California, Illinois, and New Jersey, many high schools have remained as separate school districts with their own boards of education, divorced legally from the elementary school district. The typical four-year high school, commencing with the ninth grade, has also remained a more practical arrangement for graduates from rural, small, eight-grade school districts. Long tradition too has favored the four-year school. Today the rise in the number of new middle schools, for combinations such as grades 5 to 8, is also increasing the need for more four-year high schools, which are often comprehensive secondary schools, described earlier.

Vocational and Technical Schools. Vocational and technical schools constitute the most rapidly growing sector of secondary education from the standpoint of enrollment and expenditure. Enrollments in these schools have more than doubled during the past twenty years, and expenditures have increased approximately seven times during the same period. Many more new vocational and technical schools

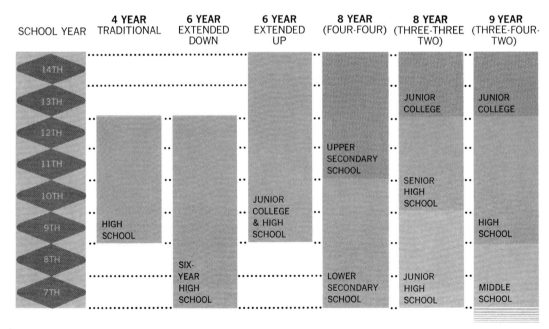

FIGURE 8-3 Organizational patterns of secondary education. These are the more common patterns of secondary education, although many other variations and combinations of these patterns exist. In many districts, the middle school—or intermediate school—is often regarded as a division between elementary and secondary education and a part of neither. The middle school sometimes includes the sixth year.

are being constructed each year. Some vocational and technical schools are post-secondary institutions. These post-secondary schools are described in Chapter 9.

The secondary-level vocational and technical schools have been developed to meet the nation's insatiable appetite for technically trained manpower and to provide appropriate educational opportunity for employment in the trade and technical vocations for students uninterested in academic programs. Some of the programs of studies in these schools are terminal programs and others are preparatory to advanced post-secondary technical education.

The curriculums of the vocational and technical schools vary widely and are usually well adapted to the particular labor needs of the regions which they serve. Many of these schools prepare students for trades such as appliance repair, automobile mechanics, drafting, electrical construction, machineshop operation, radio and television servicing, welding, refrigeration, heating, practical nursing, chemical technology, marketing, data processing, computer technology, nuclear technology, accounting, and secretarial and clerical work. Many of these schools also offer basic education in the physical sciences, social sciences, mathematics, and language arts because these subjects are important for all broadly educated citizens and also because the physical sciences, particularly, constitute the academic basis for technical study. Some vocational and technical schools offer only technical education and permit students to attend comprehensive high schools for their academic studies. Some enroll only juniors and seniors who have completed the required basic education in comprehensive high schools during earlier years.

Most vocational and technical schools offer extensive tests of students' interests and aptitudes as well as vocational counseling service to help students make the wisest possible vocational choices. Many of these schools are open year-round and offer, in addition to the usual day classes, night classes, for persons who must work during the day while preparing for their vocational advancement at night. Most of them also offer programs for adults. The graduates of these schools usually have little difficulty in finding employment.

Many of these schools are known as "area" vocational or technical high schools because they are commonly supported by the various school districts in the county or area which they serve, often under the jurisdiction of the county school office.

Of course, many comprehensive high schools offer their own vocational-education programs, but these programs are much less varied and extensive because of the great costs involved.

The federal government has stimulated the development of vocational education through the Smith-Hughes Act of 1917, the National Defense Education Act of 1958, and the Vocational Education Act of 1963.

The place of vocational and technical education in the school curriculum is discussed more fully in Chapter 14.

Specialized High Schools. Although the comprehensive high school and the general vocational-technical school are the two basic types of secondary schools, there are quite a number of distinctive and excellent specialized schools, particularly in the large cities. San Francisco's Apprenticeship and Journeyman School, New York's High School of Music and Art and its Maritime High School, Brooklyn's High School of Automotive Trades, the Interlochen Arts Academy, and Miami's Technical High School are examples of such specialized schools. Many states have instituted statewide systems of specialized trade and technical schools at the secondary level.

Three-year Senior High Schools

While patterns vary, the three-year high school, with grades 10 to 12, is usually linked organizationally with a junior high school, with grades 7 to 9. Often the size of the legal school district, the nature of the attendance units, the condition of the existing buildings, and the philosophy of the administrators and the board of education are factors affecting the type of secondary school organization. With the advent of the junior high school, it was assumed by many that institutions of higher education would not be overly concerned with the content of its last year—the ninth grade. Thus it was thought that more orientation, wider experimentation, and greater latitude would be possible for the ninth-grader in the 6-3-3 organization, with a junior high followed by a senior high. However, the long arm of accrediting associations and the continuing concern of colleges over the preparation of incoming freshmen have reduced curricular freedom and educational experimentation for ninth-graders in the junior-senior high school combination. Furthermore, today's ninth-graders—educationally, psychologically, and physiologically—belong with the tenth-, eleventh-, and twelfth-grade students rather than with seventh- and eighth-grade pupils.

Junior High Schools

Types. The most common form of junior high school organization is the three-year unit comprising grades 7 to 9 as part of a 6-3-3 system of organization. In this organization the junior high school is regarded as a separate unit, with its own curriculum, schedule, and administration, though not always with its own building. However, this arrangement is being challenged increasingly by the middle school, which is composed commonly of grades 6 to 8 or 5 to 8.

Another form of organization is the 6-6 pattern, a plan in which grades 7 to 9 are combined with the upper three secondary years to form a six-year high school in a single unit. Several unified districts operate two-year junior high schools, comprising grades 7 and 8 only, with grade 9 included in the senior high school. A few school systems maintain other variations, but most of the remainder have 8-4 plans, with no junior high school. The larger the school district, the greater has been the frequency of separate junior high schools. Most seventh- and eighth-grade students are now enrolled in some form of secondary school program. The particular pattern of the organization is of less consequence than its ability to fulfill the unique purposes proclaimed for the junior high school years.

Purposes. The junior high school was created to serve three distinct needs: to smooth the transition from childhood to adolescence, to ease the articulation between the child-centered elementary school and the subject-centered high school, and to permit students to explore various fields of study in preparation for later educational and vocational choices. Proponents of the junior high school believe that neither the elementary school nor the traditional four-year high school adequately serves the needs of early adolescents, who are significantly different from both prepubescent and late-adolescent youth. Early adolescence is a crucial period of development. The physical, emotional, and social strains of these turbulent years are legion.

Programs. The junior high school curriculum continues the development of basic skills started in the elementary school with emphasis on developmental and remedial reading. It emphasizes the tremendous changes taking place in the world and how the adolescent can cope with these changes. It also stresses democratic values and ideals to guide students into socially acceptable and personally satisfying behavior.

The junior high school provides a variety of exploratory educational experiences in such fields as art, music, homemaking, and industrial arts, as well as in the academic subjects, and it helps the student to elect courses more confidently in later years. It brings the more adequate guidance and other pupil personnel services of the secondary school to bear upon the problems of early adolescents. If the faculty is well prepared, it has the special understanding required to relate class instruction to the unique needs of the early adolescent. Unfortunately, many junior high schools are that in name only, failing to adapt their instruction, services, and facilities to the functions their school was designed to serve. Junior high schools are too often housed in cast-off senior high school buildings ill-suited to their needs. Junior high school teachers sometimes regard their positions as less prestigious than the senior high school assignments to which they aspire.

Private Secondary Schools

Private high schools, prep schools, academies, and other secondary educational institutions included in the general discussion in this chapter are very numerous.[7] One in ten secondary school students is enrolled in a private school, including (1) parochial high schools, (2) independent schools, (3) private technical schools, and (4) street academies.

Parochial High Schools. Parochial high schools, supported by various religious denominations, constitute by far the largest sector of private secondary schools, enrolling approximately 75 percent of the students attending nonpublic schools. The largest number of parochial schools, more than 2,000, are supported by the Roman Catholic church. Their

[7] *Lovejoy's Prep School Guide*, published annually by Harper & Row, Publishers, Incorporated, New York, lists approximately two thousand of the many independent, private, nonpublic college preparatory schools in the United States.

enrollment constitutes approximately 75 percent of the students attending parochial schools. Lutheran and Jewish secondary schools are next in frequency, although they are much less numerous than Roman Catholic schools. Parochial high schools are maintained to provide greater emphasis upon spiritual growth and to propagate the faith of the church that supports them. Chapter 1 describes the educational philosophy that commonly shapes these schools.

Enrollments in the Roman Catholic parochial schools began to decline in the mid-1960s, although the decline has been much less marked in the secondary schools than in the elementary schools. A decrease in the availability of state and federal funds for private schools followed the 1971 U.S. Supreme Court decision. This arrested the growth of church-supported schools.

Many parochial schools have launched new programs emphasizing special assistance to disadvantaged Negro, Oriental, and Mexican-American students. Some parochial schools have worked out cooperative programs with public schools in which the students' secular study is taken in the public schools, while study in sectarian subjects is offered by the parochial schools.

Independent Schools. Most of the remaining 25 percent of secondary students attend private day schools. A much smaller number attend private boarding schools. The private day schools vary widely in quality. Many of the better private day schools have sprung up in the suburbs. Their curriculums are usually restricted to academic studies, since their function is largely college-preparatory. Many of them offer education of fine quality within their limited purpose.

Within the last decade a great number of private day schools have been thrown together hastily and inexpertly in the Southeastern states and in the Northeastern metropolitan areas as a haven for families who prefer that their children not attend desegregated school systems. Such schools often function without adequate faculties and facilities, so that their service is both expensive and poor. They can be found in abandoned stores, church basements, and even private homes. They usually lack accreditation and are often poorly administered.

The most famous independent schools are the old prestigious private boarding schools, such as Phillips, Exeter, Choate, and Lawrenceville. These are well-endowed institutions with faculties, campuses, and facilities that would rival those of many

small colleges. The typical private boarding school enrolls between 300 and 600 students with annual tuition fees equal to those of many colleges. Here one can still find teen-agers reading Cicero in the original, going to bed at 10 p.m., and wearing coats and ties. Most of these schools are very old, and some date back to the seventeenth century. They are characterized by small classes, carefully chosen students, and college-preparatory curriculums, which give them the name "prep schools." Separate boarding schools formerly served either male or female students, but now many of them are becoming coeducational. Many of these schools are recruiting black students from the ghettos and subsidizing their education with scholarships. Some of them, such as the Francis W. Parker School in Chicago, are progressive in their educational philosophy, while others are conservative. Many of these schools, like small private colleges, are suffering severe financial strain as the costs of fine quality education outrun the revenues. As public schools improve in quality, many prep schools are losing much of the advantage they once enjoyed over public schools as guaranteed passports to college. Many of the new generation of youth don't yearn for the cloistered life-style of the private boarding school. As the headmaster of Vermont Academy put it, "They are weighing the confinement of the boarding school against staying home with girls, booze, pot, and cars." Many prep schools are shedding their old-school-tie image for one more in tune with the Aquarians. Some observers predict that private boarding schools will gradually disappear from the scene. They are important, not because of their numbers, but because of the select quality of their graduates and because the quality of their practices often influences educational thought generally.

The future of both day schools and boarding schools could be assured if the voucher plan were to become widespread. In this scheme, public revenues are distributed, not directly to public schools, but to parents in the form of vouchers to be deposited with either public or private schools as chosen by parents for their children's enrollment. This proposal has precipitated a storm of controversy and is discussed in Chapters 1 and 16.

Private Technical Schools. Several thousand private vocational, technical, and special-ability schools on

The Interlochen Music Camp and Arts Academy (Michigan) is one of the many private schools which offer education with special emphases to a great many youths.

the secondary level teach trades to, and develop the talents of, teen-agers and adults who have not finished high school or who seek "retreading" in another trade or vocation. These secondary schools offer instruction in a wide variety of fields. The Interlochen (Michigan) Arts Academy, established in 1962, was America's first coeducational boarding school for talented arts students in grades 8 to 12. Atlanta, Georgia, is the home of the National Professional Truck Drivers Training School. Countless cities have private schools of beauty culture, often bearing the lofty title of "college" or "university."

Street Academies. A new kind of private school is springing up in several large cities. Known variously as "street academies," "continuation schools," "second-chance schools," and "adopted high schools," they have one thing in common—they are an alternative to the failure of urban public high schools to meet the needs of ghetto youth. Clearly many divergent youths cannot find their way successfully through the highly structured comprehensive high school with its emphasis on uniform and sometimes repressive standards. The academies accept students, usually public school dropouts, at their own level regardless of their problems or lack of success in conventional schooling. They emphasize education which is "only a step from the sidewalk," oriented toward the reality of ghetto life-styles. The street academies are extremely flexible and operate a freewheeling curriculum that accommodates the individual needs and interests of students. They are informal and stress deep personal involvement of

adults with youths. This type of educational experience may be the last chance for the thousands of teen-agers who drop out of city high schools every month. Street academies offer to many of these young people their first taste of success and sense of personal worth.

If there is such a thing as a "typical" street academy, it consists of perhaps fifteen to thirty students, three teachers, a street worker, and many part-time instructors, some of them corporation executives, social workers, student teachers, Teacher Corps personnel, and ministers. It is housed in an abandoned store in an urban ghetto. Its students, usually black, respond to its emphasis upon black identity and black pride.

Some of the street academies are financed by grants from private foundations, most notably the Ford Foundation and the Rockefeller Foundation. Many are "adopted" by private industries, such as McGraw-Hill, Union Carbide, IBM, Continental Can, Chase Manhattan Bank, and General Electric. They look upon these academies not simply as a charitable undertaking but also as a means of rehabilitating persons who may become employable in their in-

Street academies, often adopted by private industries, provide informal education more relevant to the needs and life styles of those students who are not responsive to traditional schooling.

dustries. This benefaction by industry abrogates the charge that the capitalistic system is interested only in the exploitation of people. Not all the academies adopted by industry have been successful, but those which emphasize work-study programs with real opportunity for respectable employment appear to enjoy the greatest success. Some of the street academies have established cooperative relationships with public schools to share in their resources.

Two of the most famous street academies are the Harlem Preparatory School in New York and the Christian Action Ministry Academy in Chicago. Harlem Prep, under the dynamic direction of its black headmaster, Edward Carpenter, has been successful, not only in rescuing dropouts but also in preparing many of them for successful admission to eminent colleges. Carpenter attributes Harlem Prep's success in reclaiming lost youth to the teachers' "unshakable faith that the students can make it." Carpenter also credits many of the school's white benefactors, or "fat cats" as he calls them, for their support of the school. Sponsored originally by the New York Urban League and Roman Catholic Manhattanville College, Harlem Prep is housed in a remodeled supermarket.

The heart of Harlem Prep's staff is its "street workers"—young men and women, black and white, who live in the neighborhood and literally go into the streets to rescue their young wards. They often take homeless teen-agers into their apartments to help them kick drugs. The street worker has been described as "motivator, counselor, friend, father, disciplinarian, and companion" of the ghetto youth.

The Christian Action Ministry Academy in Chicago is also proving that public school rejects can learn. Supported by an alliance of Protestant and Catholic churches, it sets its sights on anyone, male or female, who wants to come, whether he can be prepared for college or not. Four out of five of the boys admitted have police records. Many of the students demonstrate remarkable gain in academic achievement as well as creative talent in such elective fields as art, drama, sewing, journalism, music, social problems, and photography. The climate is markedly freer than in most public schools, and the few basic rules are drawn up by the students: no weapons, marijuana, or alcoholic beverages allowed in the building, and no swearing, out of respect to the sisters; and "any brother who fights another brother will suffer the consequences."

Despite their rapid growth, these "second-

chance" schools are able to accommodate only a small percentage of the lost youths who need help. It is hoped that these schools will demonstrate to the public schools that many youths who cannot make it in the regimented traditional school can nevertheless find success in schools which are willing to adapt to the students rather than the other way around. It is further hoped that these novel schools will become the prototypes for many other such institutions to be established by both the public school systems and private enterprise.

Other Types

Summer Schools. While the "summer school" is not a special type of school organizationally, it is a special program, covering an abbreviated period of six to eight weeks, rather than a semester or a year, and operating on a more concentrated schedule of double or multiple periods.

Various factors have stimulated the great growth of, and accelerated attendance at, summer schools for secondary school students. Federal and state work laws restricting employment for youth and labor union regulations regarding the minimum age of members are two factors discouraging teen-agers from seeking summer employment and encouraging them to attend summer schools. Many talented teen-agers use summer school work to hasten their graduation date or to accumulate extra credits. Some students take summer school classes to make up "flunks," to do remedial work, or to benefit from courses not generally available during the regular year, such as driver training. In many instances secondary school summer sessions give teen-agers "something constructive to do."

The Economic Opportunity Act enables some high school juniors and seniors to attend summer sessions away from home on college and university campuses. For example, in the initial stages of the project Upward Bound, some high school juniors and seniors complete two months of residence on the university campus and attend classes on the high school level. In their free time they are permitted to audit college classes. In addition to the academic programs, the students participate in recreational and musical activities. To broaden their fields of knowledge, they tour industries, cultural centers, and governmental offices in the college area. Coun-

Upward Bound programs have been successful in helping more high school students find their way into higher education.

seling services continue after the close of the summer session.

Upward Bound programs have been remarkably successful. Their participants have been admitted to college at a higher rate (80 percent as compared with 65 percent of all high school graduates) and have attained approximately the same grade averages and retention in college as their peers. However, Upward Bound programs are still too few to accommodate more than a very small fraction of students with potential who should be helped. The Kerner Commission on Civil Disorders recommended that Upward Bound be expanded substantially as a means of reducing the alienation of our youth.

Under the Elementary and Secondary Education Act, some sixth-graders attend high schools in the summer. This type of project, called "Running Start," is designed to familiarize prospective high school students with the difference between elementary school and high school and to orient them to high school procedures.

These and other programs have stimulated summer programs in secondary schools across the country and have helped to encourage a few school systems to institute year-round school programs which may eventually become far more commonplace.

PRACTICES

Several salient characteristics of modern secondary education are presented here through brief descriptions of current practices in (1) organization and administration, (2) curriculum and teaching-learning procedures, and (3) personnel.

Organization and Administration

Generally, with few exceptions, the high school is a subject-centered, departmentalized, graded organization. Recently there has been a trend toward longer school days and longer school years. As a result of the general increase in population and the reorganization of school districts, there has been a trend toward larger, as well as more, high schools.

One interesting innovation in secondary school organization has been the rise of the "school within a school" concept. This idea is manifested architecturally in the campus-style secondary school plant. A number of partially self-contained units, each housing a few hundred students, exist as satellites near but apart from a central service unit, which includes such common facilities as administrative offices, auditorium, cafeteria, library, and gymnasium. "Also called the 'little school' or 'house plan,' it is designed to recapture the intimacy and individual attention of the small school, while retaining the greater efficiency and more extensive facilities of the large school."[8]

Modern secondary schools are becoming larger. The urbanization of our society has resulted in higher densities of population in metropolitan areas and larger numbers of students in school-

[8] Mauritz Johnson, "Research and Secondary Education," *Educational Forum*, vol. 31, p. 297, March, 1967.

Modern architecture combines beauty, creative design, and utility in secondary school buildings that depart radically from stereotyped buildings of the past.

attendance areas. The reorganization of school districts has resulted in the merger of many smaller school systems with small high schools into a single school district with a few large high schools. High schools with enrollments in excess of one thousand are common, and in metropolitan areas, high schools with student bodies in excess of two thousand are not uncommon. Although large size is no guarantee of quality, large high schools do permit broader educational programs and service at more reasonable costs per student.

The integrated, comprehensive secondary school, including a broad spectrum of vocational-technical-occupational programs, is envisioned in the concept of the "secondary education park".

The secondary education park is an organizational innovation which is specifically designed to provide a synthesis between the objectives of integration and educational quality. . . . [It is] a secondary school with three distinct characteristics: large size, comprehensiveness, and internal decentralization.[9]

These plans for spacious parks are described in detail in Chapter 15.

More secondary schools are being organized by county and intermediate administrative units. State boards of education and their state departments are becoming more aggressive in promoting statewide programs of secondary education. Regional associations that accredit secondary schools are stressing qualitative standards as well as revising quantitative measures.

[9]J. Alan Thomas, "The Secondary Education Park: Value Synthesis in Urban School Systems," *Administrator's Notebook*, vol. 14, pp. 1-4, November, 1965.

Curriculum and Teaching-Learning Procedures

The continuing explosions of knowledge and the radical revolutions in technology are producing many changes in the curriculum and in the methods and materials of instruction in the secondary schools. Curriculum research and instructional innovations have been stimulated by federal fiscal grants through the National Defense Education Act and subsequent legislation. National professional organizations, regional educational laboratories, and independent foundations are also catalytic agents producing numerous curricular changes through experimentations and innovations. These curricular changes are described in Chapter 14.

The nation's growing concern for the maximum intellectual development of its gifted students prompted many innovations such as the downward extension of advanced subject matter, the enrichment of content, and the offering of advanced-placement courses. The latter, particularly, has been one of the most remarkable and significant changes in the secondary school. Under this plan, begun in 1956 by the College Entrance Examination Board, college-level courses are being offered to bright high school students who, upon successful completion of examinations, receive advanced standing or actual college credit. Students from nearly a thousand high schools take the courses annually for credit in approximately a thousand cooperating colleges and universities. Some high school students are able to enter college as sophomores.

However, these trends toward more rigorous academic discipline in the early 1960s were challenged in the late 1960s and early 1970s by a new educational emphasis. The civil rights movement quickened the nation's concern about equal educational opportunity for minority groups who often found subject-centered education irrelevant to their interests and needs. The war on poverty demanded that high schools become more responsive to the realities of economic disadvantage and prepare students from low-income families for better employment opportunities. These forces tended to make secondary school curriculums more viable and more student-centered.

The curriculum of the comprehensive high school is being broadened to include many new courses and much more substance, with greater emphasis upon vocational education. Among the newer course offerings are environmental education, education about drug abuse, sex education, world culture, international relations, economics, sociology, psychology, philosophy, education, electronics, computer training, astronomy, space science, earth science, public issues or problems, the Bible as literature, religious literature, and many languages rather new to high school curriculums, such as Italian, Japanese, Chinese, and Russian. International cleavages and competition have resulted in greater emphasis on the study of the values, ideals, and accomplishments of representative governments, often in comparison with other political and economic systems, notably communism.

The methods and materials of instruction are changing. Teaching methods are emphasizing both the intrinsic and extrinsic values of knowledge. For example, the teaching technique of "simulation" or "gaming" is being used increasingly. Simulation helps to bridge the gap between the reality of the world and the academics of the school. Group games force students to cooperate with their teammates and to study and understand their opponents. Games force attention to the learning activity itself, since winning the game, not grades, is its own reward. Various plans are used to provide students with more time for independent study, work in small groups, and work-study programs.

Procedures for scheduling students are changing. In the large high schools, high-speed computers help match students, instructors, courses, and classrooms. Many schools have class periods longer than the conventional fifty-five minutes. Some administrators employ "modular" scheduling, where a one-hour period is divided into modules from fifteen to thirty minutes in length for such varied activities as teaching, group discussion, conference, and study. Obviously, more modules are used for laboratory work. In some schools the old multiple-class scheduling is used, in which an instructor teaches more than one subject in the same room to different groups. Some elective courses are now being scheduled after regular school hours, on Saturdays, or during summer sessions. More secondary schools should keep their libraries and laboratories open evenings and Saturdays under supervision.

The Commission on the Experimental Study of the Utilization of Staffs in Secondary Schools, sponsored by the National Association of Secondary

Small-group instruction relates learning more effectively to the particular needs and interests of students. Here an employee of Bell Telephone serves as a volunteer tutor of high school students.

School Principals, has helped to develop creative models of deploying personnel, time, space, and other resources for more effective instruction in secondary schools. It has promoted the use of varied student grouping patterns, especially small groups, independent study, team teaching, flexible scheduling, teacher aides, greater reliance on community agencies as instructional resources, and educational technology. With the support of a grant from the Danforth Foundation, thirty-four public and private high schools across the country have been selected to serve as models in the demonstration of the effectiveness of these stratagems and, it is hoped, according to the National Education Association, to "help to provide the pattern for twenty-first-century education."

Students

The most dramatic change in high school students in recent years has been their increased disposition toward activism. Student activism, spawned first on college campuses, has now become commonplace among the nation's high schools. More than two-thirds of the secondary schools have experienced some form of student protest, ranging all the way from peaceful expression of discontent to riotous actions resulting in loss of life. In some high schools police or security guards regularly patrol the halls. Some high schools have had to close temporarily until order was restored. Although the frequency and violence of student protest are greater in large urban high schools, many suburban and rural communities have not been spared. Indeed, the incidence of unruly student activism has been greater in high schools than in colleges. High school outbreaks appear to be more spontaneous than college disorders. Confrontations in high schools are more frequently between student and student, student and teacher, and student and administrator, while college confrontations more commonly center on student protests against "the establishment" and society. Many observers of student protest note that high school activists tend to be more radical than college protesters. The far greater number of high schools than colleges creates larger potential frequency for activism in the high schools.

Student activism in schools is manifested in many forms and born of many issues. In most cases students have presented lists of grievances or demands to school authorities without violent action. Clearly this form of protest is very much within the American tradition and should be encouraged. But, as students often point out, such peaceful protest is too often ignored by school authorities. In many cases students are then moved to more militant action, such as the publication of underground newspapers, demonstrations, sit-ins, boycotts, or strikes. These actions, if they are nonviolent and do not disrupt the rights and safety of other students, are very much within the tradition of protest in our society even though they may be in violation of school regulations. When student activism results in riotous behavior, such as mass fights among students, assaults on teachers and principals, and destruction of school property, the problem is of an entirely different order and the use of force in restraining the rioters is justifiable.

But many school authorities and citizens fail to make these important distinctions. Obviously when schools take the same hard line against conscientious and responsible students seeking genuine school reform through peaceful action that they take against anarchists trying to destroy schools and society, the responsible students may be driven into the arms of the anarchists. In many communities, student activists are organizing to mobilize student power more effectively.

A host of local, state, and national commissions have been organized to study student activism in high schools and to advise school systems on how they should respond. One study, conducted by the Syracuse University Research Corporation for the U.S. Office of Education, reported that racially integrated high schools are more likely to experience disruption than those that are almost all white or

black. It also found that high schools with large percentages of black enrollment are less likely to be disrupted if they also have high percentages of black faculty members. In the larger high schools, racial issues were the cause of disruption in more than 50 percent of the protests.

What other issues precipitate protests? Certainly the issues vary in time and place, but in general they include the slow pace of schools' response to the great social problems of our time; the irrelevance of the school curriculum to the real world of the students; the overly protective climate of schools in dealing with adolescents who are now maturing more rapidly; the dehumanization of schools and other institutions particularly as they become larger; unilateral decision making by the same teachers and principals who teach the importance of citizen participation in a democracy; harsh disciplinary actions; rising expectations of youth and society of their schools; discourtesy of some teachers and administrators; the contagious effect upon high school students of successful militancy by college students, teachers, and other adults; instruction which has encouraged youths to quicken their concern and their response to social injustice; the growing tendency of the courts to insist that students have the same constitutional rights of nondisruptive protest as adults; the natural turbulence of adolescent life; and the general phenomenon of civil disobedience and violence which has come to characterize much of man's life throughout the world.

These broad social forces are often particularized in high school students' protest around such issues as student dress codes; suspension of students for disciplinary reasons; personal indignities to students imposed by other students, teachers, and administrators; discrimination against students; censorship of student publications; insufficient number of black teachers, counselors, and administrators; excessive administrative control of student government; absence from the curriculum of black studies and other instruction of interest to students; restrictions on the use of automobiles by students; and constraints upon freedom of movement and activity within the schools. No single list of grievances can be complete. Certainly it must not be presumed that all high schools are guilty of all these allegations.

How should high schools respond to the discontent of students? First, it seems clear that the problem must be seen as a search for redress of the legitimate causes of protest rather than for the suppression of protest. The latter course is still too alluring to too many teachers and administrators. Second, high schools must extend the parameters of student participation in goal setting and policy making so that schools can indeed accommodate the legitimate interests and ideals of students. Third, better channels of communication and problem resolution must be maintained so that students can find within the organization the means for relief from discontent and thus preempt the need for violent activity. Fourth, the school curriculum should be reoriented toward the reality of the world and the fateful and controversial issues that confront mankind. Fifth, citizenship education should be redirected toward helping students to acquire a better sense of responsible citizenship, to understand and respect the democratic faith in rational, nonviolent stratagems for change, to discern the difference between civil disobedience and lawlessness, to accept the will of the majority with the same grace that they accept the rights and protections of government, to understand that without public order freedom and security are impossible for all, to acquire a sense of morality in dissent, and to understand when civil disobedience is moral and when it is immoral.

Schools cannot really inveigh against student protest until they have given students rich opportunity to confront in an open and scholarly way the imperfections which they see in school and society. For students, the school is the part of the establishment which is most meaningful to them. Unless the school becomes a laboratory for the practice of responsible democratic citizenship and makes itself a paragon of the best of the democratic heritage, we cannot in good conscience objurgate student protest. In sum, student activism should not be viewed as a tragic circumstance that must be subdued at all costs but rather as an opportunity to mobilize both students and educators to the challenging task of improving educational experience in ways that are meaningful both to students and to society.

Many high schools are moving in this direction. Student government is being reformed to respond more effectively and more powerfully to students' expectations. Students are being given more freedom in the determination of their programs of studies and the content of their courses. In many schools letter grades, hall passes, dress codes, censorship of student newspapers and assembly programs, searches of lockers, and other constraints and indignities are being eliminated. Grievance procedures and other equitable means for resolving disputes are being established. Ombudsmen are appearing in some schools to help students cut through red tape and misunderstanding. School administrators and teachers are struggling to create more open climates in which behavior can become more authentic and satisfying. But the problems are by no means resolved, and indeed they never will be. Deep controversies continue to exist in many schools: strident voices from some quarters call for more freedom for students, while others believe that schools are too permissive. The problems and issues of student activism at all levels of the educational spectrum are discussed more fully in Chapters 1 and 11.

High school dropouts—actual and potential—are receiving much attention from educators, sociologists, politicians, religious leaders, and others. Many high schools are revamping their curriculums, student groupings, and scheduling of classes so as to reduce the number of potential "pushouts"—students who might be expelled because of academic failures or administrative rulings as well as both married and unmarried girls who become pregnant. Teaching-learning procedures include extra remedial instruction, after-school study centers, volunteer or paid tutorial work by college students, summer school for underachievers, purposeful cocurricular activities, and early identification of potential dropouts. Many of these activities are supported by the Dropout Prevention Program funded by the Elementary and Secondary Education Act.

Besides the numerous government-supported programs, there are many private projects. For example, the National Association of Manufacturers is sponsoring a nationwide program of basic education for dropouts, with an offer of jobs to those who stay in the program to its end. This program, called MIND (Methods for INtellectual Development), is being conducted with private capital from many participating industries.

More teen-age drinking, drug abuse, and promiscuity have created many problems for all, especially for the student himself. Guidance services have been strengthened substantially to help youth come to grips with both academic and personal problems. "Crash pads" and other types of rehabilitation services are springing up in schools to help young drug addicts kick their dangerous habits. Many other student personnel services dealing with health, sensitivity training, job placement, and college placement are also being developed.

PROBLEMS

During the past dozen years particularly, the American high school, like all sectors of education, has been the target of vigorous criticism. Although critics do not always agree on either the nature of the faults or the means for correcting them, several problems are commonly underlined. One of the most inherent criticisms is that the high school curriculum is not relevant to the realities of life or the interests of students. It is also contended that high schools are overadministered, being preoccupied with order, control, and routine. High schools are allegedly unresponsive to student expectations.

When high schools functioned primarily to prepare students for college and when students who could not meet the academic standards could drop out and find worthwhile employment, our society could perhaps afford the luxury of secondary schools addressed primarily to the needs of the more academically talented. However, within the last decade we have become persuaded that secondary education must meet the needs of all youth. The old academic model of secondary education with arbitrary academic standards was not appropriate for the 25 percent of students who once dropped out. This poses the problem of redesigning secondary programs and practices to accomplish what neither this nation nor any other nation has previously attempted—namely, universal secondary education that is responsive to the needs and interests of all youths. This challenge poses problems of curriculum reform, teaching method, student personnel practices, counseling, finance, and administration.

These problems are particularly manifested in urban school systems where racial cleavages exacerbate the circumstances. Overcrowding and underfinancing also combine to complicate the problem, especially in the cities. As noted earlier, student unrest often contributes to a climate of anxiety which inhibits learning. These factors have their effect on teacher morale. Experienced teachers frequently opt for reassignment in other schools

where the climate is more serene, thus denying good teaching to the students who need it most.

These problems, although difficult, are not hopeless. There is reason for cautious optimism that secondary schools will continue to respond in many of the ways described earlier in this chapter.

FUTURE

During the past two decades particularly, American public education has been the subject of widespread study and criticism. The high school has been the center of vigorous scrutiny, criticism, and redevelopment. It is apparent that American secondary education is undergoing substantial modification.

The trend is in the direction of more flexibility, variety, openness, informality, and accommodation to the individual differences of a much more cosmopolitan student body that no longer excludes the poor and the nonconforming. Greater variations in student groupings, faculty deployment, graduation requirements, academic standards, curriculum content, and school facilities are already evident in such new arrangements as flexible scheduling, differentiated staffing and team teaching, ungraded instructional groups and "phasing" which permits grouping of students not by grade levels but by ability to grasp the subject matter. Probably the greatest educational development of the near future will be far more widespread use of new instructional technology in secondary education, discussed in Chapters 14 and 15. It is also likely that secondary education of the future will be less "classroom-bound," as schools discover the instructive potential of public and private community agencies.

Although the concept of the comprehensive high school appears sound, many unorthodox schools, such as schools without walls, street academies, and others yet to appear, will probably proliferate to accommodate students who are not responsive to conventional schooling. The American dream of secondary education for all youth is rapidly being realized and may reach its culmination during the 1970s.

SUMMARY

Secondary education reaches a larger proportion of youth in the United States than in any other country, currently enrolling more than 90 percent of youths of high school age. Federal aid programs, such as the Economic Opportunity Act of 1964 and the Elementary and Secondary Education Act of 1965, are helping to increase high school attendance and to reduce the number of dropouts. The median number of years of schooling completed by adults over 25 years of age is beyond the equivalent of high school graduation.

The historical calendar in this chapter chronicles many significant dates in the development of secondary education, which has gone through four major stages, distinguished by the institutions that characterized them: (1) the Latin grammar school, (2) the tuition academy, (3) the free public high school, and (4) the comprehensive secondary school.

Secondary education serves many purposes. It provides general education for all, prepares gifted students for college, and provides practical preparation for the problems of life that will confront those who do not attend college. Several classic statements have been made on the purposes of secondary education.

There are many types of secondary schools, among them the general, comprehensive, high school; the vocational-technical four-year high school; the three-year senior high; the three- or two-year junior high; the technical postelementary school; the street academy; and, in between elementary and secondary education, the middle school.

One in ten secondary school students is enrolled in a private high school. The majority of private high schools are parochial schools. Independent private secondary schools are often leaders in educational innovations.

The organization of secondary schools is increasingly characterized by largeness, with semi-autonomous "little schools" within the larger schools, and by much more openness, flexibility, and variety in scheduling, grouping, staff deployment, and academic standards. Their curriculums are becoming more rigorous for the gifted students, more accommodating for the handicapped, and more reality-oriented, with emphasis upon the occupational and personal needs of students who do not plan to attend college. Instructional methods are being modified to provide greater opportunity for independent study, for combinations of work and study, for educational technology, and for community-centered learning. The quickening of student activism has prompted many of these changes as well as more freedom in student personnel policies and practices.

The period of secondary education, with its emphasis on general education for all and on special preparation for practical life for those who will not go beyond secondary school, is followed by the period of higher learning, which offers a wide variety of opportunities for continuing institutionalized education. These opportunities for higher education are presented in Chapter 9.

Suggested Activities

1. Prepare a report on student activism—its causes and the reforms which it suggests.
2. Visit an independent school, parochial school, street academy, or "school without walls," if there is one near your campus, and evaluate its program in terms of the needs of its students and the applicability of its program for more conventional public high schools.
3. Compare the services of a small high school with those of a large, comprehensive school.
4. Examine the certification requirements for the teachers of secondary schools in your state.
5. List the special qualifications and preparation you think a secondary school teacher should have.
6. Interview a high school principal about the most significant changes in his school in the past decade.
7. Suggest how secondary schools can better prepare students for the institutions of higher learning, which are described in the next chapter.
8. Describe, preferably after a visit, the programs of a modern area vocational-technical secondary school.
9. Describe the main provisions of the Elementary and Secondary Education Act passed by Congress in 1965, plus its amendments, and give illustrations of its effect on secondary education.
10. Prepare a report on the Kalamazoo High School case, showing the effects of court decision on the growth of high schools.

Bibliography

Alexander, William M. (ed.): *The High School of the Future: A Memorial to Kimball Wiles*, Charles E. Merrill Books, Inc., Columbus, Ohio, 1969. Projections of future secondary schools by distinguished contributors using Wiles' original essay on the high school of the future as a starting point.

Austin, David B.: "Secondary Education," in Robert L. Ebel (ed.), *Encyclopedia of Educational Research*, 4th ed., The Macmillan Co. of Canada, Limited, Toronto, 1969, pp. 1211–1217. A review of research on the scope, history, program, organization, and problems of secondary education.

Bailey, Stephen K.: *Disruption in Urban Public Secondary Schools*, National Association of Secondary School Principals, Washington, D.C., n.d. A report of a study of student disruption in high schools—the nature of the problem, its causes, and the appropriate response.

Clark, Leonard H. (ed.): *Strategies and Tactics in Secondary School Teaching: A Book of Readings*. The Macmillan Company, New York, 1968. A collection of readings presenting foundations for teaching method, approaches, and skills for the prospective teacher.

Crary, Ryland W.: *Humanizing the School: Curriculum Development and Theory*, Alfred A. Knopf, Inc., New York, 1969, chap. 7. A discussion of needed reforms in secondary schools and their curriculums to make them more humane.

Divoky, Diane (ed.): *How Old Will You Be in 1984?* Avon Book Division, the Hearst Corporation, New York, 1969. A collection of expressions of student outrage taken from high school underground newspapers.

Eurich, Alvin E. (ed.): *High School 1980: The Shape of the Future of Secondary Education*, Pitman Publishing Corporation, New York, 1970. Analyses of the condition and challenge of change, future curriculum, and special problems as conceived by noted scholars of secondary education.

Gorman, Burton W.: *Secondary Education: The High School America Needs*, Random House, Inc., New York, 1971. A blueprint for restructuring the high school, including reforms on curriculum, organization, staffing, and student personnel policies.

Hamilton, Norman K., and J. Galen Saylor (eds.): *Humanizing the Secondary School*, Association for Supervision and Curriculum Development, National Education Association, Washington, D.C., 1970. A prospectus containing

papers by ten prominent educators suggesting ways to make secondary school years a more humanizing experience.

Holton, Samuel: *Understanding the American Public High School*, Allyn and Bacon, Inc., Boston, 1969. A comprehensive survey of American public secondary education—its evolution, its present role, and possible directions for the future.

Muessig, Raymond H. (ed.): *Youth Education: Problems, Perspectives, and Promises*, 1968 Yearbook, Association for Supervision and Curriculum Development, National Education Association, Washington, D.C., 1968. A series of papers on the problems, perspectives, and promises of youth education.

National Association of Secondary School Principals: *A Profile of the Large City High School*, National Education Association, Washington, D.C., 1971. A report of a study of urban high schools—the nature of their conflicts and some suggested solutions.

National Association of Secondary School Principals: *Secondary Education in an Environment of Change*, National Education Association, Washington, D.C., 1969. A consideration of the nature of contemporary change in secondary education in relation to the changing social milieu.

National School Public Relations Association: *High School Unrest*, National Education Association, Washington, D.C., 1969. An explanation of the causes of high school students' unrest and what schools are doing to relieve the causes of unrest and handle disruptive behavior.

Ovard, Glen. F. (ed.): *Change and Secondary School Administration*, The Macmillan Company, New York, 1968, chaps. 1, 4–7. A book of readings dealing with the changing milieu of secondary education—its organization, curriculum, pedagogy, and administration.

Tanner, Daniel: *Secondary School Curriculum*, The Macmillan Company, Riverside, N.J., 1971. An analysis and evaluation of reforms and innovations in the secondary school curriculum.

Chapter 9   Higher Education

ORIENTATION

What is going on in colleges these days? Wherever people gather, this question is often asked in anguish. Concern about our colleges is widespread.

A student asks: "What are professors supposed to do if not teach? We rarely see them. Their classes are taught by graduate students, and getting an appointment with them is tougher than trying to see the mayor."

A professor complains: "They want instant, easy education without any effort on their part. Anything more than two weeks old is irrelevant. Our whole cultural heritage is set aside. They want no grades, no examinations, no required courses, no regulations, just a big academic playpen."

An alumnus inquires: "What has happened to their manners and their dress? This must be the age of the slobs."

A dean observes: "They are better educated and more mature, but I'm not sure that they are any brighter or more idealistic. I am sure that they are more arrogant, quixotic, disrespectful, and cynical than before."

A legislator says: "Why should we burden the taxpayer with higher appropriations for the colleges? Those kids are ungrateful, have no respect for property, and don't want to be there in the first place. With a little financial pinch, many who shouldn't be there anyway must get out and work for a living and those who stay could sacrifice a little and appreciate their opportunity more. We never fire-bombed any buildings in my day; we were too glad to be able to be there."

An administrator complains: "It's like an airport—faculty and students come and go and pause

Today's college students contemplate more seriously the fateful social issues of their times.

only to complain. There is nobody around long enough to build anything permanent."

The American university is unique, fragile, and beleaguered. The American university is in danger. It is extraordinarily important that students and all others understand these qualities lest, in our ignorance, we permit our universities, and with them our society, to be destroyed.

The American university is unique because it is not government, business, social organization, welfare agency, or political party. Its purpose is not to rule; not to make a profit; not to please students or faculty or alumni; not to reform society; not to correct social injustice; not to influence political action. Although it may contribute at times to these ends, it could be destroyed by serving these ends.

Although the American university should function within the democratic spirit, it is not a democracy, nor can it be, any more than a family, orchestra, or church can be.

Nor is a university a community of scholars, although it is frequently described as such. Its students are too transient. Its professors' devotion to their academic or professional fields often takes precedence over their allegiance to the university community. Its trustees and its alumni are too removed from its action. All but the smaller institutions of higher education are far too fragmented and diverse to sustain any sense of community.

What then is a university? The university is a citadel of knowledge, which it creates, disseminates, and applies. This singular function of the university is threatened when intruded upon by any other function.

Universities are threatened by those professors who are more interested in personal aggrandizement, popularity with students, or personal freedom than in the integrity and mission of the institution.

Universities are threatened by those students

who interrupt its work, destroy its property, coerce its members, or interfere with its production and dissemination of knowledge in the name of peace, social justice, or any other cause over which it has no jurisdiction.

Universities are threatened by those administrators who acquiesce to force or who refuse to negotiate just grievances, to respond to reason, or to protect peaceful protests.

Universities are threatened by trustees who are unresponsive to the call for institutional reform.

Universities are threatened by public officials and legislators who punish all students and society by exercising budget cuts against the entire university, capitalize upon campus unrest for political campaign rhetoric, and otherwise fail to distinguish between peaceful and violent demonstrators.

For the first time in our history, Americans appear to be losing faith in their colleges. This loss of public confidence in higher education threatens not only the financial welfare of colleges but their freedom as well. As Samuel Gould, former chancellor of the State University of New York warned, "A society that cannot trust its universities cannot trust itself."

Clearly the American people must come to regard their universities as citadels of knowledge, rather than as instruments of power. They must see their universities as resources which man can use in his search for a better life rather than as weapons to be controlled. They must seek to gain power from the universities rather than power over them. The people must cherish and protect these fragile institutions.

This chapter will deepen the reader's understanding of American institutions of higher education by exploring briefly their history; for one cannot understand how they came to be as they now are without knowledge of how they evolved. Among the topics considered below are the historical development of purposes of higher education; its nature and scope; the various types of colleges and universities; their governance, organization, operation, and control; their curriculums, faculties, and students; their financial circumstances; and their future. Some of the compelling issues facing higher education—the problems of open admission, response to student unrest, the appropriate purposes of higher education, and the rising costs—were discussed in Chapter 1.

FOUNDATIONS

American higher education is a blend of inheritance from European antecedents with distinctly American ingredients. The historical development of our colleges and universities from their elitist beginning to their egalitarian present is briefly sketched below and summarized in the historical calendar on page 213.

European Antecedents

The intellectual activity of the twelfth and thirteenth centuries gave rise to the university type of organization. When the number of students and professors at a church or cathedral school grew so large that it became necessary to organize a guild or *universitas* for mutual welfare and protection, then a university may be said to have come into existence.

The oldest university in Europe was Bologna, founded by a guild of students in the city of that name in northern Italy during the twelfth century. The study of law was of prime interest to medieval Italians, and soon Bologna developed a position of leadership in this field. In southern Italy the city of Salerno, a health resort, became famous for its lectures and collection of materials in the field of medicine.

In France, another medieval institution, the University of Paris, developed from a cathedral school. Naturally this school attracted a large number of students of religion. Although theology was the core, other fields, such as the arts, were stressed. Paris was the greatest of the medieval universities.

The old University of Prague, founded in 1384, was attended by students from many nations. All the early universities had a very loose form of organization, a crude type of democracy. When a group within a university became discontented, the members moved to another center, where they established a new college.

Thus emigrants from Paris established in the twelfth century the great University of Oxford. Modeled after Paris, Oxford stimulated the development of its affiliated colleges to the point where such colleges overshadowed the university and provided the prototype for the colleges of today.

Although it brought some of its early characteristics from abroad, the American university is distinctly indigenous to this country, reflecting the democracy, diversity, and dynamics of its people.

The Development of Higher Education

1636	*Harvard University founded*	*1915*	*American Association of University Professors organized*
1693	*William and Mary College established*	*1918*	*American Council on Education formed, accenting higher education*
1795	*First state university opened in North Carolina*	*1947*	*Reports issued by the President's Commission on Higher Education*
1803	*First federal land granted for state "seminary of learning" in Ohio*	*1948*	*First Fulbright scholarships opened for China and Burma*
1819	*Dartmouth College decision rendered by the United States Supreme Court*	*1950*	*Federal loans for constructing college housing included in the Housing Act*
1836	*Charter granted to Georgia Female College (Wesleyan College at Macon)*	*1958*	*Report made by President's Committee on Education beyond High School*
1837	*Coeducation started at Oberlin College, founded in 1833*	*1963*	*Federal grants and loans authorized by the Higher Education Facilities Act*
1839	*First state normal school organized in Massachusetts*	*1963*	*National Association of State Universities and State Universities Association linked in the Association of State Universities and Land-grant Colleges*
1854	*First prototype of Negro university established at Lincoln, Pennsylvania*	*1965*	*Higher Education Act passed by Congress*
1862	*Land-grant College Act passed by Congress*	*1966*	*Funds to help meet the expenses of higher education for war veterans provided by permanent GI Bill*
1876	*First graduate work begun at Johns Hopkins University*	*1968*	*First urban-oriented land-grant college, Federal City College, opened in District of Columbia*
1895	*National Association of State Universities started*	*1971*	*Carnegie Commission's report on higher education published*
1900	*Association of American Universities organized*	*1976*	*Target date set by Carnegie Commission on Higher Education for removal of all financial barriers to attending college*
1902	*First public junior college established at Joliet, Illinois*		
1911	*Division of Higher Education formed in the U.S. Office of Education*		

The European university today differs markedly from the American in that European higher learning is characterized by more restricted admission of students, less highly organized student life, more specialized study, and less complex organization and administration.

Early American Colleges

Although Harvard College was the first institution of higher learning in the continental United States, it is not the oldest in the Americas. The University of San Marcos at Lima, Peru, and the University of Mexico at Mexico City both opened their doors in 1553—eighty-three years before Harvard.

Harvard was founded in 1636 in Massachusetts. According to the Charter of 1650, its purposes were as follows: "the advancement of all good literature, arts and sciences; the advancement and education of youth in all manner of good literature, arts and sciences; and all other necessary provisions that may conduce to the education of the English and Indian youth of this country in knowledge and godliness."

During the colonial period, nine colleges were founded in the United States. In connection with the last arose the historical Dartmouth College case. The decision of the Supreme Court threw protection around higher education and stimulated the growth of colleges. All nine colonial colleges, with the exception of Benjamin Franklin's academy, were sectarian. By 1800 there were twenty-five colleges in the United States, but their enrollments were small. Not only did the president's house occasionally serve for recitations in these early colleges, but he was often the sole member of the faculty, teaching all subjects. Even in later years the faculties were small.

The history of these institutions of higher learning is interesting reading. Most of them were supported financially by grants of land or money from legislatures, by donations of money or kind, and by miscellaneous means, such as lotteries. The small liberal arts college is indigenously American, designed originally for the education of a small, socially and economically elite class.

State support was slow to develop. As late as 1860, only 17 of 264 institutions of higher learning were financed by the state. The first state university to be chartered was in Georgia; the first to be opened was in North Carolina; and Ohio was the first commonwealth to receive federal land grants to start a "seminary of learning."

Democratization of Higher Education

In 1862, during the darkest hours of the Civil War, President Lincoln signed the Morrill Act, which offered land to each state for the support of a college of agriculture and mechanical arts. As Andrew D. White, first president of Cornell University, one of the institutions founded by this act, observed, "In all the annals of republics, there is no more significant utterance of confidence in national destiny out of the midst of national calamity."

This act made possible the development of a vast system of low-cost higher education that included ultimately sixty-nine institutions—many of them America's most distinguished universities. The act stimulated the democratization of higher education by opening its doors to many students of modest means, an undertaking never before attempted by any other people.

By the latter part of the nineteenth century, the great universities, as assemblies of colleges, began to emerge. They included the college of arts as the basis for general education in support of the professional schools of business, education, engineering, law, medicine, and others. Graduate schools provided advanced study for the professions and prepared college teachers. The Association of American Universities was formed at the turn of the century to recognize and maintain the quality of graduate work. The development of coeducation, pioneered in this country, marked a radical break from academic tradition. Coeducation on the college level began in 1837, when four women were admitted to Oberlin College. Wesleyan College at Macon, Georgia, claims to be the oldest chartered college for women, established as the Georgia Female College in 1836. A few years later Antioch College, under the leadership of Horace Mann, opened as a coeducational institution. But it was the Midwestern state universities—Iowa, Wisconsin, Michigan, and others—that threw their doors open widest to women. They needed students and lacked the conservatism of the private universities along the Eastern seaboard. Columbia, Harvard, Brown, and others refused to adopt coeducation, but created affiliated women's colleges—Radcliffe, Barnard, Pembroke. Meanwhile, separate women's colleges, Mount Holyoke, Vassar, Smith, Wellesley, and Bryn Mawr, were opened.

Slowly the doors of higher education were opened to Negroes, but not very wide. The first forerunner of a Negro university was established at Lincoln, Pennsylvania, in 1854, as an institute which later became Lincoln University. Shaw University, the first school of higher education for Negroes, was opened in 1865. Many more Negro colleges were established in the Southern states following the emancipation of Negro slaves. Howard University was founded in the nation's capital in 1867. Others were established by churches. Some were public institutions. But with few exceptions, these Negro colleges were severely handicapped, as they still are today, by meager resources. The story of their survival is often the legend of a determined band of persons, mostly blacks, who saw education as the prime vehicle for blacks' escape from poverty and ignorance. Mary McLeod Bethune, for example, rose from picking cotton to become one of the leading female educators of her time. In her words, she "rang doorbells . . . wrote articles . . . distributed leaflets, rode interminable miles on dusty roads on my old bicycle, invaded churches, clubs, lodges, and chambers of commerce" in her crusade for funds for a college for the children of Negro railroad workers in squalid settlements on Florida's east coast. The college which she founded, later to become Bethune-Cookman College, rose from old crates, boxes, and odd rooms of old houses near Daytona's city dump. The rise of Tuskegee Institute is in large measure the story of its energetic administrator, Booker T. Washington, who insisted that the education of the Negro, by increasing his purchasing power and social responsibility, would benefit white and black people alike.

By opening its portals to students of modest means, to women, and to Negroes, American higher education during the latter part of the nineteenth century set the firm basis for bringing higher education to an "enormous slice of an enormous country" and removing it from the "privilege of a small elite," as C. P. Snow put it.

One of the most powerful democratizing influences in American higher education in recent years has been the rise of the junior college. A product of the twentieth century and indigenous to this country, its truly amazing growth constitutes one of the most significant developments on the twentieth-century educational scene. Since the first junior college was founded in Joliet, Illinois, in 1902,

they have been established in all the fifty states, although their growth has been most rapid in California, New York, Florida, Illinois, Washington, Georgia, Pennsylvania, Maryland, Kansas, and Michigan.

Rapid Expansion of Higher Education

Like most American institutions, colleges and universities experienced their greatest growth and development in the quarter-century following World War II. The GI Bill of 1944 and subsequent additions to it permitted more than twelve million veterans to attend high school and college. This virtual tidal wave of students strained college facilities seriously, but fortunately it stretched the capacity of colleges and universities to a point where they could accommodate more easily a second tidal wave of students two decades later—the new generation of postwar students, many of them the children of veterans. Between these two tidal waves, the colleges survived a slump in enrollments and income. As shown in Figure 9-3, college enrollments have grown enormously since the close of the war.

The sharp rise in the number of domestic students attending college and the increase in the number of foreign students replaced for all time the smugly provincial, homogeneous campus society with a cosmopolitan student body far more representative of our total society.

Largely because of their lower tuition, public institutions carried the major burden of expanding student enrollments. In California, for example, enrollment at private colleges rose by only two thousand students between 1948 and 1958, while enrollment in public institutions of higher education rose by fifty thousand.

Higher Education and Social Unrest

The image of the college as an ivory tower sanctuary of study and thought, isolated from the action of the marketplace, was shattered dramatically. Beginning with the Free Speech Movement at the University of California at Berkeley in 1964, student activism exploded on campuses across the country. The violence of student protest had made a shambles of some campuses and sent many college presidents into premature retirement or into other careers. In 1969 the cost of campus riot damages reached $9 million and insurance premiums became almost prohibitive for urban schools. By the early 1970s there was some hope that the wave of violent student activism on the college campuses had crested. The SDS and other radical student organizations had demonstrated the futility of barbarous tactics. University authorities had learned to respond to irresponsible student attacks more prudently and wisely. The report of the President's Commission on Campus Unrest, summarized in Chapter 1, helped to diagnose the problems and point the way toward relief of students' protests. The spread of open admissions policies, the introduction of black-studies programs, the elimination of ROTC programs on some campuses, the prohibition of secret government research contracts by many universities, and the expansion of student participation in the affairs of higher education all helped to reduce campus tension. Students learned that riotous actions, although effective at the moment, were self-defeating because they endangered the same individual freedoms they had sought to protect. Public opinion too had begun to harden against student violence. More and more people had come to understand that a "blueprint for revolution" was also a blueprint for counterrevolution.

Although campus unrest had not become extinct, as indeed it never can be or should be, by the early 1970s it appeared to have taken more constructive form as colleges and society began to respond more effectively to the social problems of the times. People were increasingly sharing in the

College students show little reluctance to demonstrate for student rights and campus conveniences.

hope that, as Archibald MacLeish said, "The crisis of the university may well become the triumph of mankind." Certainly higher education will never be the same again. In Chapters 1 and 11 we speak at greater length on the phenomenon of student unrest and the manner in which colleges and universities are responding to it.

PURPOSES

The various purposes of higher education are commonly classified into three major categories: instruction, research, and service. These might be spoken of as the dissemination, creation, and application of knowledge. The first two were inherited from European antecedents; the last is distinctly American. Much of the controversy about higher education is generated over conflict regarding the emphasis which should be given to each of these purposes in view of limited resources and latent conflicts of interest. Each of these purposes is considered briefly below.

Instruction

The central and most evident purpose of higher education is the instruction of students. Some controversy exists with respect to who should be instructed and in what. Should only the more able students be accepted in colleges, as is the tradition abroad, or should colleges—at least public colleges—be open to all high school graduates? If so, will there be a lowering of standards? If admission is not open to all, can it be done without discrimination on the basis of race or socioeconomic status? The question of what should be taught is, of course, a Pandora's box. Black studies? Vocational education? General education? Electives only? The list is endless. These issues are discussed later in this chapter and in Chapters 1 and 14.

Institutions of higher learning have a long-standing and worthy allegiance to the task of enriching and passing along from one generation to another that liberal and humane learning which is humanity's finest heritage. Universities have traditionally been regarded as both the generators and the repositories of knowledge. Although many other media of communication also serve to transmit the cultural heritage, the colleges and universities have been the fountainhead of what George Peabody referred to as a "debt due from the present to future generations."

Research

Many of man's great discoveries have emerged from college and university research laboratories. Dr. Selman Waksman won the Nobel Prize for his discovery of streptomycin and other antibiotics after thirty years of research at Rutgers. Professor Herman Schlesinger accidentally discovered a new kind of jet and rocket fuel at the University of Chicago. Dr. Jonas Salk's discovery of a vaccine against polio at the University of Pittsburgh was a monumental advance in medical science. Some discoveries have been made by famous men at great universities. Others have resulted from the work of little-known men from almost obscure campuses.

About three-fourths of all academic research is now financed by the government.

Some people view with alarm the participation of the university in research on the weapons of war and any research carried on in secrecy. They contend that it is inimical to the interests of scholarship to withhold the new knowledge yielded by research and inhumane to produce knowledge that cannot be shared with all mankind.

Service

Colleges and universites have served the public interest in a multitude of ways. The agricultural colleges have improved food production and have made our farming industry the model for the world. Schools of education have prepared teachers and other specialists and have helped to improve educational programs and practices across the nation and in many parts of the world. Other professional schools have supplied the nation with its clergymen, judges, editors, actors, writers, engineers, physicians, nurses, and many other professional persons. In time of national peril, the colleges and universities have participated in war service training programs and other enterprises related to national defense.

Serving the public through preparation of persons for the learned professions is commonly accepted. But what is unique to American colleges and what is highly contested is a whole array of other public services which are not universally accepted. Should the colleges and universities attempt to redress racial injustice, urban blight, environmental pollution, drug addiction? Should they prepare reserve officers for the armed forces, chemists for war-related industries, workers in nonscholarly occupations? Should they provide "farm teams" for

professional sports and entertain the public with quasi-professional athletic extravaganzas? The list is endless again. Some have contended that the colleges, in responding to this endless array of requests for public services, have transformed themselves into social service stations. Harold Taylor insists in his book *Students without Teachers* that colleges have lost their souls and their students, diverted limited talent and money from more important objectives, and thereby prostituted their true role. The fine line between appropriate and inappropriate public service is difficult to draw to the satisfaction of all. The decision is complicated when generous grants are available from government and industry, when great social issues are at stake, and when the destinies of the university and the society are so closely intertwined. This issue is discussed further in Chapter 1.

TYPES

The range of higher education is served by a diverse array of institutions, much more diverse in the United States than in other countries. This diversity—the result of the freedom of higher education, its restlessness, its competition, its geography, and its tradition—is the genesis of much of the strength of American colleges and universities. Some observers believe that some of this diversity is gradually disappearing. Although many institutions of higher education defy classification because of their multiple nature, several common types are described: two-year institutions, state colleges, liberal arts colleges, universities, free universities, Negro colleges and universities, land-grant institutions, professional schools, and graduate schools.

Two-year Institutions

The rapid rise of community colleges, junior colleges, and vocational and technical schools has been one of the most striking developments on the educational scene. Growing more rapidly than any other sector of higher education, enrollment in these institutions approximately tripled in the last ten years. Beginning in 1969 more freshmen entered two-year colleges than four-year colleges and universities. Numbering more than a thousand, these two-year institutions now enroll approximately one-third of all college students. They are located in every state of the Union. If the present trend continues, by 1978 half of all college graduates will have had their first two years in two-year institutions, and by the year 2000 two-year colleges may have taken over the first two years of college almost completely. The sharp rise in two-year college enrollment is shown in Figure 9-1.

In 1971 the Carnegie Commission on Higher Education recommended further expansion of two-year institutions to include at least 230 more new community colleges in the 1970s to accommodate at least three million students by 1980. The Commission said that each state should have a plan for developing community colleges and that the goal of providing a community college within commuting distance of practically every potential student should be attained by 1976. It also recommended the elimination of all financial barriers to attending public community colleges.

The community college is distinctly an American creation. Community colleges offer large numbers of American youths an opportunity to extend their education at minimum cost, since tuition rates are nominal and many can live at home while attending.

Certainly these institutions have reduced the alarming number of able high school graduates who formerly did not go on to college. It is clear that the universal availability of the community college is as imperative today as the availability of the high school was a generation ago.

Two-year colleges serve four primary purposes: they provide (1) parallel programs for freshmen and sophomores planning to transfer to four-year institutions; (2) terminal programs of general education for students not planning to go on to four-year colleges; (3) technical and subprofessional studies, largely vocational in nature; and (4) continuing education studies in general, cultural, and vocational education for adults. Not all two-year institutions, of course, attempt all these functions.

The types of postsecondary institutions are as varied as their nomenclature is confusing: junior colleges, community colleges, academies, extension centers, seminaries, technical institutes, trade schools, and others. Most offer two-year programs, although some offer only one-year and others offer three- or four-year programs. Although the terms "community college" and "junior college" are often used interchangeably, the term "community college" sometimes distinguishes those institutions which seek particularly to adapt their programs to the local community and as much as possible serve the educational needs of the community broadly.

One variety of the two-year college is the technical institute, institute of applied arts and sciences, or vocational and technical school. These schools are booming too, especially since 1964. Long the stepchild of our educational system, these schools now enroll over two million full-time students across the nation. Some of the schools are residential, some nonresidential. Most are public institutions. Many offer courses ranging all the way from basic literacy training to atomic theory. Although some of the students are high school dropouts, many are very able intellectually. These schools offer not only a supply of technicians for new occupations in a highly industrialized society but also an alternative for the high school graduate who is not interested in a four-year college program.

These two-year postsecondary institutions are generally of four basic types with respect to organization and support:

Local public community colleges or technical schools maintained and financed through local school districts

The two-year extension of a four-year college or university through off-campus centers

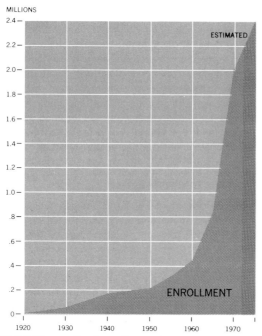

FIGURE 9-1 Total enrollment in public and private two-year postsecondary institutions. (U.S. Office of Education, Digest of Educational Statistics.)

The third type has become more common in recent years. The Carnegie Commission report questioned the first two of these three types. The first type tends to become a "stretch-out" of secondary school curriculum and an appendage of the high school. The second type tends to become strictly college preparatory, robbing the community college of its essential diversity of purposes and students. Most public community colleges are governed by an elected board of trustees and administered by a president. Virtually all are coeducational.

The majority of the two-year postsecondary institutions are public and enroll 90 percent of the students. The public institutions charge little tuition, sometimes none, and the revenue for their support is commonly divided among the state, the community, and the student. Their admissions policies are often quite liberal, and as a result they enroll many high school graduates and adults who would not be admitted to most four-year colleges.

The disadvantages of these institutions may include the loss of the maturing experience of living away from home and the danger that academic standards will be less rigorous than in four-year colleges with higher admission and degree requirements.

Because their clientele usually do not live on campus, community colleges tend to reflect in their student bodies the racial segregation pattern created by housing in their attendance areas. They therefore pose the same problems of racial integration as secondary schools.

State Colleges

Virtually every state has a system of public state colleges. Most of these institutions originated many years ago as normal schools and were later extended into state teachers colleges with four-year programs. In recent years, virtually all these institutions have become multipurpose state colleges and have dropped the word "teacher" from their name. Some of these institutions have added graduate divisions and become universities.

Liberal Arts Colleges

The liberal arts program is usually offered by two types of institutions: the liberal arts college and the division of liberal arts, or "division of arts and sciences," as it is sometimes called, of the large university. Their purposes are those of liberal education, preprofessional preparation, and some specialization. When the college is organized on a four-year basis, there is usually a gradual shift in emphasis, with the first two years devoted primarily to general education and the last two years directed toward majors or fields of concentration.

Nearly all the seven hundred or more liberal arts colleges are privately controlled. These private colleges and universities enroll only one-fourth of the total college population, a drop from 50 percent of the total college enrollment in 1949. Many of the smaller liberal arts colleges have had acute financial problems in recent years. With less access to public funds, they have had to raise their tuition sharply. Many college students have completed as much as two years of college-level work in high school, which often means that they have outgrown the curriculums of the lower divisions of these colleges.

The American landscape is dotted with approximately eight hundred "church-related" institutions of higher education. Although many carry the title "university," most of them are really liberal arts colleges. Their highest concentration is in the Eastern states. Most of them are small colleges; together they enroll less than one-fifth of all college students, and the proportion is decreasing each year. Their quality varies enormously. Approximately one-fifth of them are not regionally accredited. The term "church-related" defies generalization. It may mean that the college is owned outright by a religious denomination, that members of its board of trustees and perhaps its faculty must belong to the sponsoring church, that some of its financial support comes from a religious denomination, that its purposes reflect a religious orientation, or simply that it once had a religious affiliation that is now maintained only nominally. "Church-related" may mean any or none of these.

The organizational patterns of church-related schools vary widely. Two illustrations will reveal the diversity. The Church of Jesus Christ of the Latter Day Saints (Mormons) handles its higher education system with remarkable simplicity and effectiveness. Brigham Young University is its one and only large denominational university, owned and operated entirely by the church with no federal funds. The Mormon church then maintains religious centers near other campuses attended by a considerable number of Mormon students.

Approximately 350 of the church-related institutions of higher education are affiliated with the Roman Catholic Church, enrolling approximately 6 percent of all college students. There is an increasing trend toward more secularization in Catholic colleges and universities, notably Boston College, Fordham University, and Webster College, among others. This secularization may take the form of the inclusion of laymen on the board of trustees, displacement of familial and sacral values in the curriculum in favor of professional and secular values, or natural accommodation to students to whom denominational values are less compelling.

Increasingly, the question is raised whether sectarian colleges are necessary or, more fundamentally, whether a college with religious affiliation is a contradiction in terms. When President Jacqueline Grennan separated Webster College from the control of the Sisters of Loreto, she stated that "the very nature of higher education is opposed to juridical control by the church." One observer of the educational scene concludes that "the hard fact is that today no Catholic university stands among the leading institutions of higher education in the nation, and every Protestant church-related university that enjoys first-rank status long ago severed all but the most tenuous ties with its founding church."[1]

However that may be, it is clear that private higher education is becoming prohibitively expensive on the campuses of many church-related institutions. The courts often hold that these institutions are ineligible for federal funds when their governing boards are tied too closely to the church. With this financial plight, many of these schools face the dilemma of wanting to offer something distinctive while avoiding the danger of making themselves ineligible for either public financial support or academic respectability.

Universities

The university usually has a liberal arts college or division and a group of professional schools or colleges. The universities conduct much pure and applied research and most of the federally sponsored research in higher education. The universities enroll about two-fifths of all the students in

[1]James Cass, "Fordham University: Renaissance in the Bronx," *Saturday Review*, vol. 50, p. 52, June 17, 1967.

higher education. They are about evenly divided in terms of public or independent support.

State universities, which are usually a general responsibility of all the citizens of a state, are under one or more publicly controlled boards of higher education, elected by the people or appointed by state officials. Every state of the Union has its university or university system, and many of them are growing. The state university, with its low tuition and heavy public subsidy, is regarded as a natural and inevitable culmination of the public school system. It is a distinctly American invention. Its function is assumed to be that of supplying all the needs of society that fall within the sphere of higher education. Many state universities claim that the whole state is their campus. Several have extended their activities beyond the boundaries of the commonwealth, and many to other countries. The last decade has seen a phenomenal increase in the size of many state universities.

The University of California system of higher education spends over $700 million annually, employs more than forty-five thousand persons (more than IBM), offers ten thousand courses to more than a hundred thousand students, is spread over nine campuses, and maintains other operations at hundreds of locations across the state.

Land-grant Colleges and Universities

A land-grant college or university is an institution of higher education that has been designated by the state legislature as qualified to receive the benefits of either or both of the Morrill funds. The term "land-grant college" originated from the wording of the first Morrill Act, adopted by Congress in 1862. The act provided instruction in "agriculture and the mechanic arts, without excluding other scientific and classical studies and including military tactics."

There are now sixty-nine land-grant colleges and universities. The latest, Federal City College in the District of Columbia, which opened in 1968, is unique because of its urban location and focus. Some land-grant institutions are state universities (as in Minnesota), some have been separate (as in Mississippi), and some function as part of a private institution (as Cornell). Their locations are shown in Figure 9-2.

Today land-grant colleges constitute less than 4 percent of American colleges and universities, but they educate 20 percent of the undergraduates and grant 40 percent of the doctor of philosophy degrees in the United States. More than half of the living American Nobel Prize winners earned degrees at land-grant colleges.

The land-grant movement created many new institutions, such as the Universities of Illinois, California, and Minnesota, which serve as multipurpose state universities, and the agricultural colleges in various states. The land-grant college has been called democracy's college. It represented a liberalizing of the old classical college course, particularly in its emphasis on agriculture and home economics. The land-grant college helped to forge one of the great miracles of American technology—an astounding rise in agricultural production. There were fewer farmers in 1971 than in 1900 and the population has doubled; yet the farms are feeding the population better and are also affording massive surpluses that can be shared with less fortunate countries.

The land-grant colleges are linked with other state universities in the Association of State Universities and Land-grant Colleges.

Free Universities and Experimental Colleges

Some dissident students, after the fashion of medieval European university students, established in the late 1960s "free universities," "counteruniversities,"

"experimental colleges," "protest counterinstitutions to the unfree universities"—their titles were both quaint and inexhaustible. The Experimental College at San Francisco State College, the Free University of New York, the Washington Area Free University, and the New Left School of Los Angeles were among the better-known such institutions. Not really universities in any sense of the term, these enterprises were best known for their "extension of the curriculum" into hippie culture, political action, and community organizing. Many of the courses were addressed particularly to the poor, the black, and the "third-world" peoples. Some undertook the preposterous task of "destroying the irrelevant university." These institutions—rich in slogans, youthful enthusiasm, and Bohemian quarters but poor in intellectual substance and academic resources—did not last long. Many of their leaders were more interested in political activism and the radicalization of society than they were in learning. Those who were genuinely interested in academic reform became disenchanted with the dilettantism of the free universities and dropped out. These experiments demonstrated that although radical students could agree on their desire to rebel, they could not agree on any central purposes for these institutions. With-

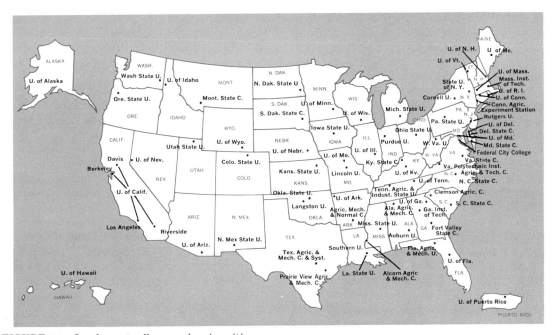

FIGURE 9-2 Land-grant colleges and universities.

out the cohesive effect of common goals, the destiny of the free universities was predictable. By 1972 they were virtually extinct.

The United States Office of Education in 1971 provided funds for a major experiment in higher education known as "University without Walls." Seventeen established colleges participate in the program, which permits a limited number of students to work toward their degrees without any of the fixed requirements normally prevailing on their campuses. A student may take some work in regular courses, switch at will to any of the other campuses, serve a supervised internship in private firms or public agencies such as the Peace Corps, or engage in independent study. The idea is based upon the progressive education doctrine of "learning by doing." It is hoped that the University without Walls will accommodate action-minded students better than the traditional university; infuse the campuses with the leavening influence of older students who have some career experience; and provide a better mix of academic study and work experience.

Negro Colleges and Universities

There are approximately 100 colleges and universities, most of them in the South, whose student bodies are predominantly black. Some of these—notably Howard, Fisk, Lincoln, Morehouse, and Tuskegee—rank among the best institutions of higher education in the country. Approximately 60 percent are private institutions, usually with religious affiliations. The remainder are state-supported institutions which enroll approximately 60 percent of the students attending predominantly Negro colleges. Stunted by financial blight, isolated from the mainstream of American society by segregation, these institutions have nevertheless provided the intellectual leadership for black people that has been so essential during the struggle for equal rights. Their alumni are found in the ranks of leaders in government, business, education, and health throughout the nation and indeed the world. Although many of their faculties are integrated, their student bodies, with the exception of Lincoln and Howard and a few others, contain only a handful of white students.

After the Supreme Court decision of 1954 calling for an end to discrimination by race in American society, many people believed that these predominantly Negro colleges should be integrated, merged

with white colleges, or phased out of existence. The prevailing view, however, was that they should continue, at least for the foreseeable future, to be predominantly black colleges continuing to meet several unique needs until the mainstream of American higher education is far better prepared to meet them. These institutions serve many black students who should have a college education but who cannot qualify for admission to other schools because of educational or economic privation. They are also needed as focal points of black awareness, black identity, black culture, and black pride in a society that is unfortunately not yet prepared to extend equal rights to all people regardless of race.

The compelling need is to strengthen these institutions so that they may better fulfill their important role in higher education. Many of them are in severe difficulty and their survival is in doubt. Some optimism springs from the fund-raising efforts of the United Negro College Fund, which was organized in 1944 to help the independent colleges serving predominantly black students meet the spiraling costs of education. Corporations and other sources of philanthropy have also been called upon to raise the level of financial support of public and private black colleges. The National Scholarship Services and Fund for Negro Students (NSSFNS) grants scholarships to talented Negro students attending college. But far greater effort will be needed to rescue many of these institutions from their dire financial need.

Many predominantly white colleges and universities are raiding the Negro colleges for their black faculty members and students. This problem is more temporary than fatal, since the reservoir of latent black intellectual talent is largely untapped.

Howard University in Washington, D.C., seems to offer a model for the redevelopment of other predominantly Negro colleges. Fifteen percent of its students are white and one student in seven is foreign. Students are attracted to Howard because of its reputation for excellence, its low tuition, and its image as a multiethnic and multiracial community of scholars. Here in microcosm may be both the model and the instrumentality for ethnic peace, an estimable service to the whole nation and indeed the world. Benjamin Mays, the eminent president of Morehouse College, has expressed this hope:

I believe that on the campuses of these colleges scholars of all faiths, cultures, and races will work together without a quota system. I believe that when the local climate is ready, students of other races will not hesitate to enroll wherever they can get a good education.[2]

Professional Schools

Since the middle of the eighteenth century, professional education has developed gradually in American colleges and universities. Separate professional schools for engineering, medicine, dentistry, pharmacy, teaching, and other professional and technical fields have developed. About three hundred of the institutions of higher education in America are professional schools. The professional schools have been created to meet career needs that are indispensable to the public welfare.

Graduate Schools

The system of American education reaches its apex in the graduate or advanced professional school. A technical distinction between a college and a university is that the former offers only undergraduate work while the latter offers both undergraduate and graduate courses. Many colleges, however, have a graduate division. In some universities, all the graduate work is centered in the graduate school. In others, graduate work is offered in the professional schools.

Beyond the baccalaureate is the master's degree, which usually requires (1) at least a year of study beyond the bachelor's degree; (2) completion of a certain number of credits or courses totaling approximately 30 semester hours; (3) examinations, both preliminary and final comprehensives, both oral and written; and (4) completion of some research project—a thesis, its equivalent, or added course work. Certain schools and departments stipulate additional requirements or permit substitutes.

An increasing number of institutions are offering an intermediate degree or diploma between the master's and the doctor's degree. This award usually corresponds to two years of graduate study. It is probable that this type of award will continue to grow in frequency and significance, since public school salary schedules and state certification agencies often recognize this level of education in regard to salary increments and certification.

Numerous doctors' degrees, such as doctors

[2]Benjamin E. Mays, "The Achievements of the Negro Colleges," *Atlantic*, vol. 217, p. 92, February, 1966. Copyright © 1966 by the Atlantic Monthly Company, Boston, Mass. Reprinted with permission.

of medicine, dentistry, or education, are offered in professional fields; and the doctor of philosophy is commonly granted in academic fields of study by graduate schools or advanced professional schools. The usual requirements for this degree are 75 to 90 semester hours of graduate study, written and oral examinations, and a dissertation or its equivalent.

Some graduate schools are awarding various certificates or degrees as substitutes for the doctorate, such as the Candidate in Philosophy or Master of Philosophy for those who have completed all the requirements except the dissertation, or the Doctor of Arts degree for students who have completed a doctorate designed to prepare its holder for teaching rather than research.

Several institutions have arranged a program and scholarships for persons who desire to study beyond the Ph.D. or Ed.D. degree.

ORGANIZATION

Articulation of Secondary and Higher Education

The gap between the completion of high school and the beginning of college was once so broad that many promising students failed to go to college, largely because of lack of money or lack of motivation. Since the nation could ill afford this lack of educated manpower, many stratagems have been undertaken to capitalize more fully on this latent talent. Several are mentioned briefly below.

Upward Bound programs identify promising high school students from low-income families and offer them college-level experiences during the summers of their late high school years without cost. This experience has helped many students to develop enthusiasm about college and to gain confidence in their ability to master college work and has eased their induction into college life. Intensive counseling services also help them to overcome the problems that might discourage their entry into higher education.

There has also been a striking growth of cooperative arrangements designed to bridge the gap between high school and college. Many colleges and universities now participate in the most significant manifestation of this trend, the Advanced Placement Program, conducted under the auspices of the College Entrance Examination Board. It has stimulated high schools and colleges to share responsibility for providing enriched and challenging academic programs for superior students and to smooth the articulation between secondary and higher education. Able students can take college-level courses while still in high school, and some enter college as sophomores, thereby saving a year of study.

Governance of Colleges and Universities

American colleges and universities are characterized by their great diversity. Although this diversity almost defies generalized description of their governance, the following statements are applicable to many.

Boards of Trustees. Public colleges are usually governed by local boards of trustees which function under the general jurisdiction of state boards of higher education with varying degrees of power over the local boards. In some states, such as New York and California, public institutions of post-secondary education comprise a single, well-coordinated, and unified system of higher education administered by a strong state board of trustees or regents. In other states, the public institutions of higher learning are an uncoordinated conglomeration of autonomous institutions. Private colleges are also commonly governed by a local board of trustees which functions rather independently of state regulations.

These boards of trustees are commonly self-perpetuating and meet infrequently, perhaps three or four times a year. They are often rather isolated from the mainstream of the campus. College trustees commonly fulfill ceremonial functions, establish general policies, approve operating and capital budgets, and appoint college presidents, and in private colleges particularly, they often play a major role in fund raising. Boards of trustees do not commonly have much to do with curricular and instructional matters, which are delegated to the president, deans, and department chairmen, along with responsibility for operational matters. Positions on college boards of trustees are often honorific recognition of distinguished alumni, businessmen, public officials, or professionals. Rodney Hartnett reported in his book *College and University Trustees* that members of college boards of trustees

are predominantly male, over 50 years of age, Republican, Protestant, white, well-to-do, and are in business and the professions. He found that less than 1 percent of college trustees were artists, musicians, writers, or journalists. However, in recent years, largely as a result of student activism and the civil rights movement, some college boards of trustees have moved to include students, young alumni, women, and members of minority groups.

Administrators. College presidents are named by the board of trustees. Their powers and responsibilities are often not well defined. Many college presidents find themselves being held fully accountable for circumstances on their campuses, but without being given commensurate authority. The general public and students often regard the college presidency as a powerful position, which in fact it is not on most campuses. On some campuses presidents are relegated to relatively minor roles. Nevertheless, the president's office is often the point of collision among conflicting demands of students, trustees, alumni, faculty, deans, and legislators. The presidents of many leading universities find the demands upon their offices intolerable. The Reverend Theodore Hesburgh, president of Notre Dame, reports that he has only one-tenth the power he had when first appointed years ago. Although he regards the diffusion of power among faculty and students as generally desirable, he believes that some resolution must be found of the conflict between the

Today's college administrators, such as Dr. Clifford R. Wharton, Jr., President of Michigan State University, shown here at a press conference, are beleaguered by complex educational, social, economic, and political issues.

dilution of the president's power and the increase in his accountability, or "no intelligent guy will want to be a university administrator." Louis T. Benezet, president of the Claremont University Center in California, presented this image of the college president in times of upheaval:

The president has been too lax; he has been too firm and unyielding; he has not listened to his faculty; he has indulged his faculty or his students; he has acted too fast; he has waited too long to act; he has called in the police; he hasn't called in the police. Whatever it is he should have done, he didn't do; whatever he shouldn't have done, he foolishly did.[3]

The turnover of college presidents (the average tenure is five to six years, considerably less than formerly) in recent years and the inability of many colleges to fill these important positions suggest that this office is becoming increasingly uninhabitable.

The administrative staffs of many colleges and universities have tripled during the last several decades to include an array of vice-presidents, administrative aides, planning and development officers, public-relations officers, government liaison officials, administrators of student services, ombudsmen, and deans. Where once "old president Smith" was attacked, now "the administration" or "the growing bureaucracy" is assailed by all as an omnipotent, impersonal, remote, unfeeling establishment.

Faculty. In the universities control of admissions, curriculum, degree requirements, faculty appointments, tenure, and student life is decentralized among the various divisions, schools, and departments. Often the faculties of the divisions, schools, and departments, rather than the administrative heads, bear the major responsibility. As one pundit once put it, "Universities are composed of an unmanageable complex of autonomous academic divisions each going their separate ways and held together only by a central heating plant." The word "university" is derived from two Latin roots, *unis* and *versom,* meaning "to make whole," "to turn into one." Certainly the term "multiversity," created by Clark Kerr, former president of the University of California, is more accurate in the contemporary scene. The degree of autonomy granted to divisions, schools, and departments varies of course among

[3] As reported in Fred Hechinger, "The College President: Damned if He Does, Damned if He Doesn't," *The New York Times,* p. 11, June 8, 1969. © 1971 by the New York Times Company. Reprinted by permission.

universities, but the general tradition of decentralization of control, particularly over academic matters, is strong within our culture. It is thought that this characteristic permits colleges and universities to respond more effectively to the unique needs of the various academic disciplines and professions and that it helps to sustain academic freedom.

On most campuses a faculty senate, along with an imposing array of faculty committees, helps to formulate institutional goals, programs, and policies. This arrangement, although democratic in spirit, is often cumbersome and slow to respond to urgent needs.

Individual professors have considerable autonomy on most campuses—autonomy with respect to what they teach, how they teach, what research they undertake, and many other aspects of their work. Many professors negotiate their own research grants directly with foundations and indeed take these grants and even their subordinates with them when they change campuses. Many professors feel more loyalty to their academic or professional fields than to their institutions. They turn out en masse when a dramatic issue arises but otherwise are content to leave the day-to-day business of university government to a small minority of their concerned colleagues who serve on the committees or senate with the administrative officers. As long as parking space and graduate student assistants are provided, such professors like to be free to do their own thing. In contrast with the college president, the typical professor has considerable authority, at least over his own domain, while assuming little responsibility or accountability for the general affairs of the institution. This arrangement is not accidental. It was so designed to sustain academic freedom and scholarship; but a worse design for institutional response to emergency and upheaval could hardly be imagined.

College faculties also flex their muscles through their organizations, particularly with respect to the conditions of their employment. The American Association of University Professors has historically served as a watchdog of academic freedom, tenure, salaries, and other conditions of employment on most campuses. Its *Statement on College and University Government* in 1966 helped to illuminate problems and improve practice in this important area. On many campuses, particularly junior college campuses, American Federation of Teachers locals have been chosen to represent faculties at the bargaining table. Indeed the AFT has mounted a major drive to organize college professors across the country. The American Association for Higher Education, an affiliate of the National Education Association, also offers membership to individual faculty members and monitors the interests of its clientele at the national level.

Students. The most significant development in higher education over the past decade is the students' sudden and successful quest for power over the affairs of the university. What should be the student's role in university government? The issue is difficult and the answers will emerge slowly and variously on most campuses. Many experts believe that the participation of students in decision making relevant to student life is crucially important and justifiable. Many believe that students should serve on academic committees and that their counsel should be sought with respect to academic matters normally decided by faculty and administration. Students, however, though they are long on interest in the university, are short on accountability. They do not have responsibility for the future, for raising funds, or for holding the university together. For this reason, some educators believe that student participation in the ritual of government usually controlled by the board of trustees would be unimportant and inappropriate. They point to the transient nature of the student population, the difficulties of identifying representative student opinion from the largely amorphous mass of students on large campuses, academic immaturity of students, and other factors. The solution to this difficult problem of determining the appropriate role of students in university government is being sought laboriously and often painfully on many campuses today. Certainly it can be said that the power of students over university affairs is increasing and that this development is in general an essential ingredient in the educative process. It can be hoped that it will serve also to strengthen higher education and quicken its response to the great social issues of our times.

Other Groups. Other groups influence college and university governance. Both state and federal legislatures exercise profound influence over colleges and universities through financial appropriations and through other legislation regulating the affairs of higher education. Alumni, particularly those who are major donors, often exercise influence directly through the conditions specified in their bequests or indirectly through trustees or administrators who are mindful of their largess and their interests. Foundations, businesses, and other benefactors also influence program development through the grants of money which they provide to universities and colleges.

In sum, the governance of colleges and universities is complex, varied, cumbersome, decentralized, and in a state of flux. Various groups are struggling to rearrange the allocation of power over university affairs, to make the university more responsive to the compelling problems of society. The central question is whether faculty, trustees, and students can act as responsible, constituent bodies to assume appropriate shares of responsibility in deciding what they want, whether they can negotiate their differences without destroying the university in the process, and whether they can support the administration in exercising the power to lead the university through the changes that are needed.[4] Some of the issues and the reforms indigenous to this problem are discussed in Chapter 1.

Operation

Faced with rising enrollments, many institutions of higher education have sought ways of maintaining the desirable qualities that accompany smallness. After the fashion of Oxford, some have established semiautonomous small colleges, each with its own faculty and student body within the larger parent body, and each drawing upon the more expensive common facilities of the parent organization. This type of organization is sometimes referred to as the "college within a college."

Valuable studies of higher education have also been conducted at the national level by the Commission on Financing Higher Education, the President's Committee on Education beyond the High School, and the President's Commission on National Goals. Several states have completed statewide surveys of their higher educational systems. Many colleges have been reorganized internally, some have achieved better coordination with other units

[4] For a more thorough discussion of the expectations of trustees, presidents, faculties, and students in university governance, see William C. Stolk and others, "Who Runs the University?" *Saturday Review*, vol. 53, pp. 53–82, Jan. 10, 1970.

of higher education, and others have entered into cooperative arrangements to avoid unnecessary duplication of facilities and faculties. Many have established smaller off-campus centers to avoid creating monstrous central campuses.

To accommodate rising enrollments and to make more effective use of time, space, and facilities, a growing number of institutions of higher education have instituted year-round schedules of three trimesters, four quarter-sessions, or other variations. Many students at universities with the conventional two-semester schedule attend summer schools, which, on major university campuses, frequently have enrollments nearly half as large as regular enrollments during the academic year. Many colleges and universities are accelerating instruction in other ways.

Segregation by sex in higher education appears headed for extinction. Such former bastions of masculinity as Yale and Princeton now admit female students. Bennington, Vassar, Smith, and Sarah Lawrence are admitting males. Harvard and Radcliffe have merged.

One of the most fateful developments in higher education has been the movement of some higher education institutions toward open admissions. This development is discussed at length in Chapter 1. By the 1970s a number of reforms were taking place in college admissions generally, even in institutions where open admission was not practiced. The reliability of both high school grades and college entrance examination scores in predicting success in college was being questioned. It was discovered that not all the students who appeared to be most promising by these measures were succeeding in college, nor were all the least promising failing. There was a growing trend in some colleges toward placing less reliance on these measures. Indeed, some colleges were abandoning the requirements of college entrance examinations and were trying to select applicants who were most likely to be favorably influenced by their particular educational programs.

Figure 9-3 charts the extraordinary increase in college enrollments resulting from two major factors: the arrival at college age of the postwar babies and the striking increase in the percentage of high school students attending college. College diplomas are more plentiful than high school diplomas were in 1945. Although the United States has only one-seventeenth of the world's population, it has one-third of the world's college students. This rise in numbers has been accompanied by increased di-

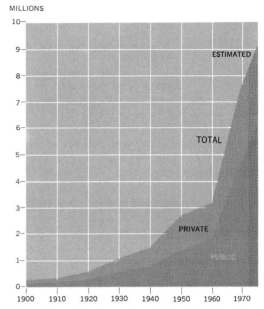

FIGURE 9-3 *Enrollment in public and private colleges and universities. (U.S. Department of Commerce, Statistical Abstract of the United States; and estimates by the authors.)*

versity of the student body. College, once reserved for the privileged few, as it always has been in other countries, is now the opportunity of the masses. Far more money is expended for higher education in this country than in all the rest of the world combined. Figure 1-3 reveals the rise in the percentage of youth between 18 and 21 in this country who are in college. The proportion will probably approach 70 percent by 1980.

Cooperative Relationships

Colleges and universities have developed a variety of cooperative relationships with other universities and various governmental agencies. Sometimes these take the form of regional associations, such as the Southern Regional Education Board, to improve educational resources through political action, cooperative research, and planning. Sometimes the scarceness of facilities prompts cooperative enterprise among universities. Many universities join to provide research capability that would be too expensive to undertake individually.

Many bilateral arrangements permit cooperation between pairs of institutions of higher education.

An example of such an arrangement, one of the oldest, is the arrangement between North Dakota and Wesley College whereby students at either institution can take courses at the other on a free-exchange basis. In an effort to strengthen Negro universities, several Northern universities have "adopted" or formed "sister" relationships with Negro colleges. For example, Brown, Cornell, Michigan, and Wisconsin universities have formed such setups with Tougaloo College, Hampton Institute, Tuskegee, and Texas Southern, respectively. This type of educational reciprocity benefits both partners through student and faculty exchanges, consultation on curriculum development, advisory conferences on administrative procedures, and joint participation in research and development enterprises.

Accreditation

In most countries of the world, colleges and universities are approved by national ministries of education. Most states in this country have provisions, sometimes perfunctory, for the approval of colleges and universities. But the accrediting agency that designates those institutions which have met required standards of quality is unique to this country. The United States is covered by a network of six regional accrediting agencies, such as the Middle Atlantic States Association of Colleges and Secondary Schools, which provide general accreditation of high schools, colleges, and universities. In addition to these general regional accrediting associations, there are a number of national professional accrediting agencies, such as the National Council for Accreditation of Teacher Education (NCATE), which accredits programs of preparation for the teaching profession. NCATE has become a powerful and constructive force in the improvement of teacher education as colleges and universities have striven to strengthen their teacher-education programs to meet the standards established by this council. The National Commission on Accrediting recognizes twenty-three professional accrediting agencies, including NCATE.

CURRICULUM AND TEACHING

Many age-old questions continue to prompt curricular conflict in colleges and universities: (1) What is the appropriate balance between general education and professional studies? (2) What should constitute a common core of general studies? (3) Where is the golden mean between required studies and elective studies? (4) Should the curriculum be addressed to social action or merely to the objective study of social phenomena? (5) Should the curriculum focus largely upon contemporary problems or upon the wisdom of mankind? The list of questions is almost endless, and we shall deal with only a few at this point.

One question centers on the choice between the free elective system and a body of compulsory general studies. The free elective system, once common throughout the country, was regarded as the essence of academic freedom, since it permitted students to study and specialize wherever they chose. Then in the 1930s a reform swept college curriculum toward required core courses in broad interdisciplinary areas of the social studies, physical sciences, and humanities to provide each student with a base of common knowledge deemed essential for the broadly educated man. Under the slogan of "relevance," the issue has arisen again. Students complain that the required courses are often poorly taught and irrelevant to their interests. Some demand the freedom to take the courses they wish and reject others, and the trend is turning toward an elective system. Stanford University has attempted to find a middle ground without returning to the free elective system. Its model would permit every freshman to have an introduction to "the nature of scholarly inquiry" in a field of his choice in a small seminar, with in-depth tutorial work with a professor. Every freshman would be exposed to some aspect of historical study to disabuse him of the myths that contemporary problems are unique and history is irrelevant. Students could select a variety of courses in several areas to gain a wide and more mature view of humanity, while avoiding the fragmentation that characterizes the free elective or "cafeteria system." This model may become the precursor of a trend in college curriculum development.

As college admissions were thrown open to larger numbers of students, many of them scarred by poverty and discrimination, the traditional ivy-covered college curriculum appeared to be inappropriate. Colleges that were satisfactory for a narrower band of academically oriented students found that the traditional curriculum was—to use a badly overworked word—irrelevant for many of the more heterogeneous breed of new students. This problem had already become familiar in the high schools a few years earlier, as noted in Chapter 8. Some critics felt that the root of the students' dissatisfaction was a basic shortcoming of the college itself: the demands which the colleges were making on their students were not sufficiently adapted to the diversity of the students and the greater differences in their career plans and life-styles. Even for academically oriented students, the new youth culture asked for education that dealt with the here-and-now practical problems, rather than with the accumulated wisdom of mankind. In one sense the clash was between the pragmatic and existentialist view of a new youth culture and the classical view that had prevailed heretofore on most campuses. Evidence for this interpretation of the clash was manifested also by the lack of student unrest in most professional and vocational divisions, where the practicality of the education offered was more apparent. Accounting, agriculture, engineering, medicine, and teaching were seen as relevant by the students in these fields, but evidently the liberal arts were considered less relevant by students. Curiously, when students were given power to determine the curriculum, they opted for something remarkably similar to what they already had.[5]

Many students were coming to college with high expectations for the expansion of their personalities. They sought deeper understanding of themselves and their fellow men, better emotional self-sufficiency, and refinement of their tastes and values. They were seeking both affective and cognitive development in institutions that had traditionally neglected the former. Some spoke of this as a "retreat from reason," a reliance on emotion and instinct rather than intellect. Many students thought degree requirements were too segmented and found little sense of unity or mastery, particularly in the general studies. The professor's podium stood on the wrong side of a broad cleavage between what was expected and what was given. Professors were mainly interested in what was taught; students were mainly interested in what was learned. These differences raised fundamental questions concerning the purpose of education (discussed more fully in Chapter 1), the proper role of the teacher (discussed in Chapter 12), and the

characteristics of a meaningful curriculum (discussed in Chapter 14).[6] The discussion here is confined to consideration of changes which resulted in some college curriculums as a result of this student concern.

Although there was great talk in the 1960s about innovations in undergraduate curriculum requirements, the American Council on Education report *Undergraduate Curriculum Trends* published in 1969 noted only relatively minor tinkering, although a few trends were spotted: a decrease in requirements in English composition, literature, and speech; an increase in the acceptance of mathematics as a science alternative; a rise in the use of proficiency examinations in certain communications subjects; and a shifting of history, philosophy, and religion from the status of required subjects to that of electives. Grades were sometimes eliminated or replaced by pass-fail grades.

In the 1970s many new electives were beginning to appear with frequency: black studies, environmental education, economics of the disadvantaged, and sexual identity, among many others. Many changes were also taking place in the mode of instruction. The marketplace and the ivory tower were joined increasingly in work-study programs. Field projects were used to take students into the community to bridge the gap between the theory of the classroom and the reality of community needs, which seemingly held so much appeal to students.

Increased use is being made of independent study and self-instructional technology in colleges generally. Motion pictures and closed-circuit television were used increasingly to expand the impact of scarce teaching talent. Educational television programs were transmitted through commercial and educational channels to students outside the college campus. The popular television series "Sunrise Semester" has provided course credit since its inception in 1963 to thousands of students and countless others on a noncredit basis. "Sunrise Semester" offers four courses each season under the direction of New York University's College of Arts and Sciences, permitting thousands of early birds to earn bona fide college diplomas through the tube.

Increased emphasis is being placed upon

[5]See Peter Schrag, "The End of the Great Tradition," *Saturday Review*, vol. 52, p. 95, Feb. 15, 1969; and Irene Tinker, "The Unprepared College Student," *American Education*, vol. 6, pp. 10–12, November, 1970.

[6]For additional discussion of the new expectations of college students, see Joseph Katz and Harold A. Korn, "The Graduates: Did They Find What They Needed?" *American Education*, vol. 4, pp. 5–8, May, 1969.

honors courses and independent study by students, freeing them, through proficiency examinations and assigned readings, from course credit requirements and compulsory class attendance.

Some institutions, notably Michigan State University and Stephens College, are endeavoring to combine living and learning by planning residence halls as centers of learning, not only as a means of more effective dual use of the same facilities but also to develop closer student-faculty relationships. Several universities are streamlining their curriculums—eliminating highly specialized fringe courses that tend to fragment education and moving toward fewer broad core courses.

The study of religion, so important in early American colleges, continues to occupy an important place in the curriculum. This is true not only in church-related schools but in independent colleges as well. Enrollment in elective courses in religion has soared at many institutions, sparked perhaps by the participation of organized religious groups in civil rights movements, the Second Vatican Council, and the writings of people like Paul Tillich and Reinhold Niebuhr. The mood of this intensified study of religion is not catechetical and doctrinaire, but rather objective and existential.

Some people felt that most of these changes were simply old wine in new bottles, that they failed to come to grips with the more compelling questions raised earlier. Many of the changes went unevaluated and produced no evidence of improvement rather than mere change. The leap from the ideal to the practical in curricular reform remains to be taken on most campuses. Joseph Schwab, a University of Chicago professor, posits the ideal rather well:

[If student leadership] could (a) be inducted into a curriculum with intellectual content which (b) included a substantial and mature practical component, which (c) existed in a community with a place for students in it, and which (d) possessed a culture identifiable with the lives of its faculty and potentially sharable by students, this small portion of the activist body might well become a saving part. They could become our finest allies.[7]

Although many American students were disenchanted by the colleges, many eminent foreign observers were not. C. P. Snow, the British author-scientist, spoke thus of his envy of American colleges and his admiration for them.

You were the first people in the world to bring higher education to an enormous slice of an enormous country and to remove it from the privilege of a small elite. . . . I have no doubt whatever that college education over the whole width and breadth of America is one of the real achievements of this world. . . .

I am far from the only foreigner who thinks highly of your system of higher education.[8]

STUDENTS

The caliber of college students is the highest in our history, according to many observers. Edmund Muskie, for example, believes that:

. . . College students today are more sophisticated than ever before, and have a greater capacity for maturity and responsibility. They have demonstrated these qualities in war, politics, social service, and other endeavors. It does not seem unreasonable that they should seek similar opportunities on the campus. If a university is to encourage its students to be active and participating members of society after graduation, that university should make it possible for students to contribute to the enrichment of campus life before graduation. . . .

Similar reports come from many campuses. Students' seriousness of purpose is manifested in subtle changes in their lives. Student newspapers, once preoccupied with such problems as the closing hours for fraternity parties, now devote space to matters of wider import. This generation of college students appears to be more skeptical of easy answers and more critical of the American social scene.

Perhaps the most important development and the most compelling conversation piece on the educational scene in the late 1960s and early 1970s was student activism. This sudden phenomenon produced a plethora of books, articles, and speeches ranging from those which viewed activism as a welcome omen for the perfection of American society to those which viewed it as barbaric nihilism. Some students described it as an existentialist revolt against the ordering of their lives. Many of the reasons for student activism were indigenous to the new youth culture; many were inherent in the society itself. The reasons were complex and are examined in greater depth in Chapters 1 and 11.

[7]Joseph J. Schwab, *College Curriculum and Student Protest*, The University of Chicago Press, Chicago, 1969, p. 35. Copyright 1969 by University of Chicago Press.

[8]C. P. Snow, "Higher Education in America," *NEA Journal*, vol. 51, p. 11, April, 1964.

Loan funds, scholarship programs, and talent searches offer precious financial help to many students. The Woodrow Wilson National Fellowship Fund and the National Merit Scholarship program, along with countless other public and private scholarships, have contributed significantly. The Ford Foundation has established a multimillion-dollar loan fund to finance four-year scholarships for worthy Negro students who could not otherwise afford college. Deferred-tuition plans help to spread the cost of college education over the entire year. Some colleges are forming cooperative arrangements with local banks and insurance companies to provide college financing on the installment plan. Many states have provided insured loan funds. Thus more students are studying now and paying later.

The college student has also become more itinerant. About one out of five entering college students is a transfer. At New York University, the largest private university in the nation, about 40 percent of undergraduate applicants are transfers from other colleges and universities. This growing mobility of students takes an estimated twenty thousand college students annually to universities abroad, in addition to the countless thousands who travel in other countries during the summer. Several hundred United States colleges now offer undergraduate credit programs abroad.

Another revolution was taking place in the private lives of students on campus. The old doctrine of the college standing *in loco parentis* was swiftly discarded in the late 1960s and early 1970s. Parietal rules that once governed the lives of undergraduates were quickly swept away on most campuses. Rules governing dormitory hours were widely discarded and housemothers and chaperons went with them. Coed dormitories became common and college men and women were free to visit each other's rooms on many campuses. It is no secret that these changes were demanded not by parents, deans, and presidents, but by the students themselves. Clearly today's American college students, their objections otherwise notwithstanding, enjoy almost as much personal freedom as do most adults not in college. The strain placed upon students who wish to be popular with other students in this permissive environment can sometimes be acute.

Various national organizations of college students compete in the struggle to represent students' interests in campus and in society. The National Students Association is the largest and the oldest and probably most representative of college stu-

dents generally. It represents well over a million students on campuses across the country. It has been a moderately liberal force in quickening the social consciousness of college students. In 1970 a group of black students, impatient with the National Students Association's stance on civil rights, broke from NSA to form the National Association of Black Students. The Young Americans for Freedom is a conservative organization of college students, numbering approximately fifty thousand students on four hundred campuses. It strives to neutralize the efforts of the more radical groups to protect colleges from disruption and violence. Certainly Students for a Democratic Society is the most strident and most controversial student organization to appear on the scene. This organization, a barbaric assortment of Maoists, Communists, anarchists, Socialists, and rowdies, is rather badly misnamed. Its avowed purpose is not to build a democratic society but to destroy it. According to its publication *New Left Notes*, "We must turn the campuses into battlegrounds. . . . Students must be persuaded that 'revolutionary violence' is needed to defeat imperialism and must reject the idea of 'control' or 'democratic participation' in 'any phase of the imperialist, racist, rotten, lying, exploiting university.'"[9] The revolutionary doctrine of the SDS has had little appeal to the vast majority of students, although its ability to foment disorder and to radicalize more moderate students in times of violence should not be underestimated.

FINANCE

The greatest problem facing colleges and universities is money. As indicated in Figure 9-4 expenditures for higher education have approximately doubled between 1965 and 1975 and the end is nowhere in sight. There are several evident reasons. Enrollment is rising and colleges lose money with each additional student enrolled. Curriculums must be extended to keep pace with the knowledge explosion. Inflation also takes its toll.

Where will the money come from? Tuition costs will continue to rise even in public colleges and universities, but, as always, they will not keep pace with the more rapidly rising costs of instruction. In

[9] "Investigations of Students for a Democratic Society," *Hearings before the Committee on Internal Security,* House of Representatives, 1970, p. 2134.

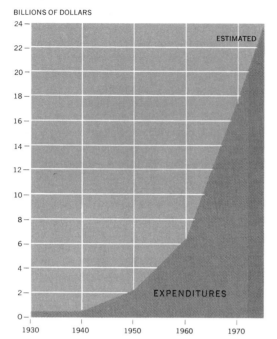

FIGURE 9-4 Total current expenditures for higher education. (*U.S. Office of Education*, Projections of Educational Statistics to 1977-78.)

fact, high as they may seem to the college student and his father, tuition rates remain one of the greatest bargains in the American economy because the typical college must receive three or four additional dollars from other sources for each one it receives in tuition.

Between 1962 and 1972, average tuition charges for undergraduates rose by one-third in public institutions and by more than one-half in private colleges and universities. The sharpest increase in tuition fees has been applied to out-of-state students in public universities. Some people believe that tuition charges should be increased substantially, particularly in public institutions, to help relieve the rising expenditures in higher education, and also believe that loan and scholarship funds should be increased to take care of the needy.

Many college officials fear that they are having to price themselves out of the market. Making students pay an increasing proportion of the costs of higher education will, if it continues, be disastrous to American society. As the Association of State Universities and Land-grant Colleges points out, "It is based on the false theory that higher education benefits only the individual and that he should therefore pay immediately and directly for its costs—through borrowing if necessary. . . . This is a false theory."

Private giving to colleges and universities amounted to approximately $2 billion in 1972. A spokesman for the Council for Financial Aid to Education estimated that this figure should reach $2.5 billion by 1975. A spokesman for the Council felt that student unrest on college campuses was not depreciating private giving, although a number of university spokesmen felt otherwise. The largest private contribution to higher education comes from parents of students.

Alumni are contributing $0.33 billion a year to their alma maters. Although exceptionally large alumni gifts are becoming fewer, many more alumni are making small contributions. The business community realizes that the prosperity of American industry is closely dependent upon the vitality of higher education. Corporations large and small are contributing millions of dollars annually. Private

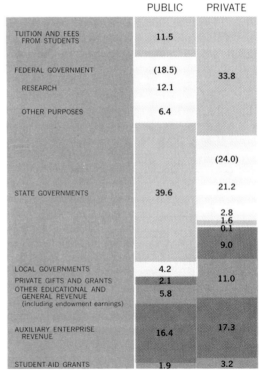

FIGURE 9-5 Sources of current fund income of public and private universities. (*U.S. Office of Education*, Digest of Educational Statistics, *Government Printing Office, Washington, D.C., 1969, p. 86.*)

foundations have made outright grants-in-aid as well as subsidies for experimentation and research. The Ford Foundation alone has made hundreds of millions of dollars available to hundreds of institutions. Billions of dollars are reaching colleges and universities through federally sponsored research, student loans, fellowships, construction loans, and other grants. However, research grants do not usually cover the full costs of the research. The National Science Foundation has made millions available to help universities to rebuild outdated research laboratories as part of the government's commitment to support basic scientific research.

With the decline of large bequests, endowment income is becoming a shrinking proportion of total university income. Some colleges have had to eat into their endowment funds to cover rapidly increasing operating expenses.

State support for higher education has more than doubled during the 1960s, but many experts believe that most states cannot continue this pace, at least not without drastic reform of their tax structures. Many of the more productive sources of taxation have been preempted by the federal government.

Chapter 2 documents the growing list of statutes enacted by the Congress for federal aid to higher education. This financial support now constitutes well over one-fourth of higher education's total budget. Some major universities receive as much as half of their revenue from Washington. In some years the federal government spends more money on the nation's campuses than all of the fifty state governments combined. Approximately half these funds go for research and research-related activities. The other half goes for student aid, books and equipment, classroom buildings, laboratories and dormitories, overseas projects, and training grants to prepare people for certain occupations. Welcome as these subsidies are, they have not been sufficient to relieve the chronic problem of colleges—the underfinancing of the general operations of the colleges. Most experts believe that even greater financial support by the federal government is imperative.

Colleges and universities have come to depend heavily on federal funds and this raises serious questions: Are interests of the federal government distracting colleges from more worthy endeavor? Has federal financial support strengthened or weakened local control of education? Has federal support strengthened the larger institutions at the

expense of the weaker? Has the curriculum become unbalanced because of the government's greater interest in the physical sciences than in the social sciences and the humanities? Should federal aid be channeled through the students or through the colleges? Should federal funds be made available to private institutions? These and other issues are discussed in Chapter 1.

The Carnegie Commission on Higher Education in its 1971 report called for massive increase in federal financial support for higher education to guarantee equality of access to higher education for youth of every economic and social class. It proposed "equal-opportunity grants" for needy students. It recommended stimulation of the flow of additional funds for student aid from other sources by matching them with federal "supplemental matching funds" to the colleges and universities. It proposed also a "student-loan bank" to provide loans to students.

By the early 1970s the financial situation on many campuses was alarming. Alumni giving, corporate giving, and public funds were not increasing sufficiently to meet the needs. Many colleges and universities were operating at a loss. Clark Kerr, chairman of the Carnegie Commission on Higher Education, spoke of "the greatest financial crisis it [higher education] has ever had."

Colleges and universities must also help themselves by effecting economies. The fiscal inefficiency of higher education is widely recognized. Needless duplication of programs and facilities by neighboring institutions must be reduced. More effective utilization of space and faculties is possible through better scheduling and year-round programming. Too many colleges do not do careful cost accounting. Toward the end of encouraging economy, the Ford Foundation has granted several million dollars to Stanford, Princeton, the University of California, and the University of Toronto to stimulate the application of systems analysis and cost-effectiveness techniques to the financial management of these institutions. These endeavors will focus upon studies of how to use academic, fiscal, and physical resources most effectively; how to computerize a number of managerial tasks; how to integrate fiscal and academic data to evaluate teaching more effectively; and how to apply cost-simulation techniques to a general university model.

Barring depression and war, this nation should

be able to afford what is needed to extend and enrich its system of higher education.

FUTURE

Some of the future of higher education can be seen by extrapolating the present; some of the change is unpredictable.

College enrollments will continue to increase. The U.S. Bureau of the Census estimates that the total number of people who have completed at least four years of college will rise from twelve million in 1970 to eighteen million in 1980. Higher education will become a logical extension of the common school movement, and within a generation virtually all able students who so desire will have access to higher education regardless of family income or College Entrance Examination scores. The combination of open admissions to public colleges and universities, the growing availability of junior colleges, and the growth of scholarship and student-loan funds will make higher education as readily available tomorrow as high school education is today.

Junior colleges will take over the first two years of higher education almost completely and there will be an egalitarian pressure to extend many of them to four-year colleges. Private institutions, particularly small private liberal arts colleges, will find themselves practically priced out of the market unless they become universities, as some are doing, or unless public funds become more widely available to them. But the distinctions among types of institutions will fade. This trend is already under way. The line between public and private institutions is sometimes hard to draw. Liberal arts colleges are becoming more like universities, and professional schools are extending their general education components. Many two-year institutions will become four-year.

It appears that the greatest growth in enrollment in higher education, after the junior colleges, will occur in the large universities in metropolitan centers. There is already a trend in this direction; three-fourths of college students are in urban institutions now. One might speculate that the problems of mass transportation, parking, urban blight, and racial tensions could reverse this trend, but we think not. These problems serve as a reminder that the climate of university life of the future will be heavily dependent upon the progress we make in redressing the malaise of an urban society.

Cooperative relationships among smaller colleges will become more common as they are driven to form consortiums, to share their stronger programs and eliminate their weaker ones, to exchange professors and students, and to make other collaborative arrangements. Student bodies of most colleges will become more desegregated, and in time, the press for segregated student centers, dormitories, black studies, and other separatist arrangements will decline.

The most critical problem of higher education will be finance. The costs are already staggering and still rising. Increases in tuition, private philanthropy, and state aid will probably not keep pace with the need. The only possible solution, in our view, lies in increased federal support for higher education. The American people have come to realize that higher education is a critical instrument of national policy in finding relief for the great social, economic, and political problems of our time; and as that realization matures, acceptance of increased federal spending in higher education will develop. Difficult decisions will have to be made regarding allocation of funds. The strongest possibility is that the federal government will make substantial aid available directly to the student after the pattern of the GI Bills, permitting him to attend private or public institutions of his choice. Comprehensive and long-range state planning of systems of higher education, common now in only a handful of states, will be necessary in order to deploy limited resources to this expensive enterprise more effectively. New modes of instructional technology will make instruction somewhat less costly, it is hoped with no great loss of effectiveness. Formal classroom instruction will be displaced in part by independent study and self-instructional devices. Year-round academic calendars will become more common to allow fuller utilization of expensive facilities.

The milieu of the colleges will continue to be affected by their encounter with the student movement. There will be more emphasis on learning, less on teaching. There will be more effort to evaluate the degree to which the student undergoes personal progress rather than being processed. The significance of the classroom will be deemphasized, while engagement with real problems will be emphasized. Progressive education will be rediscovered in higher education, as it has been in elementary and secondary schools. The range of permissible interaction between students and faculty will be broadened, and concern for the quality of this interaction will be deepened. Students are rapidly becoming the main source of initiative for reform in higher education.

It is difficult to see where the curriculum is headed. One might be tempted to extrapolate present trends if it were not known that curriculum development in higher education is cyclical. As noted earlier, required general education courses are being dropped on many campuses in favor of a kind of do-it-yourself education. Demands for current relevancy debase the currency of historical perspective. Most college students of the 1970s seem to pursue the social sciences and humanities with more determination than the physical sciences. Professions based on the social sciences also seem more alluring in the early 1970s than those based on the physical sciences. Evidently the Age of Aquarius views the physical sciences as causing, rather than solving, man's more compelling problems. The opposite of all this was true just after Sputnik, and it could become true again when a new generation of college youth contemplates the excesses of the present corrections. We think the pendulum of curriculum redirection will continue to swing and that warnings of excessive oscillation will be as unattended in the future as in the past.

Less Time, More Options, a report of the Carnegie Commission on Higher Education, issued in 1971, called for a major overhaul of the nation's higher education system. It included these recommendations which suggest the direction of future reform in our colleges:

A three-year Bachelor's-degree program
University accreditation of high schools to offer the equivalent of a first year of college
Offering a degree after every two years of higher study
Wider use of two new degrees: The Doctor of Arts and the Master of Philosophy
Reduction by one or two years of the time required to earn the Ph.D.
Availability of college-study alternatives, such as apprentices and military programs
Expansion of education opportunity for women, older people, workers, and the poor

A report on higher education financed by the Ford Foundation and published in 1971 included the following recommendations:

Reform rather than increased federal aid
Decentralization of state systems of higher education
Stimulation of college attendance by people of all ages
More imaginative educational programs for minority groups
Encouragement of work training as an alternative to only academic education

Several observers predict that the university of the future may become fairly indistinguishable from the community. It is already sometimes difficult to determine where the university ends and the rest of the world begins, as many students are taken into the community for more and more educative experiences in community action projects, work-study programs, and internships in field agencies. Both the classroom and the professor may decline in importance. The professor no longer enjoys a monopoly in his role of dispenser of knowledge in a world where television, jet travel, communications satellites, miniaturization of message reproduction, computer-assisted instruction, and other marvels of communication and travel bring almost any knowledge anywhere within reach of the student.

The dilemmas are difficult, the hazards are fateful, and the future of higher education is by no means certain, as indeed it never has been. We think our colleges and universities will change but also survive and prosper reasonably well. The walls of academe are thick.

SUMMARY

Higher education in the United States had its antecedents in European universities, but the character of our colleges and universities is distinctly American. In some respects, our system of higher education is the envy of the world. Our liberal arts colleges, public universities, and community colleges are largely indigenous to this country. The United States pioneered the democratization of higher education through its land-grant colleges in the last century and through its public community colleges and public universities in this century. Both are built on the concept of low-cost education for the many. Thus our country has been able to provide higher education for a larger proportion of its youth than any other nation. The trend in college attendance presently is sharply in the direction of community colleges, other public colleges and universities, and urban institutions.

The sharp rise in college attendance in this country has been truly phenomenal. It will continue to increase, not only because of the general rise in population but also because an increased proportion of youth are continuing their education in both undergraduate and graduate school. Some of our universities have reached an almost phenomenal size, which is the root of some of their problems.

The purposes of higher education in the United States have traditionally included instruction, research, and service. There is considerable disagreement over the relative importance of each.

Higher education is presently characterized by a number of interesting trends: greater cooperation between institutions, some reduction of differences among various institutions, an increased use of instructional technology, a greater use of independent study, more abundant financial help for students, less rigid and compartmentalized curriculums, less concentration upon general education and more upon professional and preprofessional preparation, more attention to international and intercultural education, a rise in the power of students, and vastly increased financial support from the federal government, reduction of the isolation of colleges from their communities, inclusion of more students and persons of minority groups on boards of trustees, decline in segregation by sex, and more open enrollment in public institutions particularly.

The paramount problems of higher education include the tenuous future of the liberal arts college, the preservation of quality in the face of shortages of everything but students, the growing tension between students and administrations, the further expansion of higher educational opportunity to disadvantaged minority groups, skyrocketing tuition costs, and the race between the curriculum and the explosion of knowledge, among others. Adequate financing is the most difficult problem.

In one sense, American higher education has been too successful. It has led our people, particularly students, to expect too much of our colleges and universities. Because colleges and universities have provided higher education to a larger proportion of students at a cost and on a scale never dreamed of heretofore, they have been beleaguered with responsibilities that they were not prepared to assume. Nevertheless, the outlook, in balance, is one of cautious optimism, and we are moving toward the uniquely American dream of post-secondary education for all who want it regardless of socioeconomic status.

Suggested Activities

1. Prepare an essay on "Higher Education for Negroes in America—Past, Present, and Future."
2. Prepare an essay on "The College Student's Unrest: Causes and Cure."
3. Arrange an interview with the admissions officer of a graduate school of education in a major university to discover (1) the fields of specialization available and the advanced study requirements, (2) the requirements for admission to graduate study, and (3) the opportunities for financial assistance during graduate study.
4. Interview at length someone who took his undergraduate education prior to 1955 and note contrasts between collegiate life then and now.
5. Prepare a statement of your own views on some of the major curriculum issues in higher education, such as general versus professional studies, required courses versus free electives, etc.
6. Interview a major administrative officer in your college to determine the greatest changes that have taken place on your campus in recent years and the most difficult problems presently confronting it.
7. Prepare an essay on "The Satisfactions and Frustrations of Teaching on the College Level."
8. Prepare an essay on "The Impact of Land-grant Colleges upon the Growth and Development of the Nation."
9. Read the works of Harold Taylor and Charles Frankel listed in the Bibliography, and summarize and critique their opposing views.
10. Prepare a description of the governance of the institution which you attend, including an analysis of powers held by the trustees, administrative staff, faculty, and students; also include your recommendations for reform.

Bibliography

Barzun, Jacques: *The American University: How It Runs, Where It Is Going,* Harper & Row, Publishers, Incorporated, New York, 1968. A witty and perceptive behind-the-scenes account of the operation of a university by a lifelong observer and critic of the educational scene.

Brickman, William W., and Stanley Lehrer (eds.): *Conflict and Change on the Campus*, School and Society Books, New York, 1970. A collection of 100 essays by prominent experts on the milieu of higher education administration, faculty, instruction, and students.

Campbell, Roald F., and others: *The Organization and Control of American Schools*, 2d ed, Charles E. Merrill Publishing Company, Columbus, Ohio, 1970, chap. 16. Historical development, contemporary influences, and future prospects of postsecondary education.

Carnegie Commission on Higher Education: *The American College and American Culture*, McGraw-Hill Book Company, New York, 1970. An analysis of the forces in American culture which have shaped higher education and which underlie the campus problems of today.

Carnegie Commission on Higher Education: *Between Two Worlds: A Profile of Negro Higher Education*, McGraw-Hill Book Company, New York, 1971. A discussion of how integration in higher education has posed new problems for Negro colleges, illustrated through profiles of five Negro colleges.

Carnegie Commission on Higher Education: *Breaking the Access Barrier*, McGraw-Hill Book Company, New York, 1971. A description of how community colleges have opened the doors of higher education to the masses and of the problems of survival of these institutions.

Carnegie Commission on Higher Education: *Less Time, More Options: Education beyond the High School*, McGraw-Hill Book Company, New York, 1971. Recommendations that higher education focus on learning rather than teaching and on the student rather than institution, and generally become flexible and realistic.

Carnegie Commission on Higher Education: *The Open Door College*, McGraw-Hill Book Company, New York, 1970. A recommendation of policies that should guide all aspects of community college development.

Corson, William R.: *Promise or Peril: The Black College Student in America*, W. W. Norton & Company, Inc., New York, 1970. A description of the general preconditions for revolution and the role of the black college student in social reform.

Eurich, Alvin C. (ed.): *Campus 1980*, Delacorte Press, Dell Publishing Co., Inc., New York, 1968. A collection of writings dealing with what may occur in the years from the present to 1980 on the college campus.

Frankel, Charles: *Education and the Barricades*, W. W. Norton & Company, Inc., New York, 1968. An analysis of university activism—its malaise and treatment.

Gould, Samuel B.: *Today's Academic Condition*, McGraw-Hill Book Company, New York, 1970. An analysis of current issues in higher education—finance, protest, teaching, and academic stuffiness.

Jencks, Christopher, and David Riesman: *The Academic Revolution*, Doubleday & Company, Inc., Garden City, N.Y., 1968. A description and evaluation of the relationships of colleges with the special-interest groups which founded them.

Kerr, Clark: *The Uses of the University*, Harvard University Press, Cambridge, Mass., 1969. A discussion of the university in terms of the social forces which have influenced its growth and nature.

Knezevich, Stephen J.: *Administration of Public Education*, 2d ed., Harper and Row, Publishers, Incorporated, New York, 1969, chap. 15. A description of community colleges and other postsecondary institutions.

McCluskey, Neil G. (ed.): *The Catholic University: A Modern Appraisal*, University of Notre Dame Press, Notre Dame, Indiana, 1970. Essays by eminent educators on various aspects of Catholic higher education.

Morphet, Edgar L., and Charles O. Ryan: *Designing Education for the Future*, no. 2, Citation Press, New York, 1967, chap. 9. Issues and future prospects of American higher education.

Parker, Garland G.: *The Enrollment Explosion: A Half-century of Attendance in U.S. Colleges and Universities*, School and Society Books, New York, 1971. An analysis and review of trends and developments in college enrollments in the United States in relation to national and international events from the 1920s to the early 1970s.

Smith, G. Kerry (ed.): *Stress and Campus Response*, Jossey-Bass, San Francisco, 1968. A series of essays on higher education: the social milieu, student unrest, organization, administration, teaching, and curriculum.

Taylor, Harold: *Students without Teachers*, McGraw-Hill Book Company, New York, 1969. An analysis of the causes of student unrest in the colleges and how that unrest should be mobilized for the reform of higher education.

Woodring, Paul: *The Higher Learning in America: A Reassessment*, McGraw-Hill Book Company, New York, 1968. A historical and comparative analysis of higher education and directions for the future.

Chapter 10   Adult and Continuing Education

Orientation	Continuous concerns and

Orientation
Historical development
New imperatives and
   continuing education

Continuous concerns and
   developmental tasks
Organizations and programs
Future
Summary

ORIENTATION

Increase in Young Adults. A very significant demographical development, with startling educational, social, political, and economic implications, is the growing number of young adults in the United States. Figure 10-1 predicts a possible large percentage growth in young adult population between the years 1960 and 1980. Far outweighing the substantial growth in the number of people of 65 years and older is the percentage change in the age group 20 to 34. *U.S. News and World Report* says:

Now getting under way—and certain to grow in the years just ahead—is a boom in the number of young adults. That's the age group which is going to dominate the coming decade, shaping markets for business, influencing politicians, affecting styles of living. In numbers alone young adults—people in their 20s and 30s—will outpace all other groups.

Between now and 1980, the horde of young adults will grow by 18 million, up 34 percent. People in all other age groups will increase by 9 million, or a mere 6 percent. In other words, 2 out of every 3 Americans added to the population in the coming decade will be young adults. It all stems from the baby boom in the years just after World War II. By 1980, the total U.S. population will be about 232 million and nearly one in every three Americans will be in his or her 20s and 30s.[1]

Demographic projections point to the facts that while the United States is growing older in years as a

[1]"What U.S. Will Be Like by 1980: Meaning of Population Shifts," *U.S. News and World Report*, vol. 70, pp. 70-71, Jan. 11, 1971. Reprinted from *U.S. News and World Report.* Copyright 1971, U.S. News and World Report, Inc.

A Community Action adult education program brings together adults of all ages to improve community life.

nation, a larger proportion of its population is becoming younger.

The increasing numbers of youth today and tomorrow can take heart from numerous examples of creativity and achievement in the early years of adult life. A few instances follow. William Cullen Bryant wrote the renowned poem "Thanatopsis" at the age of 16. Mendelssohn composed his overture to *A Midsummer Night's Dream* when he was 18. Einstein was 26 when he published his first statement of relativity. Thomas A. Edison obtained one-third of his 1,076 patents between the ages of 33 and 36.

For years General Douglas MacArthur had over his desk a message entitled "How To Stay Young," based upon a poem written by the late Samuel Ullman. It read in part:

Youth is not a time of life—it is a state of mind; it is a temper of the will, a quality of the imagination, a vigor of the emotions, a predominance of courage over timidity, of the appetite for adventure over the love of ease. Nobody grows old by merely living a number of years; people grow old by deserting their ideals. Years wrinkle the skin, but to give up enthusiasm wrinkles the soul. . . ."

Adult and continuing education can help the increasing number of young adults develop a real sense of "progression" rather than "regression," a spirit of "becoming" rather than "ending." As the French poet Alfred de Vigny wrote, "A fine life is a thought conceived in youth and realized in maturity."

Today's Need for Adult Education. In an earlier era, when society was less complex and living less arduous, it was perhaps reasonable to assume that one could acquire, by the age of 18, most of the education he would need throughout life. But the fantastic tempo of social and scientific change has

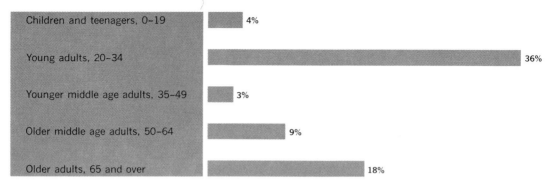

FIGURE 10-1 *Percentage increase in population, by age groups, 1970–1980. Our adult population is becoming more bimodal, with substantial increases in young and old adults and much smaller increases in middle-age adults. (Estimates are based on data from the U.S. Census Bureau, 1970.)*

vastly complicated man's existence and given unprecedented urgency to lifelong learning through adult education.

Not only is life changing, but its rate of change is quickening beyond our ability to cope with it. Consider this illustration of the extraordinary acceleration of change: Suppose that the 100,000 or more years of human existence were compressed into the last seventy years, the average life-span of contemporary man. On this scale, man would have made his first pottery at 63, begun using copper at 65, and built the pyramids at 67. He would have had the first horseback ride at 68 and entered the Christian era shortly before he reached 69. He would have discovered gunpowder six months ago, America four months ago, and the telegraph three months ago. The telephone and electric light bulb would have been developed last month; television, radar, atomic energy, and the United Nations last week. Polio vaccine, earth satellites, and commercial jet aircraft would have appeared yesterday. He would have witnessed the first walk on the moon today.

Indeed, the world has changed far more in the past ten years than it had in the previous two hundred. Moreover, it is evident that we are on the threshold of even more fantastic change. Man will soon explore the solar system, extract vast riches from the oceans, control the weather, and do other wondrous things. But the prospect of present and future change is not entirely pleasing. It will be accompanied by massive and compelling forces that have already begun to revolutionize personal and national life. In this perilous and perplexing age, in which things happen so fast, no one's education can ever be considered complete. Unfortunately, as indicated in the study *Volunteers for Learning,* conducted by the National Opinion Center under a

grant from the Carnegie Corporation, those who need adult education most do not pursue it.

Adult education is a necessity today. Varied in character and widespread in its manifestation, adult education practically eludes precise definition. In its broadest sense, it embraces all informal and formal activities which induce learning and promote better living for persons of about age 18 or older. In a narrower sense, it is organized learning sponsored by a responsible educational agency for persons beyond compulsory school age who are usually not full-time students. The broader definition would include such pursuits as reading books, listening to music, visiting museums, and traveling. As indicated below, adult education has many purposes and varied programs. Linked with adult education is the newer concept of continuing learning.

Tomorrow's Imperative: Continuing Education. Immediate adult education, with its many facets, is not enough. At the second conference on the "cybercultural revolution," Maxwell H. Goldberg stated that we need something more than adult education:

In addition we must develop a statesmanlike and imaginative long-range rationale for continuous liberal education, which seeks genetically to provide the full educational continuum of the individual's development from childhood on through the later phases of adulthood.[2]

Goldberg defines continuing education as "a way of life—namely that of a single, vital, genetic, developmental continuity."[3]

[2] Maxwell H. Goldberg, "Continuous Education as a Way of Life," *Adult Education,* vol. 16, p. 6, Autumn, 1965.
[3] *Ibid.,* p. 5.

Grant Venn, assistant executive secretary of the American Association of School Administrators, states:

Perhaps the most archaic term in education today is "graduation," which is generally thought to mean completion of a certain level of schooling. . . . No person in the future, however formally educated, can ever escape the need to learn, the need to grow, and the need to keep up with the exploding quantity of knowledge in every field. An individual citizen's economic stability, personal fulfillment, and social responsibility are enhanced by ready access to educational resources and the opportunity for formalized continuing education. . . . There is no time at which to end education. . . .

Continuing education can no longer be seen as competitive with the education of children. It is, rather, a necessary supplement to the education of all children.[4]

Education as a "developmental continuity" extends vertically and chronologically along all horizontal and sequential levels of learning from the cradle to the grave, from pre-elementary through adult learning. Pre-elementary and elementary education not only begin instruction in the traditional three Rs, but also launch the individual on the endless path of lifelong learning. As indicated in the diagram below, continuing education has a temporal axis extending through all the years of living and all the formal levels of learning.

Adult	
Higher	
Secondary	Continuous education
Elementary	
Pre-elementary	

Continuing learning also has a "circumferential dimension," with the radii of enlarging circles embracing more and more education and living. An Oriental proverb poses this pithy paradox: "The greater the diameter of light, the greater the circumference of darkness." The more one learns, the more he finds to learn. The lifelong desire to enlarge one's store of knowledge is another quantitative challenge of continuing education.

Continuing learning not only increases the quantity of wisdom—more years of schooling and greater amounts of knowledge—but can also enrich its quality. This is the axis on which real life revolves,

[4]Grant Venn, *Man, Education, and Manpower*, American Association of School Administrators, Washington, D.C., 1970, pp. 121, 122, 123, 124.

with its two poles: depth of philosophy and heights of idealism. Continuing education can help one live a life of infinite quantity and highest quality.

HISTORICAL DEVELOPMENT

Beginnings in the Ancient World. The historical roots of continuing and adult education are deeply embedded in time:

In the Western World, continuous education as a way of life goes back at least to Socrates and ancient Athens, and today the Socratic dialogue remains a major instrumentality of continuous education. Moving to the East, we find it going back in Judaic life, to the systematic adult study of the Scripture and the Rabinic commentaries. Farther to the East, continuous education as a way of life goes back, for example, to the full regimen established for the good life of the intellectually classical Hinduism.[5]

Beginnings in the United States. Although continuing education has Old World antecedents, organized adult education is very largely indigenous to American culture. The early town meetings in the New England colonies are sometimes cited as the first forms of adult education. However, education was not their primary purpose or activity. After the establishment of the republic, organizations such as the American Academy of Arts and Sciences in Philadelphia (1780), the Lowell Institute in Boston (1836), the Smithsonian Institution in Washington (1846), and Cooper Union in New York (1859) arose in the cities, mainly for the purpose of extending knowledge of the physical sciences among adults. The American Lyceum, founded by Josiah Holbrook in Massachusetts in 1831, is especially noteworthy because it eventuated in lecture-discussion groups in over three thousand towns. Although established "for the mutual improvement of their members and the common benefit of society," the principal purpose of the Lyceum was to advance the public school movement and to foster free libraries.

Numerous other pioneering movements in adult education are listed in the historical calendar. The Chautauqua Institution, founded in New York in 1874 for the original purpose of training Sunday school teachers, broadened its program to raise the general cultural level of adults, particularly in rural communities, through local reading circles, corre-

[5]Goldberg, *op. cit.*, p. 3.

The Development of Adult Education

1661	Evening schools reported in New York State	1933	TVA and WPA established, including provisions for adult education
1808	Prototype of university extension class established at Yale	1935	Social security legislation passed, giving aid to older Americans
1831	American Lyceum established in Massachusetts	1946	USAFI established officially as a permanent peacetime organization
1839	First general state law providing for evening schools enacted in Ohio	1947	National Retired Teachers Association (NRTA) formed
1859	Cooper Union opened in New York City with public forums	1951	American Association for Adult Education and Department of Adult Education joined to form the Adult Education Association
1874	Chautauqua Institution founded at Chautauqua, New York		
1883	The Correspondence University founded at Ithaca, New York	1952	Adult Leadership magazine launched by the AEA
1891	International Correspondence Schools established at Scranton, Pennsylvania	1961	White House Conference on Aging held in Washington, D.C.
1914	Federal funds for agricultural extension work provided by Smith-Lever Act	1962	Manpower Development and Training Act, providing for occupational training and retraining, passed by Congress
1924	First community (Cleveland) Organized for an adult education program	1964	Adult education stimulated by passage of antipoverty legislation
1925	Public adult education first recognized by law as part of the free schooling	1965	To coordinate federal activities for senior citizens an Administration on Aging established in the Department of Health, Education, and Welfare
1925	First educational and ethical standards for the correspondence course field established by the National Home Study Council		
1926	American Association for Adult Education formed	1969	Meeting of International Congress of Gerontology held in Washington, D.C.
		1970	Education for secondary school adults added by Congress to Basic Education Act of 1966
1928	Adult Learning, by E. L. Thorndike, published	1971	White House Conference on Aging held in three stages

spondence courses, and traveling chautauquas. Rotary, Kiwanis, Red Cross, YMCA, parent-teacher associations, public libraries, and other civic and cultural organizations trace their history in adult education activities back to the latter half of the nineteenth century.

When William Rainey Harper was president of the University of Chicago, he imported the concept of university extension education from London and Oxford, and colleges and universities began to perceive their mission in adult education. The University of Chicago, the University of the State of New York, and the University of Wisconsin established the early prototypes of university extension programs for adults. These programs centered around day-to-day—agricultural, economic, political, social, and moral—problems. The land-grant colleges, with a natural disposition toward broad public service, adapted easily to the movement. The Smith-Lever Act of 1914 stimulated the establishment of agricultural extension education. County agents, vocational agricultural teachers, and other specialists influenced millions of farm families, not only in farm practices, but also in child rearing, health, nutrition, and many cultural activities. The Smith-Hughes Act of 1917 stimulated widespread vocational education, for youths as well as adults, in the public schools. These movements in agricultural and vocational education have had a powerful impact on the development of our economy and culture. In addition, the private correspondence schools—notably the International Correspondence Schools—which sprang into being provided education to millions of Americans on a home-study basis.

Schools and teachers of adult education began to form associations. Although they were not concerned exclusively with adult education, they nevertheless served to disseminate ideas and practices about adult learning.

The Modern Era. Until World War I, adult education had been developed as an adjunct to other programs or institutions. Indeed, the term "adult education" did not come into general use in America until Frederick P. Keppel, president of the Carnegie Corporation, returned in 1924 from an inspection trip of adult-education programs in Europe. His vision of an organized movement in adult education eventuated in the founding of the American Association for Adult Education in 1926. The organization, financed in part by the Carnegie Corporation, served as a clearinghouse for ideas and resources, spon-

sored conferences and publications, and brought integrity and organization to the national movement.

The Department of Adult Education of the NEA, an important professional association of adult educators, merged in 1951 with the American Association for Adult Education to form the Adult Education Association of the U.S.A. In recent years the public school adult educators have reestablished their self-identity with the formation of the National Association for Public School Adult Education, under the joint auspices of both the National Education Association and the Adult Education Association.

Meanwhile, the federal government had engaged in several noteworthy undertakings in adult education. During the Depression years, the Works Progress Administration, the Civilian Conservation Corps, and other programs provided emergency funds for worthwhile activities for unemployed adults and out-of-school youth. One of the most striking examples of government-sponsored communitywide adult education is the Tennessee Valley Authority. The GI bills of World War II and the Korean conflict provided for the education of ten million adults who had served in the Armed Forces. The permanent GI Bill, passed in 1966, will help finance the education of many more millions of military men and women who have served more than six months of active duty. By far the most massive and significant infusion of federal funds in support of the education of adults, these GI bills have increased the nation's trained manpower markedly.

The Manpower Development and Training Act (MDTA) of 1962–1963, along with its subsequent extensions and modifications, is a specific piece of congressional legislation directed toward helping the unemployed become more employable and the employed more skillful. When it was extended to 1969, it was also liberalized to include such features as federal aid for up to two years of training in complex jobs and increased allowances for the worker in training. Recent amendments place increasing emphasis on assisting the hard-core unemployed and the undereducated underemployed. The MDTA is jointly administered by the Departments of Health, Education, and Welfare, and of Labor.

The passage of the Economic Opportunity Act of 1964 by Congress enabled many adults from minority and lower-income groups to enroll in public school adult-education classes under Title II-B of that act. These provisions became a part of the Adult

Education Act of 1966. For the 1970–1973 period, with good prospects of its continuance beyond that period, Congress added education for adults at the secondary school level to the Basic Education Act.

Powerful stimulation for the enhancement of adult education has come from numerous private foundations, such as the Carnegie Corporation and the Ford, Kellogg, and Sloan Foundations. Private industries and corporations pour billions of dollars into the education and reeducation of their employees.

Opportunities in and demand for adult education increased in 1965, when the new contractual arrangements between the automobile industry and labor unions became effective, providing for retirement as early as age 55. While coal miners have been able to retire at 55 for several years, the addition of the automobile workers and others increases greatly the number of early retirees and the need for more adult education.

Also in 1965 the federal government decided it was high time to seek to coordinate the federal activities for older citizens formerly scattered among several agencies. In the Department of Health, Education, and Welfare, an Administration of Aging was created through the Older Americans Act, including a Commissioner on Aging and an Advisory Committee on Older Americans. The new agency also supports research, administration, and training in the field of aging. The White House Conference on Aging, held under the auspices of the White House in 1971, discussed many facets of education.

From these and other stimuli a wide variety of adult education programs have arisen throughout the nation, supported by public schools and universities, industries and labor unions, fraternal orders and civic societies, the Armed Forces and other departments of government, churches, synagogues, YMCAs, and almost countless other organizations. The great growth of adult education has been one of the most striking educational phenomena of the last half-century. At least seventeen million adults are currently enrolled in organized courses, and many millions more are engaged in independent self-education.

A middle-aged housewife, her children grown, returns to college for refresher courses in education in order to resume her interrupted career in teaching. An airline pilot attends a company school to become proficient in the operation of the latest jet. A young

career diplomat, preparing for a new assignment in Peru, learns Spanish at home with the help of phonograph records. A young mother learns the art of infant care at a Red Cross class. A retired attorney finally finds time for a neglected hobby and attends an evening class in oil painting at the local high school. A young married couple learn to rumba at a local dance studio. An enterprising business executive who had to leave school early catches up on his general education by joining a "great books" discussion group. Across America, adults of all ages are engaged in the quest for richer living through lifelong learning.

Thus adult education has become established as the fifth level of our educational system—the natural culmination of pre-elementary, elementary, secondary, and higher education. Running parallel with these five formal levels of learning, as previously indicated, is the challenging concept of continuing education.

NEW IMPERATIVES AND CONTINUING EDUCATION

We mentioned earlier that changes in man's life and labor are occurring at a rapidly accelerating rate. The forces underlying these changes and the need for lifelong learning are examined in some depth.

Proliferation of Knowledge. It has been said that more new knowledge has been revealed within the lifetime of the present adult population than existed at the time of its birth. There are exciting new fields of learning scarcely identified a generation ago: group dynamics, cybernetics, astronautics, oceanography, atomic physics, aerology, and geriatrics—to mention a few. Books about science, as well as books in other fields, sometimes become obsolete almost as soon as they are published. Ninety percent of all the prescriptions written by physicians today could not have been filled twenty-five years ago. Ninety percent of all the scientists who have ever lived are alive today.

The geography of the world has been transformed since most adults received their diplomas. Scores of new nations have been formed and national boundaries redrawn. In all too many cases we can barely pronounce the names of these new nations, much less speak their languages and understand their culture, aspirations, and problems. The compelling necessity of a deeper understanding of international events provides a challenge in adult education, a challenge which we may ignore only with peril to ourselves and the rest of the world.

In education, too, the frontiers of knowledge are being advanced. Experiments in subliminal perception suggest that man is capable of learning while he sleeps. We are on the threshold of a much better understanding of the human mind, an understanding which will undoubtedly lead to more efficient teaching techniques. Electronics and automation have entered the classroom in the form of educational television, language laboratories, and self-instructional devices (see Chapter 15). Many other educational innovations are mentioned throughout this book. All these developments challenge the best efforts of our faculties to keep abreast of the art and science of teaching.

Across the nation, in all fields of human endeavor and interest, adult-education programs are placing increasing emphasis upon keeping the learner's knowledge up to date. This extension and modernization of knowledge is the central aim of adult education. Adults are responding as never before to intellectual challenges. It is quite apparent that man's thirst for knowledge is never quenched.

Basic Education. Historically, the campaign for "Americanization classes" for adults had three major objectives: to blot out illiteracy, to convert foreigners to the use of English, and to teach immigrants the American way of life. Today millions of Americans need basic education.

This fundamental education includes learning the basic tools of reading, writing, and arithmetic. As currently used by the Census Bureau, the term "functionally illiterate" denotes those with less than six years of schooling. One of the current statistics is that there are more than three million illiterates in the adult population of the United States. In Puerto Rico more than 40 percent of those aged 60 and over are illiterate.

All states give persons over age 18 who have completed less than six grades of schooling an opportunity to attend adult basic-education classes. Many have benefited from the Manpower Development and Training Act, as amended.

Federal activities are supplemented by many interesting and successful basic-education projects financed by the private sector of our economy.

Recognition of Man's Continuous Capability for Learning. Adult education has been stimulated by the growing realization that you can indeed teach

an old dog new tricks. Educational psychologists once believed that the mind was set like plaster at about 25 and that the later acquisition of new ideas was extremely difficult, if not impossible. Modern experimental psychology has exploded this myth. Edward Thorndike, Irving Lorge, and other psychologists have demonstrated that adults can continue to learn, in some respects even better and faster than children. This was corroborated by the practical experience of Selective Service during World War II and by numerous programs for continuing education which are now being provided for men and women in service. Performance on tests of mental ability improves with age, even for those who scored high in youth. It is also clear that continuous practice in learning helps adults to retain their mental powers longer. Disuse, rather than age, is the chief cause of the loss of the ability to learn.

Examples of keen mental capacity in advanced

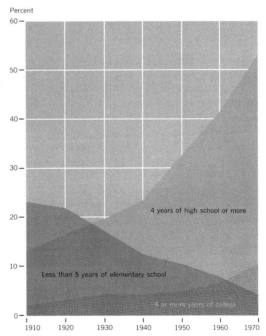

FIGURE 10-2 *Level of school completed by persons 25 years old and over. These data reveal that both the number of adults who have completed high school and the number who have completed college have doubled approximately every thirty years. NOTE: Data for 1910, 1920, and 1930 are estimations based on a retrojection of 1940 census figures. (U.S. Department of Commerce, Bureau of the Census, Current Population Reports.)*

years are legion. Winston Churchill's wartime leadership was an inspiration not only to the British but to the entire free world as well. A decade later, when he was in his eighties, he emerged as a gifted and prolific writer. Sarah Bernhardt was a brilliant actress at 77, learning new lines with the facility of a youngster. Verdi wrote *Falstaff* when he was 80 and his *Requiem* when he was 84. Voltaire at age 80 was an intellectual giant. Titian painted both the "Transfiguration" and the "Annunciation" when he was 88 and continued to accept commissions until he died, at 99.

As many a centenarian has demonstrated, it is possible to exercise keen intellectual power, despite ebbing physical vigor, even beyond the 100-year mark.

Appreciation of this never-ending capacity to learn has stimulated countless millions of adults to engage in intellectual pursuits with new vigor and enthusiasm. A lively academic interest and persistent mental exercise are undoubtedly more powerful determinants of useful adulthood than chronological age.

Impact of Automation and Technology. The story of American industry is a chronicle of miraculous invention and discovery. In 1833 the head of the U.S. Patent Office offered to resign because he felt that the limit of human inventiveness had been reached. But our advancing technology has demonstrated the folly of his prediction. And now a second industrial revolution, spearheaded by automation and advanced technology, heralds far-reaching changes in man's labor and leisure.

Machines have already taken over much of the brute work in industry. The unskilled laborer will all but disappear within a decade. The school dropout will become virtually unemployable unless he acquires vocational skills through adult-training programs. Computers and automatic control devices will handle tasks such as recording, accounting, duplicating, and reporting—more swiftly, more accurately, and more economically than human mind and hand, rendering large numbers of semiskilled workers obsolete. Even highly complex tasks will yield to automation.

The decline in the number of blue-collar workers will be accompanied by a sharp rise in white-collar workers. The urgent demand for more physicians, engineers, scientists, technicians, nurses, researchers, and other professional and

Many private industries, such as Bell Telephone, provide vocational education for adults to help reduce unemployment by training the skilled manpower they need.

semiprofessional workers is already upon us. Highly educated manpower is our most precious national resource and our most critical shortage. This shortage results not from lack of human talent but from lack of education.

The era of automation undoubtedly poses perplexing problems, for man is rapidly acquiring powers that are both fabulous and frightening. His extraordinary technology creates the possibility of a glorious world, free of hunger and drudgery. On the other hand, this same technology could usher in an era of barbarism and terror. As Stanley Casson so sagely observed, "When his practical inventiveness runs ahead of his moral consciousness and social organization, then man has equally faced destruction."

Increasing Complexity of Society. Man's social, economic, and political life is becoming progressively more complicated. Bigness and complexity are the hallmarks of his government, corporations, labor unions, mass media, political parties, and communities. Even his school systems, as reported in Chapter 5, have become increasingly large and complex. Without adequate education, his ability to understand the issues and challenges of these institutions and to direct their destiny lessens. The ordinary man becomes further and further removed from the seat of decisions. Individual responsibility and accountability can get lost in the crowd. The centralization of power also reduces man's independence and self-sufficiency. His livelihood, health, safety, prosperity, information, and happiness may be affected sharply by forces over which he has little control unless he pursues the knowledge and exercises the leadership necessary to cope with complex social organization.

Another force complicating our society is the astonishing increase in our population. While there has been a decline in the birth rate in recent years, the annual number of births is approximately the same as the total population of the United States in 1790. The increased density of population imperils human relationships, increases interdependence, generates tensions, and strains social organization. As government expands, the number of elective offices increases and ballots become so long that even the conscientious voter has difficulty knowing the candidates sufficiently well to vote intelligently. Bigness has overcome our media of mass communication—television, newspapers, movies, magazines, and advertising. Wherever he turns, man is besieged by an onslaught of advertising—exhorting, threatening, and beguiling him with the aim of getting him to buy more and more of a bewildering array of products about which it is difficult to get objective information. Other illustrations, such as the polarization of people and the generation gap, might be cited of man's increasing difficulty in exercising good citizenship, reaching wise decisions, and maintaining wholesome human relationships in the midst of a complex society. The preservation and strengthening of society in the midst of these and other encumbrances require the best continuing education that man can muster.

Protection and Strengthening of Health. The complexity of modern society adversely affects health, especially in the cities. Approximately three-fourths of our population live in cities and metropolitan areas. The air in countless cities is contaminated, almost to a critical degree at times. Congestion of population accelerates the spread of infectious diseases. Across the country water is in short supply, and numerous streams and lakes are polluted.

Especially as one grows older, ill health becomes a greater problem. However, half the chronically ill are under 45. An alarmingly large number of young men, supposedly in the prime of life, have had to be rejected for military service because of poor physical or mental health. Nearly half the hospital beds in the United States are occupied by the mentally ill. Much mental illness stems from anxieties generated by the increasing complexities of modern life, by the threat of war, and by the problems of aging. Yet, according to one authority, greater progress has been made by medical science in the past fifty years than in the previ-

ous five thousand. Obviously, there is a great gap between medical knowledge and individual health practices. Protection of health through accident prevention and the reduction of pollution are two of the goals of adult and continuing education.

The Protection of Our Free Society. As indicated in Chapter 17, today's world is deeply divided. For example, we live in a world marked by rigorous rivalry between the democratic and the Communist nations. This uneasy era of history is characterized by cleavages and competition, a succession of dangerous crises, and a continuous progression of awkward dilemmas and fateful choices.

Our people must understand that the conspicuous and unwise squandering of our riches, at a time when half of mankind is hungry, may threaten the peace of the world. How can we expect other peoples to cherish the ideal of universal suffrage when half our eligible voters fail to cast their ballots in an important election? Apathy about the quality of education, and about adult education in particular, may well deny to our people the knowledge and insights they sorely need. The individual whose education is not continuous will become dangerous to society. Despite the great advances in adult education noted in this chapter, it still lags behind social need in a time of world crisis. Clearly the preeminent challenges to education in our time are those of preserving world peace and extending freedom and justice.

Population Changes and Increased Life Expectancy. Several major changes in our population will have a profound impact upon the need for adult and continuing education.

In the first place, the population will continue to increase. The first census, in 1790, reported a total of less than four million people living in the United States. The final tallies for the 1970 census totaled more than 204 million people. Furthermore, it is predicted that by the year 2000 there may be 400 million persons residing in the United States—an exaggerated estimate according to many demographers.

Significantly, the number and proportion of adults will continue to increase because life expectancy has risen markedly over the years in our nation. The dramatic drop in our death rate is reflected in a loss of less than 1 percent of our population each year. The average man can expect to live twenty years longer than his grandparents. When today's grandparents were children, the average adult lived less than fifty years, and many children never knew their grandparents. Although the risk of death during the first year of life in the United States is higher than in any other period until the age of 65, a baby born in the 1970s has a life expectancy of more than 70 years. His offspring will probably have a life-span of nearly a century. The postwar rise in birthrates, combined with this lengthened life-span, has increased the adult population sharply. There are almost twenty million Americans aged 65 and older. The number of adults over 65 years of age is expected to double between 1960 and 1985. Furthermore, as previously mentioned and also indicated in Figure 10-1, there will be a marked increase in the number of young adults between the ages of 20 and 34.

Family-life Education. It was mentioned in Chapter 6 that the home is a very important educational institution. Each family is an informal discussion and study group.

Family-life education is one of the oldest forms of adult learning. Children learn from their parents and often teach them a thing or two. Many adult-education programs recognize the advantages of having family members study together. Husbands and wives enroll together in courses in dancing, bridge, rapid reading, swimming, classical literature, and many other recreational and intellectual subjects. Mothers and daughters take evening courses together in such subjects as nutrition, cooking, and sewing. Fathers and sons work side by side in courses in woodworking, automotive mechanics, radio repair, painting, and golf. Many parents have recaptured the great joy of sharing in the educational development of their children.

More and more, adult-education programs are including instruction in managing the family income, investments, consumer education, interior decorating, landscaping, nutrition, driver training, safety education, personal hygiene, child care, home care of the sick, and so forth. Family-life education is becoming increasingly important as more and more families become multigenerational, with grandparents and great grandparents living at home or in private nursing homes. An interesting family-life program is the Rural Family Development (RFD) of the University of Wisconsin, which applies modern behavioral theories in the mass communication field, with weekly visits by a home-study aide, and modern educational technology techniques including televised lessons given several times a day to permit optional viewing.

Parental Education. One phase of family-life education—parental education—is chosen for brief accent here because of its extreme importance, especially since the number of youths is expected to increase markedly and many will marry at an early age. Many of the young parents need marriage counseling. A husband-wife team of marriage counselors often renders real psychological and educational help to young couples about to be married, already married, or planning divorce. Parental education seeks to give parents the same opportunities that Head Start and Follow Through give their children—opportunities to catch up, keep up, and look up.

Increase in Leisure Time. Unions have been instrumental in gaining more leisure time for workers. During a strike in 1827, the Mechanic's Union of Trade Associations in Philadelphia declared: "All men have a just right, derived from their Creator, to have sufficient time in each day for the cultivation of their minds and for self-improvement." Today, the daily coffee break, the shortened workweek, and additional annual holidays and vacation days give workers more free time. For example, Congress in 1969 voted additional three-day holiday weekends. Many unions are working toward the bargaining goal of a four-day, 32-hour week. Some companies now have four-day, 36- or 40-hour weeks. Paul Samuelson of Massachusetts Institute of Technology calls the four-day week "a momentous social invention." While many workers spend extra hours "moonlighting" on another job, reduced hours of labor give other adults increased leisure time.

The earlier age at which retirement is permitted also gives millions of men and women more leisure time. Some labor-management contracts provide a bonus for employees who retire before the age of 65. The current trend is toward earlier retirement. Most persons receiving social security benefits today are under 65. Not only does retirement come a lot sooner than it did at one time, but increased longevity means that it lasts much longer, thus giving the individual worker a much greater lifetime accumulation of leisure time. New York State's significant long-term "continuing education" plan states:

Persons of all ages are searching for self-renewal and cultural renewal. For adults, the search for cultural enrichment is heightened by the dimension of increasing leisure time. Ours has always been a work-oriented society. This condition is changing rapidly. The problem of how best to use our free time matches that of how we work.[6]

Continuing Education for Women. More mechanical servants in the home and more formal pre-elementary education which takes place outside the home for at least part of the day give the modern housewife and mother more leisure time and more hours for meditation and self-improvement, including academic work. The single employed woman, with her shortened workday and workweek and the time-saving equipment in her apartment, also finds more leisure to use for personal enrichment with an informal or a formal program.

In response to the current women's liberation movement, many colleges and universities are proliferating programs for women. Supplementing the historic leadership role in education of women at the University of Minnesota and Radcliffe College in Cambridge, Massachusetts, are such programs as: Discovery at Roosevelt University in Chicago, which provides educational counseling for women and special seminars, and the College Center for Continuing Education at Sarah Lawrence College in Bronxville, New York, which offers women who have dropped out of college opportunities to earn academic degrees on the undergraduate and graduate levels.

The Plight of Dropouts. Many adults dropped out of elementary school. Almost a million students leave high school each year without a diploma. Thousands of able students desert college classrooms prematurely. Many a doctoral candidate never finishes his language or dissertation requirements.

Several federally supported programs, such as Upward Bound, are designed to reduce the number of dropouts from high school and college. After-school work activities help many remain in school. Experimental programs giving potential dropouts school credit for the on-the-job experience are being used by several state departments of education and the U.S. Office of Education. The federal government has reshaped its Neighborhood Youth Corps program for high school dropouts. The Job Corps, which came into existence in 1964 "to increase the employability of young men and women," has

brought many dropouts to learning centers, some of which have been called "trouble centers."

There are also the elderly dropouts, as indicated in an editorial in *Geriatrics:*

The dropout, long identified with young persons of high school age, is being recognized among the elderly. The aging dropout allows himself to drift out of the mainstream of life, to his disadvantage emotionally and often physically.[7]

The casualty list of adult dropouts from correspondence and night school classes is a long one each year. Especially alarming and significant for adult and continuing education is the dropout problem in secondary education. Nothing less than a Herculean effort can surmount this problem. If education is really lifelong, then young and old dropouts can, with guidance, help, encouragement, and motivation, continue to learn, for learning, like breathing, is essential to living.

CONTINUOUS CONCERNS AND DEVELOPMENTAL TASKS

Concerns in Continuing Education. Dr. Robert J. Havighurst has prepared a list of certain developmental concepts for continuing education. He has listed eight concerns that dominate certain stages of life, assigning one to each decade of the individual's "fourscore years," as shown in the following table:[8]

Decade	Years	Dominant concern
1	0–10	Coming into independent existence
2	11–20	Becoming a person
3	21–30	Focusing one's life
4	31–40	Collecting one's energies
5	41–50	Exerting and asserting oneself
6	51–60	Maintaining a position and changing roles
7	61–70	Deciding whether to disengage and how
8	71–80	Making the most of disengagement

[7] Editorial, *Geriatrics*, vol. 20, p. 90, May, 1965.

[8] Robert J. Havighurst, "Changing Status and Roles during Adult Life: Significance for Adult Education," *Sociological Backgrounds of Adult Education*, The University of Chicago Press, Center for Study of Liberal Education, Chicago, 1964, p. 17.

[6] Regents of the University of the State of New York, *Continuing Education*, State Education Department, Albany, N.Y., 1969, p. 8.

These concerns are elaborated in the developmental tasks listed below.

Developmental Tasks of Adults. Havighurst has provided another means of viewing the functions of education through his analysis of the developmental tasks that arise at certain periods in adulthood, the successful achievement of which leads to happiness:

Tasks of early adulthood
Selecting a mate
Learning to live with a marriage partner
Starting a family
Rearing children
Managing a home
Getting started in an occupation
Taking on civic responsibility
Finding a congenial social group

Tasks of middle age
Taking on adult civic and social responsibilities
Establishing and maintaining an adequate economic standard of living
Assisting teen-age children to become responsible and happy adults
Developing adult leisure-time activities
Relating oneself to one's spouse as a person
Accepting and adjusting to the physiological changes of middle age
Adjusting to aging parents

Tasks of later maturity
Adjusting to decreasing physical strength and health
Adjusting to reduced income
Adjusting to death of a spouse
Establishing an explicit affiliation with one's age group
Meeting social and civic obligations
Establishing satisfactory physical living arrangements[9]

Lifelong education programs addressed to the fundamental concerns of adult development promise mankind of all ages a richer, more satisfying life.

ORGANIZATIONS AND PROGRAMS

Adult and continuing education are being implemented in a wide variety of programs organized and administered with more diversity than any other level of education.

[9] Robert J. Havighurst, *Human Development and Education,* Longmans Green & Co., New York, 1953, pp. 9–283.

Programs for Young Adults. In the publication *Impact,* the National Association for Public School Adult Education and the American Association of School Administrators state that young adults, including undereducated dropouts and rejected military draftees, constitute one of the major groups with which education must be concerned. (Again see Figure 10-1 and also the *Orientation* section of this chapter.)

This new generation needs and demands new approaches and broader programs in adult and continuing education. Illustrations of what can be done are numerous. On the local level, the Los Angeles public schools, for example, award one out of every eight high school diplomas to an adult, mostly of the younger generation. Many states have special commissions, appointed by governors and/or legislatures, to design educational programs for out-of-school youth. The federal government has instituted special training programs for youth rejected for military service. Young adults must be and will be served in continuing education.

Public School Programs. Education for youth and adult and continuing education are fundamentally a matter of public concern. As the National Association for Public School Adult Education pointed out:

The public schools are maintained by society, are convenient to all adults everywhere, and are the agencies best equipped to provide the coordinating administrative framework, some of the physical facilities, and much of the specialized personnel to implement adult education in each community, including the programs of voluntary groups. The education of adults, therefore, is an integral and necessary service of the public school system.[10]

Begun originally in the mid-nineteenth century in a few large Eastern cities, public school adult programs at the outset centered largely upon Americanization classes for immigrants, helping millions of new Americans to familiarize themselves with the language and culture of their new homeland. As more communities opened their public schools to adults, attention was given also to the continuation of the education of adults who had dropped out of school early. Many of these programs, usually carried on in the evenings, became known as "continuation schools" or "evening schools." With the rapid rise of industrialization and

[10] *Adult Education in the Public Schools,* National Association of Public School Adult Education, Washington, D.C., 1961, p. 1.

the consequent demand for skilled manpower, vocational courses were added. In more recent years, particularly since World War II, public school adult-education programs have been conceived more broadly and include general and avocational education.

Perhaps the most common criticism of the substance of these programs has been that vocational and avocational classes have proliferated at the expense of general or liberal education, although there is some evidence of a recent reversal of this trend. In most adult programs, interest in such fields as English, foreign languages, science, and mathematics has risen sharply.

Enrollment in public school adult education programs has nearly doubled since World War II, reaching a total of nearly four million. This increasing return of adults to school is manifest in communities of all sizes and types. Many public schools are learning centers for people of all ages. Many so-called night schools are becoming opportunity schools for youth and adults, with daytime sessions and Sunday afternoon forums as well as evening sessions.

The larger the school district's population, the more likely it is to offer an adult-education program. Many public schools have joined their resources in an area organization for furnishing adult classes. For example, eleven school districts in the southern part of Kent County, Michigan, promote an areawide adult-education program. The adult programs of the public schools of the nation have helped millions of adults from minority groups. As an illustration, the schools of Dade County, Florida, have helped many Cuban refugees to further their education.

For the nation as a whole, about two-fifths of the total expense of adult education programs is met with local tax revenues, one-fifth with student fees or tuition, one-fifth with general state aid, and one-fifth with federal and state funds for vocational education. But adult education received only about 1 percent of the total expenditure for public elementary and secondary education.

The majority of instructors are drawn from the public school faculty, although lay experts are commonly employed. In many school systems these programs are planned with the help of citizen advisory groups, and sometimes they are administered by lay groups independently of the regular public school program.

More and more, public school systems must recognize and accept responsibility for the education of adults as the logical and necessary extension

of the public educational system. Clearly, the education of adults is just as compelling as the education of children in this rapidly changing world. Only one-fifth of the states provide adequate aid for adult education, with the result that many districts have come to regard adult programs, like kindergartens, as a marginal part of the total program—nice but not necessary, something that can be dispensed with at the first sign of financial difficulty. Teaching of adult classes should be regarded as a professional specialty in its own right rather than as an extra, part-time job for the weary day-school teacher. The administration of adult programs should be brought under the aegis of the regularly constituted local school authorities. Volunteer lay advisory committees, however dedicated and well-intentioned, are not adequate substitutes for well-trained and creative administrators. Finally, the curriculums of adult programs must be reconstructed to make available more academically respectable fare. Courses in the tango and fly casting are all right except when they exist at the expense of instruction in more substantive and enduring matters.

Individual Study. Perhaps the broadest type of continuing education consists in the countless and varied self-initiated, individual efforts of citizens to further their education through reading, travel, theater, radio, and television and with the help of private institutions including correspondence schools.

Private Schools. Many nonpublic institutions, including parochial elementary and secondary schools and colleges, offer local adult and continuing education courses. Many nationally known privately owned and operated schools offer instruction for adults. Besides the well-known Berlitz schools of language and the Arthur Murray and Fred Astaire dance studios, for example, schools of driver training, business education, technical education, fashion modeling, beauty culture, drama, and music are quite common. Private and public correspondence schools and colleges are important institutions for promoting individual study.

Correspondence Courses. One old and still important means of continuing one's education is the *correspondence course.* The International Correspondence Schools of Scranton, Pennsylvania, were founded in 1891. Thousands of business and industrial firms, the Armed Forces, and many of our smaller high schools use the resources of correspondence schools to bring knowledge to people who, for one reason or another, find it impractical to attend an institution of learning. Of the five hundred correspondence schools in operation, however, only about one hundred are admitted to membership in the National Home Study Council, organized in 1926 and approved by the U.S. Office of Education for nationally accrediting correspondence schools. This council, which has its headquarters in Washington, D.C., is attempting to eliminate the racketeering and fraudulent practices that have, unfortunately, characterized too many of these enterprises. Another accrediting and very creditable organization is the National University Extension Association, organized in 1915, which has a division of correspondence study and represents about seventy-five nonprofit universities and colleges that offer correspondence courses.

A comprehensive study of correspondence instruction in the United States was made with the cooperation of National Home Study Council and the Division of Correspondence Study of the National University Extension Association. Among the recommendations growing out of the survey are these:

Correspondence instruction should be integrated into the educational efforts of the United States.

The U.S. Office of Education should establish a Home Study Office. . . . The several states and the federal agencies should undertake rigorous regulation of private home study schools to prevent fraudulent operations and deceptive practices.[11]

According to the U.S. Postal Service, the number of fraudulent correspondence schools operating in this country has increased greatly. These "fly-by-night" schools usually run advertisements in want-ad columns using a job-opportunity approach as a come-on. However, most private adult schools, such as the International Correspondence Schools, have served millions of adult learners with institutional integrity and academic ability.

Colleges and Universities. As mentioned in Chapter 9, colleges and universities have long participated in programs of adult education. Approximately one hundred universities maintain a school of general

studies or extension division which offers both credit and noncredit courses for adults. The noncredit courses are often informal, have no prerequisites other than interest, and require no examinations or grades. The credit courses make it possible for adults to earn college degrees through part-time study at night. These courses are designed to increase the student's understanding of his cultural heritage, extend his vocational or professional competency, and enrich his knowledge of art, music, science, philosophy, foreign policy, or language. In many cases they are offered not only on campus but also in off-campus university extension centers. Furthermore, more than thirty universities currently offer master's and doctor's degrees in adult education.

Key leaders in the extension and enrichment of adult education are the country's community colleges. Many community colleges and others permit citizens over 65 to enroll for credit or noncredit courses without paying tuition.

Minority groups are given special attention in adult education. Navajo adults receive basic education through a program at Navajo Community College. Several hundred Cuban refugees who are graduates of universities but were prevented from

Lights from the University of Pittsburgh's Cathedral of Learning brighten the evening skies as adults attend night school there. Adults are going to night school in increasing numbers.

[11] Ossian MacKenzie, Edward L. Christensen, and Paul H. Rigby, *Correspondence Education in the United States,* McGraw-Hill Book Company, New York, 1968, pp. 230, 234.

bringing their diplomas with them have graduated from the University of Miami Retraining Center. With federal support many universities are conducting programs for the undereducated adult. The University of Notre Dame administers a program of paraprofessional training, using closed-circuit television instruction.

Related to the previous discussion on independent study is the great interest in the new "external" degree, bestowed by colleges upon persons who cannot or have not availed themselves of the regular college route, but who have acquired knowledge and skills through other sources, including on-the-job training and the ripening process of maturation, coupled with high motivation.

Certain institutions, such as the University of Oklahoma, have established a degree program for adults, bachelor of liberal studies, offered by a new academic unit, the College of Continuing Education.

Several universities, such as Michigan State University, the University of Georgia, the University of Oklahoma, the University of Chicago, the University of Notre Dame, the University of New Hampshire, and the University of Nebraska, have established excellent centers for continuing education financed by grants from the Kellogg Foundation. These centers provide fine facilities for workshops, conferences, lectures, and forums as well as classes. The University of Nebraska Center for Continuing Education embraces a Hall of Youth dedicated to serving out-of-school youth and young adults. For many years the University Center for Adult Education in Detroit has been cosponsored by the University of Michigan, Wayne State University, and Eastern Michigan University.

Universities also stress research in adult education. Many have institutes of gerontology or geriatrics or their equivalents. The Higher Education Act of 1965 established federal grants to strengthen the existing resources of higher education institutions to aid them in providing community services for adults.

Television has made it possible for universities to send both credit and noncredit courses into the homes of countless adults. Most universities conduct a wide variety of workshops, institutes, conferences, forums, and lecture series. The graduate divisions of the universities, as noted in Chapter 9, provide both preservice and in-service degree programs for advanced students in varied professional fields. In many colleges and universities, the enrollment of adults far exceeds the enrollment of undergraduates. Many universities engaged in adult education are affiliated with the Association for

University Evening Colleges and the National University Extension Association.

Through extensive research over many years, Cy Houle and other leaders in adult education have found that the more formal education an adult has, the more likely he is to be active in continuing learning. Hence a double responsibility is laid upon colleges and universities: to educate the student during his initial college experience and to reeducate the alumnus continuously.

Libraries, Museums, and Other Cultural Centers. The free public library movement, stimulated by the generous gifts of Andrew Carnegie, has made the community library almost as common as the public school in cities and villages of all sizes. Bookmobiles have brought libraries on wheels to villages and rural areas all over the nation. The public library movement finds its highest fulfillment in the Library of Congress in Washington, described by James Truslow Adams as "the one which best exemplifies the dream of the greatest library in this land of libraries." Once regarded simply as a repository for books, the modern community library has also become an information center replete with phonograph records, tape recordings, films, and other multisensory aids and equipped with reference, committee, lecture, radio, television, and periodical rooms. Many libraries conduct organized reading clubs, book-review circles, and discussion groups. The American Library Association, particularly through its Commission on Library and Adult Education, has greatly influenced the library to become an educational resource for learners of all ages.

Nationally, many organizations, such as the Adult Education Association, have a copious "library of continuing education." The New York State Library has experimented with transmitting facsimiles of valuable materials to researchers throughout the state. Many local libraries aid the adult by furnishing typewriters and reproduction facilities for public use.

Larger communities support historical, scientific, industrial, and art museums that exhibit the arts and crafts and artifacts of virtually all facets of our culture. Formal classes, lectures, seminars, and guided tours frequently enhance the educational value of these institutions.

The facilities and programs of the libraries and museums, both public and private, are steadily being improved. New standards have been developed by the American Library Association.

Many cities maintain observatories, planetariums, aquariums, aviaries, arboretums, zoological and botanical gardens, and other centers for observation and for the study of the natural sciences.

Right-to-Read Goals. When former U.S. Commissioner of Education James E. Allen, Jr., announced the "right to read" as a target for the 1970s, he attested to the need for adults to learn to read, with data such as these:

There are more than three million illiterates in our adult population. About half of the unemployed youth, ages 16–21, are functionally illiterate.

A survey by Louis Harris Associates revealed that

18.5 million Americans over 16 years of age are unable to read well enough to fill out simple application forms for: welfare benefits, driver's license, bank loans, medicaid, social security number.

Literacy levels are lower among those who are non-white, over 50 years of age, city dwellers, and of low income.

Significantly, the biggest percentage gains in literacy in recent years have been among nonwhites.

To help implement the "right-to-read" program on all educational levels, a National Reading Council has been formed and a National Reading Center established in Washington, D.C. One of the first projects approved by the U.S. Office of Education was developing standards for adult reading competence by pinpointing the basic printed materials people must use to perform necessary tasks in American society.

Continuous In-service Professional Education. As discussed in Chapter 12, the real growth of a teacher comes in the in-service years—continuing adult education which multiplies itself in the lives of the teacher and the taught. In an interesting project being conducted by Pennsylvania State University, a teacher-education trailer stops from six to ten weeks in different schoolyards. This trailer, equipped with a central computer and twelve terminals, stays open 10 to 12 hours a day, six days a week, so that elementary teachers in public and private schools can schedule professional studies at their convenience and complete them at their own pace. For teachers who cannot leave their families and homes to get additional training, the teacher trailer brings university facilities and staff to their own schoolyard.

As has been aptly said: "He who dares to teach must never cease to learn."

In-service, as well as preservice, education of professionals in the field of adult education is increasing in quantity and improving in quality. Many short-term institutes, year-long seminars, and other in-service programs under the auspices of adult-education associations, state departments of education, and the U.S. Department of Health, Education, and Welfare involve thousands of adult educational practitioners in professional training.

With the rapid advance in science and technology in all fields, professional men and women, not only at all levels of education but in many other fields such as medicine, research, psychology, industry, and banking, take courses, participate in seminars, observe in clinics, attend professional conferences here and abroad, subscribe to professional journals, and become academic addicts of lifetime learning.

Orientation and Education for Immigrants. The Immigration Act signed in 1965 augments the need for adult education, since it increases the number of immigrants who can be admitted annually. While a preference is being given to immigrants who have relatives here and who have skills needed in the United States, orientation and reeducation are still needed by today's immigrants.

The Cuban Refugee Loan program, which provides federal aid to exiled students and professionals for their continuing education, is an example of the kind of effort needed today. These long-term, low-interest loans are made through the Department of Health, Education, and Welfare. A little-known public educational institution is the Americanization School, established by Congress in 1924 as a part of the regular District of Columbia public school system. Here immigrants, diplomats, embassy personnel, and other people from nearly a hundred countries improve their English and familiarize themselves with the American way of life.

Conferences, Institutes, and Workshops. Many discussions for and by adults take place at various conferences, institutes, workshops, seminars, and short courses. An example of the countless conferences is the Michigan Conference on Employment-bound Youth. Many institutes are prolonged programs for the in-service education of employees.

The National Retired Teachers Association and the American Association for Retired Persons conduct the Institute of Lifetime Learning. When a person has completed the required number of courses, the institute issues him a certificate in the Program of Social Maturity. The Institute for Retired Professionals, located in New York City, is connected with the New School for Social Research, which offers noncredit and credit courses toward an undergraduate or graduate degree. Institutes under the aegis of an accredited educational institution have an academic climate, a professional prestige, and a reservoir of trained personnel. Funded under provisions of Title II-B of the Economic Opportunity Act, workshops have been conducted for adult educators on such subjects as the guidance of disadvantaged adults. The resources and techniques for personnel engaged in the guidance and education of disadvantaged and advantaged adults are numerous and varied.

The Aspen Institute for Humanistic Studies, founded in the late 1940s, brings business and professional men and women to this Colorado skiing resort for two weeks of "intellectual push-ups" through daily seminars dealing with a wide range of subjects.

Homes for Retired Persons. Homes and apartments tailor-made for retired persons are also mushrooming. Some of these are for specially designated groups. While the major emphases are on food, shelter, and physical care, including nursing and hospital facilities, the educational and recreational programs in many of these homes are varied, fascinating, and dynamic.

Labor Unions. Trade unions have long been active in continuing education. Basically, there are two types of labor education: instruction in matters related to union welfare and instruction in skills related to workmen's jobs. The former focuses upon the improvement of labor union organization and leadership, the strengthening of techniques of negotiation with management, and general concern for domestic and international affairs. These programs are frequently offered on university campuses. The National Institute of Labor Education, for example, consists of three 10-week institutes at Cornell, the University of California, and Michigan State University. Such institutes and courses embrace study in economics, political science, sociology, psychology, trade union history and philosophy, labor law, business organization and management, and civil liberties. Extension courses at land-grant colleges are often conducted to help labor union officers provide more effective leadership. Labor union officials are

the students at the new National Labor Relations Studies Center, established in Washington, D.C., by the Executive Council of the AFL-CIO.

The second type consists of both apprenticeship programs for beginning workers and skill-improvement programs for established craftsmen. The apprenticeship programs are the oldest and perhaps the best-known. They exist most commonly in the building, metal, and printing trades and are financed and administered jointly by employer and employee. The apprentice learns his skill by working side by side with an experienced journeyman and attending school several nights a week, his pay increasing as he progresses. The newest programs are designed to improve the skills of the experienced craftsman.

Management Concerns and Continuing Education. Labor and management both recognize the great importance of continuing education for workers. For example, a labor-management group has organized a center for job training and development. Through the American Foundation on Automation and Employment, they have jointly formed a council and established a library as a clearinghouse for information and help in developing job training programs for unions, management, and government.

Many workers trained in the first two-thirds of this century are being technologically dislocated in the last third. As previously mentioned, one authority predicts that the typical production worker in the next generation will have to be retrained occupationally four or five times in the course of his working life. A manufacturer of automation equipment has stated that automation is eliminating two million jobs a year, not only through direct displacement of workers, but also through the "silent firing" of workers who would have been employed had their jobs not been eliminated. Many in management have suggested that business concerns receive a tax credit for training new employees and retraining old ones, similar to the investment credit for improving capital equipment.

A new dimension has been added to American education by the widespread growth of educational and cultural programs sponsored by business and industrial firms. A survey by Harold F. Clark and Harold S. Sloan shows that 85 percent of the country's largest corporations have some kind of educational program in which knowledge or skills are taught according to some predetermined plan. Western Electric (ATT subsidiary), for example, has a new $5 million Corporate Education Center in Hopewell, New Jersey, not far from Princeton University. This 190-acre campus, with its residences and educational buildings, is labeled an "in-company college." Motorola, Inc., in cooperation with the Illinois Institute of Technology, has a program which makes it possible for a worker to earn a graduate degree without leaving his job.

Many programs are sponsored or supported by the federal and state governments through the Labor Department, the Office of Economic Opportunity, and the U.S. Office of Education. In 1968 the National Alliance of Businessmen launched the Job Opportunities for the Business Sector (JOBS), which pays the costs of training the hard-core unemployed. They include both contract-to-hire pledges and noncontract JOBS. The Labor Department has opened Residential Manpower Centers in major metropolitan areas, which are somewhat similar to the closed Job Corps Centers.

Managers of industry themselves must become more deeply concerned about their own continuing education. The executive dropout is thus pictured in *Dun's Review*:

In his own way the executive dropout is more burdensome to his company than the school dropout is to the educational system. He does not leave. For all intents and purposes he has taken early retirement, but he does not retire; he arrives each morning, transfers papers from the "in" box to the "out" box. Yet he has ceased to function as a mover, innovator, or contributor to the forward thrust of his company[12]

The retraining of executives, pioneered by the Harvard Graduate School of Business, is aimed negatively at slowing the process of managerial obsolescence and positively at sharpening skills and fostering new knowledge and new insights. Dean Courtney C. Brown of Columbia University's Graduate School of Business has said, "The day is coming when companies will regard refreshment of their management teams as being as important as replacing obsolescent machines."

Prison Education. Another program of informal and formal adult learning is the correctional education offered in prisons and reformatories. According to

a survey conducted by the Federal Bureau of Prisons, the typical inmate of a federal prison reads from five to ten times as many books, usually nonfiction, as the average citizen. Furthermore, many major penal institutions have academic programs from the first grade through high school graduation. The Federal City College of Washington, D.C., conducts a freshman college program in the prison complex at nearby Lorton, Virginia. Many have functional vocational programs and guidance centers. High school and college correspondence courses are widely provided. The amendments to the Library Services and Construction Act added a new title providing federal funds for libraries in state prisons.

Penological studies show that currently more than half of the persons released from prison eventually return there. On the other hand, research by the National Council on Crime and Delinquency indicates that with proper prerelease education and postrelease supervision, more than 80 percent of all convicted criminals can be trusted to remain in society as good citizens.

Many prisons are changing their basic philosophy from incarceration to liberation for learning as human beings. Indicative of the change in philosophy and nomenclature is the Buford Prison in Georgia, which has changed its name to "Georgia Training and Development Center":

Today Buford is a model many prison reformers believe all prisons should be—basically an educational institution. . . . The rock quarry has been abandoned, vocational shops hum with activity as prisoners are trained in such trades as: masonry, drafting, auto mechanics, welding, and barbering.[13]

Many adults, members of the Teacher Corps or students and teachers from nearby schools, volunteer their services in so-called "prison schools." The U.S. Department of Justice in 1971 launched a model rehabilitation program for female inmates of federal, state, and local prisons in cooperation with the United Church of Christ and Delta Sigma Theta, a predominantly Negro national public-service sorority.

With more than one-quarter of a million persons in federal and state prisons, plus those in county and local jails, the numerical potential for rehabilitation is a great challenge to continuing education. When the heavy steel gates close behind a new inmate, may he find the doors of educational oppor-

[12]Lee S. Bickmore, "The Problem of the Executive Dropout," *Dun's Review*, vol. 87, p. 34, April, 1966.

[13]Myral Alexander, "Let's Turn Our Prisons into Schools," *Family Weekly*, Sept. 20, 1970, p. 7.

tunity open to him. And when the rehabilitated person returns to society, may his fellow citizens have been reeducated to help him reestablish himself in a "new leaf" program.

Churches and Synagogues. Most religions offer important programs in education for adults, as well as for young people. These commonly include not only Saturday and Sunday morning classes, but also informal forums and discussions often held on weekday evenings in the homes of church members. Churches of all denominations have broadened the scope of their educational enterprise to meet a wide range of religious, cultural, and social problems, with considerable emphasis upon home- and family-life education. Many churches have organized leadership training classes to strengthen the work of church offices and teacher-training courses to help church school faculties improve their teaching. Many denominations have come to realize that their programs must include a large measure of both religious and secular education for parishioners of all ages.

Related to churches and synagogues are the YMCAs and the YWCAs. A YMCA or YWCA may offer courses for members or nonmembers in such areas as golf, judo, karate, yoga, skiing, skin and scuba diving, and dancing. Some of these courses are coeducational. Many coeducational programs for youths and adults are being offered by the Young Men's and Young Women's Hebrew Association in New York, the largest Jewish center in the United States. The decrease in the number of Catholic schools and the resultant increase in the number

The informality and variety of adult education are illustrated in this YMCA "class" in music for street people in Pittsburgh.

of Christian Doctrine Classes for pupils attending public schools has led to the training of numerous adult lay leaders.

Clubs and Organizations. Foreign visitors to this country have often noted the disposition of Americans to form clubs. Alexis de Tocqueville, the distinguished French scholar, wrote that "Americans of all ages, all conditions, and all dispositions constantly form associations . . . associations of a thousand kinds—religious, moral, serious, futile, general or restricted, enormous or diminutive." The Adult Education Association classifies organizations active in adult education into the five general categories discussed below; the authors have added a sixth category.

First, many *voluntary associations* operate educational programs for adults through their local, state, and national units. Women's clubs, such as the League of Women Voters, the Junior League, business and professional women's clubs, and the American Association of University Women, attract women of all interests and ages to lectures, seminars, forums, and classes on an endless variety of topics of general interest. Men, too, find that a host of organizations, such as the Lions, Rotary, Kiwanis, and the YMCA, feature lectures and other programs which are focused upon contemporary problems and events of general interest.

Second, various *educational associations*, such as the Council on National Organizations for Adult Education, the American Association of Adult Education, the Adult Education Association of the U.S.A., the National Association for Public School Adult Education, the American Foundation of Continuous Education, the National Retired Teachers Association, the American Library Association, the National University Extension Association, the American Association of Junior Colleges, and many others, are concerned primarily with the advancement of adult education.

Third, *associations in related professions*, national organizations such as the American Medical Association, the American Society of Newspaper Editors, the National Association of Manufacturers, the American Management Association, and the Telephone Pioneers of America, as well as local associations of people in all the professions and major occupations, meet regularly and provide a vital channel for the continued education of their members along professional lines. They frequently undertake to provide information to the general public, hoping to influence opinion.

Fourth, *specialized interest groups* exist in every area of public concern. Parent-teacher associations advance adult understanding of problems of education and child development. The National Safety Council's educational programs have the worthy purpose of reducing accidents. The Forty-plus clubs, Senior Citizens of America, XYZ clubs, and Golden Age clubs have been formed to help older citizens adapt to the problems and challenges of advanced age. The American Civil Liberties Union addresses itself to the challenge of maintaining and strengthening the civil liberties of our people. The American Legion and the Veterans of Foreign Wars are interested in the strengthening of our national defense and in the well-being of our armed forces and former servicemen. Chambers of commerce carry on studies, discussions, and other programs intended to increase business in their communities and to advance the general economic well-being of our society. Scores of other examples could be cited.

Fifth, among the many interesting and helpful clubs are those organized by *special disability groups* to help themselves by helping others similarly afflicted. Alcoholics Anonymous is an outstanding example. Neurotics Anonymous is modeled along similar lines. Many groups are organized to help drug addicts. Volunteers in Probation, Inc., is a national foundation, with state and local groups, promoting the use of *very inspirational personalities* in helping rehabilitate youths and others who are court cases. The members of the Diabetes Association help one another, and individually and jointly seek the assistance of medical doctors. Many physically afflicted painters are members of the Association of Handicapped Artists.

The sixth group includes a growing number of *federal organizations and workers*—specialists, field agents, and teachers in such organizations as the Civil Defense Commission, the Department of Agriculture, the U.S. Office of Education, and the Atomic Energy Commission. These workers often have common interests with workers in the other groups mentioned above.

The exact number of voluntary associations carrying on adult-education programs is indeterminate. One authority estimates that there are 100,000 persons engaged as full-time teachers in, and directors of, the education programs of these six categories of voluntary associations, in addition to five million part-time teachers and discussion-group leaders. The part-time teachers are an important component of these adult education programs, helping greatly through their voluntary efforts to reduce the financial burden of their programs. These informal, problem-centered adult-education programs reach into every neighborhood and every public interest, constituting a vital element of society's progress in providing lifelong learning.

Reading: Periodicals, Books, and Other Media. Involved in studying individually is the continuous process of personal reading. In fact, the most universal medium of adult education is *reading*. It provides for everyone, through books, newspapers, and periodicals, a ready and inexpensive access to wide realms of knowledge. The choice of reading matter is kaleidoscopic. Newspapers reach the front porches of most American homes, bringing up-to-date news, editorials, and feature stories relating to community, state, national, and world affairs. The rise in television viewing and the decline in the number of newspapers printed, however, suggest that newspapers are becoming a less significant medium of adult education than they once were.

Magazines and other periodicals are used widely in adult education, both in organized study groups and in individual reading. No other nation enjoys such an abundance of periodicals, ranging all the way from lewd and licentious magazines to beautifully illustrated and well-written journals dealing with every aspect of human experience. About fifteen thousand different magazines are published annually. Nearly every hotel lobby has a magazine stand. On commercial airliners, in doctors' offices, in student lounges, in community libraries, and in living rooms—almost anywhere that people assemble—one finds an attractive array of magazines.

The book is one of the oldest and most effective media of adult learning. It is estimated that we add about 800 million new volumes to our bookshelves each year. Paperback books have enjoyed a mercurial rise in sales. One million paperbacks are sold daily from the racks in bookstores, newsstands, drugstores, supermarkets, and department stores. Library book circulation is increasing three times as fast as our population. Book clubs like the Book-of-the-Month Club and the Literary Guild have helped to extend the scope and raise the level of adult reading, as have a number of book-based discussion groups such as the Great Books Program, the World Politics Program of the American

Foundation for Political Education, and the American Heritage Discussion Programs of the American Library Association. Through the ages the book, perhaps more than any other medium, has been the fountainhead of knowledge for learners of all ages. As Carlyle said, "After all manner of professors have done their best for us, the place we are to get knowledge is books. The true university is a collection of books."

Supplementing books are related audiovisual materials. For example, over one-quarter of a million families have used "Art Seminars in the Home," sponsored by the Metropolitan Museum of Art in New York. This program, designed to bring instruction into the homes of those who seek enlightenment about great art, provides illustrative materials and guidance and is comparable to a series of coordinated museum lectures on art.

Older Citizens' Day Centers. Day centers for senior citizens are springing up all over the United States. Through their own self-government thousands of senior centers give oldsters opportunities for growth in self-discipline and cooperation with others.

Multisensory Materials and Media. Chapter 15 describes more fully the impact of films, television, radio, and other audiovisual means of education for adults as well as youngsters. Although television has drawn many people away from theaters, it has brought films into millions of living rooms. Educational films, in increasing numbers and improved quality, join commercial films in bringing to the theater, classroom, and home an exciting vista of life and nature. Filmstrips and slides record the marvels of man's accomplishments. The film projector has become as commonplace as the blackboard in adult education classrooms.

In the last two decades television has become an important medium of education for learners of all ages. Commercial channels bring many programs into countless classrooms and homes. Nonprofit educational television channels help millions of adults to make up for what they missed in their earlier education by offering courses which range all the way from elementary reading to college-level instruction. This new electronic blackboard, through direct telecasts, closed-circuit programs, and video tapes, is rapidly becoming one of the most powerful and convenient media of adult learning. The cassette can be a powerful tool in retooling the minds of adults.

Adults find radio and recordings useful in their

pursuit of education. The high portability of transistor radios has brought the world of sound to the farthest reaches of man's travel. Although disc jockeys and talk shows have preempted much radio time, a number of excellent educational programs remain on some wavelengths. Records, long recognized as a valuable medium for the appreciation of music, now offer re-creations of great moments in history as well as instruction in foreign languages.

Travel. As indicated in Chapter 17, more Americans go more places more often than people of any other land. It is estimated that the typical American travels more than 5,000 miles a year. Over $1\frac{1}{2}$ million Americans, young and old, go abroad yearly. Twenty-five thousand students and educators study and teach abroad each year. Seminars and conventions, tours and cruises, for business and pleasure, inexorably draw our people across mountains, plains, oceans, and continents and thus into closer communication with their neighbors around the world. "The world is a great book," said St. Augustine, "of which they who never stir from home read only a page." But many millions do see the rest of the pages vicariously through illustrated armchair travel talks given by those who have gone places and seen things. Pretravel seminars are increasing in popularity for those who contemplate trips here and abroad.

The Division of Continuing Education Service of the University of Michigan, in common with many other universities, arranges educational travel tours that go beyond the travel-beaten paths of yesterday's tours and "encounter" crucial world problems, especially the problems of developing countries where the explosive issues of the future are being determined.

Discussion. Discussion is certainly the oldest medium of adult education, dating back as far as human communication itself. Free discussion is so vital to democracy that it is guaranteed in the First Amendment to the Constitution. An excellent antidote for bias and dogmatism, discussion which brings together the ideas and experiences of different people helps individuals fo find deeper meanings and gain wider perspectives. Discussion helps people to identify with one another and to unite for effective group action on common problems. Small wonder that man is so prolific in establishing discussion groups, small and large, organized and informal, addressed to almost every aspect of human experience.

Preretirement Preparation and Education. There is a real need for preretirement counseling, as more than thirty-five million Americans will retire in the 1970s. Ideally, retirement planning should begin when a worker starts his career. Many persons, middle-aged and older, are increasingly concerned about advance planning for rewarding years in retirement. With retirement in some industries permitted at age 55 and with social security payments available to some in their early sixties, preretirement planning has greater relevance and urgency than ever before. Just as a student prepares for his academic graduation and for his entrance into the world of work, so a worker with foresight prepares for his promotion from full-time labor and entrance into a fuller life of leisure and learning.

Governmental Agencies. Attention was called in Chapter 2 to the various educational programs conducted by the executive branches of the federal government. As previously mentioned, federal and state prisons invariably provide educational programs for inmates. Postal workers, policemen, FBI agents, Internal Revenue Service officers, diplomats, and a whole army of civilian employees of federal, state, and local agencies attend specialized classes supported by various branches of government.

One of the largest government-supported educational programs for adults is conducted by the Armed Forces. The United States Armed Forces Institute enrolls thousands of servicemen in correspondence courses.

The Cooperative Agricultural Extension Service has been described as the largest rural adult education agency in the world. Supported by the cooperating services of the state colleges of agriculture, county agents, and the U.S. Department of Agriculture, this program reaches an estimated 15.6 million farm families and covers a wide range of subjects, including farm production, home economics, home and family life, health, marketing and distribution of farm products, conservation of natural resources, social relations, and general culture.

The historical calendar in this chapter and those in Chapter 2 and Chapter 16 list several federal congressional acts that have helped to stimulate and implement adult and continuing education programs. Throughout this chapter there have been numerous references to various adult education programs sponsored by local, county, state, and federal agencies. Two of the most important have been the Manpower Development and Training Act, originally passed by Congress in 1962, and the Adult Education Act of 1966, which shifted responsibility for the Adult Basic Education program from the Office of Economic Opportunity to the U.S. Office of Education.

FUTURE

Adult education in this country has been characterized by a spontaneity, informality, and diversity of sponsorship that have made it adaptable to a vast spectrum of needs. However, this circumstance has resulted in a patchwork pattern which lacks central purpose and overall planning. Carried on, as we have seen, by a motley miscellany of public agencies, industries, civic groups, churches, and labor unions, adult education has developed haphazardly along the route of its sponsors' self-interests. This disunity of purpose and program has been deplored by many thoughtful education leaders.

Malcolm S. Knowles, another pioneer in adult education, states that a new comprehensive philosophy and theory of adult learning and a new coherent technology of adult teaching are being developed for the future under the label of "andragogy":

What we know is pedagogy, which is a word that comes from the same stem as "pediatrics"—the Greek word "paeda," meaning child. All education has been equated with pedagogy—the art and science of teaching children. . . . The fact is that most adult teaching has consisted of teaching adults as if they were children. This has been our hamstring.

We have learned that adults are different from children as learners in certain very critical ways. And we have been developing a new technology—methods, techniques, and materials—that is tailored to these unique characteristics of adults as learners. Furthermore, we have started, first in Europe and now in America, to give a new label to this technology to distinguish it from the technology of pedagogy. The new label is "andragogy," which is derived from the Greek word "andrus," meaning "man" or "grownups." . . . This new technology of andragogy—the art and science of helping adults to learn—is based on certain crucial assumptions about the differences between children and adults as learners. . . .[14]

With this new philosophy and appropriate teaching-learning-living techniques, adult education be-

[14] Malcolm S. Knowles, "Andragogy: Not Pedagogy," *Adult Leadership*, April, 1968, pp. 350–353.

comes "andragogy"—teaching adults as men and women, not as children.

The future of adult education will be affected markedly by great changes in the composition of its clientele—the adults—and their future needs in continuous learning. Three of the population shifts are briefly mentioned below.

This chapter commences with data on the large number and high percentage of young adults in the years ahead. The 1970–1971 *Occupational Outlook Handbook* states:

While training requirements are rising, eight out of ten jobs to be filled in the 1970 decade will be open to young workers with less than a college degree. . . . The growth in the labor market will really be a story of young men and women between 16 and 34 who will account for about two-thirds of the net increases in workers in the nine- teen-seventies.

Their needs for continuing vocational, technical, and professional education are obvious. Furthermore, with the 18-year-old getting the vote, civic and political education for young voters will need more stress in the future.

Another change in the population, as previously mentioned, is the substantial growth in the number of older adults. It was predicted at the 1971 White House Conference on Aging that there will be an estimated thirty-three million people age 65 and older by the year 2000. This number is expected to increase to fifty-five million by the year 2011. This age group will have unique needs in education and reeducation.

A third population change, predicted by the Veterans Administration, is that in less than eighteen years the number of American men 65 and older who are veterans of military service will constitute a fifth of the total aging population of the United States. The survey states "by 1995, out of every four males over 65, three will be veterans." The so-called "permanent" GI Bill and related educa- tional and rehabilitating provisions will be subject to modifications as the years go by.

Another trend in adult education is a new sense of unity and integration. UNESCO has an active International Committee for the Advancement of Adult Education. The Galaxy Conference on Adult Education, held recently in Washington, D.C., was the first joint meeting of twenty major associations concerned with adult and continuing learning. The consensus of the conference was that the United States needs a national policy on adult education, called "the neglected educational stepchild." A con-

ference-related blue-ribbon panel of experts, headed by former Secretary of Health, Education, and Welfare Arthur Fleming, recommended the fol- lowing nine imperatives in a unified approach to adult education:

Eliminate educational deficiencies of American adults,
Strengthen adult education efforts of community colleges and universities,
Provide adult programs in humanities and in public affairs,
Improve financial support,
Provide continuing education for the poor,
Integrate education into the traditional educational process,
Urge national non-governmental organizations to strengthen their role,
Increase public awareness of the importance of lifelong learning,
Achieve more federal support and coordination.

In connection with the last-listed imperative, coordi- nation is sorely needed, as the federal government alone has 250 programs dealing with adult education.

The future holds the promise of better-prepared adult educators. There will be a rapid expansion of professional training for adult educators, as the field becomes increasingly professionalized. More universities will offer undergraduate and graduate courses and degrees for adult educators. Greater emphasis will be placed on the study of gerontology, geriatrics, and various factors related to adult ob- solescence and renaissance. Research will continue to broaden our knowledge of adults and how they learn.

This will lead to newer and better ways of teaching and learning, including self-instructional devices, improved audiovisual methods, simulation techniques, sociodrama, and other tools and tech- niques in educational technology. In its 1970 report, the Commission on Instructional Technology fore- casts the possibilities of computers in adult educa- tion:

It appears that computer-based access to self-assessment as well as instructional material has particular useful- ness at the continuing education level. Areas of weak- ness or gaps in knowledge are likely to be individually different, and a professional who is already at work may be much more comfortable in private than in public.[15]

[15]Sidney G. Tickton, *To Improve Learning: An Evalua- tion of Instructional Technology*, R. R. Bowker Company, New York, 1970, p. 357.

Educational "hardware" and "software" properly used have many possibilities in continuous learning. Residential workshops, educational camps, forums, television discussion groups, and community-development projects will contribute interesting new programs. Adult-education faculties will become more highly skilled as more universities provide preparation for this important specialty.

Significant progress in adult-education programs sponsored by the public schools cannot be made without increased financial support. A study of the financing of adult education by the Adult Education Association concluded that very few communities could sustain adequate programs through fees and tuition. Clearly, increased financial support from public funds—local, state, and national—is needed.

Certainly much that goes on in the name of adult education suffers from a lack of serious purpose. It is probable that in the future adult education will transcend the pedestrian and immediate needs of man and come to grips with the more fateful social, economic, political, and cultural challenges of our time. Already there is a strong indication of this tendency.

It is also evident that the spectacular expansion of adult education will continue. Our growing population, increased leisure time, and greater longevity all reinforce this trend. Although public schools and colleges will continue to expand their role in lifelong learning, the importance of other agencies will continue to grow even more dramatically. It is almost impossible to find any enterprise of major size in American life that does not operate an educational program of some sort. If this trend continues, more than half the education of adults in this country will soon be provided by agencies other than traditional schools and colleges. Does this result from the default of school systems in meeting the educational needs of adults and therefore dictate an expansion in public school programs? Or is it both natural and desirable that many agencies should devise their own programs to meet the educational needs of their clientele? Both possibilities are likely. Certainly public school programs have been grossly inadequate in most communities. The nation has fallen far short of the recommendation of the American Association of School Administrators for "a comprehensive and diversified educational program for all adults as an integral part of every school system."

The number of public school systems offering adult-education programs will undoubtedly increase. Institutions of higher education will serve more adults, not only formally, through study programs on campus and at extension centers, but also informally, through such media as television, workshops, and conferences. The community college will play an increasingly important role and will make college-level adult education more widely available geographically. On the other hand, it seems abundantly clear that the public schools and colleges can never, and should never, attempt to provide in full the kaleidoscopic variety of instruction of interest to all adults, much of which is now being provided more appropriately elsewhere.

Undoubtedly, adult education will become the fifth level of education. Then the teaching of those things needed only in adult life will no longer be the responsibility of the other four levels. Adult education will widen its scope through continuing education and will improve its performance through the pursuit of excellence, thus capitalizing on America's most priceless commodity—human resources, at all ages.

Edwin W. Brice, former director of adult education for the U.S. Office of Education, has stated that this nation is on the verge of an expansion and enrichment of adult education on a scale "beyond description and comprehension." A new study, *The Learning Force*, conducted by the Educational Policy Research Center at Syracuse, New York, envisions in the near future a time when more Americans will be educated "outside" rather than "inside" school walls. Their research indicates that by 1976 more than eighty-two million adult Americans are expected to participate in educational programs outside the traditional school system, compared to sixty-seven million students expected to be involved in traditional schooling by that time. Adult education will become a huge industry.

SUMMARY

Adult and continuing education is to a degree indigenous to our culture. Its growth has been stimulated by voluntary associations, private foundations, government, and schools and colleges, and a great variety of learning opportunities for adults has resulted. In its fullest conceptualization, adult education embraces all the formal and informal learning activities of persons beyond compulsory school age. New imperatives such as the proliferation of knowledge, the recognition of man's continuous capacity for learning, automation and technology, the dangers of pollution of environment and of polarization among people, the increasing complexity of society, population growth and changes, and the plight of school dropouts underline the importance of dynamic and effective educational resources for people of all ages.

This continuing education is characterized by a diversity of organization and program. Public schools, libraries, and public colleges and universities represent the public sector of this effort. The fastest-growing and least visible sector of adult education is the vast program carried on by business and industry. Labor unions, governmental agencies, churches, museums, clubs, and other organizations across America enroll persons of all ages and with all interests in an endless variety of intellectual, vocational, recreational, and cultural pursuits. Millions of other adults follow their insatiable quest for knowledge independently, through courses, reading, discussion, travel, movies, television, and radio.

The most urgently needed improvements in adult education include a better definition of purpose and program, better coordination and planning, stronger academic substance, strengthened public school programs, greater financial support from public funds, and better faculties and administrators.

Expanded, diverse, informal, uncoordinated, underfinanced, and need-centered—such is contemporary continuing education.

A celebrated former professor of English, William Lyons Phelps, once said that the concept of youth as the best time of life is based on a false premise. As an old Spanish proverb states, "Gray hairs are but the dust from the road of life." Indeed, "the art of aging is merely another chapter in the art of living."

As John Dewey, in his eighties, stated, "One is sustained and soothed, even in the midst of feebleness and defeat, by a sense of the enveloping whole." *Pedagogy*—the science of teaching the *child*—will increasingly be supplemented by *andragogy*—the art of continuous education of *man*.

Suggested Activities

1. Illustrate the relationship between adult education and continuing education.
2. What are some of the modern imperatives demanding continuing education?
3. Review the development of education for adults
as summarized in the historical calendar in this chapter.
4. Discuss the role of the public school in the education of adults.
5. List all agencies in your community which are directly or indirectly connected with adult education.
6. Write a brief history of some aspect of adult education, such as the labor colleges.
7. Describe one of the federally financed programs in adult education.
8. Report on one of the scientific investigations of the learning ability of adults.
9. What are some implications for education of the fact that the nation's population is growing older?
10. List desirable qualifications for a teacher of adults. Do you possess these qualifications?
11. As a young reader, what are your preretirement and retirement plans and your goals in your own continuing education?

Bibliography

Adult Education Association of the U.S.A.: *Handbook of Adult Education in the United States*, The Macmillan Company, New York, 1970. Helpful resource volume for an overview of adult education.

Aker, George F.: *Adult Education Procedures, Methods and Techniques*, Syracuse University Press, Syracuse, N.Y., 1965. An overview of adult education programs, organization, and teaching methods.

Axford, Roger W.: *Adult Education: The Open Door*, International Textbook Company, Scranton, Pa., 1969. The challenge of adult education.

Continuing Education, State Education Department, Albany, N.Y., 1969. Statement of policy and recommendations by the regents of the University of the State of New York for a ten-year program of continuing education.

Holden, John B.: *Education in the States: Nationwide Development since 1900*, National Education Association, Washington, D.C., 1970, chap. 7. An overview of adult education and the role of the public schools.

Houle, Cyril O.: "Adult Education," in *Encyclopedia of Educational Research*, 4th ed., Collier-Macmillan Limited, Toronto, Ontario, 1970, pp. 51–57. Review of research and thought on adult education.

U.S. Office of Education: *A Lifetime of Learning*, Government Printing Office, Washington, D.C., 1969. A description of three of the lifetime learning programs administered by the U.S. Office of Education.

Venn, Grant: *Man, Education, and Manpower*, American Association of School Administrators, 1970. A history and analysis of education's relationship to manpower development.

PERSONNEL RESOURCES

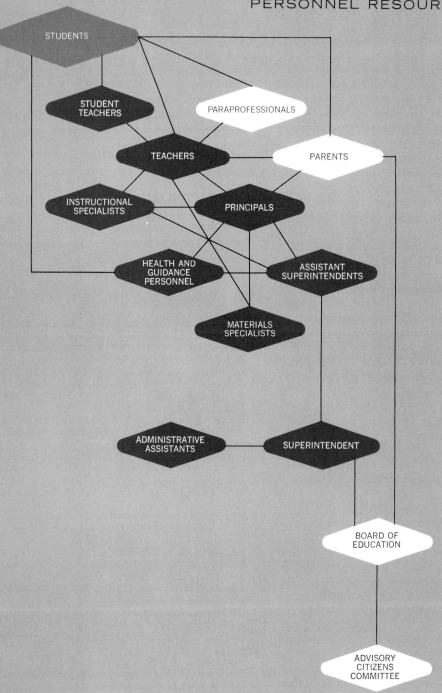

Part
Four
Personnel
in
Education

Education is essentially a *human* enterprise involving interpersonal interaction among students, teachers, administrators, and citizens. One person in every three in the United States is actively engaged in the "knowledge industry" in one role or another.

As the picture on page 266 suggests, the child is the focus of the major persons who influence him—teachers, parents, principals, and other school personnel. The school exists primarily for the student. The child grows and develops in at least four dimensions: physical, mental, social, and spiritual. Many children are atypical—they deviate from the norm sufficiently to warrant special consideration and treatment. Modern society treasures the child, be he gifted, normal, or atypical (Chapter 11).

Among the persons who exert an abiding influence upon the child is the teacher. The student and the teacher are joint partners in learning and teaching. The teacher is not an automaton but a human worker, who should be well educated and professionally alert. Teaching is becoming more of a profession. Standards for selection, as well as preservice and in-service education, are being elevated. Teacher-welfare provisions are being improved (Chapter 12).

The classroom teacher, however, is but one of the numerous persons engaged in education in the United States. Special teachers, administrative and supervisory officers, educational personnel from other professions, and other nonteachers contribute to the education of the well-rounded pupil. The opportunities to serve in educational work are numerous and varied. Persons not interested in direct classroom teaching can find many opportunities for other significant service. The teaching profession offers to persons with keen minds and warm hearts a satisfying opportunity to improve the human condition while enriching one's own intellectual and interpersonal growth (Chapter 13).

Chapter 11   Students

ORIENTATION

stu-dent (stoo'-dənt, stū'-) 1. n. one who studies, [< Latin studēns, apply oneself to studying; (originally) being eager]

The dictionary does not tell us what students should be eager about. Scholarly inquiry? Peace demonstrations? Drugs? The end of pollution? Racial equality? More elective courses? The elimination of grades? Better cafeteria service? Student representation on governing boards? During the long history of education, students have been eager about these and a great many other issues. Contemporary students in schools around the world are no exception, all the way from the upper elementary grades through the graduate schools. Their eagerness is manifested sometimes in responsible and wise struggle to participate in the improvement of their own educational experiences; sometimes in senseless assault on fellow students and other citizens and in destruction of property.

Some people regard student activism as a very dangerous threat to our free society, and there is unquestionably some element of danger in undisciplined and violent protest. Others regard student activism as one of the most powerful and hopeful forces for the improvement of the human condition. The authors accept the more optimistic view.

If one can believe that the excesses of student protest—weird hairstyles and manner of dress, unconventional life-styles, and resort to violence, for example—are juvenile aberrations that man commonly experiences in the turmoil of passing from injustice and inhumanity to a higher level of civilization, then the phenomenon of student activism can

Intellectual diligence is revealed at all ages.

be seen in more reasonable perspective.[1] Much more fundamentally, we are witnessing a profound shift toward a new humanism and existentialism in our values, a shift that is being led in part by our youth. As John Gardner points out, "The first task of renewal in the moral sphere is always the difficult confrontation of ideal and reality, precept and practices, and young people are very well fitted to practice this confrontation."[2] We are witnessing a ground swell of students who are eager to question orthodoxy, expose injustice and inhumanity, care about their fellow man around the world, search for accommodation between the material and the human components of our culture, reverse the trend toward exploitation and pollution of the environment, make the economic and political systems more responsive to the people, and expose the ambivalence of society between its professed and its manifest values. Surely all these ventures are very much within the spirit of our republic. If our youths press us to move more quickly or more honestly, we should help them sustain those efforts. If we can discount the hyperbole and vulgarity of some of their rhetoric and action and grasp instead the virtue of their aspirations, we can mobilize this powerful force and reduce their alienation from society. In the long perspective of history, it seems reasonable to predict that the more violent phases of this confrontation will be terminated when hope and progress become more evident to the young. Educators and other citizens must find authentic and effective means of

[1] We cannot view the epidemic of drug and narcotic usage so hopefully, however. For so many, the decision to use addictive drugs is an irreversible one that robs them forever of mental and physical health, and even life. It can hardly be viewed as a temporary aberration of little consequence.

[2] John W. Gardner, *Self-renewal: The Individual and the Innovative Society,* Harper & Row, Publishers, Incorporated, New York, 1965, p. 17.

267

sustaining young people's constructive drives while retarding their unwholesome thrusts. Both the schools and society can be expected to emerge from the struggle as much healthier institutions, and young people will be better prepared to be teachers and parents of the generations which follow.[3]

The quest for social and political reform is contemporary with the rapid development of new instructional methods which can sustain the educative component of the struggle. As pointed out in Chapters 14 and 15, marvelous new media of instruction are capable of bringing to all students everywhere any knowledge that exists anywhere. The computer and programmed instruction make it technically possible for the schools to accommodate to the needs, interests, and abilities of individual students and thereby to make learning both relevant and viable for all. New instructional techniques, such as sensitivity training and simulation, permit more effective instruction in interpersonal relations and introspection. New insights into the nature of learning, as described later in this chapter and in Chapter 14, suggest that the student's ability to learn can be significantly improved. McVicker Hunt, one of the foremost scholars in this field, believes that the general level of the IQ could be raised by 30 points. By the end of this century we may be working with students whose median IQ is 130. Neurological research at the Brain Research Institute at U.C.L.A. points to enormous abilities latent in everyone, except those with brain damage, and suggests the almost incredible proposition that the ultimate creative capacity of the human brain may be infinite.[4] Consider the powerful impact upon society of the next generation of students who will operate routinely at intellectual levels which we associate today with only the honor students. They will not only be brighter and far better informed but equipped also with much higher powers of analysis, abstraction, and reasoning. All children who are not brain-damaged will learn to read. If we can meanwhile relieve the cruelties of poverty, overpopulation, malnutrition, and disease, we can reduce not only the task of special education but also the alienation

[3] For an elaboration of this point of view, see Fred T. Wilhelms, "Tomorrow's Students," *National Elementary Principal*, vol. 49, pp. 5–10, April, 1970.

[4] For further discussion of this possibility, see Herbert A. Otto, "New Light on the Human Potential," *Saturday Review*, vol. 52, pp. 14–17, Dec. 20, 1969.

of the poor by opening more equal opportunity to them. Technically, these goals are not unrealistic. However, the necessary reeducation of teachers, administrators, and school boards may be a formidable matter.

These then are some of the more persuasive reasons for optimism in the outlook upon student unrest. We realize that with another set of assumptions a dismal image of the future of youth and society would be projected. We also realize that the picture which we draw is neither easy nor foreordained. If our vision is to be realized, it must be sustained by the most enlightened and patient pedagogy which our readers can muster. The task is enormous and difficult, but it is the most bracing and fateful challenge which man can discover anywhere.

Since the phenomenon of student activism pervades educational institutions, it is also covered in Chapter 1 where the appropriate response of schools to student activism is discussed more fully; in Chapters 8 and 9 which deal with student activism particularly in secondary schools and colleges; and in Chapter 14 where the implications of student activism for curriculum reform are discussed.

Let us turn now to somewhat broader consideration of the phenomenon of student activism—the nature of students who engage in it and the educational reforms suggested by it. In the remainder of the chapter we shall examine human growth and development and the demands which both normal and exceptional students place upon the schools and colleges. The causes, the cures, and the consequences of student activism are legion. The student movement is spoken of variously as a youth revolt, a new youth culture, a third-world movement, a crisis in disbelief, a generation gap, a quest for student power.

STUDENT ACTIVISM

Students in Contemporary Culture

Adolescence is a period of turbulence in human development. It comprises the difficult period of transition from childhood immaturity and dependence upon adults to adulthood and personal independence and responsibility. The transition from dependence to independence is fraught with difficulties, especially in a culture in which adolescence is artificially prolonged at the same time that young people are maturing more rapidly. Moreover, America is characterized by adoration of youth. A

Informality of dress, posture, and learning is characteristic of today's students.

child- and youth-centered culture tends to reinforce young people's sense of self-righteousness. The adult generation of parents and teachers has encouraged youths to be critical of the social, economic, and political milieu, as an essential characteristic of education. It is not surprising then that young people sometimes receive the impression that they are not supposed to be satisfied with anything. Adolescence has always been a troublous mixture of idealism and insecurity and is even more so in contemporary culture.

We are told that today's youths are brighter, better educated, more aware, and more idealistic than earlier generations. Certainly improved education and communication have made them far more aware of and knowledgable about the world than any previous generation.

Many more youths are remaining in high school than before and a great many more are attending college, including many who are not well prepared for the rigor of college work. As Bruno Bettelheim points out, contemporary education, both in the home and the school, teaches very little self-discipline, while college education requires a considerable amount of self-discipline. Consequently many college students hold the unrealistic view that schools should hand over knowledge and skills easily and instantly without the rigors of penetrating and disciplined thought. Bettelheim believes that there is widespread but unwise feeling that if students do not do well in school, the failure must lie with the school, not with the students; thus the educational system is regarded as the enemy be-

cause it withholds from them the education which they think could be so easily given.[5]

But the question of their idealism may be another matter. Historically speaking, youthful idealism has often been a capricious force which has set in motion countervailing violent forces, often abetted by youths themselves, which contradicted their own aims and quickened their own demise. As Elliot Carlson has pointed out, youth movements have tended to transform youths into what they fear most, and they seem to be presiding over their own dissolution and enjoying it, perhaps because their crusades are more romantic than intellectual, more ends in themselves than means to an end.[6]

Clearly this is not the first generation of youth to have discovered virtue. Today's youths appear to be hung up with hypocrisy, just as adults are. They are outraged, and justly so, by the slaughter of wars, but they never protest the slaughter on American highways which claims twice as many victims as the war in Southeast Asia and to which they contribute far more than their share. They crusade against pollution of the environment while a frightening and growing proportion of them pollute their own bodies more swiftly and surely with drugs and narcotics. They resent epithets directed at them, but their sensitivities are not disturbed by the obsenities which their peers hurl at others. They are sometimes more stimulated by slogans than by rational thought. They do not accept the responsibilities and constraints of good citizenship with the same grace that they accept the rights and protections of the government which they protest. They often construe administrative response to intolerable provocation as repressive authority, failing to realize that without public order there can be no protection and no rights for any citizen. By pointing to the hypocrisies of adults they seek to expiate their own. They claim to be heartsick at brutalities in American life but are blandly unconcerned about brutalities committed in the name of the "revolution." Some of them set fires and throw bombs in their crusade against violence and injustice. While holding themselves virtuous, they sometimes see the majority of adults as a cruel, apathetic, and heartless mass of

[5] Bruno Bettelheim, "The College Student Rebellion: Explanations and Answers," *Phi Delta Kappan*, vol. 50, pp. 511–512, May, 1969.
[6] Elliot Carlson, "History's Lesson to Radical Students," *Wall Street Journal*, vol. 119, p. 8, Jan. 31, 1969.

uninformed people encumbered with total guilt and presumably total corrective power for all the ills of society. They are commonly encumbered by shallow historical perspective in viewing the complex problems of their times. They often urge extraordinarily simplistic and immediate solutions to formidable problems. They seem to have unreasoned faith in isolationism and unilateral disarmament in a world teeming with hostilities. Many youths are quixotic, passionate, dogmatic, intolerant, unreflective, apprehensive, and anxious. Clearly this characterization is not valid for all of them, for they, like all Americans, manifest diversity in their values and aspirations. In sum, like all generations before them, they are engaged in the task of discovering the golden mean between freedom and responsibility, but in a milieu characterized by perhaps unprecedented uncertainty and hazard.

The circumstance of youth's ambivalence is not improved by the overreaction of some adults who vilify them and demand greater repression, thereby escalating the polarization of youths and adults and widening the gap of communication and accommodation. Some adults see the protest of youth as the prelude to anarchy or communism and respond with unreason. Some adults fail to realize that not all youths can be characterized as dangerous revolutionaries.

The eminent sociologist Robert Havighurst has represented schematically the diversity of adolescent values in the diagram presented in Figure 11-1, which depicts the relatively small proportion of radical activists of both the extreme left and the extreme right. Some of the activists of the New Left are affiliated with Students for a Democratic Society, an organization which, by its own pronouncements, is dedicated to the destruction of our government and an eventual revolution with Communist goals. The radical left is composed largely of revolutionary Communists or anarchists who have no interest in improving representative government, no commitment to academic freedom or the preservation of civil liberties. They are interested in destroying representative government and replacing it with a totalitarian form of government under Communist rule. They are interested in power, not reason. They know what they are against but not what they are for. Many of them are truly rebels without a cause. Although many of these extremists are bright, they are often persons who are incapable

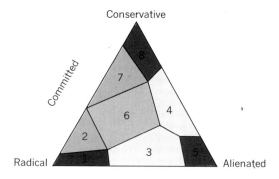

Per Cent	Category
5	1. Radical Activists (New Left)
15	2. Concerned Liberals
10	3. Hippies and Yippies
10	4. Uncommitted
5	5. Amoral Hostiles
35	6. Common Man Complacents—Squares
15	7. Concerned Conservatives
5	8. Reactionary Activists

FIGURE 11-1 *Varieties of youth. [From Arthur M. Kroll (ed.), Issues in American Education: Commentary on the Current Scene, Oxford University Press, New York, 1970. Copyright © 1970 by Oxford University Press, Inc. Reprinted by permission.]*

socially and emotionally of participating effectively in collaborative or competitive effort under a free-enterprise economic system and a representative democratic political system. These New Left activists are too few, too fragmented, too impoverished ideologically, too dictatorial, too smug, and too uncivilized in their tactics to threaten either seizure of government or the conversion of the majority. However, they are capable at times of precipitating reactionary and repressive response from administrative and legislative authorities and perhaps triggering a rightist counterrevolution which may threaten to radicalize concerned liberals and other groups of students. We would do well to remember that there has always been a small percentage of persons bent on destroying society and that many of these youthful revolutionaries abandon this movement as they grow more moderate in later years.

Too many adults lump together rational peaceful dissenters with political activists, revolutionaries, old-fashioned bullies, drug pushers, and vandals. The proper response to these various elements should be quite different—but teachers, administrators, and juvenile authorities sometimes fail to make this crucial distinction.

The militancy of some black students is the

cause of special concern among many people. However, the great majority of black students want exactly the same for themselves as the majority of white students: an equal opportunity in education, employment, and housing and an escape from discrimination and oppression. Only a small percentage of blacks, like a small percentage of whites, wish to destroy society; and most of these would abandon the radical movement if they could be persuaded that there is a less violent way of securing justice.

Figure 11-1 reveals that there is a group of youths in the radical right approximately equal in size to the group in the radical left. They advocate the suppression of civil liberties and arbitrary, quasi-fascist governmental response as protection against the New Left.

There is no reason to believe that either the extreme left or the extreme right activists, both dedicated to the destruction of traditional American values, are enjoying much success in recruiting a significant number of youths to their banners. This is an extremely important point and one which is easily overlooked by some adults who become almost paranoid in their fear of the activists. This fear is often exacerbated by the mass media, which appear disposed to magnify the image of the radicals.

As Havighurst's illustration reveals, the sectors of nonrevolutionary but concerned liberals and concerned conservatives are approximately equal. The largest single sector of the youth culture, according to Havighurst, is the "common-man complacents," whose orientation to society is compatible with the adult culture, or at least not actively hostile toward it. The remainder of youths are divided among the hippies, many of whom have withdrawn, at least for a while, from the culture to create a subculture of their own; the uncommitted, who, while not withdrawn, stand aloof from the controversy; and the amoral hostiles who are spoken of commonly as delinquents, or criminals in more extreme cases, who promote no cause other than their own selfish hedonism and despoliation of society.

Schools' Response to Student Activism

How should schools respond to student dissent? The response to student activism is as complex and difficult as are the causes of the phenomenon. This question is dealt with at length in Chapter 1, and only a brief discussion is necessary here. First,

schools must distinguish clearly between students who are interested in constructive reform and revolutionary activists who are bent on the destruction of schools and society. Schools must respond firmly but fairly with whatever action is necessary to constrain students who wish only to destroy education, to circumscribe academic freedom, to deny access to those who wish to study, and to endanger life and property. Without these protections of the public order, no citizen can enjoy freedom. Second, schools must respond thoughtfully to the many demands which are advanced by nonviolent, rational, and concerned student activists. Many of the demands which they call for are quite compatible with the reforms which enlightened educators like Rousseau, Dewey, and others have long advocated—greater student participation in the governance of student affairs, curriculum reform in the direction of more relevancy to contemporary life, open examination of controversial issues, repression of discrimination against minority groups, elimination of arbitrary standards of achievement for all students regardless of ability, relaxation of unreasonable regulation of student conduct, elimination of harsh punishment, and the full extension of civil liberties and the protections of the Bill of Rights to all students. The areas in which reform is needed are legion. Charles E. Silberman states, "The tragedy is that the great majority of students do not rebel; they accept the stultifying rules, the lack of privacy, the authoritarianism, the abuse of power—indeed, virtually every aspect of school life—as The Way Things Are."[7] Third, schools should recognize that instruction in good citizenship is a primary responsibility of the school. Educators can complain about the poor citizenship of students only after the schools have become an object lesson to students and to all society in how the establishment demonstrates the best of its democratic heritage. Students should be permitted to exercise meaningful citizenship in the governance of their own schools. Schools should be man's best laboratory for the discovery and practice of responsible citizenship and a powerful example of how a free society provides within the establishment the means for the refinement of that society through rational and nonviolent thought and action—the essence of democratic government.

[7] Charles E. Silberman, *Crisis in the Classroom*, Random House, Inc., New York, 1970, p. 155.

HUMAN GROWTH AND DEVELOPMENT

Christianity and many other great religions revere the inherent worth of every human being. This doctrine holds that each person should have every opportunity for the fullest possible self-realization and for the competence needed to deal with the problems that arise in life. Education in a democratic society holds the prime responsibility for seeing that each individual develops to this maximum of his potential. Modern educational thought holds that this potential can be increased through good teaching. American education is founded on the belief that mass education does not deny respect and care for the individual, that quality and quantity in education can coexist. American education assigns no superior status, only greater responsibility, to intellectually gifted students. It seeks to arouse in all students a profound sense of self-respect and personal integrity.

In his last State of the Union message, President Kennedy noted:

We need to strengthen our nation by investing in our youth. The future of any country which is dependent upon the will and wisdom of its citizens is damaged, and irreparably damaged, whenever any of its children are not educated to the full extent of their talents, from grade school to graduate school.

During the Nixon administration a new National Center for Child Advocacy was established in the Department of Health, Education and Welfare's Office of Child Development. The task of the Center is to promote the benefits for children recommended by the White House Conference on Children.

Understanding the Learner

To teach a student is to understand and respect him. Since his earliest recorded history, man has been engaged in the study of children and youth. The story of educational progress is, in large measure, the story of deeper understanding of the learner. In recent years the behavioral sciences have yielded new knowledge of the growth and development of children and youth. This understanding points the way toward better adaptation of the school to the unique needs of the student and toward more effective teaching.

Recent studies have revealed the increasingly important contribution which the life sciences and the physical sciences (chemistry, biology, physics, and physiology), along with the social sciences (psychology, sociology, and anthropology), are making to knowledge about the growth and development of living things.

Principles of Human Development

The understanding of children is fundamental to the task of teaching them. Complete understanding is never reached, but increased understanding is achieved through study of the expanding body of knowledge concerning child growth and development. Certain generalizations can be made from this knowledge:

1. **Human behavior is influenced by many complex and often obscure factors. One of the most powerful factors is the student's home environment. Behavior is based upon past experiences, shaped by present circumstances, influenced by hopes and plans for the future, and initiated by some sort of motivation. Motivation is a powerful influence upon learning.**
2. **Learning is a natural but not always enjoyable process, although the capacity for learning varies widely among individuals. One fails to learn because some impediment has arisen to obstruct his learning. Frequently, faulty teaching is an impediment.**
3. **Each person is unique. He not only differs from others but is in a constant process of change himself. Individual differences increase as children grow older.**
4. **All persons have some potential for growth and development. This potential can be increased by good teaching but is influenced by the socioeconomic circumstances of the learner.**
5. **The entire human organism is involved in learning and development. Mental development cannot be considered in isolation from the learner's physical, social, and emotional well-being.**
6. **Human growth is continuous but not constant. Various developmental stages are discernible among students, but rates of growth vary. Learning tasks must be attuned to the individual learner's readiness and stage of development.**
7. **Students are influenced greatly by the values of the groups to which they belong. During the early years of life, their families may be a powerful educative force. As students become increasingly detached from family life in later years, peer group identity and loyalty become increasingly influential on their development.**
8. **Many agencies other than schools have powerful impact upon what is learned—mass media of communication, commercial and industrial establishments, the church, among others. The home and the school bear neither full burden nor full responsibility for human growth and development.**
9. **Classroom learning is largely the result of the teacher's behavior in initiating and guiding student activities,**

in reinforcing the learner's responses, and in sustaining student involvement in the learning process.

10. The social milieu of the learner's life is a crucial factor in shaping both the desire and the opportunity to learn. Therefore extending the opportunity and conditions of learning is a social, economic, and political matter, as well as a pedagogical matter.

Facets of Growth

A student has not one but several ages. He may have simultaneously a chronological age, which is his actual span of life in years; a mental age, which determines his ability to perform certain intellectual tasks; an educational age, which usually denotes his academic level of achievement; a physical age, which ranks him among his colleagues in terms of such matters as stature and weight; an emotional age, which may be revealed in his affective behavior; a social age, which depends greatly upon his experiences with people; a vocational age, which may provide much of the drive for completing his studies; and an avocational age, which in an activity like stamp collecting may place a sixth-grader high above a college student. Unevenness may exist in these various ages in the same student, especially if there is poorly synchronized growth among the different systems of the body. The Bible, in this account of the early life of the Great Teacher, gives us an excellent description of all-round growth and development: "And Jesus increased in wisdom and stature, and in favor with God and man" (Luke 2:52). He increased in wisdom (mentally), in stature (physically), in favor with God (spiritually), and in favor with man (socially). The teacher and parent should promote this four-dimensional growth, each facet of which is discussed in the sections which follow.

Mental Development. One of the most important facets of human growth from the standpoint of the school is mental development. The growing mind is an integral part of the growing organism. Normal mental development is dependent upon wholesome physical, emotional, and social development. This important point was not recognized in early theories of psychology and is still missed by many critics who fail to appreciate the importance of the school's attention to the total development of the child. Pleas for exclusive concentration by the school on the mental development of the child—without regard for his physical, social, and emotional well-being—are not in accord with modern knowledge of psychol-

ogy. A hungry or frightened child cannot learn effectively. Before mental development can take place, it is often necessary for the school to help the child to acquire a sense of security and belonging, a feeling of personal importance.

Intelligence may be defined as the *capacity* for learning. It must be emphasized that intelligence is an important factor, but not the only factor, affecting the learner's progress in school. Alfred Binet, the French psychometrician and pioneer of intelligence testing, believed that intelligence could be modified through training. Maria Montessori, the Italian pioneer in early-childhood education for the disadvantaged, believed that intelligence could be improved through enrichment of the child's environment. Although both of these views are now rather commonly held among educators, it was not always so. For many years after Binet and Montessori, the general view was that intelligence was determined by heredity and that it remained constant throughout life. A number of recent investigations suggest that it is possible under certain conditions to accelerate the rate of mental growth. For example, gains in the intelligence quotient have been registered in cases where students have had the benefit of nursery school education or where mentally retarded children have received special class instruction. One reviewer of research concludes that it is likely that the greatest hope for a decline in the frequency of mental retardation will come from a serious attack on poverty and its concomitants—unemployment, deteriorated housing and physical environment, and poor and inappropriate schooling.[8] The evidence suggests that this improvability of the intelligence cannot take place after late adolescence or adulthood. The mutability of intelligence is not universally accepted. In 1969 Arthur Jensen provoked controversy on this question when he insisted that intelligence is a stable, genetically determined quality not much affected by environment. (See Chapter 1 for further discussion of Jensen's conclusions.)

Piaget's general theory of intellectual development helped to clarify our understanding of intelligence and learning. Piaget projected a sequence of stages of learning that are related to age. He believes that the sequence of these stages holds true

[8]Zena Stein and Mervyn Susser, "Education for Socially Disadvantaged Children," *Review of Educational Research*, vol. 40, p. 64, February, 1970.

for all children but that the ages in which the learning stages evolve depend upon the native endowment of the child and the quality of his environment. Piaget's construct is both a nature and a nurture theory of intelligence, a point of view which is rather widely accepted now.

Intelligence, as the capacity for learning, is commonly measured in terms of mental age. When mental age is divided by chronological age, the IQ obtained provides a measure of rate of intellectual growth. Thus a 10-year-old child with a mental age of 12 would have an IQ of 120 (12 divided by 10 and then multiplied by 100 to avoid the inconvenience of decimals). Intelligence is commonly regarded as a single trait, and we apply single labels, such as bright or dull, to individuals. But various studies, particularly those of L. L. Thurstone and J. P. Guilford, reveal that there are a number of different components of intelligence—verbal comprehension, space comprehension, memory, perception, recall—as well as overall intelligence and that both the specific and the general can be measured.

Without normal maturation, that is, the changes in the characteristics of an individual resulting from intrinsic development, training may be of little or no avail. Differences in heredity appear to establish the rates of maturation which cannot be overcome by teaching. Thus maturation determines both the rate and the limit of an individual's learning ability.

The child's academic achievement is commonly measured by standardized tests whose results are expressed in terms of normal achievement for students of a given age. This measure is sometimes referred to as "educational age." By comparing the learner's educational age with his mental age, it is possible to determine whether or not his achievement is commensurate with his capacity.

Physical Development. By far the most significant aspect of physical growth with respect to learning is the development of the central nervous system, since it is the mechanism for learning. It comprises the brain, spinal cord, and nerves. People do not function anywhere near their intellectual capacity. The central nervous system, it is estimated, contains approximately thirteen billion neurons, but the ordinary man probably uses no more than one billion in his lifetime. Today neurologists, pharmacologists, and biological and medical researchers are learning more about the functioning of the central nervous system. During the prenatal period the human or-

ganism develops from a single cell into a complex system capable of many activities. The spinal chord, nerves, and lower portion of the brain are relatively mature at birth, but the cerebral cortex, the locus of learning and complex behavior, continues to mature. Birth, therefore, is not really the beginning of life and growth, but rather an important change in the environment of the human organism.

After birth the infant grows very rapidly in height and weight. However, this rate of growth is vastly slower than that which occurs during the prenatal period, and the rate actually slows down progressively from birth to maturity. Legs grow more rapidly than the trunk and head during infancy. The brain also grows quite rapidly. Muscles grow fast during infancy, and many complex physical skills, such as walking and talking, are acquired during this period.

Gradually the rate of physical growth in children decelerates until about 9 to 13 years of age, when another spurt of growth continues for two or three years. For the first decade of life boys and girls grow at about the same rate. But puberty overtakes girls earlier than boys, with the result that girls from 11 to 15 are heavier and taller than most boys of the same age. At 15 or 16, girls' rate of growth slows markedly, while boys continue to grow until about age 20. After 20 most people continue to grow in weight but not in height.

During surges of growth, children need greater energy to sustain the growth itself. During these periods they find it more difficult to study and to withstand strain. This is often a difficult period for their parents and teachers, as well as for the children. Anything which disturbs a child or youth may interrupt his growth. When a child fails to grow or loses weight, something is interfering with his normal well-being and is cause for alarm. On the other hand, spurts of growth occur at slightly different times for different children. If this is not understood, normal periods of slow growth may cause undue alarm. Proper education can help to sustain sound physical growth and motor development.

Tallness and shortness are partly hereditary. Environment and nutrition also have an effect upon growth. Studies seem to indicate that each generation is slightly taller and healthier than preceding generations. There are still many aspects of human physical growth which are not understood.

Social and Emotional Development. Children mature socially and emotionally as well as physically and mentally. Social and emotional maturity are related to other facets of development. For example, children of advanced mental maturity tend to be more advanced socially and are larger and stronger physically as well. However, this is a general rule to which there are many exceptions.

As the child becomes a member of a large and more complex group, he becomes more aware of and responsive to others. The rugged individualist gives way to the social conformer. He learns to be more sensitive to the feelings of others and more cooperative in groups. He forms strong attachments to peer groups and participates more effectively in team sports, gangs, clubs, and other cooperative activities.

As the child reaches puberty, he acquires greater understanding and acceptance of himself. He develops more confident relations with both peers and adults. While he still needs guidance and support from the family, he is becoming less dependent upon his parents. However, puberty presents a special social problem, since girls mature more rapidly than boys during this period. Boys and girls of the same age and in the same class in school have quite different attitudes toward the opposite sex. Girls at this age are quite interested in boys, who—alas!—are likely to hold girls in disdain. Fortunately, this situation does not continue for long.

Many sociologists have called attention to the limitations imposed upon the social and emotional development of young people by the generally feminine climate of the classroom. Particularly in elementary schools, the majority of teachers are women, and the social climate of the classroom is maternal. At home too the influence of the mother is usually more pervasive than that of the father. Boys often feel that they must reject the intellectual, moral, and aesthetic values which are taught by women and join a masculine cult of anti-intellectualism. The boy's predominantly maternal climate may teach him that such commodities as brains, enjoyment of the arts, love of one's fellow man, serenity, and order are unmasculine. Some argue that passive narcissism is bred by the normative world of the American boy. One obvious antidote for this problem is the employment of a much larger proportion of men teachers in elementary schools.

As adolescence is reached, boy-girl relationships become more mature. But rapid sexual maturation poses new problems. Relationships with the opposite sex pose problems for some teenagers. Adolescence is a turbulent period of development. Physical growth is rapid—sometimes too rapid from the standpoint of poise and grace.

To them, it is a castle under construction; to educators, it is the development of social and psychomotor skills.

The adolescent yearns for the independence of adulthood, but at the same time may be frightened by the prospect of it. In modern society the family has generally less impact on youth's values than it did when youths were an integral part of a productive family unit. Children and youths are no longer well integrated into patterns of adult life. Their association with adults tends to be more superficial and divested of meaning. This isolation from adult life drives young people more and more to peer groups and contributes to their alienation from adult culture.

The difficulties of adolescence are exacerbated by the withholding of adult prerogatives from youths, who are maturing more rapidly than earlier generations. Without the right to sit on bodies governing schools and colleges, the right to enter certain kinds of employment, and the right to help determine their own destinies in many ways, young people are increasingly alienated from adult society. Overprotected and overindulged with material things, many young people, particularly in suburban areas, are "kept" people well into their teens. Their resentment of these and other circumstances has prompted the estrangement of many youths from adult society and stimulated their militancy, use of drugs, and other behavior discussed elsewhere in this chapter.

Adolescence is characterized by a strong need to conform to the mores of peers. Habits of dress and talk and other behavior are powerfully influenced by the gang, often to the consternation of parents. Adolescence is indeed a period of turbulence and stress. If parents and teachers find difficulty understanding adolescents during this period, it is not odd, because in all probability teen-agers do not understand themselves. This is not to say that adolescence is psychopathic—only that it must be recognized by both adults and youths as an agonizing period of maturation for many, a time of conflict between childhood and adulthood which is both necessary and healthy.

The social development of children and youths can be strengthened immeasurably by the school. Both social and emotional behavior are learned. Fine schools do not leave social development to chance. They accept society's expectation that the school should guide and encourage this development. Opportunity is given children within the school program to develop wholesome understandings of and relationships with others.

The student's self-esteem or self-concept is a very important factor in his maturation. From nursery school to graduate school the student is searching for an answer to that ubiquitous question: "Who am I?" He is in constant search of personal identity and the meaning of life. He is striving to find his purpose in life. This search becomes increasingly difficult in a world with weapons of mass destruction, wars, urbanization and high densities of population, strident stimuli of the mass media, and the lure of drugs and narcotics as means of escape from distressing reality. He may be anxious over his success in school, particularly when schools set arbitrary standards of achievement which may be unattainable or irrelevant in his view. Schools can help to relieve this identity crisis by demonstrating that they really care about each human being, by accommodating to the individual differences of each student, by establishing viable and realistic expectations of students, by helping them deepen their understanding of themselves, and by wholeheartedly joining the students in their quest for identity.[9]

[9]For further discussion of this problem, see Stanley Coopersmith and Jan Silverman, "How to Enhance Pupil Self-Esteem," *Today's Education*, vol. 58, pp. 28–29, April, 1969.

Development of Moral and Spiritual Values. Robert Havighurst has identified five stages of character development:

1. The amoral, impulsive stage during which the person follows his impulses with no sense of morality. This stage usually prevails during the first year of life.
2. The egocentric, expedient stage during which the person is still primarily interested in satisfying his own desires but modifies this selfish behavior for the sake of personal safety or making a good impression on others. This behavior is normal between the ages of 2 and 4.
3. The conforming stage, between the ages of 5 and 10 commonly, in which the person is strongly motivated to conform to the demands and expectations of the people with whom he lives.
4. The irrational conscience stage, also normal for children from 5 to 10 and beyond, in which the person strives to satisfy without criticism the moral teachings of parents and teachers. A kind of rigid and unexamined morality prevails.
5. The rational conscience stage, beginning in adolescence, in which emotional and intellectual independence is sought through one's own reasoning and acceptance of moral values.

The moral development of some persons is arrested short of the last stage, and they never reach mature moral behavior. Most persons have in their makeup some aspects of all five stages of moral character development.

Havighurst believes that schools can influence the development of morality by providing teachers who are exemplars of good moral character and by providing more opportunities for reflective thinking, particularly during high school years, on social problems and historical events which hinge on moral choices.[10] Research studies suggest that schools generally have not had much impact upon the values which youths acquire in life.

The mass media report distressing evidence of deterioration of our morality—the rising rate of crime, family disintegration, and violence, for example. Our values are being severely tested by hostilities among nations, dislocations caused by technology, the population explosion, racial oppression, and social cleavages. People have traditionally looked to their schools as the prime instrument, next to the church, for improving the moral fiber of society.

Actually, there is no complete solution that is acceptable to all in this dilemma. Inevitably, the

[10]Robert J. Havighurst, "What Research Says about Developing Moral Character," *NEA Journal*, vol. 51, pp. 29–30, January, 1962.

public schools are caught in the center of opposing charges. Some will complain that they are godless, while others will insist that they must remain that way. In any event, it can be agreed that it is important for public schools to inculcate high moral and ethical standards of conduct in young people and, at the same time, to avoid sectarian indoctrination. Even within the constraints imposed by the United States Constitution, it is possible for the public schools to endeavor to inculcate such standards of conduct in students.

CREATIVE STUDENTS

It is sometimes assumed that the term "creative" is synonymous with "mentally gifted." Although it is true that for certain activities a minimum IQ is prerequisite, creativity does not appear to be a function of intelligence, nor is it measured by intelligence tests. Research suggests several capabilities which seem to characterize gifted students. First, gifted students are adept at "divergent thinking," that is, they resist premature closure on a single solution to a problem but instead entertain mentally a variety of possible solutions which they weigh carefully before selecting the best. Second, creative students are able to discern more complexity in whatever they are doing. They are challenged by complexity and seek to find order in it. Third, creative students place greater reliance on intuition and hunches and trust their nonrational mental processes.[11]

Project Talent and the Institute of Personality Assessment and Research at the University of California, along with other organizations, have directed their attention to the identification and nurture of gifted students. This is an important enterprise because all of society gains from the efforts of a relatively few highly creative persons. It is important that schools understand the nature of creativity, identify potentially creative students who come from all strata of society and all races, and develop the kind of stimuli and support that will help creative students to develop more fully. Many critics of education believe that schools typically not only fail to nurture creativity but, worse yet, stifle creativity in students by rewarding conformity. Creative students are often nonconformists. They are generally more productive in independent study than

[11] For further discussion of the nature of creativity, see Frank Barron, "The Dream of Art and Poetry," *Psychology Today,* vol. 2, pp. 19–23, 66, December, 1968.

in group activities and they achieve most when instructed by creative teachers. The Association for the Gifted, a part of the Council for Exceptional Children, is the preeminent organization for teachers interested in the education of gifted students.

MENTALLY GIFTED STUDENTS

Concern for the mentally gifted child is by no means new. Nearly a century ago, Thomas Huxley wrote that ". . . the most important object of all educational schemes is to catch these exceptional people and turn them to account for the good of society." Eminent educational psychologists, such as Lewis Terman, Paul Witty, Jacob Getzels, Phillip Jackson, and others, have been concerned with the education of gifted children for decades. But the recent explosion of technological advancement has focused new attention dramatically upon the shortage of top manpower and has precipitated vigorous academic talent hunts. The great intensification of interest in finding and developing top intellectual talent is one of the most significant and widespread developments of the current decade.

Who Are the Mentally Gifted?

There is no universally accepted definition of the mentally gifted—sometimes referred to also as the "academically talented" or "superior." For example, one writer defines the term to include the upper 3 percent of the school-age population; another's definition would include the upper 25 percent of all children. Perhaps the most common concept of the academically gifted child would include those with IQs exceeding 125 or 130, although intelligence alone is not an adequate measure of giftedness. These learners can be identified by standardized intelligence tests, such as the Revised Stanford-Binet or the Wechsler Intelligence Scale for Children; by their marks; and by teachers' judgments. The term "giftedness" can be applied, of course, to a variety of talents. A child may be gifted in reading but not in art.

Intellectually, the gifted student is, of course, capable of learning more fully and more rapidly. However, his superior capacity for learning is not automatically sustained without appropriate education. Indeed, one of the tragedies of life is the failure of many gifted students to realize their full potential because of inadequate educational experience. The gifted student possesses superior ability in reasoning and generalizing. He can deal more easily with abstract ideas. He may or may not have a positive attitude toward school, depending on the nature of his school. He tends to be more creative and inquisitive. The gifted student has a higher vocabulary level, superior memory, and a longer interest span and is more persevering. He is more capable of independent study and usually has more varied interests. He is likely to be more interested in nonfiction than in fiction and outgrows children's literature earlier. He reads omnivorously, and his mental agility leads him to explore many fields.

Providing for the Mentally Gifted

Good teachers and good schools have always sought ways of identifying and encouraging able students. On the other hand, many teachers have found it easy to become preoccupied with helping slow learners and have assumed that the bright students would take care of themselves. Without much effort on their own part or on the part of the teacher, these students have usually met academic standards geared to the average ability of the group. However, in too many instances they have not been challenged to the full measure of their ability. Too often they have become indifferent.

Many proposals have been advanced for caring for the gifted in school. Most procedures can be classified into three basic patterns: grouping, acceleration, and independent study.

Grouping according to academic ability was once widely practiced, but then fell into disrepute on the grounds that it fostered an educational elite, encouraged undesirable feelings of superiority or inferiority among students in the upper and lower groups, denied future leaders an opportunity to associate with their future followers, and was undemocratic. In some cases superior students are grouped in separate classes. In some city school systems, special high schools have been established for the gifted. The trend at present, which seems to be consistent with the recommendations of experts, is toward grouping superior children together for part, but only part, of the day in the same school with other children. Since most children are not equally gifted in all areas, some schools have developed flexible groupings. Thus a child may be in an advanced science group, an average art group, and a lower group in physical education. A student may move to a higher or lower group at any time. In this way inflexible cleavages between able and less able students are not fixed, and each group is made up of students of relatively equal ability in a given subject. Primary teachers, of course, have practiced this type of grouping for many years. Grouping makes it possible for the teacher to work with a narrower range of ability.

Acceleration is an arrangement by which the gifted child advances through school more rapidly than others. This may be accomplished by early admission to kindergarten and first grade, by going through an ungraded school in less time than others, by skipping grades, by completing high school work early and undertaking college-level work in high school, or by advanced placement in college. One argument favoring acceleration is that it permits students to complete college and undertake careers and marriage earlier in life. Since the early twenties are the most productive and creative years for many people, it is argued that entry into a career should come as early as possible. The usual argument against acceleration is that an accelerated student's social and emotional maturity may not be commensurate with that of his older classmates.

Independent study is an arrangement whereby the gifted student is neither segregated nor accelerated but rather is given extended work, usually performed on his own initiative, beyond that expected of average students. This arrangement is less disruptive of the school organization. Also it means that the gifted child receives a larger total amount of education than is possible under an accelerated program, since his years of schooling are not cut short. Through such independent study gifted students may go either further or deeper than the remainder of the class. They may do extra work in the same area in which the class is working, such as research or creative writing, beyond that expected of others. Or they may work at a level in advance of the rest of the class, such as studying elementary algebra in a junior high school general mathematics class.

Many claims and counterclaims are made for each of these patterns. Such evidence as already exists indicates that all three patterns show considerable promise and that superior youngsters are able to profit from any of the arrangements. It is important that a plan or combination of plans best suited to the individual school, its students, and its faculty be undertaken. Experience and research have identified several crucial aspects of the problem of educating the talented:

1. **Better means of identifying intellectually gifted pupils are needed.**
2. **Much more must be known about the nature of giftedness and about the creativity, critical thinking, personality, and value concepts associated with it.**
3. **More experience with, and better evaluation of, curriculums, organization, and methods of instruction for gifted students are needed.**
4. **The nature of society's impact—its attitudes and values—on the nurture of giftedness must be investigated.**

Much interesting experimentation in meeting the educational needs of the gifted is under way. Several governmental and nongovernmental programs help to identify talented youths and provide them with financial assistance in higher education, such as the National Merit Scholarship Program, the Science Clubs of America, and the Presidential Scholars program. Unfortunately, however, many scholarly high school students do not go to college. Among the organizations supporting the study of gifted students and developing better programs for educating them are the National Association for Gifted Children and the National Education Association's Project on the Academically Talented.

HANDICAPPED STUDENTS

Great advances have been made in the improvement of education for handicapped children during the last decade, although this problem is by no means conquered. This progress has been quickened by greatly increased funds for the education of the handicapped, better understanding of the nature of education for the handicapped, and more effective new approaches to the instruction and care of the handicapped.

Beginning with the passage of the Fogarty-McGovern Act in 1958, the Congress has enacted a number of bills to enrich educational opportunity for exceptional children. These programs, administered largely through the Bureau of Education for the Handicapped in the U.S. Office of Education, include provisions for research on mental retardation, training programs for special education teachers, model demonstration schools for children with various handicaps, development of instructional materials especially designed for handicapped children, regional resource centers to supply consul-

tative help and to demonstrate special teaching methods, and programs of early intervention in the lives of pre-elementary children to reduce the impact of handicap during the most formative years.

Sidney P. Marland, U.S. Commissioner of Education, in 1971 deplored the fact that less than half of the nation's six million handicapped children of school age were getting the special education they needed. He urged the adoption of a national goal to provide full educational opportunity for every handicapped child in the nation by 1980. The Commissioner contended that "it is unjust for our society to provide handicapped children with anything less than the full and equal educational opportunity they need to reach their maximum potential and attain rewarding, satisfying lives."

This accelerated inquiry and experimentation in the education of the handicapped prompted a new orientation to the problem. In an earlier time, educators were disposed to focus upon the causes of students' handicaps and stereotype them accordingly. The constraints imposed upon their learning by their handicaps, sometimes exaggerated, were impressed upon both students and teachers. This tended to become a self-fulfilling prophecy for many. Children with hearing difficulties, for example, were sometimes called deaf and subtly persuaded that they could not function normally. Small wonder that they succumbed. Other children with undetected brain damage that did not necessarily impair their learning seriously were labeled "mentally retarded." Teachers and parents often expected too little or too much of them. If too little was expected, the children fulfilled the expectation. If too much was expected without appropriate accommodation by the school, frustration and possible psychological damage were added to the student's handicap. If the child's handicap inconvenienced the classroom teacher, he sometimes shirked the responsibility by rationalizing, "This child doesn't belong in this room." Many handicapped children were placed in special education classes where they became more handicapped through exclusion from the broader experiences of the regular classroom. Thus the handicapped label, once applied, tended to condition the child's entire life even though the handicap usually applied to only a part of his activity. In sum, the focus of this concept was upon causes and limitations of the handicaps and the accommodation of the child to the limitations rather than upon maximizing the student's remaining capabilities.

Many schools failed to realize that students with severe physical handicaps, even brain damage, were still quite able intellectually. Physical, emotional, and social disabilities, unless extreme, need not inhibit learning. With modern educational methods and materials, it is increasingly possible for children to be educated in the conventional classroom by properly trained teachers, unless the student's impairment is too severe. It has also been discovered that the identification of disabilities in early childhood and appropriate intervention in the child's environment can reduce the effects of the handicap. To illustrate, when autistic children have difficulty interacting with teachers and other children, their education is impeded and their handicap in life compounded. But many autistic children have little difficulty interacting with the impersonal talking typewriter, particularly in the pre-elementary school years. As a result of this happy circumstance, they often are able to learn to interact with other people and their handicap is reduced. Early identification of children with disabilities often prompts early clinical treatment of correctable conditions before the handicap accumulates and emotional problems result. Much of the educational response to the alleviation of disabilities in early-childhood education has been prompted by the Handicapped Children's Early Education Assistance Act, passed by the Congress in 1968.

The relief of handicaps caused by physical and emotional disabilities has been quickened by the merger of educational, psychological, and medical resources in the identification and treatment of handicapped children. Many school systems are developing clinical resources within the school consisting of educational, medical, psychological, and other special persons and agencies closely coordinated with the classroom. Many students with severe physical problems who in earlier years would have been assigned to residential schools for the blind or the deaf are now increasingly attending regular school classrooms for part of the school day but spending the remainder of their time in special education facilities designed to help them reduce the impairment of their disability. In this new view, the medical or psychological cause of the learning impairment becomes less important, while the modification of the learner's behavior in such a way as to condition him for intellectual training becomes

more important. Professor Hewett of the University of California at Los Angeles explains it in this way:

Rather than view the emotionally disturbed child as a victim of psychic conflicts, cerebral dysfunctions, or merely academic deficits, this approach concentrates on bringing the overt behavior of the child into line with standards required for learning. Such standards may include development of an adequate attention span; orderly response to the classroom; the ability to follow directions; tolerance for limits of time, space, and activity; accurate exploration of the environment; and appreciation for social approval and avoidance of disapproval.[12]

Instructional technology has also helped the school to accommodate more effectively to the needs of the handicapped. For example, electronic amplification devices reduce the handicap of hard-of-hearing children. Programmed instruction and computers permit far greater accommodation to the individual differences of students with various learning disabilities. Innovations in school architecture and school buses permit physically handicapped students much more mobility. Many other examples could be cited.

Perhaps the most important factor is the classroom teacher. The achievement of students with disabilities can be quite remarkable when guided by a teacher with adequate knowledge, compassion, and skill. We will speak of these skills at greater length in the pages which follow.

Despite the trend toward including in the regular classroom many children formerly assigned to special education classes, some students have disabilities so severe that special education facilities are still necessary for them. We turn now to a consideration of four categories of handicapped children—intellectually impaired, physically handicapped, emotionally handicapped, and socially and culturally handicapped—while reemphasizing that only those students who suffer extreme handicaps in any of these categories are necessarily in need of education in special classrooms, although many may need special accommodation in regular classrooms.

Intellectually Impaired Students

It is very important to distinguish between two types of subaverage intellectual functioning: students with neurological handicaps and students who are

[12] Frank A. Hewett, as quoted in Joseph Stocker, "Help for Hangups," *American Education*, vol. 5, p. 7, June-July, 1969.

otherwise mentally retarded. The former may be bright and capable of normal academic progress, while the latter are not. The distinction is imperative if the neurologically handicapped are not to be relegated to the same fate as the others through the neglect of the schools, as indeed a great many are.

The Neurologically Handicapped Students. The term "neurologically handicapped" is used with reference to persons with any impairment of the central nervous system, whether mild or severe, whether congenital or the result of accident. The term "minimal brain dysfunction" excludes the more severe neurological disorders such as cerebral palsy and epilepsy. The incidence of brain dysfunction in children is increasing, amounting to an estimated proportion of one in ten among school-age children. It is estimated that remedial facilities in schools are available for less than one in twenty of the children so affected, a tragic circumstance.

Neurological dysfunctions can result from several causes: injury to the fetus, poor prenatal care, injury during birth, oxygen deprivation, malnutrition, chemical or blood irregularities, genetic inheritance, illness of the expectant mother, or a blow on the head during early childhood. Recognizing and responding to the tricky symptoms are more important than discovering the causes. Often the symptoms are not manifested until the child enters school. The symptoms may include such things as erratic performance in schoolwork, easy distraction of attention, swift changes in mood, and clumsy psychomotor skills. Although the victim is often above average in intelligence, he may fall further and further behind in school unless appropriate special remediation is provided. Inept in his play, he may be rejected by his peers. Eventually he may assume that he is worthless, give up on himself, and compound his miseries by social and emotional maladjustment. Many delinquents and criminals emerge in later years from this group of brain-damaged people.

Although more research and experimentation are needed to yield a fuller understanding of the medical and educational rehabilitation of the neurologically handicapped, many of them would be capable of fairly normal educational progress and social adjustment even with present knowledge. Some schools are demonstrating remarkable success in reaching these students, but fewer than 10 percent of the teachers needed for this work have received the special preparation necessary. The Association for Children with Learning Disabilities (ACLD) is an organization for parents and profes-

sionals, with many local chapters striving to increase public understanding of learning disabilities and to increase school and community services to these impaired youngsters.

Within recent years there has been a remarkable confluence of educational, medical, neurological, and psychiatric energy and expertise in dealing with children with learning disabilities. This new collaboration among the professions is yielding far better understanding and remediation of the problems of learning disability. Much of this new understanding and better practice in the field of learning disability offers promise for the improvement of learning for all students.

There are several forms of neurological impairment. The most common form is dyslexia, which affects perhaps as many as 10 percent of the early school population to one degree or another. It is regarded as a genetic, neurological dysfunction that results in imperfect directional sense. The dyslexic child reverses letters, words, and numbers: "b" becomes "d," "left" becomes "felt," and "42" becomes "24." His auditory perception may be similarly distorted. Without special instruction, he is likely to have difficulty learning to read and may suffer emotional disorganization as a result of his academic frustrations. Early diagnosis and treatment of this problem are essential. We mention dyslexia here because there is little general awareness of this particular disability in most schools. Also, too few reading clinics are presently helping the dyslexic child. There is far too much public and professional ignorance of this dysfunction, which affects $2\frac{1}{2}$ million children. With proper diagnosis and remedial services, the problem could be solved almost completely.[13]

Neurological impairment is of course manifested in many other ways. The overactive minimally brain-injured student has poor impulse control and tends to be overtly disruptive in class. The autistic minimally brain-damaged child tends to be withdrawn, uncommunicative, and pathologically shy. These children simply have learning problems although they may appear to be intellectually dull. Without understanding of the roots of the problem psychiatric help is often not effective. Relief must be found instead in behavior modification to reduce

[13] For further discussion of this disorder and what neighborhood schools can do to help students, see Benjamin H. Pearse, "Dyslexia," *American Education*, vol. 5, pp. 9-13, April, 1969.

the learning problem in appropriate educational placement, in individualized counseling, and in tutoring.

Mentally Retarded Students. The term "mental retardation" is commonly used to cover a wide diversity of below-average intellectual functioning. For purposes of our discussion, we will exclude the students with neurological dysfunctions discussed earlier. Mental retardation is no longer regarded as a condition which is easily diagnosed. Robert Havighurst estimates that perhaps as many as half the students now treated as mentally retarded could have developed normal intelligence if they had had treatment in early childhood.[14]

The retarded student's mental age and IQ suggest the limitations of his abilities of association, comparison, comprehension, generalization, and symbolization as compared with those of the normal child. His limited vocabulary and reading skills handicap him in learning other subjects. His attention span is short, and he forgets easily. Tragically, he falls further and further behind his age norm as he grows older.

The mentally retarded student has less ability to learn from experience, to take in all the elements in a complex situation, to foresee consequences, and to form judgments than the normal person. He is less capable of making adequate social adjustments and often becomes a behavior problem. Most mentally retarded students closely resemble normal students of corresponding chronological ages in physical appearance.

Retarded students' needs, desires, and emotions are greatly intensified, resulting in more crying, laughter, fighting, talking, and physical activity than characterize the average student. They tend to become frustrated by the difficult demands placed upon them by school and society. Many of these antisocial behavioral patterns result from the student's impairment and should not be interpreted by the teacher as willful negativism. However, even these shortcomings should not be regarded as immutable. The potentiality of most mentally retarded students can be raised through good teaching.

Some of the characteristics listed above may be detected through age-grade progress reports, close observation by the teacher, and case studies. A rule-of-thumb judgment must not be final. Both physical and mental examinations should be given in most cases to be sure that the apparent mental retardation is not in reality the manifestation of some physical disability such as poor hearing.

Mentally retarded children are commonly classified into three groups: the educable, the trainable, and the custodial.[15] While the lines of demarcation between these groups are not absolute, the educable are generally regarded as those with IQs between 50 and 75, approximately 3 percent of all children. The trainable are those few children whose IQs are below 50 but who are capable of some learning. Custodial children, extremely few in number, have IQs below 30 and are practically incapable of any learning. The Children's Bureau estimates that of each one thousand persons, thirty are mentally retarded. Of this thirty, approximately twenty-five are educable, four are trainable, and one is custodial.

Educable students are increasingly included in regular classroom instruction rather than in special education classes as a result of recent more open and optimistic views of the potentialities of the mentally retarded. These students have attenuated cognitive development. Some experts believe that by attacking the emotional, social, and motivational aspects of the problem, educable students can become capable of greater academic achievement than was heretofore expected. New instructional materials created especially for the educables, along with better instructional methods, have had a significant impact upon the education of these students. Materials and content must be within the range of the educable child's capacity if they are to be meaningful to him. Materials should be closely related to the child's environment and experience. Assignments should be within his range of ability. As much as possible he should be given extra help. Since slow learners have particular difficulty with verbalization and abstractions, television and other visual aids are particularly helpful.

Trainable pupils are those who are unable to profit from regular classroom experience but who will not need to spend their lives in institutions. With appropriate instruction, trainable pupils are often capable of learning to take care of themselves, to make a reasonably adequate social adjustment, and to learn simple occupational skills. Many, however, are not able to become occupationally self-sufficient. Some trainable children are enrolled in special ungraded classrooms in public school systems. Others are provided for in residential schools for the men-

---

[14] Robert J. Havighurst, "The Educationally Difficult Student," *National Association of Secondary School Principals Bulletin*, vol. 49, p. 110, March, 1965.

[15] The term "slow learner" is sometimes loosely applied to all children of less than average mental ability.

tally deficient. Although most public schools once rejected these children, more and more districts are recognizing their responsibility for the care of trainable pupils and are establishing appropriate programs.

Custodial children are so limited in intelligence that education is out of the question for them. They usually require close supervision and care at home or in a mental institution especially for the care of the mentally retarded.

Many mentally retarded youngsters are further handicapped in life by parents who are unwilling to accept their child's mental handicap. Frequently parents are ashamed and perhaps even nourish feelings of guilt because of their children's shortcomings. They may try to isolate the child from association with others to hide their shame. Or they may threaten the child by exhorting him to achievement of which he is hopelessly incapable. When this happens, emotional disturbances are compounded with mental retardation. Unfortunately, some teachers are not as sympathetic to and understanding of mentally retarded youngsters as they should be. Like all handicapped children, they must be accepted for what they are and helped to achieve up to their level of ability, however modest it may be. The National Association for Retarded Children was founded to help achieve this end. The federal government and its officials have manifested much interest in discovering the causes of retardation and in working for its prevention and cure.

Physically Handicapped Students

Several types of physically handicapped students require special consideration: (1) visually handicapped students, (2) deaf and hard-of-hearing students, (3) speech handicapped students, and (4) crippled and health-impaired students.

Visually Handicapped Students. Visually impaired students have the same basic educational needs as students with normal sight. Visually impaired children belong in the regular classroom, unless their impairment is severe, since the general education curriculum is appropriate for them. Many of the techniques which a teacher should use with visually impaired students also enhance the learning of all students.

The alert teacher is on the lookout for behavior that is symptomatic of poor vision: frequent mistakes with words or figures; inability to study without eye discomfort; complaint of headaches; peculiar head positions, squinting or frowning; holding

books too close to the eyes; ability to see objects at a distance more clearly than those at close range; inability to see objects at a distance; redness and swelling of the lids; inflamed or watery eyes.

Any symptoms of defects discovered by the teacher should be reported for further examination, diagnosis, and remedial treatment by an expert. It is estimated that one in every four school children needs some eye care. Medical treatment obviously is the first provision. The educational treatment of blind and partially sighted pupils varies according to the degree of visual acuity. The degrees are the blind, the partially sighted, and those with eye difficulties that can be corrected readily with glasses. The last group is not usually considered visually handicapped.

Most blind children are educated in special state-operated schools. A few city school systems operate their own schools for the blind.

Partially sighted pupils are those with vision of 20-70 or less after correction. Some systems maintain special classes for them. However, partially sighted youngsters should be educated in regular classrooms. It is important for the teacher to be aware of such handicaps and make appropriate adjustments in classroom organization and procedure. For example, the partially sighted student should be located so that his desk receives adequate light. He should be located near the front of the room so that he can see the teacher and chalkboard as easily as possible. The teacher should verbalize material on the chalkboard and state explanations and instructions clearly so that visually impaired students are not disadvantaged. It is important that partially sighted students use their vision within reasonable limits because unused vision tends to be lost. Teachers and other students should avoid giving too much help. Safety can be a problem particularly in fire drills or in unseen hazards in the school or on the playground.

The teacher's physical contact with a visually impaired student can communicate the warmth that a smile or eye contacts give a child with normal sight. Realistic understanding and accommodation rather than pity should characterize the relations of the teacher and other students with the visually impaired student.[16]

---

[16] For further discussion of the classroom accommodations that the teacher may make to help the visually impaired student, see Lou Alonso, "The Child with Impaired Vision," *NEA Journal*, vol. 56, pp. 42-43, November, 1967.

New media of instruction have helped visually impaired students to overcome their handicaps in the regular classroom. Typewriters and books with large type are available. Braille typewriters have reduced the time needed to produce instructional materials for partially sighted students. Thermoform and variform processes can reproduce braille materials quickly and inexpensively. Voice tapes and other audio equipment help to reduce the student's dependence upon visual communication. Relief maps, embossed materials, magnifiers, and many other materials are now widely available.

Deaf and Hard-of-hearing Students. The primary problem in the education of those who have never heard speech is the unavailability of the normal use of language as a vehicle of communication. Even the hard-of-hearing often have difficulty with language development, which handicaps their acquisition of the basic skills. Deaf children require education in special classes. Hard-of-hearing students whose disability is not too great can be educated in the regular classroom if adequate accommodation is made for them.

The teacher should be alert to the following as possible symptoms of loss of hearing: failure to respond to calling of a name, cocking of the head to one side, failure to follow directions, looking in a direction other than the source of sound, watching others and following their movements, frequent requests for repetition of a word or phrase, faulty pronunciation of common words, speaking in an unusual voice, inattention, restlessness, aggressiveness, apathy, daydreaming, earache, discharge from the ear, and persistent mouth breathing. Teachers may note this unusual behavior but not recognize it as symptomatic of hearing loss. The easiest and surest way of identifying students with impaired hearing in one or both ears is through the use of the audiometer. Perhaps half of all hearing damage and subsequent school failure could be prevented by early detection and remediation. The hearing-impaired student needs medical care. Progressive deafness comes on so gradually and so insidiously that it frequently escapes notice until it is too severe to be corrected.

Children with residual hearing are usually given auricular training by means of electronic aids, such as the radio ear, an instrument that magnifies the human voice so that the pupils can hear the words of the teacher. Every desk is equipped with a headphone and a rheostat so that each pupil can adjust the intensity to his own need. The Verbotonal method of instructing deaf and hard-of-hearing students, developed recently by Peter Guberina, a Yugoslav scientist, appears to be quite promising. Communication in the Verbotonal method takes place through the sensory nervous system other than auditory channels with the help of special equipment which helps deaf children learn to "hear" through the interpretation of sound vibration and to speak by translating the sound vibrations into language. Above all, the student needs to acquire confidence in his ability to live with normal people in a world of sound.[17]

Speech-handicapped Students. Children with speech impairments consitute by far the largest group of physically handicapped students in the nation's schools. Speech defect has been defined as any acoustic variation from an accepted speech standard so extreme as to be conspicuous in the speaker, confusing to the listener, or unpleasant to either or both. Among these defects are stammering and stuttering, lisping, lalling, cluttering, nasality, thick speech, baby talk, hoarseness, foreign accent, and defects caused by organic difficulties.

Undesirable personality traits may accompany poor speech. An enfeeblement of the general health or extreme nervous excitement may aggravate the condition of a confirmed stammerer or stutterer.

Because of speech defects a child may not display his normal ability and may thus be falsely rated low in mentality. Hence teachers should seek to identify pupils with speech difficulties and to understand the major causes of the trouble.

The classroom teacher, through his daily contacts with the pupils, is the usual avenue for locating speech defectives. Schools should employ speech therapists who make periodic surveys of all children and undertake speech-correction treatment with those having speech difficulties. However, the demand for speech therapists outruns the supply.

A very common but fallacious observation is that a child will outgrow a speech defect. Lisping tends to cure itself, but other defects are more deep-seated and complex in origin. These require the attention of the specialist. Many speech problems which have no organic origin can be corrected in the primary grades through the encouragement of teachers who refuse to accept as normal the continuation of baby talk beyond the early years of

[17] For further information, see Hazel Rothwell, "What the Classroom Teacher Can Do for the Child with Impaired Hearing," *NEA Journal*, vol. 56, pp. 44–46, November, 1967.

childhood. Perhaps no group of physically handicapped children can be helped more completely than those having speech defects. According to many case studies, speech-correction treatment has improved the personalities of antisocial pupils. In order that such changes can be effected, the student must be more than a passive participant in the process; he must have the will to improve, plus courage, patience, and perseverance. The classroom teacher should in no way threaten or ridicule the student who has a speech impairment. Teachers should encourage him to speak despite his difficulty. It is important also to enlist the help of parents and suggest ways in which they can encourage more wholesome speech development in an anxiety-free home environment.[18] Listening to a recording of his own voice aids the student in improving his pronunciation. Very often speech impairment can be reduced by helping the student to develop the ability to listen skillfully to the spoken language of others. Using a mirror to watch one's own speech is also helpful.

Role playing and drama work give impetus to speech correction. Habits of independence and self-confidence are also assets. Participation in creative speech classes and choral speaking can make the voice quality of both handicapped and normal children more pleasing and effective. Attention by the teacher to his own speech will help decidedly to improve the imitated utterances of the pupils.

The human values of speech reeducation cannot be overemphasized. People are prone to make allowances for the blind, the deaf, and the crippled in limb, but not for those crippled in speech. A child who stammers, for example, may actually be punished for reciting. Even though he knows his lesson, he is often a source of merriment to his comrades, a torment to himself, and an object of sympathy to his teacher.

Crippled and Health-impaired Students. Paradoxically, modern medical science has decreased the incidence of some types of physical disabilities while increasing others. The scourges of polio, osteomyelitis, rickets, and nonrespiratory tuberculosis have been virtually eliminated, and the crippling effects of other disorders, such as epilepsy, have been reduced. But medical science is also saving more defective babies at birth and in infancy. Birth

[18] For more information, see Evelyn Y. Allen, "What the Classroom Teacher Can Do for the Child with Speech Defects," *NEA Journal*, vol. 56, pp. 35–36, November, 1967.

and congenital deformities constitute the largest single category of disabled children. Heart and circulatory defects are approximately ten times as common now as they were a decade ago. Highway and other accidents are increasing the incidence of crippled students. Many students from low-income families are the victims of malnutrition. The incidence of venereal disease is increasing among adolescents. During this decade many classroom teachers, along with the general public, have become much more knowledgeable about such disorders as cystic fibrosis, nephrosis, muscular dystrophy, anemia, hemophilia, and cerebral palsy.

Some crippled or health-impaired students are so severely handicapped that they must be educated at home either through personal tutoring or through radio, television, two-way radio-telephone, and other electronic means of communication. Other students are educated in special schools or special classrooms of regular schools when their physical disability is too severe for the regular classroom. Most states now provide special financial subsidies for the transportation of these students and for the special educational facilities and instruction which they may require. Many advances in the design of self-propelled wheelchairs, school buses, school furniture, and school buildings have given crippled children more freedom of mobility, more self-reliance, and better access to the educative experiences which normal children enjoy.

As is the case for all handicapped students, the school should seek to modify its organization and regimen to accommodate these students in the regular classroom unless their disability is too severe. However, exaggerated program modifications or overprotection can deprive the student of normal opportunities to adjust to his environment, to establish satisfying social relationships, to face problems and risks, and to develop self-control. The attitudes of teachers and students toward these handicapped persons are vital. Realistic and understanding attitudes must displace the old wives' tales in dealing with a student seized by an asthmatic or epileptic attack or insulin reaction. The teacher should also know the parameters of his physical impairment and have accurate knowledge of what he can and cannot do, of symptoms which can serve as warnings of flare-ups, and of the measures to be taken when serious symptoms are manifested. In many cases the teacher will need the help of medical and psychological services to provide expert advice in serious circumstances. Many physically impaired students suffer from excessive absence from school and from discontinuity in their education if they are transferred frequently from the regular classroom to the special classroom or to hospital schools or homebound instruction.

It is quite important that the teacher strive to reduce the social and emotional impact of the student's condition lest secondary handicaps compound the student's physical disability and encumber his adjustment to life. New educational technology is helping to relieve the physically handicapped student from dependence upon conventional materials that he may have difficulty coping with. For example, an electric typewriter can be equipped with a covered keyboard with holes into which a student with psychomotor skills too poor for an ordinary typewriter may insert an unsharpened pencil or a dowel.

All schoolchildren should have annual physical and dental examinations so that disorders may be identified and corrected early. Unfortunately, many school health examinations are too superficial to detect maladies, particularly in their incipient stages.

The advances in instructional technology, new insights into teaching methods appropriate for the physically handicapped, and the support of medical and psychological resources can help physically impaired students to fill productive occupations and enjoy satisfying lives, thereby reducing their burden upon themselves and upon society. Thus the higher costs of educating these students is returned.[19]

Emotionally Handicapped Students

According to the National Institute of Mental Health, more than ten school-age children per hundred suffer some form of emotional disorder, two need psychiatric services, and less than one is getting it. More than half a million children are brought before the courts each year for juvenile delinquency, many of them suffering from emotional disorders. The suicide rate among the school-age population has more than doubled within the past decade. Admissions to juvenile mental hospitals are increasing about three times as fast as the total juvenile population. The number of mentally ill persons in the nation exceeds

the number of patients suffering from any other malady; they occupy almost half of the hospital beds. In many cases drug addiction is rooted in emotional disorder. These are indeed frightening statistics.

Frequently the causes of mental illness and emotional disorder can be traced to early childhood, and since many of the symptoms appear then, early identification and treatment of disturbed persons is crucial. But only 10 percent of the nation's school systems have programs and resources to help children with mental handicaps, and most of these deal with mental retardation rather than emotional disturbances. Many counties have no mental health clinics, and very few communities provide an acceptable standard of services for mentally ill children. Many disturbed children are sent to the adult wards of state mental institutions, where they stay for the rest of their lives. It is no wonder that the Joint Commission on Mental Health of Children concluded that this country's failure to alleviate mental disorders is creating a "quiet emergency" of growing and serious proportions.

Disturbed students manifest various forms of atypical behavior. Their behavior may be aggressive, such as provoking fights, defying authority, destroying property, or disrupting class; or it may be more passive, such as withdrawal or daydreaming. Many school dropouts, delinquents, and criminals come from the ranks of the emotionally disturbed. These people often have normal or superior intelligence, but their emotional disturbance usually makes them so disorganized or antisocial that they cannot adapt to the expectations of the school or society. A study of dropouts from Harvard University revealed that nearly half of those who leave do so for psychiatric reasons. Many of them are bright students who see their identity threatened by competition with other bright students. This feeling of inadequacy causes depression and is related to the rise in drug usage and communal living. The report concludes that colleges focus primarily on the intellectual development of students and ignore their emotional development.

The ordinary classroom teacher is not prepared to practice therapy to correct emotional disorder. Emotionally impaired students should be referred to the school psychologist. Diagnosis and therapy of psychotic and neurotic children require the specialized service of the clinical psychologist or psychiatrist. But in many schools the number of referrals to these specialists is far greater than they can handle, and only the most severe cases receive treatment.

[19] For further information, see Frances P. Connor, "What the Classroom Teacher Can Do for Crippled and Health-impaired Children," *NEA Journal*, vol. 56, pp. 37–39, November, 1967.

A new orientation to the field of mental health has come about during the past decade. The trend is away from a medical orientation centered on clinics, hospitals, and individual therapy and toward treatment in the schools and the "educational model." The new direction is sometimes spoken of as "community mental health," in which the total resources of the community are mobilized. It seeks to widen the impact of the limited number of mental health workers by (1) treatment directed toward groups (as in family and group psychotherapy), (2) early detection, diagnosis, and treatment of children before emotional impairment becomes too severe and difficult to treat, and (3) prevention of mental illness.

The skillful teacher can help to prevent mental illness by maintaining an environment that threatens students' mental health as little as possible. A wholesome interpersonal relationship between teacher and student is the first essential. For some, school is the only place in the world where there is any chance for real security, affection, and encouragement. For such a child, having a relationship with an adult who cares about him is therapeutic in itself. The student must enjoy at least some measure of success if he is to be at peace with himself and his fellow man. Rigid marking and promotion practices and arbitrary standards of achievement which are beyond their reach tend to condemn some children to failure. Repeated failure breeds mental disorder. Thus the primary goal is to encourage the child to proceed at a pace that is comfortable for him in dealing with assignments that interest him and are within his capability. In this way children can be helped to gain approval and self-respect, the prime antidotes to emotional disorder.

Teachers can help children with latent emotional disorders to anticipate crises and strengthen their "stress immunity." Students can be encouraged to express negative feelings rather than to suppress them and find a scapegoat to attack. Role playing and other forms of sociodrama can be used to help students relieve themselves of hostility and aggression in a nonthreatening setting. In sum, the teacher should strive to prevent as much emotional disturbance as possible through humane teaching methods. Or perhaps, as someone has put it, the teacher's job is to comfort the troubled and trouble the comfortable. In any case, it is less burdensome for the teacher to try to prevent emotional disturbance in the classroom than to try to deal with its aftermath.

Many of the causes of emotional disturbance, however, lie outside the classroom, and teachers

usually have little control over these forces.[20] The National Mental Health Act has helped states, counties, and cities by subsidizing psychiatric services and establishing the National Institute for Mental Health. These programs have transformed many emotionally handicapped persons into self-sufficient, productive, confident citizens and have thus repaid their cost to society many times over.

Socially and Culturally Underprivileged Students

Our nation—like all nations, only less so—numbers in its midst socially and culturally handicapped people: in our case, sharecroppers, migratory farm workers, immigrants, exiles, and slum residents. Robert Coles, a research psychiatrist, speaks of these as "the children the schools have never served" and "the wanderers we would rather not see." Although socially and culturally maladjusted students come from all races, the vast majority are Negro, Puerto Rican, Chicano, American Indian, and Eskimo. Much of the literature on culturally disadvantaged students focuses on Negroes, but studies show that poverty with its related social, cultural, and psychological consequences is the common denominator of the disadvantaged.

The maladjustment of the underprivileged to society has been multiplied and complicated by technological revolution. Modern agricultural machinery has dislocated many from their employment on farms and forced them to migrate by the thousands to urban centers, where their chance for employment is not much better. Many socially and culturally underprivileged students come from families that are highly mobile. Changing schools can be a psychological and social problem for any student, and it is compounded when moving is frequent. Leaving friends and familiar teachers can be as wretched an experience as the loneliness of a new and unfamiliar school and community. The problem can be complicated when the new student is not properly placed academically in his new school.

Industrial automation has vastly reduced the need for unskilled labor in metropolitan centers as well as in rural areas, making many virtually unemployable. In a technological economy a strong back and a willing heart are no longer enough for

[20] For further discussion of what classroom teachers can do to reduce emotional disturbances, see William C. Morse, "Disturbed Youngsters in the Classroom," *Today's Education*, vol. 58, pp. 31–37, April, 1969.

self-sufficiency. The complexity and congestion of urban living, often combined with racial discrimination in housing and employment, add to the misery of the urban poor. They often congregate in overcrowded, dreary, unsightly, and unhygienic ghettos, where schools and social agencies are grossly inadequate in terms of both quality and quantity. These slum neighborhoods are often characterized by crime, delinquency, dope addiction, alcoholism, sickness, broken homes, and violence. When children's homes are culturally deprived, their parents uneducated and apathetic about education, and their schooling unrelated to their most pressing problems, it is small wonder that they have difficulty learning.

Middle-class persons often assume that the culture of poverty or of racial minorities is largely pathological. Such is not always the case. These subcultures are often characterized by family lifestyles that are highly organized; relative freedom from strain, self-blame, and parental overprotection; abundant good humor and enjoyment of the company of others; and informality. But under conditions of abject poverty and neglect, students may either withdraw from life or become aggressive. Those who withdraw sit silently in school until they can drop out. For them the conditions essential for learning are destroyed. They see only hopelessness in their lives. Learning is virtually impossible for them until hope, self-confidence, and trust have been restored. Other children react to deprivation with aggressive behavior. Since they have not yet lost hope, they attack other students, teachers, the school, or the community. They can still communicate but do so on their own terms. Since they still have hope, they seek unorthodox channels of achievement which are often incompatible with institutionalized mores because the schools do not appear to be responsive to their needs.

The orientation of the school's teachers, students, and curriculum to middle-class values and products may seem unreal and meaningless to disadvantaged children from lower-class families. It was once commonly believed that these underprivileged young people failed to learn in school because of the inadequacies which they brought to school from their home environment. Many of them do not have the advantage of the "hidden curriculum" of middle-class familes where they are read to, taken on trips, talked with, and given other educative experiences. Handicapped by inadequate language development, disadvantaged children have

Life is not without its problems, even for very young learners.

difficulty in learning to learn at school under conventional instruction. Their crowded homes often fail to provide a quiet and convenient place for study. Often they are malnourished and lacking adequate medical care. If their parents are undereducated, they lack exemplars of school success. Since they are often disposed to express emotions in movement rather than words, and since they try to excel in toughness or athletic skill rather than academic skill, they often have difficulty accommodating to the conventional school setting. Although these factors probably contribute to difficulty in learning in conventional schools, a more defensible contemporary view is that the school, not the child, is responsible for this failure in that it does not accommodate to the child's particular needs. This failure of the school has been categorized as (1) the failure to match teaching method with children's different learning styles, (2) the failure to use material that is related to their knowledge or background of experience, and (3) the failure to use materials and methods that engage their feelings.[21] To illustrate,

[21] Gerald Weinstein and Mario Fantini (eds.), *Toward Humanizing Education: A Curriculum of Affect*, Frederick A. Praeger, Inc., New York, 1970, pp. 21–22.

instructional materials written in "hip" language are useful in gaining their interest. Materials that deal with the milieu of the inner city rather than the suburban scene which is common in most school books can attract their attention better. And learning experiences which involve physical activity are more compatible with their learning styles.

Schools must expand and enrich the social and cultural experiences of these children to compensate for the barrenness of their homes. They must be given more than the usual opportunity to assume constructive social roles within the school.

The school curriculum must be closely attuned to the real-life problems and aspirations of children if school is to have any meaning for them. Strong programs of vocational education can help them to acquire job skills and strengthen their feeling of self-sufficiency. Above all, they need to see the relation of education to life. Chapter 14 speaks at greater length of the curriculum modifications which are being made to meet the needs of these students.

Many cities have initiated programs of compensatory education for socially, economically, and culturally disadvantaged children and youths in the inner city. These compensatory programs, as their name implies, attempt to compensate for children's disadvantages by offering them special educational experiences and services. They may include the use of mental health teams of child psychologists, psychiatric social workers, and home and school visitors who help to identify the children and institute remedial and preventive treatment. Stronger ties between the home and the school are sought to generate parental understanding and support for the child. Very often the child is incapable of learning until the more serious dysfunctions in the home are relieved. All too often the schools alone are incapable of meeting the needs of the more severely handicapped. Social agencies, churches, social and civic groups, child-guidance centers, juvenile courts, the police, youth centers, and various other governmental agencies are imperatively needed to help relieve the out-of-school roots of slum children's problems. Parental education and pre-elementary programs such as those described in Chapter 6 are quite important.

The most seriously maladjusted must be removed from their own school environment and placed in correctional institutions for their own good, as well as for the welfare of other students who may actually be endangered by their presence.

However, it must not be assumed that all socially and culturally deprived children come from families that are low on the socioeconomic scale. Some

children of middle- and upper-class parents are also victims of homes that are socially and culturally barren—homes without fine books, music, or art or in which they are given no motivation to learn. Broken homes, brutality, parental hostility, apathy toward education, and other ills are not the exclusive legacy of poor families.

The socially handicapped child is seldom popular in school, and school is seldom popular with him. The frequency of his absence, failure, and dropping out is high. Several studies indicate that socially disadvantaged students typically have four basic concerns: acceptance (fears about self-adequacy), data (a deep sense of depersonalization and isolation), goals (loss of identity, a feeling of not knowing who they are or what they want from life), and control (a deep feeling that they cannot get themselves to do what they want to do or cannot exert any significant influence on their worlds).[22] Thus a major thrust of the school's attack upon the learning problems of socially disadvantaged students must be directed toward their affective development—their feelings, their attitudes, and their interpersonal relations. Other aspects of the education of the poor and the minority groups in our society are discussed in Chapters 1, 2, 5, and 14.

Clearly the most important variable in the education of disadvantaged youngsters is the teacher; his attitude toward socially and culturally disadvantaged students is most important. It is easy to imagine that children of the ghettos—often not well scrubbed or well mannered, at least by middle-class standards—are somehow inferior. If they do not respond to conventional instruction, it is easy to imagine that they are intellectually inferior. Kenneth Clark, an eminent educator, asks to what extent underprivileged children do not learn because their teachers do not believe they can learn, do not expect them to learn, and do not help them to learn. Clark believes that children who are treated as if they are uneducable invariably become uneducable. One is reminded of Goethe's admonition: If you treat an individual as he is, he will stay as he is, but if you treat him as if he were what he ought to be and could be, he will become what he ought to be and could be. Samuel Shepard, an early pioneer in the improvement of schools in the inner city in St. Louis, explains that teachers must be convinced that beneath the dirt, bad language, tardiness, and even

[22]Leland P. Bradford, Jack R. Gibb, and Kenneth D. Benne, *T-Group Therapy and Laboratory Method*, John Wiley & Sons, Inc., New York, 1964, pp. 280-282.

recalcitrance of any student is the unique and infinitely precious human being whose inherent dignity renders him worthy of our most sincere respect and efforts to bring his potentiality to the fullest possible development. Shepard emphasizes that it is imperative that the schools send children home every day liking themselves better than when they came in the morning.

Teachers must be helped to meet disadvantaged children on their own ground. This does not mean that standards should be compromised or children condescended to; indeed, they should be held to high but attainable standards of work. It does mean that the teacher must recognize the standards of the culture from which these students come and turn these standards to educational advantage. The effective teacher must understand the culture of poverty, must know the conditions under which his students live, and must develop teaching methods that are compatible with their unique styles of learning. Clearly the prime attribute of the teacher is respect for the disadvantaged child because this is the key to winning his respect and cooperation.[23]

Drug-handicapped Students

Although the effects of many drugs and narcotics on the human mind and body are not fully understood, there can be no question that many drugs and narcotics have deleterious effects on the body. Aerosol sprays, if inhaled, can freeze the esophagus, congest the lungs, and cause almost immediate suffocation. Certain "mind-expanding" drugs can damage brain tissues irreparably. LSD can cause insanity, induce suicides, damage chromosomes, and destroy the health of children yet unborn. Overdose of some narcotics can cause almost instant death. Aside from the physical hazards, drugs and narcotics are capable of causing psychological damage; they permit one to escape from the problems of life by taking a pill or smoking a weed, and they may thereby prevent him from attaining full emotional, social, or intellectual maturity. Most drugs are capable of disturbing mental processes and behavior sufficiently to expose the user and others to additional hazards in ordinary activities of life, such as driving a car.

Many reasons are advanced to explain the use

of drugs and narcotics by young people: the pressures of schoolwork and life in general, boredom or dissatisfaction with life, the blandishments of pushers or peers who use drugs, the impact of commercial advertising of household drugs as chemical solutions for all kinds of unpleasantness, inability to escape addiction after an experimental usage, compulsion to find ever better "trips" from more powerful drugs, the sheer euphoria or enjoyment which drugs produce temporarily, among others. Many but certainly not all drug users find themselves inadequately prepared emotionally to deal with the problems of life and look forward to the escape which tranquilizers, amphetamines, barbiturates, hallucinogens, or narcotics provide. However, this escape is temporary and illusory and often deflationary over the long run. Too often it becomes only a rigid defense against growing up.

What can schools and society do to relieve the problems caused by the abuse of drugs and narcotics? A volume would be required to answer this complex question fully, if indeed such an answer is possible. In a more general sense, schools should help to quicken students' enjoyment of life, decrease their boredom with life and school, reduce academic pressures to a manageable point, help them acquire a sense of self-realization and fulfillment, and help them find deeper meaning and excitement in life through more authentic and wholesome experiences such as music, art, athletics, and other physical, aesthetic, and social activities. In sum, schools should strive to remove the causes of drug and narcotic abuse.

Schools should provide students with more authentic information about drugs and narcotics. Many of the early efforts at drug-abuse education were based largely upon fear, exhortation, and folklore. The instruction often exaggerated the consequences of some of the less harmful drugs and detracted from its credibility. Young people need objective and reliable information about the physical and psychological effects of drugs and narcotics, the risks which are involved, and the help which is available to victims of excessive drug use. Chapter 14 discusses drug-abuse education at greater length.

Schools should facilitate the detection and referral of victims of drug abuse. Some high schools have established "crash pads" for emergency treatment of students who have "freaked out." The "crash pads" are usually staffed with a nurse, a psychiatric technician, and student aides. Psychiatrists and psychiatric social workers are sometimes available. Schools without on-site emergency help

[23] For further discussion of effective stratagems in the education of ghetto children, see Gertrude Noar, *Teaching the Disadvantaged*, National Education Association, Washington, D.C., 1967.

should establish "hot-line" counseling and referral services to outside agencies that are capable of providing emergency help for students who are in danger from drugs. Unfortunately virtually all communities lack sufficient resources for the treatment of drug addiction. Certainly the rehabilitation of students addicted to hard drugs is a task well beyond the capability of schools.

Teachers, administrators, and counselors must become far more familiar with the drug and narcotic problem so that they can discuss the problem more knowledgeably with students both individually and in classes. If teachers fail to distinguish between drugs and narcotics, between the addictive and the nonaddictive, between the symptoms and the cause of drug abuse, they can soon become ineffective in teaching and counseling. Better counseling service is needed to help many youths find worthwhile alternatives to drug usage. Students should be able to level with their teachers and counselors on such problems with impunity and with the assurance that they are being understood. Lines of communication should be kept open, and students should be free to confide in teachers and parents. Scare tactics should be avoided. Schools should undertake programs of adult education so that parents too may understand the phenomenon more fully and react more sensibly when their children use drugs or narcotics. Finally, teachers should strive to become well-adjusted citizens, demonstrating that it is possible to lead full and satisfying lives without resort to chemicals. Young people are searching for models of human conduct and have the right to find them on school faculties. Teachers and parents who are themselves "turned on" by life without recourse to drugs or narcotics are probably the best preventatives.[24]

Pregnant Students

The number of teen-age pregnancies is increasing annually. Many college, high school, and even some junior high school girls become mothers out of wedlock. The number of illegitimate births among persons of all ages has tripled in the last quarter-century. The number of pregnant girls who have abortions is not known. Both married and unmarried teen-age students have a high school-dropout rate.

[24] For further information on how schools can help, see Theodore J. Miller, "Drug Abuse: Schools Find Some Answers," *School Management*, vol. 14, pp. 22–31, April, 1970; George Demos, "Drug Abuse and the New Generation," *Phi Delta Kappan*, vol. 50, pp. 214–217, December, 1968; "Students and Drug Abuse," *NEA Journal*, vol. 58, pp. 36–50, March, 1969.

Until fairly recently it was not uncommon for schools to deny enrollment to married students and to pregnant girls. Some school districts still do. Indeed this practice was once common among colleges years ago.

More than half of the school districts still make no special provision for pregnant students. For many years the only formal education available to pregnant girls was instruction at home conducted by the school district or programs conducted in maternity homes by social agencies.

However, more and more school districts, particularly larger school districts, are establishing special educational programs for pregnant girls and young mothers who have not completed their high school education. These programs may be found in regular high schools as supplemental to the conventional curriculum or, more commonly, in special centers established for this unique purpose. The better programs focus upon three major objectives: (1) to increase the chances of normal pregnancy and childbirth and to protect the health of the infant and its mother, (2) to help the girls solve the personal problems which have led to or resulted from pregnancy and to help direct them toward a satisfying future, and (3) to help girls keep up with their schooling during pregnancy and thereby increase their chances of continuing their education after childbirth. Courses in prenatal care, nutrition, and infant care are commonly instructed by teams of obstetricians, psychologists, nurses, and nutritionists.

Many courts are decreeing that the right to an education should not be qualified by motherhood or early marriage. All school districts should make the best possible provisions to assure that young parents may continue as students during this sometimes difficult period.[25]

FUTURE

The future of students and their learning is difficult to predict. Some have taken the pessimistic view that by the year 2000, half the human race will have been lost through the scourges of drug abuse, environmental pollution, and overpopulation. A positive view is also possible, however: that these threats will be reduced and that modern science will con-

[25] For further discussion of this problem and examples of how school districts and communities are meeting it, see Marion Howard, "School Continues for Pregnant Teenagers," *American Education*, vol. 5, pp. 5–7, January, 1969.

tinue to make life healthier, safer, and more productive for children and youth.

Insofar as learning is concerned, it has already been demonstrated that planned intervention in the environment of early childhood can raise intelligence quite markedly. When this stratagem becomes commonplace, the academic achievement of students will rise remarkably. New educational technology may make possible much more efficient and effective instruction and may create the capability of reaching many handicapped or disadvantaged students in ways far beyond the capability of present classrooms. New developments in the field of biochemistry suggest that it may someday be possible to transfer learning from one human being to another through the transplantation of tissues. "Memory pills," although still experimental, may build better brains through chemistry. The science of eugenics may reduce greatly the number of malfunctioning babies. The nation's assault on poverty may eventually remove the disadvantages of the poor. Better teacher-preparation programs, such as those pioneered by the Teacher Corps, will help teachers deal more effectively not only with the disadvantaged but with all students. In any event, the study of students and the manner in which they learn will remain the essence of educational thought.

SUMMARY

Student activism has focused intensified attention upon the nature of student growth and development, the role of young people in society, and the educational reforms which are needed to make education and life more meaningful and satisfying. Many schools are responding by distinguishing more carefully between revolutionary activists who are interested only in the destruction of society and responsible nonviolent students who seek legitimate educational reform.

The individual student is of surpassing worth in our society. Thus schools must seek to understand each child and to stimulate his development up to his full capacity.

Each child is unique. His behavior is influenced by varied and sometimes obscure factors. Children vary widely in their ability to learn, but virtually all children are capable of some learning. A child's development is dependent upon his total organism—mental, physical, social, and emotional. A teacher must understand and be concerned about all aspects

of growth. Although general patterns of growth are discernible, children vary widely in the rate and extent of their growth.

Recent educational developments have helped us understand that the intellectual capability of most students can be raised through good teaching. They have helped us understand that learning is a complex phenomenon greatly influenced not only by the school but also by the home environment, the peer group, the mass media of communication, and the entire social milieu. Modern educational thought has also focused attention on the entire human organism and revealed that intellectual, emotional, physical, and social development are interdependent. Modern research and experimentation have given us new insights into the creative and mentally gifted students. Greater effort is being made to identify these students early and to challenge them to the full measure of their abilities. This consists usually of enriching their program, accelerating their progress through school, grouping them for instruction with other gifted students for part of the school day, and permitting them to undertake independent study to extend their academic inquiry.

Advances have been made recently in the improvement of the education of handicapped students, although this problem is by no means conquered. These advances have been quickened by the allocation of federal funds for research and experimentation. This effort has changed our concept of education of the handicapped from one of stereotyping handicapped students and focusing upon their limitations and helping them to accommodate to and accept these limitations to one of maximizing the handicapped student's capabilities by modifying the learning environment to accommodate him more fully. New instructional method and materials are helping to reduce impaired children's learning difficulties. Medical science, psychiatry, social work, and other professional fields are joining their efforts more effectively toward this end. Many more handicapped children are being included in the regular school classroom, at least for much of their education, rather than consigned to special education classes.

Great advances are being made in overcoming the handicaps of neurological, physical, emotional, social, and cultural impairment. The problems of relieving the scourge of drug abuse among students, however, are legion and show little sign of improvement. Exciting developments in biochemistry, genetics, medicine, and learning theory raise the hope that teaching and learning may become extraordinarily more effective before the end of the century.

Through local, state, national, and international agencies, such as city councils, the state departments of education, the U.S. Office of Education, the Office of Economic Opportunity, the Council for Exceptional Children, and the American Personnel and Guidance Association, better services can be developed for socially maladjusted as well as other pupils.

The most powerful factor in the educational development of all children—normal and handicapped alike—is the teacher. Schools need teachers who are capable of developing in the classroom a climate that is as free as possible from devastating pressure upon students; teachers who can perceive and respect the individual differences of students; teachers who can vary the learning experiences and expectations of the school to fit the needs of each child; teachers who can recognize and nourish each spark of talent, however modest it may be; and, above all, teachers who can demonstrate a sense of affection and respect for each human being. We shall speak more of the crucial role of the teacher in the next chapter.

Suggested Activities

1. Prepare an essay on the topic "Student Activism—Causes and Appropriate School Response."
2. Study some of the literature on mental health in education, pressures on children, and related topics; then prepare a "Guide for Classroom Teachers in Protecting the Mental Health of Students."
3. Read references in the bibliography dealing with children of poverty and analyze your own potential for teaching children from slum communities.
4. It is said that more teachers leave teaching or fail to enter teaching because they cannot—or fear they cannot—maintain discipline than for any other reason. List the considerations and strategies which you consider most important for effective classroom control of students by the teacher.
5. Interview a rehabilitation counselor to learn modern methods of working with handicapped children.
6. Explain means by which the classroom teacher may discover and nurture latent interests and unique talents of children in the regular classroom.
7. Study carefully one exceptional student, keeping a careful record of all pertinent data, and compare

his characteristics with those associated with average pupils of the same age.
8. Suggest the most effective ways in which the mentally gifted child can be nurtured in the regular classroom.
9. Describe the ways in which the mentally retarded child can be helped most effectively in the regular classroom.
10. Prepare a "Guide for Classroom Teachers in Identifying Potential Dropouts and Reducing the Causes of Their Disaffection with School."

Bibliography

Dennison, George: *The Lives of Children*, Random House, Inc., New York, 1969. A moving, perceptive book on the lives of children, which should be read by all teachers and prospective teachers.

Duvall, Evelyn Millis: *Today's Teen-agers*, Association Press, New York, 1969. Practical advice for parents and adults who work with youth.

Harshman, Hardwick W. (ed.): *Educating the Emotionally Disturbed*, Thomas Y. Crowell Company, New York, 1969. A book of readings to help teachers deepen their understanding of how emotionally disturbed students can be dealt with effectively in school.

Hentoff, Nat: *Our Children Are Dying*, The Viking Press, Inc., New York, 1967. Stern criticism of how metropolitan high schools disenchant youth, written by a sensitive and humane high school principal.

Holt, John: *How Children Learn*, Pitman Publishing Corporation, New York, 1967. Interpretation of how children learn, drawn from warm and understanding observation of children.

Jersild, Arthur T.: *Child Psychology*, 6th ed., Prentice-Hall, Inc., Englewood Cliffs, N.J., 1968. Classic textbook on child growth and development.

Kavanaugh, Robert: *The Grim Generation*, Trident Press, a division of Simon & Schuster, Inc., New York, 1970. A portrayal of students of various types in their search for new values in a changing society and an analysis of campus turmoil.

Kozol, Jonathan: *Death at an Early Age*, Houghton Mifflin Company, Boston, 1967. A national best seller about the deleterious effects of inner-city schools upon ghetto students, written by a teacher.

Martin, Peter, and Allan Cohen: *Understanding Drug Use*, Harper & Row, Publishers, Incorporated, New York, 1971. An analysis of the drug problem written by a school administrator and a physician.

Piaget, Jean, and Barbel Inhelder: *The Psychology of the Child*, Basic Books, Inc., Publishers, New York, 1969. A synthesis of forty years of work by experts on child development from infancy through adolescence.

White House Conference on Children: *Report to the President*, Government Printing Office, Washington, D.C., 1970. Reports and recommendations from the 25 forums of the White House Conference on Children.

Chapter 12   Teachers

ORIENTATION

We assume that you read this book because you are reflecting on teaching, possibly as a career for yourself. Many people have reflected on teaching and teachers. We include some of their reflections here to stimulate your own.

If you become a teacher, by your pupils you'll be taught.
—*Anna, in* The King and I

No man can reveal to you aught but that which already lies half asleep in the dawning of your knowledge. . . . If he is indeed wise he does not bid you enter the house of his wisdom, but rather leads you to the threshold of your own mind.

—*Kahlil Gibran,* The Prophet

I had, out of my sixty teachers, a scant half dozen who couldn't have been supplanted by phonographs.
—*Don Herrold as quoted in*
A Treasury of Humorous Quotations

He who can, does. He who cannot, teaches.
—*George Bernard Shaw,* Man and Superman

But where's the man who counsel can bestow, Still pleas'd to teach, and not proud to know?
—*Alexander Pope,* Essay on Criticism

Where else would a handsome and very young man put his arms around me and ask, "Do you know that I love you?" Where else could I walk up and down the aisle and have warm little hands touch me? Where else could I have the privilege of wiggling loose teeth and receive the promise that I may pull them when they are loose enough? Where else could I eat a soiled piece of candy from a grimy little hand and not become ill?
—*Anonymous*

To me, a teacher is a person with a touch of immortality. . . . The desire to teach is a deep-seated one and permeates the hearts and souls of thousands upon thousands who have never given conscious thought to entering the profession. We all teach in one way or another, and

in such activity we find unusual and almost mysterious satisfaction. . . . Why does this happen? Because we all sense, directly or indirectly, consciously or unconsciously, that to leave a vestige of oneself in the development of another is a touch of immortality. Through this we live far beyond our span of mortal years. Through this we find new and more impelling reasons for being, for populating this earth.
—*Samuel B. Gould, from an address at an Antioch College Assembly*

Her former pupil found her late one afternoon and paid some small part of the debt he owed her in the coin which is the treasure of all good teachers—the gratitude of a former pupil for an important lesson well taught.
—*Harold C. Hand, in* Why Teach?,
edited by Louise Sharp

Men have sought and still seek an elixir of youth. I've found it as a teacher of junior high school science. Teaching has made it possible for me to enjoy the fun, excitement, wonder, humor, intensity, and sensitivity of youth while enjoying the benefits of mature adulthood (whatever these may be).
—*Christopher R. Vagts, in* Why Teach?,
edited by Louise Sharp

What indeed is the good teacher if not a well-informed lover? . . . To teach is to love. And in the final analysis we learn only from those whom we love . . . the most important of all qualities in the world. . . . This is because the most important of all desires of a human being is the desire to be loved, and at the same time to love others.
—*Ashley Montagu,* Education and Human Relations

Teachers everywhere have as important a role to play as politicians and diplomats. . . . One of the most important tasks of the teacher, as I understand it, is to bring to clear consciousness the common ideals for which men should live. These common ideals have a force which unites.

—*U Thant, from an address*

A good teacher is first of all a good human being— someone who in personality, character, and attitudes exercises a wholesome and inspiring influence on young people.
—*Norman Cousins, in* Why Teach?,
edited by Louise Sharp

Teaching is preeminently an intellectual encounter.

Given a mastered subject and a person committed heart and soul to teaching it, a class accustomed to think, attend, and be led; the result will be, under God, as near to the discourse of men and angels as it is fit to go.
—*Jacques Barzun*, The House of Intellect

In this chapter we consider further the second most important element in the educational equation—the teacher. And we discuss the question: "Should I teach?" Some of the lively issues relating to teachers and teaching are also discussed in Chapter 1.

DEVELOPMENT

The Colonial Era

The history of teaching in America begins with the very founding of the colonies. As the early colonists struggled to establish settlements, they built first log cabins, then churches, and then schools. In many communities in colonial America, education was based upon religion; church and school were generally seen as one.

Many of the teachers—or schoolmasters, as they were then called—were ministers, ministers' assistants, sextons, or men preparing for the clergy. These early schoolmasters often led the church choir, read the Scriptures, played the organ, taught the Sunday school classes, tended the sick, conducted wedding and funeral services, and not infrequently dug graves. This custom set the tradition that is manifest even today, the expectation that the teacher's character should be exemplary. Some of the colonial schoolmasters, such as the famous Ezekiel Cheever, were the most eminent and learned men of their community. In other communities where the influence of the church was not so great or where capable men were in shorter supply, schools were sometimes taught by indentured servants, by cripples, and occasionally by rogues and drunks. The schoolmaster had no formal preparation for teaching, no knowledge of psychology or pedagogy. In many cases he was not much better educated than the older scholars whom he attempted to teach. The curriculum consisted of what he wanted to teach—perhaps Greek, Latin, English, good manners, and the principles of the Christian faith.

The Early Nineteenth Century

With the rise of the free public school movement in the nineteenth century, the need for more teachers and better-prepared teachers became evident to some of the educational leaders of the time. In 1823 Reverend Samuel R. Hall established at Concord, Vermont, a private academy with a model school attached for the training of teachers. A few years later Hall wrote his *Lectures in School Keeping*, the first book on pedagogy published in this country. Through the energetic efforts of Horace Mann, the first public normal school for the training of teachers was opened in Lexington, Massachusetts, in 1839, and two more followed within the year. Through the leadership of Henry Barnard, who had studied teacher-training institutions abroad, more normal schools and teacher institutes were established in the neighboring state of Connecticut. Other states followed, and by the mid-nineteenth century the professional education of teachers had begun, however primitive it may have been by today's standards. Many of the early students at normal schools attended for only one term.

Gradually it became apparent to educational leaders that teachers had to be *prepared* over a period of years, rather than *trained* during an eleven-week term or a summer session or two. The quality as well as the quantity of instruction had to be altered. Instead of equipping the prospective teachers with a bag of tricks, it was necessary to teach them how to guide the growth and development of children. For this purpose an institution with a higher rank than a two-year normal training school was needed.

Institutes were held once or twice a year to help teachers in service. These institutes consisted usually of demonstration lessons, forums for the discussion of practical problems of teachers, and oratorical performances by visiting lecturers. Horace Mann's influential annual reports and *Lectures on Education* had a wide impact on teaching practices. The certification of teachers was at first a local matter. Teachers were sometimes given oral examinations, often by laymen, as a basis for certification. Good moral character, ability to keep order, and knowledge of subjects—mostly in that order—were the prime criteria for the certification, which was sometimes scribbled on the back of an envelope and which had to be renewed annually. Gradually oral examinations gave way to written tests, and permanent certification became more common.

The Development of the Teaching Profession

1794	First formal teachers' organization, Society of Associated Teachers, organized in New York City	*1946*	National Commission on Teacher Education and Professional Standards launched by the NEA
1823	First private normal school started in Vermont	*1946*	World Organization of the Teaching Profession started (1952 WCOTP)
1827	First state legislation provided for training of teachers in New York	*1947*	National Retired Teachers Association formed
1838	First state normal schools established in Massachusetts	*1948*	Three teacher-education groups merged into the American Association of Colleges for Teacher Education
1843	Authority to issue state certification for teachers established in New York	*1954*	National Council for Accreditation of Teacher Education made operative
1845	First state teachers' associations begun in New York and Rhode Island	*1958*	Loans to future teachers in public elementary and secondary schools made available by the National Defense Education Act
1857	National Teachers Association formed, later the National Education Association (NEA)		
		1959	Ford Foundation grant of $9 million made to strengthen teacher education
1893	Normal school of Albany, New York, made Albany State Teachers College and empowered to grant degrees	*1961*	Collective-bargaining rights gained by New York City teachers, triggering similar movements across the country
1896	First statewide teacher-retirement system adopted in New Jersey	*1963*	The Code of Ethics of the Education Profession adopted by the NEA
1904	National Catholic Education Association formed	*1963*	Conant's survey of teacher education and his recommendations published in The Education of American Teachers
1909	First state teacher-tenure law passed in New Jersey		
1916	American Federation of Teachers organized as an affiliate of the American Federation of Labor	*1966*	Segregation of teachers in its state affiliates terminated by action of NEA
		1966	Training begun for volunteers in the National Teacher Corps
1917	American Association of Teachers Colleges formed	*1967*	Education Professions Development Act approved by Congress
1930	National Survey of Teacher Education authorized by Congress		
		1972	Teacher demand in United States equaled by supply for first time in a third of a century
1938	National Organization of Future Teachers of America organized		

Teaching conditions in the early nineteenth century were primitive. Textbooks and other instructional materials were practically nonexistent. School buildings were austere. Classes were large: sixty or a hundred students in one room were not uncommon. One-room schools were the rule, except in the cities, and teachers taught students ranging in age from 6 to 17 in the same room. Discipline was harsh and the rod was not spared. Many teachers prided themselves on their mastery of the art of corporal punishment. The salary for men was about $20 a month, plus room and board, and women teachers' salaries were typically half that amount. Many teachers were still not well trained. A large number were young and immature, and few planned to make a career of teaching.

The Late Nineteenth Century

By the latter part of the nineteenth century, several significant milestones en route to professionalization had been reached. In 1857 the National Teachers Association, now the National Education Association, was organized by forty-three teachers gathered in Philadelphia. It adopted a charter proclaiming its dual purposes: "to elevate the character and advance the interests of the profession of teaching, and to promote the cause of education in the United States." At first women teachers were not admitted, but the professional organization movement, which was to play a significant role in the maturation of teaching, was under way despite the absence of female members.

Education departments began to appear in major colleges and universities. The first part-time chair devoted to professional training was established at New York University in 1832; the first permanent chair, at the University of Indiana, in 1852. The first important steps toward the professionalization of teacher preparation had been taken. The study of pedagogy became more serious, and professional literature began to appear. Supervision of teachers—quite primitive at first—was undertaken as a means of improving practice in the schools. Comprehensive written examinations were established as a basis for more rigorous certification, and the more incompetent candidates were turned away. Courses of study, textbooks, globes, maps, and other instructional matters were improved and became more plentiful.

The Civil War took many men teachers from their classrooms, and many failed to return. Their places were taken by women, who soon outnumbered their male colleagues. Elementary school teaching became almost exclusively a female undertaking, and more and more women found positions on high school faculties as well. Teachers' salaries were still dismally low, and the increased feminization did little to improve them.

The Twentieth Century

The twentieth century brought further reform to the profession. Colleges and universities assumed more responsibility for the preparation of teachers, particularly of high school teachers. The emphasis shifted from narrowly vocational teacher *training* toward more professional *preparation*. Four-year preparation programs, stressing both general and professional education, began to emerge. Normal schools were transformed into teachers colleges and played an important role, particularly in the preparation of elementary teachers. Laboratory and experimental schools, often affiliated with teachers colleges and universities, were established to demonstrate superior methods and to provide clinical facilities for student teachers.

Responsibility for the certification of teachers was gradually assumed by the states, and teachers' examinations were replaced by requirements for the completion of prescribed courses. Teachers' salaries were gradually improved, and pension, retirement, and sick-leave benefits began to appear. Local and state teachers' associations grew in number and influence and had a powerful effect upon the improvement of working conditions and economic benefits for teachers.

The federal government has become increasingly concerned with teacher education. For example, in 1967 Congress passed the Education Professions Development Act. This is a landmark, for it coordinates all federal programs bearing on teacher education.

Despite its relatively brief history, teaching has made remarkable progress in professionalization. Much remains to be done, but progress is accelerating. Thus, each new generation of teachers is at once the beneficiary of a rich professional legacy won for it by a prior generation and, through its own dedication, the benefactor of successive generations of teachers.

PRESERVICE EDUCATION

Preservice education includes such factors as the recruitment and selection of students for the teaching profession, the in-college education of these candidates, their certification upon meeting the necessary standards, and their placement in teaching positions.

Recruitment and Selection of Students

Teacher Supply and Demand. For the first time since World War II the supply of teachers began to equal the demand in the early 1970s. The shortage of elementary and secondary school teachers was especially severe during the first two decades following World War II. Several factors had contributed to this shortage: the sharp rise in school enrollments during this period, the low birthrates during the Depression of the 1930s—the generation from which new teachers were recruited—low salaries for teachers, and the insatiable demand for educated manpower in many other learned occupations in an age of expanding technology. By the mid-1960s the outlook for a better balance between supply of, and demand for, elementary and secondary school teachers had improved somewhat. The increase in birthrates had at last slowed down by the late 1950s, resulting in a less rapid rise in elementary and secondary school enrollments. The postwar crop of babies swelled the colleges and universities, giving the nation a far greater pool of young people preparing for learned occupations. The percentage of these college graduates entering teaching had also risen slightly. Moreover, the age of automation had greatly reduced the number of workers required for production work and had released more breadwinners for social service occupations such as teaching.

By the early 1970s, a number of other forces helped to increase the supply of teachers. Through collective bargaining at the local level and lobbying at the state level, teachers' organizations exerted powerful pressure upon the improvement of salaries and conditions of work. Many persons, particularly men, who earlier would have left teaching after a few years, were now finding it a more attractive profession. School enrollments receded at the elementary level, thereby reducing the demand for elementary teachers. Nevertheless shortages of

teachers persisted in certain sectors of the educational scene, particularly in early-childhood education, special education, vocational and technical education, and higher education, especially in community colleges.

Recruitment. During the period of shortage of teachers, efforts were made to attract more and better persons to the profession. The Education Professions Development Act (EPDA) of 1967, discussed more fully in Chapter 2, added a substantial measure of federal funding for the recruitment, preparation, and continuing professional development of teachers and other educators. EPDA permitted for the first time a comprehensive understanding of the national manpower situation in education. The act provided funds for the stimulation of preparation in fields that were in short supply, mentioned above, as well as teachers of disadvantaged and handicapped children as part of the war on poverty and underprivilege. Some observers believe that EPDA may become the most significant federal influence upon the development of the profession of education. EPDA has brought together under one jurisdiction responsibility for the administration of various provisions for teacher recruitment and preparation authorized by earlier acts described in Chapter 2—low-interest loans for college students entering teacher-preparation programs under the National Defense Education Act, the Teacher Corps program under the Higher Education Act, and fellowships for graduate study for persons pursuing careers in higher education authorized by the same act. Many states have established scholarship and loan programs for those going into teaching. Several private philanthropies, such as the Woodrow Wilson National Fellowship program, provide fellowships for persons preparing for teaching.

The problem of recruiting teachers is not entirely that of subsidizing the future teacher's preparation. Young people must first be attracted to teaching as a career. The Future Teachers of America, under the auspices of the National Education Association, enrolls high school students in local chapters to help them become more familiar with career opportunities in teaching and learn how to enter the profession. At the college level, future-teacher groups are organized as chapters of the Student NEA. These campus chapters and state student education associations are integral parts of the Student NEA on the national level.

Within the past decade, the proportion of teachers who are married, the proportion under 30 years of age, and the proportion of male teachers have grown substantially. Thus dies the stereotype of the old-maid schoolmarm.

The Negro population is another sector of the manpower pool that should be attracted to teaching in far greater numbers. Black people have been tragically underutilized in all the learned professions. For years it was felt that the professional preparation of black teachers was substandard, as indeed it appeared to be when measured by examinations that were standardized on a population of white, middle-class culture. Many urban districts have abandoned the use of arbitrary cutoff scores on the National Teacher Examination as a prerequisite for inclusion on employment eligibility lists to encourage the employment of more teachers from minority races. The Education Professions Development Act stimulated the recruitment of more educators among persons from low-income families, many of them blacks. Most colleges and universities have increased loan funds and scholarships targeted for people of minority races. Discrimination on the basis of race has subsided markedly, resulting in far greater employment opportunity in education for nonwhite Americans.

A source of teachers is Peace Corps volunteers. More than half of these "practical idealists" have served as schoolteachers in their host countries. In a broader sense, all of them have been teachers, whether in classrooms, hospitals, or laboratories. More than half of the returning Peace Corps workers have enrolled in colleges and universities, many in programs of teacher education. These workers are likely to have a powerful commitment to education for intellectual and emotional reasons forged in their dealings with the harsh realities of life; they see education as the key to the improvement of the human condition. Having worked with the underprivileged abroad, they have a unique capability for doing so in their own country, at the very time that this nation has mounted a major war on poverty and underprivilege at home.

Another force in increasing the supply of teachers has been youth's own disposition to turn increasingly toward social service occupations, particularly teaching, in their quest for the improvement of the human condition. Young people are coming to realize that the crusades against war, poverty, ignorance, pollution, racial discrimination, and the other great social problems are best waged in the schools. Many of these idealists are finding the Teacher Corps the vehicle for their entry into teaching. Teaching is no longer regarded as an occupation for those who can't do anything else but rather as one of man's most compelling occupational challenges. As a result, the lure and the status of the teaching profession have been strengthened. In an opinion poll of a national sample of public school teachers, less than one teacher in eight felt that teachers had low prestige in the community in which they worked. There is good reason to believe that the nation's recent renaissance of interest in its educational establishment has helped to improve the image of the teacher in American society. Hopefully, teachers themselves may increasingly regard their profession as sufficiently worthy to encourage others to enter it.

Vigorous recruitment enlarges the pool of manpower from which teachers are selected. We turn our attention now to the problems of teacher selection.

Selection. The selection of teachers takes place at many points: the selection of students for admission to teacher-education programs and later the selection of those who will be graduated and certificated to teach; the selection of candidates for teaching positions; and the selection of probationary teachers who will be continued into tenure positions.

Selection of teachers is difficult because the evidence regarding those characteristics demonstrably related to success in teaching is not as decisive as one might like. Teaching ability is a complex constellation of talents that are not easily sorted out, defined, and measured. National associations of school administrators, classroom teachers, and school boards combined their efforts to review the research findings on indicators of successful teaching and published their conclusions in an excellent publication entitled *Who's a Good Teacher?* In brief, this study reports the following conclusions:

There is only slight relationship between intelligence and rated success as a teacher although a minimum level of intelligence is certainly important.

Mastery of subject matter, although important, is not a major factor in teaching performance.

Good grades in college are consistently related to effective teaching.

Teachers with the most professional knowledge tend to be the more effective teachers.

Teachers who have had professional preparation are generally more effective than those who have not.

Teachers' rated effectiveness at first increases rather rapidly with experience, levels off at five years and beyond, and shows little change for the next 15 or 20 years, after which it tends to decline.

Teacher effectiveness is not significantly related to the socio-economic status of the teacher.

Differences in sex account for little of the difference in success among teachers.

Differences in marital status account for very little difference in teaching effectiveness.

Differences in aptitudes are of little value in predicting success in teaching.

Differences in attitudes account for little of the variation in effectiveness among teachers.[1]

A monumental review of research on teaching effectiveness sponsored by the American Educational Research Association revealed that some of the more promising approaches to predicting success in teaching are derived from studies of the teacher's behavior in the classroom.[2] These approaches, although useful to the researcher, are usually too sophisticated to be of much value to the harried school administrator in selecting teachers. In general it can be said that the selection of candidates for teaching positions in schools is still in a rather primitive stage and will remain so until we know far more about the measurement and prediction of teaching success than we do presently. Much of the difficulty arises from disagreement over what constitutes "good teaching," a term that virtually defies definition, agreement, or measurement.

Types of Teacher-education Institutions

The institutions for educating teachers have been (1) normal schools, (2) teachers colleges, (3) departments of education, and (4) schools or colleges of education.

Normal Schools. The first normal schools were established in order to prepare teachers for the elementary schools. Students were admitted on the basis of their elementary school records. The cur-

[1] American Association of School Administrators, Association of Classroom Teachers of the NEA, National School Boards Association, *Who's a Good Teacher?* National Education Association, Washington, D.C., 1961.
[2] N. L. Gage (ed.), *Handbook of Research on Teaching*, Rand McNally & Company, Chicago, 1963, chaps. 6, 10.

riculum was usually a year in length and contained very little of what is now considered professional education. Normal schools in the United States have disappeared in name and function. Historically, the normal schools were important institutions.

Teachers Colleges. These are usually single-purpose, degree-granting institutions. Nearly all states of the Union once established teachers colleges or state colleges with teacher education as one of their functions. Whereas the old normal school trained teachers for elementary service only, the teachers college spread its offerings to include the education of secondary school and special education teachers.

Most of the teachers colleges have been transformed into multipurpose state colleges or universities, although teacher education remains the most dominant component for most of them. Their curriculums have been broadened to include more general education. By 1972 the authors could identify only eight remaining teachers colleges. The best-known of these, Teachers College of Columbia University and George Peabody College for Teachers, are really not single-purpose institutions, despite their names.

Departments of Education. The liberal arts college and many of the newer state colleges usually include a division known as the education or the psychology department, and some have both. The requirement, in terms of hours of education and psychology, is about the same as the minimum in teachers colleges. Student teaching is coupled with this program. In some universities, work in education is organized as a department. In others, teacher education is a function of a department within a larger division, such as social sciences or liberal arts. In a few, the whole institution serves as a department educating teachers.

Schools or Colleges of Education. Professional work in education at state and private universities is usually centralized in a separate entity, the school or college of education. It may accept students at the beginning of the freshman year, at the end of a period of general education in the sophomore or junior year, or for graduate work. The history of the University of Michigan, one of the first American universities to offer education courses, illustrates the evolution of schools of education. Its first permanent chair in this field, established in 1879, was called the Science and Art of Teaching; in 1921 it gave way to a School of Education, coordinate with the other prefessional schools. Most teachers today are prepared in private and public liberal arts colleges and universities.

In-college Education for Teaching

Major Curricular Beliefs. The National Council for Accreditation of Teacher Education prepared a working statement entitled "The Teacher Education Curriculum." It contains the following major beliefs

regarding in-college preparation for teachers: "The curriculum for teacher education should be attractive to capable students who seek a good basic education for themselves and adequate preparation for a professional career."

The statement also includes the following major convictions:

All teachers should be well-educated persons.

The curriculum should produce an area of subject-matter concentration for each teacher.

Teachers should have specific preparation for their specific responsibilities.

The curriculum should include a well-organized program of professional work, including laboratory experiences.

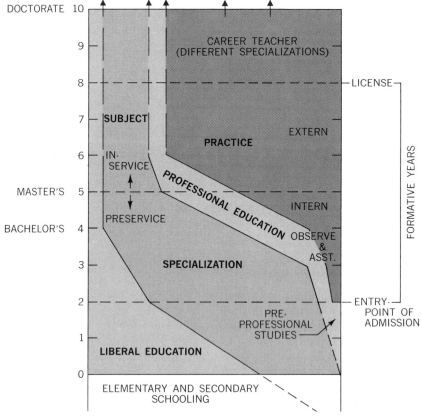

FIGURE 12-1   *A design for teacher education. This design shows the ideal mix of liberal education, specialization, professional education, and practice through an eight-year program extending from entry into college until licensure. The second year of college becomes a common point of formal entry. Practice begins immediately and is broadened after preservice study, which is merged into in-service education. Liberal education is extended through the entire career. (Reprinted from National Commission on Teacher Education and Professional Standards,* The Real World of the Beginning Teacher, *National Education Association, Washington, D.C., 1966, p. 13. Copyrighted by the National Education Association, 1966.)*

These beliefs are usually implemented through curricular programs in at least three areas.

The teacher is an interpreter of the general culture; hence his preparation must include general education. He teaches some specialized subject or generalized field; hence he needs subject-matter or field preparation. He teaches a variety of students; hence he takes professional work in education and psychology. He also needs supervised practice in his art. These four areas—general or liberal education, subject-field specialization, professional education, and practice in teaching—are illustrated in a model design of teacher education in Figure 12-1.

General or Liberal Education. Fundamentally, liberal education includes the social sciences, the natural and physical sciences, and the humanities. The teacher works in a broad profession and not a narrow trade. He is responsible for the general education of young Americans—the workers and citizens of tomorrow. Therefore, teachers are expected to have a rich cultural background.

Specialized Education in Subjects, Fields, or Levels. Prospective teachers should complement a broad cultural and general education with specialization in the subjects, fields, or levels in which they expect to teach. For teachers in elementary school, the preparation is usually in terms of grade levels and the subjects and fields, although academic specialization by elementary school teachers is becoming much more common and is required in some states.

Professional Education. Usually, the requirements in specific professional education are stated in terms of semester hours. The median requirement is twenty-four semester hours for elementary teachers and eighteen semester hours for secondary school teachers. Most teacher-education institutions go beyond the legal minimum. In some colleges this professional work is concentrated in the last year or two, but in the majority it is spread over the upper three years. For some it is concentrated in a fifth year, as will be indicated later. For some it is diffused over several years.

Directed observations, case studies of students, and activities in preparation for student teaching are essential phases of professional education because they include actual experience with children. As has been repeatedly stated, the verb "to teach" has two

accusatives—the student, and the subject. Some knowledge of students can be acquired through observation, practicums, and direct student teaching.

Supervised Practice in Teaching. One of the most important aspects of preservice education is experience as a student teacher. "Student teaching" or "practice teaching" as it may be termed, gradually inducts the prospective teacher into the full responsibility of the teaching-learning activities under the skillful guidance of a supervising, or helping, teacher and the college's director of student teaching and his faculty colleagues.

A higher level of experience for future teachers is provided through internships comparable to those in medicine. In addition to the fact that it very vitally integrates the theoretical and practical aspects of the student's education, internship has many other significant values. It gives the beginning teacher a chance to spend the first year in a superior school under conditions conducive to growth, it provides guidance and supervision at the time they are most needed, it makes possible a gradual transition from student to teacher, and it serves as a period of testing and probation. These values and others are derived from internship plans now conducted jointly by many institutions of teacher education and cooperating schools. These internships are often found in curricular patterns such as the five-year programs. Half-time graduate study is often combined with a half-time paid internship, terminating in a master's degree.

Nearly all teacher-education institutions provide facilities for students to experience actual teaching, either in the campus laboratory school or in off-campus schools. The laboratory school and student teaching, both on and off campus, play increasingly dynamic roles. The national organization in this field is the Association for Student Teaching, organized in 1920. It has helped to promote functional off-campus learning-teaching experiences in the public schools.

Curricular Patterns in Teacher Education. The four areas of teacher education—general or liberal education, specialization in subjects or fields in which the student expects to teach, and professional work, including student teaching—are organized in various patterns. There is considerable disagreement over the merits of each. Actually, this disagreement is part of a larger quarrel over the proper balance among these four areas in the total preparation program. Figure 12-1 illustrates a model design for teacher education.

Conant, in his book *The Education of American Teachers*,[3] called for drastic changes in teacher education.

Some of Conant's recommendations are controversial. Several of them—more selective recruitment of teachers, more flexible preparation programs, greater emphasis upon general education, liberalization of certification requirements, strengthening of student teaching, emphasis upon full-time study, and better-controlled periods of probationary service—are in harmony with reforms in teacher education under way in many places. Some of his other recommendations are subject to spirited controversy and have not been adopted on any widespread scale. They should not be.

A weakness of Conant's study is that it lacks a basic philosophy of education; it never faces the question of what kind of education we should prepare teachers to render. Without this kind of philosophical backdrop, discussion of teacher education is largely spurious, as the following parable reveals so poignantly:

Greeting his pupils, the master asked:
"What would you learn of me?"
And the reply came:
"How shall we care for our bodies?"
"How shall we rear our children?"
"How shall we work together?"
"How shall we live with our fellowman?"
"How shall we play?"
"For what ends shall we live? . . ."
And the teacher pondered these words, and sorrow was in his heart, for his own learning touched not these things.[4]

George Denemark, recent president of the American Association of Colleges for Teacher Education, has identified ten weaknesses of teacher education which demand reform:

[3]James B. Conant, *The Education of American Teachers*, McGraw-Hill Book Company, New York, 1963.

[4]J. Crosby Chapman and George S. Counts, *Principles of Education*, Houghton Mifflin Company, Boston, 1924, frontispiece.

1. Inadequacies and irrelevance of much that presently constitutes the general or liberal education component.

2. The hostile academic atmosphere in which teacher education is conducted.

3. Lack of conceptual framework for teacher education.

4. Simplistic views of teaching and teacher education.

5. Inadequate interlacing of theory and practice.

6. Continued acceptance of the single model, "omnicapable" teacher.

7. Low standards for selection and retention of students in teacher education.

8. Schedule rigidities and cumbersome procedures for curriculum change.

9. Absence of student opportunities for exploration and inquiry.

10. Schizophrenic role expectations for teacher education departments.

Problems of Teacher Education. The problems confronting teacher education are legion, and space permits brief mention of only a few. Teacher education is generally underfinanced. According to a study by the U.S. Office of Education, the average cost of educating teachers is less than $1,000 per student per year, while the cost of educating physicians and other professionals is commonly ten times that amount. Most colleges and universities have badly shortchanged their schools or departments of education. Moreover, four out of five of the nation's future teachers, according to the report, are being educated at institutions which are rated C or D on the scale of faculty salaries of the American Association of University Professors. Some of this underfinancing is being relieved slightly by new federal funds for teacher education.

Perhaps the greatest shortcoming of teacher education has been its general inability to prepare teachers who are capable of providing effective instruction for children from economically depressed neighborhoods. These are the children who need superb teaching most. One out of five American children attend schools that cannot attract and hold well-trained teachers because of the isolation of the schools in rural areas or because of despair bred in urban ghettos. These children are not incapable of learning, but it takes more professional skill to reach them. Undernourished, underprepared, and often hostile to conventional schooling, they require patient and imaginative teaching. Many of them are of minority races and have difficulty responding to teachers of white middle-class culture who are inexperienced in interracial relations. Teacher Corps trainees are of course the shining exception to this generalization. These sensitive young people complete teacher education addressed specifically to the education of poverty children. Their success in slum schools derives from their capacity for love, openness, and sense of humanity. But there are not enough of them. The preparation of more and better teachers for educationally and economically disadvantaged students is surely one of the prime educational challenges of our time. Just as we arrange for the best surgeons to perform the most difficult surgery, so we must arrange for the most skillful teachers to guide the education of children whose learning is most difficult. We have not done that heretofore. Our slum schools have been staffed in large part by teachers who remain after the more attractive schools have made their choices.

Another problem of teacher education is the ambivalence between the education courses and the real world of classroom teaching. Preservice preparation and in-service education are usually not well articulated. The American Association of Colleges for Teacher Education (AACTE) has named six vital issues confronting teacher-education institutions. The AACTE intends to direct its attention toward these issues in an effort to continually upgrade the quality of teacher preparation in the United States. The six issues cited are:

1. **The crisis of confidence in higher education among the public and its legislative representatives**
2. **The crisis of the fragmentation of governance in higher education**
3. **The problem of balancing higher education's traditional role as a citadel of knowledge and its function as an agent of social change**
4. **The urgent need for a system of curriculum change which will adequately reflect societal needs and realities**
5. **The problem of appropriately defining the roles of school systems and colleges in teacher education**
6. **The problem of business and industry involvement in teaching and teacher preparation**

The major problem of teacher education is no longer the quantity of graduates but the quality of graduates.

Level of Teacher Preparation

Much has been said in recent years about the undereducation of the nation's teachers. Nevertheless, there is substantial evidence of a dramatic

improvement in the American teacher's professional qualifications, even during the time of acute teacher shortage. Between 1950 and 1972 the proportions of elementary school teachers with four years of college preparation rose phenomenally from 50 to almost 94 percent. At the secondary school level, less than 1 percent of the teachers have had less than four years of college-level education. The public school teacher without a college degree is rapidly disappearing. Nearly all states now require the bachelor's degree for teacher certification. Approximately one-third of all public elementary and secondary school teachers hold the master's degree, and the proportion is constantly rising. This steady improvement of the nation's teaching force, even during periods of rapid growth in school enrollments and manpower shortages, is clearly one of the most heartening signs of wholesomeness in our educational system.

Accreditation of Programs

The National Council for Accreditation of Teacher Education, organized in 1954, was recognized in 1956 by the National Commission on Accrediting "as the sole national agency for accreditation of teacher education." This Council (NCATE) is autonomous with regard to the policies and procedures it follows. It is not a branch of any organization. Its purposes are not merely accreditation, but improvement of teacher education.

Although Conant and others have been critical of the National Council for Accreditation of Teacher Education and have called for sharp reduction of its influence, a comprehensive study of the NCATE by the National Commission on Accrediting gave little comfort to its critics. Although the study made several recommendations for the improvement of the structure and operation of the NCATE, it expressed faith that this Council is rendering a vital service in strengthening the quality of teacher-education institutions.

Certification of Teachers

The certificate of a teacher serves to give status; to protect its holder against unfair competition with unqualified teachers; to control the granting of licenses; to provide a means for the improvement of instruction; to yield information on which a continuous inventory of teachers and their qualifications may be based; to authorize the payment of salaries; and, most important, to protect society from inadequately prepared teachers.

A license, certificate, or permit to teach in the elementary and secondary schools is required in all states. Four years of college-level preparation is required by virtually all states for certification of teachers. Approximately half of the states require an oath of allegiance and a certificate of good health. Most of the states require a statement of recommendation of the candidate for certification by his college or employing officer.

Many states are moving toward improved certification practices, such as:

Elimination of substandard or emergency certificates

Four years of approved teacher preparation with a bachelor's degree as a minimum and with a fifth year as soon as possible

A minimum of 15 semester hours of professional work including student teaching

A probationary period of not less than three years under professional guidance

Discontinuance of permanent or life certificates

Centralization of general certification in a state agency

Reciprocity between states in certifying qualified teachers

Greater emphasis on qualitative competencies and professional growth

Increasing responsibility for teacher-education institutions through an approved program approach to accreditation and certification

More simplicity and less specificity in certification requirements

Increase in the number of state professional practices acts in which teachers exercise more responsibility for setting certification standards

The National Commission of Teacher Education and Professional Standards, a division of the National Education Association, seeks to help states strengthen their teacher-certification standards and publishes periodically a *Manual on Certification Requirements for School Personnel in the United States.*

Placement of Teachers

There are two phases of teacher placement: the collection of candidates' credentials and the appointment of selected candidates to actual positions.

Collection of Credentials. School administrators look to four possible sources for the identification of candidates for positions in their schools: (1) noncommercial teacher-placement agencies, (2) commercial teacher-placement agencies, (3) recommendations of candidates by acquaintances of the superintendent, and (4) unsolicited applications by candidates.

Teacher-education institutions maintain the most important noncommercial agencies for placing their graduates and alumni. Probably more than half of all beginning teachers find their first position through college or university teacher-placement offices. Many school systems arrange appointments for interviews with candidates through these offices and regularly interview student teachers. Most teacher-education institutions offer placement services to their students and alumni at no cost. Some charge a small service fee to handle the processing of credentials. College placement offices are in a good position to render effective service for several reasons: they usually have a personal interest in, and acquaintance with, their students; they have ready access to the student's records, his professors, and his cooperating teachers; because they are nonprofit, their interest in the quantity of their placements need not interfere with the quality of their services; they usually maintain close contact with the school systems they serve and can offer valuable information to the candidate about the quality of these schools and their personnel practices; and they can offer valuable career counseling service to their clients.

The candidate should prepare his credentials carefully and file them with the placement office early in his senior year. He should become personally acquainted with the placement director or a member of his staff. He should state clearly the kinds of positions he will accept and identify the geographic areas in which he might not wish to be placed. Many beginning teachers lack adequate understanding of the whole employment process and the ability to assess their own potential realistically. Their professors can be helpful in solving any such problems. The Association for School, College, and University Staffing (ASCUS) enrolls most of the placement offices of teacher-education institutions and attempts to promote greater effectiveness in helping teachers find employment.

A number of state departments of education and state education associations maintain teacher-placement services on a nonprofit basis, although they may charge a small registration fee. Most of these agencies provide service for nonmembers or nonresidents of the state as well as for members and residents. However, the services of these agencies are not widely used by school districts. These agencies will be most useful to teachers seeking employment out of state and beyond the region normally served by their own college placement offices.[5]

In 1967 the formidable powers of the computer were brought to bear on the teacher-recruitment task through two nationwide centralized clearinghouses for teacher referrals. NEA-SEARCH is a central computerized staffing service, sponsored by the National Education Association, that matches candidates with vacancies in educational institutions at home and abroad. Teachers interested in obtaining a new position supply information about their qualifications, minimum salary requirements, range of geographic availability, and other relevant matters, which is stored in the electronic memory of the computer. School administrators in search of teachers fill out a questionnaire which gives the computer information about the specifications of the vacancy, such as required professional qualifications and salary available. The computer quickly matches candidates and vacancies and prints out a list of names and addresses of suitable candidates for each vacancy. The computer's job is done at this point, and the subsequent processes of checking, evaluation, and negotiating are undertaken by employee and employer. A small registration fee is required of NEA-SEARCH candidate-registrants, and another small fee for each candidate's name is charged to the employer.

The Association for School, College, and University Staffing, in collaboration with the College Placement Council and the General Electric Corporation, has established another nationwide computer-based teacher-referral system known by the acronym FILE (Fast Index Location Educators). FILE is a clearinghouse through which college teacher-placement offices may register seniors and alumni of their institutions at no cost to the candidate. Here, too, the computer attempts to match vacancies with available candidates on a nationwide basis. These two services result in more efficient referral of

[5] Lists and addresses of state education departments and state education associations offering placement services are given in the pamphlet entitled *Locating a Teaching Position*, published by the National Education Association.

candidates to employers; help teachers of all ages find more acceptable opportunities in public and private schools, colleges, and universities; and permit employers to identify a better supply of candidates. The student can obtain further information about NEA-SEARCH and FILE from his college placement office.

A small percentage of school systems utilize the services of commercial placement agencies. The smaller the school system, the more likely it is to recruit candidates through commercial teacher-placement agencies. These private agencies typically charge 5 or 6 percent of the candidate's first-year salary for their services, in addition to a small registration fee. Many of these commercial placement agencies subscribe to the standards and ethical practices established by their parent organization, the National Association of Teachers Agencies. Addresses of commercial teachers' agencies are given in their advertisements, which appear frequently in the journals of the National Education Association, the American Federation of Teachers, and the various state education associations.

Nearly all school systems welcome unsolicited applications from candidates interested in positions in the particular district. Thus in most school systems, it is appropriate for a candidate to submit a letter of application for a teaching position without knowing of a particular vacancy. More than half of all beginning teachers are self-recruited in this manner and receive their first appointment without reference by a placement office. The larger the school system, the easier it is for a candidate to locate a position in this manner.

Teaching candidates may at times feel annoyed by the complexities of filing their credentials and proceeding through the recruitment and selection processes. However, this experience provides an excellent opportunity for the candidate to make some valid judgments about the quality of the potential employer. Those districts which handle the recruitment and selection of candidates in a careless and superficial manner will most likely deal with all personnel matters in the same way. On the other hand, those districts which select teachers with care are demonstrating their concern about selecting the best possible people for their faculty, a concern that is likely to be manifested in all their relations with teachers. The importance of genuine care and thoroughness on the part of both candidate and employer in the appointment process can hardly be overstated.[6]

Appointment to Position. The appointment of teachers—a power that should be carefully exercised—is usually made upon the basis of credentials, record in college, participation in extracurricular activities, personality, personal interview, and experience.

The best practice in the employment of personnel is, first of all, for the board of education to adopt a set of sound personnel policies, recommended by the superintendent and staff. In consonance with written and accepted policies, the board of education officially appoints teachers recommended by the superintendent.

CONTINUING PROFESSIONAL DEVELOPMENT

The knowledge explosion has encompassed the world of classroom teaching just as it has all man's learned endeavors. The educator whose professional knowledge and skills are not up to date becomes not only increasingly obsolete but downright dangerous to society. The teacher never "completes" his education. Throughout his career he is in pursuit of fuller knowledge—general education, specialized education in his subject-matter field, and professional education. This continuing professional development is sometimes spoken of as "in-service education." We prefer the broader term "continuing professional development."

This stimulation toward fuller knowledge, unsurpassed in any other occupation, represents one of the great satisfactions and attractions of teaching. It is known that many people with vigorous intellectual curiosity are attracted to teaching because of its incitement to constant inquiry.

[6]Candidates for teaching positions will find the following publications helpful in providing information on locating positions and promoting their candidacy: U.S. Office of Education, *Teaching as a Career*, Government Printing Office, Washington, D.C., 1971; Sam Adams and John Garrett, Jr., *To Be a Teacher*, Prentice-Hall, Inc., Englewood Cliffs, N.J., 1969; Paul J. Gelinas, *So You Want To Be a Teacher*, Harper & Row, Publishers, Incorporated, New York, 1965; National Education Association, *Teaching Career Fact Book*, Washington, D.C., 1972; T. M. Stinnett, *Professional Problems of Teachers*, The Macmillan Company, New York, 1968, chaps. 5 and 6; Laurence D. Haskew and Jonathan C. McLendon, *This is Teaching*, Scott, Foresman and Company, Glenview, Ill., 1968, chap. 9.

The National Society for the Study of Education, which devoted one of its yearbooks to in-service education, stated the following purposes for in-service education:

To promote the continuous improvement of the total professional staff of the school system

To eliminate the deficiencies in the background preparation of teachers and other professional workers

To give much needed help to teachers who are new in the particular school and to those who are entering a new responsibility or a new field of work in the profession[7]

Induction of New Teachers

The orientation and induction of new teachers are not well managed in most schools, judging from the severe drop in morale among first-year teachers.

What are the reasons so many become disenchanted almost as soon as they begin? A conference of the National Commission on Teacher Education and Professional Standards addressed itself to this problem and reported some of its findings.[8] It called attention to the fact that many beginning teachers are assigned to subject-matter fields or grade levels for which they are not prepared. Often the beginning teacher is assigned to the least desirable classes or schools or is given the most unattractive club sponsorships, which veteran teachers can escape because of their seniority. In many cases their collegiate preparation has been too abstract and their student teaching has taken place in the bracing environment of the better-financed and better-administered school systems in middle-class communities. Small wonder that they are quickly frustrated and disappointed when they find themselves, a year later, teaching in run-down and overcrowded schools with poor materials and equipment and being neglected by administrators and supervisors. Many of them are ill-prepared to cope with the problems of instruction and discipline that are thrust upon them. Often they are unfamiliar with school regulations and routines. Most beginning teachers have not yet become familiar with their instructional materials and have not developed a backlog of lesson plans from which they can draw. Everything

[7]National Society for the Study of Education, *In-service Education*, The University of Chicago Press, Chicago, 1957, p. 13.

[8]National Commission on Teacher Education and Professional Standards, *The Real World of the Beginning Teacher*, National Education Association, Washington, D.C., 1965.

is new to them, and they have not had time to develop confidence and security in their teaching style. Many of them work in self-contained classrooms in isolation from more experienced colleagues who could help them. When these conditions prevail, it is not surprising that many young teachers lose heart.

Enlightened school systems are searching for ways of helping beginning teachers more effectively. Some districts begin a systematic program of orientation as soon as they are hired. Newly hired teachers are given copies of their textbooks, courses of study, and other instructional materials in early summer so that they may become familiar with them before the opening of school. Orientation meetings are held to introduce them to their superiors and colleagues, to familiarize them with the buildings in which they will work, and to acquaint them with the resources that they may call upon when they encounter difficulty. School procedures are explained to them, and they are given help in preparing for the opening of school. Orientation is viewed as a continuing process that lasts at least throughout the first year of teaching. Group and individual conferences are held with new teachers during the year to provide clinical help with their problems as they see them. Good schools reverse the traditional practice by giving beginning teachers lighter and easier assignments than normal until they have had an opportunity to gain experience and confidence.

Despite these enlightened practices, which appear increasingly in better schools, many new teachers will continue to work in less fortunate circumstances. We can offer only this assurance for them: Be patient and persevering. Although a great many inexperienced teachers become disconsolate and leave their posts after a year or two, many of them, were they to persevere longer, would overcome their insecurities and disappointments and find teaching a satisfying occupation.

Supervision of Teaching and Learning

Supervision is now thought of as the means by which organized help is provided for the teacher to stimulate his continuous professional development. It was not always so. In its earliest form, supervision was conceived as a means of quality control of teaching through classroom inspection and arbitrary prescriptions for improved practice. Although this approach may have been appropriate in the days when teachers were not well prepared, it makes far less

sense today, although, alas, it is still far too common in traditional school systems. In better schools today, supervision is seen as enlightened professional leadership in improving the total teaching-learning situation. It seeks to stimulate self-anaylsis and guide the teacher's self-direction. Its strategy is not to inspect and control, but rather to release and coordinate the creative abilities of teachers. In many schools, the title of "supervisor" is being displaced by "helping teacher." The mood of this modern concept of supervision is cooperative, nondirective, supportive, flexible, and problem-centered. Although it may include classroom visitation, its emphasis is upon cooperative analysis and evaluation of teacher behavior and collaborative efforts to find means of improving teaching. Its strategy is that of studying and improving curriculum and instruction broadly.

The methodology of supervision today has also been broadened. It includes individual and group study of the day-to-day problems of teachers, often through action research. Workshops focusing upon the real problems of teachers frequently provide outside consultants expert in dealing with the problems under consideration. Curriculum development projects provide opportunity for teachers to learn more about learning and teaching as a by-product of program development. Many schools grant released time to teachers to observe master teachers at work as a means of acquiring better methods for themselves. Never before has there been such intensive effort on so many fronts toward the improvement of the teaching art. Opportunities for continued professional development for the teacher are truly exciting.

TEACHING PROFESSION

Teacher Welfare

We turn our attention now to several of the more important aspects of the financial welfare of teachers: salaries, fringe benefits, tenure, and retirement.

Salaries. Clearly one of the most important hallmarks of wholesomeness in any profession is the adequacy of the salaries of its members. Society has a way of judging the eminence of an occupation by the salaries it pays. On this criterion, teaching in this country did not fare well until recently. It was not until 1961 that the average salary of teachers exceeded the average salary of employees in manufacturing, most of whom are nonprofessionals. The average salaries of the federal government were substantially higher than the average salaries of elementary and secondary school teachers until the 1970s. The average starting salaries for male college graduates employed in private industry exceed the average starting salaries paid teachers. Nevertheless, over the past decade the average annual salaries of the instructional staffs in public elementary and secondary schools have increased rather sharply, beginning with the advent of widespread collective bargaining by teachers in the 1960s. There are, of course, great variations in salaries scheduled and paid to teachers across the nation, although these differences are gradually being reduced. For example, the average teacher's salary in California is almost twice the average teacher's salary in Mississippi.

More than half the states have enacted legislation to mandate minimum salaries for teachers throughout the state. These mandated minimums tend to be lower than the minimum salaries actually paid in most local districts. Most local districts have adopted their own salary schedules, commonly after negotiation with the local teachers' organization. Table 12-1 illustrates a fairly typical teachers' salary schedule. To a large degree it determines automatically the initial base salary, the amount and number of annual increments (vertical column), the amount and number of increments paid for advanced academic preparation (horizontal column), and of course

TABLE 12-1   EXAMPLE OF PART* OF TEACHERS' SALARY SCHEDULE (PITTSBURGH, PENNSYLVANIA, PUBLIC SCHOOLS: TEACHERS' SALARY SCHEDULE, 1972)

Step	Bachelor's degree	Master's degree	Master's degree plus 30 credits
1	$ 8,500	$ 8,900	$ 9,500
2	8,900	9,300	9,900
3	9,400	9,800	10,400
4	9,900	10,300	10,900
5	10,500	10,900	11,500
6	10,800	11,400	12,000
7	11,200	12,100	12,700
8	11,800	12,600	13,200
9	12,200	13,300	13,900
10	12,800	14,200	14,800
11	13,600	15,100	15,700

* Additional salaries are scheduled for higher levels of preparation, including the Ph.D., up to $16,300.

the maximum salaries to be paid teachers in each classification. The schedule illustrated in Table 12-1 is a single salary schedule, as nearly all are, since it prescribes a single schedule for both elementary and secondary teachers. An index-type schedule, which establishes an index or ratio for each horizontal and vertical classification, often relates the salaries of administrators and other specialists to the base salary for teachers. Thus the index schedule automatically adjusts the salaries of all professional employees (the superintendent is commonly excepted) to any change in the base salary for teachers. These salary schedules are usually supplemented by scales prescribing extra pay for duties outside the classroom, such as the supervision of extracurricular activities.

Several trends are discernible in salary schedules: fewer but larger annual increments, more gradations of advanced academic preparation, more index-type schedules, and the elimination of distinctions based on sex, marital status, and level of teaching assignment. Many school board members and laymen and some teachers yearn for salary policies that recognize variations in teachers' performance on bases other than years of service and graduate study credit. The issues related to salary policies are discussed in Chapter 1. Differentiated staffing patterns, discussed later, and team teaching are creating distinctions in salary on the basis of differentiated status and responsibilities among teachers in these patterns of collaborative teaching.

When public school teachers' organizations began to bargain collectively with school boards in the 1960s, salaries rose much faster than before, and fringe benefits also improved. Teachers' salaries were quite attractive to women in comparison with salaries paid in other comparable occupations, particularly when the nine-month work year was taken into account, although many men still found more attractive salaries in other learned occupations. In general, the greatest gains were realized in large districts. Regional differences in teachers' salaries were reduced somewhat. Some districts started a trend toward eleven-month contracts for teachers.

Perhaps the greatest weakness in public school salary structures is the depressed level of maximum salaries in many districts. In most learned professions, the difference between beginning salaries and maximum salaries is much greater than it is in teaching. The organized teaching profession's general insistence upon lockstep salary schedules without differentiation of salary with respect to quality of performance has helped to constrain the level of maximum salaries.

Fringe Benefits. Perquisites of employment, commonly referred to as "fringe benefits," are becoming increasingly common in most fields of employment, including teaching. Virtually all teachers enjoy a guaranteed annual wage. Many people are fond of calling attention to the long vacation periods that teachers enjoy, and this is, in itself, an attractive feature of teaching. However, the fact that the teacher's relatively short work year serves also as a depressant on salaries makes this a mixed blessing.

Long-term leaves of absence are another fringe benefit offered to teachers by some states and by many local districts in other states. Known as "sabbatical" leaves because they are customarily available every seventh year, these leaves are intended to permit teachers to engage in full-time advanced study, to travel, to participate in exchange teaching, to render service to professional organizations, or to seek restoration of their health, among other activities deemed in the best interests of schools. Nearly half of the states have laws either permitting or mandating leaves of absence for teachers for specified reasons, such as those mentioned above. Sometimes the laws specify that partial salary must be paid to the teacher on leave; others allow this to be decided by the local district.

Most school systems provide some sort of paid sick leave for teachers. Some school districts permit unused sick leave to be accumulated without limit. In many districts the amount of sick leave with pay that may be accumulated depends upon the length of the teacher's service. Most districts permit a few days' leave with pay annually for death or serious illness in the immediate family. Some districts permit a few days' leave with pay each year for religious holidays or for personal reasons. Many districts permit unpaid leaves of absence for maternity. The larger the school system, the more likely it is to provide group life insurance, hospitalization insurance, medical-surgical insurance, major medical insurance, liability insurance, and tax-sheltered annuity plans. Fringe benefits for teachers are being extended because more and more school systems recognize the importance of these indirect emoluments in attracting and holding educated manpower, as the organized teaching profession has insisted upon them at the bargaining table.

Tenure. Fundamentally, tenure laws are enacted to serve the learner and the public, protecting them from teachers who are intimidated by fear of dismissal. Prior to passage of such laws, many teachers were dismissed arbitrarily because of their political,

religious, or other beliefs. Thus tenure helps to protect the academic freedom of the learner and the teacher. However, these laws should not be drawn so tightly as to discourage the dismissal of incompetent, immoral, or unprofessional teachers. The National Education Association has framed certain basic principles that should guide tenure legislation and policy. Provisions vary among the states, resulting in annual contracts, permissive contracts for more than a year, continuing contracts, or permanent tenure. With the increased protection of collective bargaining and grievance procedures, there is a growing feeling among school board members that tenure laws should be repealed.

Retirement. Responsibility for the retirement of teachers began in cities and local districts. All but a few of the local plans have been absorbed by statewide retirement or pension systems. All states and dependencies except Delaware now have state-mandated plans by which the state, the local district, and the teacher share the costs of retirement. The greatest weakness of current plans is that the benefits are usually inadequate and there is little reciprocity among the states so that a teacher can lose much of his retirement equity when he moves into many states. A few associations and cities have established homes for retired teachers who are indigent. Many public and private school and college teachers benefit from the retirement provisions of the Social Security Act. Many teachers retired from one institution obtain employment in another school or college. The National Retired Teachers Association, an affiliate of the NEA, offers its members many services including subscription to the *NRTA Journal* and its news bulletins, hospital-surgical-medical insurance, nonprofit drugs and travel services, residence for retired teachers, nursing home programs, and a fully staffed hospitality center in St. Petersburg, Florida.

Professional Ethics for Education

A profession can rise no higher than the code of ethics it adopts and uses daily. Among the groups with whom teachers come in contact in their work are the board of education, administrators, supervisors, teachers, nonteaching staff, pupils, parents, and the community. Teachers are frequently confronted with ethical problems: "Should one accept gifts from his students?" "Should one discuss another teacher's weaknesses with a parent?" "Should one support a school policy that he does not believe in?" "Should a teacher disregard his contractual obligation with a district to accept a better position two weeks before the opening of school?" As guides to the ethical behavior of teachers, codes of ethics have been evolved by state associations and the National Education Association. The NEA adopted in 1963, and subsequently revised, the Code of Ethics of the Education Profession. This code has been adopted by all the state associations and is subject to extensive review every five years. We strongly urge the reader to study it carefully and to use it as a guide for his professional conduct. The American Federation of Teachers' Bill of Rights for Teachers should also be examined.

Professional Organizations

Membership and participation in professional organizations can help educators to continue their growth. In some areas of the world—for example, Canada—membership in the professional teachers' organization is required by law. In the United States, generally, freedom is accorded the teacher to join or not to join a professional organization.

Educational organizations may be classified by primary objective, such as the promotion of childhood education (Association of Childhood Education); by subject fields (the National Council of Teachers of Mathematics); by major function, such as the accrediting of schools (National Council for Accreditation of Teacher Education); by the significance of leaders in education (Horace Mann League or John Dewey Society); by academic level of institutions, such as elementary schools (Los Angeles Elementary Teachers Club or National Society of College Teachers of Education); by religious affiliation (National Catholic Education Association or Association of Hebrew Teachers Colleges in America); by labor affiliation (American Federation of Teachers); or by scope, such as geographical areas (Memphis Education Association, Illinois Education Association, or National Education Association). Because of their simplicity, the geographical classifications—(1) local, (2) state, (3) national, and (4) international—are utilized here as a framework for outlining the professional educational associations.

Local Organizations. Teachers are not organized in some communities, but nearly all public and private school teachers do belong to a state or national educational organization of some sort. Many belong to several. This banding together serves many purposes. The Association of Classroom Teachers of the NEA states that it is the peculiar function of local teachers' organizations to provide teachers with an opportunity to understand the problems of their respective communities and to acquaint the public in each community with the needs of its teachers and its schools. In the local education association is found the growing edge of the organized teaching profession. It is the unit of organization that has wielded powerful influence for improved conditions of employment through collective bargaining with local school boards.

State Organizations. Local units may be organized as parts of some larger whole, such as the county or state associations. Many of these are determined by fields, as social studies teachers; by grade levels, as elementary school teachers; or by function or personnel, as city superintendents. The main core of organized professional activity within the state, however, is the statewide, all-inclusive society, which is usually known as the state education association, state teachers' association, or state federation of teachers. The usual purpose of these organizations, as indicated in their state journals and as reflected in their activities, is to perform on a statewide basis what the local groups seek to do. There is a major emphasis on professional improvement of the members; the advancement of teacher and student welfare; service to the schools and communities in the state, particularly through legislation; and active cooperation with the associations of other states and national associations.

The state organizations exercise more influence on educational policy and practices than the local or national associations, probably because, under state systems of educational control, the most important decisions affecting education are made at the state level.

National Organizations—General. The *Educational Directory*, prepared periodically by the U.S. Office of Education, lists numerous educational organizations whose names begin with the word "National" or "American." All these and many others are nationwide in scope. Although most of them represent some special field, they are permeated with large elements of common interest. In recent years many national agencies have made critical analyses of particular aspects of American public education.

National Education Association. This national, all-inclusive educative organization is also the largest teachers' association in the world. It was organized in 1857 as the National Teachers Association. The name was changed to the National Education Association in 1907, when it was incorporated under a special act of Congress. By 1972 membership in the NEA had reached approximately 1.2 million.

In brief, its purposes are these:

The National Education Association is dedicated to the upbuilding of democratic civilization and is supported by the loyal cooperation of the leaders of the United States to advance the interests of the teaching profession, promote the welfare of children, and foster the education of all the people.

It renders two kinds of services. First come those services which reach the members directly, such as *Today's Education,* which has the largest circulation of all professional journals, and other publications, as well as conventions of the association, its departments, and allied organizations. These help to promote personal growth and educational research and to build up the common mind of the profession. The second type of service is indirect. Like the values which the citizen receives from his taxes, these benefits are often overlooked. An important function of the association is to develop a high level of public understanding of education and a desire for good schools. It aims to elevate the character and advance the interests of the teaching profession and to promote the cause of education in the United States. It is not, however, an agency of the federal government.

The National Education Association was once an all-inclusive voluntary organization of teachers and administrators in pre-elementary, elementary, secondary, higher, and adult education. However, collective bargaining by classroom teachers intensified cleavages between teachers and administrators, resulting in the withdrawal of principals and administrators' organizations from direct affiliation with the NEA to autonomous status only loosely associated with the NEA. This same development has been common in many state organizations.

Policies are determined by the representative assembly coming from all over the United States each summer in connection with the annual convention. This body consists of delegates elected by state and local organizations of teachers. The administration of the affairs of the association is handled by this representative assembly, a board of trustees, an executive committee, and a board of directors. The professional and clerical staffs, work-

ing under the direction of the executive secretary, are housed in the association's building at 1201 Sixteenth Street, N.W., Washington, D.C. The organization of the NEA is shown in Figure 12-2.

The NEA is an independent organization unaffiliated with labor unions. It favors professional negotiations as a means of improving the profession. It endorses the invoking of "sanctions" against school systems where professional negotiations are unsuccessful in obtaining better salaries and improved working conditions. In many instances it has also condoned strikes by teachers.

The story of this important national organization is told in *NEA: The First One Hundred Years,* published by the NEA and written by Edgar B. Wesley for the centennial celebration in 1957.

American Federation of Teachers. This national organization is affiliated with the AFL-CIO but is relatively autonomous with respect to its program and policy. The AFT contends that education has traditionally had its greatest support from organized labor and the affiliation with the AFL-CIO offers a strong power base for correcting the economic and political injustices from which education allegedly suffers. The federation has the following two main objectives:

1 To consolidate the teachers of the country into a strong group which would be able to protect its own interest.

2 To raise the standard of the teaching class by a direct attack on the conditions which, according to the federation, prevent teaching from reaching its desired status. Among these conditions are lack of academic freedom and civil liberty and the absence of self-determination of policy and of democratic control.

The story of the American Federation of Teachers is told in a publication by its Commission on Educational Reconstruction entitled *Organizing the Teaching Profession.* The official organs of the AFT are *The American Teacher* and *Changing Education.* The federation maintains standing committees on the following: academic freedom, democratic human relations, pensions and retirement, protection of teachers' rights, state federations, taxation and school finance, vocational education, working conditions, adult and workers' education, child care, and educational trends and policies. The American Federation of Teachers has drawn up a Bill of Rights for Teachers, as was mentioned on page 312.

The federation has launched a drive to unionize college professors. Administrators are not permitted membership in the AFT on the grounds that they represent management rather than labor in the classic cleavage between employer and employee. Many of the AFT locals and AFT membership are found in city school systems. The United Federation of Teachers, the New York City local, was the first teacher organization to win collective-bargaining rights in a large city school system. The membership of the American Federation of Teachers has been approximately one-fifth as large as that of the National Education Association. Although the American Federation of Teachers and the National Education Association are presently locked in a very competitive and sometimes acrimonious rivalry for

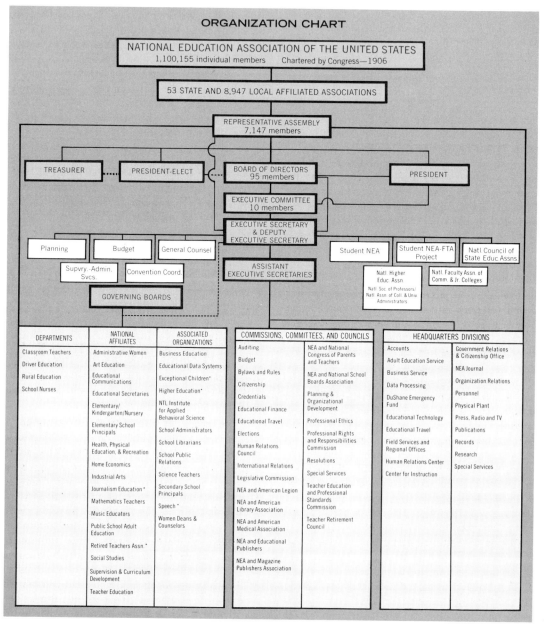

FIGURE 12-2 *Organization of the National Education Association. (National Education Association, "Organizational Chart," NEA Handbook, 1970–71, The Association, Washington, D.C., 1970, p. 18.)*

membership and support of the nation's teachers, there have been overtures toward the merger of the two organizations. This competition and the issues relevant to it are discussed in Chapter 1.

Organizations of Black Educators. Several organizations of educators, most notably the Black American Teachers Association and the National Association for Afro-American Education, bring together educators interested in strengthening educational opportunity for black people, improving professional opportunity for black teachers, and promoting black cultures and Afro-American studies.

National Catholic Education Association. Educators in Catholic schools and colleges commonly hold membership in the NCEA, founded in 1904. This organization maintains four regional offices and a headquarters in Washington, D.C. Through this association, Catholic educators meet for the exchange of ideas, interpret their efforts to the public, cooperate with other organizations, conduct research, and otherwise strengthen educational practice for Catholic parochial schools and colleges. The NCEA publishes the *National Catholic Education Association Bulletin.*

Other Religious Organizations. Most of the other major religious faiths, particularly those which operate church-related schools, also maintain educational associations for educators and others interested in sectarian education in their faith.

Professional Fraternities and Honor Societies. The *Education Directory of Education Associations,* published by the U.S. Office of Education, lists 158 national professional fraternities, honor societies, and recognition societies. The more prominent ones for educators are Kappa Delta Epsilon, Alpha Delta Kappa, and Pi Lambda Theta for women, and Phi Delta Kappa and Phi Sigma Pi for men.

International Organizations. As is indicated in Chapter 17, many organizations listed in the *Educational Directory* contain in their titles the word "World" or "International." The NEA has an active Committee on International Relations. Many countries were represented in the World Organization of the Teaching Profession, which was organized in Glasgow, Scotland, in 1947 and reorganized as the World Confederation of Organizations of the Teaching Profession in 1952 at Copenhagen. This organization has been recognized by the United Nations as an official consultative body.

TEACHING PERSONNEL

By far the largest number of educational workers are teachers. The major types of teaching personnel described here are (1) classroom teachers, (2) team teachers, (3) special classroom teachers, (4) teachers in federal jurisdictions and foreign countries, and (5) teachers of teachers. Other persons engaged in education work are discussed in Chapter 13.

Classroom Teachers

Although there are numerous private and parochial schools, the public school system affords the largest number of teaching positions. Classroom teachers are found in nearly all the institutions mentioned in Chapters 1 to 5, namely, international, national, state, county, and local systems. They work in all the academic levels considered in Chapters 6 to 10, namely, pre-elementary, elementary, secondary, and higher institutions, and in adult and continuing education.

Team Teachers

Teachers may be assigned to the same group of students for all or most of the school day, as in the self-contained classroom most commonly found in the elementary school, or to several classes in the same subject-matter field or group of fields, as in the departmentalized organization typically found in high schools and in a number of elementary schools. Both of these patterns of organization and their variations are described in Chapter 7.

Although this term "team teaching" is often used loosely to identify a wide variety of collaborative activity, essentially it means that several teachers—usually three to seven—are combined in an instructional team under the general direction of a team leader. The team may be organized vertically to include various subjects on one or two grade levels. The form is a flexible one, and it permits teaching teams to vary widely. Team teaching represents an effort to use the teacher's time and talents more effectively. The group arrangement permits each member of the team to specialize in some particular aspect of instruction and to give more time to planning, preparation, and evaluation. No longer isolated in the traditional classroom, teachers in teaching teams have more opportunity to see their colleagues at work and to improve their own skills in the process. During some of the school day one teacher may lecture to several combined classes, permitting other teachers to give more time to planning, study, counseling, remedial work, and other tasks.

Another pattern of collaborative teaching effort, differentiated staffing, has attracted considerable attention in recent years and promises to become an exciting trend. Figure 12-3 illustrates one model of differentiated staffing. This plan differentiates the assignment, responsibility, status, and salary of teachers on the basis of variations in their preparation, competence, experience, and interest in some form of collaborative group-teaching enterprise. It also commonly utilizes subprofessionals and nonprofessionals, such as teaching interns and teacher aides. These distinctions in assignment are usually accompanied by differentiation in rank, such as master teacher, senior teacher, staff teacher, associate teacher, teacher aide, resource-center aide, and lab assistant, as in the Temple City, California, prototype. Each position has a different salary range and educational requirements.

The advantages claimed for differentiated staffing include (1) more effective utilization of teaching talent, (2) differentiation of pay on the basis of responsibility and talent rather than lockstep advancement through years of experience, (3) encouragement of good teaching techniques, such as flexible scheduling, better match-up of learning resources with learners' needs, and better individualization of instruction, (4) more incentive for the advancement of good teachers within the ranks of teaching through much higher salaries and professional challenge for talented teachers.

Special Classroom Teachers

The special teachers are those who deal with (1) particular types of students, as the exceptional; (2) special methods or instructional media; (3) specialized subjects or fields, as vocational education; and (4) special institutions, as hospital schools. Two are discussed here.

Teachers of Special Students. Chapter 11 centers around the two major types of students, namely, the normal and the atypical. The former, because of their natural resourcefulness, ability, and ambition, may succeed in school and life despite their teachers; but the disadvantaged students may be further handicapped in a marked degree because their teachers are inefficient or not specially educated for their particular task. The atypical students, espe-

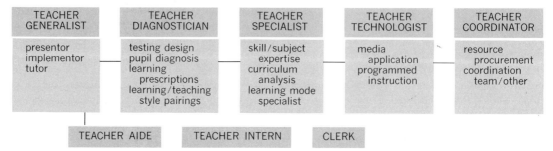

FIGURE 12-3 Models of differentiated staffing. (From Fenwick W. English, "Differentiated Staffing: Refinement, Reform, or Revolution?" ISR Journal, vol. 1, Fall, 1969, p. 229.)

cially those severely handicapped, need teachers expert in the special areas pertaining to the major types of exceptional students described in Chapter 11. The laws of most states stipulate that teachers of exceptional children must have specialized preparation and certificates.

In addition to special preparation, the teacher of handicapped children should have patience, a sympathetic and thorough understanding of the principles and facts of physical growth, buoyant optimism, and a healthy social philosophy. There is a shortage of teachers of handicapped students. To increase the supply of such teachers, however, the federal government has provided many generous scholarships for special education teachers. In view of the specialized preparation, the exacting nature of the task, and the special state aid for such children, the salaries of these special instructors are usually higher than those of the regular classroom teacher.

The National Teacher Corps has created a new type of educational specialist—the teacher of children from impoverished families. Heretofore, most teachers have preferred not to serve those who need them most, namely, children for whom learning is most difficult and unappealing. Many teachers have felt unprepared to teach children who are almost of another culture. The National Teacher Corps was created to recruit and prepare teachers for this task. A number of universities have developed special programs that prepare teachers and administrators to serve in slum schools. These programs are designed to help future educators understand the problems of children in such schools and accept the responsibility for helping those students who are, as someone has described them, "those 'other' Americans who are largely invisible to middle-class society." Teachers who are successful in this work must be endowed with wholesome attitudes toward people of minority races, a tolerance for vulgar language and unconventional behavior, the ability to be firm without being domineering or ingratiating, ingenuity in the fine art of pragmatic teaching, and, above all, an abundant respect for all human beings, however humble their origin. This is indeed a rigorous set of qualifications, but many returning Peace Corpsmen and Teacher Corpsmen have them, as do many other young students. Such teachers must be found because their task is the most compelling and the most difficult in the entire educational system—that of returning to the mainstream of American society, through education, those people who have been most alienated from it.

Teaching requires the desire and the ability to relate effectively to human beings.

Teachers in Special Schools. Thousands of teachers are employed in special schools, such as church and Bible schools, technical schools, correctional institutions, experimental centers, and hospital schools. The last are briefly mentioned here.

Some hospital schools are in private institutions, whereas others are in municipal or state hospitals. Such teaching renders three types of services: therapeutic, vocational, and general educational. It seems reasonable to expect that states will give increased financial and moral support to this type of teaching and that many positions will have to be filled in the years to come.

Teachers in Federal Jurisdictions and Foreign Countries

Many teachers are employed or supervised by the federal government. Many persons teach in the federal reservations and in the territories, dependencies, and special areas in and outside the United

States. In some of the dependencies, only natives or resident people are employed as teachers.

Many opportunities to teach away from home are provided by exchange teaching. Exchanges in teaching personnel are made between cities and between countries, usually for one-year periods. Information on reciprocity in teaching positions is available in *Teacher Exchange Opportunities*, which may be obtained from the U.S. Office of Education in Washington, D.C., and from the Institute of International Education in New York. Chapter 17 describes several of the opportunities for international teaching, including the Peace Corps.

Teachers of Teachers

Thousands of persons are engaged in teaching teachers, in state colleges, teachers colleges, and departments and schools of education in colleges and universities. Among the positions are those held by associate teachers or supervisors of student teachers and teaching interns in teacher-education institutions or in affiliated schools, and by members of the various departments in colleges and universities, especially in the education and psychology departments. Opportunities for this work are thus available on all academic levels, from preservice education of prospective nursery school teachers to in-service education of faculty members in graduate schools.

The Training of Teachers of Teachers, or Triple T programs, funded by the U.S. Office of Education, as the title suggests, concentrates attention on the in-service improvement of professors of education and liberal arts professors, media specialists, and public school people as trainers of student teachers and teacher interns. The emphasis of the Triple T programs is to encourage university faculties and public school faculties to join hands in bridging the gap between preservice and in-service education, between the universities and the public schools, between subject matter and method, between the professors of education and professors of academic disciplines, and between educational concepts and learning theory. These teachers of teachers are mastering many new techniques such as microteaching, which consists of subjecting samples of teaching behavior to videotape recording so that the teachers may review and analyze their performance in the light of good teaching theory and practice. The supreme challenge in teacher education lies in the unsurpassed opportunities to spread one's influence, since an instructor of prospective or regular teachers potentially reaches thousands of students.

FUTURE

Our view of the future is essentially optimistic. It is derived from projections of forces already under way in education. We believe that the prestige of the teacher in American society is rising and will continue to do so. Although Americans have always spoken of the importance they attach to education, their commitment to the educational enterprise and to teachers has not always reflected a deep concern. Finally our people have come to recognize that education is the fundamental vehicle of social, economic, and political progress. The nation is finally turning to education as the fountainhead of progress in dealing with the great problems of our times.

Many changes will continue to make the teacher's environment more satisfying. Imaginative architectural design and interior decorating will make school buildings more pleasant and comfortable for teachers as well as students. Flexibility in scheduling and programming will give teachers more control over the use of their time. New instructional methods, greater use of subprofessionals, and new plans of teacher utilization, such as differentiated staffing, will make the teacher more productive, give him more status, and relieve him of many of the more pedestrian tasks.

The nation's teaching force will become increasingly cosmopolitan. Heretofore the vast majority of our teachers have been drawn from the middle-class stratum of society. More young people from both the upper and the lower socioeconomic classes are entering teaching, stimulated in part by the appeal of antipoverty programs, civil rights movements, and the deeper sense of commitment and responsibility among young people. The proportion of male teachers will continue to rise. As racial discrimination recedes, school faculties will become increasingly multiracial. Thus the stereotype of the American teacher as the young, timid, unmarried, middle-class female is becoming obsolete, and the trend will be accelerated until school faculties reflect the same melting-pot character that we have commonly noted in student bodies. As a consequence of this, schools will never be the same. We hope that this more cosmopolitan teaching force will leaven the middle-class ethos of our schools and make them more acceptable to students from low-income families. Tomorrow's teacher will be more intelligent and better educated. This "new breed of professionals" is more self-assertive, more vigorous in the pursuit of full professional prerogatives, and more capable than any of its predecessors of doing a first-class job. Better trained, more self-confident, with stronger career commitment, and more conscious of their professional dignity, they will continue to press for full professional stature. Many boards of education and school administrators, once complacent about their cavalier treatment of acquiescent young female teachers, are encountering this new breed of teachers around the negotiation table. We believe that their drive toward fuller participation in the decisions affecting their work is long overdue in many communities. We hope that they will assume the responsibilities of the profession as readily as they do its privileges, and that teachers and boards of education will negotiate collectively in a more civilized manner than they currently do in many communities.

The proliferation of studies and experimentation in teacher education will inescapably bring fundamental improvement to the professional preparation of the teacher. The artificial line between preservice education and in-service education will become obscured. As has long been true in other professions, the responsibility for professional education in teaching will be shared increasingly by both the teacher-education institutions and school systems. Much more emphasis will be given to in-service education in the future. The theory of the college program and the realities of the public schools will be joined in teacher preparation and continuing professional development. The colleges and universities will work in closer relationship with the school systems in easing the new teacher gradually into full professional responsibility under the joint guidance of the professor of education and the school administrator.

The role of the teacher will become more highly specialized. The typical teacher of the future will not be viewed as the one and only purveyor of information for a self-contained group of students throughout the day. With increased use of team teaching, computer-assisted instruction, instructional technology, differentiated staffing, teacher aides, and a corps of school psychologists, counselors, remedial teachers, and other supporting specialists, the classroom teacher will concentrate his talents and energies more directly upon fewer and more discrete teaching tasks. With this increased specialization will come increased professional stature and remuneration. Differences in teaching rank, perhaps after the fashion long extant in colleges, will become more common in public schools.

The isolation of the teacher from society will be reduced. As schools are called upon to serve as instruments of social purpose, the interaction between schools and communities will be quickened. This trend is evident in the antipoverty programs, in which schools are forced to cooperate more fully with community agencies. This will reduce both the teacher's isolation and his autonomy. It will create frictions and dilemmas, but in the long run it should strengthen both school and community.

The organized teaching profession appears to be moving rapidly toward maturity. Many states have granted teacher organizations the right to negotiate with boards of education for improved conditions of work. The remaining states will rapidly follow this trend and thereby accelerate the attractiveness of the profession. An increasing number of states have enacted "professional practices acts" which grant to teacher organizations more legal power in defining competence, fitness, and professional conduct and in adjudicating alleged violations of professional standards and practices through professional standards boards. Thus the organized professional is gradually winning in various ways more autonomy and control of its destiny. Teaching has not yet reached full status as a learned profession, but the move is clearly in that direction.

These are some of the more important trends we see in the teaching profession. They will not occur overnight. Neither are they unmixed blessings. Without doubt they will be accompanied by cleavages and frustrations. Nevertheless, the long-term outlook is one of cautious optimism, we believe. In any event, these trends will quicken the sense of high adventure that will surely characterize the American teacher in the latter part of the twentieth

Teaching requires concern for the organized profession, as manifested by this teacher's participation in a meeting of the board of education.

century, as he occupies more fully than ever the real frontiers of social progress.

SHALL I TEACH?

Values and Satisfactions in Teaching

We all want to do those things which seem important to us, and we develop our own sets of values out of our experience; but each occupation, too, has its own set of inherent values which it tends to impose upon its workers. When these occupational values are compatible with our own values, we experience a sense of satisfaction and worthwhileness in our work. Through purposeful employment, then, one progresses toward his most valued goals in life, for work provides a major means to their realization. In searching for a career, then, one must ask: "What values and goals do I seek in life? What do I hope to achieve in life? In what occupation can I pursue my aspirations most effectively?" Let us consider some of the unique aspirations that can be realized through teaching.

Teaching offers singular opportunities for the realization of many important, intrinsic values in life. It enables—indeed requires—the teacher to engage in a never-ending pursuit of knowledge himself. The world of the teacher is a world of learning. The opportunity for self-education for those of insatiable intellectual curiosity is unmatched in any other profession. It is in the education of others that the teacher finds the secret of his own education. The teacher's role in educating others is becoming increasingly profound. We have traditionally thought of the teacher as a dispenser of information. Today he must be conceived as something far more than that. The knowledge explosion has forced upon us, fortunately, a new concept of the teacher. It is no longer possible to dispense during the school years all the knowledge that the student will need in his lifetime, so we have come to stress "learning how to learn" as the essence of modern education. Thus the new role of the teacher becomes that of stimulating the learner's curiosity, sharpening his powers of independent intellectual discovery, and strengthening his ability to organize and use knowledge on his own initiative—in short, helping the learner acquire lifelong powers of self-education.

The modern teacher has often been spoken of as an exemplar of fine scholarship, a model scholar whom students may emulate, the very embodiment of his discipline. This new role of the teacher as

exemplar, far more profound than his role as mere dispenser of information, extends the impact of the teacher on the modes of thought and methods of study of the student throughout his lifetime. Thus the teacher is sustained by the challenge of implanting this important intellectual vestige of himself in others. To help in guiding another generation's chance to grow is perhaps the noblest form of human expression. This is immortality beyond compare and is as near to having a share in eternity as one can come in this earthly setting. This is indeed a difficult task.

Many teachers are attracted by the intellectual challenge of the task. Others choose to become teachers because of their fondness for working with people in a very personal manner. This close interpersonal relationship is manifested in both heartaches and joys. The heartaches include the discouragement of trying to teach students who will not or cannot learn well, the futility of trying to overcome the deep scars that society has imposed upon some children, and the heavy toll on one's conscience imposed by this awesome responsibility for so many young lives.

People wish to be engaged in socially useful work. Throughout this book, we have stressed the paramount importance of teaching. There are people who believe that teaching is surpassed in importance by no other occupation.

Personal Qualities of Teachers

Throughout this chapter reference has been made to the personal qualities that teachers must have. Table 12-2 lists qualities of behavior which are effective in teaching and corresponding qualities which are ineffective. The World Confederation of Organizations of the Teaching Profession has summarized well the most essential qualities of the effective teacher:

The teacher must possess high personal qualities of an intellectual and ethical character. The teacher in his personal life as well as professional life must always be aware that he is a model for the pupils. The love of children, faith in his vocation, personal devotion and commitment are equally indispensable, as is courage in all difficult situations. Patience, intellectual curiosity, critical thinking and tolerance are also essential because the teacher must in his work respect the child in his charge and help him to develop his individuality. These qualities must be supported by good physical and mental balance, a sense of humor, and enthusiasm which will develop in the class a relaxed and peaceful climate of learning among the students.

TABLE 12-2   *GENERALIZED DESCRIPTIONS OF CRITICAL BEHAVIORS OF TEACHERS*

Effective behaviors	Ineffective behaviors
Is alert, appears enthusiastic	Is apathetic, dull; appears bored
Appears interested in students and classroom activities	Appears uninterested in pupils and classroom activities
Is cheerful, optimistic	Is depressed, pessimistic; appears unhappy
Is self-controlled, not easily upset	Loses temper easily, is easily upset
Likes fun, has a sense of humor	Is overly serious, too occupied for humor
Recognizes and admits own mistakes	Is unaware of, or fails to admit, own mistakes
Is fair, impartial, and objective in treatment of students	Is unfair or partial in dealing with students
Is patient	Is impatient
Shows understanding and sympathy in working with students	Is short with students, uses sarcastic remarks, or in other ways shows lack of sympathy with students
Is friendly and courteous in relations with students	Is aloof and removed in relations with students
Helps students with personal as well as educational problems	Seems unaware of students' personal needs and problems
Commends effort and gives praise for work well done	Does not commend students; is disapproving, hypercritical
Accepts students' efforts as sincere	Is suspicious of students' motives
Anticipates reactions of others in social situations	Does not anticipate reactions of others in social situations
Encourages students to try to do their best	Makes no effort to encourage students to try to do their best
Classroom procedure is planned and well organized	Procedure is without plan, disorganized
Classroom procedure is flexible within overall plan	Shows extreme rigidity of procedure, inability to depart from plan
Anticipates individual needs	Fails to provide for individual differences and needs of students
Stimulates students through interesting and original materials and techniques	Uninteresting materials and teaching techniques used
Gives clear, practical demonstrations and explanations	Demonstrations and explanations are not clear and are poorly conducted
Is clear and thorough in giving directions	Directions are incomplete, vague
Encourages students to work through their own problems and evaluate their accomplishments	Fails to give students opportunity to work out their own problems or evaluate their own work
Disciplines in quiet, dignified, and positive manner	Reprimands at length, ridicules, resorts to cruel or meaningless forms of correction
Gives help willingly	Fails to give help or gives it grudgingly
Foresees and attempts to resolve potential difficulties	Is unable to foresee and resolve potential difficulties

SOURCE: David G. Ryans, *Characteristics of Teachers,* American Council for Education, Washington, D.C., 1960, p. 82.

These are noble qualifications for the exemplary teacher. James Russell Lowell recognized the importance of nobility in the exemplar when he wrote:

Be noble, and that nobleness that lies
In other men, sleeping but never dead,
Shall rise in majesty to meet thine own.

SUMMARY

The professionalization of teaching is little more than a century old. The more important milestones in this development are listed in the historical calendar in this chapter. During its development, teaching progressed from a primitive, relatively unskilled trade to an occupation requiring vocational training and finally to a profession demanding thorough, specialized preparation.

The growth and development of our schools were handicapped until the 1970s by a serious shortage of qualified teachers, which resulted from rising school enrollments and disadvantageous income and conditions of work. Within the last decade

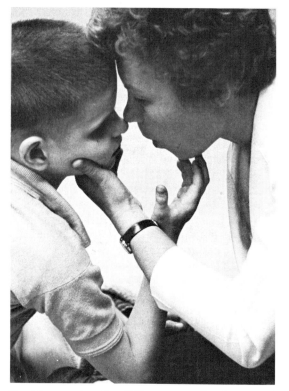

Teaching requires the abiding concern for the cares of individual children.

the lot of the teacher has improved greatly, largely through the militant actions of teachers themselves, who have forced boards of education to join them at the bargaining table in bilateral determination of salaries and conditions of work. With these successes the profession has become more attractive. Many more persons have entered and remained in teaching, and the supply of teachers has now exceeded the demand.

Teacher education has been subject to intensive criticism and study in recent years and is presently undergoing substantial redevelopment in many institutions. The four components of the teacher's education are general education, specialized education in his teaching fields, professional education, and student teaching. There is wide variety among teacher-education institutions in terms of the relative importance attached to each component and the manner in which each is structured into the preparation programs. There is a distinct trend toward elevation of the level of teacher preparation through more stringent certification requirements.

The preparation of the teacher is viewed increasingly as a continuous process that extends throughout his tenure, with preservice preparation and in-service education increasingly merged.

The induction of teachers into employment has not generally been well handled, as evidenced by the extraordinarily large number of teachers who drop out of teaching after a few years of service. Many schools are attempting to improve their programs of orientation and supervision to provide more help and encouragement for new teachers.

Supervision of teaching is changing gradually from an inspectorial type of quality control to a more cooperative, nondirective, supportive, problem-centered approach that seeks to further the teacher's self-improvement. Many more resources are being made available to encourage the continued professional development of the teacher, which becomes increasingly imperative because of the rapid development of curriculums and methodology.

The economic position of teachers has improved rather substantially during the past decade. Fringe benefits, such as leaves of absence, sick leaves, life and health insurance programs, and retirement provisions are being improved as schools seek to compete with other occupations in recruiting educated manpower.

There is a wide proliferation of associations for teachers at the local, state, and national levels. The greatest proportion of teachers hold membership in state associations, most of which are affiliates of the National Education Association, which enrolls approximately five times as many members as its rival, American Federation of Teachers. These two organizations are presently engaged in a highly competitive drive for ascendancy in the representation of teachers.

Although the vast majority of teachers are assigned to individual classes, the deployment of teachers is changing through the increased use of team teaching and differentiated staffing. The number of teachers of special classes and special subjects and in special schools is increasing. Particular emphasis is being given to the recruitment and preparation of teachers of children from low-income families.

It is likely that the nation's teaching force will enjoy greater remuneration in the future as the nation commits its resources more fully to the important task of strengthening education. The teaching force will become increasingly cosmopolitan as more persons from upper and lower socioeconomic classes, from minority races, and from upper age groups enter teaching. The professional competency of the teaching force will be strengthened as better persons are attracted to the profession, as the quality of teacher-education programs is upgraded, and as in-service development resources are improved. The outlook for teaching as an attractive profession is optimistic. It is to be hoped that the profound challenge of teaching as an occupation of great social consequence, of increasing financial reward, of greater self-realization will attract more young men and women of keen mind and warm heart who see in teaching the most promising avenue for the improvement of the human condition.

Suggested Activities

1. Study the literature on differentiated staffing and prepare a report which summarizes its essential elements and the advantages which are claimed for it.

2. Prepare a report on "What It Takes to Teach Poor Children."

3. Read Bel Kaufman's Up the Down Staircase *and summarize the major lessons which it holds for teachers.*

4. Review reports of studies of first-year teachers and of teacher dropouts and summarize in order of importance those reasons which appear to explain teachers' disenchantment with their teaching positions.

5. Prepare a set of specifications derived from your reading of this chapter against which you might evaluate a school system in which you are considering employment.

6. Make a critical self-evaluation to determine whether you should enter or remain in the teaching profession.

7. Study an NEA report of teacher supply and demand and make a report on those fields which are most undercrowded and most overcrowded.

8. Summarize the changes that have taken place in the teacher-education program of your college or university in the last decade.

9. Review the research on teacher evaluation and teacher selection and summarize your findings.

10. Describe the best elementary or secondary school teacher you know.

Bibliography

American Association of Colleges for Teacher Education: *Teachers for the Real World*, Washington, D.C., 1969. Argument for radical reform of education—the nature of schooling process, systems which control educational policy, and institutions which prepare teachers.

Carlton, Patrick, and Harold I. Goodwin: *The Collective Dilemma: Negotiations in Education*, Charles A. Jones Publishing Company, Worthington, Ohio, 1969, parts I and II. A book of readings on the range of issues relating to collective bargaining in education.

Ebel, Robert L. (ed.): *Encyclopedia of Educational Research*. The Macmillan Co. of Canada, Limited, Toronto, 1969, pp. 1–7, 154–159, 330–342, 353–354, 488–494, 1005–1008, 1008–1016, 1376–1384, 1410–1443. A comprehensive review of research on academic freedom, college faculty characteristics, economic status, professional organizations, education certification, and the effectiveness and roles of teachers.

Elam, Stanley (ed.): *Improving Teacher Education in the United States*, Phi Delta Kappa, Bloomington, Ind., 1967. An anthology of papers by leading educators recommending reforms in teacher education.

National Education Association, National Commission on Teacher Education and Professional Standards: *The Teacher and His Staff*, National Education Association, Washington, D.C., 1969. A symposium of statements on the future roles of the teacher and the supporting staffs for classroom teachers.

National Education Association, Research Division: *Economic Status of the Teaching Profession*, National Education Association, Washington, D.C., 1972. This annual publication reviews the salaries paid and scheduled in public schools, colleges, and universities and compares them with income in comparable occupations and with prices and family budgets.

———: *Teacher Supply and Demand in the Public Schools: 1972*, National Education Association, Washington, D.C., 1972. A report of an annual study of teacher supply and demand by grade levels, subjects, and geographic regions.

Postman, Neil, and Charles Weingartner: *Teaching as a Subversive Activity*, Delacorte Press, Dell Publishing Co., Inc., New York, 1969. Plea for inquiry and iconoclasm rather than lecture, exhortation, and recitation in the classroom.

Rousculp, Charles G.: *Chalk Dust on My Shoulder*, Charles E. Merrill Books, Inc., Columbus, Ohio, 1969. Warm and witty description of the rewards and frustrations of teaching by a teacher with twenty years of experience.

Stinnett, T. M. (ed.): *The Teacher Dropout*, Peacock Publishers, Ithaca, N.Y., 1970. Exposition of the causes and cures of teacher dropouts.

Stinnett, T. M.: *Turmoil in Teaching*, The Macmillan Company, New York, 1968. A history of the struggle between the NEA and the AFT in the organization of the teaching profession.

Chapter 13   Other Educational Personnel

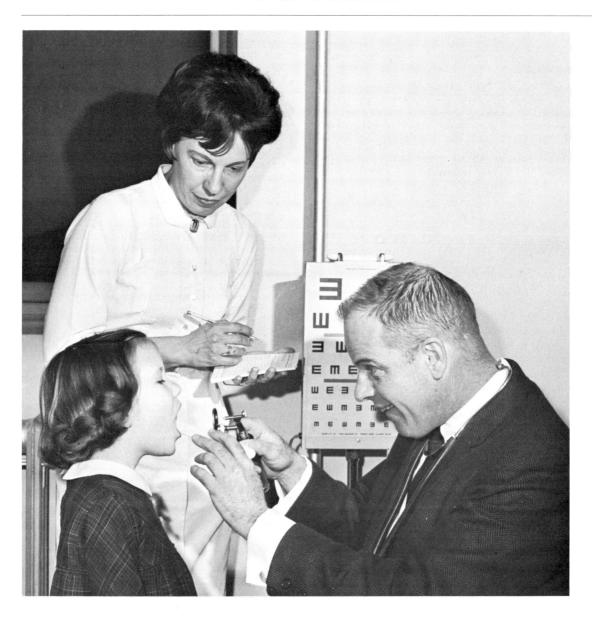

ORIENTATION

Ombudsman (ahm-BOODS-mahn). This Swedish word signifies "agent," "deputy," or "representative." This office, which had its origin in Sweden in the year the American nation was founded, was modified in 1809 when the Swedish Crown appointed an officer, known as the *Justitie Ombudsman*, who received citizens' complaints against royal officials.

In the United States recent years have witnessed many proposals for creating an office akin to that of the Swedish ombudsman. Hawaii was the first state government to adopt the plan. Several large cities and some counties have adopted measures for institutionalizing the handling of complaints. As indicated in the research report *The Ombudsman in Education*,[1] very few elementary and secondary schools have ombudsmen. However, several colleges and universities have created the office of ombudsman, or an intermediary post similar to it, for employees and students. The President's Commission on Campus Unrest, under the chairmanship of William W. Scranton, former governor of Pennsylvania, in its 1970 report, underlined "the crisis of understanding" as the underlying cause of campus unrest. The potentialities of campus ombudsmen are being explored on many campuses today. The work of the ombudsman is one of the newer fields open to those who wish to serve society in the widening spectrum of education.

[1]Educational Research Service, *The Ombudsman in Education*, National Education Association, Washington, D.C., 1970.

Many professions contribute their services to the modern school program.

Other Educational Personnel. A study financed by the Carnegie Corporation and reported in 1970 by Charles E. Silberman was not delimited to classroom teachers per se. For many positions of significance, classroom teaching is a prerequisite, but many persons in educational work are not directly engaged in full-time teaching. As stated by Silberman:

If our concern is with education, we cannot restrict our attention to the schools and colleges, for education is not synonymous with schooling. Children and adults learn outside as well as—perhaps more than—in school. To say this is not to denigrate the public schools. . . . Nor is it to denigrate the colleges and universities, which for different reasons occupy a position of great and growing importance. It is simply to give proper weight to all the other educating institutions in American society: television, films, and the mass media; churches and synagogues; the law, medicine, and social work; museums and libraries; the armed forces, corporate training programs, boy scout troops.[2]

No one can overestimate the importance of the teacher in the classroom, but neither should he ignore or forget the million and more other educational workers in the United States. They are contributing members of a supportive, differentiated, and auxiliary staff in and outside schools and colleges.

Supportive, Differentiated, and Auxiliary Staff. The supportive staff assists and reinforces the work of the classroom teacher. Teaching is no longer a "one-man job." The processes in teaching and learning call for many specialists and generalists. The supportive staff usually consists of: certificated educators, professional noneducators, paraprofessionals, and others. To the question "Why should

[2]Charles E. Silberman, *Crisis in the Classroom*, Random House, Inc., New York, 1970, p. 5.

the classroom teacher have a supportive staff?" the Association of Classroom Teachers answers:

Learning experiences of children are enhanced.
Teacher effectiveness is enhanced.
Services of administrative and supervisory school personnel are enhanced.
Professional prestige of the classroom is enhanced.
Teacher retention and recruitment are enhanced.
The public image of the school is enhanced."[3]

Related to the concept and practice of supportive members is that of differentiated staffing. This, too, is an outgrowth of team teaching. The National Commission on Teacher Education and Professional Standards (NCTEPS), a prime mover in promoting differentiated staffing, defines it as follows:

Differentiated staffing is a plan for recruitment, preparation, induction, and continuing education of staff personnel for the schools that would bring a much broader range of manpower to education than is now available. Such arrangements might facilitate individual professional development to prepare for increased expertise and responsibility as teachers, which would lead to increased satisfaction, status and material reward.[4]

The professional power of a school staff can be multiplied by uniting in the diversification of duties. However, there are many arguments pro and con in regard to differentiated staff.

There are many patterns or models that schools use in implementing the concept of differentiated staffing. The Temple City Unified School District (California) uses a technostructure that places major emphasis upon: (1) teaching, (2) curricular, and (3) organizational responsibilities, as the modes of differentiation, with secondary emphasis on (4) learning theories as a base of diversification.[5] One differentiated staffing model depicts: (1) master teacher, (2) teacher instructors, (3) noncredentialed instructional and technical assistants, with (4) a supportive staff of specialists, such as those dealing with curriculum, media, logistics, guidance, testing, and research.[6] Organizational models for differentiated staffing are often tailor-made to fit the local school system. Whatever the pattern for providing maximum benefits for pupils, many interesting and challenging positions are opening for those who want to support the educational process in differentiated roles. One of the growing fields for auxiliary staff is that of teacher aides, described later in this chapter.

Recruitment and Placement of Personnel in Education. The search for talent in educational work has to be broadened. More persons of ability should be recruited from minority groups for service in teaching and nonteaching positions. Some progress has been made in recent years.

More Negroes are being appointed or elected to responsible positions in American education and allied fields. For example, in the state of Michigan, the State Board of Trustees of Michigan State University appointed Clifton Wharton, Jr., as the first Negro president of a major American university. In the same state John W. Porter became the first black State Superintendent of Education when he was selected unanimously by the State Board of Education. An Indian has been appointed Chief of the U.S. Bureau of Indian Affairs, which aids in the education of the descendants of "the first Americans." "Viva la Raza," "the silent minority," is finding its voice in seeking educational positions for Latin-Americans. Increasingly the recruitment and placement of personnel in teaching and nonteaching positions are crossing the barriers of color.

The barrier of sex is one being torn down too in the 1970s:

Women, the largest group of minority workers, are actively seeking to reduce the inequities in opportunities for career development. New organizations . . . are being established to deal with opportunity for equal employment. During the 1960 decade the racial attitudes of Americans have been examined. Now is the time for us to examine our attitudes toward women.[7]

The National Education Association has urged the congressional adoption of an "equal rights for women" amendment to the United States Consti-

[3] Association of Classroom Teachers, *The Classroom Teacher Speaks on His Supportive Staff*, National Education Association, Washington, D.C., 1967, p. 16.

[4] *Education USA, Differentiated Staffing in Schools*, National School Public Relations Association, Washington, D.C., 1970, p. 1.

[5] Fenwick English, "The Differentiated Staff: Education's Technostructure," *Educational Technology*, vol. 10, pp. 24-27, February, 1970.

[6] James L. Olivero, "The Meaning and Application of Differentiated Staffing in Teaching," *Phi Delta Kappan*, vol. 52, pp. 36-40, September, 1970.

[7] Lorraine Eyde, "Eliminating Barriers to Career Development of Women," *Personnel and Guidance Journal*, vol. 49, p. 25, September, 1970.

tution and an end to a "consistent pattern" of discrimination against women by school boards. Efforts are being made to increase the number of women in local, county, state, and federal administrative positions in education. Nonteaching as well as teaching appointments should be made defensible on the bases of personal and professional qualifications rather than sex or color. The central concern in the placement of all educational personnel ought to be the individual student to whom the members of a differentiated staff relate effectively in school and in society.

Unfortunately, the emphasis in recruitment of personnel has been unbalanced, limited to the customary and established positions for classroom teachers; the wide range of educational activities in which careers have been established or are now emerging has not been revealed. This has tended to inhibit social progress and to drive away from educational service many talented persons.

Several hundred different positions are now found in education. Approximately fifty types of educational work are mentioned briefly in this chapter. Teaching personnel, especially classroom teachers, are described in Chapter 12. The pages that follow in this chapter are concerned primarily with persons engaged in educational work other than full-time classroom teaching: part-time teachers and semiteachers, administrators and supervisors, personnel from other professions, other nonteaching personnel, and unpaid personnel.

PART-TIME TEACHERS AND SEMITEACHERS

Thousands of educational workers in the supportive staff do not devote a full school year or their entire time to teaching. Those who are not administrators may be grouped in three categories, namely, (1) part-time teachers, (2) personnel workers, and (3) other specialists. Various persons within these groups are described briefly.

Part-time Teachers

Substitute Teachers. Work opportunities for many persons, particularly married women, are afforded by part-time instruction in the form of substitute teaching. Occasional teachers should be carefully chosen according to definite standards. The fact that an unemployed person who taught twenty years ago

needs a few dollars should not be the sole basis for selection. The candidate for substitute teaching is usually required to fill out and file with the superintendent of schools an application blank giving data as to education, ability, past experience, and certification. The applicant is also subject to an oral interview before being placed on the eligibility list. Adequate preparation is essential, since in one day a poor substitute may undo a week's work of the regular teacher. Research studies indicate that the typical substitute teaches extensively in subjects and grades not authorized by his certificate. Hence a large number of qualified teachers should be on the school's substitute roster.

Other Part-time Teachers. Others who give a portion of their time to instruction include special teachers employed for only a part of a day or week on a regular schedule. For example, a special music teacher may work a few hours daily; in college, a specialist from the business world may teach an economics class, or an expert surgeon may serve part time as a special lecturer in certain aspects of surgery. Teaching provides part-time employment for many persons.

Many married and unmarried mature women are entering or returning to teaching or other educational positions—part time. A national organization, Catalyst, based in New York City and founded in 1962, seeks ways in which mature women can combine family responsibilities with work in positions that match their abilities. Catalyst's most outstanding achievement is in placing mature women in part-time positions in education. For example, in some schools two teachers share a single full-time position, one working the morning session and the other the afternoon. Studies such as *Part-Time Teachers and Their Work* indicate that teachers who work part of the day meet with wide acceptance among pupils, parents, and community. Despite the current surplus of teachers in certain fields, there is still a dearth of well-qualified instructors in specific areas, where part-time teachers can render distinctive services in all levels of education.

Personnel Workers

This chapter and the two preceding deal with personnel in American education, including students, teachers, and other workers. Obviously, many employees are especially delegated to tasks concerned almost entirely with the human or personal agents in education. This very important group, segregated here as personnel workers, includes (1) directors of certificated and classified personnel, (2) visiting teachers or counselors, (3) attendance personnel, (4) guidance personnel, (5) placement personnel, (6) directors of student personnel, (7) deans of boys and men, (8) deans of girls and women, (9) international advisers, and (10) recreational leaders. These groups are singled out from a larger number for special emphasis in the succeeding pages.

Directors of Certificated and Classified Personnel. One of the newer positions in education is that of director or assistant in charge of certificated workers, such as teachers, and of classified personnel, such as custodians. The increase in the size of school systems and colleges and the development of the concept that human resources are of extreme importance in education have led to the employment of a director of adult personnel.

Among the many duties usually assigned to the director of personnel are these: preparing job descriptions, recruiting the best human resources, conducting the preliminary interviews, administering tests, recommending employment, establishing employment conditions conducive to growth and efficiency, orienting new staff, compiling cumulative personnel data, and assisting in preparing staff communication media.

Home and School Visitor. The home and school visitor is a vital part of today's complex educational system. He is a professional social worker whose job is to act as a liaison between the school and the homes of children with problems. He aids the school in selecting the proper type of class and educational program for the child, and he helps the members of the family in their efforts to solve the problems connected with the child. A home and school visitor may encounter problems in the areas of medicine, vocational rehabilitation, retardation, emotional disturbance, crisis situations, and problem behavior in the school.

Attendance Personnel. Among the employees of the school district are full-time or part-time census enumerators and attendance officials. Sometimes the same person, who may also be engaged in teaching, performs the duties of both. In earlier days these employees were called "truant officers." Current practice favors a title such as "attendance worker," since it emphasizes the positive philosophy of improving the attendance of all pupils rather than the negative and often temporary remedy. The modern objective implies the willingness of school authorities to adjust the program to the student's peculiar needs, interests, and abilities. It also suggests the importance of discovering and correcting, as much as possible, the causes of nonattendance.

Guidance Personnel. Marked improvement in school attendance results from the adoption of guidance programs. Many persons are employed in this work, which involves studying an individual; learning his capacities, needs, and interests; guiding his efforts; and then seeing him through until he obtains a position and succeeds in it. Guidance ought to be systematic and functional so that students will not make important educational decisions, vocational choices, and life adjustments on the basis of mere guesses, false assumptions, or meager information.

The American Psychological Association has recognized three different levels at which counselors function. On the first level are part-time counselors, who carry on some counseling in connection with their other duties in schools, industries, churches, or social agencies. On the second level are psychological counselors, who must have the equivalent of two years of graduate training and probably a master's degree. On the third level are counselor-psychologists, who would be expected to have completed a longer period of graduate work leading to a doctor's degree. Workers at most levels are desperately needed today.

One type of specialized counseling is vocational counseling, which has been defined as the process of assisting the individual to choose an occupation, prepare for it, enter it, progress in it, and retire from it. The work of the vocational counselor is outlined by the National Vocational Guidance Association, which lists the following specialized activities: study of the individual through interviews, school records, questionnaires, examination and tests, and employment records; study of occupations through surveys and compilations of literature; interviews with groups and individuals; employment certification and placement; follow-up services; and related activities, such as club work.

A guidance position of growing importance in the elementary schools is that of "instructional diagnostician," who combines the functions of counseling, diagnosis, prescription, instruction, and evaluation.

Instant telephone counseling for troubled teen-agers is available continuously from some guidance centers for students who want help with personal problems and "hang-ups" of all kinds.

A growing area of counseling is occasioned by the "open-door policy," the "liberal admission programs," or both, of colleges and universities. The marked increase in community colleges with an open-door policy and the direct admission of community college graduates into many institutions of further education demand vanguard counselors who relate students to the broader and higher horizons of continuing educational opportunity.

Increasing national attention to educational and personal guidance has been stimulated by Congressional appropriations. For example, the National Defense Education Act, the Elementary and Secondary Education Act, and their revisions and extensions have helped improve and expand the preparation and in-service education of guidance personnel at all educational levels.

Placement Personnel. Junior placement or employment for youth is becoming an increasing responsibility of the schools. In many cities the junior consultation service for out-of-school youth is also sponsored by the public schools. All placement workers have certain basic duties, whether they perform them in a school, social service agency, or state employment service. The duties include analyzing jobs, registering and interviewing applicants, classifying registrants, receiving employers' orders, selecting and referring applicants to prospective employers, verifying placement, following up the employees, doing field work to contact employers, keeping records, preparing reports and statistical data, and continuously evaluating.

The placement worker's stock-in-trade is information about the world of work. Furthermore, he has to establish numerous contacts with school staff members, parents, school psychologists, employers, and community agencies. He must have as varied an occupational background as possible, with prolonged training and education in the same disciplines that are required of other professional personnel who are dealing with human beings in their individual and social adjustments.

The National Advisory Council on Vocational Education, noting that colleges and universities have operated placement offices for years, laments the fact that very few secondary schools have employ-

ment offices. The Council states that high school placement offices "must become universal." The task of placement personnel at all educational levels is being increasingly recognized as a necessary one, and placement work is coming to be regarded as a challenging career that requires standards, certification, and supervised internship.

Directors of Student Personnel. In some large school systems and in many universities, there are directors in charge of the overall relations among and with all the students. This position may be in lieu of, or supplemented by, those of dean of boys and dean of girls.

Deans of Boys and Men. Many counselors for male students are called "deans of boys" in the high schools and "deans of men" in the colleges. In the secondary school, some titles are "dean of boys," "vice-principal," "assistant principal," "administrative assistant," "boys' adviser," "boys' counselor," "director of guidance," "coordinator," "class adviser," and "guidance teacher."

The outstanding qualifications for deans in secondary schools are special training in guidance; a knowledge of adolescent physiology and psychology; a liking for, and sympathetic understanding of, teen-age boys and their problems and possibilities; the ability to aid in the solution of individual problems; the art of inspiring confidence and respect; and plenty of patience. Usually a master's degree is required. Among the responsibilities are attendance problems, vocational guidance, curriculum development, discipline, food and clothing for needy students, interviews with parents and prospective employers, supervision of leisure-time activities, and individual counseling.

Deans of men are found in most colleges and universities. Paramount among their many duties is that of counseling. The National Association of Student Personnel Administrators is one of the many professional organizations.

Deans of Girls and Women. The guidance of students is sometimes assigned to people of their own sex. Obviously, the administrative and supervisory responsibilities of the position vary with the size and type of school. The qualifications for deans of girls and women are similar to those for deans of boys and men. Deans of girls and women have a national association, which is a department of the National

Education Association. This National Association of Women Deans and Counselors holds annual meetings.

The tasks of deans of women and of men have become increasingly difficult but also important in these days of student activism and of changed mores in and out of dormitories and on and off the campus.

International Advisers. As indicated in Chapter 17, there is a great increase in the number of foreign students and teachers coming to the United States and of American learners going overseas, and many universities have added the position of counselor, director, or dean of international services. The duties of most of these international advisers fall in the category of personnel services. In addition to the regular personnel functions performed for all students, this advising service provides immigration information, community contacts, curriculum counseling, special sight-seeing trips, and assistance in language problems. The international advisers also assist American students and staff going overseas. Several universities have launched a program for the preparation of so-called "foreign-student advisers." Interest in exchanging ideas on the international exchange of persons, and a nationwide desire to improve international advising, led in 1948 to the establishment of the American Association of Foreign Student Advisers.

Recreational Leaders. The inextricable relationship between recreation and education is evidenced in the similarity of their objectives. In many communities, school authorities have incorporated play and leisure-time activities into the program at preschool, in-school, and postschool levels. The practice of providing for community recreation as part of a broad educational program is growing. Many communities have recreation in conjunction with school services. Although most communities do not supply the recreational-educational workers, the joint programs are steadily increasing in number.

Other Specialists with Semiteaching Duties

Among the many specialists engaged in semiteaching are those in the fields of (1) curriculum,

(2) technology, (3) multimedia education, (4) radio and television, (5) research, and (6) public relations.

Curriculum Personnel. Several state departments and institutions of higher learning and many city school systems employ persons especially trained in curriculum procedures. Such a worker is usually designated as "director of curriculum," "assistant superintendent in charge of the curriculum," "curriculum coordinator," or "director of surveys." The advent of team teaching has created such new posts as those of team-teaching leader, team curriculum specialists, and team supervisor.

Educational Technologists. The new technology in education described in Chapter 15 affects the curriculum personnel and the teachers and creates a number of new educational specialists. The Commission on Educational Technology in its 1970 report to the President and the Congress of the United States writes:

Technology can achieve its fullest potential in schools and colleges only with technical and paraprofessional support—"media coordinators" serving as advisors on the use of instructional technology, experts on the production and procurement of instructional materials, plus specialists in many different disciplines working with teachers in research and development.[8]

More specifically the following are some of the positions that are and will be necessary to implement the new educational technology:

Many school systems will probably need an "educational engineer" to supervise and to coordinate the work of the communication specialists. Ideally, the educational engineer will have general knowledge of technical aspects of communication engineering and general professional knowledge of instruction. . . .

The installation of computers will require the employment of programmers—people who can talk to the computers. . . . The programmers' skill will be narrow but precise and important, and will require a moderately high intellectual level.

Their work will be supervised by specialists in computer-assisted instruction who are capable of linking computer capabilities with the problems of curriculum and instruction. These specialists will articulate the work of technicians and teachers and will themselves be experts in both technology and pedagogy.

The most sophisticated specialization to emerge from educational technology may be that of "systems analyst."

[8]Commission on Instructional Technology, *To Improve Learning,* Government Printing Office, Washington, D.C., 1970, p. 57.

The position of system analyst has no precursor in public school organizations. . . . Its incumbent will sit at the nexus of communication and the locus of decision making in the school system. He will bring an intellectual discipline to decision making. . . . The present short supply of systems analysts is jeopardizing the full and rapid application of systems theory to educational administration.[9]

The periodical *Educational Technology* and other technical and educational publications detail the job descriptions of many specialists and paraprofessionals in this fertile field of the future. It is significant that the NEA Department of Audiovisual Instruction has changed its name to the Association for Educational Communications and Technology. The first National Educational Technological Conference was held in 1971. In 1973 is scheduled the completion in Chicago of the thirty-four-story Educational Facilities Center, where educators and laymen can see and touch teaching tools designed and used by educational technologists.

Multimedia Managers. An important field related to educational technology is audiovisual education. This field has expanded so widely that the audiovisual director of yesteryear is becoming a manager of multimedia machines and materials. While the chief accent of this director is still on audiovisual aids, such as slides, filmstrips, motion pictures, radio, and television, he recommends the purchase and use of many other multisensory aids, including tactile teaching tools, such as charts made by students and teachers, and teaching machines. He is a specialist in the instructional materials of the curriculum and sees equipment and materials as teaching-learning tools—means for the achievement of the ends of education. This specialist is also known as the "coordinator of instructional materials" or "the director of the instructional materials center," encompassing all instructional media. This function is also assumed in many schools by the librarian whose training has been expanded to that of media manager.

Radio and Television Specialists. The technical fields of radio and television are given special attention here because these two mass-communication media are also teaching tools with a promising

[9]AASA Committee on Technology and Instruction, *Instructional Technology and the School Administrator,* American Association of School Administrators, Washington, D.C., 1970, pp. 135-136.

future. Many radio stations on and off the campuses have full-time or part-time educational program directors and producers.

Educational television (ETV), directed primarily toward the home, and instructional television (ITV), slanted to the classroom, represent major innovations. As finances and facilities increase, and as programs improve, there will be great demand for instructional and educational television specialists in schools and colleges.

Research, Development, and Diffusion Workers. Early school administrators were guided primarily by guess, intuition, and practical experience earned often by dint of trial and error. Today, federal, state, county, and local educational divisions and other agencies ferret out pressing problems, subject them to research, develop programs based on their findings, and then diffuse the results to others.

Many persons are engaged in research, full-time or part-time, under the auspices of the U.S. Office of Education. In 1969 its Bureau of Research became the National Center for Educational Research and Development. The Elementary and Secondary Education Act of 1965 markedly changed the characteristics of federally sponsored educational research and coupled it with development and diffusion, in the new "Research, Development, and Diffusion" (R, D, and D) program. A projection of educational R, D, and D manpower needs indicates that:

ESEA-created agencies (e.g., educational laboratories, ERIC clearing houses, Title III centers, R and D centers) are creating a demand for new types of R, D, and D professionals in sizeable quantities. . . . A changing employment pattern will establish education R, D, and D as fields which require full-time career commitment. Program staff will commit themselves to new career lines, to a continuing avenue of investigation or endeavor, and to a particular location or team for an extended period. Project staff carry on their R, D, and D work as an activity ancillary to their permanent career line (e.g., instruction), as a discrete activity of definite duration (e.g., 18 or 24 months), and are often able to move themselves and their project to a different location.[10]

It is estimated that more than two thousand research workers, full-time or two-thirds-time, will be em-

[10]John E. Hopkins, "Educational R, D, and D: Manpower Projections and a Proposal," *Phi Delta Kappan,* vol. 50, p. 584, June, 1969.

ployed on programs by the U.S. Office of Education alone. It is also projected that fifty thousand educational research workers will be needed in the United States as a whole. Relatedly, the Research and Policy Committee of the Committee for Economic Development has recommended that a Commission of Research, Innovation, and Evaluation be established under a charter by the Congress as an independent, nongovernmental agency, empowered to receive both public and private funds.[11] Such a proposal, if implemented, would require several thousand more research workers and supportive staff.

The departments of education in the fifty states and territories are employing an increasing number of research workers, statisticians, computer operators, writers, and other related personnel dedicated to the advancement of education through research, development, and diffusion. The more than three thousand county and intermediate school districts are also increasing their research and follow-up activities.

Locally, the formal research of a school system is usually conducted or summarized by an administrator or a professionally trained research worker, known as "director of research." Such directors are generally located in the large school systems that also employ a supportive staff in this field.

Increases in research personnel are anticipated in many other settings, e.g., institutions of higher education, private foundations, business and industry, private educational research agencies, and professional organizations, such as the educational research services sponsored by the American Association of School Administrators and the Research Division of the National Education Association. Many research workers are members of the American Educational Research Association, the Association of Institutional Research, and the International Association for the Advancement of Educational Research.

In line with the federal accent on the development after research, the U.S. Office of Education has changed the name of its Bureau of Research to the National Center for Educational Research and Development, which includes the Office of Program

Planning and Evaluation, the Office of Information Dissemination, and the National Center for Educational Statistics. A nongovernmental organization established in New York City in 1970 a New Center to Provide Research and Consulting, with the initial support of the Carnegie Commission on Higher Education, the Ford Foundation, and the Clark Foundation for Educational Testing.

One of the issues in research today is that of institutions of higher education doing classified research for the United States government. A sample negative statement of policy is that adopted by the University Council of Illinois State University declaring the university "will not enter into any contract supporting research for the purpose of killing, maiming or incapacitating human beings through chemical, biological or other types of military warfare."

Directors of Public Relations. Abraham Lincoln once said, "With public sentiment nothing can fail; without it nothing can succeed." To win and hold public sentiment and support, many schools and colleges have added part- or full-time directors of public relations. Although classroom teachers are the key persons in creating public understanding of schools, it is desirable, especially in the larger schools, to have a director of public relations. He is the coordinator of a broad program which seeks to promote the interest, support, and participation of citizens in the educational program. He helps to plan special publicity projects designed, for example, to win the taxpayers' support for a new building program, but his chief continuing concern is the daily use of two-way communication. Most public relations directors have developed year-round programs to reduce the credibility gap between school and community. Increased efforts are being made to reach minority groups, especially through home visitations.

The media employed represent a wide spectrum: letters, house organs, brochures, report cards, newspapers, student and faculty publications, radio, television and other multimedia aids, including the telephone. "Answering" and "record-a-comment" telephone services are used by some school systems. Many directors have established "rumor clinics." The National School Public Relations Association has proposed "Educational Public Relations Standards—for Programs—for Professionals." The director of public relations is a valuable member of the administrative team in schools and colleges.

[11] Research and Policy Committee, *Innovation in Education: New Directions for the American School*, Committee on Economic Development, New York, 1968, p. 20.

ADMINISTRATORS AND SUPERVISORS

Thousands of positions of an administrative or supervisory nature are available in American education, particularly for persons with experience, leadership, and initiative. Contrary to general belief, these positions do not exclude women. Many county superintendencies are held by women; grade school principalships and supervisory work are shared by women and men. However, few city superintendencies or high school principalships are held by women. One of the recommendations of various manpower studies is that more effective use be made of outstanding women in administrative positions.

Among the persons engaged in an executive capacity are (1) superintendents, (2) principals, (3) supervisors of instruction, (4) department heads and administrative deans, (5) presidents, and (6) other administrators, including business and building officials.

Superintendents of Schools

On the basis of the main geographical divisions, the superintendents of schools are (1) local, (2) county, or (3) state, whereas the chief school superintendent for the United States is known as the Commissioner of Education. American education also employs many assistant superintendents in both public and private education. A person must have two years of education beyond his bachelor's degree before he can be admitted to membership in the American Association of School Administrators. Several states now require three years of graduate study for certification as school superintendent, and many require two.

Local Superintendents. The multiple, difficult, and yet challenging duties of the city superintendent of schools are listed in Chapter 5. His main function is to serve as the chief administrative officer of the board of education. He is usually called the "city superintendent of schools," but in some instances he is designated the "community high school principal" or the "supervising principal."

The AASA, in a recent study listed in the bibliography at the end of this chapter, reported that the typical superintendent of schools

Is 49 years old
Was 29 years old when appointed to his first administrative position

Has been a teacher (commonly secondary) and a principal
Holds a master's degree with post-master's work
Holds an undergraduate major in social sciences (rather than in physical education, as is commonly believed)
Is male (almost without exception)
Works about 58 hours per week, including three evenings
Grew up in a small town or rural area
Plans to continue in the superintendency until retirement age is reached
Would select the superintendency again if he had to make a career choice again
Thinks the position of superintendency is rising in importance
Thinks the position is more difficult to handle than it was formerly

County Superintendents. Nearly all the three thousand counties in the United States have a chief educational officer, usually designated the "county" or "intermediate district superintendent of schools." The duties and qualifications of these superintendents are enumerated in Chapter 4.

State Superintendents. The usual tasks of the chief state educational officer are mentioned in Chapter 3. Quantitatively the fifty state administrators exert great power as they direct the work of more than thirty-three thousand staff members. As in the case of the county superintendents, political affiliation is sometimes a determining factor in the selection of a state superintendent or commissioner of education.

Assistant Superintendents. Since good administration involves the delegation of responsibility, a large system employs not only an executive but also a staff or assistants. School-district reorganization has resulted in fewer but larger districts, prompting the development of many well-paid positions for assistant superintendents in charge of curriculum, personnel administration, public relations, business management, and buildings and grounds.

Principals of Schools

The unit of education that means the most to children, parents, and the community is the individual school, of which the principal is the head. Principals constitute by far the largest group of administrators. These positions range all the way from teaching principals in small schools to principals of immense schools. There are elementary school principals, high school principals, and evening school principals. In some cases, particularly when they have charge of both elementary and secondary education, they are known as "supervising principals." Many large districts employ assistant principals. A master's degree and successful teaching experience are usually required.

In many private schools the head educational administrator is known as the "headmaster." The headmastership or principalship is a position of large responsibility. The principal is the person to whom teachers are directly accountable. Ideally, the principal should be responsible for the total educational program in his school, as well as a member of the administrative team in the cooperative development of systemwide program and policy.

There is a trend toward increased professionalization of this important post. The two major organizations contributing to the in-service education of these administrative men and women are the National Association of Elementary School Principals, and the National Association of Secondary School Principals.

Supervisors of Instruction

Many educators are engaged in instructional supervision, which has been broadened to involve the entire field of teaching and learning, deepened to reach down into a functional philosophy of education, and elevated to higher qualifications. Six major functions of this work, according to an analysis of duties performed by supervisors, include study of the student, in-service education of teachers, conduct of curriculum investigations, preparation and installation of courses of study, selection of textbooks and preparation of materials of instruction, and conduct of the public-relations program. Most of these duties call for teaching experience and special preparation. The typical supervisory positions are those in elementary schools, secondary schools, and other educational institutions. Many counties and all state departments of education also employ supervisors. Supervision on all educational levels helps to implement the objectives of education by improving both teaching and learning. The major professional organization serving these specialists is the Association for Supervision and Curriculum Development, an NEA affiliate.

Department Heads and Administrative Deans

Heads of Departments. The large secondary schools have semiadministrative officials known generally as "heads of departments." For example, studies such as those of the NEA Educational Research Service indicate that the practice of having department heads in senior high schools is markedly more prevalent in the larger school systems, with enrollments of 100,000 or more pupils. To them are delegated details of administration and supervision within their fields of instruction. Many high schools with only a few hundred students designate heads for the larger departments, usually English, social science, and business education.

Most institutions of higher learning have heads of departments or directors of academic divisions. The qualification for such positions is usually a doctor's degree and teaching experience in the area. The main task of heads of departments in all educational institutions is to improve instruction through aiding members of the department and cooperating with others on the staff and in administration.

College and University Deans. As discussed under *Personnel Workers*, high schools and institutions of higher learning have student deans. The deans mentioned here are academic and administrative officers in colleges and universities. The liaison officer between departments and between them and the president of the institution of higher learning is usually the dean. Some universities have several: a dean of instruction, an administrative dean, and deans of women and men. These officers must possess at least a master's degree, several years of teaching experience, and administrative ability. In very few institutions the position of dean is a highly centralized administrative office. The dean's office often combines teaching with administrative duties. With the recent rapid development of graduate work, many colleges and universities have added a graduate division under the direction of a graduate dean or a chairman who has a doctor's degree.

Presidents of Educational Institutions

More than 2,500 presidents direct the colleges and universities of the United States. Many of them have charge of private or parochial institutions, but a large number are directly engaged in public education, particularly the presidents of community junior colleges, state colleges and universities, and land-grant colleges.

Presidents of Community Colleges. The executive officer of the community or junior college, especially if it is linked with the high school, is usually known as the "principal" or "superintendent." His duties are similar to those of a local superintendent of schools, although technically he is president or dean of the institution. A growing practice in community colleges is that of officially designating the chief administrative officer as "president."

Presidents of Colleges and Universities. Among the crucial and well-paid positions in American education are college and university presidencies, several of which are held by women. A presidency is not, however, a bed of roses devoid of thorns. Says one president in a caustic vein, "A college president is so harassed by the time-consuming minutiae of administration and finance that he cannot be an educator."

In an age of student unrest on the campus, faculty demands for participation in decision making, taxpayer complaints about costs, alumni aggressiveness in athletics, trustee dictation in policy, union demands for workers, and governmental requirements in paper work, the president of an institution of higher learning is constantly besieged with pressing problems. Hence, there is a trend toward following the practice of business and appointing several vice-presidents to whom details are delegated. The president, as captain of the team, has, despite his many worries, an unexcelled opportunity for educational leadership and for a permanent influence upon many areas of American life.

Following student uprisings on many campuses, beginning at the University of California at Berkeley in 1965, there has been an unprecedented series of presidential resignations from what has become a very difficult administrative position on many campuses. An extended discussion of the problems of college administration is found in Chapter 9.

Other Administrative Officers

The list of administrative officers in schools, colleges, universities, and other educational organizations is long and varied. Two of the many officials engaged in administrative or supervisory activities relating to money and materiel are (1) business officials and (2) buildings and grounds officials.

Business Officials in Educational Institutions. Since education is a big business involving an annual expenditure of several billion dollars and an invested capital of many billions more, obviously schools and colleges must be run on a businesslike basis. The business official in the small school is usually the superintendent, who works with the board of education in solving the financial problems of the district. In the large schools a business manager, an assistant superintendent in charge of business, or a board secretary carries the major financial responsibilities.

The ideal business manager has a practical background and teaching experience—a sharp business outlook and an educational point of view. There is a dearth of well-educated persons with teaching and business experience plus personal assets to qualify them for the office of assistant superintendent of schools in charge of business. A similar lack of well-educated business officers is evident in colleges and universities. Organizations such as the Association of School Business Officials, and many other organizations, are seeking to improve business personnel and procedures in schools and colleges. As indicated in Chapter 16 the field of educational finance calls for numerous well-trained personnel.

Buildings and Grounds Officials. The business aspects of education embrace the care and maintenance of buildings and grounds. Usually in the large city systems and in the colleges, both public and private, a separate administrative officer, such as the superintendent of buildings and grounds, is in charge. His duties are to supervise repairs, make inventories, direct the maintenance and operation of the plant, improve the grounds, and assist in the planning of new structures. Practical experience, such as having worked as a building contractor or in the building trades, aids in the successful execution of these duties. As considered in Chapter 15, the erection, operation, and maintenance of educational buildings call for well-equipped personnel. Many building officials are members of the Council of Educational Facilities Planners.

PERSONNEL FROM OTHER PROFESSIONS

Most educational workers are teachers and administrators, but doctors and lawyers may also perform school duties. Among the other professional workers mentioned in the succeeding pages are (1) librarians, (2) health personnel, (3) business and building personnel, (4) lawyers, (5) negotiators, and (6) other professional workers such as psychologists, sociologists, social workers, directors of religious education, and consultants. Paraprofessionals are also discussed below.

Librarians

The library is indeed an indispensable educational and social institution in a democracy. The role of libraries and books is treated further in Chapter 15; attention is here directed to librarians.

Librarians are employed (1) in schools and colleges, (2) in public libraries, (3) in combined school and public libraries, and (4) by other public and private agencies.

School and College Librarians. A broad cultural background, enthusiasm, approachability, tact, poise, and understanding are indispensable traits for school librarians, who are being recognized as important members of the faculty.

Many institutions in the United States now provide thorough library education. Today a school librarian should have a college education and at least one year of library school training. In several states he must also possess a teacher's certificate or special state certificate. The School Library Manpower Project, initiated by the American Association

The school librarian plays a crucial role in guiding learning.

of School Librarians, reveals that in schools having outstanding programs of unified library and audio-visual services the heads of the library media centers hold master's degrees.

Colleges and universities offer many opportunities for training and experience in library services. Federal loans, grants, fellowships, and traineeships are available for educating librarians at all academic levels through the Higher Education Act, which also provides funds for library research and demonstration.

The U.S. Office of Education estimates that approximately five million pupils attend schools without the services of a librarian. Unfortunately, elementary school libraries are the last to be recognized for their importance in lifelong learning. Most elementary schools today are sorely in need of libraries and librarians. Many junior high school and high school libraries are unorganized and inadequately staffed. The Elementary and Secondary Education Act provides federal funds for school library resources, textbooks, and other instructional materials.

Public Librarians. The status of the public library as an educational institution has long been established in America. The federal government has granted funds for improving libraries in one-fourth of the United States—rural territory—which was without any kind of library service. Additional library personnel and equipment, especially for bookmobile services for rural areas, are urgently needed. Much equipment, several services, and many rooms have been added to public libraries through the Library Services and Construction Act, passed by Congress. The greatest need is for librarians.

Combined School and Public Librarians. Some persons work in public libraries controlled by boards of education. The Educational Policies Commission envisioned the ultimate unification of all public educational activities, in communities or areas of appropriate size, under the leadership of a public education authority.

Other Librarians. Many public and private agencies other than schools, colleges, cities, counties, and states employ librarians. Among these are foundations, research associations, private firms, educational associations, settlement houses, hotels, hospitals, and other agencies that promote reading and research.

Health Personnel

The school health program is composed in whole or in part of the following services: health instruction, health examinations, medical attention, communicable-disease control, promotion of mental health, provision of healthful environment and regimen, and health supervision of teachers and employees. To perform these services well, a large and varied health team is needed, including (1) a physician, (2) a dentist, (3) a nurse, (4) a health educator, and (5) a nutritionist.

Physicians and Dentists. Ever since the city of Boston, faced with an epidemic of dreaded diphtheria, initiated in 1894 a program of school health inspection, the physician has assumed an important role in education. School dentists, too, have a real role in the health program of the school.

The health of the pupils is not the responsibility of the school physician alone; all doctors may promote this cause through participation in campaigns for immunization against contagious diseases and in their daily duties as family physician. In their private practice the physicians, especially the pediatricians and psychiatric workers, have numerous heavy educational responsibilities devolving upon them.

The school physician or dentist, whether a full-time or part-time employee of the board of education or the city, has educational obligations, such as emphasizing to the pupils and parents the importance of proper care of the body. He should have a thorough understanding of the school health program. Inspections by the school dentist or doctor do not take the place of a careful and thorough examination by the family dentist or physician.

Nurses. School nurses usually devote part of their time to preparing instructional materials; giving individual health instruction and examinations; interpreting the results of the examinations to parent, child, and teacher; and maintaining an inventory and follow-up of illnesses in the school population. Success in this field requires certain natural qualifications, such as a genuine liking for children. In addition, school nurses must have high professional and educational qualifications. It is significant that a number of men are now entering the field of nursing, which was formerly made up almost entirely of women. The courses vary in number of years of study: licensed practical nurse, one year; associ-

ate degree in nursing, two years; registered nurse, three years; bachelor's degree in nursing, four years; and graduate work in nursing education, five and more years.

Health Educators. A position that is increasing in number and significance is that of health educator or coordinator. Many state departments, county boards, and local school systems employ personnel experienced in health and education to work with nonschool children, pupils, parents, teachers, nurses, doctors, and dentists. The professional preparation usually required is training and experience in health and teaching, with the technical degree of master of public health. Some health educators are doctors of public health.

Nutritionists. In connection with school and college home economics departments, lunchrooms, and residence halls, many educational institutions employ nutritionists, dietitians, or both, full or part time.

Business and Building Personnel

In addition to the business manager and the buildings and grounds superintendent, previously mentioned as administrators, schools and colleges employ other members of the business and building professions on a part-time or full-time basis. Those who are considered professionals are (1) accountants and auditors, (2) educational program auditors, (3) architects, and (4) engineers.

A specialist in speech instruction helps this young learner.

Accountants and Auditors. Thousands of accountants are employed in educational work periodically or full time. Often these officials are businessmen or educators who have specialized in educational finance. Usually the chief auditor or accountant is a C.P.A. (certified public accountant).

Educational Program Auditors. In his pioneering work, *Budgeting in Public Schools*, published in 1936, Chris A. DeYoung urged the appointment of auditors "trained in accounting and in education":

An audit should be more than a prosaic report on expenditures and receipts. The school audit, like the school budget, differs from the commercial type in that it is based on the educational program. . . . There is a dire need for educational auditors. . . . Schools of education and commerce should assume aggressive leadership in preparing these experts. Improvement of the current accountancy practices can be hastened by the appointment of educational auditors in the state departments of education.[12]

The leading spokesman today for "accountability," Leon Lessinger, carries this basic concept further and expands it as follows:

The ideas of audit, performance contracts, developmental capital, and educational escrow accounts contribute the rather basic, primitive attributes of the concept of accountability for learning results. . . . The Independent Accomplishment Audit (IAA) relies upon outside judgment of results or accomplishments.[13]

The essential parts of this meaningful and potentially professional concept of audit are presented later in this volume in Chapter 16. The central figure in the application of this new educational technique is the "educational program auditor."[14]

Architects. Large city systems and some state departments employ full-time school architects. Some architectural firms specialize in school and college buildings, and others have a department of educational architecture. The definite relationship of buildings to the curriculum makes school architec-

[12] Chris A. DeYoung, *Budgeting in Public Schools*, Doubleday, Doran & Company, Inc., New York, 1936, pp. 450–451.
[13] Leon Lessinger, "Accountability in Education," *National Committee for the Support of Public School News*, February, 1970, pp. 4–6.
[14] W. Stanley Kruger, "Program Auditor: New Breed on the Educational Scene," *American Education*, vol. 6, p. 36, March, 1970.

ture extremely important. The school architect must have a thorough knowledge of modern education so that the building he designs will facilitate the education of the pupils (see Chapter 15). The leading organization for school and college architects is the Council of Educational Facility Planners.

Engineers. Most educational buildings are in the charge of engineer-custodians. In the small systems, the persons who direct the maintenance, operation, and care of school plant and properties are often called "janitors." In the large systems, engineers are assigned to definite tasks in terms of their specialties, such as mechanical or electrical work, usually after having passed civil service examinations.

Legal Personnel

Law is the basis for most school transactions; hence the significance of the legal profession in education. Among those engaged in school law work are (1) lawyers and (2) other legal advisers.

Lawyers. Most full- or part-time legal positions in education are available only to persons who hold a bachelor of laws (LL.B.) degree and membership in the bar. The Association of American Law Schools and the Council on Legal Education of the American Bar Association maintain certain standards for approving law schools. The typical law curriculum has had marked leanings toward the needs of private practice and has not given much emphasis to the needs of the schools. Many law schools and teacher-education institutions offer courses in school law.

Other Legal Advisers. Many state departments have legal advisers who may or may not hold legal degrees but have studied both school and general law. Their business is to help interpret the laws affecting education. Occasionally lawyers who specialize in certain areas of law are called upon for school service. The National Organization on Legal Problems of Education, organized in 1956, has helped to stimulate research in law affecting education. The *Yearbook of School Law* provides an annual compilation of school-law information.

Negotiators. The era of educational negotiations is here. The recent enactment of laws concerning negotiations between controlling boards of education and teachers and professors has accelerated the demand for lawyers who specialize in the rights and responsibilities of employers and employees. The new militancy in the educational profession seeks to gain for instructors some of those bargaining rights which workers in the private sector have enjoyed for many years under the supervision of the National Labor Relations Board. Since many states now have statutes permitting or requiring boards of education to "bargain" with their employees, the need for negotiators qualified in law—both written (constitutions and statutes) and unwritten (court decisions and traditions)—is great. Negotiators need not be attorneys. School administrators often serve as negotiators for their boards, and local classroom teachers often negotiate for the teachers' organization.

Persons skilled and experienced in collective negotiations will undoubtedly be added as a new group of specialized personnel in education, especially for large school systems, state departments, and organizations such as those of professional educators. In 1970 the Association of Educational Negotiators was organized in Washington, D.C., consisting of employee-relationship directors and others who work around the bargaining tables. *The Law and Teacher Negotiations* is a large index book for those concerned with day-to-day issues and problems of collective negotiators in public education.[15]

Mediators, Fact-finders, and Arbitrators. The substantial number of impasses in collective bargaining in school districts has increased the need for outside, third-party experts in resolving conflicts. Mediators are commonly used in impasses to enlighten the process of negotiation by helping the parties themselves reconcile their differences through more skillful negotiation, somewhat in the manner of a marriage counselor. Should mediation fail, fact-finders are often called to make their own independent appraisal of the dispute and the arguments on either side and then recommend their own solution. Their recommendations are only advisory but often carry a lot of weight in molding opinion. As a last resort short of litigation, arbitrators or arbitration boards are often used to resolve disputes, much as a referee would in a sports contest, by simply rendering a decision which is usually binding on both parties and which may have the force of law.

These personnel are presently in short supply

[15] Donald H. Wollett and Robert H. Chanin, *The Law and Teacher Negotiations*, Bureau of National Affairs Books, Washington, D.C.

in education. These positions beckon persons who are skilled in resolving disputes with equal justice to both sides and who are very knowledgeable of educational policies and practices, particularly staff personnel administration. Although knowledge of school law is helpful, it is not necessary that mediators, fact-finders, and arbitrators be attorneys.

Other Professional or Semiprofessional Workers

Among the many other professionals or semiprofessionals engaged in educational work are (1) school psychiatrists and psychologists, (2) school sociologists, (3) school social workers, (4) security personnel, (5) educational consultants, and (6) workers in religious education.

School Psychiatrists and Psychologists. Many schools and colleges are employing psychiatrists and psychologists in an effort to treat causes rather than symptoms of unusual behavior by students and to retard mental illness. Part-time psychiatric services are offered in hospitals, universities, foundations, or other agencies, such as clinics. In rural areas, a school psychologist is often employed by the county office to serve all the schools under its jurisdiction.

Clinical psychologists are increasingly in demand. Groups such as the Association of Consulting Psychologists and the Division of School Psychologists of the American Psychological Association have helped to establish and elevate standards for clinical psychologists and for their training programs. The National Committee for Mental Hygiene has also made recommendations.

School Sociologists. At present the nation's schools employ few sociologists. Courses in sociology, particularly in the secondary schools, would be far more functional if a sociologist were engaged to make actual community contact through social surveys and other means. The school has too long tried to insulate itself against direct community service. Administrators have been likely to think in terms of education but not of society. A crying need exists, therefore, for educational sociologists who seek the improvement of society as a whole rather than merely that of the schools. In addition to excellent personal qualifications, the educational sociologist should possess at least a master's degree. A doctor's degree is usually required for university duties in this field or for the teaching of sociology courses.

Harvard University has initiated a new doctoral program called "Education and Social Policy," aimed at producing planners, analysts and researchers for educational-social careers in all geographical areas from the local school district to the U.S. Office of Education.

School Social Workers. Social responsibility is the keynote of twentieth-century legislation. In its publication *Social Services and the Schools*, the Educational Policies Commission states that ". . . the schools, in particular, are obligated not only to see and provide for their educational responsibilities to the community but also to cooperate in providing welfare services that are closely related to education." The task of social workers is economic and educational as well as social.

The social worker of today is a trained member of a profession, usually holding one or more college degrees. Their social services may include child welfare, family welfare, community organization, institutional work, parole, probation, psychiatric social work, public assistance, unemployment relief, social group work, social research, visiting teacher work, and the teaching of social service. The "community agent" who works with all people in the school area is becoming more common in educational sociology. Efforts are being made to humanize the school with person-to-person contacts in the community.

Security Personnel. During the past decade of dissension and disturbance there arose across the nation a greatly increased demand for security personnel, employed by schools and colleges. These security aides, many of whom have been trained as policemen, are assigned to middle schools, high schools, and colleges in order to protect the institutions from intruders, to guard educational buildings and equipment, and to serve as interpreters and, if necessary, active agents of law enforcement. The New York City school board, for example, employs several hundred security aides whose duties include watching school entrances, checking visitors, and patrolling corridors. Night watchmen, deputized as police officers, patrol many school sites and college campuses.

In a pilot program in Grand Rapids, Michigan, the Board of Education and the City Police Department joined in assigning a police officer to a middle school to work with counselors, teachers, parents, and students in designing and implementing an eighth-grade unit for enriching the social studies program by helping the individual student to develop human relations skills and positive attitudes toward his responsibilities for law observance in a democratic society.

The continuing and accelerating increase in vandalism and disturbances in schools has precipitated the formation of another organization—the International Association of School Security Directors.

Educational Consultants. Many school systems and universities employ various educational consultants or specialists on a part-time basis. Most such employees come from colleges and universities or private firms that specialize in advisory services. They usually work with a board or committee in the local community, the state, or the nation on short-term or long-range educational problems. They seek to analyze systematically the educational problems, to design alternative solutions in the form of programs, to supplement plans, and to evaluate the procedures employed. Some specialize in fund raising, development work, plans for buildings, and public relations. The development of regionalism in education has resulted in the appointment of many federal and state consultants on large-area bases between and within states.

Workers in Religious Education. The parochial schools and denominational colleges have a clear-cut obligation to teach religion. Furthermore, both public and secular institutions of learning are giving more courses "about" religion. Many instructors are needed for these purposes. Usually the requirements for collegiate positions are graduation from a theological seminary and practical experience in preaching, teaching, or religious educational work. The seminaries of the land are expanding and need many professors. Many colleges employ a chaplain who ministers to the spiritual needs of the student body and faculty. Many positions are available for directors of religious education or teachers in churches, cathedrals, and synagogues. Many teachers find a special challenge in overseas service as educational missionaries. Catholic, Protestant, and

Jewish schools are exchanging staff members and becoming more ecumenical in their cooperative efforts. The work of campus ministers is also becoming more unified and consolidated in larger geographical areas.

Paraprofessional Personnel

Teaching Aides. Among the "paraprofessional" personnel (those who work alongside the professionals) in education are aides. They free classroom teachers from some subprofessional, routine tasks, so that they have "more time to teach." Hence a growing number of schools and colleges employ subprofessional personnel such as teacher aides, theme readers, laboratory assistants, and clerical aides. Teacher aides, often used in connection with team teaching, are sometimes also employed to relieve teachers of large classes from nonprofessional or semiprofessional tasks.

These aides perform such tasks as arranging instructional materials; reading aloud and storytelling; arranging bulletin board displays; supervising bus loading; helping with field trips; scoring objective tests; and supervising study halls, lunch periods, and playgrounds. Such aides often have some higher education, and often they are young persons aspiring to teaching careers. Some schools employ theme readers or lay readers to assist English teachers in the massive task of correcting students' compositions. These readers are often housewives with college majors in English who enjoy this part-time work. Similarly, college graduates with backgrounds in science are sometimes employed as laboratory assistants to science teachers. A number of schools employ secretarial and clerical aides for their faculties. These aides keep attendance and other class records, make out routine reports, handle lunch money, score objective tests, answer correspondence, cut stencils, file materials, and perform other secretarial and clerical tasks.

Teaching aides are used on all educational levels, from pre-elementary education, where they might serve as helpers in Head Start programs, to graduate education, where they may function as teaching assistants.

The U.S. Office of Education has launched a professional program to bring "bright, ambitious, deeply concerned people from low-income communities into the schools." The Career Opportunities

Program (COP) begins with teacher aides and technicians on the first rung of the ladder. Through in-service experiences and academic college courses, these aides can climb the career ladder to become assistant teachers, interns, and eventually fully certificated teachers.

OTHER NONTEACHING PERSONNEL

The vast array of nonteaching workers not definitely ranked as professionals include (1) school clerks and secretaries; (2) food service workers; (3) building service personnel; (4) transportation personnel; (5) educational editors, publishers, manufacturers, and sales personnel; and (6) others employed in education. Each of these groups is described briefly.

School Clerks and Secretaries

Countless opportunities for educational work are available in the field of clerical and office service. Typists, stenographers, secretaries, bookkeepers, and similar employees can and do perform many tasks of an educational nature, thus releasing administrators and teachers for purely professional duties.

An important school business official, especially in the East, is the school board secretary. Secretaries should be provided for every administrator, especially the county superintendent, in the number needed to relieve him and his professional assistants from clerical duties. Many attendance clerks are needed in public schools. Obviously secretaries, as well as all school employees, should be appointed upon strict professional bases rather than because of political influence or nepotism.

The National Association of Educational Secretaries is developing a service program that seeks to make the secretarial position in the school system a professional one, requiring specialized training and experience.

Food Service Personnel

Ever since the days of the Great Depression of the 1930s, when the federal government started the school lunch program, the demand has been steadily increasing for competent food service personnel. The antipoverty programs of the 1960s added another meal—breakfast—for millions of children. The school cafeteria and lunchroom and the university dining halls can be powerful factors in the educative processes of physical and social growth. Much care must be exercised in the selection and training of a manager for the school cafeteria and lunchroom and the university food service.

Building Service Personnel

During the early colonial days, most teachers performed the housekeeping duties in the schools, a practice that still exists in many rural communities. Today the schools and universities employ numerous caretakers and assistants with specific titles and definite responsibilities, such as engineer, painter, cleaner, carpenter, mower, electrician, and playground caretaker. In most systems, however, these duties devolve upon one person, who in the past has usually been called the "janitor." The more acceptable nomenclature today is "school custodian" (man) and "school matron" (woman). Whatever the term, the modern school requires from its custodian less manual labor but more knowledge and skill than formerly.

Custodians must be trained in the installation and care of delicately adjusted equipment and various machinery. This practical training is being expanded by colleges, universities, state departments, and other agencies. Eventually preservice and inservice training will be required of all custodians. Some systems give a civil service examination for prospective custodians. Among the great hindrances to the improvement of school maintenance and operation personnel have been too frequent political interference in their appointment, insecurity of tenure, lack of retirement allowance, low pay, and inadequate recognition. A custodian may get signal recognition in a tangible way:

Set in the wall of the main corridor of a public school in a small town in Iowa is a bronze tablet bearing, in low relief, the heroic likeness of a man and the inscription—"He gave thirty-two years of faithful service to the youth of this community." From the dedicatory program we learn the tablet was placed "by its hundreds of donors with the belief that all those who shall frequent these halls in the years to come will be inspired, as we who present it were inspired by him."

Cafeteria workers are among the variety of nonprofessional school personnel.

This superior personage, so memorialized, was not a member of the board of education; he was not a superintendent; not a principal; nor an exceptional teacher, but the school janitor or custodian.

The janitor or custodian is usually one of the many forgotten men and women who daily serve youth in school.

Transportation Personnel

Transportation has developed into a major educational enterprise, particularly in states that have adopted larger units of administration and in city school districts that use busing as a means for securing better racial balance. Most states are now paying part of the costs of conveying pupils, and most local districts have added the school bus driver to their payroll.

Some school districts use students, parents, and faculty members as part-time bus drivers. Sometimes a bus driver helps with the practical highway experience for students in driver education. The large systems, which own a fleet of buses, employ various mechanics in their garages and repair shops. School transportation has developed to such significance that specific qualifications and training have been set for those engaged in this all-important work of bringing pupils safely to the teachers.

Educational Editors, Authors, Publishers, Manufacturers, and Sales Personnel

Thousands of persons who render educational services are employed in the publication of textbooks, in the manufacture of educational supplies and equipment, and in sales work.

Educational Editors, Authors, and Publishers. One aspect of textbook publication is editorial work. In addition to the editors, numerous persons are employed as directors of educational research service with publishers of textbooks. The work of field consultants for a textbook company is largely professional and includes such activities as lecturing or making informal talks to groups, training teachers in service, and holding conferences with various kinds of committees and individuals. Opportunities for women, especially teachers, are multiplying in the textbook field. A challenging task for all educators, especially for classroom teachers, is that of writing articles and books for publication. The prep-

aration of children's books is now an enormous enterprise that employs a great many educators. Contrary to general belief, those who enter the publishing and editorial field do not lose their educational status.

Sales Personnel. Many persons are engaged in selling schoolbooks, supplies, and educational equipment. Undoubtedly the best textbooks, educational supplies, and educational equipment in the world are made in America. These are available as teaching tools for American schools, but unfortunately the best is not generally used. Restricted budgets and the apathy of the general public account in part for this situation. Then, too, many classroom and laboratory teachers are not acquainted with the wide variety and high quality of modern educational materials. Promotional and sales personnel, traveling to schools, colleges, educational exhibits, and state and national conventions, spread the news of improvements. The best preparation for this salesmanship is teaching and business experience.

Others Employed in Education

Workers in Nonschool Organizations. Many educational, recreational, and professional organizations employ thousands of trained workers. For example, UNESCO, the Red Cross, the Youth Department of the Jewish Agency with its summer in kibbutz overseas program, the YMCA and YWCA, the National Congress of Parents and Teachers, the Boy Scouts and Girl Scouts of America, the 4-H Clubs of America, educational fraternities and sororities, educational foundations, state and national educational associations, and countless other groups draw heavily upon the teaching profession for their personnel. Most industrial corporations maintain extensive educational programs for their employees and sometimes for their families. The Arabian American Oil Company, for example, maintains a complete school system for Americans in Arabia. The Armed Forces also operate a vast educational program, hiring many professional educators both at home and abroad. The Peace Corps and VISTA need many types of educational workers.

Challenging Career Services in Education. The improvement of many nonteaching positions requires more than higher standards of recruitment. These positions, especially for clerks and stenographers, must become career services if they are to enlist adequately trained personnel. The term "career" as used here means a lifework in an honorable occupation which one normally takes up in youth with the expectation of advancement and pursues with happiness and profit until retirement. School service in both public and private institutions should be so organized and conducted as to constitute a continuous, challenging career.

Though the role of some employees in education may appear insignificant, each professional or nonprofessional worker, from the chief executive officer of the educational institution down to the lowest-paid day laborer, can make a direct and significant contribution to American education.

UNPAID PERSONNEL

This chapter concludes with a discussion of the role of the unpaid persons who labor for education. The main groups are (1) members of boards of education, (2) lay advisory committees in education, (3) alumni, (4) students, (5) parents, and (6) educational volunteers.

Members of Boards of Education. Chapter 5 includes an extended discussion of the important role of members of school boards or boards of education.

Many men and women serve also on other boards of education of various types, such as county and state boards of education. Examples of the latter are the state retirement board, the state certification board, the state board of education having general jurisdiction over public elementary and secondary schools, and the group selected or appointed to work with the presidents of colleges and universities, both public and private.

A significant movement in recent years has been the development of more lay control in parochial colleges and universities, as well as in church-related local school systems. Another trend, growing out of student activism on the campuses, is the addition of students to the membership of governing boards of colleges and universities. The average age of trustees on these boards is being lowered. More women are appointed to boards. These men and women serve unselfishly the cause

of education, and they donate millions of clock hours and dollars to their tasks. Just as teachers have local, county, state, and national organizations, so do the board members. Jointly, they spearhead lay leadership in learning.

Lay Advisory Committees in Education. Lay advisory committees in education are not new. The local board often appoints an advisory committee of citizens to help with school policies. These lay groups, selected by the board of education or by community groups, bring the citizens back into educational partnership with the board, the superintendent of schools, and the teachers. This total team marshals lay leadership on the side of better education. They may be short-term committees, assigned a specific project such as a building program, or long-span groups, delegated a continuing constructive challenge.

Many states have advisory lay boards, such as a commission on higher education or a school problems advisory committee. The National Center for Citizens in Education, the National Council for Better Schools, and the National Committee for the Support of Public Schools stimulated the formation of lay groups to study education and to make recommendations to the boards recognized in law. It must be borne in mind that these groups are not superboards and that the official agencies have the legal authority for making final decisions affecting education.

Alumni. Among the unpaid part-time educational workers are the alumni of schools, colleges, and universities. Many alumni have strong emotional attachments to their schools. They help their alma maters in recruiting students, especially those with athletic and academic abilities; in seeking talented staff members; in publicizing the institution; and in soliciting and donating funds. Billions of dollars have been contributed privately by alumni to their alma maters.

These unpaid workers are often assisted or directed by paid alumni staff members. Many institutions of higher learning hold membership in the American Alumni Council. The Manhattan Tracers Company of America is one of the commercial organizations that help educational institutions locate their lost alumni.

Students. This has been aptly called the "age of students." Students have an increasing role in their own education. As previously mentioned, some students are now serving education on the governing boards of colleges and universities. Permitting voting at the age of 18 adds to the responsibility of students in selecting persons for the governance of their educational institutions. As indicated in Chapter 14, students at all levels govern their cocurricular activities. Students, especially in higher education, are being given more responsibility in developing relevant curriculums and in evaluating them and the instructors. At many universities students are voting members of every major faculty committee. Many students serve as paraprofessionals in schools. Many tutor disadvantaged students in a one-to-one relationship. Thousands serve as members of "the environment guard." The role of students in the educational process is discussed in greater detail in Chapter 11.

Parents. One of the current criticisms of education is that parents have abdicated their rights and responsibilities and have assigned too much to teachers. Education is too important to be left entirely to paid professional personnel. The perennial partnership of parent and teacher must be promoted. Each needs the other, and the pupil needs them both.

Parents can assist teachers in various ways. The parents are the child's first tutors and as such can ready him for school; then they can supplement and support the work of the teacher. No teacher seeks to supplant the parent. Many schools utilize class mothers to assist in routine classroom chores.

The local, county, state, and national groups most concerned with volunteer leadership for parents are the parent-teacher associations. On the countrywide level, the main organization is known as the National Congress of Parents and Teachers and has its headquarters in Chicago. This organization merged in 1970 with the National Congress of Colored Parents and Teachers. It is the largest volunteer organization in the world, with more than twelve million members, and is still growing.

A descriptive brochure, *A Teacher's Guide to the P. T. A.*, is published by the National Congress of Parents and Teachers. It states that the national, state, and local associations are governed by four basic policies. In brief, these policies affirm that the organization (1) shall be educational and shall develop its program through conferences, committees, and projects; (2) shall be noncommercial, nonsectarian, and nonpartisan; (3) shall work to improve

the schools without seeking to direct their administration or control their policies; and (4) shall cooperate with other organizations and agencies having common interests. Parents and teachers can promote a paying partnership that brings rich rewards for children.

Educational Volunteers. In addition to the donated services of the groups mentioned under *Unpaid Personnel*, many more men and women volunteer their services to education. For example, the various local programs in Head Start, in the national war on poverty, have demonstrated the worth of dedicated volunteers. Many local groups, such as the School Resource Volunteers in Berkeley, California, organize their willing workers. Many states have helping organizations, such as Michigan's CAPE (Citizens to Advance Public Education). The National School Volunteer Program, financed by the Ford Foundation, helps large city school systems with their volunteer organizations.

Another example of a national organization at work in the communities across the nation is Volunteers in Probation, Inc., which has stimulated thousands of mature persons to volunteer their services in the reeducation and rehabilitation of persons brought to courts of justice.

Volunteers range from teen-agers to the elderly. Many youth in college fraternities and sororities donate services in tutoring disadvantaged pupils. Usually the tutors are helped as much as the children they seek to serve. More and more retired teachers and professors are donating their time and tested talents.

Parent volunteers often help with nonprofessional school chores.

SUMMARY

Personnel management is extremely important in education, which has a huge task force engaged in human engineering. More than a million men and women are employed in educational positions other than straight classroom teaching, in which another two million and more work. Careers challenge the talents of nonteachers in a hundred and more types of positions. Hence recruitment for education should not be limited to classroom teachers. The best human resources need to be enlisted for all types of educational work.

Among the semiteaching personnel in differentiated staffing are part-time teachers, such as substitutes; off-campus leaders, such as extension workers; personnel people, such as guidance and placement officials; and other specialists, including curriculum and research directors and educational technologists.

Many positions in the higher-salaried group are of an administrative and supervisory nature. These positions are found at all educational levels, from pre-elementary through adult learning. Administrators should be the servants and not the masters of education.

From professions other than teaching come many educational workers, such as librarians, doctors, dentists, nurses, accountants, architects, lawyers, social workers, religious-education directors and consultants.

Among the other nonteachers employed in education are teaching aides, clerks, secretaries, food service personnel, custodians, bus drivers, authors, publishers, salesmen, and day laborers. Many institutions employ a director of nonacademic employees.

Education is too important to be left to those who receive direct compensation. Among the unpaid persons who labor for learners are five major groups: members of boards of education, lay advisory committees in education, alumni, parents, and educational volunteers. The perennial partnership of parents and teachers must be promoted. The interested parents, the child's first tutors, supplement the work of the talented teacher. No teacher supplants the pupil's parents. Lay participation must be marshaled with professional leadership in a spirit of teamwork for the welfare of the learner and society.

Suggested Activities

1. List arguments pro and con for differentiated staffing.
2. Investigate the opportunities for training as a school librarian.
3. Find out what qualifications your state requires for city, county, and state superintendents of schools.
4. List some of the advantages and disadvantages of being a school principal, supervisor, or head of a department.
5. Describe the work and qualifications of an educational technologist and instructional designer.
6. What are some of the duties of teacher aides?
7. List the duties of a school or college business manager.
8. Explain some of the functions of a school psychologist. What are some of the desirable qualifications of a psychologist?
9. Discuss the importance of transportation services in education.
10. What are the duties of an educational program auditor?
11. Describe the type of educational work other than teaching which might interest you.

Bibliography

American Association of School Administrators: *The American School Superintendent*, American Association of School Administrators, Washington, D.C., 1971. A survey of the public school superintendent—his experience, preparation, career line, working conditions, and his views of the position.

American Association of School Administrators: *Profiles of the Administrative Team*, American Association of School Administrators, Washington, D.C., 1971. Descriptions of various public school administrative positions and their responsibilities.

Association for Supervision and Curriculum Development: *Supervision: Emerging Profession*, National Education Association, Washington, D.C., 1971. Symposium of articles on the professionalization of supervision.

Cronbach, Lee J., and Patrick Suppes (eds.): *Research for Tomorrow's Schools: Disciplined Inquiry for Education*, The Macmillan Company, New York, 1969. Statements from the Committee on Educational Research of the National Academy of Education, with a concluding section on pressing problems that need scholarly consideration.

Department of Audiovisual Instruction: *Jobs in Instructional Media*, National Education Association, Washington, D.C., 1969. A comprehensive analysis of jobs performed in the field of instructional media, plus a list of two-year colleges giving paraprofessional training in this field.

Guerney, Bernard G., Jr., (ed.): *Psychotherapeutic Agents, New Roles for Non-professionals, Parents and Teachers*, Holt, Rinehart and Winston, Inc., New York, 1969. A discussion of the role of paraprofessionals, parents, and professionals in helping youth.

Hersey, John: *Letter to the Alumni*, Alfred A. Knopf, Inc., New York, 1970. A letter to the alumni of Yale (and other institutions) giving an analysis of today's college students and of the revolution they seek.

National Association of Elementary School Principals: *The Assistant Principalship in Public Elementary Schools*, Washington, D.C., 1970. Part of a survey of the so-called "forgotten man" in the school..

National Association of Secondary School Principals: *The Principalship: Job Specifications and Salary Considerations for the 70s*, National Education Association,

Washington, D.C., 1970. A discussion of the role and conditions of employment of the principalship for the future.

Rauh, Morton A.: *The Trusteeship of Colleges and Universities*, McGraw-Hill Book Company, New York, 1969, chap. 7. A review of recent history of student activism and its impact on trustee responsibility.

Wollett, Donald H., and Robert H. Chanin: *The Law and Teacher Negotiations*, Bureau of National Affairs Books, Washington, D.C., 1970. An indexed how-to-do-it book for those interested in collective negotiations.

Wright, Betty Atwell: *Teacher Aides to the Rescue*, The John Day Company, Inc., New York, 1969. Suggestions for using teacher aides, with some case histories.

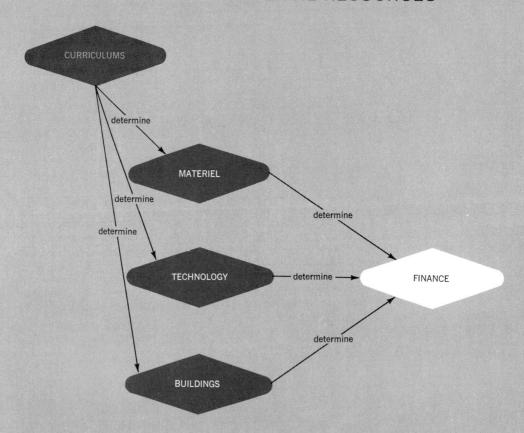

MATERIAL RESOURCES

Part Five

Provisions for Educational Materials and Environment

Effective education requires a planned educational program, instructional materials, and an environment in which teaching and learning may be sustained. The program, materials, and environment are shaped by the educative process, and the educative process in turn is shaped by the program, materials, and environment.

The educational program for the school consists of the curriculum and the cocurricular activities. The curriculum includes all the experiences that students have under the guidance of the schools. The modern curriculum is developed cooperatively by academicians, educationists, administrators, teachers, and students. The objectives of the curriculum are determined by the needs of the students and the needs of society. Society in turn is influenced by the nature of the school curriculum. One of the most fruitful ways of understanding a society is to study the curriculum of its schools and colleges.

Indeed, many of the cleavages of society are manifest in the divergent views which people hold regarding their schools. The development and improvement of the curriculum and of the cocurricular programs constitute a continuous and often controversial undertaking (Chapter 14).

In order to work effectively, the teacher and the students need supplies and equipment. They must also have a place to use these tools. The school grounds and buildings constitute the workshop or laboratory of American education. The modern school building is intimately fitted to human needs—physical, educational, psychological, and aesthetic. Modern educational buildings are needed in many communities and on college campuses (Chapter 15).

The curricular and the cocurricular activities, the supplies and the equipment, and the grounds and buildings are made available through large expenditures for education. Revenue for school operation is generated from local, state, and federal sources. Expenditures for education are not a cost—they represent a long-term investment (Chapter 16).

Chapter 14   Curriculum

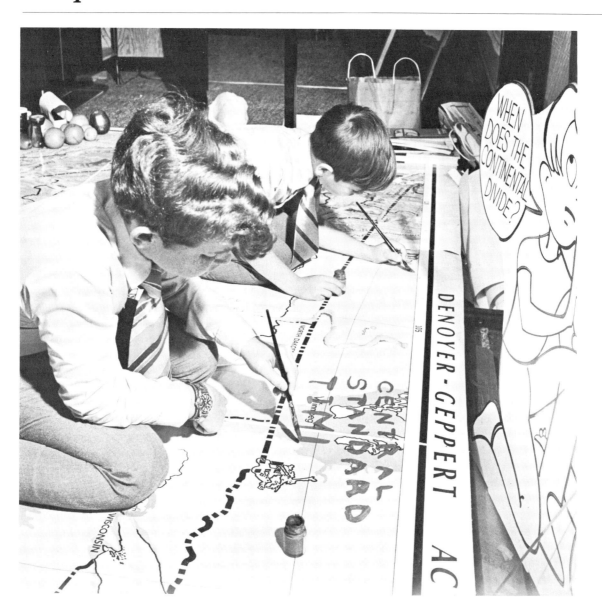

ORIENTATION

CUR-RIC-U-LUM (kə rik′ yə lem) n. in its broadest sense, the organized experiences that a student has under the guidance of a school; in a more precise sense, a systematic group of courses or sequence of subjects required for graduation or certification in a major field of study. [< Latin, curriculum course, chariot < currus, chariot, currere, run]

Many students believe today, perhaps with good reason, that the Latin derivation is still appropriate, that the curriculum is indeed a racetrack. Others, who question its relevancy to modern life, might prefer to regard it as a runaround.

A 10-year-old acquaintance gave us the most succinct definition we have heard: "the stuff kids learn." Any society has great interest in what kids learn because what they learn, or fail to learn, influences the future of the society. The reaction is reciprocal, since the values and aspirations of a society also influence the school curriculum. Thus the school curriculum becomes the locus for much of the controversy in educational thought. School auditoriums have been filled by citizens, some demanding that sex education be stopped, while others insist that it be continued. Students have boycotted schools, insisting that the stuff they are forced to learn is irrelevant. Offices of college deans have been occupied by students demanding the introduction of black studies. Some school boards have forbidden instruction in communism, the Whiskey Rebellion, the United Nations, German, and evolution. State legislators have enacted laws requiring the public schools to offer instruction in such matters as the evils of alcohol, humane treatment of animals, and the heroics of General Pulaski. The federal

The modern school curriculum is enriched by interesting instructional materials.

government has appropriated millions of dollars to stimulate improved instruction in drug abuse, vocational education, environmental education, agricultural science, Russian, and a host of other academic and professional fields.

Interest in the school curriculum is quickened during periods of social, political, and economic turbulence. In present times, many forces have combined to intensify interest in "the stuff kids learn": racial injustice, poverty, international cleavages, population expansion, urbanization, technological revolution, proliferation of knowledge, new life-styles of youth, among many others. Thus the schools of a free society continue the endless process of adaptation to the shifting needs of the individuals and the society which they serve.

The major issues related to the curriculum are discussed at greater length in Chapter 1.

FOUNDATIONS

Milieu of Curriculum Change

Curriculum construction was a simple task in the primitive life of early American schools. Preelementary schools did not exist. The common schools stressed the four Rs—reading, 'riting, 'rithmetic, and religion. High schools emphasized the college preparatory curriculum, consisting largely of classical studies. College courses of study offered a combination of liberal and professional education suited to a relatively simple agrarian society and economy. Adult education, at least on an organized basis, was virtually unknown. In those days it was generally assumed that the curriculum of the schools at all levels was built upon the separate academic subjects. These subjects were organized around the academic disciplines—English, other languages,

The Development of Curriculums

1633	In a prototype elementary school, established in New York, the four R's—reading, 'riting, 'rithmetic, and religion—given major accent	1903	Child-centered curriculums in progressive education stimulated by John Dewey in The Child and the Curriculum
1635	The first Latin grammar-secondary school primarily for those going to college begun; classical languages and English emphasized	1904	Insight into development and needs of adolescents provided by G. Stanley Hall's book Adolescence
1751	Secondary school curriculums broadened for college- and non-college-bound youth, with opening of Franklin's academy	1908	Scale to measure educational achievements designed by E. L. Thorndike
1837	School curriculums criticized and vitalized through work of Horace Mann in Massachusetts	1917	Vocational education in secondary schools stimulated by federal assistance through the Smith-Hughes Act
1876	Curriculums in graduate work first initiated at Johns Hopkins University	1918	Seven Cardinal Principles of Education formulated by the Commission on Reorganization of Secondary Education
1880	First manual training high school opened in St. Louis	1918	Progressive Education Association formally organized
1893	Emancipation of secondary schools from domination of college entrance requirements recommended in Report of the Committee of Ten	1924	One of the first textbooks on curriculum, How to Make a Curriculum by F. Bobbitt, written
1895	National Herbart Society, forerunner of the National Society for the Study of Education, founded; educational thought on curriculum and teaching widely influenced by its yearbooks	1926	Simple, hand-cranked device, prototype of modern teaching machines and programmed learning, invented by B. F. Skinner
1895	Better correlation of studies in the elementary school recommended in Report of the Committee of Fifteen	1931	Unit method of teaching and learning advanced by H. C. Morrison in The Practice of Teaching in the Secondary School
1898	Herbartian method, with five formal steps in teaching, presented by C. A. McMurry in Elements of General Methods	1932	Eight-year Study of the Commission on the Relations of School and College launched by the Progressive Education Association
1899	Elective principle in secondary schools recommended by the Committee on College Entrance Requirements	1945	Association for Supervision and Curriculum Development established as a merged organization

1945	Life-adjustment movement, designed to meet the "imperative needs of youth," initiated by the U.S. Office of Education	1963	Vocational education programs and facilities further enhanced through the new Vocational Education Act
1950	National Science Foundation created by Congress	1964	First prototype of Individually Prescribed Instruction (IPI) launched in Pennsylvania school
1951	Advanced placement programs developed to give high school students advanced credit on entering college	1965	Creativity and innovations in curriculums stimulated through Projects to Advance Creativity in Education (PACE) and other experiments financed through the Elementary and Secondary Education Act
1951	Current curricular reform movement initiated by work of University of Illinois Committee on School Mathematics	1965	Federal grants and loans for promoting the arts and humanities in schools and colleges provided through the National Foundation on the Arts and Humanities
1952	Educational television (ETV), with a national potential, born when the Federal Communications Commission reserved over two hundred channels for noncommercial use	1966	Regional research and development centers and educational laboratories established by the U.S. Office of Education
1956	Conservative educational philosophy and programs sharpened by establishment of the Council for Basic Education	1967	Experimental national assessment of education actively launched in thousands of classrooms with the aid of "measuring instruments"
1958	Cooperative research program launched by the U.S. Office of Education "to improve courses of study at all educational levels"	1968	Various prototypes of new technology-based instructional systems widely field-tested
1958	Through the National Defense Education Act (NDEA), federal funds made available for curriculum work in several teaching fields in elementary, secondary, and higher education	1970	National Reading Center established and advisory National Reading Council appointed
1959	Conant's widely read book The American High School Today: A First Report to Interested Citizens issued (updated in 1967)	1970	Educational thought on instructional method and classroom climate widely influenced by Silberman's book Crisis in the Classroom.
1960	First volume published on the subject of programmed learning	1970	Drug Abuse Education Act passed by Congress
1961	Goals for continuing education chartered in Adult Education: A New Imperative, published by the Adult Education Association	1970	Environmental Education Act passed by Congress
1963	National Education Association's Center for the Study of Instruction launched as a follow-up of the Project on Instruction	1971	NEA-sponsored National Foundation for the Improvement of Education launched

mathematics, science, history, geography, and so forth. The courses of study included as much of the content of the subject field as could be taught to students. The function of the school was almost exclusively the transmission of organized knowledge.

The twentieth century introduced changes in curriculum organization and teaching methodology. The rise of systematic study of human growth and development, the psychology of learning, and educational sociology brought new understanding of the student and the learning process.

During the first third of the century, the school curriculum was relatively stable. However, the Great Depression precipitated grave economic and social problems such as unemployment, poverty, and alienation of many people from the social and political system. The 1930s was a decade of social and economic reform under the New Deal. The educational philosopher and historian George Counts was asking *Dare the Schools Build a New Social Order?* in a book which bore that title, or must they simply transmit the old cultural heritage? Counts' beliefs would be fairly compatible with the aspirations of many of today's less radical student activists, but his position at that time aroused bitter controversy among those who preferred for the schools a position of neutral detachment from the issues of the times. John Dewey, William H. Kilpatrick, and other advocates of progressive education enjoyed considerable credibility during this period of social and economic disorder. The latter part of the 1930s witnessed the high-water mark of progressive education as some schools—never a large proportion of them—addressed their curriculums to the compelling reality of the times. "Experience-centered" and "problem-centered" were fashionable concepts for the organization of educational activities around real-life problems. In the late 1940s and early 1950s, similar concepts such as "persistent life situations" and "life-adjustment education" were still oriented largely toward the progressive education doctrine that education is life. Coverage of subject matter became less important than the application of selected knowledge to problems that were important to the learner and society. Despite the folklore to the contrary, these progressive education doctrines, which were essentially learner-centered rather than subject-centered, never really permeated educational practice to a very significant extent.

During World War II and the cold-war period

that followed, the nation's anxiety over the threat of fascism, and later communism, was manifested by critics concerned about un-American doctrine in the curriculum. Self-appointed censors examined textbooks for subversive doctrine, usually under narrow definitions of Americanism. More constructive critics, such as Conant in his *Education in a Divided World* and Counts in his *Education and American Civilization*, stressed instead an education that would strengthen the classic faiths of truly free society and thereby make democracy more fit to survive in its fateful competition with totalitarian regimes.

The dramatic advent of Sputnik in 1957 suddenly precipitated an unanticipated set of issues relevant to the nation's technological rather than ideological capacity to vie with foreign powers. Critics focused now upon the contribution that education should make to the physical security of the nation and the exploration of space. Rickover, for instance, in his *American Education: A National Failure*, argued for a hard, "no frills" curriculum and stressed predominant attention to the gifted learner. Bestor, Koerner, and others insisted that it was time to emphasize rigorous study of essential subjects. It was both an essentialist and an elitist philosophy of education which stressed academic virtuosity, particularly for college-bound students. The National Defense Education Act of 1958 manifested this renewal of faith in essentialism by providing funds for the improvement of instruction in the physical sciences and other subject fields related to defense.

The emphasis was upon the subject-centered curriculum at all levels of education. There was new pressure for the teaching of subjects as such, for beginning some of them at earlier grade levels, and for stressing the structure of the subject itself. This was accompanied by a demand for more difficult courses of study and more rigorous academic standards, particularly for the academically talented.

These proposals for reform in curriculum and instruction had hardly been enunciated in the 1960s before new forces in society were pressing for a return to neo-progressivism in education. The age of science and technology was being overtaken by the age of Aquarius. The civil rights movement raised new dilemmas by calling attention to the problems of undereducation and underemployment and the underprivilege which results. The common school was now criticized by the common man for its failure to meet the needs of his children. The preeminent educational issue became that of reducing the underprivilege of minorities through better education. The social sciences and humanities, which were not only neglected but sometimes even suspect during the post-Sputnik era, were now rediscovered because some of the nation's most perplexing problems—race relations, human rights, and crime—were essentially social problems. The Great Society turned to education as the fountainhead of progress for the improvement of the great social and economic problems of the times. Schools which had overreacted to the demands for intellectual rigor and attention to the gifted now turned their attention increasingly to the problems of the disadvantaged.

By the mid-1960s, the issue was focused not so much on whether the schools were tough enough, but rather on how they could produce intellectual excellence while at the same time accommodating students disenchanted by programs unattuned to their abilities and needs. The rigorous subject-centered and defense-oriented curriculum was considered irrelevant, indeed anachronistic, by a new youth culture that was more existentialist than essentialist in its outlook toward life, more intuitive than rational in thought process, more quixotic than deliberate in its selection of problems, and eager for activism rather than detachment in confronting the challenges of their times.

Conant, Bestor, Koerner, Rickover, and other essentialist reformers, all but ignored in the new crusade for humanism in education, were replaced by a new breed of romantic reformers—Goodman, Friedenberg, Holt, Kozol, and Silberman, among others—who insisted that schools should accommodate to the learner, rather than the other way around. They insisted that affective development was at least as important as cognitive development; that the neglect of the social sciences and humanities should be redressed; that the curriculum should be essentially student-centered rather than subject-centered; and that fun was more important than rigor in learning. The watchwords of curricular reform in the early 1970s became "relevancy" and "humanism." The elitist philosophy of the post-Sputnik era was replaced by a more egalitarian view.

Many writers spoke of the post-Sputnik years in education as innovative and revolutionary. Many innovations were adopted, sometimes thoughtfully but more often compulsively and unwisely. Many great new "breakthroughs" were hailed with fanfare, only to disappear quietly a few years later. One diligent observer of the educational scene, John Goodlad, concluded, after visiting many schools, that the reforms and innovations espoused during this

period were not conspicuously present in very many schools. The reader is therefore cautioned that the changes in curriculum described here are more characteristic of leading educational thought than of educational practice.

Curriculum change continues, as indeed it must in any viable culture. The historical calendar in this chapter lists some of the more significant developments in the evolution of the curriculum. Dates of other significant events in special teaching fields are given in other chapters. Many of the more crucial issues of curriculum development are explored in Chapter 1. In the pages which follow in this chapter, more attention will be given to the forces which have precipitated these changes and the nature of the emerging curriculums.

Impact of Committees and Other Organizations

The educational scene in this country is characterized by an endless succession of various committees and organizations that recommend changes in the school curriculum. Curriculum development has been greatly influenced by the reports of some of these groups. Some of the important efforts and their effect are described briefly.

Committees. The *Report of the Committee of Ten,* published in 1893, marked the attempt to emancipate secondary schools from the domination of college entrance requirements and facilitated a liberalization of high school courses of study to meet the needs of non-college-bound youths. The *Report of the Committee of Fifteen,* two years later, recommended better correlation of studies in elementary education. The Committee of Nine on the Articulation of the High Schools and Colleges appointed, like the other two, by the National Education Association, recommended in 1911 that the completion of practically any broad, well-planned high school curriculum should be accepted as preparation for college. The Commission on the Reorganization of Secondary Education followed to study the reorganization of high school subjects. This commission formulated in 1918 the famous Cardinal Principles of Secondary Education reviewed in Chapter 8.

Educational Policies Commission. The Educational Policies Commission, now defunct, has been a dynamic influence through the years in the improvement of school curriculums. In 1940, its publication *Education and Economic Well-being in American Democracy* stressed curriculums that prepare youth for productive labor, give them an understanding of the economic system, teach them about conservation of natural resources, and acquaint them with principles of wise consumer buying and saving. A year later, in *The Education of Free Men in American Democracy*, it advised a nation on the threshold of war of the kind of curriculums needed to prepare children and youth for the responsibilities of citizenship sorely tested by the threat of totalitarian countries. Its statement *Education for All American Youth* in 1944 proclaimed that all youth should have access to a broad, well-balanced curriculum to equip them for an occupation, prepare them for citizenship, stimulate their intellectual curiosity, generate in them an appreciation of ethical values, and offer them a fair chance to pursue happiness. In 1949, in anticipation of the anxieties of the cold war, the Educational Policies Commission asked, in its pamphlet *American Education and International Tensions*, for education to meet the challenge of fear, economic uncertainty, psychological tensions, and international understanding. Its pronouncement in 1957, *Higher Education in a Decade of Decision*, recommended that college curriculums be designed to stimulate individual self-realization, transmit the cultural heritage, and facilitate the application of knowledge to real-life problems. In 1960 it published *Contemporary Issues in Elementary Education* and pleaded for an elementary curriculum better attuned to the interests, needs, and capabilities of children. In 1962 it published *Education and the Disadvantaged American* and made a plea for more educational opportunity for underprivileged youth. Three years later it spoke again of the problems of disadvantaged pupils in *American Education and the Search for Equal Opportunity*; it pleaded for extended pre-elementary programs for children from low-income families, a more humanistic school environment to reduce children's hostility toward learning, and strengthened relations between school and community. The commission terminated its significant work in 1968.

National Education Association. Various affiliates of the NEA have engaged in significant study of school curriculums and have issued influential pro-

nouncements. The Association for Supervision and Curriculum Development, particularly, has influenced curriculum development through its annual conferences, its research studies, and its journal *Educational Leadership*. The titles of some of its publications suggest the focuses of its interests in curriculum improvement:*Balance in the Curriculum; Freeing Capacity to Learn; Human Variability and Learning; Leadership for Improving Instruction; Curriculum Change: Direction and Process; A Curriculum for Children; Curriculum Decisions: Social Realities; Curriculum Materials 1970; Early Childhood Education Today; Ethnic Modification of the Curriculum; Humanizing the Secondary School; The International Dimension of Education; Student Unrest: Threat or Promise?; To Nurture Humaneness: Commitment for the '70's; The Unstudied Curriculum: Its Impact on Children; Youth Education: Problems, Perspectives, Promises; New Dimensions in Learning; Perceiving, Behaving, and Becoming: A New Focus for Education; What Are the Sources of the Curriculum?; The Junior High School We Saw; New Curriculum Developments; Strategy for Curriculum Change; Theories of Instruction; The New Elementary School; Supervision: Perspectives and Propositions;* and *Influences in Curriculum Change.*

In 1959 the National Education Association commissioned the National Committee of the NEA Project on Instruction to provide guidance in the redevelopment of school curriculums and instruction in the aftermath of the near national hysteria over Sputnik. Several of its publications, particularly *Deciding What To Teach, Planning and Organizing for Teaching,* and *Schools for the Seventies,* identified and clarified the issues, reviewed curriculum research and development, and made a number of influential recommendations relative to the content and structure of the curriculum, classroom organization, instructional method, and decision making in curriculum development.

In 1971 the NEA initiated the National Foundation for the Improvement of Education to mobilize research and experimentation for the improvement of instruction and learning. The Foundation integrates the various enterprises previously existing in the various departments of the NEA and mobilizes the resources of state and local NEA affiliates more effectively in curriculum research and development.

The *Handbook of Research on Teaching,* published in 1963 by the American Educational Research

Association, was a monumental compendium of research findings on teaching method and related topics.

Other Professional Organizations and Learned Societies. Many other professional associations and learned societies have helped to give direction to curriculum builders. Some are described in detail later in this chapter. Among the others is the National Society for the Study of Education, whose various yearbooks have focused upon significant aspects of school improvement. The now defunct Progressive Education Association conducted a memorable eight-year study of progressive education curriculums in selected high schools. The Commission on Life Adjustment formulated the much-maligned concept of education attuned to the real-life needs of youth. The American Council on Education, through its various studies and commissions, such as the American Youth Commission, has brought scholarly research to bear upon the more important problems of curriculum reform. The Council for Basic Education, a leading exponent of essentialism, has emphasized the importance of much more rigorous standards and curriculums organized around subject matter. Phi Delta Kappa, an honorary fraternity for men in education, has influenced school curriculums through its various conferences, monographs, and particularly through its excellent publication *Phi Delta Kappan.* The various regional accrediting associations have influenced both high school and college curriculums in those institutions which have sought to raise their standards of instruction to merit accreditation. This list is illustrative rather than exhaustive.

Several presidential committees, conferences, and commissions have issued influential statements pointing the way toward curriculum improvement at all levels of education. The findings of the White House Conferences on Education, the President's Committee on Education beyond the High School, the President's Science Advisory Committee, and the President's Commission on National Goals have been referred to in other chapters.

Educational Foundations. Educational foundations have also had a significant impact upon program development at all levels of education. The Ford Foundation has stimulated innovations in teaching methodology, principally team teaching, educational television, learning laboratories, and self-instructional devices. It has also encouraged changes in

the curriculum of teacher-preparation institutions and helped to strengthen the curriculums in liberal arts, science, engineering, and public and international affairs in colleges and universities. The Kellogg Foundation, Carnegie Corporation, Rockefeller Fund, and Sloan Foundation have funded various enterprises in curriculum improvement, particularly in the professional schools.

Another national organization, IDEA, an acronym for Institute for the Development of Educational Activities, was launched in 1966 to help get proved educational practices adopted by more schools. Funded by the Kettering Foundation and directed by John Goodlad, IDEA is gathering promising new concepts for the improvement of elementary and secondary education.

A great many other educational foundations and organizations have provided the funds necessary to extend the educational frontier in virtually all areas of school curriculums at all levels of education. The National Safety Council has stimulated improvement of safety education in the public schools. Driver education has been subsidized by the American Automobile Association. Health education and accident prevention have been primary concerns of the major insurance companies. Many other examples could be cited.

Contributions of Scholars

In addition to the individuals mentioned elsewhere in this chapter, countless others have contributed to the development of the contemporary curriculum. G. Stanley Hall's classic study *Adolescence*, published in 1904, had a marked effect on the high school curriculum by revealing more cogently the nature and needs of youth of secondary school age. Charles W. Eliot, a former president of Harvard, greatly changed college curriculums and worked for the elective system which is now being carefully scrutinized. Edward L. Thorndike, through his productive research at Columbia University, threw new light on the learning processes and capabilities of children, youth, and adults. Arnold L. Gesell, formerly of the Yale University Clinic for Child Development, for more than forty years studied youngsters and how they learn. His observations affected the curriculum for pre-elementary and elementary school children. Jean Piaget, the Swiss educationist, through his empirical studies of children added much to our insight into the learning process and how it can be sustained through effective teaching.

The educational philosopher John Dewey, whose prolific writings are discussed at some length in other chapters, had perhaps the greatest influence of any single writer and teacher upon our understanding of the nature of learning and instructional method. Harold Rugg, W. W. Charters, William H. Kilpatrick, among many others, were eminent contributors to educational thought in curriculum theory. Kimball Wiles and Hollis Caswell brought scholarship to the study of the processes of curriculum development. Lawrence Cremin chronicled the history of curriculum development in American schools. Harry Broudy and John Palmer's *Exemplars of Teaching Method*, John Holt's *How Children Fail* and *How Children Learn*, John Goodlad's *The Changing School Curriculum*, James Conant's several works on American high schools and junior high schools, and Jerome Bruner's *The Process of Education* were especially noteworthy contributions to the development of school curriculums during the 1950s and 1960s. Martin Mayer's best seller, *The Schools*, noted outstanding curricular practices in strong American and European schools and has had considerable influence upon educational thought, especially among laymen.

In 1970 Charles Silberman's book *Crisis in the Classroom* called attention to oppressiveness and joylessness of school classrooms caused by the schools' preoccupation with order, routine, and control. He indicted the "tyranny of the lesson plan" and the schools' failure to develop students' capacity to learn for themselves. He urged educators to think seriously about the purposes and consequences of their pedagogy and its effect upon children. Here is one of Silberman's major conclusions:

Schools can be humane and still educate well. They can be genuinely concerned with gaiety and joy and individual growth and fulfillment without sacrificing concern for intellectual discipline and development. They can be simultaneously child-centered and subject- or knowledge-centered. They can stress esthetic and moral education without weakening the three R's. They can do all these things if—but only if—their structure, content, and objectives are transformed.[1]

[1] Charles Silberman, *Crisis in the Classroom*, Random House, Inc., New York, 1970, p. 208.

One powerful influence in curriculum reform in elementary and secondary schools has been the involvement of professors of the academic disciplines. Once content to remain aloof in their ivory towers and criticize the state of elementary and high school instruction, these academicians have finally recognized their own responsibility for educational improvement. Realizing that the quality of education in colleges and universities is inevitably linked with the quality of previous learning, they have hastened to close the gap between research findings in the academic fields and the teaching of these fields in the public schools. Many conferences, research projects, trial demonstrations, and experiments have brought together the academicians and the educationists, who were once content to go their separate ways. They have now joined hands in unprecedented numbers with elementary and secondary school teachers. The results have been remarkable.

Stimulation of Federal Support

In Chapter 2, attention was called to the federal financial effort in education. Many federal acts have been born out of national concern in times of crisis.

Title III of the Elementary and Secondary Education Act of 1965 provided for the creation of supplementary centers and services to help local school districts enrich their school curriculums. These programs, commonly known as PACE, seek to encourage flexibility, innovation, and experimentation in curriculum and instruction. It is hoped that each center will be designed to meet the needs of the particular school community.

The Elementary and Secondary Education Act authorized several regional laboratories designed to stimulate and disseminate exemplary instructional methods and materials. These laboratories are typically confederations of universities, school systems, and other educational organizations. Some of these laboratories have had important impact on curriculum and instruction. One of the more influential of these laboratories, the Educational Development Center (EDC) located in New England, is a merger of the Institute for Educational Innovation (IEI) and Educational Services, Inc. (ESI). EDC has brought together eminent professors from the arts and sciences and school teachers to create new courses of study in basic subjects complete with textbooks and supporting audiovisual instructional materials. EDC is reportedly the largest organization devoting itself entirely to curriculum research and development.[2] Many other examples of private and public enterprise in the development of curriculum and instructional materials could be cited.

Contributions of Private Industry

Publishers of textbooks and other instructional materials have for many years influenced school curriculums. One educator said, "Let me write your textbooks, and I will have written your curriculum." Over the last two decades many large manufacturers of electronic equipment have purchased publishing firms to join the manufacture and distribution of educational hardware and software. This trend, which has stimulated the development of educational technology, is discussed in Chapter 15. One example of industry's contribution in the development of educational technology is the Westinghouse Learning Corporation's Project PLAN. PLAN is a systematic specification of educational objectives tailored to meet each student's special aptitudes, interests, and patterns of learning. A computer stores these data and presents "teaching-learning units" tailor-made for each student according to his needs and achievement. The computer also monitors his progress and feeds back evaluation of his work. PLAN has been widely tested in the field and promises to have widespread impact on the whole development of computer-assisted instruction.

New Insights into the Nature of Learning and Creative Intelligence

The interest of psychologists in the study of learning is not new. Thorndike, Terman, Gesell, Piaget, and others have long explored the nature of learning and its implications for instruction and curriculum organization. Harvard professor B.F. Skinner's pioneering work in learning theory has established the basis for teaching machines and other devices for programmed learning. It has also cast important light upon the orderly, sequential presentation of content, which is basic not only to programmed learning but also to efficient and systematic ordering of all courses of study. It has forced teachers and re-

searchers to raise fundamental questions about the objectives of teaching, the nature and order of materials to be learned, the function of evaluation and reward in learning, the adaptation of the curriculum to individual differences, and other important facets of the entire educative process.

Many other investigators have turned their attention to the nature of intelligence, seeking to learn more about the nourishment of creative thought and discovery in education. Through such investigations have been established the methodological bases for the new curriculums in mathematics and the natural sciences, which are described later in this chapter. Although much remains to be learned about the phenomenon of learning and intelligence, it is clear that modern man is on the verge of new insights into the human mind that will lead to further changes in education through new curricular structures and the organization of more effective learning experiences.

Proliferation of Knowledge

The past quarter-century has been characterized by a wondrous expansion of knowledge. The school textbooks used by most parents of today's college students failed to mention advanced placement courses, polio vaccine, space satellites, teaching machines, transistors, tape recorders, electronic computers, astronauts, NATO, Orlon, cortisone, team teaching, the National Science Foundation, and the Department of Health, Education, and Welfare. Far less academic substance had to be fitted into the curriculum in those days, although the school day and year were almost as long as they are today. No longer can one "complete his education," although both the term and the idea were common a generation ago. This pressure of new knowledge has forced educators to look for more compact means of organizing programs of study, to prune out the irrelevant and obsolete, and to focus upon content that is most conducive to continued independent learning.

Influence of Educational Technology

A society whose industry has been revolutionized by technology must expect a similar transformation in its schools. Educational technology is discussed

[2] For further discussion of this important organization, see James D. Koerner, "EDC: General Motors of Curriculum Reform," *Saturday Review*, vol. 50, pp. 56–58, 70–71, Aug. 19, 1967.

at length in Chapter 15. Here we simply call attention to three illustrations of how this new technology is affecting curriculum and instruction. The miracle of television has brought the world of instantaneous sight and sound into the classroom as it has into the living rooms of the nation. Thanks to the linkage of television with Telstar, it is now technically possible to bring any knowledge anywhere in the world into any classroom. The computer now makes it technically possible for schools to realize the long-sought goal of full individualization of instruction for each student. Computer-assisted instruction permits each student to carry on a sort of tutorial dialogue that is responsive to his particular capabilities and achievements. Finally, the application of systems analysis to the educational program permits schools to plan and design curriculums adapted specifically to their own objectives, to monitor the costs and benefits more precisely, and to choose more wisely among the various curriculums and instructional modes. Clearly most of the impact of educational technology upon the curriculum lies in the future.

OBJECTIVES

One of the ageless educational questions, the one central to all others, is: "What is the purpose of education?" If this question could be answered to the satisfaction of all—as, of course, it never will or should be—practically all other educational issues could be resolved. Is it the purpose of education to transmit subject matter? To reform society? To encourage individual self-realization? To develop better citizens? To train more productive workers? To build better attitudes and values? To improve intergroup and international relations? Is it all of these, or none of these?

The Association for Supervision and Curriculum Development has stated five philosophical positions that have been taken in response to the question: "What is the purpose of education?"

Position 1. *The primary responsibility of the school is intellectual development. Intellectual development is conceived as mastery of subject matter through exposition by the teacher, use of texts, drill, recitation and examination. Education is concerned primarily with building in the learner a storehouse of information, skills and values which may be useful to him at some later time.*

Position 2. *The primary responsibility of the school is intellectual development. Intellectual development is conceived as being directed toward creative problem solving, the use of education as a tool, the fostering of curiosity, experimentation, and the reorganization of ideas. However, schools should not waste valuable time on the practical arts, the development of social skills, or problems of personal adjustment. Other agencies such as the church, home, and YWCA and YMCA can do these important jobs.*

Position 3. *Intellectual development is the primary responsibility of the school, but the individual is an integrated organism. Growth is interrelated. Emotional health, personal-social adjustment, group process skills, and physical vitality all contribute to and are essential to intellectual effectiveness.*

Position 4. *All areas of development are important in and of themselves. Schools should educate for life. Students need all-around development—social, emotional, intellectual, and physical. The public schools are in a better position to do these jobs effectively than is any other institution, although the value of contributions by homes, churches and other agencies is recognized.*

Position 5. *The academic emphasis is appropriate to only a small portion of the student body. For many, general problems of life, particularly the immediate, practical, personal needs of the pupil, are the appropriate subject matter. Vocational skills are of primary importance. Intelligence is developed and utilized by such pupils in relationship to these practical problems of living.*[3]

These points of view reflect various positions on a continuum ranging from essentialism (position 1) to progressivism (position 4) and life adjustment (position 5). Obviously the curriculum one finds most satisfactory depends heavily upon the philosophical position one takes in his definition of education. The reader is referred to Chapter 1 for a more extended discussion of educational philosophies.

One's educational philosophy establishes the values and priorities from which a statement of educational objectives can be derived. Obviously, it is impossible to design or evaluate a curriculum until educational objectives to be realized through the curriculum have been specified.

Examples of statements of educational objectives are legion. The authors rather like the set of ten objectives listed below, which were established to guide the Quality Education Project in Pennsylvania. Quality education should help every child:

[3] Robert S. Fox, "Balance and the Problem of Purpose," *Balance in the Curriculum*, Yearbook of the Association for Supervision and Curriculum Development, National Education Association, Washington, D.C., 1961, pp. 51-52.

Acquire the greatest possible understanding of himself and an appreciation of his worthiness as a member of society.

Acquire understanding and appreciation of persons belonging to social, cultural and ethnic groups different from his own.

Acquire to the fullest extent possible for him, mastery of the basic skills in the use of words and numbers.

Acquire a positive attitude toward the learning process.

Acquire the habits and attitudes associated with responsible citizenship.

Acquire good health habits and an understanding of the conditions necessary for the maintaining of physical and emotional well-being.

Find opportunity and encouragement to be creative in one or more fields of endeavor.

Understand the opportunities open to him for preparing himself for a productive life and should enable him to take full advantage of these opportunities.

Understand and appreciate as much as he can of human achievement in the natural sciences, the social sciences, the humanities and the arts.

Prepare for a world of rapid change and unforeseeable demands in which continuing education throughout his adult life should be normal expectation.[4]

These goals are general statements of objectives to guide the development of the total school curriculum. In recent years great emphasis has been placed upon the formulation of *behavioral objectives* for units of work. The advent of programmed instruction has made behavioral objectives quite essential to the programmer, who must know in terms of the student's *behavior* exactly what the unit of work is expected to accomplish. Abstract words such as "understanding," "skill," and "attitudes"—although unavoidable in generalized statements of curriculum objectives—are not adequate for the planning of study units or precise evaluation of student progress in programmed instruction. Behavior is overt and observable and measurable, even though the more generalized goals or objectives are the ultimate goal. These two examples of behavioral objectives are illustrative:

Identifies and reads decimal fractions to hundredths.
Subtracts with no borrowing up to three digits.

The specification of behavioral objectives by classroom teachers is important, even though programmed materials are not in use, for the same

[4]"Ten Goals of Quality Education," *Pennsylvania Education*, vol. 119, p. 19, September-October, 1970.

reasons stated above. That many teachers proceed without them in no way denies their importance.[5]

It is impossible in a dynamic society to develop educational objectives that are universally applicable or perpetually enduring. Each school system must subject its objectives to continuing scrutiny just as classroom teachers must do for the instruction which they offer.

PRINCIPLES

A common practice in the initiation of programs for curriculum development is to prepare a list of basic principles or guiding assumptions. This initial attack provides a unified point of view and a basis for consistency of action among the educational workers as they develop curriculums. The following list reflects the authors' preferences with respect to (1) the nature of the curriculum and (2) the procedures of curriculum development.

The Nature of the Curriculum

The Curriculum Should Be Rooted in a Philosophy of Education. As stated earlier, school systems and individual teachers must consider certain fundamental questions relative to the purposes of education and must specify rather clearly in terms of the learner's behavior the educational objectives which should be accomplished through the curriculum and instruction if the school is to be effective. Without a philosophic rationale, important decisions may be made on spurious considerations and the curriculum is less likely to be coherent and consistent. A well-defined philosophy of education will also help to establish priorities. Clearly this philosophy of education should be developed cooperatively by the faculty, administrators, board of education, and students.

The Curriculum Should Accommodate a Wide Range of Individual Abilities and Needs of Students. The doctrine of individual differences among students is axiomatic, and it is important that the

[5]For further elaboration of the importance and use of behavioral objectives, see Robert L. Ebel, "Behavioral Objectives: A Close Look," *Phi Delta Kappan*, vol. 52, pp. 171-173, November, 1970.

curriculum be sufficiently broad and flexible to provide meaningful educative experience for students with quite varied interests and abilities—students who are preparing for college as well as students who are preparing for trades, gifted students who learn easily and quickly as well as other students who learn with more difficulty, students who can learn through independent study as well as students who need close supervision.

Four general approaches to the individualization of instruction are illustrated in Figure 14-1: individually prescribed instruction, self-directed study, personalized instruction, and independent study. Many schools use adaptations and combinations of all four categories.

The vertical organization of the curriculum should permit continuous progression of all learners, but at various rates of progress differentiated according to their abilities. Ungraded and multigraded organizations are useful patterns for achieving this ideal. Programmed instruction offers a technological device by which instruction may be adapted more effectively and efficiently to the individual needs of learners.

The Curriculum Should Be Life-centered, Shaped by Both Present and Future Needs of the Individual and Society. Considerable debate has raged over the issue of whether the curriculum should simply transmit the cultural heritage of the past or address itself to the contemporary and future needs of the culture. There is also the issue of whether the curriculum should be subject-centered, child-centered, or community-centered. Fortunately, these are not mutually exclusive choices, despite contrary claims by many critics of the curriculum. Figure 14-2

shows a schematic view of these issues. The vertical dimension of the figure illustrates the issue of the individual's needs versus the needs of society. One might take the position that schools are established by society to serve its needs—such as increased production, better race relations, reduction of poverty, and improved national defense posture, among others. Or one might contend that the primary function of education is to nurture the development of the individual learner in relation to his personal needs: self-realization, self-understanding, and self-expression, among others. The first orientation is primarily social; the latter primarily psychological. We take the position that it is both unrealistic and unnecessary to take a categorical stand on one of these two positions; the real issue centers around the relative emphasis to be given to the needs of society and the needs of the individual. Both are essential. In our view, the individual can realize himself as an individual only in relation to the society in which he lives. The learner and society are constantly interacting and being shaped by each other. Any curriculum that considers only the demands of society or only the needs of the learner fails to come to grips with the dynamics of this interaction.

The horizontal dimension of Figure 14-2 represents the issue of whether the curriculum should present only the cultural heritage of the past or include consideration of contemporary and future needs of the learner in society. The classical realists contend that the function of the school is to transmit the cultural heritage of the past, not reshape present or future culture. The reconstructionists, existentialists, and others, on the other hand, contend that the primary function of the curriculum is to help citizens reconstruct and improve society in the present and the future. The former view conceives the curriculum as something static and suggests that the adult

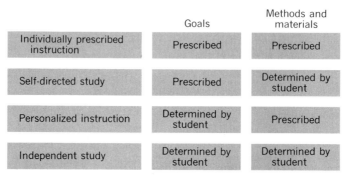

	Goals	Methods and materials
Individually prescribed instruction	Prescribed	Prescribed
Self-directed study	Prescribed	Determined by student
Personalized instruction	Determined by student	Prescribed
Independent study	Determined by student	Determined by student

FIGURE 14-1 *Comparison of modes of individualized instruction.*

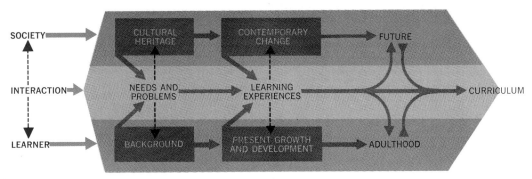

FIGURE 14-2   *The curriculum in relation to the learner and society.* (*Willard S. Elsbree, Harold J. McNally, and Richard Wynn*, Elementary School Administration and Supervision, *3d ed.*, *American Book Company, New York, 1967, p. 83.*)

needs of today's children can be predicted and provided for from what we now know. But the speed of social change and the rapid growth of knowledge suggest that today's curriculum cannot provide for the learner all the knowledge that the future will require. Yet one can hope that the school curriculum, by confronting the learner with current problems, will provide him sound modes of thought, processes of inquiry, and patterns for the organization and application of knowledge, thereby permitting him to "learn how to learn" throughout life. In the authors' view, education should address itself to the entire time continuum. It should give attention to the social heritage and the learner's background and then look to both the contemporary and future needs of the society and the learner. Thus the curriculum must be broad and comprehensive.

The Curriculum Should Be Well-balanced. As noted elsewhere in this chapter, various components of the curriculum have been emphasized and others neglected. Special-purpose federal aid, prompted by various crises and designed to stimulate curriculum development in certain subjects, has contributed to this situation. Ideally, a sound curriculum is one in which the several subject fields are kept in reasonable balance in terms of time allotments, money spent for research and development, and prestige associated with them.

The Process of Curriculum Development

Certain principles should govern the development of the curriculum in a free society because the quality of the curriculum is highly dependent upon the wisdom of the process which produces it.

Curriculum Building Should Be a Cooperative Enterprise. In local, statewide, or national programs, cooperative effort is essential in curriculum work. One postulate of democracy is that persons enjoy those things which they have helped to build. This is doubly true in regard to the curriculum of the school. Local school faculties should have the freedom and authority to make decisions about how to teach and what to teach, within the limits of state and local requirements. Effective curriculums are the fruit of collaborative work by teachers, curriculum specialists, academicians, consultants, and to a more limited degree, students and citizens.

Evaluation Is Essential for Curriculum Improvement. The results of student achievement, as well as other measures, are necessary to appraise the effectiveness of the curriculum and instruction. Although the measurement of cognitive development is a fairly well-refined science, the measurement of the affective objectives of the curriculum is much more difficult. The National Assessment for Educational Progress, sponsored by the Education Commission of the States, is an ambitious effort to gather normative data from a national sample of students' achievement, which provides schools with data which will permit comparison of the effectiveness of the curriculum and instruction with national norms.

Curriculum Support Systems Should Be Adequate. Curriculum development is handicapped in many schools by the lack of adequate resources, placing too much responsibility upon the harried classroom teacher who has little time for curriculum improvement. Fine school systems provide experts in curriculum theory and method on their own staffs, who are supplemented as needed with consultants from intermediate district offices, state departments, regional laboratories, and other organizations. Some teachers are employed on twelve-month contracts so that they will be available during the summer months for curriculum development work.

Various material resources are also important. More and more good schools are providing curriculum materials centers which stock sample textbooks and other instructional materials and often produce their own materials when commercial materials are inadequate. Testing programs, counseling services, child-study centers, reading clinics, and many other ancillary services are needed to support the modern school program. These services are discussed in Chapter 13. Other material resources, such as planetariums, learning laboratories, television facilities, and science laboratories, are discussed in Chapter 15.

Curriculum Development Should Be a Systematic Process. One of the hallmarks of a fine school system is the deliberate, systematic, continuous attention which it devotes to the development of the total educational program, as opposed to the sporadic, incidental, intuitive approach to program building which still characterizes too many schools. The application of systems theory is refining the process of curriculum development even more thoroughly.

ORGANIZATION

The organization of learning experiences in the curriculum is very important because it affects the effectiveness of teaching and learning.

Types of Curriculum Organization

Curricular patterns range from the traditional type to extremely experimental types. Five of the curricular patterns, with alternative designations, are (1) subject or traditional, (2) correlated or fused, (3) broad fields or areas, (4) core or common learnings, and (5) experience or functional curriculums. These types, which are not mutually exclusive and have numerous variations, are illustrated in Figure 14-3.

The Subject Curriculum. This is characterized by a large number of subjects taught independently of

one another. Most of the student's time is spent in learning from books and other written and printed materials in various subjects in which the accumulated wisdom of experts in that field has been recorded. The emphasis is upon the learning of subject matter selected long before the students appear in the classroom.

In such a curriculum, history, geography, and civics usually are isolated subjects. A modern variation of the subject curriculum began to emerge in the late 1950s. It is spoken of as the "subject-discipline curriculum" and emphasizes not the memorization of information but the perception of the structure of the subject field—its concepts, modes of inquiry, and organization of knowledge. It was prompted by the impossible load of the growing subject matter, the desire to give students a mode of inquiry that would permit them to study the subject on their own initiative after mastering its structure, and to help students gain a fresh and enriched view of the nature of general education. Its disadvantages include its failure to relate to real-life problems, such as pollution, which do not come wrapped up in a single subject field; its failure to integrate knowledge from several subject fields; and its difficulty to apply in fields outside the physical sciences where knowledge is not readily organizable.[6]

The Correlated Curriculum. Here the underlying ideas are those described for the subject curriculum. The starting point is subject-matter-set-out-to-be-learned. The correlated curriculum can be carried out in numerous ways, which can be conveniently arranged on a scale. At the bottom would be located the casual and incidental efforts to make relationships between subjects. At the top of the scale would be located the conscious and definitely planned efforts to make effective relationships between subjects. Among the correlations may be those between subjects within a field, as social science, or between subjects within two or more fields, as English and history. Subjects may be fused so that boundaries disappear.

The Broad Fields Curriculum. This is composed of a few fields rather than a large number of small subjects. In broad fields, under the subject philoso-

[6] For further discussion of the subject-discipline organization, see Arthur W. Foshay, "How Fare the Disciplines?" *Phi Delta Kappan*, vol. 51, pp. 349–352, March, 1970.

phy, the learning area is restricted, although definitely broader than what would be expected as a summation of various subjects. In broad fields, under the experience philosophy, the learning area is greatly increased. Examples of these broad fields or areas are social science and the language arts.

The Core Curriculum. This includes subjects or a common body of experiences required of everyone, but with variability of content and activities to meet the varying needs of individuals. The term "core" is used to cover a wide range of types of curriculum

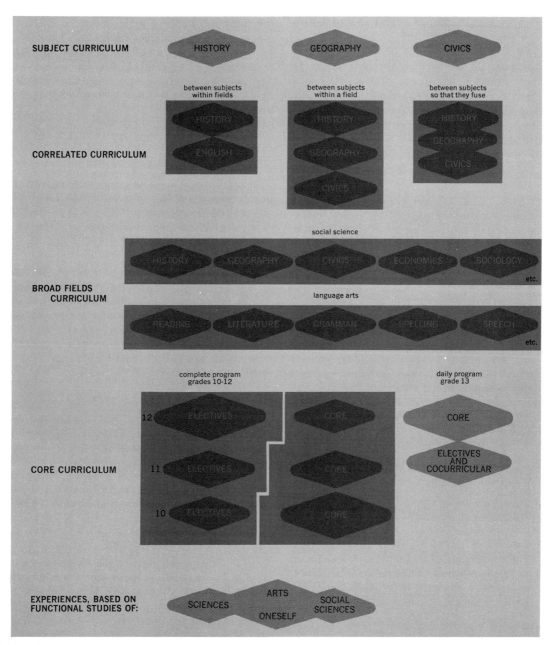

FIGURE 14-3 Major types of curriculums.

practice. Part of the work in the senior high may be a basic core running through grades 10, 11 and 12 with variable time allotments. A certain portion of each day may be devoted to the core, or common learnings.

The Experience Curriculum. This type of curriculum is very compatible with progressive, reconstructionist, and existentialist philosophies of education because learning is thought of as the reconstruction of experience. The curriculum is made up, at least in part, of students dealing directly with problems or circumstances in the cultural milieu, very often problems of their own selection. These might include the study of water pollution or urban renewal through direct observation and analysis in the community; acquiring skills in creative writing by publishing a school newspaper; or gaining an understanding of international relations by participating in a mock session of the United Nations General Assembly. The hallmark of the experience curriculum of course is learning by doing—either in real-life settings or in simulated reality.

Experience-centered curriculums may range between curriculums that are largely predetermined and structured by school authorities to almost completely spontaneous and unstructured activities which characterize the street academies, alternative schools, schools without walls, or "free universities," as they are commonly spoken of. Many contemporary educational reformers regard the experience curriculum as the best response to the alienation of youth and to the demand for relevance in education. Two educators, for example, state the following conviction:

It is more relevant to engage young people in a study of the problems of the larger culture in which many of their own problems have their origin. The culture of most significance to the young consists of those aspects that are problematic—that is, the large conflicts and confusions which translate into the conflicts and confusions of individuals.[7]

The advantages of the experience curriculum are that it can obviously be made more relevant to the concerns of students, it can stimulate a high degree of motivation, it can contribute directly to

[7]Lawrence E. Metcalf and Maurice P. Hunt, "Relevance and the Curriculum," *Phi Delta Kappan*, vol. 51, p. 361, March, 1970.

the improvement of the human condition, and it can mobilize knowledge from several academic disciplines to bear upon a problem. Its major disadvantages are that it can be very time-consuming in relation to what is learned, that it can produce serious gaps in one's general education by focusing large blocks of time upon very limited aspects of the world of knowledge, and that it may lack intellectual rigor, particularly if too much responsibility is placed upon the student for his own learning. Although most schools build part of their curriculums upon the experience curriculum (driver education, typewriting, and debating, for example, can hardly be taught otherwise), few schools other than the so-called "open schools" base their curriculums entirely upon experience.

Types of Instructional Systems

The discussion above dealt with patterns of curriculum organization. We consider now various types of instructional systems. There are no standard means of classifying instructional systems. They might be classified on the basis of the deployment of students in the system: (1) group instruction and (2) individualized instruction. They might be classified on the basis of the deployment of responsibility for directing the instruction: (1) teacher-mediated instruction, (2) computer-mediated instruction, and (3) student-mediated instruction or self-instruction. These two sets of categories are overlapping. The categories rarely exist in pure form. We shall discuss both sets of categories.

Group Instruction. We are all familiar with various types of group instruction which have prevailed almost entirely until recent years. Students are grouped in various sizes on the basis of chronological age, reading ability, academic interests, intelligence, or various other criteria. The obvious advantage of group instruction is that it is more economical of the teacher's time than individualized instruction. Its disadvantage is of course that it fails to accommodate individual differences in the learner.

Individualized Instruction. Mark Hopkins on one end of the log and the student on the other is the classic illustration of individualized instruction. This kind of private tutoring was prohibitively expensive in most cases until programmed learning reduced the teacher's involvement in the process. Various modes of individualized instruction are discussed

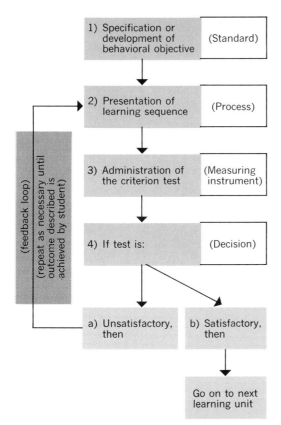

1) Specification or development of behavioral objective	(Standard)
2) Presentation of learning sequence	(Process)
3) Administration of the criterion test	(Measuring instrument)
4) If test is:	(Decision)
a) Unsatisfactory, then	b) Satisfactory, then

(feedback loop)
(repeat as necessary until outcome described is achieved by student)

Go on to next learning unit

FIGURE 14-4 Sequence of a task in programmed instruction. This figure illustrates the essential elements in a sequence of programmed instruction. When the feedback loop is present and offers remedial instruction, the program is "branched." Without this loop, the program is "linear." (Reprinted from American Association of School Administrators, Instructional Technology and the School Administrator, *The Association, Washington, D.C., 1970, p. 40.)*

earlier in this chapter and in Chapter 15. Various models of programmed instruction are now in fairly common use in schools and colleges. Figure 14-4 illustrates the sequence of a programmed instructional task. Individually Prescribed Instruction (IPI) was developed by the Learning Research and Development Center at the University of Pittsburgh and tested in the field in the Baldwin-Whitehall School District beginning in 1964. By 1971 IPI materials were available in elementary school language arts, mathematics, social studies, and science.

The essential procedures of the IPI instructional system include:

Diagnose student's strengths and weaknesses with tests.

Prescribe instructional tasks built upon behavioral objectives and tailored to the individual's needs.

Analyze the student's progress with the instructional task through tests.

Apply guidance or tutoring as needed to assure mastery of the task.

Administer test to confirm mastery.

Repeat the cycle with the next set of learning tasks.

IPI is based upon the following instructional stratagems:

Help each student proceed at his optimal rate in progress toward well-defined instructional tasks derived from specific educational objectives.

Involve each student actively in learning activities that are wholly or partially self-directed and self-selected.

Engage the student in evaluating the quality and rapidity of his own progress toward mastery of the instructional tasks.

Encounter various instructional modes and materials best adapted to his particular needs and learning style.

Assessments of the IPI program to date indicate that it yields generally higher achievement for students than is common in conventional instruction. IPI has been discussed at some length here because it is one of the most widely used and carefully developed programs of individualized instruction developed so far. It promises much wider use in the years ahead and may one day be regarded as one of the most significant developments in instruction in our history.[8]

Various other programs of individualized instruction are also noteworthy but can be mentioned only briefly here. Project READ, developed by Behavioral Research Laboratories, is also widely used. Project PLAN, developed by the Westinghouse Learning Corporation, was described earlier. Educational Systems for the Seventies (ES'70), initiated by the U.S. Office of Education, comprises a number of school systems across the country, which are pioneering various instructional systems that are highly individualized and which are likely to become prototypes for the future. Many others are in various stages of development.[9]

[8]For further description of IPI, see Diane Divoky, "Individually Prescribed Instruction," *The Nation's Schools*, vol. 84, pp. 44-46, November, 1969.

[9]See John C. Flanagan, "How Instructional Systems Will Manage Learning," *The Nation's Schools*, vol. 86, pp. 65-69, 120, October, 1970.

Individualized instruction is noteworthy generally for many reasons. It may eventually realize that age-old dream of adapting instruction rather precisely to the needs, interests, abilities, and learning styles of each individual. It may obviate conventional marking systems which are usually so dysfunctional. It will prevent learners from falling hopelessly behind in their schoolwork and render obsolete the concept of failure and the practice of nonpromotion. It will stimulate research on how students learn and deepen our understanding of how they may be instructed more effectively. It will help students undertake responsibility for their own learning and make them less dependent upon the instructor. Small wonder that most educators are viewing the development of individualized instruction with approbation. Its chief disadvantage is that the costs will remain fairly prohibitive for most districts until the economies of mass production can be realized.

We will consider now the three basic types of instructional management systems: teacher-mediated, computer-mediated, and student-mediated instruction.

Teacher-mediated Instruction. Conventional instruction has been almost entirely teacher-mediated. The teacher selects the instructional materials and methods; the teacher dispenses the knowledge through lecture, discussion, and assigned readings; the teacher evaluates the results. In short, the teacher manages virtually all the options within the parameters set by the school district.

Computer-mediated Instruction. The computer is being used increasingly to store and analyze data concerning the student's learning needs, problems, styles, and progress; to prescribe appropriate instructional tasks; to score and feed back the results of his work; to monitor his progress; and, in short, to handle many of the logistical instructional tasks formerly assumed by the teacher. Many programmed instructional systems, such as PLAN, mentioned earlier, are dependent upon the computer. These systems are commonly spoken of as "computer-assisted instruction" (CAI). The computer eventually will make it financially feasible to handle the great burden of data processing which is generated by programmed instruction, which in turn provides for the individualization of instruction.

Computer-assisted instruction, manifested by this teletypewriter, permits better individualization of instruction.

CAI is discussed at greater length in Chapter 15. Figure 14-4 illustrates a typical sequence of programmed learning.

Student-mediated Instruction. Man has always been engaged in certain learning activities which are independent of the teacher and the computer. Independent study is becoming increasingly common in many schools during part of the school day. As noted earlier, few if any schools utilize computer-mediated instruction or student-mediated instruction exclusively, and teacher-mediated instruction still predominates in most schools. The ideal instructional program utilizes all three management systems.

Developments in Subject Fields

Modern curriculum development can be understood best when considered in relationship to specific subject fields. These developments in both content and method are summarized here.

Language Arts. Language skills, particularly reading, are basic to all other learning. It was estimated in 1970 that 7 million students cannot read well enough to make full progress in school; that 8 million adults are functionally illiterate; and that 25 million jobholders are denied advancement because of reading difficulties. To relieve this tragedy, President Nixon in 1970 launched a Right-to-Read project designed to help virtually all children learn to read. The project functions under the direction of the National Reading Center, a private, nonprofit educational corporation which contracts with the U.S. Office of Education on reading-improvement projects. This enterprise is augmented by regional reading centers and is advised by a National Reading Center.

Controversy has raged for many years over the relative advantages of the phonic method of reading instruction versus the "look-say" method.[10] In the former, students are expected to associate the spoken sounds of letters with their printed symbols. In the latter method, students are expected to recognize whole words through association with pictures which illustrate the meaning of the word, clues from the context in which the word is used, or other intuitive means. Educationists and authors of reading books have traditionally overwhelmingly preferred the "look-say" or meaning-emphasis method, while critics of reading instruction, such as Rudolph Flesch in *Why Johnny Can't Read* and Jeanne Chall in *Learning to Read: The Great Debate*, have argued for greater emphasis upon the phonic approach. The evidence appears to favor the phonic method, which was not customarily used in most basal reading series before the debate.

Several new phonic approaches to reading have been devised. Hay and Wingo have developed a system, *Reading with Phonics*, in which the simpler phonetic sounds are taught first to provide a basic reading vocabulary, with more difficult sounds coming later. Caleb Gattegno has developed an ingenious simplification of reading instruction, *Words in Color*, in which the various multiple sounds of the same letter are represented by distinctive colors. The Initial Teaching Alphabet (ITA), illustrated in Figure 14-5, was devised by Sir James Pitman, an English headmaster. ITA consists of forty-four symbols, each with a distinctive single sound, thereby conveying all the different sounds of the English language. This eliminates the confusion of multiple sounds for the same letter, phonetic inconsistencies,

[10] For further discussion of this controversy, see Patrick Groff, "Jeanne Chall Revisited," *Phi Delta Kappan*, vol. 51, pp. 162–165, November, 1970.

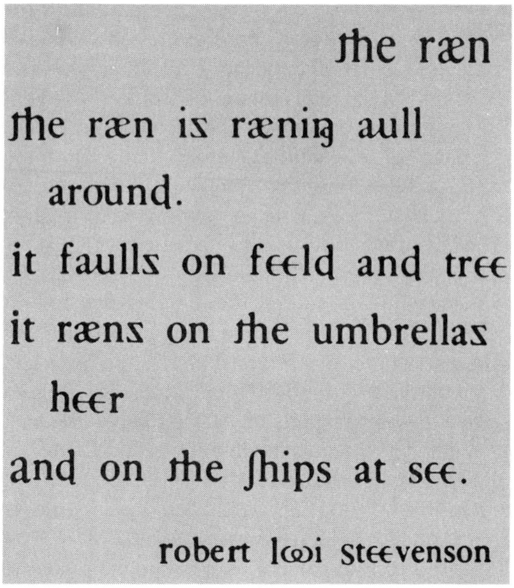

FIGURE 14-5 Example of the Initial Teaching Alphabet.

and different capital and lower case symbols for the same letter. After gaining reading mastery with ITA, students appear to have little difficulty later in mastering the twenty-six conventional letters of the English language. Some reading systems attempt to combine the phonic system with the word recognition system. The Children's Television Workshop began a new series of programs in 1971 designed to help elementary school children learn to read, stressing "decoding strategies" which emphasize the relationship between the printed and the spoken word.

In many elementary schools the basic language skills—reading, handwriting, spelling, grammar, creative writing, and listening—are no longer taught as disparate subjects, but are fused into a language arts core curriculum. This strategy offers many advantages. For example, the relationship between intonation in spoken sentences and punctuation of written sentences is more easily perceived when the two are taught together. Children can learn to develop their own creative writing skills by studying writing styles used in literature. Thus creative writing, study of literature, language games, and other devices are displacing the traditional abstract, dull, rote learning of grammar.

In the high schools and colleges, the "new English" has triggered controversy between its proponents and traditionalists. Traditional instruction has emphasized explanation of correct usage of English through the application of rules of grammar and parts of speech. Transformational grammar, characteristic of the new English, emphasizes construction of different kinds of sentences through the use of diagrams not unlike chemical formulas. This approach is very compatible with the translation of languages by computers. Presumably the new English helps students read and write better. Its opponents claim that it is abstract, difficult, and frustrating for students.[11] The science of linguistics is being applied to the teaching of all languages. Much of this work has been stimulated by the Center for Applied Linguistics of the Modern Language Association. Knowledge of linguistics helps students learn foreign languages more readily.

Three central components of the language arts curriculum are being recognized: language, literature, and composition. Increasing emphasis is being given to the latter two, which have been neglected in more traditional curriculums. The National Council of Teachers of English (NEA) is the major professional organization of English teachers.

Social Studies. Curriculum improvement in the social studies has been less deliberate than that in the physical sciences in spite of the fact that mankind's most compelling problems—peace, international understanding, race relations, urbanization, and social justice—look largely to the social sciences rather than to the physical sciences for solution.

Representatives of the social sciences cannot agree on whether history, geography, sociology, economics, and other disciplines can be taught more effectively as separate subjects or combined into an interdisciplinary format. Some emphasize the importance of combining the social science disciplines into a multidisciplinary approach to such topics as "governing," "consuming," and "exchanging"; others insist that the student can acquire a comprehensive view of society only through the perspective of specialized study of each of the social science disciplines.

Several of the major weaknesses of social

studies curriculums have long been apparent. World history courses have given far too little attention to the non-Western world, a serious shortcoming in view of the rising importance of the Asian, African, and South American countries. The contribution of Negroes to our national civilization and their disadvantaged position in American society has been badly neglected until recently. Geography has been largely physical geography with too little emphasis upon its human and economic facets. Citizenship education has commonly been preoccupied with dreary study of the mechanics of government rather than the values, rights, responsibilities, and behavior essential to effective and responsible citizenship. Data released by the National Assessment of Educational Progress revealed that many students lack fundamental understanding of the essential obligations of good citizenship. The behavior of many student radicals raises serious questions about the effectiveness and relevance of citizenship education.[12] Many other weaknesses could be cited.

Newer concepts from the fields of sociology, economics, political science, anthropology, and the other behavioral sciences are now finding their way into the high school social studies curriculum. For example, the American Sociological Society has developed Sociological Resources for the Social Studies (SRSS), which consists of a one-semester high school course in sociology, a series of paperbacks containing readings in sociology, and "episodes" which stimulate the discovery and application of sociology to the social problems of mankind.[13] Similarly, a new course in geography, "Geography in an Urban Age," has been developed by the Association of American Geographers. The course is addressed to the theme of why people live and work where they do and how they adjust to their surroundings. It includes urban, economic, cultural, and political geography of the United States and the world and stresses the inquiry method of learning. Oceanography and earth sciences are being emphasized. Black studies, discussed later, are a significant and sometimes controversial addition to high school and college curriculums.

---

[11] See Seamus McGrady, "What You Should Know about the New English," *School Management*, vol. 12, pp. 57–61, October, 1968.

[12] See Richard Wynn, "What Ever Happened to Citizenship Education?" *The School Administrator*, pp. 15–16, September, 1970.

[13] For further description of this course, see Thomas Switzer and Everett K. Wilson, "Nobody Knows the Trouble We've Seen: Launching A High School Sociology Course," *Phi Delta Kappan*, vol. 50, pp. 346–349, February, 1969.

In higher education, colleges and universities have broadened and deepened instruction in the social sciences—particularly in the behavioral sciences, sociology, anthropology, geography, and public affairs. Instruction about the international aspects of the social sciences has been strengthened, and several schools of international affairs have been created to prepare more Americans for public service at home and abroad. Area study centers on Africa, the Far East, and Latin America bring several social science disciplines together in an investigation of the problems and cultures of specific areas.

Perhaps the most significant development in the social studies at the college level has been the increased trend toward interdisciplinary study in which the social sciences are interrelated by experts in the individual fields of specialization. Many of the undergraduate social science courses have been fused into broader core courses to reduce narrow compartmentalization. Much more work remains to be done in social studies curriculums at all levels before they will have been refined to a point adequate to our rapidly shrinking and anxious world.

The tempo of redevelopment of the social studies curriculums will undoubtedly accelerate in the years ahead. Fifty or more groups in the United States are now working on the improvement of instruction in the social sciences, although there is little evidence of any unification of their efforts. The National Council for the Social Studies (of the NEA) is the umbrella organization for social studies teachers, supplemented by other organizations of teachers in specific subjects, such as geography and history.

Natural Sciences. The curriculum in natural sciences has changed drastically during the past decade. Elementary school science, once restricted largely to nature study, now stresses the identification and solution of simple scientific problems, exposure to the method of scientific inquiry, and the performance of simple experiments.

The redevelopment of elementary school science programs has been stimulated by the University of Illinois Elementary School Science Project and the Commission on Science Education of the American Association for the Advancement of Science, among others. The AAAS program emphasizes the basic skills essential to learning science, such as observation, classification, inference, and prediction. Four major areas of content are emphasized:

the universe, the structure and reaction of matter, the conservation and transformation of energy, and the interaction between living things and their environment. Science kits, portable laboratories, and even little cyclotrons are now commonly found in elementary schools. More advanced concepts are taught earlier, and the various branches of the physical sciences are often fused at the elementary level.

But the main transformation of the science curriculum is taking place at the high school level. Much of the early pioneering emerged under the impetus of the National Science Foundation, an agency of the federal government created in 1950 "to develop and encourage the pursuit of a national policy for the promotion of basic research and education in the sciences." National Science Foundation funds and grants from the National Defense Education Act have provided much more sophisticated science equipment for high schools across the nation. Overarching concepts of science, the logical structure of scientific knowledge, and the unity and interrelationship of the branches of science are being stressed. The science curriculums are becoming more unified, better coordinated, and more sequential. Science is being fused with other fields such as health and safety education. With respect to methodology, the shift is from reading and listening to problem solving, experimentation, and deduction. Advanced courses are being created for gifted students, and more time is being devoted to science in the schedule.

The physics curriculum has been the target of major redevelopment, stimulated in part by a decline in student enrollments at a time when the nation needs more physicists. Two developments have been noteworthy. The Physical Science Study Committee (PSSC), headed by Professor Zacharias of Massachusetts Institute of Technology, stressed the study of thermodynamics, solid-state physics, nucleonics, radioactive isotopes, reactors, nuclear energy, quantum theory, aerospace science, rocketry, and principles of propulsion. The Harvard Project Physics (HPP), which emphasizes humanistic rather than preprofessional training, emphasizes concepts of motion, motion in the heavens, energy, waves and fields, and models of the atom and the nucleus. In a sense it attempts to bridge what C. P. Snow referred to as the "two cultures" of the sciences and the humanities.

The Biological Science Curriculum Study (BSCS), created in 1959 by the American Institute of Biological Sciences, has led the reform in biology instruction at both the elementary and secondary levels. Instead of the old parade of plant and animal life with endless names, more emphasis is now placed on the unity and conceptual framework of knowledge of the plant and animal world. Biochemistry reveals the ubiquitous connection between life and nonlife. Microbiology, evolution, homeostasis, genetics, and radiation biology are sometimes included. The modern biology curriculum places greater emphasis upon molecular and cellular biology than upon classical biology. Great use is being made of laboratory work.

In chemistry, too, the new approach emphasizes the interrelationship of knowledge in chemistry through the concept of chemical bonds, pioneered by the Chemical Bonds Approach (CBA) group. Another enterprise, the Chemical Education Materials Study (CHEMS), emphasizes the atomic-molecular nature of substance. Both the CBA and the CHEMS approaches rely heavily upon laboratory experimentation as the prime method for learning. Both of these organizations have developed special textbooks, laboratory manuals, films, and models particularly adapted to these instructional approaches. The ninth-grade general science course has taken on greater academic respectability with the inclusion of introductory work in the space sciences, astronomy, meteorology, earth sciences, and other fields.

The pollution of air and water and the abuse of our natural resources have quickened the nation's interest in how man can preserve life through environmental education. This has been stimulated by

The laboratory plays an increasingly important role in education, not only in the chemistry class shown here, but in other subject areas as well.

the National Environmental Policy Act, and by the various organizations interested in conservation, wildlife, forestry, and health, with the support of many industries and governmental agencies. The preservation and improvement of our environment has become a compelling crusade for many students at all levels of schooling. Environmental education is really multidisciplinary in nature, including the study of ecology, conservation, biology, geography, law, agriculture, forestry, political science, and even history. Economic, political, social, and cultural considerations are clearly involved. The trend is to weave study of environmental education into established courses and to stress learning through direct observation of the environment and student participation in action-oriented field projects. The emphasis on environmental education is manifested from the elementary school through the graduate school.[14]

The purposes of science education have been reconceived to include the provision of scientific facts and information; the development of understanding and capability in the use of the scientific method for problem solving; the encouragement of scientific attitudes and habits of thinking; and the exploration of new fields of interest and appreciation. The study of science is now regarded as an integral part of general education. In most schools it is no longer an elective field of specialization only for those who need it for advanced work, but rather a required part of the general education of all students growing up in a world of scientific revolution. The National Science Teachers Association (of the NEA) includes teachers from the various fields of science.

Mathematics. Stimulated by the National Defense Education Act, a veritable revolution has taken place in the arithmetic and mathematics curriculums of the nation's schools. Although not universal, the changes are rapidly gathering acceptance and the results appear meritorious. The "new mathematics," as it is called, was spearheaded even before the NDEA by the University of Illinois Committee on School Mathematics in 1951 by Max Beberman. Various other groups followed. The School Mathematics Study Group (SMSG), begun in 1958 under the direction of Edward Begle of Stanford University, is perhaps the most extensive project. Patrick Suppes, also of Stanford, has developed computer-

[14]See "Environmental Education," *Today's Education,* vol. 6, pp. 21-25, October, 1970.

assisted tutorial programs in mathematics. The National Council of Teachers of Mathematics (NEA) has also provided leadership in the improvement of instruction in mathematics.[15]

Many advanced concepts are now introduced quite early. In the lower grades and sometimes in kindergarten, number concepts and spatial relationships are taught through the use of a set of rods first developed by Georges Cuisinaire, a Belgian teacher. The blocks or rods are of different colors and vary in length from 1 to 10 units. The shapes and colors of the blocks enable young children to deduce and prove basic numerical relationships, such as square roots, and to understand the rationale of multiplication, division, addition, and subtraction within a few months. Number sets, which form the primary basis for the new mathematics, are introduced as early as the fourth grade. Emphasis is placed upon deductive thinking and symbolic logic, which students use as tools in learning and in organizing knowledge. A sense of discovery of mathematical principles and generalizations is evoked. Young children reportedly learn and enjoy fairly difficult abstract ideas that help them see the overall structure of mathematics.

At the high school level, the ninth-grade general mathematics course has been replaced by more advanced work in algebra. In the senior high school, the old compartmentalization of courses is broken down; algebra, geometry, and trigonometry are fused. Some of the old content, such as solid geometry and logarithms, is eliminated or reduced and replaced by the study of probabilities, statistics, functions, and matrices, along with Boolean algebra and binary number systems, the language of the automatic computer. In some schools students are given the opportunity to work with computers. Some advanced high school students master calculus and other college-level subjects. The colleges, too, have moved toward the abandonment of the old college algebra courses, now rendered obsolete in many cases by the achievement of college freshmen. More advanced work is now possible at the college level also.

The main emphasis of the new mathematics is its stress upon the unity and the structure of the science; a systematic, logical organization of mathematical concepts; its utilization of self-discovery

[15]See Marilyn N. Suydam, "Continuing the Math Revolution," *American Education*, vol. 6, pp. 26–30, January–February, 1970, for further description of the various math projects.

of principles and relationships; and its employment of symbolic logic and deductive thinking. First used experimentally in several schools, the new mathematics has been revised and presented in new series of mathematics textbooks ranging from the fourth grade through the high school years. Some critics of the new system ask whether abstract mathematics is being emphasized at the expense of applied mathematics. However that may be, students apparently enjoy the new approach, show far more understanding, and display greater achievement than was once considered possible.

Foreign Languages. Development of foreign language curriculums has been stimulated by the National Defense Education Act and the work of the Modern Language Association. The impact of these efforts has been felt at the elementary as well as the secondary level. The number of elementary school students studying other languages increased rapidly during the middle 1960s but has recently been declining. Spanish and French are the languages most commonly offered, frequently as early as the third grade and, in a few schools, in kindergarten. FLES, Foreign Languages in the Elementary School, is the name commonly given to this educational movement. There is reason to believe that younger children learn to speak other tongues with less inhibition and more fluency than is possible later. It is also argued that acquaintance with another language is an essential part of one's general education, a cultural experience to be begun early in life. Most instruction in the elementary school is at the conversational level only. Many educators are still uncertain of the value of foreign language instruction at the elementary level.

In response to the nation's increasing responsibilities around the world and its desire for deeper international understanding, foreign language study at the secondary level has been expanded. A wider range of languages is available in most high schools—Spanish, Latin, French, German, Italian, and Russian commonly are offered. A few high schools and many colleges are teaching the languages of the non-Western world, notably Arabic and Chinese. But the biggest revolution here has been in teaching method. The tedious old grammar-translation method, with its heavy emphasis upon mechanics, is preceded by an audio-lingual method. Hearing, speaking, reading, and writing are undertaken in that order, in distinction to the traditional order in which students often failed to learn to speak the language after two years of grammar for grammar's sake.

Modern foreign language instruction is placing more emphasis upon the science of linguistics. Attention is being given to language as a form of communication and as a means of understanding other cultures. In colleges, too, enrollment in foreign language courses is expanding, and many languages, particularly non-Western ones, have been added to the curriculum. The emergence from schools of more Americans with four-, and even eight- and ten-year, sequences of study of one or more languages promises to make our nation more capable of dealing intelligently with other peoples of the world in governmental, business, educational, and cultural exchanges.

The Humanities. The humanities are commonly regarded as those "humane studies" which humanize man. Narrowly defined, they include language, literature, history, religion, art, music, and philosophy. Broadly defined, they include dance, drama, creative writing, photography, jurisprudence, archeology, and any other humanizing study. With the exceptions of literature and history, discussed earlier, the humanities have been badly neglected in most school curriculums until recently. The post-Sputnik hysteria prompted emphasis upon defense-related subjects, primarily the physical sciences. However, the social unrest of the past decade, and the students' resolute search for meaning, purpose, love, and beauty in life, excited interest in the humanities. Although most high schools offer courses in music and art, they are usually elective and offered only one or two periods per week.

Much of the schools' instruction in the arts has been banal and rudimentary. The purpose of the arts in education has been widely misunderstood by both lay persons and educators. Until recently at least, many have regarded music, drama, dance, sculpture, poetry, painting, and many of the other humanities largely as entertainment—nice but not necessary. Yet the humanities offer the vehicle by which man can raise the aesthetic tone of his community and home, elevate his mind and spirit above the banality of his environment, and prevent himself from "growing up absurd," as Paul Goodman has phrased the plight of youth in a depersonalized

society. The humanities are also superb media for the nurture of perception, communication, creativity, self-expression, and imagination, so highly prized by contemporary society. And many view the arts as intellectual disciplines in their own right.

Music education in the high schools has traditionally emphasized the production of student musicians and vocalists for school bands, orchestras, and choruses. Unless the student's musical talent is sufficient to promise him a place in the marching band or the varsity chorus, it has all too often been neglected. In many communities it is assumed that performing musicians should arrange for private lessons at their own expense. In the elementary school, too, music is taught as if it had no purpose other than entertainment and recreation, something to be done for relaxation after the study of more academic subjects. Music is taught too often in isolation from the sources of both high art and genuine folk art, and the relationship of music with other forms of art and literature is often missed.

The true purposes of music education must be more clearly understood. These include the development of musical competence—the ability to sing, to play instruments, and to read music; musical understanding—the ability to perceive musical structure, style, harmony, and rhythm; taste in discerning quality in musical performance and composition; and appreciation of music as both art and literature.

Fortunately, there is increasing reason for optimism concerning the improvement of music education. The rising popularity of folk singers has more than doubled the sale of guitars within the last decade. The American Music Conference speaks of the "return of music-making as an important part of family self-entertainment." It is estimated that more than twelve million students now play some type of musical instrument. New methods of music instruction emphasize simplified technique, enabling the student to play simple compositions early and avoiding, except for the serious performer, many of the tedious exercises that can discourage budding musicians almost before they begin to practice. Students are also encouraged to create simple musical compositions and find therein an avenue for creative expression and self-realization.

Fine arts education has also been popularized by emphasizing simpler techniques that permit the beginning student to experience the pleasure of accomplishment early. The media have been broadened to include not only drawing and painting but sculpture, ceramics, plastics, woodcarving, linoleum-block printing, silk-screen printing, photography, and graphic arts. Facilities have been enhanced through better laboratories, studios, creative centers, and workshops. Creativity rather than perfection is stressed. Stereotyped methods of instruction are giving way to more permissive approaches in which children are encouraged to express themselves freely and imaginatively. Experimentation is encouraged in the studio of today. Many fear that this undisciplined sort of self-study has left the student with an insufficient knowledge of fine art, undisciplined artistic techniques, and a low level of aesthetic taste. Certainly an effort should be made to develop greater understanding and appreciation of art, not only as a source of beauty but also as a form of communication and expression.

One of the most promising developments in education in the arts has been the trend toward fusion of instruction in the arts and other humanities. High school students in many states may participate in the new humanities courses, which draw upon knowledge from English, social studies, art, and music to promote understanding of universal issues such as man's relation to God, truth, the natural world, beauty, society, and freedom. World culture courses are becoming more common in colleges and high schools particularly. The history, art, music, literature, language, religion, and other cultural heritages of people in other lands are studied, not only for the humanizing impact of cross-cultural studies, but also for their contribution to international understanding.

Religion is also finding its way into the school curriculum, not in devotional Bible reading and prayer, which were banned by the Supreme Court, but in consideration of the Bible as literature and history. Religion and culture, the world religions, comparative religions, and the history of religious thought are being included increasingly in school and college curriculums. Educators hope that these studies will quicken the younger generation's interest and knowledge of religion as a humanizing force in man's eternal quest for the good life. This development is somewhat handicapped by the lack of adequate instructional materials and teachers.

The strengthening of curriculum development and instructional method in the arts and other humanities is being stimulated by several agencies. The creation of the arts and humanities branch of the U.S. Office of Education has helped to bring new vitality to education in these important areas.

The study of other cultures, as in this unit on Puerto Rico, is being emphasized to promote better intercultural understanding.

The Music Educators National Conference, the National Art Education Association, and affiliates of the NEA in other fields in the humanities are also active in the improvement of curriculum and instruction.

Health and Physical Education. The importance of good health is readily apparent. Sound health practices tend to increase life expectancy, to deepen one's satisfaction with living, to reduce the financial burden of medical bills and loss of income during illness, and to improve physical appearance. Perhaps not so evident is the positive relationship between a student's physical fitness and his academic achievement. The World Health Organization has defined good health as "a state of complete physical, mental, and social well-being, not merely the absence of disease and infirmity."

There is good reason for concern about the health and physical fitness of the nation's youth. The rise in drug addiction and in venereal diseases are two cases in point. Various studies have revealed that American youth rank far behind youth of other countries in physical fitness tests. President Kennedy pointed out the shocking lack of physical stamina and health among American children and youth. He emphasized that "it is of great importance that we take immediate steps to insure that every American child be given the opportunity to make and keep himself physically fit—fit to learn, fit to understand, to grow in grace and stature, to fully

The well-balanced curriculum includes opportunity for physical development as in this coeducational gym class.

live." Toward this end he appointed the White House Conference on Health and Physical Fitness, which launched a nationwide enterprise to strengthen health and physical education.

Perhaps the most ambitious investigation of health education in the nation's schools was reported in the *School Health Education Study*. It recommended that the following components of health education be given greater emphasis in health curriculums: alcohol education, community health programs, consumer health education, environmental hazards, health careers, international health activities, nutrition and weight control, sex and family-life education, smoking, and venereal disease education.[16]

What is the scope of an adequate program of health and physical education? Clearly, a good program is multidisciplinary in nature. Its scope is broad and includes such diverse areas as the nature of

[16]Elena M. Sliepcevich, *School Health Education Study*, National Education Association, Washington, D.C., 1964, pp. 6–7, 20, 24, 38–39.

disease; the importance of good nutrition; the awareness of environmental hazards; the prevention of accidents; health and medical care programs; first aid; intelligent selection of health products and services; driver education; community health services; recreation; physical exercise; motor skill development; sex education; understanding of the hazards of alcohol, tobacco, drugs, and narcotics; and mental health.

Many high school and college students conspire to skip physical education classes, which are often a dull routine of undressing, dressing, roll call, dodgeball, undressing, showering, and dressing, under the supervision of a coach who is more preoccupied with the fortunes of the school's interscholastic athletic teams than with the physical development of all students. The physical education activities often include only competitive team sports, which most students will not long continue in adult life, rather than recreational pursuits such as dancing, golf, tennis, skiing, or swimming which can be enjoyed later in life. Budget pressures often constrain the facilities, faculties, and time necessary for a well-balanced physical education program compatible with the needs and interests of individual students. When the costs of a new school building must be trimmed, the swimming pool is invariably the first facility to be sacrificed. The American Association for Health, Physical Education, and Recreation, an affiliate of the National Education Association, attempts to improve the scope and quality of health and physical education in the schools through conferences of teachers, research studies, and a wide variety of publications.

Vocational and Technical Education. A renewed interest in vocational and technical education has been generated by dramatic advances in technology, by the need for skilled manpower created by automation, and by the plight of large numbers of underprivileged youths out of school and out of work. One-fourth of the young men and women who become 18 each year are not sufficiently educated to be employable. These youths constitute a serious economic and social liability. It is essential that we make vocational educational opportunity available to all so that they may experience the dignity, satisfaction, and self-sufficiency that comes from a productive role in society.

The objectives of vocational education have been defined to include imparting an understanding of industry and its place in our culture, the discovery and nurture of talent in technical fields and in the applied sciences, the development of career consciousness and occupational orientation, the development of technical problem-solving skills, and the provision of a basic facility in the use of common tools and machines. The Smith-Hughes Act and subsequent enactments, such as the Vocational Education Act and the Manpower Development and Training Act, stimulated the growth of vocational education in many fields, but the belief is growing that the curriculums have become stereotyped and are in need of thorough restudy and reconstruction.

There is obviously no single best curriculum, because vocational education must be adapted to the needs of industry and to the resources of the local school system. Many districts are handicapped by their small size. Vocational education programs require expensive, highly specialized shops and laboratories. Further, the great proliferation of skilled jobs reduces the high school's ability to meet the needs of all the fields. Its effort, in many cases, is limited to the craft level (in such semiskilled trades as carpentry, plumbing, auto mechanics, printing, electrical trades, metal trades, and business education) and to providing junior high school youth with broad exploratory experiences and a general introduction to the more common semiskilled occupations. Real technical education, in most cases, requires a one- to three-year sequence of postsecondary education.

The National Advisory Council on Vocational Education has called for several major improvements in vocational education:

Recognition of the importance of vocational education as an integral part of education
Vocational education should include part-time employment as a regular part of the curriculum as well as employment services and follow-up counseling for those who drop out
Priority attention should be given to the disadvantaged students without separating them from the mainstream of education
Parents and students should be encouraged to participate in the design of vocational education programs
Residential vocational schools should be established for those who need them

As described in Chapter 9, many community colleges and technical institutes have helped to expand the nation's capacity for the preparation of technicians, which the age of automation demands

in ever-increasing numbers. Vocational education at the adult level must also be expanded to accommodate workers whose jobs are eliminated or whose skills must be updated as a result of automation.

There is controversy about whether vocational education should be provided in separate vocational high schools or included as part of the program of the comprehensive high school. Some believe it should be offered largely in postsecondary schools. In either case, the vocational curriculum too often suffers from the low prestige ascribed to both the students and the teachers engaged in it.

Several trends in vocational education are noteworthy. Earlier opportunity to explore the world of work is being provided in junior high schools and even in some elementary schools. More vocational educational opportunities are being made available to girls. More courses are oriented toward the jobs of the future. Courses are being clustered around broad occupational fields, such as health, business, and electronics, rather than in more narrow specializations. Schedules are being devised to permit students to enter and finish at their convenience apart from the traditional academic year. Fewer programs are considered terminal or dead-end. Work-study programs are being expanded to permit students to earn while they learn and to gain practical on-the-job experience related to their classroom or laboratory instruction. Junior high school industrial arts courses are being transformed from mere "shop" courses, where bookcases and tie racks are made, into real study of the history and theory of industry and technology as well as development of skill in designing and building projects that sharpen their mechanical and engineering talents.[17]

The American Vocational Association is the professional association for teachers of vocational education. Its conferences, meetings, research, and publications have helped give direction to the improvement of education for the world of work.

Other Multidisciplinary Studies. Three other fields of multidisciplinary study have commanded major attention during recent years: black studies, sex education, and drug education.

[17]For more extended discussion of these trends, see Velma A. Adams, "Vocational Training: Still for Someone Else's Children?" *School Management*, vol. 14, pp. 12–15, September, 1970.

The term "black studies" is rather ambiguous. Since it is a recent development, curriculums still vary widely in scope and substance. Roscoe Brown, director of the Institute of Afro-American Affairs at New York University, defines black studies as "the examination of the culture, history, and social, economic, and political influences of black people in Africa, the Caribbean, and the United States."

Although most educators look forward to the day when Negro history and culture will be fully integrated into the curriculum, many agree that the emphasis of separate courses is presently necessary to overcome the neglect of the Negro in the traditional curriculum. Black studies are prompted by the need to redress this injustice, to help black students gain a greater sense of awareness of their culture, and to help both black and white students gain deeper understanding of the problems of race and the means for their alleviation.

Los Angeles, for example, has introduced courses in Afro-American history, Afro-American literature, African studies, and Swahili. Most other city school systems, and even school districts with all-white student bodies, have also added black studies to their curriculums. Some states have mandated the inclusion of black studies in public school curriculums. Many colleges have introduced courses in black studies and some have created special academic departments or centers of black studies.

Several problems complicate the development of black-study programs. The lack of adequate instructional materials is being overcome as authors and publishers collaborate in this task, but the shortage of qualified instructors endures. Black students seem to prefer black instructors in this field and qualified black instructors are not readily available except by raiding the faculties of the Negro colleges. Some black-study programs, thrown together hastily in response to student confrontations, lack quality and coherence. Many college programs are still inadequately funded. In some cases enrollment is declining. Controversies arise regarding the control of the black-studies programs in universities. On some campuses militant minority groups struggle for control of these programs as a base for political action and a training ground for revolutionaries. These and other issues are discussed in Chapter 1. It is hoped that black studies will sustain the scholarship necessary to help blacks assume leadership in the liberation of their race and to help students of all races reduce social injustice.[18]

Sex education is another special field of education that cuts across various academic fields—social studies, biological sciences, and health education. Because of its multidisciplinary character, questions arise concerning the proper location of sex education in the curriculum. It may be offered as a separate subject, correlated with the subject areas mentioned above, or included in the health education curriculum. Many authorities prefer the latter.

Although some people still hold nineteenth-century attitudes regarding sex education and some even see it as a communist plot to degrade our morality, many other people are agreed that it is vitally needed; that most homes and churches are not doing the job; and that school is the logical agency. The sharp rises in teen-age marriages, premarital pregnancies, venereal disease, and abortions have helped to quicken people's concern for sex education. It must not be assumed that these problems will be greatly reduced by classroom instruction in a society where sex is exploited by the advertising and entertainment industries.

A comprehensive program of sex education includes far more than a biological treatment of human reproduction. Spoken of commonly as sex and family life education, the better programs deal with sexuality in its broad social, physical, psychological, and moral context; with its relationship to personality development and social relations with peers and family members; and its impact upon physical and mental health. These considerations are subject to great controversy in a pluralistic society, making sex education a delicate field of instruction that is frightening to many teachers and anathema to some citizens. It may be boring to students if it is not taught with intelligence, tact, and honesty. One of the problems has been the unavailability of teachers who are adequately prepared for the task. Publishing companies are now preparing better instructional materials, and various professional organizations are attempting to provide training pro-

[18] For further discussion of the progress, problems, and issues in black studies, see National School Public Relations Association, *Black Studies in Schools*, National Education Association, Washington, D.C., 1970; Eugene D. Genovese, "Black Studies: Trouble Ahead," *Atlantic*, vol. 223, pp. 37–40, June, 1969; and DeVere E. Pentony, "The Case for Black Studies," *Atlantic*. vol. 223, pp. 82–89, April, 1969.

grams for teachers. The trend is to extend sex and family-life education into the elementary schools for young students who still have the frank and objective curiosity of children and have not yet developed all the emotional distractions that appear with puberty. The home economics curriculum, or "homemaking," as it is sometimes called, in most high schools commonly offers instruction in various aspects of family life including marital relations and sex education.[19]

Drug education is another multidisciplinary field of study that has assumed compelling importance because of the frightening spread of drug abuse. Teen-age deaths from heroin are growing. It is estimated that drug addicts cost the nation more than $1 billion per year in drug-control programs and robberies which they commit to support their addiction. Once the problem of the ghetto, drug abuse has now spread in epidemic proportions to suburban and rural areas. Various aspects of this problem are discussed at length in Chapters 1 and 11. We shall consider here the problems and progress in drug-abuse education while realizing that both drug rehabilitation and drug prevention require many other resources beyond the school curriculum. It is hoped that sound programs in drug education can help to prevent drug abuse. Many of these programs have been extended into the elementary schools, since the beginning of experimentation with drugs sometimes begins before adolescence. Many authorities believe that ninth grade may be the most effective time for concerted drug-abuse education, although the program should be continued throughout the high school and college years.

At first "crash" programs in drug education were attempted. These often consisted of lectures in the school auditorium which attempted to arouse students' fear of drug usage. These approaches proved to be futile and are being replaced by programs which avoid moralistic positions in favor of scientific explanations of the physical and psychological effects of drugs on the human organism, information on sources available to assist students with problems relating to drugs, and information on the legal aspects of drug usage. These seem to be the topics of most interest to students. More and more use is being made of outside resources— pharmacists, physicians, lawyers, scientists, and,

[19] For further discussion of the problems and progress in sex and family-life education, see Ian Forman, "Sex and Family Living," *American Education*, vol. 5, pp. 11–13, October, 1969.

especially, rehabilitated former drug addicts. The last appear to be especially effective because they "have been there." Small informal group discussion sessions which permit students to ask questions appear to be helpful. This approach helps to clear up many of the misconceptions which both students and teachers have about drugs. Sometimes student organizations are enlisted to sponsor the programs. For example, several Westchester (New York) school systems have programs in which high school seniors undertake projects to dissuade younger students from taking drugs. These stratagems utilize the concept that peers have more influence than adults on adolescent behavior and values. Many of the programs include consideration of tobacco and alcohol as well as narcotics and other drugs. Good films and other instructional materials are becoming increasingly available through the National Clearinghouse for Drug Abuse Information and the National Institute of Mental Health. The Drug Abuse Education Act, the National Institute of Mental Health, and the U.S. Office of Education, as well as many state governments, have provided funds for the training of teachers in the fundamentals of drug education. Clearly the development of educational programs that are effective in preventing drug abuse is a paramount imperative in education, as attested by resolutions to this effect enacted by nearly every professional educational organization in the nation.[20]

COCURRICULAR ACTIVITIES

Having discussed the academic sectors of the curriculum, we turn our attention now to that ancillary— but nevertheless important—sector of the curriculum commonly spoken of as cocurricular activities, extraclass activities, or student activities.

Formerly the curriculum was so rigid, formal, academic, and dominated by the teacher that any informal, semiacademic, student-initiated undertaking was labeled as extracurricular. The latter included all those student enterprises which were not a part of regular classroom activities. They were usually under the direction of the school but were conducted at the close of the school day. Their growth was due largely to the dullness and monotony of the regular curriculum.

[20] For further discussion of drug education, see "Drugs and the Educational Antidote," *The Nation's Schools*, vol. 85, pp. 49–52, 127, April, 1970.

Fortunately, the term "extracurricular" is disappearing. In many schools the old extracurricular activities are assuming a prominence and function almost parallel with the curricular undertakings. These activities are increasingly included within the regular school day, making it difficult to distinguish between what is curricular and what is cocurricular.

Goals

Cocurricular or extraclass activities serve a number of worthwhile educational goals, sometimes more effectively than the formal curriculum.

Satisfaction of Unmet Needs. Some cocurricular activities are initiated to satisfy certain drives among students not satisfied by the formal curriculum, which is usually controlled largely by school authorities. Student sit-ins, student action groups, clubs, and social organizations, for example, are often organized to express concerns or attack problems or form fellowships which are not sustained by the curriculum. In some cases these enterprises may be anathema to school authorities. The formation of student activities to give expression to these drives offers a wholesome relief from the frustrations of the constraints of the curriculum and authority of the school.

Reinforcement of Student Interest in School. Many students develop strong interests in extraclass activities which sustain their commitment to remain in school or to pursue their academic studies more vigorously. Various studies have shown that participation in extraclass activities tends to quicken student interest in the more formal aspects of their schooling. A common characteristic of school dropouts is their lack of participation in cocurricular activities. Membership in some organizations, such as the National Honor Society and other honorary societies, is conditional upon superior academic accomplishment.

Education for Democratic Living. Most cocurricular activities place upon students a major responsibility for their management. This experience requires students to practice group decision making, to consider the rights and responsibilities of others, to understand the necessity for order and justice, to assume the mantle of leadership or the discipline

of followership, and, in general, practice good citizenship. If schools are indeed the laboratory in which good citizenship is learned and practiced, then the cocurricular activities must be the most fertile fields for citizenship development. Student government organizations are especially well suited for this experience if students are indeed given real responsibility in important decision making in school affairs. Virtually all cocurricular activities offer real potential for putting the creed of citizenship into deed as long as the activities are not too closely supervised by the faculty.

Enrichment of Interpersonal Relations. Cocurricular activities provide experience in group activities which depend for their success very often upon effective interpersonal relations. Sports demand cooperation and teamwork. Many racial and other prejudices have been lost on the playing fields as teammates are bound together in common cause. Musical groups, clubs, fraternities, and other social groups help students to overcome self-consciousness, to engage in social interaction, to acquire the social amenities, and to assume greater concern for their fellow man.

Exploration of Vocational Possibilities. Many vocational alternatives can be explored in cocurricular activities through experiences that are not provided commonly in the regular curriculum. Many high school and college athletes have developed talents that have led to professional sports. Musical and drama clubs have often been the springboard to careers in professional entertainment. Participation in the Student National Education Association has helped many students explore careers in education and examine their own qualifications for these careers more wisely. Many cocurricular activities reveal latent talent that might otherwise go undiscovered.

Wiser Use of Leisure Time. The squandering of leisure time in worthless or even harmful pursuits is tragic. Cocurricular activities can help young citizens develop hobbies or other recreational pursuits that can enrich their lives, improve their surroundings, and quicken their sense of well-being long after formal schooling is over. Schools can promote the worthy use of leisure time through what Thomas Briggs called "teaching people to do better those desirable activities that they will do anyway."

Many lifelong avocational interests have been discovered and enriched in cocurricular activities.

Development of Sound Character. Many student athletes have learned the lessons of good sportsmanship on the playing fields. Student officers of school organizations have experienced the responsibilities of public trust and financial stewardship. Editors and reporters for student publications have learned to reconcile freedom of the press and responsible journalism and acquire some literary taste. Group activities force students constantly to exercise their moral judgments, to set standards of behavior, to reconcile individual aspirations with the welfare of the group. The opportunities for character development in a sound cocurricular program are even more abundant than those in the formal curriculum because students have more opportunity to make important decisions and more responsibility for their actions in extraclass activities.

A caveat is important at this point in the discussion. We have been speaking of the goals of cocurricular activities and illustrating the achievement of these goals in rather platitudinous terms. In balance, we must recognize that cocurricular activities are sometimes miseducative. Fraternities, while extolling the high ideals of brotherhood, are commonly clannish and discriminate in their membership on the basis of race or creed or both, thereby reducing the opportunity for the improvement of racial and religious understanding. The pressure upon interscholastic athletic teams for victorious seasons sometimes prompts unethical practices and the exploitation of student athletes, thereby compromising the virtue of the institution. The coercion of administrative authorities of student activities, particularly the school newspaper, sometimes teaches unintended lessons in how special interest can constrain the freedom of the press in school and society. The rejection of democratic principles by Students for a Democratic Society offers a tragic object lesson in how some students can deny the very goal which is specified in the title of the organization. Many other examples should be cited. These are indictments, not of cocurricular activities per se, but of the frailties of the human beings who engage in these or any other enterprises.

Program

The numerous organizations and the complex interrelation of the various cocurricular activities make

it difficult to group them, since many may be classified properly under several headings.

Class Organizations. An old and prevalent cocurricular activity is that of class or grade organizations. These groupings are found all the way from the kindergarten through higher education. The class usually elects a president, a vice-president, a secretary, a treasurer, representatives to the student council and other organizations, and a class sponsor or sponsors from the faculty. These class officers, along with various committees, assume responsibility for the social affairs of the class, participate in various ceremonial functions such as commencement, and represent their classmates in student government and often in advising school administration on various matters.

Student Government. Student government offers great opportunity for the practice of democratic principles and the development of effective citizenship. Various forms of student government—student councils, student courts, student senates, interfraternity councils, student-faculty committees—exist in most high schools and colleges. Many elementary schools have also introduced limited forms of student government. Many of these student government organizations function well and realize the goals intended. However some schools place so many restraints upon eligibility for membership that they fail to represent the entire spectrum of the student body. Some school administrators are reluctant to share any real authority with student government organizations, and some faculty sponsors supervise their affairs so closely that these organizations serve very little function other than to delude students and create a facade of democratic school organization. Hopefully these circumstances are exceptions rather than general characteristics of perhaps the most important extraclass activity in the school.

School Clubs. Most cocurricular activities may be classified as clubs. Nowhere in the school life is more freedom and variety displayed than in the names of the clubs. Their vast variety testifies to the individualistic interests of youth as well as to its gregariousness. Through a wide variety of organizations, the school seeks to interest each student in at least one meaningful cocurricular activity in which the desideratum is not mere membership but active and voluntary participation on the part of the boy or girl. Emerson once said, "We send our children to the master but the boys educate them." School clubs, an outlet for the urge to gregariousness, should have definite educational and recreational values.

Journalistic Activities. The most common form of student publication is the newspaper. Many elementary school papers are mimeographed, whereas in the larger high schools and colleges the papers are printed. Often in elementary and small secondary schools the students and teachers cooperate with the local newspaper in producing a school page. At least half of the secondary schools have some form of news organ. The school newspaper today is an important agent in the transmission of ideas and school spirit. Through this medium many young people first learn the privileges and responsibilities involved in the freedom of the press in a democracy. Significantly, the principals of the schools usually rank the newspaper as the most important activity outside classes.

The yearbook is usually an expensive publication. In many quarters justification for its costly existence is seriously questioned. The yearbook, once the only publication in most schools, is now being subordinated to the school newspaper, although its archival function will always give it a place in the program.

The current emphasis upon unleashing creative efforts and developing literary interests of pupils has focused attention upon school magazines and similar avenues for expression. These periodicals, issued in duplicated or printed format, constitute outlets not only for literary creativeness and insight, but also for expression through drawings, cartoons, and photographs.

Some student journalists in some high schools and many colleges have become sufficiently creative in their choice of language and vigorous in their criticism of the establishment to discomfort school administrators and school boards. In some cases these student journalists have been expelled from their offices, had their writings censored, or school funds withdrawn, practices which are generally frowned upon by the courts. In some cases these enterprising journalists have gone underground and published "independent newspapers" which are distributed to students, posing a new dilemma for the harried school administrator.[21] Although school authorities should not sanction libel and obscenity in school publications, most schools should be very prudent in placing other restrictions upon student publications. Students can learn responsible journalism more effectively in an atmosphere of freedom than an atmosphere of constraint.

Musical Organizations and Activities. Music is the center of many curricular and cocurricular activities. Singing is often combined with acting, as in operettas, and with instrumental accompaniment, as in a cantata. The music groups are naturally interested in both performing and listening. A separate music appreciation club may be organized for non-performers who are unable or unwilling to produce music but who, as consumers, are desirous of raising their level of music appreciation.

The chief vocal organizations, either curricular or cocurricular, are glee clubs—boys', girls', or mixed. Their chief objectives are recreation, entertainment, and appreciation. Their origin may be traced to the old singing schools.

The instrumental groups most frequently formed in secondary schools are bands and orchestras. Smaller groupings, such as string ensembles, present chamber music, whereas harmonica and other instrumental clubs meet the music hobby interests. The various musical organizations may contribute jointly to a public program or festival, the latter usually being given outdoors. The widespread popularity of rock music has spawned many small groups of student musicians which feature well-amplified guitars and uninhibited vocalists.

Speech Activities. Generally school dramatics are handled either in regular classes or through cocurricular activities. The major productions or one-act plays may be promoted by a local drama club or a chapter of National Thespians or by the junior or senior class. Usually the work is divided among various committees for costuming, lighting, scenery, and advertising. The drama coach may encourage the more backward students to self-expression through acting; he may even contribute to the legitimate stage through the development of latent histrionic talent in his pupils. Many by-products accrue from drama, including the extensive reading of many

[21] For an interesting collection of articles taken from student underground newspapers, see Diane Divoky (ed.), *How Old Will You Be in 1984?* Avon Book Division, The Hearst Corporation, New York, 1969.

plays and the practicing of clear enunciation. The school drama helps students to see, to hear, to act, to construct, and to write their own plays.

Forensic activities include debates, poetry reading, extempore speaking, choral reading, telecasting, radio speaking, role playing, panel discussions, and forums. Writing original speeches appeals especially to students who possess creative literary talents and who hope thereby to inform, impress, or persuade the audience to thought or action. Debates constitute the chief activity in the field of public speaking. Debates help students to think logically, to organize materials carefully, to cultivate mental alertness, to analyze an argument critically, to promote reliance upon facts and research rather than prejudice, and to develop a lifelong interest in socioeconomic and governmental problems. Debate and discussion are the breath of democracy.

Play and Athletic Activities. Children love to play. The recess period, with its opportunities for games, is often cherished more than the regular three R's. Often the outside-class activities of schools and colleges that receive the major share of financial support and the largest amount of publicity are of an athletic nature. A well-balanced physical education program in secondary schools and colleges includes athletics, in addition to the regular programs for guidance and instruction in health and physical activities.

Athletics include intramural and interscholastic sports. The intramural sports program may also include several schools within a city. Intramurals, as distinguished from interscholastic sports, encourage maximum participation by local boys and girls. The intramural program seeks to maintain many sports for the sake of all students rather than for the sake of a few athletic teams. It is directed toward developing lasting recreational interests and sport skills in people who must live in a highly industrialized civilization.

Critics find fault with huge football stadiums, large gate receipts, larger expenditures, postseason games, salaried athletes, athletic scholarships, lax scholastic requirements for athletes, long practice sessions, game schedules that take athletes away from their studies, and high-salaried and overzealous coaches whose tenure depends upon the production of winning teams. Some of these criticisms are discussed in Chapter 1. Despite these accusations, interscholastic athletics continue to flourish. Conscientious efforts are being made to eliminate or reduce the evils in the system.

Social Organizations and Activities. A well-balanced educational program fosters the social development of students. This goal is achieved in large part through the cocurricular program. In the elementary school, parties and other simple social affairs are held during the school day. In high schools, social activities are usually an important part of virtually every extraclass organization. There are banquets for the athletic teams, musical groups, casts of plays, and other groups. There are dances sponsored by the various classes and mixers, parties, and picnics sponsored by the school. These affairs help the student to feel at home in a social environment and give him a lifelong appreciation for the little niceties, the social techniques, and the pleasurable amenities so necessary in a civilized world. School parties, properly supervised, promote simple pleasures and platonic relationships between boys and girls and help counteract the present undue emphasis upon commercialized amusements. Unfortunately, for some students the socializing process is carried to excess through too many social affairs, which often begin too early in an adolescent's life. Many schools have established parents' committees to help establish and enforce reasonable policies.

There are many social organizations in colleges and universities, although fraternities and sororities are regarded as the major socializing institutions on most campuses. Building upon the pageantry of ancient Greece, these Greek-letter organizations began to appear on the campuses in the 1830s to fill the social and emotional void which many students felt. Fraternities are seen variously as a refuge from university authority, a partial solution to the college housing problem, a bastion of brotherhood and good fellowship, the locale of glamorous but clannish social life, the power structure of campus politics, and a source of support for good scholarship. Although fraternities' discrimination in membership and their revelry are sometimes the source of embarrassment to colleges and universities, fraternities have changed very little through the years. They have displayed an amazing resiliency which demonstrates that they do indeed fulfill a vital social need on most campuses. Many fraternities and sororities are rendering educational and social services through numerous volunteer programs.

Auxiliary Organizations and Activities. Ancillary to the curricular or cocurricular programs are the following: assemblies and programs, commencements, social activities, school lunch, camping and outdoor education, scouting, and miscellaneous activities which are far too numerous to mention.

In the early days the assembly was a period of devotional exercises, perhaps an outgrowth of the college chapel. The Supreme Court's ban on Bible reading and prescribed prayers has altered this function, although silent meditation and nonsectarian spiritual invocation are still common in many schools.

The purposes of the assembly, the "town meeting of the school," include orientation into school life, cultivation of school spirit, unification of the entire school, dissemination of general information, inspirational help, opportunity for students and faculty to appear before an audience, all-school special convocations, installation of student council, and cultivation of effective listening and courteous audience habits.

Commencement means more than the mere handing out of diplomas to graduates after they have listened to an orator. These modern programs center attention on the students and help to enlist community interest in the school and the results of its work. Important parts of the older graduation programs, such as class history, will, poem, and prophecy, are scheduled on class night during commencement week.

Camping and other forms of outdoor learning, teaching, and living rank high in character-building potentialities. Various educational organizations have long recognized the value of outdoor education, especially camping. Charitable associations sponsor camps for the underprivileged, and private ones often cater to the well-to-do, but millions of youth do not enjoy outdoor living. Hence many school systems seek to provide outdoor education and camping as curricular and cocurricular activities.

Growing in favor are the school-sponsored educational trips. These afford students the opportunity to visit local, county, state, and national sites. A favorite destination for senior classes is Washington, D.C.

Among the hundreds of other cocurricular activities found in American educational institutions are alumni organizations, student speakers' service bureaus, correspondence and personnel exchange with students in foreign countries, visitation of other schools by students, community fund drives, and social service work, particularly at Christmas. The organization and administration of these activities constitute a major task in American education.

Advisement of Cocurricular Activities

The success of many extraclass organizations may be traced in large part to faculty advisers or sponsors. Although the sponsor should not assume the dominant role, nevertheless he should exert a real influence. Some general qualifications for faculty advisers are an understanding of youths and their interests and problems, the ability to win the confidence of both youth and parents, the capacity to lead and to follow, a willingness to be identified wholeheartedly with the organization and to put in extra hours of work in its interest, high standards of personal conduct and morals, a sense of humor, alertness to what is going on outside as well as inside school, and a good sense of values in the expenditure of time, money, and talents. Besides these general requirements, the directors of certain groups need specialized training, for example, for journalistic, athletic, and music events. There is no set pattern for faculty advisers. On the whole they must possess the quality of "teaching as though they taught not," while bearing constantly in mind the purposes for which the activity is designed.

How shall the advisers be chosen? Usually the procedure involves selection by the principal, election by the students, or a combination of these. For example, students may choose an adviser from a recommended list. Often the advisers for activities that call for technical training are appointed to that task when employed by the board of education and superintendent of schools. Advisers and students should be happy and congenial in their cocurricular relations.

Student Participation

A goal in extraclass work is that of universality—all students in the school participating in at least one cocurricular activity. This necessitates promotion and stimulation, preferably by the student body. A corollary is the principle that participation must be restricted. These are two parts of the same basic idea that cocurricular activities must be regulated in order to avert the danger that the pendulum for some students will swing to the extreme of nonparticipation and for others to that of overparticipation. Two methods of curtailing the ambitions of the overzealous or talented individual are a point system and a program of majors and minors. The former assigns to each activity a specified number of points and stipulates the maximum permitted each student. The latter divides activities or offices into majors and minors, each student being restricted to a specified number.

FUTURE

Several forces that will have major impact upon the development of the curriculum are fairly evident: discovery of new insights into the nature of learning; the compelling need for humanizing school experience; the growing capacity of the school for accommodating individual differences; and the increased capability of building coherence and continuity into the curriculum. We shall consider each of these briefly.

It is clear that we really know very little about the phenomenon of human learning, notwithstanding the vigorous attention which researchers have devoted to this task over the years. It is also clear that sound pedagogy and curriculum development must be rooted in learning theory. The curriculum reform of the 1950s and early 1960s focused upon subject matter in the academic fields. The academicians who led this undertaking soon discovered what curriculum specialists had long understood: that curriculum cannot be developed without reference to the developmental characteristics of the learners. As John Holt explicates so clearly in his books *How Children Fail* and *How Children Learn*, the manner in which children think and learn must be regarded as organizing principles for the curriculum. Fortunately intensive investigation is now being directed toward the science of human learning and development. The subject-oriented academicians have joined with the behavioral scientists to bridge the objects of the verb "to teach"—the learner *and* the subject. This advance has been stimulated by the development of programmed instruction, which depends so heavily upon understanding of modes of learning as well as upon the structure of knowledge. Instructional programmers have learned the hazards of ignoring either. Observation, research, and experimentation in human learning have been sustained by the work of many educationists such as Holt, Piaget, Pressey, Dewey, Skinner, and Bruner and by many organizations such as the regional educational laboratories, PACE, IDEA, and the NEA's National Foundation for the

Improvement of Education. Massive research in neuropsychology and biochemistry directed toward learning and memory almost stagggers the imagination when its impact upon teaching and curriculum is considered. Work in these fields suggests that the information gap between the science of learning and the science of teaching may be reduced eventually, to the great advantage of students. The fascinating science of brain chemistry suggests that man may eventually be able to inject memory into people through drugs and to relieve learning dysfunctions in retarded students and senile persons by altering their brain chemistry. These discoveries, derived for experimentation with lower animals, are still many years distant from application to human beings. However, their application to man may one day revolutionize our concepts of curriculum and learning.[22]

The hallmark of proposals for educational reform in the early 1970s has been the demand for humanizing the school. As noted earlier, the post-Sputnik reformers were primarily interested in the learner's cognitive development in defense-related subject fields. Some of their reforms were counter-productive with respect to the development of the learner's affective development—his tastes, his values, and his emotions. The curriculums which they produced were not very relevant to the personal needs and interests of students and the sometimes harsh reality of the milieu in which they lived. As John Goodlad noted, "The schools do not, in general, foster man's creative talents, nor grapple with his great ideas, nor relate these ideas and talents to the contemporary environment where man's dramas are continually re-enacted." By the early 1970s many books were calling for humanizing the schools by adopting a spirit of reverence for children and youth.[23] The alienation of many students from school and society quickened interest in developing school programs and practices that were at least as concerned with the human spirit as they were with cognition. The new educational

[22] For an account of this research, see G. Unger, "Chemical Transfer of Learning?" *Today's Education*, vol. 58, pp. 45–47, February, 1969.

[23] See, for example, Charles E. Silberman, *Crisis in the Classroom*, Random House, Inc., New York, 1970; Ryland W. Crary, *Humanizing the School: Curriculum Development and Theory*, Alfred A. Knopf, Inc., New York, 1969; and Herbert R. Kohl, *The Open Classroom*, Vintage Books, Random House, Inc., New York, 1970.

reform, prompted in part by the youth culture as well as by the compelling social problems of the times, is at this writing in very early development. The movement of open education, evolving in England for half a century, will become increasingly common in American schools. Open education is a new way of thinking about children, learning, and curriculum. Open education has been described in these terms:

It is characterized by openness and trust . . . spatial openness of schools . . . time is open. . . . The curriculum is open to significant choice by adults and children as a function of the needs and interests of each child at each moment. . . . Perhaps most fundamental, open education is characterized by an openness of self. Persons are openly sensitive to and supportive of other persons. . . . Feelings are exposed, acknowledged and respected. Administrators are open to initiative on the part of teachers; teachers are open to the possibilities inherent in children; children are open to the possibilities inherent in other children, in materials, and in themselves. In short, open education implies an environment in which the possibility for exploration and learning of self and of the world is unobstructed.[24]

A massive thrust toward the humanization of schools through the model of open education, should it come, as we think it will, would have profound effect upon the school and its curriculum. The humanities would finally acquire the stature in the curriculum that the physical sciences formerly preempted. In universities, the professions related to the social sciences—teaching, social work, and theology, for example—would at least equal in prestige the professions related to the physical sciences—engineering and medicine, for example. In elementary and secondary schools, marking systems, report cards, graded school organization, retardation, special education, and compensatory education will be rendered obsolete. Much more learning will take place outside the schools through direct participation in the larger community. The concept of student failure will be replaced by the concept of varying rates of student success in learning. Class schedules, student regulations, courses of study, room assignments, school hours, examinations, and many other artifacts of the educational scene will be radically transformed and perhaps discarded in some cases. Probably open education will degener-

ate into sloppy permissiveness and wistful romanticism at the hands of educators who do not understand it well. Genuine open education requires of teachers rigorous consideration of what learning is, which learning is of most worth, and what pedagogy really is.

The thrust toward individualization of instruction will accelerate markedly in the 1970s. This trend is quite compatible with the humanization of education because learning can hardly be humane if it is not attuned to the needs, interests, and abilities of the individual student. Individualization of instruction, sometimes spoken of as "adaptive education," was really not feasible, except at enormous expense, under traditional modes of instruction and learning. The linkage of programmed instruction with computer-assisted instruction through programs such as PLAN, described earlier, now makes the individualization of instruction technically possible. However, it will be several years before it becomes financially feasible for most school systems. Unless differentiated staffing suffers the same fate as team teaching, this new method of deploying teachers and students more effectively will also enhance the individualization of instruction. Independent study, minicourses, flexible grouping of students, and nongraded school organization will also be employed more commonly as stratagems for individualizing instruction.[25]

The future will hold greater promise for the development of continuity and coherence in the curriculum. Harold Shane defines this goal as "an unbroken chain of ventures and adventures in meaningful learning, beginning with early childhood education . . . [and] extended through postsecondary education and on into later-life education."[26] Many educators agree that the future requires far more fundamental consideration of the purposes of education, priorities of education stated as goals, better assessment of progress toward these goals, and more vigorous experimental comparison of alternative ways of achieving these goals. The application of systems theory and management to curriculum development may or may not succeed in bringing order, system, coherence, and continuity

---

[24] "Informal Education," *The Center Forum*, vol. 3, p. 1, July, 1969. A publication of the Center for Urban Education.

[25] For an extensive discussion of the future of individualized instruction, see Harold E. Mitzel, "The Impending Instruction Revolution," *Phi Delta Kappan*, vol. 51, pp. 434–439, April, 1970.

[26] See Harold G. Shane, "A Curriculum Continuum: Possible Trends in the 70s," *Phi Delta Kappan*, vol. 51, pp. 389–392, March, 1970, for an extension of this concept.

to the school curriculum.[27] Although experts differ in their opinions of the ultimate effectiveness of the application of systems theory and analysis to curriculum development, they are agreed that its application is still some years distant. The romantic educational reformers would regard the application of systems analysis to the curriculum as antithetic to open education. To our minds, it is too early to reach convictions on these issues; the returns are not yet in. In any case, school curriculums will be affected to a degree by prototype instructional systems such as Educational Systems for the 70s, described earlier. Also, the National Assessment of Educational Progress will provide far better evaluative data to support the improvement of curriculums and instruction.

The new curriculum development enterprises have commonly recognized the importance of the teacher in the implementation of the new courses of study. Curriculum change, if it is to permeate the educative process, necessitates a change in teacher performance. Thus increasing attention is given to institutes, workshops, and courses for the instruction of teachers in the design and use of the new methods and materials. These in-service development activities have often resulted in the invigoration of the teacher in the new curriculums and higher standards of teacher performance. Clearly the future will place far greater burdens upon the teacher to keep pace with accelerated change in curriculum and instruction.

Immediately upon his appointment as U.S. Commissioner of Education, Sidney Marland called for an end of the general education curriculum in the nation's high schools, condemning it as neither vocational nor academic. He advocated elimination of the term "vocational education" in favor of "career education" to end the false dichotomy between things academic and things vocational. He urged educators to prepare all high school students to become either usefully employed immediately after graduation or to go on to further formal education. He pointed out that only half of the high school graduates now get "career education"; the remainder get what he termed "irrelevant general educa-

[27] For different views on the possibility of systems theory's being successful in school applications, see American Association of School Administrators, *Instructional Technology and the School Administrator*, Washington, D.C., 1970, and Anthony G. Oettinger, *Run, Computer, Run*, Harvard University Press, Cambridge, Mass., 1969.

tion." This recommendation, if fully implemented, would result in a profound change in the curriculums of most high schools.

SUMMARY

Through the combined efforts of many agencies—so typical of a society as pluralistic as ours—great advances are being made in American education. The federal government, the learned societies, the professional associations, the educational foundations, the academicians, the educationists, the administrators, the teachers, and the critics—all have participated in the effort to improve the school curriculum at levels, albeit their participation has not usually been well harmonized.

The curriculum has been defined as the sum total of the experiences the student has under the direction of the school. Education has been defined as the transmission of the accumulated knowledge of human civilization and its application to contemporary and future problems of the individual and society. This concept emphasizes the life-centered curriculum, which includes the learner and society and the knowledge necessary for the full realization of both. It holds that education, ideally, is more than subject, more than the individual learner, more than society. Education is life itself.

A revolution has been taking place in the American school curriculum during the past two decades. Far-reaching changes, precipitated by forces on the domestic and world scene, have already taken place in many schools, and even more dramatic reformation is in prospect.

Curriculum reform in the 1950s and early 1960s was characterized by an essentialist, elitist philosophy of education, which emphasized a subject-centered curriculum oriented almost exclusively toward cognitive development. More recently an existentialist, humanistic, and egalitarian view of education has helped to bring the subject and the learner, the cognitive and the affective, into better balance. The latter view has stressed the importance of freedom, success, and happiness in schooling.

The development of programmed instruction has forced attention systematically upon both the learner and the subject: the manner in which students think and learn; and the fundamental principles, broad concepts, unity, and general structure of knowledge in the various subject fields. Although much remains to be discovered in the phenomenon of learning, new insights into the human mind promise profound change in curriculum and instruction. The development of educational technology not only offers new media of instruction but provides greater capability for the individualization of instruction.

Ungraded school organization, independent study, flexible scheduling, minicourses, and an openness of space, time scheduling, facilities, and curriculum have helped schools to accommodate individual student differences more effectively.

The various types of curriculum organization include the subject curriculum, the correlated curriculum, the broad fields curriculum, the core curriculum, and the experience curriculum.

The curriculum is being viewed as a continuing sequence from the kindergarten through the graduate school, and substance is being moved among the once inviolate educational levels—pre-elementary, elementary, secondary, and higher. Continuity is the key word. Logical sequence of content through many grade levels, rather than disparate layers of unrelated content, is being sought. This search for continuity has resulted in organizational changes that permit a flexible progression of students, each at his own pace, up the educational ladder. The ungraded school, honors courses, and advanced placement are manifestations of this trend.

Effort is being made to apply systems theory to produce curriculums that are better related to educational goals, more coherent, and more effectively evaluated.

Curriculum reform was focused largely upon the physical sciences, mathematics, and foreign languages in the years immediately after Sputnik. In the years following, increasing attention was given to the social sciences and the humanities. Sex education, black studies, drug education, and environmental education assumed great importance in response to acute problems in these domains. Vocational education was also expanded to meet the manpower needs of our industrial society and to maximize the employability of youth.

It is clear that the curriculum is undergoing more careful scrutiny and more fundamental change than at any other time in our history. It is still far too early to assess the value and impact of this change. The problem of building a curriculum adequate to the vast and complex needs of a rapidly changing world is difficult, frightening, and exciting, but the future promises more dramatic and far-reaching transformations in the school curriculum.

Suggested Activities

1. After further reading on the topic, write an essay on "Open Education and the Needs of Youth and Society."

2. Discuss the relationship between the individualization of instruction and school organization.

3. Explain the controversies that surround black studies and establish your own position.

4. From your own experience with them, list the major advantages and disadvantages of cocurricular activities.

5. List the major current criticisms of the school curriculum and indicate your agreement or disagreement with each.

6. Prepare a comprehensive review of recent curriculum reforms and instructional innovations in your field of teaching.

7. Examine as many of the documents listed under Foundations *in this chapter as you can and then formulate your own set of major purposes of education.*

8. Prepare an essay on the progress and problems of curriculum development in your teaching field or at your grade level. Consult the bibliography below.

9. Read the seven philosophical views of education in the section on curriculum in Chapter 1. Select the one that accommodates your views best and explain the reasons for your choice.

10. Make a critical examination of a given school's course of study in your field or at your grade level.

11. Describe some major curricular developments in your fields of study in college.

Bibliography

Billett, Roy O.: *Improving the Secondary School Curriculum,* Atherton Press, Inc., New York, 1970. A statement of the problems, objectives, and programs of the secondary school curriculum.

Crary, Ryland: *Humanizing the Curriculum,* Alfred A. Knopf, Inc., New York, 1969. An analysis of the social milieu and its implications for the reform of school curriculums.

Dressel, Paul L.: *College and University Curriculum,* McCutchan Publishing Corporation, Berkeley, Calif., 1970. A description and evaluation of contemporary curriculum trends and issues in higher education.

Dworkin, Martin S. (ed.): *Dewey on Education: Selections*, Teachers College Press, Teachers College, Columbia University, New York, 1959. A collection of John Dewey's writings related to the learner and the curriculum.

Goodlad, John I., and M. Francis Klein: *Behind the Classroom Door*, Charles A. Jones Publishing Company, Worthington, Ohio, 1971. A collection of material from many schools to reveal current change in instruction and curriculum.

Hack, Walter G., and others: *Educational Futurism, 1985: Challenge for Schools and Their Administrators*, McCutchan Publishing Corporation, Berkeley, Calif., 1971. A forecast of the future of educational programs and their support systems.

Hicks, William V., and others: *The New Elementary School Curriculum*, Van Nostrand Reinhold Company, New York, 1970. A description of curriculum theory, processes, and practices for elementary schools.

Holt, John: *What Do I Do Monday?*, E. P. Dutton, New York, 1971. Suggestions to help classroom teachers make their classrooms and the curriculums more open, flexible, and humane.

Kerensky, V. M., and E. O. Melby: *Education II—The Social Imperative*, Pendell Publishing Company, Midland, Mich., 1971. A bold design of an educational program centered in community life and capitalizing more fully upon the human potential for learning.

Kohl, Herbet R.: *The Open Classroom*, Vintage Books, Random House, Inc., New York, 1970. A sad but realistic account of how rigid teaching and inflexible school curriculums turn off young people; a plea for an open classroom and school environment.

McClure, Robert M. (ed.): *The Curriculum: Prospect and Retrospect*, National Society for the Study of Education, University of Chicago, Chicago, 1971. A scholarly review of the past development, current trends, and future prospects of the curriculum.

National Education Association, Association for Supervi-

sion and Curriculum Development: *To Nuture Humaneness: Commitment for the '70s*, National Education Association, Washington, D.C., 1970. An analysis of the new goals in society and the need for a more humane purpose in the educational program.

National Education Association, National School Public Relations Association: *Black Studies in Schools*, National Education Association, Washington, D.C., 1970. An overview of the pros and cons on black studies, progress being made, and case descriptions of high school programs.

————: *Environment and the Schools*, National Education Association, Washington, D.C., 1971. A description of the best programs in environmental education and the views of expert authorities.

————: *Individualization in Schools: The Challenge and the Options*, National Education Association, Washington, D.C., 1971. A description of some of the best prototypes of individualized educational programs.

————: *Reading Crisis: The Problem and Suggested Solutions*, National Education Association, Washington, D.C., 1970. A roundup of the best discoveries and solutions to the problems of reading instruction.

Rogers, Carl: *Freedom To Learn*, Charels E. Merrill Books, Inc., Columbus, Ohio, 1969. A scholarly but interesting version of the ideal conditions for learning, drawn from a lifetime of experience by the eminent educational psychologist.

Silberman, Charles E.: *Crisis in the Classroom*, Random House, Inc., New York, 1970. An important indictment of the oppressiveness and joylessness of school classrooms, with recommendations for improving education.

Van Til, William: *Curriculum: Quest for Relevance*, Houghton Mifflin Company, Boston, 1971. A collection of readings on curriculum including criticisms, analyses, and predictions by leading educators.

Chapter 15   Educational Materiel and Technology

ORIENTATION

Instructional Technology: Definition. The U.S. Commission on Instructional Technology uses two definitions of "instructional technology":

In its more familiar sense, it means the media born of the communications revolution which can be used for instructional purposes alongside the teacher, textbook, and blackboard. . . . In order to reflect present day reality, the Commission has had to look at the pieces that make up instructional technology: television, films, overhead projectors, computers, and the other items of "hardware" and "software" (to use the convenient jargon that distinguishes machines from programs).

The second and less familiar definition of instructional technology goes beyond any particular medium or device. In this sense, instructional technology is more than the sum of its parts. It is a systematic way of designing, carrying out and evaluating the total process of learning and teaching in terms of specific objectives, based on research in human learning and communication, and employing a combination of human and nonhuman resources to bring about more effective instruction. The widespread acceptance and application of this broad definition belongs to the future.[1]

Both of these definitions—the narrow, as exemplified by a single piece of equipment, like a computer, and the broad, as represented by an overall "systems approach"—permeate this chapter on educational technology and materiel.

Materiel in Education: Major Types. Stone, brick, cement, glass, steel, wood, and other construction

[1] Sidney G. Tickton (ed.), *To Improve Learning: An Evaluation of Instructional Technology*, vol. 1, R. R. Bowker Company, New York, 1970, p. 7.

Special education teachers receive in-service education in a mobile computer-assisted instructional system.

materials can serve society in beautiful and functional educational *buildings*. Likewise, the steel in file cases, the glass in school microscopes, and the wood in the violins in the school orchestra make useful instructional *equipment*. The iron filings in the chemistry laboratory experiment, the limestone in the chalk for traditional blackboards, the rubber in erasers—these, too, though short-lived, serve as useful school *supplies*. The *buildings*, with their equipment and supplies, must have a location, a *site*. These are the materiel in education discussed in this chapter. Educational technology is more than the sum of its materiel and machines. Futhermore, it requires skilled teacher-technicians and others with expertise in educational technology.

As indicated in Chapter 14, "Other Educational Personnel," the demand for educational technologists is increasing rapidly. One of the most dramatic and consequential developments in education has been the rapid appearance of a great variety of new instructional materials and equipment. Referred to variously as a "technological revolution in education," "instructional technology," "new media," and "educational automation," this development has brought to the school an interesting and, to some, frightening array of mechanical and electronic hardware that promises literally to revolutionize education.[2]

A great technological gap exists between new, available teaching tools and outworn teaching techniques. The current bottleneck in computer-assisted instruction (CAI), states Prof. Patrick Suppes of Stanford University, is not technological but pedagogical—it concerns devising ways of individualizing

[2] Willard S. Elsbree, Harold J. McNally, and Richard Wynn, *Elementary School Administration and Supervision*, 3d ed., American Book Company, New York, 1967, p. 434.

instruction and designing curriculums suited to individuals.

At an international symposium on technology and society, held at the Center for the Study of Democratic Institutions, Prof. Emmanuel G. Mesthene, director of Harvard University's Institute of Technology and Culture, said: "The malaise of our age is that our power increases faster than our ability to understand it and use it well. But, that, surely, is a challenge to be wise, not an invitation to despair."[3] Innovations in education are invitations to use appropriate new machines and to retool teaching techniques, which are evolving in the historical development of educational technology.

DEVELOPMENT OF EDUCATIONAL TECHNOLOGY

The historical development of certain aspects of educational technology in America, such as books and television, is discussed later in this chapter under specific headings. A general overview is presented here. An interesting and significant historical study of the evolution of educational materiel and technology is Charnel Anderson's *Technology in American Education: 1650-1900*. Some of his historical findings, grouped according to three rather well-defined periods, are abstracted and supplemented here, with a fourth period—the twentieth century—added.[4]

1. Colonial Period. Almost all school supplies were handmade in colonial times. The pens were goose quills, and each family supplied the children with homemade ink. The hornbook was a one-page primer, showing the alphabet, the digits, and sometimes the Lord's Prayer, fastened to a piece of board and covered with a thin, transparent sheet of horn. Writing paper was rough and dark. Textbooks were crude; materials were poor, and the prices were high. The ABC primers were widely used in colonial times. The first American textbook of any importance—*The New England Primer*—was bound by hand. Illustrations in books were used sparingly, and drawings and engravings were very crude.

[3] Jeanne Riha, "Controlling Man's Brain Children," *Rotarian*, vol. 109, p. 29, December, 1966.

[4] Charnel Anderson, *Technology in American Education: 1650-1900*, Superintendent of Documents, Washington, D.C., 1962. (First published by the National Education Association as Occasional Paper No. 1, July, 1961.)

The typical one-room school building was built of logs. School furniture tended to be more crude than the buildings; benches, for example, were made of backless split logs. The colonial schools had no blackboards, slates, or maps, although some flourishing schools could boast of owning a globe.

2. From the American Revolution to the Civil War. During this seventy-year period, from 1791 to 1861, a great deal of school apparatus was added. The steel writing pen made its appearance in classrooms. The abacus, known by many names including "arithmetican," came into general use during this period and offered a new dimension in math instruction. In the more progressive schools, maps were extensively used.

Webster's "blueback" speller, the *Elementary Spelling Book*, gave rise to a whole hoard of imitations. The first texts to rival it seriously were the famous *McGuffey Readers*. While Webster and McGuffey dominated the textbook movement, several other books made new technological contributions. The technique of map coloring to indicate elevations was introduced. Illustrations were now prepared from copper plates, which the artist made from photographs.

School architecture and furniture improved. The buildings still consisted of one room, although the monitorial school of the 1840s added separate rooms for recitations. Early desks in this period were only sloping shelves built against the walls on three sides of the classroom. Later, combination desks were introduced. The earliest reference to a blackboard dates from 1809. By the 1840s, blackboards darkened many classroom walls. The hyloplate and slate blackboards came in the last half of the nineteenth century. Local schoolteachers often made their own blackboards. Slates for pupils were slowly introduced into American schools, and globes began to be regarded as essential items.

3. From the Civil War to 1900. A significant revolution in attitude toward educational technology occurred during this period. The new educational apparatus introduced after the 1860s, once regarded as novelties, now were ranked as necessary educational implements. This attitude was so widely accepted that states passed legal statutes to enforce the purchase of equipment. Furthermore, after 1860 there was a veritable flood of new educational publications, in the form of pedagogical journals, reviews, and weeklies. The states began to publish their own journals to keep the teachers informed, producing a wave of interest in educational technology and teaching techniques. The international exhibitions did much to disseminate knowledge about educational equipment and supplies.

Technological advances in papermaking brought better-quality paper into the classrooms at lower prices. In 1861 Eberhard started a factory in New York, thus introducing the pencil industry into America. Lead and slate pencils were priced very reasonably. Printing from movable type became rather obsolete and was replaced widely by stereotyping and then by electroplating. There was some improvement in bookbinding. Illustrative materials steadily improved. Offset printing and color work came in. Numerous devices were invented to help the pupil learn to read.

A real visual aid introduced in this period was the "magic lantern," which projected pictures on a screen. The marriage of photography and projection techniques had produced a professional "brainchild." Another interim aid for education was the hand-held stereoscope. Using a single optical apparatus and two photographs, the stereoscope added a "third dimension" to teaching.

The main architectural innovation during the decade following the Civil War was the introduction of more space and comfort into school buildings, plus a trend away from the austere, if not severe, appearance that had characterized them in the past. Toward the end of the nineteenth century, it became evident that some schools were too elaborate, ornate, and wasteful in construction. An era of standardization set in. School furniture continued to improve. The long, benchlike desks and seats of the period before the Civil War gave way to dual or separate desks.

4. Twentieth Century. The first seven decades of the present century witnessed more changes in educational materiel and technology than the centuries that elapsed since the first Latin grammar school was founded in 1635. A few of the many advances are mentioned here, and others are discussed later in this chapter.

During this century "audio" was added to "visual," and much audiovisual equipment was produced. Sound was added to silent motion pictures. Filmstrips took on a new dimension with the addition of sound attachments or accompaniments, such as disks and tape recorders. Then television came into the classroom, bringing both pictures and sound. About two-thirds of all schools and colleges now are in areas covered by ETV, and satellites in the

sky—"the fourth revolution"—beam instantaneous pictures and simultaneous sound from far-off lands to the worldwide classroom. Firsthand pictures of the moon appear on the classroom screen. School and college students may soon see closer pictures of the planets. The laser light in the university laboratory burns many times brighter than the light at the sun's surface. Educators are approaching the "age of enlightenment" through twentieth-century instructional technology.

The architecture of educational buildings now accents beauty and function. Countless classrooms are carpeted, which adds beauty and enhances acoustics. Central air conditioning and communication systems affect each student. Round-the-clock surveillance of mechanical equipment in many schools and colleges is achieved by "electronic watchdogs." Educational parks are resulting in enlarged school sites and expanded school functions. Educational furniture is tailor-made to fit the learner and the learning situation. Individual study carrels have replaced the double seats of yesteryear. The lonely librarian has become the director of a learning center, teeming with many media and learners. The third-grade reader has been expanded into a library of books. Teaching machines marshal electronics in the service of education. Educational equipment is no longer stationary; the bookmobile has road companions in the traveling art studio, the mobile history laboratory, and the trailer teacher-education laboratory.

A broad and bold breakthrough in educational technology has taken place in the second third of this century—and new aspects of it will continue to appear. A few examples of national scope follow. In 1969 was created in the U.S. Office of Education a new Office for Instructional Resources, with responsibility for a new Bureau of Library and Educational Technology. In 1970 the first volume of the report of the Commission on Instructional Technology was published.[5] In the same year the American Association of School Administrators issued the report of its Committee on Technology and Instruction.[6] In 1971 was held the first national conference on educational technology and the first annual exhibition of equipment and materials in this rapidly

[5] Tickton, *op. cit.*

[6] Stephen J. Knezevich and Glenn G. Eye (eds.), *Instructional Technology and the School Administrator*, American Association of School Administrators, Washington, D.C., 1970.

developing field. The year 1973 is the date scheduled for the completion in Chicago of the thirty-four-story Educational Facilities Center designed to facilitate viewing and purchasing of the materiel of modern education.

Throughout the history of American education the major teaching-learning tool has been the book, which is discussed below in some detail.

BOOKS

Historical Development

The Role of Print in Education. "What is the greatest invention in human history?" There are many answers to this question, but for education there is only one: "The greatest invention is printing." The first press in the territory now included in the United States was set up at Harvard College, Cambridge, Massachusetts, by Stephen Daye in 1639. In the three hundred and more years that have elapsed since that time, the relationship between the printing press and institutions of learning has been vital. The Association of American University Presses, Inc., reports a booming book business. Furthermore, in a single year, according to *Publishers' Weekly*, more than thirty thousand new books or new editions of old books are printed in the United States, many of which are textbooks. The publishing of educational books and other materials today constitutes a big business.

Early American Textbooks. The evolution of schoolbooks, briefly mentioned earlier in this chapter, forms a fascinating chapter in the history of our schools. *The New England Primer*, an example of the small, moralistic textbook used in the colonial days, is said to have taught millions to read and not one to sin. *McGuffey's Readers* taught the Bible and morals by means of interesting stories. America's textbook best seller—over one hundred million copies—was the *Elementary Spelling Book*, the "blueback" speller of Noah Webster.

The four main influences in the development of modern school books were child psychology, textbook publication as a specialized industry, the improvement of printing and binding, and research by authors and publishers.

The Textbook in Modern Education. The number of textbooks published in the United States has doubled in the last decade. In recent years there has been a marked trend toward the merger of textbook publishing companies seeking the economies that result from broader distribution of their products. Also, companies that published only elementary school books are joining with others that published only high school or college books so that an articulated sequence of books throughout all educational levels can be produced and marketed together. Some textbook firms are merging with manufacturers of electronic educational equipment.

Textbooks have been widely criticized on a number of grounds. Some claim they are too radical, others that they are too conservative. Certain patriotic groups have launched periodic attacks on textbooks, especially on those used in the social studies. They insist that many books tend to instill either an un-American point of view or at least a discontent with democracy and private enterprise. However, when New York State established a textbook-review commission to examine allegedly subversive books, only a handful were referred to it.

Other critics contend that school textbooks are too conservative or unprovocative. Jacques Barzun, in *The House of Intellect*, said that

. . . the textbook writer must defend his words and views [against the classrooms where local prejudices and sacred illiteracies obtain] squaring his mind with those anonymous critics who are often his inferiors in learning and sense.

Many insist that there is too much timidity in the writing and publishing of materials not only on democracy but on many controversial issues.

One of the problems with textbooks until recently has been their neglect and mistreatment of minority groups. There are now signs of breakthroughs on all academic levels in promoting real understanding of minority groups in our textbooks. For example:

. . . The multi-ethnic or integrated elementary textbook is a relatively new phenomenon. The integrated elementary textbook in social studies, when used by an able, well-prepared teacher whose respect for the minority-group child pervades the classroom atmosphere, . . . can be a powerful weapon against this insularity and lack of understanding of the peoples which have helped to make this America.[7]

[7] Robert D. Price and Thelma L. Spencer, "Elementary Social Studies Textbooks and Their Relevance to the Negro Child," *Social Studies*, vol. 61, p. 173, April, 1970.

Obviously, textbooks and other reading materials should recognize the contribution of all to all from the wars of the colonial days through the modern civil rights revolution and the women's liberation movement.

The old question whether the textbook shapes the curriculum or vice versa is similar to the question about the chicken and the egg. It seems evident that there is interaction; the textbook does indeed have quite an influence upon the curriculum, but curriculum change also helps to shape what is published. There are unfortunately some teachers who use the textbook as the sole source of material and the major medium of learning. There are others who use no single book, drawing instead upon a variety of materials including textbooks, periodicals, and reference sets. Most teachers probably use textbooks fairly wisely as a valuable, but certainly not the sole, source of information. The use of programmed books and materials is increasing markedly.

Workbooks, sometimes misused as a form of busywork by some teachers, once developed a bad name. However, they have the advantage of helping busy teachers to adapt assignments to the varying abilities and interests of individual students. Many workbooks have been designed recently on the basis of programmed instruction, described later in this chapter, presenting knowledge in orderly, sequential form and permitting the student to proceed at his own rate. Workbooks and student manuals are often prepared and sold in conjunction with a companion textbook. Some are especially designed to facilitate the student's note-taking. Others are prepared for use in the physical sciences as laboratory manuals.

But the biggest boom in the school book industry is the miraculous rise of the paperback. One publisher predicts that half of all school textbooks will be in paperback form within a decade. The paperback book is less expensive than the clothbound, permitting the instructor to require more extensive reading, an important advantage in literature classes, for example. Its lower cost also permits the student to mark it up and to retain possession of it, thus acquiring early the nucleus of his own library. The paperback is fresh, clean, germ-free, and possibly more up to date than the clothbound book passed along year after year. Its disadvantages include its less durable nature and often poorer technical quality. Many schools enroll students in paperback book clubs, and a growing number operate their own paperback bookstores. Robert Escarpit, in his UNESCO-published volume entitled *The Book Revolution*, states that the mass-circulation paperback book is the most important cultural development of the second half of the twentieth century. Approximately one-third of a billion paperbacks are sold annually.

Curtis G. Benjamin, former president of the McGraw-Hill Book Company, has made in *Saturday Review* observations related to books in education:

The paperback explosion actually has been more helpful than hurtful to hardcover publishing. . . . Teachers began some years ago to move away from the conventional textbook as a monolithic instructional instrument. . . . During the 1960s there occurred an astonishing explosion of nonliterary books.[8]

Books other than textbooks are discussed later in this chapter in connection with libraries.

In summation, as to the important role of textbooks, the American Book Publishers Council, in its publication *Books in the Schools*, stated:

The single most effective means for stimulating learning, it is generally agreed, is to surround children with books from their preschool years in the home through their school careers . . . the door that reading and books can open to the whole range of human knowledge and experience must be swung wide in our classrooms.[9]

The American Educational Publishers Institute has produced a motion picture with the tenable title *Textbooks: The Second Most Important Influence*—the first being teachers.

Selection and Purchase of Books

Selection of Books. A few states maintain a policy of statewide selection of school books by a state textbook commission which adopts a book for each subject for all schools of the state. A larger number of states have textbook commissions which approve a number of books from which local districts may make their choices. But the practice of leaving the selection entirely to the local district is growing.

[8]Curtis G. Benjamin, "Book Publishing's Hidden Bonanza," *Saturday Review*, vol. 52, pp. 19-21, 81, Apr. 18, 1970.

[9]James Cass (ed.), *Books in the School*, American Book Publishers Council, New York, 1961, pp. iii, iv.

More than half the states now follow this policy. It permits adaptability to local needs and interests. Furthermore, it permits participation in selection by the teacher.

When textbooks are selected locally, the most common practice is for a committee of teachers to examine available books and recommend a choice. In this way teacher and pupil interests, needs, and likes are made known and given consideration. Obviously, the educational interests, needs, and capabilities of the pupils must be given priority in the writing, publishing, and selection of textbooks.

The two general techniques in evaluating textbooks prior to their adoption are subjective and objective appraisal. Usually both are employed. The one is a casual examination of the book or books, often preceded by a sales talk by a representative of a book company or by the receipt of a letter or descriptive folder. The other technique is a more painstaking scrutiny by means of a checklist, scorecard, or guide for textbook analysis. Guides for textbook analysis usually contain information about the following major items: authorship, date of publication, suitability of content, organization, vocabulary burden, readability, methods of teaching and learning, teaching aids, pupil helps, format (such as illustrations and physical attractiveness), and miscellaneous details. Content, suitability, and format are the three most important factors.

The format or mechanical construction of the book is an important factor. The physical appearance is affected by the size of the page and the book and by the binding, cover, paper, illustrations, type, spacing, and margins. Modern textbooks are more attractive, appealing, and durable than their earlier counterparts. Modern books are more readable and contain more and better-organized subject matter. Most of the changes in format and content have been effected through the joint efforts of teachers, administrators, librarians, authors, researchers, and publishers. The American Institute of Graphic Arts, through leading book designers and printers, has launched a nationwide campaign for better-looking books—books that please the eye as well as the mind.

Storage of Books. One of the many impending changes in book information storage and retrieval, especially in libraries, is that of miniaturization.

What the transistor is to radio and television, high reduction photography is to the printed page. By photographing materials at very great reductions onto a small, transparent film card called a microfiche, this process at first was able to transfer a whole book onto a single card. With advanced technology, however, it is now possible to print six books on a single 3″ × 5″ card.[10]

Distribution of Books. Virtually all the public schools of the nation provide textbooks free to students. In some cases the cost is borne by the local district, in others by the state, and in a few by both. The purchase or rental of textbooks by students is not fully in accord with the democratic concept of supplying free education and free instructional materials. In a 1970 decision the Supreme Court of Michigan ruled that local school districts must furnish school pupils with free textbooks and certain supplies.

A further factor in the distribution of school books was added when the Elementary and Secondary Education Act was passed by Congress in 1965. While private schools do not receive the federal grants for instructional materials, nevertheless textbooks and other printed and published materials are made available to private school students and teachers on a loan basis. This loan arrangement also applies to elementary and secondary school resources and materials for libraries.

Educational Libraries and Learning Centers

Their Role in Education. The modern educational library in school and college is a learning and materials center. The library ought to be the heart of the school or college, with arteries running into each room, and capillaries to each pupil. The plan of extensive reading requires much supplementary material. Therefore, administrators and teachers should be familiar with the library and competent to guide pupils in its use.

Elementary and secondary schools should have a close and cooperative relationship with public and private libraries. In some large cities and in many small districts, the school library is operated as a branch of the city or county system and draws freely on the larger collection of books. Rolling libraries

[10]John Tebbel, "Libraries in Miniature: A New Era Begins," *Saturday Review,* vol. 54, p. 41, Jan. 9, 1971.

and bookmobiles are increasing in number and in services to rural areas. Tennessee is one of several states where the county circulating library system has proved very successful. Several school districts cooperate in the establishment of a central library system whereby the books obtained are made available by a well-planned system of circulation.

On the college and university levels, the library is the heuristic hub with its academic branches serving as spokes radiating to the distant rim of the universe. In answer to the question "What can a library be?" Thomas R. Buckman, Northwestern University's head librarian, writes:

It is a source of ideas for change and a workshop in which they may be developed and refined. It is for problem solvers who want to design a new society. The library is also an instrument for personal inquiry. Organized collections of books and manuscripts have for centuries been in the mind-expanding business, long before LSD, and with far fewer hazardous side-effects. . . .

It should be a place for independent, course-related study where students, on their own, may range widely over recorded knowledge as well as using the methodology of their discipline—a place in which they may test and strengthen their ideas in solitude, where much of real learning occurs.[11]

The federal government cooperates fiscally in improving libraries, librarians, and their services. For years rural libraries have been receiving federal support. Some of the more recent acts which contain provisions for enhancing libraries are the Higher Education Facilities Act (1963), the Library Services and Construction Act (1964), the Higher Education Act (1965), and the Elementary and Secondary Education Act (1965). In addition, various amendments to these original acts have extended aid to libraries. For example, in 1966 former President Lyndon B. Johnson signed the Library Services and Construction Act amendments, which authorized the program for five additional years, and added two new titles providing for interlibrary cooperation and for special libraries in state institutions, such as hospitals and prisons.

Instructional Materials Center. The advent of the new technology has brought a significant change to some school libraries. In addition to their role as depositories of books for students, they may also include teaching machines, programmed materials,

[11]Thomas R. Buckman, "What Can a Library Be?" *Northwestern Report*, vol. 1, pp. 7–8, Fall, 1970.

collections of professional books and magazines for teachers, a store of sample school textbooks, and a file of instructional materials including units of work, courses of study, sample lesson plans, and other curriculum materials. Some schools have combined their audiovisual centers with their libraries. Thus films, slides, pictures, mock-ups, models, and exhibits join books, newspapers, and periodicals in what is often referred to as an instructional materials center. Some libraries have tape-listening centers, music centers, and programmed services, and some use computers and data processing to facilitate circulation.

Evaluation of School Library. A satisfactory book collection for a library should rate fairly high on the following points: number of titles, balance of distribution, appropriateness for school purposes, and recency of publication. Modern education requires a well-balanced library in every building as a central opportunity for extended reading experience. A joint committee of the American Association of School Librarians and the newly named Association for Educational Communications and Technology collaborated in preparing *Standards for School Media Programs.* The implementation of standards such as these and others of the American Library Association will have a great impact on libraries and educational technology, as the role of the librarian changes from providing mere media to that of stimulating the learning environment.

OTHER MATERIALS AND EQUIPMENT

Space does not permit a detailed list of all the supply and equipment items other than books that are found in a modern school. The two types singled out for emphasis are (1) ancillary reading materials and (2) technological aids to learning.

Ancillary Reading Materials

The Dictionary. An important book, which should receive special attention in all educational institutions, is the dictionary. A large dictionary placed on a bookshelf or desk in the front or rear of the room is not adequate. Each pupil ought to have an attractive dictionary gauged to his level and at hand for steady use. This may be supplemented by larger lexicons available for the group. Extensive reading and frequent reference to a dictionary help to develop a copious vocabulary and fine discrimination in meanings.

Newspapers. Students are interested in newspapers. Today thousands of classrooms contain newspapers. Many teachers employ the news, magazine, financial, and sports sections as means of general knowledge enrichment; they depend upon the book review, magazine, theater, movie, art, music, radio, television, science, travel, and hobby sections for cultural guidance and enrichment.

Magazines. Allied with the use of newspapers is that of magazines and periodicals. Many schools subscribe to publications such as *Our Times, Reader's Digest, My Weekly Reader,* and *Scholastic.* The current emphasis on candid photography and pictorial sections in popular magazines brought about the introduction of these aids into the school. It is obvious that the school must give attention to the selection and use of periodicals. For example, the producers of television's successful children's show "Sesame Street" distributed two million copies of each issue of *Sesame Street Magazine*—a four-color periodical of comic-book size—to disadvantaged children.

Other Technological Aids in Education

Globes. This is a global age literally and figuratively. Supersonic jet planes make any part of today's world no farther away than tomorrow morning. The manufactured globe is a simple but significant symbol of this shrinking world of which the classroom is a part. As a teaching tool it possesses great versatility, especially with attachments showing man-made moons and God-created constellations.

Planetariums. There are several types of planetariums, which have become popular in this modern space age. The "orrery" (named after the astronomer Charles Boyle, fourth Earl of Orrery) is an apparatus showing the positions and motions of bodies in the solar system by balls moved by wheelwork. The term "planetarium" is also applied to a domed room made to represent the sky. A multilensed instrument in its center projects the sun, moon, planets, and stars, and displays their apparent motions in a realistic space environment. It is an astronomical aid in such related subjects as mathematics, science, space education, and, of course, astronomy itself. It has many possibilities for integration with other subjects.[12] Many municipal and community planetariums are available for educational use.

Maps. The United States is a land with millions of maps. In addition to the maps on globes, many others are available as teaching tools. These visual aids include a mite map made of a first-grade classroom; a sketch of each school building; a master plan of the entire campus, with its long-term projections for the future; the community map; the county plot plan; the state survey; the national resources locations; and the worldwide maps. The International Geophysical Year emphasized the important role of maps. There is an endless variety of realistic resources available to the teacher in many fields of learning, ranging from the small, inexpensive plan made by students to the large, expensive, manufactured wall map. A new dimension in teaching social studies is the "action map"—a large map covering many square feet—used on the classroom floor. On this kind of map, whether commercially produced or made by the students and teacher, students can write, walk distances, and do artwork.

Slides. Maps are also available for projection on the screen or chalkboard. Countless other slides, both commercially manufactured and made in the classroom, enhance learning by tailor-making pictures to fit the discussion or unit. Many grade and high school and college students have access to colored slides available for group sharing.

Films and Filmstrips. Under the stimulation of the National Defense Education Act, the number of educational film and filmstrip libraries has grown at an astonishing rate. They have made the pages of history come alive and have brought everything from great symphonies to space flights to the eyes and ears of the school child. Slow-motion photography permits the examination of phenomena that happen too fast to be perceived by ordinary vision. Time-lapse photography speeds up the blooming of

[12]H. Bruce Geiger, "How to Integrate Planetarium Usage into the Educational Program, *Nation's Schools,* vol. 85, pp. 112–113, May, 1970.

a flower or the growth of a plant so that an event that might take several hours or months to materialize can be seen in a few minutes.

While most educational movies were once 16-mm width, the 8-mm type is increasing in popularity, due in part to lower costs. Films are usually designed to visualize a single topic, or a specific technique, or as part of a broad "film-mediated instructional unit." The 35-mm filmstrip is also widely used as a visual aid. It presents still photographs and is especially useful for showing charts or diagrams. Many teachers prepare their own filmstrips.

A significant development is the textbook-movie-filmstrip package, in which a motion picture is correlated with a textbook and its showing is followed by a tailor-made filmstrip which visually reinforces learning. Educational television has also stimulated the production of films for telecasting to large audiences. Film sets covering an entire course in physics or history are being marketed. One enterprising producer is at work putting an entire high school curriculum on film. Live educational telecasts are frequently stored on film or video tape for reuse.

Tapes—Audio and Audiovisual. The tape recorder has become a helpful home-study machine and a schoolroom necessity. Various firms and educational institutions prepare and sell or rent individual tapes or several in a series. As a corollary to "speed reading," an illustrative experiment at the University of Michigan with taped lectures shows that learners can speed up their listening too. While a professor may normally lecture at a rate of 150 words a minute, university students can absorb oral presentations at the rate of 250 words a minute.

The videotape recorders and recordings are widely used in educational institutions at all academic levels including adult education. Some of their features are instant playback, closed-circuit television, recording of broadcast programs, and ease of storage. Videotapes, perfected by the television networks, are being used increasingly, for example, in the reproduction of paintings and in scientific developments. An illustration of educational use on the elementary school level is the series of fifteen-minute videotapes entitled "Patterns in Arithmetic" (PIA), developed with the aid of the U.S. Office of Education. Many audio tapes have been developed for college use, such as Sound Seminar Tapes, which augment lectures, stimulate discussions, and promote individual study and enjoyment.

Radio. The Federal Communications Commission allocated numerous channels for noncommercial, educational FM (frequency modulation) service, with its static-free, high-fidelity bands. Increasing in use is the audio correspondence course, the lesson material for which is broadcast. Through the addition of the so-called "fourth R" (radio), many rural schools are losing their one-teacher status. Many large schools have installed central sound systems.

Educational Television. It has been estimated that one-third of the nation's school children receive part of their school learning via television. The U.S. Office of Education states that two-thirds of all students enrolled in American schools and colleges are in areas covered by educational television. In addition, many adults take television credit courses, which are becoming increasingly available. The United States Office of Education estimates that today four out of every five persons are within viewing range of educational television. This is a tremendous development since 1963, when federal funds first became available to establish and expand educational television stations. Since that date more than a hundred ETV stations have been activated and over seventy-five expanded.

There are four basic types of educational television: commercial network programs, local educational television stations, telecasts from airborne transmitters, and closed-circuit systems within school districts or colleges.

Commercial network television programs, such as the popular "Sunrise Semester," are viewed by adults at home. Although most of these programs carry no academic credit, a few do. Live news programs, documentaries, dramatizations, travelogues, musical presentations, and other telecasts have brought the world of sight and sound into our living rooms and added immeasurably to our education. The tragedy of commercial television, on the other hand, is that the truly educational fare is badly out of balance with a mishmash of dramas featuring violence and revolting commercials. Nevertheless, the miracle of television has opened a wondrous window to the entire world and indeed to the universe.

The Ford Foundation has proposed to the Federal Communications Commission the use of satellites to deliver electronic teaching nationwide. COMSAT has done this for several years on an international scale, through Telstar and Lani Bird. Satellites have carried television cameras into outer space and have enabled man to perceive hitherto unknown aspects of the universe, such as a closeup view of the moon's surface.

The arrangement which allegedly will eventually have the most profound impact upon schools and colleges is the closed-circuit television system within a local school system or college. In a closed-circuit arrangement, live or taped telecasts originating in a studio within the school system are piped simultaneously to the separate schools through a coaxial cable. The cables and other installations are expensive, but the school system has complete control over the facilities and can adapt the programming to its own needs, an advantage that is largely lost in regional telecasting. Hagerstown, Maryland, installed the first system of this sort with the help of an initial grant from the Ford Foundation and now maintains a closed-circuit system which serves all the pupils in its schools. Hagerstown's closed-circuit educational television has made it a showplace. Other local closed-circuit systems have since been installed in schools and colleges. One of the most advanced examples of instructional technology has been constructed at the University of Texas Dental Branch in Houston, which has a 100-student-position, individual-use, individual-process system. It is an operational three-dimensional television system.[13]

Local stations, such as WQED in Pittsburgh, the first community-owned educational television station, have grown in number since 1950. Stimulated by grants from the Ford Foundation, these stations have obtained additional financial aid from school systems, other foundations, state educational agencies, community groups, private philanthropies, public fund drives, and, more recently, the federal government. At least two dozen local school systems operate television stations. In Newburgh, New York, an instructional network reaches public as well as parochial schools. New York's Catholic archdiocese offers instructional television to many schools. More than 125 additional noncommercial stations beam programs into countless classrooms. Local stations are producing many educational programs.

The most successful educational television program has been the much-acclaimed "Sesame Street," which is designed to sell learning to preschoolers. The Educational Testing Service states that "Sesame Street" has shown that television can be used effectively to teach 3- to 5-year-old children simple facts and skills. It won the Peabody Award as the best children's show. The Nielsen ratings indicate that it has reached more than half of the twelve million estimated children in the nation between the ages of 3 and 5. This five-day-a-week program has over three hundred outlets on commercial and noncommercial television stations. It has been funded by both private and public agencies. Produced by Children's Television Workshop, it has a thoroughly integrated cast of children and adults, plus a large cast of puppet characters each with its own personality. Carl T. Rowan, in his syndicated newspaper column, wrote: "Sesame Street is one of the most important programs since TV was invented. Because if these youngsters can be taught effectively through "the tube" we may be able to break the vicious circle that lets poverty and ignorance perpetuate themselves, generation after generation."[14]

A 30-minute new elementary school show was launched in 1971 by the Children's Television Workshop for children 7 to 10 years old, with special emphasis on reading and reasoning for pupils in the second grade.

How well has educational television done the job? Certain conclusions are fairly evident. According to a review of approximately four hundred research studies, it is clear that students generally learn about as well with instructional television as they do in the typical classroom setting. The overall verdict in most studies has been "no significant difference," at least as far as standardized achievement tests are able to measure. Television teaching appears to be most successful in the elementary school. At the secondary and college levels, the traditional classroom appears to produce slightly better results. Although there is great variation in attitudes, elementary school pupils and teachers appear to like instructional television more than high school and college students and teachers, who favor it less and sometimes oppose it.

As evaluated by the Commission on Educational Technology, ITV does not get a high mark on its report card:

Instructional Television has made little impact on American education. Commitment to the use of televi-

[13]Rudy Bretz, "An Independent-access Instructional Television System," *Educational Technology*, vol. 10, pp. 17–22, December, 1970.

[14]Carl T. Rowan, "School Gap Bridged by ETV Show," *Grand Rapids Press*, vol. 78, p. 9B, Dec. 28, 1969.

sion is generally lacking on the part of administrators and teachers. While individual systems can claim some success, the simple imposition of television on traditional administrative and educational structures is usually disappointing. The medium itself cannot be blamed, however; the major reforms necessary are much more basic than a single medium.[15]

It is somewhat surprising that educational television has failed to demonstrate more marked superiority over the conventional classroom, since the best teachers are usually chosen for the telecasts and are given generous time and help in lesson preparation and the best facilities and materials.

Television Cassette. A potentially powerful instrument for education is the television cassette, which permits a viewer and listener to choose his own program as he might select a phonograph record and a related motion picture:

The potential for a revolution in quality is enormous. With a player and a clutch of cassettes, a viewer can ignore commercial TV's rigid timetable and standardized fare. He can watch whatever he likes, including films he makes himself, and he can see it a lot more sharply than the fuzzy images of most broadcast TV.

In the schoolroom . . . cassette TV could easily touch off a small revolution in the ways of learning and teaching. Using cassettes instead of rigidly scheduled TV lessons, teachers could choose their own subject air time for instruction. They could stop the show to answer questions from the class, go over the trickier sections as often as they like in slow motion and send their pupils away with cassettes to study at home. With home recording videotape systems the pupils, in turn, could create their own cassette reports to hand in as homework. . . . Technologically this is all within sight now.[16]

The future tense in learning-teaching technology is pregnant with possibilities for the birth of many a "brainchild" such as the television cassette.

Phonograph and Records. Despite the growing popularity and use of modern teaching tools such as cassettes, the phonograph of yesteryear is still a good teaching machine. Long-playing, stereophonic, unbreakable, unscratchable records are easy for pupil and teacher to use. The repertory of records includes many high-quality educational and cultural programs. Records made by students or teachers can also enhance motivation and learning, especially for shut-ins.

[15]Tickton, *op. cit.*, p. 150.
[16]From "A Good Revolution Goes on Sale," by Edward Kern, LIFE Magazine, Oct. 16, 1970, © 1970 Time Inc.

Cameras. In some schools elementary students have been motivated to improve their speaking and writing abilities by reporting on observations made with an inexpensive camera using black-and-white film and their own eyes and ears. Some movie cameras make possible low-cost sound-on-film recording, putting sound-film production within the reach of most schools. Many schools and colleges are now producing some of their own instructional films. Hidden in many an instant duplicating machine is an obscure camera which produces copies with high fidelity and clarity for classroom use. The thermocopier produces transparancies and master copies for dittoing from printed pages and from originals made by the teacher. As mentioned later in this chapter the costs of vandalism and thefts in educational buildings have caused many institutions of higher education to install electronic monitoring devices within buildings. They are usually closed-circuit television operations, with cameras located in strategic places, such as cashiers' offices and libraries. Many schools sponsor camera clubs as cocurricular activities, academic subjects, or adult education noncredit courses.

Programmed Instruction. Programmed instruction—variously referred to as "autoinstruction" or "automated instruction," self-instruction, programmed learning, and teaching machines—is one of the most remarkable new forms of pedagogy on the scene. Psychologist Sidney Pressey in 1926 invented a simple hand-cranked device, an early prototype of the modern teaching machine, which rewarded the student with a piece of candy for each right answer. The modern teaching machine was pioneered largely by B. F. Skinner, professor of psychology at Harvard.

The term "programmed learning" and its synonyms are used loosely to describe a wide variety of instructional devices. Their prices range all the way from $5 to $150,000. Some of the more primitive ones are not very different from the old-fashioned workbook. At the other extreme are enormously complex pieces of expensive equipment. In one device, for example, the student is shown a scene, map, or other visual presentation of a problem on a television screen. The machine poses questions, which the student answers by punching a keyboard wired into an electronic computer. The computer responds "right" or "wrong." A student who receives "wrong" may press a button marked "help," whereupon the computer decides, from the nature of the error in his answer, what kind of additional information he needs to resolve his confusion. When the remedial material has brought sufficient insight to the student, he punches the "aha" button, and the computer returns him to the main body of questions and answers. The linking of the computer to the teaching machine opens vast and sometimes magnificent vistas of the possibilities of this mechanical partnership.

In a more common and less expensive type of teaching machine, a question appears in a window, and the student records his answer, either by writing his response on a roll of paper inside the machine or by punching a key which records his answer on a tape. The machine then presents the right answer after the student's answer has been cranked to a position behind the window where he can no longer change it. This protection against "cheating" after the correct answer is revealed is one of the essential features of the machine. The student's answers are permanently recorded and scored. After each question, he is presented immediately with the correct answer, which is not the case with most classroom tests and homework assignments. Thus learning is immediately reinforced. Subject matter is presented in a sequence of short units or "frames," which a student must answer before moving ahead. The material is arranged in an orderly sequence of ideas, beginning with simple ideas and progressing gradually up to more complex concepts and their applications. Difficulty is introduced gradually, and clues or "prompts" are given to suggest correct responses. The programs tend to be deliberately redundant, repeating the same thought in different language to reinforce learning. It is this systematic, cumulative sequence that distinguishes programmed learning from old-fashioned drill of disjointed fragments of knowledge. Either a brief unit or an entire course can be programmed. Figure 15-1 illustrates a section of a programmed lesson.

The programming of academic substance has become a highly refined art and represents one of the unique strengths of this medium. Programmed material is thoroughly pretested and revised in the light of how children learn, rather than how teachers think material ought to be organized. This process yields valuable insights into the proper organization of substance for natural, orderly learning and promises to aid the overall improvement of teaching and curriculum construction. In some cases a "linear se-

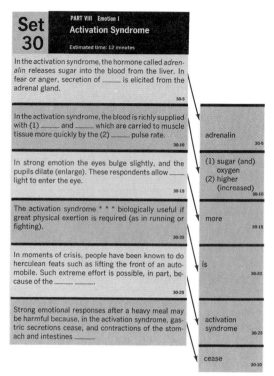

FIGURE 15-1   Sample sequence from a programmed lesson. In programmed lessons, the answer to a question at hand is not revealed to the learner until he has responded to the question and turned ahead to the next frame, at which time the answer to the completed question is revealed immediately, as indicated by the arrows. (From James G. Holland and B. F. Skinner, The Analysis of Behavior: A Program for Self-instruction, McGraw-Hill, New York, 1961, pp. 208–209.)

quence" presents just one route of questions and answers for all students to follow. But some of the more sophisticated programs include a "branching" arrangement, which presents to the student who answers incorrectly some additional information that will help him discover the correct answer. One incorrect multiple-choice response would send a student along one branch; another incorrect answer, along another branch. This arrangement is obviously an effort to accommodate individual differences.

Programmed instruction is currently undergoing extensive trial and development. Quite a variety of models have been developed. Many textbook publishers have moved into the production of programmed texts. Much of the recent enterprise in production of programmed materials is stimulated by grants to schools from funds provided by the National Defense Education Act, Elementary and Secondary Education Act, and their amendments.

Several universities have set up centers for experimentation and research in programmed learning, such as the University of Pittsburgh's Learning Research and Development Center. The National Education Association's Technological Development Project has directed attention to programmed learning as well as to other facets of instructional technology. The Center for Programmed Instruction in New York, a nonprofit organization dedicated to this effort, publishes a newsletter, *Programmed Learning*. The monthly periodical *Educational Technology* contains many articles on programming and describes numerous tools and techniques for facilitating the teaching and learning processes.

Geary A. Rummler, a former president of the National Society for Programmed Instruction, evaluates programmed instruction as follows:

In addition to the increasing use of programs, there is a wide and imaginative use of quasi-programmed instruction systems which take advantage of many of the control and presentation features of programs. . . . However, programmed instruction is no doubt having its greatest impact by providing training people with a set of principles and a process which is basic to all training. The process of systems and behavioral analysis, instructional design, development and validation is well on its way to being the process followed in all training. . . .

In summary, programmed instruction is alive today and well—and busy solving problems. In fact, in areas where people have human performance problems to solve, and expect results for dollars invested, programmed instruction is flourishing.[17]

Will programmed instruction eventually replace the teacher? The answer seems clearly in the negative. It will assist the teacher greatly when wisely and properly used, but even its most ardent supporters make no claims that it will replace the teacher. Kenneth Komoski of the Center for Programmed Instruction points out, "Programmed instruction cannot teach the entire curriculum for the simple reason that it cannot educate a person."

Role of Computer in Educational Technology. The report of the Commission on Educational Technology states:

The computer has three main uses in education: it is a research tool; it is a management tool; and it is a teaching-learning machine.
1. As a research and study tool, *especially in higher*

[17]Geary A. Rummler, "PI—Where the Action Is," *Educational Technology*, vol. 10, p. 31, July, 1970.

education, computers have been in use since the mid-1950s. Today faculty and students in many disciplines are increasingly exploiting the computer's power of computation, data processing, problem solving, and simulation. . . . Recently the computer has been playing an increasing role in the development of information-retrieval system for research purposes. Information-retrieval services for educational needs—to date, highly specialized—are beginning to appear. . . .
2. The extensive use of computers for management *purposes in higher education, particularly in larger institutions, is not surprising, considering bulging enrollments and increasing amounts of data to be processed. Administrative uses of the computer vary from the fairly straightforward keeping of scholastic records to the more complex problems of forecasting future buildings and staff requirements via simulation techniques. . . . In elementary and secondary schools, the computer's use is less widespread, but growing. . . .*
3. Computer-assisted instruction, *although it dominates the headlines, has to date had much less impact on education, both quantitatively and qualitatively, than the other two uses of computers. Despite the claims that the computer is a highly flexible teaching-learning machine, the predominant application thus far of CAI in schools and colleges is for drill and practice. . . . The more creative modes of computer-assisted instruction—tutorial, inquiry, and simulation—are used much less frequently.*[18]

Because of its great potential, computer-based instruction is discussed further.

Computer-based Instruction (CAI). One increasing use of the computer's capabilities is in the instructional processes at all levels of learning. A prototype of this new development is the classroom designed by the System Development Corporation and known by the apt acronym CLASS (Computer-based Laboratory for Automated School Systems). Each of the pupil stations receives simultaneous automated instruction in sequences and at levels adapted to the needs of each learner:

The computer makes an almost limitless amount of information available to the learner and teacher. It provides an almost infinite capacity to adapt to the individual needs of countless students when linked with instructional media. . . . It can carry on instructional dialogues with many individual students simultaneously. Although much refinement and further development are necessary in its adaptation to instruction, its total capabilities are almost unimaginable.[19]

[18]Lawrence Parkus, "The Computer," in *To Improve Learning: An Evaluation of Instructional Technology*, R. R. Bowker Company, New York, 1970, pp. 73-75.
[19]Elsbree, McNally, and Wynn, *op. cit.*, p. 450.

Figure 15-2 illustrates a model of a computer-based program.

Patrick Suppes of Stanford University, who directed the Stanford Computer-Assisted Instruction Projects, was quoted in an article in the periodical *American Education* as saying:

I view computer-assisted instruction as having, roughly speaking, three stages. First is the development around university centers where there's a lot of various types of technological and technical and research talent. The second stage is the demonstration projects in school systems. The third stage occurs when school systems make this an integral part of some of their curriculum.[20]

Many schools and colleges are using the computer as a catalyst to accelerate curriculum changes.

Data-processing Equipment. Another kind of laboratory in many educational institutions is the statistical workshop with its data-processing machinery. Many large local school systems and numerous colleges and universities have installed data computers and related hardware. With fiscal aid from the National Defense Education Act, most state departments of education have installed equipment to facilitate handling the huge amounts of data gleaned from the annual and periodic reports of schools and colleges within the state. The tabulation, interpretation, dissemination, storage, and retrieval of educational data necessitate much equipment and many talented technicians. In 1965 the Association of Educational Data Systems (AEDS) was formed. A national center on educational data processing has been established in the headquarters of the National Education Association in Washington, D.C. The U.S. Office of Education, the official national clearinghouse, is a leader in data processing for education. An example of how "datamation" helps educators is the Uniform Migrant Student Record Transfer System with a computer bank at Little Rock, Arkansas. This data-processing equipment and service provides background information on any migrant child within twenty-four hours. These data help school and health officials to keep track of migrant children as they travel from state to state with their parents.

The Overhead Projector. The overhead projector is a versatile device that is being increasingly used in the classroom. It permits the direct projection onto a screen of charts, drawings, pictures, or printed materials from a book, without first transforming them into slides. It also projects the instructor's writing directly onto a screen as he solves a mathematics problem, corrects an English theme, balances a chemical equation, or fills in a map, making it unnecessary for him to turn his back to the class, as he must when he uses the blackboard.

Talking Typewriter. The new talking typewriter is another example of a miracle machine in instructional technology. Acronymed SLATE (Stimulated Learning by Automated Typewriter Environment), the talking typewriter has a remarkable capacity to teach reading and other curricular subjects:

This ingenious device consists of an electric typewriter, a sound mechanism, and a digital computer. The student types letters and words and immediately sees the printed characters and hears the letters and words pronounced by the machine. From a master console the teacher can program words and sentences so that the keys on the typewriter are rendered inactive except for those which, when struck in proper sequence, will print the programed words or sentences and pronounce them for the student. A student's own spelling list can be programed in the machine. . . . Each student's work can be monitored by the teacher at a master console.[21]

The computer-assisted instruction, the talking typewriter, and many other modern, miraculous machines are ushering in the "electronic age in education." Many of the teaching tools of educational technology are housed in learning laboratories.

Learning Laboratories. A learning laboratory involves a special kind of programmed learning that has had a great impact on the educational scene. It is discussed separately because of its singular physical form. It had its beginnings during World War II, when the Armed Forces wanted thousands of servicemen to acquire conversational command of other languages in a hurry. Since 1958 its development has been stimulated by funds from the National Defense Education Act and other legislation such as the Elementary and Secondary Education Act, which subsidizes such equipment. The language laboratory, an early prototype of the learning laboratory, is essentially a marriage of the science of linguistics and electronic programmed learning. A complex set of sounds, put together in successive stages and in logical habit-forming sequence, enables the learner to gain command of the spoken language. Known as the "audio-lingual" or "aural-

---

[20] Marilyn N. Suydam, "Continuing the Math Revolution," *American Education*, vol. 10, p. 29, January-February, 1970.

[21] Elsbree, McNally, and Wynn, *op. cit.*, pp. 450-451.

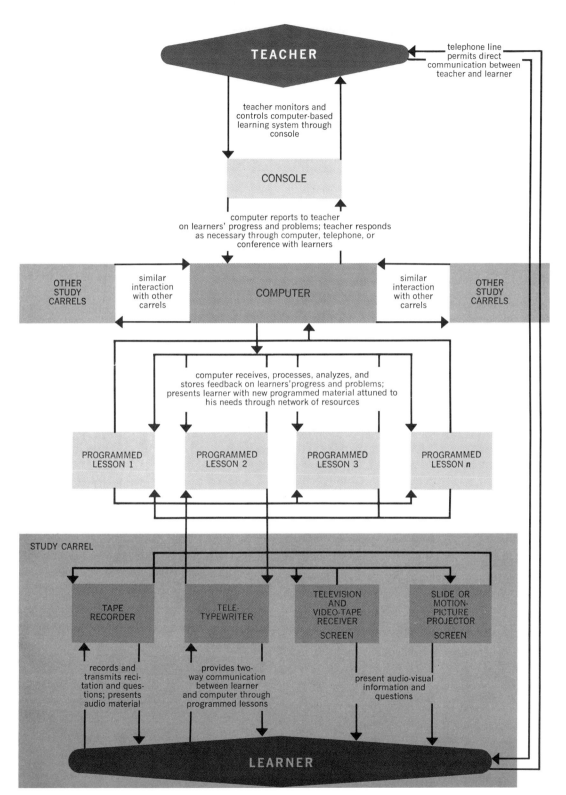

FIGURE 15-2 Model of a computer-based instructional system.

oral method" because of its emphasis upon listening and speaking, the language laboratory has reversed the old order of language mastery into this sequence: listening, speaking, reading, and writing. The language laboratory's contributions concern only the first two of these.

Physically the learning laboratory consists of an eggcratelike pattern of private cubicles equipped with tape-recording and listening equipment tied into a central monitoring system through which the student and teacher can communicate. The cubicles provide privacy, eliminate distractions, and reduce the student's self-consciousness about reciting on tape. The method also permits individualization of instruction, since students may work on different subjects and at different levels. It permits the teacher to tune in on any student's work or to play back at his leisure the student's recorded work. Learning laboratories can be used either for organized instruction of a class group or for independent, individualized study. Some laboratories contain a variety of embellishments such as a jukebox-type arrangement whereby the student can dial his tape recordings of more advanced difficulty or previous tapes for review, as he is ready for them.

What is said to be the largest language laboratory in the nation is the School of Letters and Languages at the University of Kentucky. A total of 210 students can be accommodated in individualized booths at one time. Students dial numbers on selectors and instantly hear on the headphones lessons on many aspects of various languages.

Simulation and Educational Games. Simulation implies the creation of reality-centered instructional settings, with real-life problems to be solved.

While traditional childhood games provide little more than social experience, modern educational games are designs for specific practice in communications, problem-solving, scientific inquiry, information management, and decision making. As a tool in training, simulation has four crucial characteristics: it starts with an analogous situation; it provides for low risk input; it feeds back consequences symbolically; and it is replicable . . . providing an opportunity for iterative procedures in arriving at best solutions.[22]

Simulation, which proved to be a useful technique in placing men on the moon, is providing break-

throughs on the educational scene. Since Berne wrote his best seller *Games People Play*, educators have written many articles and books, such as *Games to Improve Your Child's English*, *Learning through Games*, and *Simulation Games in Learning*. While playing games and play environments have always markedly influenced the mental, physical, and social growth of children, now games, simulation techniques, and role playing are having a direct impact on the intellectual learning, academic attitudes, and social strategies of youth and adults. An illustration is the so-called "Life Career Game," in which teams of learners play the roles of hypothetical characters, make tentative life decisions for them, and then evaluate the success of the characters.

School and College Buses. An expensive and functional instrument for most schools and many colleges is the educational bus, used for transporting students. Approximately seventeen million students are transported on school days. The total annual expenditure for buses and busing approximates $1 billion a year. The National Transportation Safety Board, a unit of the federal Department of Transportation, issued new standards for school bus inspections in 1971. Changes in school bus design may follow later, although improvements are constantly being made by manufacturers. The occupant death rate for school buses is only one-fourth that of regular buses.

Related to direct educational technology are two developments in student busing. One is the use of computers in scheduling bus routes and students.[23] The Ohio State Department of Education has a data bank on each of the thirteen thousand school buses in the state. Another teaching tool is exemplified in the use of headsets for each student in the bus, allowing him to select from several channels and thus hear tapes dealing with his school studies. Listening to lessons en route to school enhances learning.

"Micro" Developments. Among the many big developments in educational technology are some small things—such as microfilms and microfiche—which can compact big ideas and visual patterns into a small space. Just as the tiny transistor has helped to revolutionize industry, so some of the smaller bits of educational technology are needed

[22]Isabel H. Beck and Bruce Monroe, "Some Dimensions of Simulation,"*Educational Technology*, vol. 9, pp. 45–46, October, 1969.

[23]"Computers Making Getting There Easy," *American School Board Journal*, vol. 158, pp. 37–39, November, 1970.

to fill in the spaces. One of the "micro" techniques that uses smaller-than-usual units of time and materials is "microteaching."

Microteaching. The technique of microteaching was started in 1963 by a team of Stanford University professors in anthropology, medicine, and education. Today it is used in more than half of teacher-educating institutions. *School and Society* briefly describes it as follows:

Microteaching puts a teacher on camera to apply a specific skill by teaching a short lesson of about 10 minutes to a group of about five pupils. This scaled down version of a classroom situation gives microteaching its name.

The teacher watches himself on videotape replay after the session and evaluates his performance. Next he prepares another lesson and tries again on camera. The goal is to master specific skills through self-observation and practice. . . .

For the inservice training of teachers, microteaching has been combined with instructional films, handbooks, and evaluation forms into short self-instruction lessons called "minicourses." These courses are designed to help teachers change their behavior in the classroom.[24]

Howard F. Hjelm, head of the Office of Education laboratories, states that the success of microteaching "shows that scientific knowledge about the teaching process, based on intensive research efforts, can produce major improvements in classroom teaching."

Mobile, Computerized In-service Teacher Education. In addition to microteaching there are many large "vehicles" for enhancing in-service teacher education. Many teacher-education institutions are bringing continuing education programs and facilities to the teachers in or near their own schoolyards. An illustration is the mobile van used by the College of Education of Pennsylvania State University to bring computer-assisted instruction to teachers in special education. The mobile operation is placed by diesel tractor in various remote locations in the Appalachian region for periods of six to eight weeks. The expanded van is equipped with sixteen instructional stations. The instruction is individualized so that sixteen teachers can react independently and also interact simultaneously with the computer and the instructor.

[24]"Success with Microteaching," *School and Society*, vol. 98, p. 200, April, 1970.

Special Education: Instructional and Learning Aids for the Handicapped

In Chapter 11 there is a discussion of the various types of handicapped learners. Here is a brief account of some of the many instructional aids available to enhance the learning of these disadvantaged learners.

Pioneering work in "visual English" has been done by the National Technical Institute for the Deaf at Rochester Institute for Technology. This system permits visual communication by means of lipreading, sign language, or both. A special dial telephone switching system handles video as well as voice signals. Transmission is possible over ordinary telephone lines.

A blind learner can sit at his individual terminal and receive computer-assisted instruction. The teletype produces raised printed messages for sightless persons, and an audio capacity can be added.

"Braille machines" are being built to pick up signals on ordinary magnetic tape and play them back in patterns of raised dots—letters and numerals in the braille alphabet—on an endless plastic belt. The braille user can add his own notes to the magnetic tape.

A new type of polyethylene paper permits blind persons to communicate readily by writing and reading conventional letters and numbers rather than braille. An oversized, automatic ball-point pen or blunt pencil raises characters a few thousandths of an inch above the paper's surface so that they can be identified by touch.

Books with large type, such as 18 point, relieve eyestrain, tension, and fatigue and reduce headaches for many whose eyesight is deficient or deteriorating with age.

The U.S. Office of Education, the National Geographic Society, and the Alexander Graham Bell Association joined resources to produce a new magazine, *World Traveler*, for teen-agers with language or reading handicaps.

The American Printing House for the Blind has long been the primary source of development, distribution, and evaluation of educational aids for the visually handicapped.

Closed-circuit television is being developed for partially sighted children and adults.

Hearing aids have improved markedly. The General Auditory-Vibratory Experience Translator helps many nearly deaf people sense vibrations by touch or pressure. Motion pictures with numerous captions and titles on the film help the deaf to enjoy movies.

The University of Southern California has developed television programs for teaching adult migrant farmers and their families and for training Teacher Corps interns. Among the videotapes made are some for teaching English to Spanish-speaking adults.

Teleclasses connect the teacher in telephone conference hookups with physically handicapped learners who, because of injuries, heart conditions, muscular dystrophy, or other diseases, are temporarily or permanently unable to attend regular classes in school.

One simple machine projects an instructional film on a small individualized screen and plays an accompanying record or tape.

Highly interesting and difficult programmed materials can be used to challenge the bright students.

Many bright pupils with "learning difficulty" (LD) profit by motor experiences and other technological aids that can be provided by machines.

Many bright students who suffer from the neurological disability known to medical science as "specific dyslexia" are helped by the type-reader method of reinforcing word skills through carefully designed drills on a special typewriter.

A multimedia program kit, *Improving the Instruction of Culturally Different Learners*, prepared by the Division of Technology of the National Education Association, contains black-and-white and color filmstrips, a leader's guide, audio tapes, and reference scripts to help teachers learn to understand and help students who are culturally different.

Federally aided Instructional Materials Centers (IMCs) and Regional Media Centers (RMCs) have experimented with many types of technological aids for the handicapped.

The U.S. Office of Education has helped develop many media for special students—gifted or otherwise.

Obviously, the aim of the many machines and tools for individualized instruction is to help handicapped learners to proceed at their own rates. In short, "In many respects the role of educational technology in special education will parallel general education, but with one important difference. Since the student's need is greater, the utilization of tech-

nology will be greater, except where cost is a major restraint."[25]

Systems Approach to Educational Materiel and Technology

As a summation of the foregoing discussion on numerous selected types of educational materiel and technology, mention is made of the broad-gauge "systems approach." Edward E. Booher, chairman of the McGraw-Hill Book Company, states:

. . . Another force which will affect our future will be the application of the systems concept to instruction and instructional materials. A considerable mystique has grown up around this term, but in reality there is nothing complicated or mysterious about this. It simply means that more than ever before we are defining the objectives of instruction for a given person in a given subject and then utilizing in a rational manner all of the tools available in the wide field of instructional materials to meet those objectives.

This systems approach of viewing a problem as a set of interrelated, interdependent parts which "work together for the overall objectives of the whole" is also being applied to the planning and erection of educational buildings, discussed later in this chapter. "The systems approach, when applied to building problems, results in a process whereby resources and needs can be related effectively to performance, cost and time. . . . A systems approach to buildings can take place either with conventional products or newly developed ones."[26] The American Association of School Administrators has published a helpful volume, *Systems Approaches in Education*, which covers many details of the systems approach, applied not only to supplies and equipment but also to other phases of educational administration.

Selection, Purchase, and Use of Materials

Many principles and procedures are involved in the selection, purchase, and management of materials. Supplies and equipment should be selected in terms of the educational program of the school. Therefore, teachers should be consulted as to the need. An NEA research study indicates that "almost three-fourths of the nation's public school teachers take part in

[25] Donald Perrin, "Educational Technology and the Special Child," *Educational Technology*, vol. 10, p. 142, November, 1970.

[26] Ezra D. Ehrenkrantz, "The System to Systems," *CEFP Journal*, vol. 8, pp. 4–5, November–December, 1970.

the selection of instructional materials at the school building, local school system, or state level of decision making."[27]

Ethics in Handling School Supplies and Equipment. To improve the selection of school supplies and equipment and to maintain a high professional standard of conduct, a code of ethics has been developed by the Education Industries Association. The National School Supply and Equipment Association, in existence for more than fifty years, has restated its purposes to read: "To advance the interests of the industry through the voluntary action of the members, to formulate and develop solutions of the problems affecting the industry as a whole, and to promote service to educational institutions." These codes and goals should be supplemented by a nationwide code for school teachers, professors, and administrators, relative to the selection, purchase, and handling of textbooks, supplies, and equipment. For example, some administrators, teachers, and professors have a penchant for collecting free textbooks by asking publishers for samples, under the pretext of possible adoptions.

Purchase of Supplies and Equipment. Former U.S. Commissioner of Education Harold Howe II warned against "an unfortunate combination of sophisticated machinery and unsophisticated buyers." In 1967 a new service to guide buyers of instructional supplies and equipment was established. It is the Educational Products Information Exchange (EPIE), located in New York City. It issues a monthly periodical, *Educational Products Report*, which analyzes and categorizes information on specific educational products. Using a computer system to process, disseminate, and retrieve data, the Exchange "uses technology to cope with some of the problems created by technology." Purchasers can be helped by such other informational aids as *The Learning Directory*, a seven-volume work, published by Westinghouse Learning Corporation. It describes more than 200,000 separate materials and tools of educational technology.

Use of Educational Technology

Administrators and teachers should take advantage of technically accurate and professionally useful

[27]"Selection of Instructional Materials and Equipment by Teachers," *NEA Research Bulletin*, vol. 70, pp. 14–16, March, 1970.

devices like the audiometer, which is the best-known way of testing the hearing of pupils; the light meter, which is an accurate measure of the foot-candles of light in any part of a room; and the electric test-scoring machines.

An increasing trend in planning new and renovating old buildings is to provide a materials and equipment center, where facilities for making teaching-learning supplies and equipment for classroom use are located. Materials centers are equipped with such items as hammers and saws, lettering outfits, cardboard for posters, paint and brushes, metal supplies, and dozens of other production items for making learning more meaningful in the classrooms.

Curriculum libraries and materials centers are becoming more common, particularly in larger districts. In these centers sample textbooks in all fields from many publishers are kept in one place for all to use. Other instructional materials, such as films, tapes, tests, manuals, and many others, are kept in one central location to be more easily available to all.

More important than the storage of acquired tools and instruments of educational technology is, of course, their use. As indicated in Chapter 13, trained manpower is needed in the field of educational technology: "Media specialists, assisted by technicians and aides, make unique and vital contributions to the scheduled educational program of the school. Staff in sufficient number and with a variety of competencies is an indispensable part of the functional media center."[28] In writing on the "limitations of technology," The Committee on Technology and Instruction of the AASA states:

Technology can't determine values or goals, nor can it define purposes. Technology cannot overcome bad utilization of its potential. *Its effectiveness rests on the adequacy of human and fiscal resources. . . . It should be stressed once again that technology is a means to an end in instruction. Its value lies in its contributions to improvement of learning and financial savings. If it fails to improve human learning or if costs far exceed alternative approaches to more effective instruction, then it is questionable, indeed. The worship of technology for the sake of technology is self-defeating.*[29]

[28]American Library Association and National Education Association, *Standards for School Media Programs*, American Library Association, Chicago, 1969, p. 7.
[29]Knezevich and Eye, *op. cit.*, pp. 28, 30.

These observations apply also to the remaining section of this chapter dealing with sites and educational buildings.

SITES

The school building should be intimately fitted to the grounds, but formed and fashioned to human needs—practical, psychological, and aesthetic. The structure ought to be planned as a unified collection of functional relationships, erected in such close relationship with its surroundings and so fittingly furnished that its beauty charms the students, who breathe into the architect's creation the breath of life.

School Building Needs

An NEA research study indicates that many school buildings are old and obsolescent.[30] The findings show that only one teacher in eight was teaching in a school building that was less than five years old; one in eight was teaching in a building fifty years old or older; and one in one hundred was teaching in a structure at least eighty years old. The mean of the building ages reported was twenty-two years; the median fifteen years. Many of these buildings cannot be readily adapted to the tools and techniques of modern educational technology described in this chapter. "The standard closed door, 30 × 30 classroom, in its cloistering of students with a single teacher, has probably done more to impede the implementation of progressive interaction programs than any other single factor. Traditional buildings have placed a heavy burden on change."[31] Many new facilities are needed to serve youth through modern educational technology—a need that cannot be met in many old buildings.

Furthermore, the nation's schools and colleges are witnessing a great shortage of educational facilities due to increases in enrollments. A few examples are cited from the 1970 census returns, which show that enrollments of 5-year-old children in public school kindergartens rose from 64 percent in 1960 to 78 percent in 1970. While elementary

school enrollments are declining, from 36,600,000 in 1970 to a possible 35,500,000 in 1975, it is estimated that this decline is temporary and that the last half of the 1970s decade will again witness an increase. The 1970 census also shows that 90 percent of 16- and 17-year-olds are in school—up from 83 percent in the 1960 census. Furthermore, a dire facility need is represented by the spectacular rise in college enrollments. It is estimated that the number of college students will increase from 7,200,000 in 1970 to 9,100,000 in 1975. Also the burgeoning enrollments in adult and continuing education will continue to climb in view of the statistic that the United States may have a population of 400 million by the year 2000 in contradistinction to the 204 million recorded in the 1970 census. As former President Lyndon B. Johnson stated in 1965, "In the next thirty-five years we must literally build a second America—putting in as many houses, schools, apartments, parks, and offices as we have built through all the time since the Pilgrims arrived on these shores." By the year 2000 this nation must erect more educational buildings than have been built in the first three and a half centuries of our history as a society that prizes education. This calls for immediate, and especially long-term, planning.

Long-term Master Plans for Facilities

The selection and development of sites and the planning and erection of educational buildings constitute a long-span proposition. Since a new structure usually involves bonded indebtedness, it is necessary to project the estimated cost ten to twenty or more years in the future. This is not unwarranted, since the building may be used for fifty years or more. Hence, extensive long-range plans for sites and buildings must be developed far in advance of actual needs.

Each individual building is part of the ultimate master program, which should embrace three essential and integrated phases, namely, (1) the educational plan, (2) the expenditure program, and (3) the financing plan.

Educational Plan. School buildings and sites are merely facilitating media for the instructional process. Hence, written educational specifications are a necessity for the building-to-be. Functional planning demands that educational aims of the school be translated into an actual, workable program for the architect and that his drawings and specifications then be checked with it.

[30]"Age of School Buildings Where Teachers Teach," *NEA Research Bulletin*, vol. 48, pp. 80–81, October, 1970.
[31]Spencer B. Cone, "Technology and Its Potential for Educational Facilities Design," in *Facility Technology: Catalyst for Learning*, Council of Educational Facilities Planners, Columbus, Ohio, 1969, p. 4.

Expenditure Program. Costs fluctuate with the price of materials and labor. Building costs will probably continue to rise generally. Some critics have complained that too much money is spent on school construction. Surely some money has been wasted. On the other hand, false economy is often practiced. Inexpensive materials which are not durable or which necessitate high maintenance costs have often been used.

Financing Plan. The erection of new school buildings or the rehabilitation of old structures is usually financed by the community through the pay-as-you-build plan or some means of borrowing. Because the former method calls for payment out of the current school budget, it is used sparingly and only in large cities. The second plan calls for either long-term or short-term bonds or loans. It is recommended that bonds not extend over a period longer than twenty years. Usually the erection of a building is preceded by a school election that authorizes the board of education to bond the district.

A marked trend is paying some of the building costs from the state treasury as part of the minimum foundation program. Typical state grants include stimulation aids, flat grants, emergency aids, continuing grants, equalization grants, loan funds, and money from state building authorities or commissions.

The federal government has manifested much interest in helping to finance the costs of educational buildings. As indicated in Chapters 2 and 16, the federal government has allocated multimillion-dollar sums for educational equipment, building equipment, and buildings and sites for schools and colleges, both public and private.

Private agencies and individuals are also interested in financing school and college buildings. Many buildings are the gifts of groups and individuals. The Ford Foundation in 1958 allocated several million dollars for the establishment of the Educational Facilities Laboratories, an independent, nonprofit organization concerned with research and experimentation in school and college facilities. Over fifty years ago the National School Supply and Equipment Association was organized with the twin goals of helping industry and rendering services to educational institutions. A more recently established agency, the Learning Resources Institute, seeks to promote economy and efficiency in educational materiel.

Site Selection and Use

Selection of Site. The school site—its size and dimensions, the character of the grounds, the location of the building, and the amount of space for parking, play, and sports—is of fundamental importance, since it conditions not only the development of an adequate recreation program but also possible additions to the existing school plant.

Sociological factors affect the selection of most school sites today. The impact of the civil rights movement has affected and will affect the selection, use, or even abandonment of some school sites. The earlier site-survey technique of drawing spatial and demographic circles to circumscribe the area to be served by a school site and facility is generally unsuited for planning sites today. The 1954 decision of the United States Supreme Court banning discrimination in public schools; the 1964 Civil Rights Act, providing for the withdrawal of federal support from any community or school district in which racial discrimination is practiced; the awakened conscience of America; and the continuing agitation of the disadvantaged have placed sociology and human welfare in the formula for selecting school sites.

Environmental factors in today's technological world affect the selection of school sites. For example, the Los Angeles school district had to close some of its school buildings because of extreme noises and vibration caused by jet-age airplanes.

Size of Sites. Most school sites are too small. Even in rural or suburban communities where farmland can be purchased rather inexpensively, many elementary schools have a fenced-in area so small as to prohibit a game of baseball. The grounds around many secondary schools are hopelessly inadequate, especially in terms of parking facilities. Furthermore, the modern program of health and physical education requires several additional acres. The Council of Educational Facility Planners suggests these recommendations for minimum site areas: for elementary schools, 5 acres, plus an additional acre for every 100 pupils of ultimate enrollment; for junior high schools, 20 acres, plus an additional acre for every 100 students; and for senior high schools, 30 acres, plus an additional acre for every 100 students of peak enrollment. Thus a senior high school of 1,000 pupils would have a minimum site of 40 acres.

Theoretically there is no acreage limit to the size of a school site. As indicated in Chapter 5, the entire local community should serve students, teachers, and research workers as an educational laboratory. The resources of the whole community need to be tapped for learning potentials. Local institutions such as hospitals, banks, post offices, churches and synagogues, city and county government buildings, and other tangible and intangible assets enlarge the locus of learning beyond the actual "schoolyard." As to enlargement of sites for universities, James C. McLeod, dean of students at Northwestern University in Evanston, Illinois, which expanded its campus by spreading into Lake Michigan, says: "Expansion of the campus is not nearly as important as expansion of the minds."

Educational Parks. Related to site selection and the next section on educational buildings is the educational-park concept in modern education. A brochure prepared by the Educational Park Project of the Center for Urban Renewal, now a Regional Educational Laboratory, thus defines this concept: "An educational park clusters educational facilities in a campus-like setting, utilizing centrally organized common facilities, and drawing its student body from the whole community." In the same brochure there is a brief summary of some of the advantages of the educational park:

For education. *Educational park facilities widen the opportunity for enrichment of curriculum to serve more adequately the needs of the individual child on an economically feasible basis for the community. . . .*
For the student. *He finds stability in attending school in the same setting as long as his family lives in the community; he has continuity of guidance throughout his school years. . . .*
For the teacher. *He can teach in his field of specialization and can grow professionally as a teacher by becoming the master teacher in his professional field and teaching less-experienced teachers. . . .*
For the administrator. *Educational park facilitates the hiring of teachers into one cluster of schools. . . .*
For the community. *Educational parks can become the cultural center of the community. . . . Desegregation also is a result of the reorganization of the school system into educational parks. . . .*[32]

[32]"Educational Parks," Center for Urban Education, New York, no date, pp. 1-4.

Architects and city planners have long urged the pressing need for land banks, parks, and new types of public and private ownership, including public and private schools. The public and especially educational administrators are becoming convinced of the need for open spaces or places to help cleanse air and to provide room for recreation and leisure. The federal Department of Housing and Urban Development (HUD) has an active division known as "Open Space and Urban Beautification Division." Several school districts have received federal funds for furthering school park plans and facilities. Many educational parks are being built without regard to existing boundary lines, thus facilitating desegregation.

As an example, the public schools of the District of Columbia have developed "flexible educational park planning formats for the district, serving students from pre-kindergarten through high school as well as adults on around the clock and around the calendar basis." The plan of the new educational park in Wilmington, Delaware, consists of four major centers: (1) a career development center, (2) an urban center for innovation and continuing education, (3) an opportunity center for mentally handicapped children, and (4) a center for creative and performing arts.

Community Playgrounds. The school's program for leisure should be integrated with the community's needs. The facilities in and out of school must be planned with an eye not only to future generations of students but also to adults in the community.

A neglected phase of school and community life is the summer program. Too many schools are closed for two or three months, the very time when they might be well used. Articulation of all community efforts in the development of a twelve-month program of education and recreation includes a flexible, unregimented vacation plan for children of all ages from all schools.

Landscaping and School Gardens. Much importance must be placed upon the aesthetic influence of the school site. The beautification and upkeep of school grounds and buildings may be the responsibility of a standing committee from the board of education, a teacher-pupil committee, or a special group from the parent-teacher association. Appropriate landscaping helps to soften the building and hide some of the ugliness of foundations. Daily contact with a beautiful school framed in a natural setting is uplifting and beneficial to all. The wonders of nature upon the school premises, such as trees, shrubs, grass, and flowers silently unfolding their splendors, may initiate a program for beautifying the entire community.

BUILDINGS

A visitor to a stone quarry asked three laborers what they were doing.

"What are you making?" he said to the first workman.

"I am making four dollars an hour," he replied.

"And what are you doing?" the visitor inquired of the next man.

"I am cutting a stone," he answered.

"Now, what are you making?" he asked of the third laborer.

"I am building a school," he replied with a gleam in his eye. "This stone that I am cutting is to be a part of a beautiful building that will serve my children and their children's children."

The first worker thought primarily in terms of money. The second saw only materiel. But the third was motivated by morale: he had a vision of the service that materials can render to youth and society in the form of an educational building.

Continuing with the words of an educational architect, Spencer B. Cone, chairman of the Committee on School and College Architecture of the American Institute of Architects: "There are new demands to architectural design—dimensions related to people, behavior, and the multi-sensory qualities of space and environment—dimensions related to human values and to the disciplines of new technologies."[33]

Building Programs

Major Steps in a Building Project. On the selected sites are erected school and college buildings, which usually follow three major phases of development:

1. Preparing educational specifications. The philosophy of the educational institution, the fundamental purposes of the building, the curriculum and the cocurricular activities to be programmed therein, the types of educational technology and teaching-learning procedures to be employed, and the projected enrollment of pupils to be housed are presented by the chief administrator to the

[33]Cone, *op. cit.*, p. 4.

board of education or board of control. When adopted, these give professional guidelines to the architect.

2. Making drawings and building specifications. The architect and his staff of specialists prepare complete drawings and written building specifications for materials and workmanship. These also form the bases for budgeting the costs and letting the contracts for construction.

3. Constructing the building. The third and final phase is the actual building of the structure on the selected site under supervision and according to the educational and building specifications.

Obviously the educational buildings erected are of various types.

Types of Construction. In addition to classifications as to style of architecture, buildings are also grouped in terms of degree of fire safety—A, B, C, D, and E. Type A buildings afford the greatest protection, since the gross structure and interior are of fire-resistive materials.

One development in architecture is dimensional coordination of building materials and equipment, popularly known as modular or unit construction. Four inches was determined as the optimum size for the standard module. Products are so designed that their dimensions, plus the required joint, fit the 4-inch dimension (or multiples thereof) in the modular grid.

Types of construction materials defy classification; they are extremely varied, including directional glass blocks, pressed wood, colored plastics, hard and spongy rubber, and many metallurgical miracles. Factory-fabricated materials, including artificial turf for university stadiums, are used in increasing quantities. Many schools employ structural materials and architectural designs indigenous to the particular region.

Schools are also grouped according to condition. Some are brand-new, some are rehabilitated or modernized, and many are merely old structures in need of rehabilitation or elimination.

As to shape, school buildings are often erected in the form of the letters T, I, U, N, B, E, H, X, or O, or combinations or modifications thereof. Each shape possesses distinctive advantages and limitations. Buildings may have three degrees of enclosure: the closed, the semi-open with porch or patio effect, and the enclosed but unroofed play space. Some schools have playgrounds on the roof.

"Open-space schools," which are not in the shape of letters, are increasing in number.

The continuing effort to devise educational containers which mold themselves to the fluid activities within, instead of the other way around, has led to a new and burgeoning phenomenon in schoolhouse architecture: the school without inner partitions . . . packages of unbroken space containing anywhere from three to five regular-size groups of children and teachers.[34]

Height varies from one story, the prevailing height of many elementary school buildings, to skyscraper structures in universities. Some buildings spread out over an entire city block.

The building of superior educational facilities is of course a highly technical task requiring the cooperative efforts of administrators, curriculum consultants, educational technologists, engineers, building architects, landscape architects, health specialists, contractors, lawyers, and experts in air conditioning, lighting, and sanitation.

Characteristics of a Good Educational Building. Buildings can have personality. The essential qualities of a good school structure include (1) educational adequacy, (2) safety, (3) healthfulness, (4) efficiency, (5) economy, (6) expansibility and contractibility, (7) flexibility, (8) durability, (9) utility, and (10) beauty. The first three of these characteristics are discussed briefly below.

Educational Adequacy. An educational building is a huge teaching tool. It must be adequate to the educational task. The building and environment must enhance education. Hence, as previously mentioned, written educational specifications for the building should be prepared by the chief administrator and staff. Just as educational objectives are needed for the curriculum, so educational specifications must be prepared for the school building in which the curriculum functions. Consultants often assist in converting curriculum requirements into spaces for learning.

Safety. No school in the United States can be certain that it is entirely free from the threat of disaster. School administrators, school boards, and college officials are expected to see that students are protected, as far as possible, against disasters of all

[34] *Profiles of Significant Schools: Schools without Walls,* Educational Facilities Laboratory, New York, 1965, p. 3.

kinds. School architects are drawing plans for buildings which provide maximum protection against radioactive fallout.

Related to safety is the convenience factor in providing building facilities for the handicapped learner. Following World War II many colleges and universities started designing not only teaching-learning tools for the physically handicapped, but also modifications in building facilities. The University of the State of New York, with a grant from the U.S. Vocational Rehabilitation Administration, has prepared a very helpful publication, *Performance Criteria for Making Facilities Accessible to the Handicapped.* The criteria give consideration to special needs of the blind, deaf, paraplegics, amputees, and hemiplegics, as well as those with cardiac conditions.

Another aspect of safety of buildings is their protection against vandalism and destruction. The 1960s witnessed many instances of the willful destruction of educational buildings by vandals. Hence many educational authorities have taken added antivandalism precautions. For example, the University of Florida at Miami has installed a $200,000 system of devices to keep students, demonstrators, burglars, and vandals out of key buildings. Many public schools have installed plastic windows to reduce vandalism. The costs of repairs caused by vandalism run to over $1 million in some large school systems. Furthermore, as indicated in Chapter 16, insurance rates for schools and colleges are soaring. The National Fire Protection Association states that

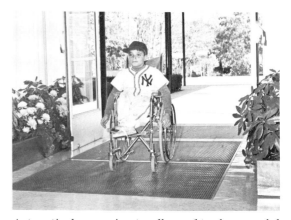

Automatic door-opening treadles, safety-glass paneled doors, and other modifications of school buildings permit physically handicapped students to receive their education with others in school rather than alone at home.

a substantial factor in the increased costs of insuring educational buildings is incendiarism. Vandalism increases the cost of education and should be eliminated.

Healthfulness. Only one aspect of healthfulness need be mentioned here: "eye health," which is being accorded increasing care in schools and colleges. Is the student getting enough light and is he getting the right kind of lighting? The conventional 70 footcandles as measured by a light meter was the suggested standard for years. But in 1970 the Illuminating Engineering Society, the official standard-setting professional group, changed the minimum standard to 70 equivalent sphere illumination (ESI) footcandles, a standard which stands for the actual glarefree level of lighting assisting the reader.[35]

Evaluation of Educational Buildings, Sites, and Equipment. Evaluation should be made in terms of purposes. Two general questions to ask in the evaluation of school facilities are these: "How effectively do they promote the instructional process?" and "How do they protect the health of the pupils and teachers?" In many school districts an independent survey of buildings is made to determine strengths and weaknesses. A scorecard or checklist is usually employed in evaluating physical facilities.

A very important test in evaluating a school building is the utilization of the plant. The percentage of utilization is calculated by determining the number of periods when each room might be utilized and then checking that number against the number of periods when it is actually in use.

Evaluation of a public school building should also include utilization by the community. The building is not an island. The school is not merely located in a community; it is an integral part of it. In the forty-ninth state, Alaska, schools have long been centers of economic, social, and recreational life for young and old. Educational plants ought to be designed not merely for youths but for all learners.

Equipment for Buildings. Some of the criteria for good buildings also apply to the equipment installed in it. The criteria of healthfulness, for example, can

be applied to many types of equipment. The two singled out here for accent are lighting and seating.

Gradually, organizations like the National Society for the Prevention of Blindness, the Illuminating Engineering Society, the Council of Educational Facility Planners, and the American Institute of Architects are making the public conscious of eye health. Many classrooms lack adequate and appropriate lighting, either natural or artificial. "Better light for better sight" means basically the admission of abundant natural light through careful, efficient window planning and through the controlled use of artificial lighting when needed.

Modern movable classroom seating is in sharp contrast to the screwed-down double desks of yesteryear. A special report in the *CEFP Journal,* entitled "New Directions in School Furniture," states:

Lately, some of the new trends in teaching . . . particularly open-space planning, individualized instruction, team teaching, and variable groupings . . . have started breaking up rigid seating patterns, demanding variable responses from classroom furnishings. Single units of chair and desk as one, not bolted to the floor, have helped. Various table shapes with loose chairs enable variable-ratio discussion and work groups to exist. . . . Analysed by teaching function— rather than for its discipline or maintenance function— the resulting design becomes a tool for instruction rather than a corral to assist discipline.[36]

Buildings and equipment wage a perpetual battle against the elements of water, wind, sun, and extremes of temperature. A school-painting renaissance is needed in many communities. Paint, usually regarded as a mere protection, is an integral part of a structure. The use of bright color, an essential part of Egyptian architecture, has been revived. Many large school systems and colleges have specially trained maintenance men for carrying on needed renovations. Teachers and pupils, through cooperation with the administration and the custodial force, can make decided contributions to effective and economical operation and maintenance of the school equipment, plant, and grounds, as well as to their beautification.

Figure 15-3 illustrates an interesting example of modern school plant planning.

[35]John C. Gardner, "How Much Light Is Enough?" *American School and University,* vol. 43, pp. 14–15, January, 1971.

[36]"New Directions in School Furniture," *Council of Educational Facilities Planners Journal,* vol. 8, p. 1, July–August, 1970.

FUTURE

This chapter closes, as do the others, with a forward look—a brief recital of some of the trends discernible now and on the horizon of educational history. These trends in educational technology are grouped according to (1) educational materiel and equipment and (2) educational sites and buildings.

Educational Materiel and Equipment

Teaching-learning tools will help accelerate the rate of change in the seventies, as projected by Alvin C. Eurich:

My prediction for the seventies is that in the next ten years we will see more basic changes in the schools and in education generally than have been made in our entire history. . . . Whereas change proceeded arithmetically in the sixties, we are . . . entering a period when the rate of change will approach geometrical proportions.[37]

Future trends that will help to accelerate such change are indicated here for a few of the specific tools of educational technology.

Books. An editorial, entitled "Civil Rights and White Textbooks," in the *Negro History Bulletin* presents a challenge to textbook writers:

The major unfinished task of our democracy is the efface-ment and erasure of false ideas about Negroes produced by books in the minds of American people both black and white. Basic to status on equality of treatment are not only the courts and the legal action but there is also a great need for the development of an improved and truthful image—not an exclusive white one.[38]

The trend in the writing and illustrating of textbooks on all academic levels is definitely in the direction of more and better material dealing with all minority groups.

Television. As the most pervasive and persuasive teaching-learning tool, educational television—"Sesame Street," for example—offers for the future many exciting and versatile possibilities, in school and at home. Television, supplementing (1) the home and (2) the school, is becoming the third educational system in the United States. One reason why this is happening is that motion-picture cameras, video tape recorders, cassettes, and other audiovisual instruments are becoming more portable.

Computers in Education. Students in educational institutions and at home will use computers increasingly and more widely in what may help to trigger a real revolution in educational technology. In his challenging book *Computer Revolution,* Edward A. Tomeski states:

Computer technology has advanced in the past several years considerably beyond the user's ability or capacity to utilize the advances. This means that there is a vast untapped potential in the existing and soon-to-be-available computer equipment and software (programs that provide the automatic instruction phase to computer processing).[39]

This observation is particularly applicable to the role of the computers in education. In the wave of machines for the 1970s, for example, is a large-scale computer that can make three million calculations per second. The "maxi," "midi," and "mini" machines will affect markedly educational programs and practices on all academic levels. For example, a recent research study of the Carnegie Commission on Higher Education and the National Science Foundation, entitled *The Emerging Technology: Instructional Uses of the Computer in Higher Education,* reveals the high potential of computers in the important area of learning.

As to the present and future role of computers in education, McLuhan briefly summarizes thus:

Central school computers can now help keep track of students as they move freely from one activity to another whenever moment by moment or year by year records of student progress are needed. This will wipe out even the administrative justification for schedules and regular periods, with all their antieducational effects, and will free teachers to get on with the real business of education.[40]

In general, the major trends for using technological teaching tools are clear: the reevaluation of educational goals, more research in teaching-

[37] Alvin C. Eurich, "Recommendations for Changing the Urban Schools," *Bulletin of the National Association of Secondary School Principals,* vol. 55, p. 186, January, 1971.

[38] "Civil Rights and White Textbooks," *Negro History Bulletin,* vol. 33, p. 5, January, 1970.

[39] Edward A. Tomeski, *The Computer Revolution,* The Macmillan Company, New York, 1970, p. 121. Copyright by The Macmillan Company, 1970.

[40] M. McLuhan and G. B. Leonard, "The Future of Education," *Look,* vol. 31, p. 25, Feb. 21, 1967.

learning theories, and more experimentation with the hardware and software of educational technology in order to make more efficient use of the better-educated instructional personnel working with tomorrow's youth and adults. Furthermore, technology can develop better systems for feedback from citizens and students and thus enhance public relations and fiscal support.

Educational Sites and Buildings

Sites. The trend is toward selecting sites well in advance of need. A striking trend, especially since the 1954 Supreme Court decision ruling discrimination in the schools unconstitutional and the 1964 passage by Congress of the Civil Rights Bill, has been a more careful consideration of the socio-economic factors in locating school sites. Equality of opportunity for minority groups, population movements, air-contamination factors, expressway plans, and urban renewal developmental activities will greatly affect the choice of school sites.

A growing trend is toward the cooperation of school and community in establishing joint playgrounds. The development of educational parks, especially for secondary schools, is an effort to provide for the integration of students and for comprehensiveness in offerings, plus quality education. In this mobile age, large-area vocational schools, community colleges to which students commute, and car-infested university campuses need more site space for parking.

School and college sites will be larger and linked more closely with community resources. The physical environment in the immediate and surrounding area will be thoroughly inventoried before purchase. The Environmental Education Act, which became federal Law in 1970, provides grants for the planning of outdoor ecological study centers. Educational institutions, especially colleges and universities, will play important roles in the next phase of the "technological revolution," as they seek to clean up the environment and to develop techniques for recycling and reusing waste materials and old educational supplies and equipment, producing a more attractive and healthful environment for all.

The sites for many learners will be established institutions in the community, such as churches, synagogues, business and industrial plants, and welfare institutions. Furthermore, students' homes will become learning stations, for it will be easier

to transport information to the student than to have him travel long distances.

Educational Buildings. In linking together the numerous tools of educational technology, and in erecting new educational buildings, the "systems approach" will be used more widely. The unusual name "charette" is being applied by innovators to a technique in planning future educational buildings:

An "Educational Facilities Charette" is a technique for studying and resolving educational facilities development problems within the context of total community planning needs. The technique requires a majority representation of community residents and community leadership direction of a multidisciplinary group. . . . Primary emphasis is given to educational facility and program as the natural catalyst for revitalization of the whole community.[41]

Figure 15-3, with the photographs accompanying it, illustrates some of the trends that are taking place in school building construction.

Many schools, especially pre-elementary and elementary, will implement the concept of "joint occupancy," which means combining schools with housing, commercial businesses, and community services and facilities such as municipal or county office buildings. Many public and private schools will share some of their facilities. With the closing of many Catholic schools, some of their buildings and sites will be bought or leased by public school boards. With inflation and the high costs of new construction, many older educational buildings will be renovated for use.

There is a trend to name some public schools in memory of prominent Americans—benefactors of mankind—from minority groups. Two of the many examples are the Martin Luther King, Jr., Elementary School in Schenectady, New York, named after the distinguished Negro minister and civil rights leader; and the Hostos Community College in the Bronx, New York, the first continental United States institution of higher education to be named after the Puerto Rican educator and revolutionist Eugenio Maria de Hostos.

Related to educational technology and future trends is the proposal of President Richard Nixon that the United States "create a National Institute

[41]William W. Chase, "The Educational Facilities Charette," *Educational Technology*, vol. 10, p. 20, June, 1970.

1. Individual study carrels are used by students, shown here picking up their individually prescribed instructional tasks. The individual differences of students are thereby accommodated.

2. The teachers' planning facility provides space—commonly missing in many schools—for teachers to plan and organize their work. Shown here is a teaching team in the unified arts at work.

3. Instead of corridors, which are commonly unused except at brief intervals, the commons areas here not only accommodate traffic but can be used also for instructional purposes, such as the French class shown here. Carpeting throughout the building permits students to sit on the floor in comfort.

4. The instructional materials center is the heart of the school—both structurally and educationally. In this large open area in the center of the school, students, teachers, and instructional materials flow freely.

5. A modern audiovisual center serves the latest electronic media, such as the video-taping of a lesson here either for instant replay or for later review.

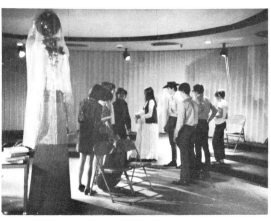

6. Versatility and flexibility are built into the structure through multipurpose facilities such as this combination planetarium and theater.

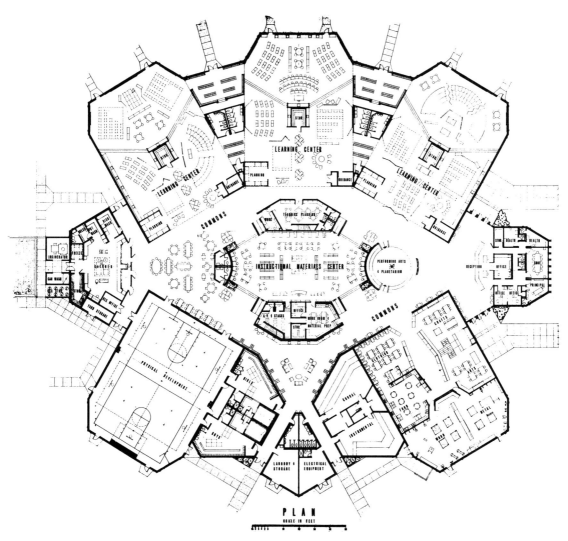

FIGURE 15-3 Floor plan of Patapsco school, with an overall view. The award-winning Patapsco Middle School in Howard County, Maryland, illustrates many excellent concepts in school design: accommodation of students' individual differences, maximum utilization of space, effective accommodation of a wide variety of instructional materials and media, and versatile use of facilities. Notice the open spaces, the large learning centers (rather than smaller traditional classrooms), the relatively few stationary partitions, the use of shapes other than rectangles, and the windowless construction. The six photos at the left illustrate the use of various facilities shown in the floor plan above.

for the Educational Future to serve as a clearing-house for ideas in elementary and secondary education and explore the possibilities that modern science and technology are making available to education."

Humanizing Educational Technology. The future presages increased concern about the personal and social problems associated with the burgeoning use of educational technology. One of the dangers is the depersonalization of the teacher and the student. The galaxy of gadgetry in education must be outshone by the greatness of the teacher or "guru."

Charles de Carlo, director of automation research at International Business Machines, says:

In terms of educational technology, I do not believe the idea of a completely depersonalized teaching machine to replace the teacher. I do think educational technology can be used to bring information to a child or to a grownup. I do think it can be used in a behavioristic way to teach skills. But, in the long run, the kind of education that is going to make the world more than a mechanical world has to take place between people.[42]

SUMMARY

The history of changes in educational technology as they relate to supplies, equipment, sites, and buildings can be roughly divided into (1) the colonial period, (2) the period between the American revolution and the Civil War, (3) the period between the Civil War and 1900, and (4) the twentieth century. Currently educational technology is on the threshold of producing a revolution in education. In examining the historical development of educational technology, with its wide scope and latent power, one becomes prone to believe the message in the title of David McReynold's recent book, *We Have Been Invaded by the 21st Century.*

Although human resources rank first in American education, appropriate physical properties must be provided. Supplies, equipment, sites, and buildings markedly affect the work of the teacher and learner. Starting in 1958, Congress recognized the realistic role of teaching tools and their use by granting federal funds for equipment for science, mathematics, foreign languages, guidance, and

evaluation. Such teaching tools are, however, merely means for facilitating and improving the teaching-learning process. All academic aids may prove sterile unless used intelligently.

The greatest educational invention is printing. The four main influences in the development of modern textbooks were psychology of learning, textbook publication as a specialty, improvements in printing and binding, and rigorous research by authors and publishers. Next in importance to the teachers are the textbooks. Therefore, the selection, adoption, purchase, and use of these books are of extreme importance.

The school or college librarian must like pupils and love books and seek to bring the two together. Librarians today are becoming multimedia specialists. The federal projects for libraries have stimulated book services for youth and adults.

Ancillary reading materials include: dictionaries, workbooks, newspapers, magazines, and tests. Television has become one of the most dramatic and promising instructional media to burst upon the educational scene. Audiovisual aids used today include globes, maps, slides, films, tape recorders, radios, computers, cassettes, laser holographs, and other electronic equipment.

The grounds, buildings, and equipment for schools and colleges decidedly affect learning-teaching possibilities. The school sites of yesteryear were often selected because they were not usable for other purposes. Modern plans for sites and buildings are long-term, embracing the three integrated phases of educational, spending, and financing plans. Improvement in the selection of sites has been accelerated in recent years. Modern socio-economic factors complicate the process of selecting sites for tomorrow's schools. Many school buildings are community centers. Modern schools and colleges are built on a greatly increased number of acres. A beautiful school framed in a natural setting is uplifting to pupils, parents, and public.

Each individual educational building should be a part of a long-term master program. Systems approaches, employing technological tools and know-how, and community charettes are used in the planning and construction of many new buildings. Educational buildings may be classified on such bases as style, shape, degree of safety, life of plant, and purpose of the program.

Among the important items of furnishing for schools and colleges are a good lighting system and satisfactory seating. Modern schools provide play space and also parking facilities. The planning and

[42] Irving A. Falk (ed.), *Prophecy for the Year 2000*, Julian Messner, a division of Simon & Schuster, Inc., New York, 1970, pp. 88–89. Reprinted by permission. Copyright © 1970 by Irving A. Falk.

use of schools and colleges in the community, state, and nation are permeated by the philosophy of cooperation expressed in the first three words of the Constitution of the United States, "We, the people." Schools and colleges are basically not buildings but people. Efforts are being made to emphasize "people" and to minimize the dangers of dehumanizing education through educational technology, which is merely a means toward the end of helping students and teachers in learning, teaching, and living.

Suggested Activities

1. Discuss the following statement: Modern technology is on the threshold of producing a revolution in education.

2. What effects will programmed instruction have on teachers and learners?

3. Give the historical evolution of some aspects of educational materiel and technology, such as textbooks or educational television.

4. Contrast an old textbook with a modern one in the same field.

5. Visit a modern learning laboratory and describe how it differs from a traditional school library.

6. Prepare a bibliography of the best paperback books available as supplementary readings in your field of teaching.

7. Examine or prepare a scorecard for evaluating a textbook in your major field.

8. Write a report on "The Computer in Modern Education."

9. Describe one of the newer teaching-learning tools, such as cassettes.

10. What special technological tools are available in special education?

11. List some radio and television programs that have an educational emphasis.

12. List the changes in school building construction that have been prompted by new instructional methods such as ungraded classes, multiple grouping, television, team teaching, programmed instruction, and audiovisual aids.

Bibliography

Borton, Terry: *Reach, Touch, and Teach,* McGraw-Hill Book Company, New York, 1970. The role of technological tools in providing a more humane and human environment for learning.

Council of Educational Facilities Planners (ed.): *Guide for Planning Educational Facilities,* Columbus, Ohio, 1969. The creation of schools from concept through the evaluation.

Drucker, Peter F.: *Technology, Management & Society,* Harper & Row, Publishers, Incorporated, New York, 1970, chap. 11. Some notes on the relationship of the technological revolution to technology, science, and culture.

Engelhardt, Nickolaus L.: *Complete Guide for Planning New Schools,* Parker Publishing Co., West Nyack, New York, 1970. Helpful volume with coverage from kindergarten through twelfth grade, and many suggestions for higher education facilities.

Knezevich, Stephen J.: *Administrative Technology and the School Executive,* American Association of School Administrators, Washington, D.C., 1969, chap. 5. The implications of technology for educational staffing patterns and organizational arrangements.

——— **and Glen G. Eye:** *Instructional Technology and the School Administrator,* American Association of School Administrators, Washington, D.C., 1970, chap. 1. Some basic perspectives on technology and instruction.

Kohn, Sherwood: *Experiment in Planning an Urban High School: The Baltimore Charette,* Educational Facilities Laboratory, New York, 1970. An experiment in participatory democracy (charette) in the planning of a new high school.

———: *The Early Learning Center,* Educational Facilities Laboratory, New York, 1970. A brochure introducing and accompanying the motion picture "The Early Learning Center," describing the new Montessori School of Stamford, Conn.

Minor, Ed, and Harvey R. Frye: *Techniques for Producing Modern Visual Instructional Materials,* McGraw-Hill Book Company, New York, 1970. Methods and processes in producing audiovisual teaching aids.

Skinner, B. F.: *The Technology of Teaching,* Appleton Century Crofts, New York, 1968, chaps. 3-4. Discussion of teaching machines and the technology of teaching by a pioneer in the field.

Tickton, Sidney G. (ed.): *To Improve Learning: An Evaluation of Educational Technology,* R. R. Bowker Company, New York, 1970, part 1. Major recommendations of the Commission on Instructional Technology, as reported in vol. I. (See also the 1971 report, vol. II, part 4, dealing with practical considerations for instructional technology.)

Tofler, Alvin: *Future Shock,* Random House, Inc., New York, 1970, chap. 19. Recommendations for positive technological goals for the future.

Tomeski, Edward A.: *The Computer Revolution: The Executive and the New Information Technology,* The Macmillan Company, New York, 1970, chap. 9. Vast untapped potential in the existing and soon-to-be-available computer equipment and software.

Venn, Grant: *Man, Education, and Manpower,* American Association of School Administrators, Washington, D.C., 1970, chap. 2. The role of education in a technological society.

Chapter 16   Educational Finance

The trouble with a cheap education is that we never stop paying for it.

Consider the roots of poverty.

Half of the kids in the primary grades won't finish high school. In America today, one out of three high school students won't graduate.

If the dropouts don't wind up as delinquents or criminals (and their chances are ten times greater than average), they'll wind up with a family.

But with less chance to earn the money it takes to support a family.

The chances are two to one that a man with less than eighth-grade education will earn $3,000 or less. Too little to support a family.

So while we can skimp on dollars for education, we'll spend the money we save—and more—supporting the people who don't have the education they need.

Good schools with good teachers and good facilities can produce good citizens.

Which is why money spent on education represents the best investment we can make.

An investment that never stops paying.

Sources for information contained in this message on request.

This message is sponsored by the **Copier Duplicator division of the Addressograph Multigraph Corp.**
As businessmen who have a stake in education.

First, because we are deeply involved in ways to use communications technology to improve the quality of American education. (For instance, the Multilith offset press has been used in programs that serve to recapture the interest of potential high school dropouts and help prepare them for gainful employment.)

Second, because we believe America's future—and ours—is no better than the future of American education.

If you would like more information on how educators are using the products of the Copier Duplicator division to improve their schools—or if you'd like reprints of this message—write Addressograph Multigraph Corporation, 1200 Babbitt Road, Cleveland, Ohio 44117.

ORIENTATION

Students and Educational Finance. Students today realize that education is an attractive, desirable, and even necessary investment. For example, as indicated in Figure 16-1, an investment in a college education can add almost a quarter of a million dollars to one's lifetime earnings. To many graduates the personal and social satisfactions of earning a college degree far outweigh the fiscal rewards.

Consumer credit—long a feature of American life—is now extended for purposes other than the purchase of a home or durable goods. It is a techique widely used today to invest in education and to ensure the future. Many educational institutions have "study now, pay later" or "college credit" programs for helping students defray expenses while studying. Significantly, the trustees of Yale University adopted in 1971 the principle of allowing students to pay for their tuition over a period as long as thirty-five years after graduation. Under such a plan, a student begins after graduation to pay the college or university a percentage of his earnings for the deferred tuition. There are also many private tuition plans. A favorite form of assistance in many educational institutions is a "financial aid package," consisting of a scholarship, a loan, and a job on or off the campus.

College and university counselors or staff members in charge of financial aids annually assist thousands of students in arrangements for paying for their college education, which is indeed a good investment.

Many industries are concerned about the high cost of cheap education, as illustrated by this public-service advertisement.

Education: A Good Investment. As the public-service advertisement on the opposite page tells us, "The trouble with a cheap education is that we never stop paying for it" and conversely, "Money spent on education represents the best investment we can make." Charles Benson, a noted authority on school finance, lists the following dividends on the investment in education:

One of the most easily measured benefits is financial: the more education a person has, the more money, on the average, he earns. [See Figure 16-1.]

With few exceptions, the higher the level of education, the broader the range of job opportunities one has to select from. This is a good thing in itself: most people like to choose their jobs from among a variety.

Education provides a hedge against the risk of unemployment in an era of rapid technological change.

Persons with higher levels of education are more likely to own their homes than are persons with lesser amounts of schooling.

A person's future family is likely to be happier as a result of the education he has acquired.

Just as in the case of benefits to students, the return on educational expenditures to business takes several forms.

Educational expenditures not only lead to bigger markets for business men but also serve to reduce production costs.

Schools are providing the talent pool from which private industry will recruit personnel.

Citizens benefit from research, the quality of which in great part depends upon the quality of the educational system.

As they earn substantial salaries they pay substantial amounts of taxes to support our defense establishments and other types of public activity.

The last—and most important—social benefit of education, however, is the preservation of our free, highly productive, democratic society.[1]

[1] Charles E. Benson, *Education Is Good Business*, American Association of School Administrators, Washington, D.C., 1966, pp. 1-48.

In short, one's investment in education benefits directly and indirectly himself, his family, his state, his nation, and, as indicated in the next chapter, the whole world.

The evolution of the modern multibillion-dollar educational investment of the 1970s is traced briefly through the past three and a half centuries under *Historical Foundations* and in the related historical calendar of fiscal events.

HISTORICAL FOUNDATIONS

Early Development of Educational Finance. Lotteries and similar games of chance were legitimate means of raising money for schools and colleges in colonial America. These indirect and painless ways of obtaining funds took the place of direct taxation. Then, too, much education was financed through charity. Direct gifts by individuals and groups to semipublic or charity schools enabled many poor children to obtain some pauper schooling. Churches, through their denominational schools, have always financed the education of many children. Barter, the exchange of commodities and services, has been used frequently even in the present century. One commodity was wood. In lieu of money a parent furnished the equivalent in wood to keep the schoolroom warm in winter. The teacher often boarded around, receiving his board and room in exchange for part of his services.

The Battle for Publicly Supported Education. Cubberley[2] used the term "battle" to describe the efforts to win public funds for education. It was indeed a prolonged war, in which the major victories may be recorded as follows:

1. Permission to communities to organize a school district and to levy a local tax for schools on the property of those consenting
2. Local taxation extended to all property, regardless of consent
3. The organization of school districts made easy, and mandatory on proper petition
4. Small state aid to all organized school districts to help support a school

[2]E. P. Cubberley and Walter C. Ells, *An Introduction to the Study of Education*, Houghton Mifflin Company, Boston, 1933, p. 478.

5. Compulsory local taxation to supplement the state aid
6. Permissive, and later compulsory, township or county taxation to supplement the district taxation
7. Larger and larger state support, and assumption of public education as a state function
8. Extension of the taxation idea to include high schools as well as elementary schools

The historic decision in the extension of public support for high schools was rendered by the Michigan State Supreme Court in 1872 in the Kalamazoo High School case. This milestone and many others are listed in the historical calendar in this chapter.

Twentieth-century Educational Finance. The historical calendar also reveals great activity in the financing of education in the current century.

One of the early events after the turn of the century was the establishment of the first publicly supported junior college in 1902. The Smith-Hughes Act, later incorporated in the Vocational Education Act, markedly influenced the development of vocational and agricultural education. The original GI Bill stimulated the education of returned veterans and helped to trigger an enrollment explosion in higher education. Then in 1958 came the epoch-making multibillion-dollar National Defense Education Act.

The historical calendar reveals many innovations in principles and practices in educational finance during the decade of the 1960s. The Civil Rights Act of 1964, for example, provided for the withdrawal of federal funds from any school district practicing discrimination. This law has profoundly affected the financing of education. In the same year the Economic Opportunity Act provided initial funds for equalizing opportunities through compensatory education and other means, especially for minority groups. Direct payments to parochial and private schools were authorized by the State of Pennsylvania, a provision which was later held unconstitutional by the U.S. Supreme Court. In the 1960s decade the restriction of property ownership as a qualification for voting in school bond election was overruled by the U.S. Supreme Court.

Thus far in the 1970s more educational history was made by such unusual acts as Congress overriding a President's veto of educational appropriations. For the first time a private educational firm was awarded a "performance contract" by a public school system. The President's Commission on School Finance, reporting in 1972, will influence principles and practices for many years to come.

FISCAL PRINCIPLES

As a backdrop for the discussion of fundamental fiscal principles undergirding American education, we relist here the perennial partnerships, discussed under *Foundations* in Chapter 2, that education forms with democracy, society, equal opportunity, economic well-being, individual excellence, and morality.

Several related principles, basic to the financing of American education, are presented here; however, they are neither automatic nor all-inclusive.

Educational Finance Is Broader than Public School Finance. The title of this chapter, "Educational Finance," was chosen deliberately to accent the broad scope of our topic. As indicated elsewhere, "education" is a more inclusive term than "schooling." Furthermore, the expenditures for education beyond pre-elementary school, elementary school, and high school represent a substantial amount of money. Finally, as indicated in the preface, private and parochial schools and colleges, also called "independent institutions," are included with the public schools as part of the American educational system. In a letter to General Breckenridge in 1821, Thomas Jefferson said of the educational program he envisioned for the state of Virginia, "Let us keep our eyes steadily on the whole system." This remark, applied then to one state, was paraphrased by President Kennedy, in one of his messages to Congress, to apply to the educational system of the union of fifty states and dependencies. Educational finance is a really powerful means for enhancing the educational opportunities of all Americans.

Educational Finance Must Be Related to the Total Pattern of American Economy. The second tenet may be termed the "principle of economic interdependence." Teachers and administrators in schools and colleges and other forms of education must see the financing of education in relationship to the problem of support for public and private functions and services of all types.

For example, public school finance, as stated above, is only a part of educational finance, which in turn is only a part of the larger whole, namely, public finance. The fact that public school finance is a part of public finance is illustrated in the distribution of the tax dollar in any community. The implications

of this fact are far-reaching. Since the school is only one of the many enterprises supported by the public taxation, schoolmen may well approach their own isolated interests from the broad view of *public* rather than *school* financing. Other general activities, such as those of fire and police departments, aim at goals similar to those of education—they seek to protect the individual, his property, and his rights. Education, in the long run, serves as a form of insurance for which the public ought to be both willing and able to pay. The individual benefits of education have long been recognized. Its social increments are being recognized more and more.

Educational Finance Should Be the Servant of Education and Society. Many states and communities have millage and debt limitations which make finance virtually the master of education. Finance should function as the servant, not as the master, of education and society. The child is more important than the dollar. In many school systems, however, money is the dictator, and education is the slave. The opposite condition is likewise unfortunate, for lavish spending brings financial disaster to the school district and the allied taxing units. Educational finance helps to give a learner the best education possible within practical limits.

Educational finance serves not only schools and colleges but also society. It is a social as well as an economic factor. The social motive, thus far subordinated, now bids fair to assume a larger control in public education. Educational finance is indeed the servant of society as well as the handmaiden of education. As the late Walter Reuther, president of the United Automobile Workers, said, "Education is the most important thing for the United States to develop in its attempt to create a great society." As indicated under *Orientation*, expenditures for good education are indeed sound investments—for both the short and the long term—in a strong society. The investment power of education is illustrated in Figure 16-1.

Increased Responsibilities Must Mean Increased Costs. Those who are prone to cut the educational budget with one hand and to give the schools and colleges increased responsibilities with the other should realize that the two are incompatible. Among the major causes of the rise in educational expendi-

The Development of Educational Finance

1633	A town school established and a school tax levied by the Dutch in New York	*1917*	Federal funds for vocational education provided through Smith-Hughes Act
1643	Earliest record found of rate bills or tuition fees for support of schools	*1931*	Federal aid recommended by National Advisory Committee on Education
1693	Massachusetts towns given the legal power to levy school taxes	*1933*	Emergency grants for education initiated by Congress during the Depression
1785	Land set aside in the Northwest Territory by the Ordinance of 1785, beginning federal aid for education	*1944*	Original GI Bill, with federal subsidies for veterans' education, enacted
1795	First state-supported university— University of North Carolina— opened	*1946*	National School Lunch Act passed by Congress on permanent basis (extended and expanded in Child Nutrition Act of 1966)
1795	First permanent public school fund established in Pennsylvania	*1946*	Financing of Fulbright program for international exchanges approved by Congress
1819	Inviolability of charters of private colleges established by Dartmouth College decision	*1953*	Council for Financial Aid to Education established as nonprofit organization to encourage voluntary support of higher education
1821	First free public high school organized in Boston	*1958*	Educational Facilities Laboratories established with aid of Ford Foundation
1834	Free elementary education first adopted by the state of Pennsylvania	*1958*	Epoch-making National Defense Education Act enacted by Congress
1862	Morrill Act, creating federally supported land-grant colleges, signed by President Lincoln	*1962*	National Committee for the Support of Public Schools organized
1867	First major philanthropic foundation in the United States established by George S. Peabody	*1963*	First state law specifically providing funds for compensatory education to aid culturally disadvantaged children passed in California
1869	First state law providing some financial aid for school busing approved by Massachusetts	*1963*	Higher Education Facilities Act, including funds for undergraduate and graduate facilities, passed by Congress
1874	Taxation for secondary schools upheld in Kalamazoo (Michigan) case		
1902	First publicly supported junior college established at Joliet (Illinois)		

1964	Civil Rights Bill passed by Congress, containing a provision for the withdrawal of funds from any school district practicing discrimination
1964	Economic Opportunity Act passed by Congress, with special provisions affecting education
1964	Funds provided for the public schools of New Hampshire by the first state lottery in the United States
1965	Federal grants made in Appalachian Regional Development Act, including supplementing costs of constructing educational facilities
1965	Elementary and Secondary Education Act passed, providing some services and loans for private schools
1965	Higher Education Act passed by Congress
1966	Federal authorization, but no appropriations, voted by Congress for the International Education Act
1966	Permanent GI Bill passed by Congress, including financial aid for schooling
1967	Education Professions Development Act adopted by Congress
1969	First federal grants for undergraduate student research made by the National Science Foundation
1969	Restriction of property ownership as a qualification for voting in school bond elections banned by U.S. Supreme Court
1969	First federal grants awarded for development of educational radio stations
1969	A private educational firm awarded, for the first time, a "performance contract" by public schools (Texarkana, Arkansas) to provide academic instruction for its students

1970	Presidential veto of federal educational appropriation measure overridden by Congress
1970	GI educational benefits substantially expanded and increased by Congress
1970	Supplemental federal funds provided by the President to help predominantly black colleges, their students, and staff
1970	Largest of all federal-aid-to-education grants ever appropriated approved by Congress in the passage and three-year extension of Elementary and Secondary Education Act and amendments
1971	Direct public aid to private schools ruled unconstitutional by U.S. Supreme Court
1971	Decision rendered by the U.S. Supreme Court approving the "supermajority" laws in states that require more than a majority of "yes" votes for approval of school bonds
1971	Property tax as major means of school support ruled unconstitutional by California Supreme Court
1971	First national nonpublic school federation, the Council for American Private Education, formed to promote the interests of private schools
1971	State law passed in Maryland to provide scholarship funds for students in nonpublic elementary and secondary schools
1972	Report of Presidential Commission on School Finance published
1973	Target date set for implementing the "comparability" concept in federal legislation
1976	Target date proposed by Carnegie Commission on Higher Education for removal of all financial barriers to higher education

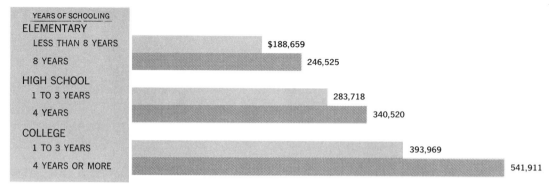

FIGURE 16-1 *Estimated lifetime earnings of males in relation to years of schooling completed.* (*U.S. Office of Education,* Digest of Educational Statistics, *1969.*)

tures are (1) a decline in the purchasing value of the dollar, (2) an increase in enrollments, (3) an increase in the size of the educational tasks, especially in the relatively expensive junior college years, and (4) higher standards of educating, akin to today's higher standards of living. The first causal factor is primarily monetary. The last three are educational in nature and account for a large share

BILLIONS OF DOLLARS

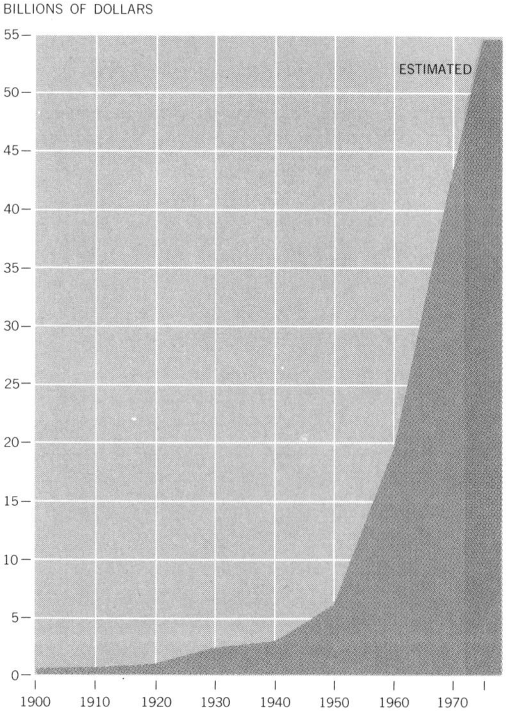

FIGURE 16-2 *Total current expenditures for public and private elementary and secondary schools.* (*U.S. Office of Education,* Estimate of Educational Statistics; *and estimates by the authors.*)

of the enlarged costs. The extension and enrichment of educational services call for expansion in school revenue.

The Costs of Inadequate Education Are High. Figure 16-2 reveals the soaring costs of public and private elementary and secondary schools. Those who complain about the high costs of good education should reckon the higher costs of inadequate preparation. In an address dealing with excellence in education presented at a meeting of the American Jewish Committee, Hubert Humphrey stated:

How much longer will we continue to save pennies by cutting educational expenses, only to lose dollars through the inevitable economic and social consequences of inferior or insufficient schooling? The loss of only one year's income due to unemployment is more than the total cost of 12 years of education through high school. Failure to improve educational performance is thus not only poor social policy, it is poor economics.

The high cost of inadequate education is directing more attention to the economic loss and social waste of dropouts at all educational levels. The dropout's loss of personal self-esteem is also an important psychological factor and often leaves permanent mental scars. Educational deprivations and inadequacies are very costly.

Educational Opportunity and Burden Should Be Equalized. On the federal and state levels, one of today's tenets is equalization programs. Strayer and Haig in 1923, building upon Cubberley's earlier dissertation, were the first to give a clear-cut picture of the equalization principle. Their analysis, and later the analyses of Paul R. Mort and others, interpreted this principle as the complete equalization of the burden of a satisfactory minimum educational program below which no locality could be allowed to go, but above which any locality would be allowed to rise by means of local support. In contradistinction to the payment-for-effort or matching principle, the operation of the equalization plan tends to shift to more able communities some of the undue burden carried by the less wealthy localities (see Figure 16-7). Most states today have a state-local partnership foundation program in which the commonwealth bestows more on the schools which have less in fiscal resources. Local school districts should receive enough state aid to relieve the local property tax and thus provide enough local tax leeway to adapt to peculiar local needs. On the other hand, complete financing through state aid preempts local responsibility for finance and undermines local initiative. For this reason also, most experts on school finance want boards of education to be fiscally independent, that is, free from fiscal dependence upon other units of local government.

In brief, the equalization principle means that governmental agencies collect educational funds where the money is and spend the money where the pupils are. Every man's property and income must be taxed to educate every man's child. Even though a man chooses to send his own children to a parochial or private school, he is not exempt from contributing his support to the education of all children. The golden rule in educational finance is, "Thou shalt educate thy neighbor's children as thine own."

Initially this idea of equalization was applied to small areas, as the county and state. Now the old slogan "The wealth of the state must educate the children of the state" is being supplemented with the clause "and the wealth of the United States must be used to equalize the education of all the children in the nation." Furthermore, the phrase "all the children in the nation" implies that more adequate educational opportunities and greater financial

Underfinancing of education is manifested in many ways such as this overcrowded music class jammed in a corridor (left) and this obsolete and Spartan classroom (right).

support should be provided for disadvantaged, exceptional, or atypical children, since their learning opportunities, as in the case of the blind, are below par, and the costs of their instruction are above average. American public education will not be genuinely democratic until there is nationwide application of the principle that opportunity and burden shall be equalized for all learners. As former United States Commissioner of Education Harold Howe II has stated: "In order to equalize educational opportunity for America's children, the school must provide resources equal to the task, not equal resources for each child."

Educational Expenditures Can Help Reduce Poverty. The so-called Great Society legislation was designed in part to increase the quantity and improve the quality of education available to all segments of society. Its special focus, however, is on economically and culturally deprived persons—the disadvantaged. More than $2 billion is being spent annually for educational programs planned especially for persons of all ages in impoverished areas. The target group is students from low-income families.

The booklet *Education: An Answer to Poverty*, published jointly by the U.S. Office of Education and the Office of Economic Opportunity, from both of which federal funds are available for remedial or compensatory education, states in part:

Why is America so concerned about improving the education of children of the poor? . . . We have learned that poverty and ignorance go hand in hand. We have learned that the modern variety of "hard core" poverty has something in common with elegance and security of wealth. It is inherited. America is newly committed not only to relieving the dependence of millions of families on public welfare and unemployment compensation, but to breaking the chain of dependence that passes from old generations to new.[3]

"Compensatory" education seeks to "compensate" for the backlog of neglect and unmet needs of the disadvantaged by spending extra funds for, and giving more thought to, their teaching. More schooling, and thus more potential earning power, must be given to those with little education. This means more than extra dollars per pupil for edu-

[3]U.S. Office of Education and Office of Economic Opportunity, *Education: An Answer to Poverty*, 1966, p. 5.

cating the disadvantaged—it calls for quality education in integrated schools.

Public Education Should Be Fiscally Free for All Learners. Basic to the financing of public education is the democratic concept of free education. How long education should be provided at public expense is a debatable question. Practices vary markedly among the states, but there is general agreement that children should be educated through high school at public expense. Some authorities would extend tuition-free schooling through the junior college years. This does not mean that everything is free. Many costs are hidden. There is disagreement about the elements that should be provided without cost to pupils. For example, in the education of rural high school pupils, some states furnish only tuition, whereas others include free transportation, textbooks, or board of pupils in lieu of transportation. Many states have set up what is called a defensible minimum program to be furnished tuition-free to all pupils. Along with the American Bill of Rights, including guarantees for freedom of speech, of religion, of the press, and of assembly, there goes a dictum that American public education shall be free to all pupils. The emancipation proclamation in educational finance precludes dependence upon charity, fees, and tuition. Free public education is the American's birthright in each community and state and in the nation as a whole. The Adult Education Act of 1966 provides some funds for continuing education of adults. Furthermore, the Carnegie Commission on Higher Education has set the target date of 1976 for the removal of all financial barriers to higher education.

Local Citizens Should Contribute Some Fiscal Support and Much Interest. Although the main responsibility for the support of public education should rest with the fifty state governments, the local communities must continue to bear some of the burden for financing education. The schools can thus be kept closer to the taxpayers, who are citizens of the immediate local community. Even when districts are merged and large consolidations are formed, local citizens' advisory groups can recommend budgets to the official board of education and take an active interest in the school, the pupils, the staff, and the facilities. However, the proportion of school costs now borne by the local communities is too high in most states.

The State Should Be Primarily Responsible for Public Education. The Tenth Amendment to the Constitution of the United States made education primarily the responsibility of the individual states (see Chapter 3). Hence the support of public education became mainly a matter of state concern. Today every state makes some contribution from its revenues to the support of public schools through many types of funds, some of which are described later. An inconsistency exists, however, between the legal intention to provide the state support and the many cases of neglect and inadequacy. For the nation as a whole, state governments supply only about 40 percent of the cost of schools. Furthermore, the method of distributing such aid is an important factor. Despite arguments for federal support of public education, the fact remains that the individual states will have to give more assistance to schools and colleges.

The Federal Government Is a Fiscal Partner in Education. As recorded in the historical calendar in this chapter, the federal government adopted the Northwest Ordinance in 1785 and reaffirmed it two years later. This ordinance clearly postulated: "Religion, morality and knowledge being necessary to good government and the happiness of mankind, schools and the means of education shall be forever encouraged." In implementation of this policy, the first public lands were given to education in Ohio in 1803. The calendar lists some, but not all, of the many financial grants given directly to schools and colleges and given indirectly through the U.S. Office of Education (see Chapter 2). Private education, too, especially on the college level, has shared in some of the money grants.

While the federal government dedicates only about 8 percent of its income to education, it has manifested an increasing fiscal concern about schools and colleges under the permissive "general welfare" clause of the Constitution. Some of the newly developing countries, such as Cambodia, imbued with a zeal and vision for education, are spending at least 25 percent of their national budget on schools and colleges. The United States government is a paying partner in the fifty states and in many other nations, but unfortunately, education has a low federal priority here at home.

However, financial aid to education from federal and other sources is merely a monetary means toward an educational end. As President Lyndon B.

Johnson stated: "Nothing is more dangerous than the easy assumption that simply by putting more money into schools we will emerge with an educated, trained, and enlightened nation." Value judgments must be made in order to improve education.

"Lighthouse Schools" Can Indicate Better Practices through Their Richer Resources. Related to federal and especially state financing is the principle of adaptability. According to this rule, espoused ardently in his graduate classes and emphatically in his writings by the late Paul R. Mort, the state tries to keep schools wholesome and vigorous by preserving local initiative and utilizing other devices. Its early application consisted of a program of fiscal rewards to a community for supporting its schools. This reward-for-effort device is being modified because in practice it gives the most help to the rich districts. The modern interpretation of this principle makes it possible for wealthy districts to use their wealth in going far beyond the foundation or equalization level guaranteed to all schools. These better-financed schools, or "lighthouse schools," as they are sometimes called, help point the way to future progress for all schools.

Educators Should Be Held Responsible for Performance. One of the "in" words in education that may soon rival "relevancy" is the shibboleth "accountability." As briefly defined in the Glossary in the Appendix of this book, "accountability" is "the responsibility of an educational agency to be held answerable to the public for its performance." This concept of accountability in education is not new. Many writers in educational finance textbooks of yesteryear have stressed the need for "educational auditors" and fiscal responsibility.

The recent impetus to this concept of accountability was triggered by the Coleman Report, published in 1966. This educational survey, published under the title *Equality of Educational Opportunity*, was made by the U.S. Office of Education at the request of the Civil Rights Act administration. This report clearly indicated that "input" in education is not an accurate measure of how good schools are. The survey found, for example, that, despite equal inputs in dollars, there was great disparity in resultant skills in schools attended by whites and those attended by blacks.

The significance of the Coleman report in connection with educational accountability lies in the demonstration of how federal resources can be applied through the U.S. Office of Education to gather comprehensive data about the state of educational affairs."

It was inevitable that the Coleman report should generate attempts to assess success in other areas of education. It was no surprise, therefore, that in 1968 the proposal for national assessment of what schools were accomplishing in respect to learners' achievement . . . found fertile soil. . . . Plans came to fruition in 1969 when student achievement testing in areas of science and citizenship, two of the ten areas to be stressed, was begun. . . .[4]

In his 1970 "Education Message" President Richard M. Nixon stated:

From these considerations we derive another new concept: accountability. *School administrators and school teachers alike are responsible for their performance, and it is in their interest as well as the interest of the pupils that they be held accountable. . . . We have, as a nation, too long avoided thinking of the productivity of schools.*

Leon M. Lessinger, one of the chief promoters of accountability, states:

Accountability is the coming sine qua non for education in the 1970's. How to engineer accountability for results in public education is the central problem for the education profession. . . . Accountability is the product of a process. Performance contracting is one process for which accountability is the product.[5]

Performance Contracting Can Be One Means of Promoting Accountability. As indicated above by Lessinger, contracting for performance is *one* way to implement accountability. Again, performance contracting is not new. Such contracts have long been used in educational administration for such services as lunch programs, custodial care, and maintenance of equipment and buildings. As Lessinger states: "At its most primitive level the process works like this: A public authority grants money to a local, educational agency to contract with private enterprise to achieve specific goals within specific periods for specific costs."[6]

As an illustration, the Texarkana Dropout Pre-

vention Program, which was initiated in 1969, first brought into national focus the practice of making the nonpublic contractor completely responsible for the success or failure of an educational project. Various patterns of contracting for performance are taking shape.

The principle and practice of performance contracting may prove to be a mixed blessing: "Teachers organizations are already warning their members that involvement of private enterprise in school accountability efforts could increase industry's voice in educational policy and reduce teacher influence."[7] Performance contracting is one way and only one way of implementing the concept of accountability.

Cost-benefit and Cost-effectiveness Analyses Help to Evaluate in Educational Finance. In the Glossary (see pages 483ff) are also found these two definitions: "Cost-benefit analysis" is "a means of comparing the costs of a particular undertaking with the benefits it is expected to yield." "Cost-effectiveness analysis" is "a means of analyzing the extent to which an undertaking accomplishes its objectives in relation to its cost in comparison with alternative undertakings."

Additional information on these principles is supplied from the printed report by the Commission on Instructional Technology:

Cost-benefit and cost-effectiveness analysis are used in the . . . systems analysis in order to choose among alternatives for reaching the desired objectives. The best alternative is the one which has the highest ratio of benefits to cost. Cost-benefit, the broader category, includes cost-effectiveness, which may be measured concretely in dollars or valid test scores. In addition, cost benefit includes such aspects as enjoyment or recreation, which may be deeply felt but defy precise qualification.[8]

A specific illustration is provided from the field of adult education:

Using the single criterion of income increase, the potential benefits of the Adult Basic Education program are about four times the annual costs. The potential benefits are truly exciting when any sort of estimate is made of the huge payoffs to the community from the other factors which have not been quantified or considered in this estimate of benefits.

[4]Leslie J. Mauth, "'Accountability': New Stress in Education," *Torch,* vol. 44, p. 7, January, 1971.

[5]Leon M. Lessinger, "Engineering Accountability for Results in Public Education," *Phi Delta Kappan,* vol. 52, p. 217, December, 1970.

[6]*Ibid.*

[7]"Accountability: The New 'In' Word," *The Shape of Education for 1970-71,* National School Public Relations Association, Washington, D.C., 1970, p. 20.

[8]Sidney G. Tickton (ed.), *To Improve Learning: An Evaluation of Educational Technology,* R. R. Bowker Company, New York, 1970, p. 88.

Another benefit of Adult Basic Education can be almost anything that a man or woman takes away from an educational experience. It is difficult to quantify pride, self-esteem, or confidence. It is impossible to measure the joy and satisfaction that comes to a mind at long last awakened.[9]

The benefits in measurable tangibles and incalculable intangibles are factors in evaluating costs in educational finance.

Education Should Be Economically Administered. Every school system must practice economy at all times. Groups as well as individuals should heed the advice of Ralph Waldo Emerson "to make money spend well." The term "economy" is often misunderstood, since there are false and true economies. Educators and laymen must distinguish between retrenchment and economy. Retrenchment is merely a reduction in expenditures. Genuine economy is effected through intelligent spending and vigilant administration. Benjamin Franklin wrote, "Human felicity is produced not so much by great pieces of good fortune that seldom happen, as by little advantages that occur each day."

Fiscal Management of Education Cannot Be Identical with That of Private Business. As indicated at the beginning of this chapter, education is a big business. Hence a common fallacy is to liken the fiscal management of education to that of private business. Especially unfortunate is this enforced metaphor when applied to public schools. Although both strive after economy and efficiency, they differ decidedly. In the first place, public education is a public matter, and business is mainly private. Then, too, the basic aims of education and of business are not identical, for although money is invested in both public education and private business, the major objective of the latter is quarterly cash dividends, whereas the former seeks long-time returns in character, personality, skills, and the changes wrought in the child through growth and development. A business, although employing many people, is run for the special benefit of a few stockholders; public education is conducted cooperatively for the benefit of all members of society. Of course, the public schools and other educational institutions can profit much from observing private business, even though they are dissimilar in philosophy and function.

[9] *A Lifetime of Learning*, Government Printing Office, Washington, D.C., 1969, p. 10.

Personnel in Fiscal Management Should Be Well Trained and Honest. Both business and school officials advocate that those engaged in fiscal management be well trained. The persons handling educational finances should have specific training for their jobs. The school treasurer, the superintendent, the business manager, or whoever is in direct charge of school or college finances should be versed in the theory and practice of business accounting. Such personnel should also be professionally trained educators. Increasingly, superintendents of schools, business managers, and other staff members are taking courses in educational finance and business management.

The personnel should be not only efficient but also impeccably honest. As a precautionary and custodial measure, all persons who handle school money should be bonded. The staff is usually trustworthy, but unfortunately the schools and colleges are tempting objects for despoliation by greedy politicians and racketeers.

Expenditures for Public Education Should Be Recorded and Reported. A person may be careless about recording his personal receipts and expenditures, but he cannot be so with public money, which must be accounted for meticulously and honestly. The receipt of money and its expenditure should be registered promptly and accurately. Records ought to be kept in a fire-resistive vault and subjected to scientific scrutiny through periodic audits.

Fiscal Planning Is Necessary for Education. Educational welfare necessitates fiscal planning. Education of a child calls for a long-range master plan, not only because he requires twelve to sixteen years of schooling, but also because much of the cost is often borne by one school district. Long-range planning for education is an attempt to substitute intelligent forecasts for the opportunism of a laissez-faire philosophy. Effective long-range forecasting must rest upon improvement in the short-term fiscal plan, that is, the annual budget.

BUDGETING

The budget is a very important instrument in education, and the budgeting process applies many, if not all, of the basic principles of educational finance, previously mentioned.

Evolution of the Budgeting Process

Pioneer Studies and Writings in Educational Budgeting. The earliest doctoral study of public school budgeting was made by John W. Twente and published in 1923. The second nationwide survey was made by Chris A. De Young and published in 1932. Both of these surveys revealed that budgeting was then "in the kindergarten stage" of development. In 1936, after a follow-up study, De Young published the first graduate textbook in school budgeting. In presenting the triangular concept of the school budget, Figure 16-3, he stated:

The ideal school budget contains three parts: 1) the work *plan, which is a definite statement of the educational policies and program; 2) the* spending *plan, which is a translation of the accepted policies into proposed expenditures; and 3) the* financing *plan, which proposes means for meeting the costs of the educational needs.*[10]

Much pioneering work in educational budgeting was done by such college professors as Arthur B. Moehlman, Nickolaus L. Engelhardt, and John Guy Fowlkes. From these earlier works and pioneering efforts of thousands of school administrators, the modern concept of the Planning-Programming-Budgeting System evolved gradually.

Newer Planning-Programming-Budgeting System (PPBS). The Glossary in the Appendix defines PPBS as "an application of systems analysis to the allocation of resources to various competing educational purposes and needs through systematic planning, programming, budgeting, and evaluation." This budgeting system was initiated by a commercial firm, du Pont Company. Robert S. McNamara, then United States Secretary of Defense, later transplanted this budgetary system to his department. In 1965 President Lyndon B. Johnson directed the adoption of this modern approach to planning and budgeting in the federal government. The U.S. Office of Education, which had initiated a nationwide study of the possibilities of PPBS in educational reform, awarded in 1968 a three-year contract to the Research Corporation of the American Association of School Business Officials: "To provide an

improved method for determining the quality and cost of the product of education as a means toward improved management of educational and fiscal resources." After the three-year study, the Research Corporation issued budgeting "guidelines" which are available from the Government Printing Office. The guidelines aid in setting educational goals, identifying and allocating resources, developing programs, considering alternatives, using detailed methods of allocating and accounting, and evaluating results. While the Research Corporation developed the conceptual design for the integrated budgetary system, the public schools of Dade County, Florida, served as a demonstration of an operational system. The Research Corporation more aptly calls this sophisticated budgeting program "Educational Resources Management System." The first textbook on PPBS applied to schools, written in 1968 by Harry J. Hartley, bears the title *Educational Planning-Programming-Budgeting.*[11] Whatever the title, budgeting systems are becoming more prevalent as annual and long-term fiscal programming.

Progress of the Annual School Budget

Budgeting in public education may be divided into four major steps: (1) preparation, (2) presentation and adoption, (3) administration, and (4) appraisal.

Preparation of the Budget. Budget building is a continuous job. The starting point is the development of objectives—behavioral and academic—and an implementing educational program that help make the budget a professional document rather than a statistical report. This educational emphasis in school accounting is made possible through the cooperation of all staff members and the board of education. The preparation of the educational specifications is inextricably linked with the development of the spending and financing plans for the budget, and with appropriate alternatives and their cost benefits and effectiveness possibilities.

Presentation and Adoption of the Budget. After the budget has been prepared in tentative form, it is usually presented to the board of education and to other legal and extralegal groups. Fiscal publicity is important in the broader program of public rela-

---

[10]Chris A. De Young, *Budgeting in Public Schools,* Doubleday, Doran & Company, Garden City, N. Y., 1936, p. 7.

[11]Harry J. Hartley, *Educational Planning-Programming-Budgeting,* Prentice-Hall, Inc., Englewood Cliffs, N J., 1968.

tions. Various techniques aid in interpreting the school budget to the board of education, the school personnel, and the general public. After the budget has been presented with interpolations, it is legally ratified by the proper body or bodies, such as the board of education and the city council, or by the people in some states.

Administration of the Budget. After the estimated figures have been transferred to the school accounting books as initial entries, the budget is ready to be administered. It functions not as a dictator but as a definite guide for the economical and efficient conduct of the schools.

Appraisal of Budgets and Budgetary Procedures. One means of appraising budgets and budgetary practices is the audit of expenditures and educational results. Then there is also the objective appraisal of the format and content of the document itself as an instrument for building public relations. But most important is the evaluation of the outputs in sound learnings and desirable changes in students. This annual budgeting process can best be appraised in relation to a long-term budget extending several years into the future.

Long-term Educational Budgets

The annual budget has many items with long-term implications and obligations. Hence long-term budgeting is a necessity in education. A common impression is that long-term budgeting involves making a forecast for a period of five or ten years

and then, at the end of that time, making an evaluation and preparing a new long-term budget. That is *periodic,* not *continuous,* long-term planning. Continuous long-term budgeting for education uses the correction technique of adjusting forecasts annually or periodically. This is budgeting constantly ahead in the light of recent developments, and always several years in advance of the annual budget. Large corporations, such as telephone companies, public utilities, and others, have long used the budget and related data in extending their projections a decade or more into the future.

Both long-term and annual budgeting procedures, whether developed by means of a modern planning-programming-budgeting system or more traditional techniques, can be classified as developing the three interrelated programs previously mentioned, namely: (1) planning educational programs, (2) calculating expenditure outlays, and (3) inventorying resources as possible receipts.

DEVELOPING EDUCATIONAL PROGRAMS

The base of the budget triangle, as indicated in Figure 16-3, is the educational program. Before the administrator and his staff can estimate expenditures and receipts, the educational plan must be formulated. These educational specifications form the work program of the school or college. In general, the nature of this work plan is conditioned by the educational philosophy held by the administrator, the

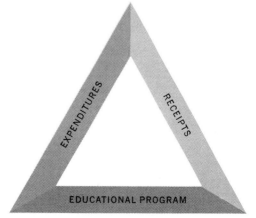

EARLY FORM   TRADITIONAL TYPE   MODERN BUDGET FOR SCHOOLS

FIGURE 16-3 Modern budget for schools.

staff, the board of education, and the community or clientele. Philosophic principles and educational concepts need to be crystallized into specific educational objectives. Just as the objectives form an integral part of the curriculum, so, too, educational goals should be the mainspring of the budget. The implementation of these objectives through proposed programs of action makes the educational budget a professional document. These educational programs are discussed in other chapters of this book. The remainder of this chapter is devoted to the other two parts of the budget triangle: expenditures and receipts.

EXPENDITURES

Classification of School Expenditures

The U.S. Office of Education has prepared a standard accounting classification form for schools. The major headings and subheadings are as follows: administration, instruction, attendance and health, pupil transportation, operation of plant, maintenance of plant, fixed charges, food services, community services, capital outlay, debt service, and outgoing transfers.

Cost of Public Education

Where the School Dollar Goes. Teachers and administrators are frequently asked, "Where does the school dollar go?" "How is the money spent?" The classroom teacher, as an agent in the public relations should be fortified with facts so as to be able to answer such questions intelligently. Obviously, the dollar is not spent in the same way in every school system. Two extremely variable items listed are debt service and capital outlay.

For the entire United States, the percentage distribution of the school dollar for current expenditures is revealed in Figure 16-4.

Annual Cost per Pupil in Average Daily Attendance. The percentage distribution of the school dollar is not the only way of calculating school costs. Another method is to figure the cost per capita for an area as large as the United States or as small as a local school district. The basis for determining these unit costs is usually the average daily attend-

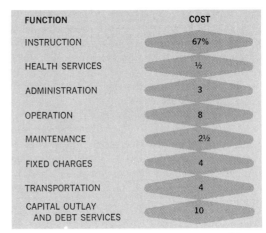

FUNCTION	COST
INSTRUCTION	67%
HEALTH SERVICES	½
ADMINISTRATION	3
OPERATION	8
MAINTENANCE	2½
FIXED CHARGES	4
TRANSPORTATION	4
CAPITAL OUTLAY AND DEBT SERVICES	10

FIGURE 16-4   Where the school dollar goes. ("Annual Cost of Education Index," School Management, vol. 14, January, 1970, p. 42.)

ance (ADA), the number enrolled in school, or the total population of the United States. Current expenditures per pupil are many times as great in some school districts as in others.

Annual Cost per Pupil Enrolled and per Capita of Population. The cost of education in the public elementary and secondary schools can be calculated also on the basis of the number of pupils enrolled. This total unit cost is less than the cost per pupil in average daily attendance. Another unit, less reliable than per-pupil average daily attendance, is the cost per person in the United States. Figure 16-5 reveals the cost of education per pupil enrolled. As the nation develops a program of lifelong learning for all individuals, the cost per capita of population will be increasingly indicative of the cost of public education per consumer.

Daily Costs per Pupil Enrolled. Costs for education may also be calculated on the basis of the daily rather than the annual expenditures indicated thus far. In a typical school the costs for current expenditures average approximately $5 a day for each pupil enrolled. The cost-per-day unit for calculating school expenditures is advantageous, since it is small, easily handled, and readily understood by the man in the street.

The total expenditures do not measure the cost or the worth of education. Increasingly the public is learning to evaluate this service not in terms of dollar aggregates but by means of standards and

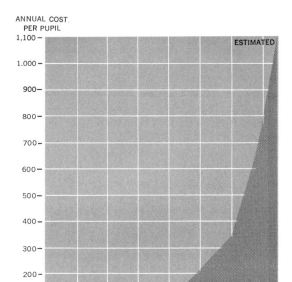

ANNUAL COST
PER PUPIL

1,100 —

1,000 —

900 —

800 —

700 —

600 —

500 —

400 —

300 —

200 —

100 —

0 —

ESTIMATED

COST (dollars)

1900 1910 1920 1930 1940 1950 1960 1970

FIGURE 16-5 Annual cost of education per student in public elementary and secondary schools. (U.S. Office of Education, Digest of Educational Statistics; and estimates by the authors.)

results achieved. The quality and quantity of educational returns must be considered as well as the nature and amount of expenditures. Furthermore, expenditures are made possible only through the receipt of adequate revenue.

RECEIPTS

Classification of School Receipts

Less uniformity is found in classifying school receipts than in classifying expenditures. Receipts are usually grouped by (1) taxing or political unit, (2) method of production, (3) accounting classification, (4) specific funds, or (5) a combination of these. Each of these methods is briefly described here.

Taxing or Political Unit. A convenient way to group estimated or actual school receipts is according to the taxing unit that provides the revenue. The main political units are local, township, county (parish), state, and federal. Patently these geographical categories overlap somewhat. For example, prop-

erty taxes may come from more than one political unit.

Method of Production. The more common forms of financing public education are listed alphabetically here: endowments, gas tax, grants, income tax, inheritance tax, interest, personal property tax, real estate tax, rentals, sales tax, subventions, and tuition. It is difficult to determine the exact methods by which all school revenue is obtained.

Accounting Classification. The U.S. Office of Education recommends major accounting classifications for school receipts, including these:

Revenue receipts
Revenue from local sources
Taxation and appropriation
Tuition from patrons
Transportation fees
Other revenue from local sources
Revenue from intermediate sources
Revenue from state sources
Revenue from federal sources

Nonrevenue receipts
Sale of bonds
Loans
Sale of school property and insurance adjustments
Income transfer accounts

Specific Funds. It has been suggested that legal stipulations separating school money into special, distinct funds be abolished. Many of these regulations, however, have long histories that fortify them against change. Rigidity in accounting is exemplified in Illinois, where school money must be separated into educational and building funds. Numerous special school funds have been created by state legislatures.

State and National Uniformity Recommended. Many other systems of revenue classification are employed. The most common practice is that of listing receipts by local, state, and federal sources. As in the case of expenditures, a combination of systems is recommended, with due regard to state laws and national uniformity, as advocated by the U.S. Office of Education in its *Financial Accounting Handbook II* (1972).

Major Means for Obtaining Public Revenue

Where the School Dollar Comes from. The source of the school dollar is an important question, for it goes to the root of the American economic system. Since school finance is a segment of public finance, the teacher and administrator are drawn into broad problems of public financing when they seek the deep sources of the dollar that the school receives. As in expenditures, there is little uniformity in receipts throughout the United States.

Figure 16-6 shows the sources of school revenue according to political units. Fifty-two percent of school funds comes from local and county sources, mainly the former. The proportion of school revenue derived from local taxes has decreased markedly in the past quarter-century, from 80 percent to slightly more than 50 percent. The consolidation of schools and the enlargement of the taxing unit to embrace entire counties cause county and local sources to coalesce. The state's share of

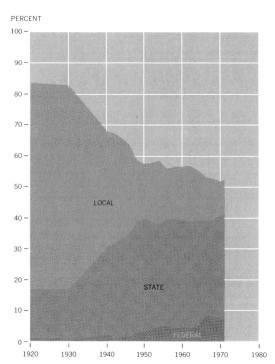

PERCENT

FIGURE 16-6　Percentage of public school revenue from federal, state, and local sources. (U.S. Bureau of the Census.)

school financing has been increasing gradually, amounting now to 41 percent. State taxes are derived largely from personal and corporate income taxes, sales taxes, and sometimes from miscellaneous taxes on gasoline, tobacco, and alcoholic beverages. The federal government's share of school expenses in 1971 was only 7 percent, although it collects over three-fourths of all taxes levied.

Taxation. Edwin A. Seligman, a noted economist, defines a tax as "a compulsory contribution from the person to the government to defray the expense incurred in the common interest of all without reference to special benefits conferred." In other words, through taxes people contribute to the cost of different services and common social purposes. The growing size of the tax bill is revealed in the statistics that in 1970, the total amount of taxes collected by federal, state, and local governments in the United States was $3,927 per family, while ten years earlier, in 1960, it was $2,264.

Since most of the support for American public education comes from taxation in its myriad forms, laymen, teachers, and administrators desire a good tax system which is not too dependent upon a single tax, such as that on property. The general property tax is becoming increasingly unsatisfactory because of the difficulty in assessing all kinds and classes of property at the same rate. Many European nations have to a large degree abandoned this method, but in America the local property tax has long been the prime source of school revenue. In an historic decision, the California Supreme Court in 1971 ruled that the local property tax was unconstitutional. The court held that it discriminated against people in poor communities where less property value per capita is available for taxation for public services, principally education. Decisions of this sort could force states to go to state property taxes or to increased sales and income tax levies, and thereby shift the basis of school financial support (and perhaps control as well) from local to state government.

Among the numerous plans for making the property tax less painful are classification of property; equalization of assessments; more economical, efficient, and honest administration in assessing, levying, and collecting taxes; and the inclusion of the property tax as a part of a broader tax base. It is the abuse rather than the use of the property tax that constitutes a menace to the schools.

The income tax, both personal and corporate,

and the sales tax are being used more widely by the states as sources of general revenue. The state income tax, which was introduced by Wisconsin in 1911, is increasingly a source of school revenue. More than three-fourths of the states have income taxes as a source of revenue. Linked intimately with the problems of broadening the tax base for school support are the issues of increasing efficiency through the consolidation of small, weak units and of reducing costs through carefully planned economies. Archaic taxing systems are not the only cause of trouble, for even where tax systems have been revised, revenues are often inadequate. Some of the difficulty lies not so much in the failure of taxation as in increased expenditures. Many schools may well give less emphasis to raising more funds to spend and devote more thought to spending money more efficiently.

Nonrevenue Receipts. As previously defined, nonrevenue receipts do not constitute a genuine source of income, since they incur an obligation that must be met at some future date. These receipts include mainly the revenue either from the sale of property and bonds or from loans. Since property is not frequently sold by the school district, attention is directed here to the common practice of borrowing money.

The prevalent ways of financing schools when cash is not available are (1) long-term obligations, (2) short-term obligations, and (3) refinancing. Illustrative of the first are the straight-term bond, which is used for a stated number of years, to be repaid or refunded at the date of maturity; the sinking-fund bond, which is made for a definite period of years, to be paid from a fund which is collected and invested during the term of the bond; and the serial bond, which is paid in installments during the period of the total bond issue.

In view of the large number of school bond issues that have been voted down by taxpayers in recent years, various court decisions are very important. The U.S. Supreme Court in 1970 ruled as unconstitutional state laws limiting voting on general obligation bond-issue proposals to real property owners and taxpayers. Laws in fourteen states were affected by this extension of the "one-man, one-vote" concept. The California State Supreme Court has ruled unconstitutional a state law mandating a two-thirds voter approval for local bond issues, including school bonds, as a violation of the equal-protection clause of the Fourteenth Amendment to

the U.S. Constitution. However, the U.S. Supreme Court reversed the California decision.

An unusual bond method of financing new school construction is that of the New York Educational Construction Fund, empowered to issue tax-free bonds without referendum for building combined school facilities and income-producing space. The private developer builds a structure containing classrooms, designed by the board of education staff, and other facilities, designed privately, such as stores, offices, apartments, or low-income housing. The rent is used to cover the land costs and payment of interest and principal.

Distribution of Public Revenue: Local, State, and Federal

The bases upon which school funds are distributed are very important. Decisions on the distribution of revenues must be made (1) at the local level with respect to distribution to individual schools within the district and for various purposes within the schools; (2) at the state level with respect to distribution of state funds to local districts; and (3) at the federal level with respect to states and with respect to purposes.

Local Funds. Local and intermediate school units, such as county, township, and city school districts, sponsor many educational projects. The county pays most of the bills for the office of the county superintendent of schools, county libraries, agricultural agents, and certain club activities like the 4-H clubs (see Chapter 4).

Local and intermediate school units promote various types of public education in addition to schooling for children. Among these activities are recreation and other phases of adult education, library and museum facilities, and special projects predicated on local needs, interests, and fiscal abilities. Local school districts supply approximately 50 percent of the revenue for educational purposes (see Chapter 5).

State Equalization Fund. As the term connotes, an equalization fund is intended to equalize educational opportunity and burden. Too often the type and amount of a child's schooling are the result of chance or geography. The child who through the felicity of circumstances lives in a school district that can tax a railroad line or a uranium company enjoys enhanced opportunities for an all-round education. The accidental meanderings of a river often determine the boundaries that demarcate superior and inferior educational opportunities. Unfortunately, in many districts throughout the United States, even when the highest permissible tax rate has been applied to areas of low valuation, the funds secured are insufficient to run the schools. Even if a model tax plan were put into effect, the poorer districts and states would still be unable to support their schools adequately.

Figure 16-7 illustrates a typical state equalization program. The state provides most of the revenue for the education of children in impoverished districts, guaranteeing that children shall not be denied a minimum educational opportunity because they were born in a poor community. Less state aid is provided in districts of average wealth. Wealthy districts often receive no or, at most, little state aid. The justification of providing state aid to districts of average or better ability is that they are given financial leeway and incentive to use local funds to enrich or extend their educational programs beyond the minimum level. The guaranteed minimum expenditure level is regarded as a floor, below which no district may go, rather than as a uniform level for all, or as a ceiling.

The amount of state aid varies widely—from 87 to 8 percent. Nearly all of the states distribute all or part of their state school funds on the basis of an equalization plan. The fifty states use four hundred different plans for distributing state revenues to education. Some of " . . . the formulas for calculating this aid are so complicated that only the experts can understand them."[12] The funds for these equalization plans are derived from statewide sources. Every state needs a program, built upon research and individually patterned, which provides for local initiative and state equalization. This forms the groundwork upon which a federal equalization program may be based. Figure 16-8 reveals the current expenditures by states for public elementary and secondary school students.

[12]James B. Conant, *The Comprehensive High School: A Second Report to Interested Citizens*, McGraw-Hill Book Company, New York, 1967, p. 20.

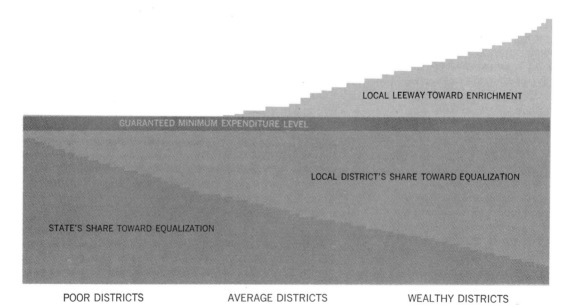

FIGURE 16-7 *State and local support of education. In poor districts, local effort to support schools produces only a small fraction of the cost of a state-guaranteed minimum or foundation program. State support is provided in an amount necessary to meet the equalization level or foundation program. In average districts, the amounts of state and local support are more nearly equal. In wealthy districts, little or no state support is needed, since local wealth is sufficient to reach and often surpass the equalization level. (Adapted from Paul R. Mort and Walter C. Reusser,* Public School Finance, *3d ed., McGraw-Hill Book Company, New York, 1960.)*

Other State Educational Funds. In addition to equalization funds, the states provide many other types of fiscal aid to schools, colleges, and other educational institutions and projects. These include funds for early-education projects; adult education; community services such as public libraries, community centers, and recreational programs; and higher education. As indicated later in this chapter, the states are large contributors to the support of higher education. M. M. Chambers, nationally recognized specialist in the financing of higher education, estimates that appropriations of state tax funds for annual operating expenses of higher education in the United States totaled $7 billion in the 1970–1971 fiscal year. The financing of higher education is discussed in detail in Chapter 9.

Federal Equalization Funds. Education is not primarily a personal benefit, like the sidewalk leading to one's home, nor is it merely a community benefit, like a streetlight. Rather, it is a boon to all. In many ways it is comparable to a city street which is also a state highway and a national route. Both the building and the maintenance of that local-state-national highway are the obligation of all people, not just of those who happen to live near or travel that route. Likewise in the building and maintenance of schools, the local, state, and national interests are merged.

Yet the very schools designed for promoting common local, state, and national welfare may fail in their task. As an illustration, witness the inability of the depressed economic areas and groups to provide proper education for their children from generation to generation. Some school districts have sixty times more wealth per child than others. Some states have a per-capita income two times as great as others. Federal funds that are or may be made available for public education should be so distributed as to guarantee equity and to correct the present glaring inequalities in the use of school funds for children of the different races. According to many fiscal experts, no sound program of local or state taxation can be devised and established which will support in every community a school system that meets minimum acceptable standards. Time can never efface the inequalities in natural resources that exist between states. Therefore, unless the federal government participates increasingly in the financial support of the schools and the related services in the less able areas, several million children in the United States and the outlying terri-

tories and possessions will continue to be denied the educational opportunities that should be regarded as their birthright. Most recommendations and proposals for federal aid stipulate positively that such grants shall not entail federal control over education. Figure 16-8 reveals the great inequalities in per-pupil expenditure among the states.

Federal equalization aid should be provided especially to needy school districts that are unable to reach a satisfactory minimum level after making a genuine effort. This issue and others in federal aid to education are discussed in detail in Chapter 1.

Federal Categorical Aid to Education. Other federally supported educational projects of nationwide and worldwide significance are the various national surveys authorized by Congress and the promotion of democratic educational systems in such countries as Germany, Austria, and Japan following World War II. Congressional grants have financed such outstanding surveys as those of secondary education, teacher education, school finance, higher education, and Negro education. Through such agencies as the Department of State and the Department of Defense, many educational experts from the United States have served as consultants in various countries abroad, and many teachers, students, and other educational personnel from foreign countries have visited and studied in the United States. In Chapter 17 are detailed many of the grants made by the United States to promote international education. As indicated in Chapter 2 and in the historical calendar in this chapter, the federal government has helped finance numerous educational projects in the United States. Their number totals over two hundred programs. Two of the congressional acts that indicate large present and future cash involvements are the Elementary and Secondary Education Act and its amendments, and the permanent GI Bill and its amendments.

Former U.S. Commissioner James E. Allen, Jr., has suggested that federal funds for education be channeled into three areas:

1. **General grants designed to help provide a national minimum level of educational opportunity and to support a broad range of educational activities at all levels**
2. **Categorical aid for special problems**
3. **Research and development of new approaches in education**

Educational research is listed by United States Commissioner of Education Sidney P. Marland as one of the priorities, along with such categorical aids as urban schools and higher education. He is urging "sweeping reform in education" that "will cost billions of dollars." When he was asked to list his top priority, he stated: "Schools must restore public trust in the schools." Public trust in our educational system is a *sine qua non* in obtaining adequate financial support for all facets of American education.

Major Types of Federal Money Legislation. In connection with federal aid to education and other purposes, it is germane to indicate the four major types of federal money legislation:

1) *Authorization bill: authorizes a program, specifies its general aim, and usually puts a ceiling on amount of money to be used in the program;*
2) *Appropriation bill: grants actual monies approved by*
authorization bills, but not necessarily the same amount—usually less;
3) *Continuing appropriation bill: joint resolution enacted when a fiscal year ends and Congress has not acted on regular appropriation bill;*
4) *Supplemental appropriation bill: appropriation designed to cover the difference between an agency's regular appropriation and amount deemed necessary for full fiscal year.*

Also, for programs whose authorization and/or appropriation are still awaiting action, Congress regularly enacts in the last few days of June before the expiration date, a "continuing resolution," which allows programs to go on for a specified time.[13]

Currently, because of the gaps between "authorization" and "appropriation" bills, there are money and time restrictions imposed by Congress. Furthermore, often the President of the United States withholds funds that have been appropriated.

In line with the social revolution occurring in

[13] American Association of School Administrators, *Hot Line*, vol. 2, p. 4, July, 1969.

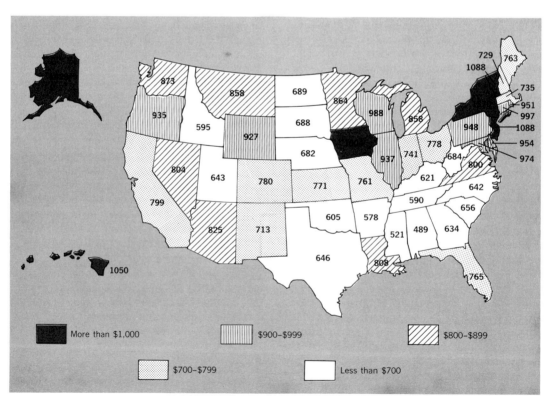

FIGURE 16-8 *Estimated current expenditure by each state for public elementary and secondary schools, per pupil in average daily attendance.* (*National Education Association, Research Division,* Estimates of School Statistics, 1970-71.)

the United States, the federal government also appropriately restricts its giving of educational funds, as indicated in the box below. This restriction appears in most publications of the U.S. Office of Education.

Discrimination prohibited

Title VI of the Civil Rights Act of 1964 states: "No person in the United States shall, on the ground of race, color, or national origin, be excluded from participation in, be denied the benefits of, or be subject to discrimination under any program of activity receiving Federal financial assistance."

PRIVATE FINANCING OF EDUCATION

The broad title of this book, *American Education,* and its contents embrace more than *public* education—*private* education is included as well. Throughout the various chapters reference is made to the important role of private education in the United States. This chapter concludes with a discussion of private financing in education, including the major facets: (1) private and parochial schools, (2) private institutions of higher education, (3) private foundations, (4) corporate enterprise, and (5) miscellaneous gifts.

Private School Support. In the early days of American history, most education was privately financed. Various religious groups started elementary and secondary schools. As state systems of public education became established and as the principle of separation of church and state emerged, most elementary and secondary education became publicly supported. However, the right of parents to send their children to private schools has been upheld by the Supreme Court. Thus private schools have become an accepted and important part of our educational system. The federal government now provides some equipment loans and services to parochial schools. About one-seventh of the elementary school population and one-tenth of the secondary school students in the United States attend private schools.

The combined annual budget of nonpublic elementary and secondary schools is almost $2 billion. Most of this is supplied by tuition from the six million students and their parents. Often the sponsoring

church or organization provides substantial sums. A survey made by the National Association of Independent Schools shows that most of these schools are experiencing financial difficulties.

Many private segregation academies have sprung up. Two factors stimulating the growth and fiscal support of these so-called "white academies" were the U.S. Supreme Court decision of 1954 ruling that racial discrimination in public schools was unconstitutional, and the passage in 1964 of the Civil Rights Bill, including provisions for the withdrawal of federal funds from any school district practicing segregation. The U.S. Supreme Court in 1971 ruled that the allocation of state funds to private schools for operating expenses was unconstitutional. These schools have been further constrained by the decision in 1970 of the Internal Revenue Service to remove the tax-exempt status from segregated schools, which stated: "We feel that a private school that is racially discriminating in its admissions policy is not meeting the broad standards of what is charitable."

So serious is the financial crisis facing the nation's private elementary and secondary schools that in 1970 President Richard M. Nixon appointed a panel of four educators, headed by Clarence Walton, president of Catholic University, to study the national situation and to make recommendations.

Private Higher Education Fiscal Support. Private support for higher education in the United States started with the founding of Harvard College in 1636. During the colonial period nine colleges were established, and all but one of these were sectarian. Today there are over a thousand private colleges and universities in operation. The financial support of higher education is discussed in detail in Chapter 9.

Private Foundation Support. The tax-deductibility of gifts to educational, religious, and numerous charitable causes "has a long and honorable history." The first major philanthropic foundation in the United States, which markedly helped education, was established by George S. Peabody in 1867. The foundation-supported Foundation Center estimates that today there are over twenty-two thousand foundations with resources of over $20 billion. John W. Gardner, former Secretary of Health, Education, and Welfare, who served for ten years as president of Carnegie Corporation, estimates that in a single year all foundation gifts to educational, charitable, and religious organizations approximate $12 billion—although the income of foundations is about 0.5 percent of federal revenue. Ford Foundation alone, as an example, has given over $2 billion to education, culture, and community welfare projects.

American private foundations are supporting education—both private and public—on all academic levels, from such pre-elementary school projects as the television show "Sesame Street" through graduate education. Federal legislation is seeking to restrict their activities and spending and in 1970 placed a federal income tax on the income from the investments of foundations. Furthermore, the threat of "death after forty years" hangs over these foundations. One of the conclusions in the "Educational Endowment Series," published by the Ford Foundation, is: "Anglo-American law has never stood for long in the path of progress, but has accommodated to changing needs. This is and should be its role and function in the field of education."[14]

Corporate Support for Education. Financial support of education, especially higher education, by business firms has increased greatly in the past decade. One major reason is the growth in the number of "matching gifts" programs sponsored by American businesses. Under the plan, when an employee of a participating company sends a gift to his accredited alma mater, or often the college of his choice, the company matches his gift to the institution. The gifts of companies take various forms. For example, many companies have become "adoptive" paying parents of schools or "street academies."

According to the Council for Financial Aid to Education, corporations contributed $375 million in support of higher education in 1969. The Council, a nonprofit research and service organization supported by many companies, stated that while the increase has been substantial, "it has decreased as a share of the total budget for higher education because the financial requirements of our colleges and universities have grown even more rapidly . . . as a result of an explosive growth in enroll-

ment and a sharp increase in costs." Joseph C. Wilson, chairman of Xerox Corporation, has well stated: "The support of higher education by business, regardless of the financial condition of a college or university, is not only inseparable from the future health of free enterprise, but inseparable . . . from the total health of the global society."[15] With more than one and a half million corporations in the United States reaping tangible and intangible dividends through their educated personnel, much more money should be made available to education on all levels by private business.

Miscellaneous Gifts to Education. An indirect annual gift to private schools and universities, as well as public ones, is their tax-exempt status; they do not pay local, state, or federal taxes. Some institutions, however, voluntarily contribute to the city for recognized services. Some school districts receive benefactions through the purchase, by private subdividers, of bonds to help build schools. Numerous other types of gifts, direct and indirect, are made to schools and colleges, both private and public.

In short, as to fiscal support, the once dark and heavy line of demarcation between private and public support is fading. In some states there has been a definite breakthrough for a measure of public financing for private schools. The involved issue of "parochiaid" and the use of "vouchers" are discussed in Chapter 1.

FINANCIAL EFFORT

To meet the goal of quality education for the nation's increasing quantity of learners, greater financial effort must be made by both the private and public sectors of American economy. Currently the United States is spending about 7 percent of its gross national product on education—public and nonpublic institutions at all educational levels. This can and should be increased soon to at least 10 percent. Since Russia, England, and many other nations spend between 5 and 10 percent of their national income for education, this is not an unreasonable expectation in the United States, the cradle of free public education.

However, as the President's Commission on National Goals pointed out, it will be difficult to

[14] William L. Cary and Craig B. Bright, *The Law and the Lore of Endowment Funds,* Ford Foundation, New York, 1969, p. 66.

[15] As quoted in L. L. Golden, "Public Relations: Holding the Line," *Saturday Review,* vol. 52, p. 73, December, 1969.

channel enough of this increased prosperity to schools without increased federal support:

The federal government has been a factor in education for almost all of our national history. But its role is changing—and where the change is taking us no one can say. No one knows how best to design the role of the federal government in education. But one thing is certain: with education playing a vastly more important role in our national life, there is no likelihood that the federal government can escape greater involvement in it. No one need be alarmed at such involvement. Our tradition of local control in education is a healthy one, but we must not let it thwart us in accomplishing important national purposes. . . . Primary responsibility for financing the schools must lie with states and local districts. But it is clear that federal support must be increased, and so designed as to offer minimum interference with state and local autonomy, and not to undermine local incentives to raise money for schools.[16]

The problem of federal aid to education is discussed at length in Chapter 1.

The American people must come to realize that adequate financing of education is not really a levy upon their pocketbooks, but rather an investment in their most priceless resource, young people. It is an investment that pays liberal dividends. As numerous studies have shown, when the level of education is increased, the level of personal and private income is increased far beyond the added costs of education. Thus education improves the people's economic well-being far in excess of its original cost. The countries with the highest standards of living are inevitably the countries with the best educational programs. It is increasingly apparent that sound education is also fundamental to national survival. A nation cannot maintain a sound defense posture in this era of international tension without large numbers of intelligent, well-trained persons in many critical areas of human endeavor.

When a person complains about the costs of education, he should remember other costs which often result largely from poor education: to support a family on relief costs three times as much; to keep a delinquent in a detention home costs $4\frac{1}{2}$ times as much; and to keep a prisoner in jail costs five times as much.

A nation whose real per-capita income, after all taxes, has risen over 60 percent in the last twenty

[16]Report of the President's Commission on National Goals, *Goals for Americans*, pp. 97–98. © 1960 by the American Assembly. Reprinted by permission of Prentice-Hall, Inc., Englewood Cliffs, N.J.

years can hardly be incapable of providing better schools. Clearly the effort that the United States makes to educate its people is not equal to its ability or its needs. Following are three pertinent statements, made by the late President Kennedy, former President Johnson, and President Nixon, respectively:

No task before our nation is more important than expanding and improving the educational opportunities of all our people. . . . We must find the means of financing a seventy-five per cent increase in the total cost of education . . . which must be of the highest quality if our nation is to achieve its highest goals.

The quality and quantity of our educational effort should be stepped up at all levels in an effort to help persons attain the background they need. . . . The nation that has the schools has the future.

When I look at American education I do not see schools, but children, and young men and women—young Americans who deserve the chance to make a life for themselves and ensure the progress of this country. . . . I am establishing a President's Commission on School Finance to help States and communities to analyze the fiscal plight of their public and nonpublic schools.

It is hoped that this President's Commission will help give a sense of direction to the future of educational finance.

FUTURE

The following are some of the many discernible trends in the financing of education in the United States:

1. Education will become an even bigger business than it is today. Education will boom as the "new dynamic of our national economy." The "knowledge industry" will surpass all others in the expenditure of American dollars.

2. Obviously, educational expenditures will increase in size and also in proportion of the gross national product. In 1970 the GNP of the United States reached the unprecedented total of $1 trillion ($1 thousand billion). In the same year the total of public and private expenditure for education was only $70 billion. Former United States Commissioner of Education James Allen, Jr., predicts that the cost of education will total $100 billion by 1980. The proportion of the gross national product that will be devoted to education will increase from the cur-

rent 7 percent to at least 10 percent in this decade. It is hoped that the federal government, as part of the post–Vietnam war "peace dividend" will dedicate a larger share of its revenue to education—both public and private. Charles W. Lee, executive secretary of the Emergency Committee for Full Funding of Educational Programs, has expressed this thought: "Probably in my lifetime, I will live to see the federal share of the educational cost rise from the present level of somewhat under 7 percent to a third or a half of the cost."

3. The Committee for Full Funding has urged that, because of the great disparity between authorizations and appropriations, "Congress appropriate the total amount of funds authorized by all federal legislation." Furthermore, the committee recommends that "all applicable legislation be amended to provide for a minimum of a three-year authorization, with funds to be appropriated one year in advance."

4. Some of the currently scattered federal programs in education will, it is hoped, be more closely aligned with appropriate educational agencies and be better coordinated. Most of the numerous federal programs in education should be consolidated. Furthermore, federal categorical grants ought to be made more flexible. Many national organizations have also suggested that in the future general aid be awarded to colleges and universities instead of present earmarked funds for construction, student aid, and other programs.

5. A current trend is to continue present forms of federal aid to education, with some added amendments and many extensions in time.

6. The demand is increasing for a federal tax credit per student for parents who are paying their children's college expenses. Also there is increasing interest in obtaining federal and state tax deductions for parents who have children in parochial elementary and secondary schools. The prospects for general adoption of the voucher plan, whereby the parent gets a voucher he can use in paying for his child's education at any approved school, are very vigorously promoted by some and contested by others.

7. As a result of the increased fiscal activity of the federal government, the U.S. Office of Education is increasing its role of dispensing educational dollars to states and local communities.

8. In the future, federal and state agencies will make greater efforts to coordinate their appropriations with the fiscal schedules of school districts.

9. The future presages an increased role for the fifty states in providing revenue for education. The Advisory Committee on Intergovernmental Relations, established by Congress to review and make recommendations on allocating functions and revenues among the various levels of government, stated that the time has come to "remove the massive and growing pressures of the school tax on owners of local property." It proposes that the states provide 90 percent or more of the nonfederal share of financing local schools, but that control remain at the local level. The trend is away from the present amounts of property tax, and toward a search for so-called "new revenue."

10. The states will develop better plans for distributing their increased share of support to intermediate and local school districts. Foundation and equalization plans will be open-ended and at a "variable level." These plans will have "built-in flexibility and dynamic equilibrium that will facilitate desirable changes." More states will modify their present state-aid formulas in the direction of the "power equalizing" approach discussed in Chapter 1, a stratagem that sends more aid to poor districts by rewarding local effort rather than local wealth.

11. Local property taxes will produce a smaller proportion of total school revenues as the constitutionality of this tax is increasingly questioned.

12. There is a growing demand that the federal tax-collecting agency return to the states and local districts some funds earmarked either for education or for general state purposes, including education.

13. A fiscal tendency is for the federal government and the states to provide ancillary services, especially for the physically and mentally handicapped and for socially and economically disadvantaged children.

14. Bitter battles for and against "parochiaid" will be fought in this decade with a shift from direct to indirect grants to private schools.

15. The number of Catholic schools and the enrollments will undoubtedly continue to decline, due primarily to financial problems, thus adding additional fiscal burdens for public schools. The U.S. Catholic Conference predicts that two million pupils will be forced to transfer to public schools.

16. Expenditures for school busing will increase materially.

17. As at all academic levels, many more billions of dollars will be needed in higher education. The American Alumni Council has stated prophetically: "No decade in the history of higher education—not even the eventful one just ended, with its meteoric records of growth—has come close to what the seventies are shaping up to be."

18. Billions will be needed to implement the social and economic commitment to universal access to post-secondary education in this decade. For example, the sums needed to implement the recommendation of the Carnegie Commission on Higher Education that 1976 be the target date for the removal of all financial barriers to higher education are staggering.

19. More funds will be needed for student aid. Some institutions will defer full payment of tuition until a decade or more after graduation.

20. More funds will be spent for the education of those at both ends of the age scale: young children in pre-elementary education and adults in continuous learning.

21. More learners and more education mean more manpower in the classroom. Higher standards for the selection and retention of teachers necessitate increased funds for personnel services. Bargaining and negotiating rights for teachers and other educational personnel will lead to more substantial increases in salary, additional fringe benefits, and pensions.

22. Fiscal administrators and governing boards of education will increasingly utilize modern accounting techniques, such as accountability, program-planning budgeting systems, and cost-benefit and cost-effective analyses, to support requests for increased funds with evidence of anticipated benefits.

23. Public performance contracts with private companies for educational services and teaching technology may be mixed blessings.

24. With the increased crises in financing, higher costs of building construction, and more borrowing, the interest on public school debt will rise from 3 cents of every dollar to 4 cents by 1976.

25. Riots and vandalism on school and college campuses may seriously and adversely affect support for education.

26. There will be much more emphasis on public and fiscal publicity in protecting the huge investment in education and in seeking increased public and private support.

27. Fortunately, industry and philanthropic foundations are increasing their private aid to education at all levels.

28. The inflation spiral, unless checked, will continue to cause hardships for learners and headaches for administrators planning budgets for current and capital expenditures for educational institutions.

29. There is a general trend toward making all American citizens more economically literate in regard to educational finance—a long-term investment in democracy for which the people should be willing and able to pay.

SUMMARY

The basic and major principles undergirding the financing of American education may be summarized as follows:

Equality of opportunity for an education, extended to all

Quality of education, sought in the pursuit of excellence

Quantity of education, extended to all Americans from pre-elementary through secondary education, plus at least two years of college for those interested and able

Extra quality and quantity of education provided for disadvantaged children, youths, and adults through compensatory education

Equalization of the burden of support, necessary to finance the desirable quality and the necessary quantity of education

These and other fiscal principles have evolved slowly during more than $3\frac{1}{2}$ centuries of American education. Education in early America was supported largely by private funds. As education became universal and compulsory, it came to be more public in its support and control. However, private elementary and secondary schools and colleges continue to exist and are an important part of the educational system. About one-ninth of the cost of elementary and secondary education and one-half of the cost of higher education are borne privately.

The budget is an important instrument for the planning and control of educational expenditures and receipts. The budget consists of three basic parts: the educational plan, the expenditure plan, and the financial plan. A master plan for budgeting, the planning-programming-budgeting system, is gradually evolving, helping to emphasize accountability in education.

The proportions of local and state support for education vary widely among the states. Most states allocate aid to the districts on the basis of need, providing larger sums for poor districts and smaller amounts for wealthier districts. This is known as "equalization aid," since it guarantees a minimum foundation of expenditures for each district, regardless of its wealth, and at the same time provides financial leeway and incentive for local districts to exceed the foundation level.

Expenditures for education have increased sharply for a number of reasons: increased school enrollments, longer attendance at schools, increased scope and quality of education, and rising costs. Further increases in school expenditures are inevitable. About 7 percent of the gross national product is spent for education. Over the last ten years the rate of increase in educational expenditures has averaged 7.5 percent—an increase twice as great as the GNP's annual growth rate of 3.7 percent. This will be increased in the years ahead to achieve both higher quality and greater quantity of education. It is reasonable to believe that our prospering economy can easily afford this kind of support for education. However, this is not likely to eventuate unless the pattern of educational revenue is revised to capitalize upon the more abundant yield of federal taxes. Recent congressional actions, indicating a trend toward changing the pattern through more federal aid, provide funds for educational television, medical schools, reducing mental retardation, and facilities for public and private colleges and universities, elementary and secondary education, and international education. There is a growing demand for more general aid to education rather than so many categorical grants with restrictions.

A striking trend in educational finance during the last half of the twentieth century has been the increased participation of the federal government. Its fiscal influence extends to all the aspects of American education—both public and private—discussed in this volume. The federal government's support of such a large number of activities raises many issues in American education, some of which are discussed in Chapter 1.

The talented Bach specialist Rosalyn Tureck has said: "In Bach the music came first, then the instrument." The same is true of the dedicated educator: Education comes first, then the instrumentalities that help make education possible. Chapter 15 and this chapter discuss two of the necessary instruments—materiel and money—used in producing the symphonic movement "American Education." This, however, does not become a masterpiece as a national work, but as part of an international symphony. Hence, the next and concluding chapter is entitled "American Education in Today's World."

Suggested Activities

1. Describe briefly the main forms of financial aid available to students in college.

2. Trace the historical development of financial support for education in the United States.

3. Give some of the important court decisions (of both state supreme courts and the United States Supreme Court) that have affected the financing of education.

4. Examine a school budget or an annual financial report and evaluate its contents and format.

5. How are parochial and private schools and colleges supported?

6. Should private industry contribute more money for education? Why?

7. Investigate the role of private philanthropic foundations in private and public education.

8. Indicate the relative importance to education of the following main sources of revenue: local, county, state, federal, and private.

9. Define and illustrate the four main types of federal money legislation: (a) authorization, (b) appropriation, (c) continuing appropriation, and (d) supplemental appropriation.

10. List the titles of the major acts of federal legislation in each of the five levels of education discussed in Chapters 6 to 10, namely: preelementary, elementary, secondary, higher, and adult and continuing education. Describe each act briefly.

Bibliography

American Association of School Administrators: *The Year-round School*, American Association of School Administrators, Washington, D.C., 1970. Exploration of financial savings and other benefits from year-round operation of schools and colleges.

Browder, Lesley (ed.): *Emerging Patterns of Administrative Accountability*, McCutchan Publishing Corporation, Berkeley, Calif., 1971. Series of articles on the economics, politics, and applications of the accountability principle in school management.

Center for the Study of Public Policy: *Education Vouchers: Financing Education by Grants to Parents*, Center for Public Policy, Cambridge, Mass., 1970. Preliminary report on the proposed system of giving parents vouchers to help parents pay for the education of their children.

Hack, Walter G., and Francis O. Woodward: *Economic Dimensions of Public School Finance: Concepts and Cases*, McGraw-Hill Book Company, New York, 1971, part 4. Public finance theory and relationship of federal, state, and local government sources of school finance.

Harris, Seymour (ed.): *Education and Public Policy*, McCutchan Publishing Corporation, Berkeley, Calif., 1969, part iii, chaps. 9–12. Discussions by various authors on educational productivity, economics of schooling, management, planning, and functions of student aid.

Hartley, Harry J.: *Educational Planning-Programming-Budgeting*, Prentice-Hall, Inc., Englewood Cliffs, N.J., 1968. The first book to apply a program-planning budgeting system to educational planning.

Johns, R. L.: *Education in the States: Nationwide Development Since 1900*, National Education Association, Washington, D.C., 1969, chap. 4. Overview of state financing of elementary and secondary education.

Johns, Roe L., and others (eds.): *Economic Factors Affecting the Financing of Education*, National Educational Finance Project, Gainsville, Florida, 1971. A discussion

of the economic basis for school finance by blue-ribbon panel of economists and educationists.

Knezevich, Stephen J., and Glen G. Eye (eds.): *Instructional Technology and the School Administrator*, American Association of School Administrators, Washington, D.C., 1970, chap. 6. Redefinition of education-industry relationships.

Lessinger, Leon M.: *Every Kid a Winner: Accountability in Education*, Simon and Schuster, New York, 1970. An analysis of performance contracting and other means of improving accountability for the performance of children in school.

Machlup, Fritz: *Education and Economic Growth*, University of Nebraska Press, Lincoln, Nebraska, 1971. An analysis of the relationship between education and the economy, with a prediction that teachers may be largely replaced by educational technology.

Muirhead, Peter F.: *How the Office of Education Assists College Students and Colleges*, Government Printing Office, Washington, D.C., 1970. Two kinds of aids administered by the U.S. Office of Education.

National School Public Relations Association: "Catholic Schools Face Crisis," *The Shape of Education for 1970–71*, Washington, D.C., 1970, pp. 24–30. Several leading Catholic educators quoted on the future of Catholic education in America.

——: *Federal Aid: New Directions for Education in 1970–71*, Washington, D.C., 1970. A short, helpful overview of federal legislation affecting education.

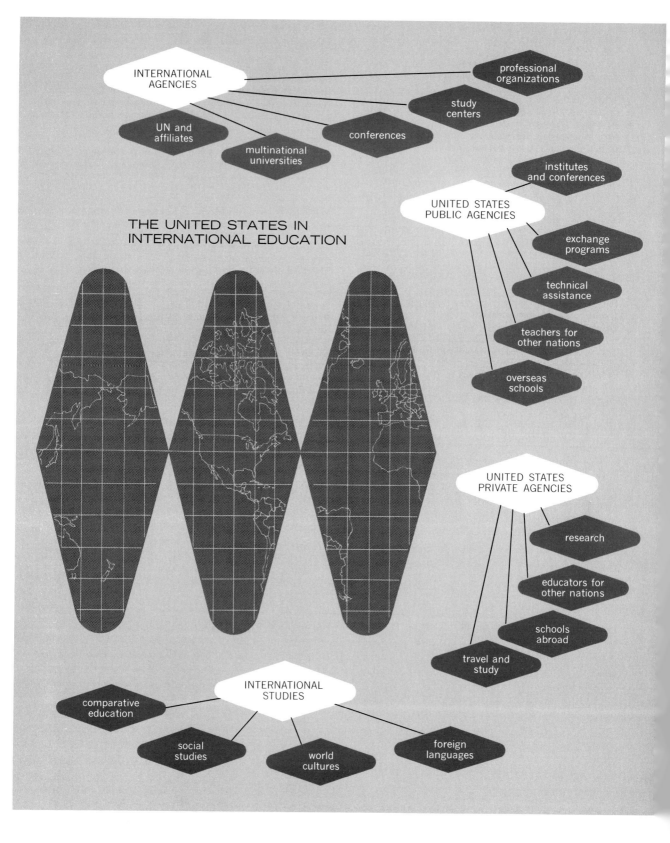

THE UNITED STATES IN
INTERNATIONAL EDUCATION

INTERNATIONAL
AGENCIES

professional
organizations

study
centers

UN and
affiliates

conferences

multinational
universities

UNITED STATES
PUBLIC AGENCIES

institutes
and conferences

exchange
programs

technical
assistance

teachers for
other nations

overseas
schools

UNITED STATES
PRIVATE AGENCIES

research

educators for
other nations

schools
abroad

travel and
study

INTERNATIONAL
STUDIES

comparative
education

social
studies

world
cultures

foreign
languages

Part Six International Education

Today's world is fraught with grave perils—overpopulation, hunger, disease, illiteracy, and wars. But man's faith in education sustains hope for reducing these scourges and drawing mankind together in a universal commonwealth of understanding, peace, and prosperity.

While education in the United States gives priority to the welfare of its own citizens, it also has an international dimension. In today's world, American educators seek to help other peoples in other lands to increase the quantity and enrich the quality of their schooling. American teachers, at home and abroad, are learning how to increase mutual understanding and to strengthen international cooperation in education.

Motivated both by altruism and by national self-interest, the United States along with other nations has developed multifaceted educational programs for implementing its international interests. Numerous programs present themselves to educators everywhere in an age of speed, space, and stress. We can hope that man will come to realize that deeper international understanding and cooperation through education are imperative in his survival.

This last chapter of *American Education* is designed to place our subject in its international setting. Entitled "American Education in Today's World," it is an account of the educational role played by the United States in the modern, worldwide drama of life.

Chapter 17 American Education in Today's World

ORIENTATION

Historians may regard man's journey to the moon as the most fateful event in human history. Man's view of himself and his fellow man has always been shaped powerfully by his view of the world, and the Apollo spacecrafts have fatefully transformed man's conception of the world and his being. Throughout his existence, man has been engaged in a tireless search for what Paul Tillich regarded as his "ultimate concern"—the meaning of life and existence. The dawning of the space age has pushed man's perception into far wider dimensions of time and space in a cosmic content. This cosmic vista may help man escape the petty prejudices and hostilities that have heretofore characterized his geocentric and ethnocentric perspectives.

Consider the reactions of the astronauts themselves to their awesome observations in space. Frank Borman, for example, concluded that "we are one hunk of ground, water, air, and clouds floating around in space. From out there it is really 'one world'." The poet and architect of UNESCO, Archibald MacLeish, viewed the Apollo flights as a hopeful summons "to see ourselves as riders of earth together, brothers on that bright loveliness in the eternal cold—brothers who now know they are truly brothers."

One is reminded of Sir James Barrie's play "The Admirable Crichton," which depicted how shipwrecked persons isolated on a desolate island quickly learned how trivial and senseless were their class and ethnic differences in comparison with their relentless need to cooperate for survival. Through-

out his existence on this planet, man has been beleaguered by his inability to live in peace with his fellow man. Recently he has been forced to question whether he will continue to dominate this planet. He is becoming persuaded that he cannot long survive in a world of ethnocentrism and chauvinism. Consider Neil Armstrong's hopeful comment upon his arrival on the moon: "One small step for a man, one giant leap for mankind." Consider also this penetrating reflection of his crew mate Edwin Aldrin after his return from the Apollo 11 flight:

We've come to the conclusions that this has been far more than three men on a voyage to the moon, more still than the efforts of a government-industry team, more even than the efforts of one nation. We feel that it stands as a symbol of the insatiable curiosity of all mankind to explore the unknown.

We hope that the sanguine views of these cosmic harbingers will help to point man finally toward a global civilization based upon the common needs and aspirations of all mankind in a ubiquitous search for the good life.

Although education is not the remedy for all of the cares of the world, it is unquestionably one of man's most potent assets. But the hour is late and the task is great; nothing short of a maximum effort will relieve what is rapidly becoming a world educational crisis.[1] Although educational systems have been expanding greatly in most countries since the early 1950s, too often the demand has outrun the resources. Even though enrollments are burgeoning (they have doubled in the last two decades in many of the younger nations), the population growth has surpassed the enrollment growth. The frightening dimension of the problem can be seen

---

Educators from many countries are brought together to share their expertise, such as this group on the Michigan State University campus, who are helping to advance educational development in Southeast Asia.

[1] For a fuller discussion of the impending world educational crisis, see Philip H. Coombs, *The World Educational Crisis*, Oxford University Press, New York, 1968.

from several sets of statistics. About two-fifths of the world's children between the ages of 5 and 14 find no schooling available. In the Arab nations and in sub-Sahara Africa, almost two-thirds of school-age young people are unable to attend school. In Asia the percentage of those unable to attend school is close to the international average of 40 percent. Many of these countries are striving to achieve universal primary education by the late 1970s, but progress so far has been disappointing.

Sixty percent of the people in UNESCO member countries are illiterate, and the number of illiterate adults in the world is increasing. Some experts in national development believe that it is hardly possible for a country to sustain substantial industrial growth when more than 40 percent of its adults are illiterate. Figure 17-1 shows the correspondence between the literacy of nations and their economic prosperity.

The crisis in education is abetted more by lack of resources than by lack of effort. In Africa, for example, most countries spend at least 20 percent of their total public expenditures for education; many spend 35 percent, and some spend as much as 40 percent. In many African countries the annual rate of increase in educational expenditures exceeds the rate of growth in national income. These countries, like many countries on other continents, are plagued by a shortage of funds, teachers, classrooms, and materials—shortages of everything except students.

Although the nature of the educational crisis varies among countries in form and magnitude, no nation is spared; the exigency exists in the rich and the poor, the large and the small, the old and the new, the industrial and the agrarian. It is no wonder that educational leaders from fifty-two countries were attracted in 1957 to the International Conference on the World Crisis in Education.

Even more cataclysmic than the crisis in education is the crisis in hunger. Each year the world's growth in population exceeds its growth in food production. Figure 17-2 illustrates this grim statistic. By the end of this century, the world's population will double, but food production will increase least in the nations with the greatest population growth. Thus the disparity between the rich and the poor countries may increase. One authority, Raymond Ewell, a chemical economist, has presented a time-table of what he calls "the greatest catastrophe in history." He warns that the serious famine already

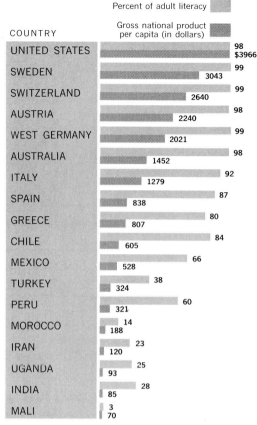

FIGURE 17-1 *Relationship between literacy and per-capita gross national product; percentages of adult literacy and GNP in selected countries, in U.S. dollars. The relationship between the educational level of a nation and its economic prosperity is evident from these data. Many countries are seeking to raise their standards of living primarily by strengthening their educational systems.* (UNESCO Statistical Yearbook, *1967*.)

evident in India, Pakistan, and China may spread to Iran, Turkey, and Egypt by the late 1970s and reach most of Africa, Asia, and Latin America by the 1980s unless present trends are reversed.

United Nations Secretary-General U Thant, in addressing the twenty-fifth anniversary celebration of the United Nations, listed these major problems of the world: the arms race, population growth, poverty, food shortages, urbanization, the squandering of natural resources, environmental pollution, and racism. He asked whether some future universal historian on another planet might say of us: "With all their genius and their skill, they ran out of foresight and air and food and water and ideas," or, "They went on playing politics until their world

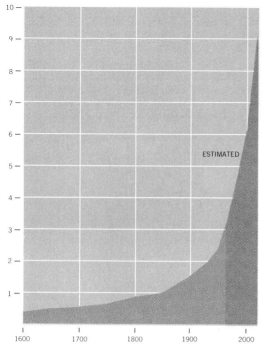

BILLIONS

10 —

9 —

8 —

7 —

6 —

5 —

4 —

3 —

2 —

1 —

ESTIMATED

1600   1700   1800   1900   2000

FIGURE 17-2 World population growth. (*Source of estimates is Herman Kahn and Anthony J. Weiner,* The Year 2000, *The Macmillan Company, New York, 1967, p. 139.*)

collapsed around them," or, "When they looked up, it was already too late."

Surely education alone cannot reverse these dreadful conditions. However, more and better education can help to increase economic productivity and prosperity. Moreover, the birthrate tends to be lower among the better-educated cultures. A prodigious extension and improvement of education around this planet are surely one of the essential forces in the attack on famine and illiteracy.

Clearly the people of the world recognize as never before the need for strengthening the educational enterprise. The demand for education by the common people of all nations has never been so clear or compelling. The fantastic successes in the exploration of space have demonstrated that by concentrating his effort and wisdom man can master some of the most complex and unyielding tasks ever imagined. Many have asked whether the same wit and determination cannot now be applied to the problems of hunger, disease, and ignorance so that man can live in peace with his fellow man and render *this* planet more secure for human existence.

HISTORICAL FOUNDATIONS

The historical calendar on pages 456–457 reveals important events related to the development of international education, which we now consider in its historical perspective.

Early Ideas on International Education

The universities of ancient Greece, where students and teachers from many lands gathered to exchange knowledge, have been regarded as the earliest progenitors of cross-cultural learning. During the Middle Ages, informal intercultural exchanges took place in the great centers of learning in Europe, Asia, and even at Timbuktu in Africa. Great teachers, such as Abelard at the University of Paris, attracted students from many lands. Other great universities, particularly those at Prague, Bologna, and Oxford, attracted many foreign students.

The Moravian educator Johann Amos Comenius might be regarded as the father of modern concepts of international education. A sensitive humanitarian, Comenius sought to end the political and religious wars that beleaguered his times. In the middle of the seventeenth century, Comenius proposed in his masterwork, *A Consultation Concerning the Improvement of Human Affairs*, a College of Light, which would serve as an international academy and office of education. He believed that this international educational enterprise could use the spread of knowledge to see that "no one nation rises against another, and that no man dare to stand up and teach men to fight or to make weapons." He believed man's highest virtue to be "supreme concord and perpetual unanimity for the well-being of the human race; as if they were one heart, or one soul of the world, made up of intellect, will, and executive faculties." The College of Light was likened to the light of wisdom which, like the light of the sun, should spread over all peoples to clarify and purify the whole human race. Comenius believed that universal schools, universal books, and a universal language would be essential to this pan-harmony through which the whole world would be enlightened. In the centuries which followed Comenius's work, Montaigne, Rousseau, Kant, Fichte, and others insisted that international educational cooperation was essential to world peace. In 1967 130 scholars from sixteen countries gathered in

The Development of Participation of the United States in International Education

1643	Establishment of a College of Light to serve as international office of education and universal academy urged by Moravian educator and churchman Comenius		*1908*	China Foundation for Education and Culture established with aid of Congress, bringing three thousand Chinese to American universities
1816	Training begun for officers from foreign countries at the United States Military Academy at West Point		*1910*	Carnegie Endowment for International Peace formed, with primary accent on international education
1840	Library of Congress program initiated for exchanges with foreign countries		*1919*	Institute of International Education established privately, accenting international exchanges
1843	Observations on schools in England, Ireland, Scotland, Germany, Holland, and France published by Horace Mann		*1922*	International conference of scholars and first major international organization to aid educational development in backward countries sponsored by Committee on Intellectual Cooperation
1849	Educational exchange service begun by Smithsonian Institution with similar agencies abroad		*1923*	World Federation of Education Associations formed in San Francisco with aid of National Education Association
1854	Observations on overseas schools published by Henry Barnard in his National Education in Europe		*1925*	International Bureau of Education established in Geneva to publish studies of comparative education, teacher education, and school organization
1899	New approach to cross-cultural education established by Englishman Cecil Rhodes through scholarships to Oxford for students from abroad		*1938*	Division of Cultural Relations established in the Department of State
1901	Mass exportation of teachers started when the first six hundred of thousands of American teachers arrived in Philippines to begin heroic service		*1938*	Convention for the Promotion of Inter-American Cultural Relations ratified (Buenos Aires)
1902	Pan American Union established to strengthen cross-cultural exchange among Western-hemisphere nations		*1941*	Division of Inter-American Educational Relations formed in the U.S. Office of Education
1908	First world center for the exchange of educational information established in Ostend by Belgian educator Edward Peeters		*1946*	United States membership in, and funds for, UNESCO approved
			1946	Fulbright program for international exchanges approved by Congress

1946	World Organization of the Teaching Profession (WOTP) organized with active participation of American educators (WCOTP in 1952)	*1962*	Bureau of International Education in U.S. Office of Education created
1946	Division of International Education, U.S. Office of Education, established	*1962*	New era in international communications and education initiated by the United States' launching of the satellite Telstar
1947	Program launched by the National Education Association to send food, clothing, and books to devastated countries and to bring teachers to the United States for visits	*1962*	The "Teach Corps" of the National Education Association organized for volunteers who serve overseas
1948	Smith-Mundt law for global program in "information and educational exchange" approved by Congress	*1962*	Education and World Affairs established by grants from Ford Foundation and Carnegie Corporation to strengthen performance of American colleges in world affairs
1949	Point Four program of technical assistance to other nations proclaimed by President Truman	*1965*	White House Conference on International Cooperation, including educational exchanges, held as part of worldwide observance of International Cooperation Year
1953	International Council on Education for Teaching started in Oxford by educators of teachers	*1966*	International Education Act approved by Congress, but its fiscal implementation postponed
1956	Comparative Education Society, to study education around the world, organized in the United States	*1968*	Institute of International Studies established by U.S. Office of Education to serve as central clearinghouse for work in intercultural education
1958	Soviet-American Cultural Exchange Agreement, to promote cultural and educational reciprocity, signed	*1968*	Design for strengthening teachers' understanding of international relations presented by The World of the American Teacher
1960	East-West Center established with federal aid at the University of Hawaii, to promote "mutual understanding among the countries of Asia, the Pacific area, and the United States"	*1970*	Four-year polycultural international liberal arts college named after the late Dag Hammarskjold opened at Columbia, Maryland
1961	Agency for International Development (AID), designed to unify and shape aid to other nations, created by Congress	*1970*	International Education Year observed by the United Nations to emphasize educational planning and improvement in developing nations
1961	Peace Corps launched by the United States for sending Americans to work abroad in education and other fields	*1972*	Permanent home for the United Nations International School opened in New York for youths from eighty nations
1961	Previous legislation consolidated by passage of Mutual Educational and Cultural Exchange Act (Fulbright-Hays Act)	*1972*	Proclaimed by UNESCO as International Book Year

Czechoslovakia to consider the applicability of Comenius's teachings to the problems of today.

These views were widely regarded as visionary and utopian at a time when nations were more enchanted by nationalistic "manifest destiny" than by a spirit of internationalism. The legends of King Arthur were more widely read than Comenius's essays, and it was not until well after the Napoleonic Wars that organized international effort in education materialized.

Early Foreign Influences upon American Education

The American nation's early educational heritage stemmed largely from Europe, whence came most of the colonists. The Pilgrims, Puritans, Quakers, Moravians, Huguenots, and other settlers brought with them from the Old World their concepts of education. The kindergarten was imported from Germany. From England came basic ideas of nursery schools, dame schools, writing schools, and Lancastrian schools, which are described in Chapters 6 and 7. The Latin grammar school was molded largely after its European forerunners, and its successor, the high school, was imported from Scotland. Harvard and other early American colleges followed the English collegiate pattern. Many textbooks were imported from England. Educational thought and practice in the young republic were influenced heavily by the writings and teachings of Comenius, Rousseau, Herbart, Froebel, and many others.

Many prominent early Americans traveled widely in Europe and transplanted promising educational practices from abroad. Calvin Stowe, at the request of the Ohio legislature, reported in 1837 on the curriculum and teaching methods of elementary schools in Europe. His reports were widely published and influenced educational thought in this country. Horace Mann was impressed by pedagogical practices and teacher-training programs which he observed in Europe, particularly in Germany; he helped to implement many of these practices upon his return through the reports he published in 1843. Henry Barnard's book *Pestalozzi and Pestalozzianism* was influential in infusing the great Swiss educator's educational thought into the stream of American education. Barnard also interpreted Froebel's educational ideas to the American people.

Barnard's other accounts of European educational practice are contained in his *First Annual Report to the Connecticut Board of Education*, published in 1839, and his *National Education in Europe*, a few years later, both of which were widely read. Benjamin Franklin's design of the first academy in this country was undoubtedly influenced by his travels and observations abroad. Among other prominent Americans who helped broadcast European educational thought to the new land were John Adams, Thomas Jefferson, and John Jay.

Beginning of International Educational Organizations

The late nineteenth century marked the beginning of organized international conferences on education. In 1851 representatives from Germany, England, France, and the United States met in London to exchange knowledge about education. In 1876 United States Commissioner of Education John Eaton presented a plan for a permanent international educational agency at the International Conference on Education held at Philadelphia. In 1880 representatives from many nations at the International Conference on Primary Education in Brussels approved a plan for a world council on education. Eleven years later, Herman Molkenboer, a Dutch lawyer, published an imaginative plan for disseminating educational information, which was later broadened to include an international council of education as a vehicle for promoting world peace. Molkenboer believed that nations could not live together peacefully until teachers were prepared to teach world understanding. Although a great many individuals joined Molkenboer's movement, it received little support from governments and eventually collapsed.

The American School Peace League was organized in 1908 as part of an international affiliation to promote through the schools the causes of international peace, the arbitration of national disputes, the elimination of racial injustices, and a more rational and humane national life and patriotism.

In the same year, a Belgian educator, Edward Peeters, created a world center for educational information at Ostend, thereby bringing to fruition the dreams of Jullien and Molkenboer. The center suffered from lack of financial support and eventually became a casualty of World War I. However, it did serve as a prototype for the International Bureau of Education, which was formed by an international group of educators at Geneva in 1925. The Bureau has published studies of comparative education, organization of national programs of education, the preparation of teachers, and various other aspects of education. Its annual conferences are now sponsored jointly with UNESCO. The United States did not officially join the Bureau until 1958.

An enterprising American educator, Fannie Fern Andrews, was the leading figure in one of the most ambitious international educational conferences conceived in the early twentieth century. Long devoted to the promotion of world peace through education, she worked tirelessly to gain the official support of governments and teachers' groups for an international council on education. Delayed by government indecision, the planning conference could not be held on the eve of the outbreak of World War I. Following the war, the partisans of international education saw in the League of Nations a new opportunity to create an international educational agency as a component of the League. Fannie Fern Andrews and her associates argued that it was important to teach young people around the world about the League of Nations and that mankind could be rescued from war only through universal schooling in the democratic ideal. Unfortunately the League was preoccupied with other problems and these efforts were futile.

Beginning of International Educational Cooperation

The twentieth century ushered in a new phase of international educational cooperation in education. Heretofore activity had been confined largely to international conferences and exchanges of educational materials. The new period quickened the exchange of educators and students and put international teams of educators to work strengthening schools in backward countries.

Cecil Rhodes, an Englishman, established in 1899 a new approach to cross-cultural education by providing scholarships at Oxford University for students from other lands. Many distinguished Americans, including Supreme Court Justice Byron White, were beneficiaries of this largess and thereby helped to deepen man's understanding of his fellow man. By the middle of the century the United States was providing scholarships for students from other lands through the provisions of the Fulbright and Smith-Mundt Acts. Some other nations have made similar contributions.

In 1901 a wonderful but unheralded event ushered in an important new development in international cooperation in education. Six hundred American schoolteachers sailed across the Pacific to become volunteer teachers in the newly occupied islands of the Philippines. Followed eventually by thousands more, they lived in modest Filipino homes, helped to construct the schools in which they would teach, and assumed many responsibilities in building the nation that took them far beyond the classrooms. Twenty-seven of them died during the first two years from the rigors of primitive life. Some of them died forty years later from the hardships of the occupation of the Philippines by the Japanese during World War II. They came, not in search of wealth and fame, but only to help a willing and deserving people find their destiny as a free and literate nation. This mass exportation of American teachers, a forerunner of the modern Peace Corps, was surely one of the most remarkable efforts ever undertaken in the realm of international cooperation in educational development. It permitted Gen. Carlos Romulo, Ambassador of the Philippines to the United States, to comment that "the American schoolteachers joined with us in creating the literacy, the knowledge, the self-confidence and the devotion to democracy on which it was possible for us to establish our Republic."

In 1922 the Committee on Intellectual Cooperation was established under the leadership of such famous scholars as Eve Curie and Albert Einstein. Among other enterprises, the Committee in 1931 marshaled resources from several cooperating nations to aid in the reconstruction of China's educational system, thereby establishing the precedent of multilateral cooperation in improving educational opportunity in underdeveloped countries.

In the early decades of this century, the United States cooperated with other nations of the Western Hemisphere in many multilateral educational endeavors. This nation participated actively in the affairs of the Pan American Union, established in Washington in 1902. The Union has been active in educational and cultural exchanges among the nations of this hemisphere. The first International Conference of the American States was held in Washington in 1910. The United States participated in the Convention for the Promotion of Inter-American Cultural Relations in Buenos Aires in 1938.

To strengthen our participation in cross-cultural

cooperation, the Division of Cultural Relations was established in the Department of State in 1938, and two years later the Division of Inter-American Educational Relations was established in the U.S. Office of Education.

Private organizations joined in the effort to mobilize American know-how in the improvement of educational systems around the world and to deepen international understanding. The Institute of International Education was established in 1919 to supply information, counsel, and direct help to universities and to exchange students, both those going abroad and those coming to this country. Four years later, the International Institute was established at Teachers College, Columbia University, a mecca for thousands of students and teachers from overseas and a catalytic agent accelerating educational improvement in countless countries. Many other private and public organizations, including missionaries of many faiths, have undertaken various kinds of educational programs designed to promote literacy, health, and other manifestations of the good life around the world.

Era of Accelerated Technical Assistance

During and following World War II, millions of American servicemen, government officials, and businessmen were thrust, for the first time in their lives, into foreign cultures and forced to come to grips with the task of building postwar understandings and relationships that would repair the ravages of war and hopefully strengthen world peace. These Americans abroad had relatively little knowledge of the non-Western world. Few spoke or read Urdu, Swahili, or Hindi.

By 1945 the United States looked out upon a world in social, political, and economic turmoil. Like it or not, this nation was thrust into a role of international leadership at a critical time in history characterized by cold-war cleavages between the bloc of communist nations and the democracies of the West. Education, at this juncture of history, was seen by the United States as an instrument of foreign policy in strengthening democracy in its fateful struggle with communism for world domination. Several widely read books, Conant's *Education in a Divided World*, Bush's *Modern Arms and Free Men*, and Rickover's *Education and Freedom*, all published within four years of the close of World War II, advanced the stern admonition that a strong educational system was the prime weapon in our free society's struggle with Communism. Americans sought not only to strengthen their domestic educational system but also to help democracy in friendly countries through the exportation of educational know-how. Thus during the cold war much of the United States' educational activity abroad consisted of technical assistance programs and scholarly exchange programs as instruments of foreign policy.

The inauguration of the Marshall Plan in 1948 provided economic aid and technical assistance for the rebuilding of war-ravaged nations and their school systems. The Point Four program, begun in 1950, continued technical assistance for many purposes, including education, and was later embraced in 1961 by the Agency for International Development (AID), described in more detail later. The Alliance for Progress, initiated in 1961 to aid in the economic, social, and cultural progress of countries in the Western hemisphere, included assistance for educational development. One of our domestic educational developments of this period, the National Defense Education Act of 1958, illustrated by its title this same concept of shoring up our national defense through education. Other significant programs of this era of technical assistance are noted in the historical calendar.

Some observers have characterized this period as an age of "cultural imperialism" in which the prime motivation was that of assuring that other governments might be fit to survive by making allies of them through education for democracy. Such motivation was not surprising at a time when one of the political leaders of the communist bloc declared that he planned to bury the United States and its democratic allies. Certainly not all of the educational enterprises of this period were motivated by "cultural imperialism." Many exchanges of students, teachers, and materials were genuinely altruistic in character, motivated largely by a spirit of global understanding which became a more propulsive purpose of international education in the 1960s and 1970s.

Era of Global Civilization

By the 1960s there was a growing conviction that the concept of education as a vehicle for national defense through "cultural imperialism" was obsolete. The new thrust in international education was new, not because it never existed before, but because it had changed in emphasis and quality. Comenius and others had dreamed of the new emphasis for centuries. Significant transformations were taking place in the world order that demanded revision of the mission of international education.

Slowly but inexorably during the 1960s man was coming to realize that the most compelling characteristic of the modern world is not its great unrest, although that is most visible, but the increasing interpenetration of the destinies of peoples and nations throughout this shrinking globe. As noted under *Orientation* in this chapter, it was now possible to see ourselves and our world through the astronauts' cameras as "riders of the earth together . . . brothers who now know they are really brothers." A new "one-world" outlook was emerging in both astronomical and ideological perspectives. Religion and secular beliefs were finding new accommodation to each other through the worldwide ecumenical movement which emphasized, as Pope John put it in *Pacem in Terris*, the "common good of the entire human family."

The proliferation of nations with nuclear power capability, along with the fantastic development of weapon-carrying missiles and satellites, helped man realize that without international cooperation he was quite capable of destroying life on this planet. Vietnam helped to convince him that war no longer served as a means of resolving problems among nations. As President Kennedy warned, "Mankind must put an end to war, or war will put an end to mankind."

On the political scene the power struggle between the democratic and communist blocs of nations was being leavened by the breakup of both blocs. The disaffection of youth around the world with chauvinism helped to accelerate the détente. The great problems of the world—poverty, malnutrition, apartheid, population explosion, and illiteracy, among others—were seen increasingly as urgent challenges to all mankind rather than as Soviet-American issues.

We have spoken of these forces because they may augur an era in history which, it can be hoped, will forge a nobler view and destiny for international education. Harold Taylor, in his book *The World and the American Teacher*, speaks of this new era and its impact upon international education:

In the most optimistic reading of contemporary history, we could now say that we have reached a stage at which

it had become necessary for the educated man to extend the dimension of his loyalty to the entire human race, and that the conception of education itself must be one which locates man intellectually in a universe described by scientists, artists, and writers, and in a cultural setting as big as the globe. To enjoy any longer the luxury of defining one's nation, one's society, or oneself in terms of pride of ancestry, social superiority, or power of destruction is not only supremely dangerous to the survival of the race, but intellectually and socially obsolete. . . . It is now the task of education, on a world scale, to put together the scattered fragments of the world's knowledge of itself in a form which can become the basis for a new kind of education in human affairs.[2]

The new argument for international education is based upon reaching common understanding among cultures and upon narrowing the gap between the have and the have-not nations—not for purposes of imperialism but rather as a means of bringing greater vitality, happiness, and freedom to all people. It is far too early to forecast the success of this spirit in international education but not too early to proclaim an avid hope that it will contribute to the United Nations' goal of "promoting social progress and better standards of life in larger freedom."

PURPOSES

For several compelling reasons, it is easy to make a case for increased emphasis upon and improved quality of American education in its international context. The reasons are related to three broad purposes:

1. **The survival of man**
2. **The improvement of the human condition in less favored communities**
3. **The cultural enrichment of man**

Indeed one might argue that the three reasons are reciprocal and inseparable. Nevertheless for purposes of discussion we shall deal with each separately.

The Survival of Man

Comenius understood centuries ago the importance of education in ameliorating international conflict.

[2]Harold Taylor, *The World and the American Teacher*, American Association of Colleges for Teacher Education, Washington, D.C., 1968, pp. 15–16.

The challenge is infinitely more fateful in the modern world than it was in Comenius's time. The world has shrunk to a point where no place on earth is more than half a day away by air. Communications satellites make it possible for much of the world to view on television, while it is happening, an event halfway around the world. As miracles of modern transportation, communication, and commerce have contracted our planet, man has become increasingly dependent upon his fellow men around the world. Isolationism is no longer an option in the modern world. For example, a new political regime in Cuba can alter the political power structure throughout the Western hemisphere and can trigger reverberations in Moscow and Washington. Civil War in Vietnam or Korea can claim the lives of thousands of American youths and prompt repercussions in Washington, Moscow, and Peking. A war in the Middle East can threaten the rich oil fields and bring the industrial might of European countries to a halt. Sensors in orbiting satellites provide an entirely new strategy for monitoring the military capabilities of other nations and prompt a whole new system of military intelligence. A book on prerevolutionary Russia can put the theme song from the movie *Doctor Zhivago* on the hit parade of countries around the world. A new fashion on Carnaby Street can change the length of hemlines in Albuquerque, Capetown, Oslo, Buenos Aires, and Tokyo. The horrendous holocaust of nuclear explosion can quicken man's determination to find an alternative to war in solving his international problems. There are many irreducible interlockings in man's affairs that require him to become more world-minded if he is to have a future on this rapidly shrinking planet.

Improvement of the Human Condition in Less-favored Communities

Man has long been motivated by altruism in his international endeavor, even though not all his overseas enterprise has been altruistic. For centuries men and women have left their homelands to teach and to minister in other ways to less privileged persons abroad, in an effort to reduce ignorance, poverty, illness, and hatred. This purpose is certainly one of the oldest in the history of international education. In the absence of all other reasons, it would be sufficient to justify vast effort abroad.

Thousands of overseas missionaries from America and other lands of many denominations and faiths—Catholic, Jewish, and Protestant—are assigned to educational work around the world. These dedicated teachers toil long hours at low salaries in all types of educational work from nursery through higher and adult education. They teach by precept and example in theological seminaries, synagogues, church schools, agricultural colleges, medical schools, teachers colleges, liberal arts colleges, and individualized programs such as the ashrama of India. These dedicated teachers, imbued with the twin ideals of service to God and man, believe earnestly in the fatherhood of God and the brotherhood of man. They seek religiously to implement the two great commandments: "Thou shalt love the Lord, thy God," and "Thou shalt love thy neighbor as thyself."

The United States fulfills a strong economic role in supporting international understanding among children, youth, and adults. For example, the United States contributes almost 40 percent of the budget for the United Nations Children's Fund (UNICEF), which was awarded the 1965 Nobel Peace Prize. Children cannot study on empty stomachs. Hence the Food for Peace program is directly related to education. Nor can children and youths learn well without books. The Book Brigade, formed by the Agency for International Development (AID), the National Academy of Sciences, and United States book publishers, supplies millions of books for learners overseas. The altruistic American citizen manifests, though inadequately, a belief in the scriptural injunction: "For unto whomsoever much is given, of him shall much be required" (Luke 12:48).

Mention has been made of the thousands of American teachers who taught in the Philippines during the first half of this century. The Peace Corps was prompted by man's motivation to help the underprivileged. Many educational consultants work abroad each year, often at considerable personal sacrifice, because they sense an obligation to be their "brother's keeper" until he is capable of keeping himself.

In a sense, this purpose is closely related to the first, the survival of mankind. Sargent Shriver, the first director of the Peace Corps, noted this relationship.

We know that the world can not be divided between the well-fed and the hungry, between the educated and the ignorant. Such an imbalance would threaten us even if there were no cold war. We can not solve this imbalance merely with grants of money or with propaganda. We have to solve it with people. The time has come in history for us to share our wealth in educated people as well as in material might.[3]

People who are ill-fed, poorly-housed, and under-educated are unable to join the family of man and thereby enjoy the blessings of economic prosperity and social equality. Disadvantaged and disenchanted, they understandably turn to violence at times as their only means of attaining the necessities of life. Wherever we can roll back the darkness of ignorance, despair, poverty, and disease, we not only extend the prosperity and freedom of other people but buttress our own freedom and security as well.

There is a destiny that makes us brothers;
None goes his way alone;
All that we send into the lives of others
Comes back into our own.

                 —*Edwin Markham*

Man's Cultural Enrichment

Consider how barren our own culture would be without the heritage of other civilizations—the works of Shakespeare, the artistry of Michelangelo, the educational thought of Pestalozzi, the inheritance of Roman and English law, the philosophy of Confucius, the social-action concepts of Gandhi, the art forms of Africa, the healing genius of Pasteur, the astronomy of Copernicus, the psychological insights of Freud, and the religious teachings of Jesus of Nazareth. Much of the progress in the exploration of space is attributable to the genius of scientists from abroad. No field of knowledge is indigenous to America, and few if any fields of knowledge are untouched by the scholarship of all nations.

A less-evident advantage of assisting other nations' educational development accrues from the insight which Americans gain into their own problems by studying similar problems abroad. For example, as the need for the use of the English language spread around the world immediately after the war, American resources were deployed to

[3] R. Sargent Shriver, "Address," *Your AASA in 1962,* American Association of School Administrators, Washington, D.C., 1962, pp. 34–35.

Education is enriched by cross-cultural contributions. Here Vinh Bang, a Vietnamese psychologist, works on an intelligence test for young children based upon the research of the Swiss psychologist Jean Piaget, who looks on with approval.

improve English-language teaching abroad. The linguistically oriented teaching techniques developed during the war for teaching unfamiliar languages were applied directly to this new task. This experience forced American educators to reexamine the pedagogy of teaching second languages and resulted in improved teaching method in foreign languages in schools and universities at home. Thus by learning how to teach the English language to non-English-speaking people, American educators became able to improve the teaching of other languages to Americans, as well as the teaching of English to Cuban refugees, Puerto Rican immigrants, Mexican-Americans, and American Indians.

Another illustration can be drawn from the field of economic development. As American economists, anthropologists, educators, political scientists, and other specialists have tackled the problems of rescuing impoverished people in poorly developed countries, they have learned to understand poverty better and to cope more effectively with the problems of poverty at home. Education may be the only asset that can be exported while enriching rather than depleting a nation's resources. Thus we may regard international educational exchange as a modern-day example of the Biblical parable about casting bread upon the water and getting it back a hundredfold. Some of the issues inherent in the purposes of international education are discussed in Chapter 1.

NATURE AND SCOPE

A half-century ago, H. G. Wells warned that human history becomes more and more a race between education and catastrophe. As noted later, some men have for centuries viewed education as man's best hope for improving the human condition on this planet. The particular kind of education most related to this task is commonly referred to as "international education." This term embraces many meanings and many different types of activities. It includes (1) the study of other people and other lands, as in elementary, secondary, and higher education courses in history, geography, foreign languages, literature, or world cultures; (2) particularly at the college level, interdisciplinary study of international relations, world affairs, foreign policy, or, more specifically, the problems of hunger, poverty, war, and illiteracy around the globe; and (3) comparative and cross-cultural study in academic disciplines and professional fields, such as anthropology, art, music, linguistics, education, medicine, political science, and many others. These are the major categories in the realm of *study* in international education. Let us consider briefly several categories in the realm of *activity* in international education. These activities include (1) programs of international cooperation in educational development and scholarly exchange, such as the work of UNESCO and the Alliance for Progress; (2) the exchange of students and teachers among countries for learning and instruction abroad, such as the Peace Corps, the Rhodes Scholars, or the Experiment in International Living; and (3) technical assistance to the development of education in other countries through foreign aid programs, such as the United States Agency for International Development or the Ford Foundation's support of library development in Asian, African, and South American countries. All these types of international education and their contribution toward man's quest in his "ultimate concern" will be examined in greater detail in the pages which follow.

PROGRAMS OF INTERNATIONAL ORIGIN

The United States participates in almost countless international education programs at home and abroad. We shall consider first some of the more important programs which are of international origin and which are sustained by multilateral support and organization.

United Nations and Related Programs

In 1945 the United States, along with fifty other nations, signed the Charter of the United Nations. The Charter is a document of such vision that every prospective and practicing teacher may wish to study it. The Preamble opens thus:

We the Peoples of the United Nations Determined
    To save succeeding generations from the scourge of war, which twice in our lifetime has brought untold sorrow to mankind, and
    To reaffirm faith in fundamental rights, in the dignity and worth of the human person, in the equal rights of men and women and of the nations large and small, and
    To establish conditions under which justice and respect for the obligations arising from treaties and other sources of international law can be maintained, and
    To promote social progress and better standards of life in larger freedom. . . .

Today the United States is linked with 126 nations in implementing the Charter of this organization, dedicated to peace.

UNESCO. The main avenue of the UN for training and educating human beings in new and old countries is the United Nations Educational, Scientific, and Cultural Organization (UNESCO), founded in 1945. UNESCO is one of the specialized agencies provided in the Charter of the United Nations and affiliated with the Economic and Social Council. UNESCO's mission is expressed in the following statement from the Preamble of its Constitution:

The Governments of the States Parties to This Constitution, on Behalf of Their Peoples, Declare
    that since wars begin in the minds of men, it is in the minds of men that the defenses of peace must be constructed . . .
    that the wide diffusion of culture, and the education of humanity for justice and liberty and peace are indispensable to the dignity of man and constitute a sacred duty which all the nations must fulfill in a spirit of mutual assistance and concern.

The statement reads almost like a passage from Comenius.

Alexander Meiklejohn said of the organization:

"Its aim is the development of that international intelligence upon which the success of any United Nations activity depends."

Official approval by the United States came in July, 1946, when both houses of Congress passed a joint resolution providing for the membership and participation of the United States in UNESCO and authorizing an appropriation. In signing the joint resolution, President Harry S Truman said:

The government of the United States will work with and through UNESCO to the end that the minds of all people may be freed from ignorance, prejudice, suspicion, and fear and that men may be educated for justice, liberty, and peace.

Technical and financial aid continues to large-scale regional programs in Asia, Africa, and Latin America. Among the many projects receiving the special attention of educators and others are those involving the creation of new teachers colleges and technical schools in underdeveloped countries and the strengthening of existing ones; the preparation of world-history textbooks; the elimination of world-wide illiteracy; the promotion of East-West cultural appreciation; the improvement of libraries, museums, and information centers; and the improvement of Latin-American education.[4]

A significant UNESCO development was the establishment in 1963 of the International Institute of Educational Planning, located in Paris. Created with financial aid from the Ford Foundation, the Institute "helps member states of UNESCO create sound, workable plans for developing their educational systems." Two of the major activities center around the development of research and the training of teachers in international education.

The United Nations General Assembly designated 1970, the three-hundredth anniversary of Comenius's death, as International Education Year in commemoration of UNESCO's massive $17 million drive to help developing countries improve their educational systems. During the International Education Year, nations were encouraged to take stock of their educational needs, undertake studies related to the improvement of education, strive to improve the financial support of education, strive for the

[4] A helpful chronology of UNESCO activities during its first twenty years is found in "Chronology, UNESCO: 1946-1966," *School and Society*, vol. 94, pp. 425-430, November, 1966. The entire special issue is devoted to UNESCO.

elimination of all forms of discrimination and inequality of treatment in their schools, and heighten international awareness of students.

UNESCO activities are reported in its various publications. The best known of these is the *UNESCO Courier*, which reaches a million and a half persons in more than 120 countries. A third of its subscribers are teachers.

United Nations International School. One of the interesting and significant facets of the educational program of the UN is its United Nations International School (UNIS) in New York City for the children of UN personnel. This school, in which many tongues are spoken, occupied a new $10 million building in 1972, made possible largely through the philanthropy of the Ford Foundation. UN Secretary-General U Thant sees UNIS as an "experiment in cultural understanding."

UNICEF. The United Nations Children's Fund was organized originally in 1946 as the United Nations International Children's Emergency Fund (UNICEF) to furnish food, clothing, and medical supplies to children in war-ravaged countries. Supported entirely by voluntary contributions from governments and individuals (almost 40 percent from the United States), UNICEF is currently helping children in more than a hundred countries, mainly in the developing areas of the world. UNICEF projects now include maternal- and child-welfare services and training, child nutrition, and control of disease. The United States Committee for UNICEF, a private, nonprofit organization set up to promote knowledge and support for UNICEF, has provided a wide variety of materials for teaching both adults and children about international cooperation.

In addition to cooperating in special schools and in UNESCO programs, the United States participates in many other educational or semieducational activities through the UN.

World Bank. The International Bank for Reconstruction and Development, which is commonly known as the "World Bank" and is located in Washington, is a specialized agency of the United Nations. It has a membership of more than eighty nations. In a major policy change announced in 1968, the World Bank directed much greater financial support to education, agriculture, and family planning—the tasks which are most directly antidotal to what we noted earlier as "the greatest catastrophe in history." In recent years the World Bank has become an increasingly important agency in the realm of international education.

International Peace Corps Secretariat

The Peace Corps, established by the United States in 1961, assumed international dimension a year later with the inauguration of the International Peace Corps Secretariat. Since its beginning, the International Peace Corps Secretariat has helped more than a dozen nations in beginning their own Peace Corps programs for service abroad. In 1970, without a dissenting vote, the UN Economic and Social Council recommended the establishment of a world Peace Corps under the jurisdiction of the UN.

Institute of International Education

The Institute of International Education, a private, nonprofit organization founded in 1919, develops and administers programs of educational exchange for students, teachers, and educational specialists among the United States and more than eighty other countries. It acts as a clearinghouse for all aspects of international education, working closely with governments, foundations, universities, corporations, private organizations, and individuals. It publishes the *Handbook on International Study for Foreign Nationals* and the *Handbook on International Study for U.S. Nationals*, which contain useful information on opportunities for foreign study, grants available, regulations, and other information of use to the student abroad. Its annual report, *Open Doors*, provides statistics on international educational exchange activities. Its headquarters building at the United Nations Plaza in New York has been a mecca for thousands of arriving and departing educators from many lands.

International Centers

A number of international centers have been established at various locations around the globe to bring persons together for the advancement of specified sectors of education. Among them is the University of Geneva International Center for Genetic Epistemology, which provides facilities where interdisciplinary teams can work together for protracted periods of time on specific problems of mental development of children under the guidance of the Swiss child psychologist Jean Piaget. The Universities Service Center established at Hong Kong in 1963, with the financial support of three United States philanthropic foundations, provides assistance and facilities for scholars of Chinese studies. Many other centers for international study, such as the East-West Center at the University of Hawaii, are located on the campuses of the major universities and colleges of the world. They serve as meccas for students and teachers from many other lands interested in acquiring the specialized knowledge accumulated in these centers.

International Professional Organizations and Conferences

The number of international professional organizations and conferences on education are legion. By far the largest is the World Confederation of Organizations of the Teaching Profession, which numbers 151 constituent teacher organizations from ninety-five countries, with a total membership representation of approximately five million teachers around the world. Its annual Assembly of Delegates brings together approximately five hundred leaders of teachers' organizations to come to grips with an agenda that covers a wide range of educational problems. Phi Delta Kappa International, an honorary fraternity for men in education, has members on all continents. Many international organizations of teachers exist in the several subject fields and teaching specializations, such as the International Reading Association, the International Graphic Arts Education Association, the International Childhood Education Association, and the International Council on Education for Teaching (ICET).

Many international conferences on education are held annually dealing with a wide variety of topics, as suggested by the following sample list: International Conference on the World Crisis in Education, International Conference on Human Skills, International Education and Teacher Education Conference, and International Moral Education Conference.

REGIONAL PROGRAMS

Many cooperative programs in international education are focused upon the needs of specific regions of the world. Several of these programs are considered briefly here for illustrative purposes. Many more could be cited. Some of the programs are supported by public funds, some by private funds, and many by combinations of public and private moneys.

Alliance for Progress

The Alliance for Progress was inaugurated in 1961 to accelerate the cultural, economic, social, and political development of nations in the Western Hemisphere. Much of the effort of this publicly financed enterprise has been directed toward education, with noteworthy results. In approximately a decade, it had helped to reduce the number of adult illiterates in Latin-American countries and had raised the school attendance of children of primary school age from 49 to 56 percent.

One of its major projects, backed by the United States Agency for International Development, has been the development of fine-quality, low-cost Spanish-language textbooks adapted to the needs and interests of nearly a million primary school students. The long-term goal of this project is to develop textbook authorship, production, and distribution capability among Latin-American countries so that they need no longer depend upon a limited supply of textbooks imported from other countries.

Afro-Anglo-American Program in Teacher Education

The Afro-Anglo-American Program in Teacher Education was begun in 1960 under the joint enterprise of Teachers College, Columbia University, and the Institute of Education of the University of London, with financial support from the Carnegie Corporation, for the purpose of preparing educators to teach in African secondary schools and teacher-training institutions. Africa, like many parts of the world, is hampered by a dearth of qualified teachers, particularly in its secondary schools. The immediate goal of the A-A-A Program is to prepare American and British teachers for interim service in Africa. Within its first decade of existence, the project had recruited and trained nearly a thousand teachers and

had helped to train an additional 1,400 Peace Corps teachers for service in nine African countries. The program's long-term goal is to strengthen African countries' teacher-training capability to meet their own needs. Toward this end, the Carnegie Corporation has made several million dollars available to African institutes of education. Some of the money is used to finance study by African teachers of American and British teaching. The program was conceived and guided by Karl Bigelow of Teachers College, Columbia University, an eminent authority on African culture and education. The A-A-A Program stands as a paragon of how educators of vision in both industrialized and underdeveloped nations can join hands across the seas to share in man's march toward a better destiny through education.

UNITED STATES PROGRAMS

We turn our attention now to the wide variety of undertakings in intercultural education which have arisen under the aegis of the United States in cooperation with other countries. These programs may be categorized as those supported by (1) federal, state, and local governments; (2) private organizations; (3) schools and colleges; and (4) individuals. Some of the more important undertakings in each of these categories are described.

Federal, State, and Local Government Programs

U.S. Office of Education Programs. The Office of Education of the Department of Health, Education, and Welfare considers international education an integral part of its mission of strengthening American education at all levels. One of its best-known, oldest, and most extensive enterprises is the exchange program administered by the Institute of International Studies. Conceived by Senator William Fulbright in 1946 and modified in 1961 by the Mutual Educational and Cultural Exchange Act (popularly known as the "Fulbright-Hays Act") and subsequent legislation, this program supports three major types of enterprises: university lecturing and research abroad by American nationals, undergraduate and graduate study and research abroad by American nationals, and exchanges of American and foreign elementary and secondary school teachers. More than 150,000 American teachers and students have received grants to teach and study abroad, usually in non-Western countries, to gather materials that will be useful in curriculum development at home in such fields as foreign languages, world cultures, political science, international relations, anthropology, and sociology. They return with deeper knowledge and understanding of the language, geography, history, and culture of the country visited, which permits them to broaden and enrich their teaching at home. In many cases their positions at home are filled during their absence by teachers whom they replace abroad. Exchange teachers are chosen for posts abroad through national competition.

The Office of Education also helps develop curriculum materials about foreign countries for all school levels, helps other federal government and state government agencies internationalize their staffs for more effective service, sponsors comparative studies of educational systems in foreign countries, provides direct services to American educators and to educators from abroad who are studying in the United States, and serves as a general resource for American academic, civic, and business enterprises.[5] These and other functions are discharged by the Office of Education's Institute of International Studies established in 1968 to achieve the following goals:

Communicate the concept that the national interest in education includes an international dimension

Increase our knowledge of the world and its people

Infuse an appropriate international dimension throughout the domestic educational program

Stimulate or support research and development projects designed to improve methods and materials for international education

Educate more specialists for international studies and services

Promote international study and cooperation

Peace Corps. One of the most interesting and effective international programs of the United States is the Peace Corps, which was established by Congress at the request of President Kennedy in 1961.

[5] For a more detailed discussion of the U.S. Office of Education's work in international education, see Robert Leestma, "OE's Institute of International Studies," *American Education*, vol. 5, pp. 5–8, May, 1969.

In signing the measure giving the Peace Corps permanent status, President Kennedy said it would "assist other nations toward their legitimate goals of freedom and opportunity." The purpose of the organization, as indicated by its name, is to advance peace through a corps of United States citizens who serve as volunteers overseas. In 1971 the Peace Corps was merged with other federal volunteer programs into a new agency called "Action."

The Peace Corps is a modern governmental application of the old ideals of service and sacrifice overseas, which have been promoted by nongovernmental missionary organizations and other volunteer groups since the founding of the United States as a new nation. The sixty foreign countries to which Peace Corps members are sent are primarily newly independent nations.

The recruitment of members for the Peace Corps in recent years has been handled almost entirely through returned volunteers, who annually visit 1,000 colleges and universities.

There is a demand from numerous nations around the world for Peace Corps volunteers. Why this demand? Former Director Shriver replied:

The fact is that new nations of the world realize that to unlock their own resources and to bring their own societies into the twentieth century, they must have education. They know that in a democratic society, as Horace Mann said, education must be open to all.[6]

More than half the volunteers have served in the Peace Corps as teachers, and half of these had had no previous teaching experience. Among the thousands of members currently serving overseas, the largest single profession represented is teaching.

What can be said of the Peace Corps' accomplishment? One criterion of the success of the Peace Corps is the testimony of the returned volunteers. Generally they feel that in addition to having rendered tangible service, they personally have gained much from the experience, especially in terms of increased understanding of other cultures and peoples.

Peace Corps alumni are much sought after. As additional inducements to attract returned teachers to their staffs, many school systems count the years in the Peace Corps toward advancement on the salary schedule and for retirement credit. Many colleges and universities in the United States have

[6] Shriver, *op. cit.*, p. 34.

granted returnees substantial scholarships for advanced study.

Clearly the Peace Corps has done much to quicken man's quest for the good life in many countries and has deepened American understanding of other cultures. On the other hand, the vaunted independence of the Peace Corps has sometimes resulted in its failure to relate effectively to American and other national programs abroad. Also, most of the Peace Corps volunteers are young, and national pride has sometimes been hurt by the efforts of such young Americans to "educate the natives," often without adequate coordination with local development plans. Some of the volunteers have been inadequately trained for their difficult assignments. These and other problems have prompted a modification of the Peace Corps in its mission to come to grips more effectively with the major problems of nation building. Joseph Blatchford, the third director of the Peace Corps, has insisted that the Peace Corps "is in puberty" and that it should start looking for more mature, more highly skilled people to help in development.

Perhaps the greatest testimony to the success of the Peace Corps has been the dissemination of the idea in other countries, as noted earlier. Some of these countries are participating in the Volunteers to America program by sending their corpsmen to the United States as teachers, social workers, community development aides, and a variety of other occupations. Truly these volunteers from other lands, like their American counterparts, are ambassadors of goodwill and understanding, demonstrating again the reciprocity which is endemic in most efforts of intercultural enterprise.

International Education Act. As part of the program during International Cooperation Year (ICY-1965), the White House Conference on International Cooperation, including educational exchanges, was held in Washington. A task force prepared proposals for new and increased programs for American participation in international education. These and other proposals were included by President Johnson in his presentation to Congress of the International Education Act of 1966, which he said was designed "to rid mankind of the slavery of ignorance." Its four purposes are as follows:

1. **To strengthen American capacity for international educational cooperation**

2. **To stimulate exchange of students and teachers with other lands**
3. **To assist the progress of education in developing nations**
4. **To build new bridges of international understanding**

Unfortunately the act has not been adequately funded by the Congress, and its potential has been greater than its accomplishment.

Other Activities of the Federal Government. Many other branches of the federal government are also active in intercultural development. The Agency for International Development (AID) in the Department of State administers many activities that relate to educational development including the provision of model textbook depository libraries in other countries, the sharing of educational materials abroad, technical assistance in the improvement of national school systems, and various seminars, workshops, conferences, and other means of intellectual exchange. The United States Information Agency provides publications, films, broadcasts, telecasts, and other media of education in many stations abroad to help other people learn more about our culture. The United States Travel Service in the Department of Commerce provides many visitors from abroad with the information about this country which they need to plan their visits. The Smithsonian Institution and the Library of Congress exchange educational materials with other nations. Many other activities of the national government in intercultural education could be cited.

State and Local Government Programs. Several state and local educational agencies have undertaken programs in intercultural education. For example, the New York State Department of Education established the Educational Resources Center in India's capital city of New Delhi to develop better human and material resources for studying about India in American schools, as well as to strengthen channels of intellectual and cultural communication between India and the United States. The Center makes curricular materials on Indian life available to American schools, provides a convenient depository for research material for use by foreign and domestic scholars of Indian culture, and holds workshops and seminars for educators interested in deepening their knowledge of India.

Many local intercultural programs exist on college and university campuses and will be described later. Some local public school systems are also strengthening their international interest through the School-to-School Program sponsored jointly by the American Association of School Administrators and the U.S. Office of Overseas Schools. In this program, American and foreign school systems are paired so that they may share curriculum materials and establish exchanges of students and teachers. The Association for the Advancement of International Education was formed in 1966 from an alliance of domestic and foreign school administrators associated with the School-to-School Program.

Private Organizations

Education and World Affairs. Founded in 1962, Education and World Affairs is a private educational organization funded in part by the Ford Foundation and the Carnegie Corporation of New York. Its primary mission is to strengthen the performance of American higher educational institutions in world affairs by teaching Americans about other cultures, conducting research, exchanging personnel, and cooperating with educational institutions and efforts abroad. The organization's major activities include consultation and participation in international education policy making with pronouncements on important issues; careful studies of key issues in international education; standing committees and regional councils on educational cooperation with countries in selected regions of the world; problem-oriented conferences with American and foreign representatives; consultation with American colleges on the improvement of their international education programs; and the dissemination of important information relevant to the development of international education. Its studies and reports have had great influence upon the organization of the Office of Education in relation to its work in international education and upon the shaping of the International Education Act. It draws upon the expert knowledge and experience of some of the most eminent American and foreign authorities in international education. Its publications are widely read and are very influential in shaping educational thought in the international dimension.

Professional Organizations. The Committee on International Relations of the National Education Association publishes instructional materials related to intercultural understanding, plans tours and provides hospitality for foreign educators visiting the United States, provides a clearinghouse service for teachers requesting information on international education, services requests on educational matters from the various embassies in Washington, and compiles information on teaching positions abroad for United States teachers. It also distributes teaching materials on UN Day, Pan-American Union Day, Refugee Year, and other events of international significance. Many local citizens' groups, such as the International Group of Memphis and the Pittsburgh Council for International Visitors, provide hospitality, plan tours, tutor visitors in English, and plan programs for foreign visitors to their cities.

The NEA's Overseas Teacher Corporation recruits many unpaid volunteers who conduct classes, workshops, and seminars abroad each year. The National Catholic Education Association, the National Council for the Social Studies, the American Council on Education, the American Association of Colleges for Teacher Education, Phi Delta Kappa, and other national professional organizations maintain active committees on international education.[7]

Private Foundations. Many American foundations have long been active in the support and encouragement of intercultural education. The Carnegie Corporation of New York, founded in 1911 as an educational foundation, has provided funds for several noteworthy enterprises, such as the Institute of International Education, mentioned earlier, the Russian Research Center at Harvard, the Commonwealth Studies Center at Duke University, and the Afro-Anglo-American Program to Train Teachers for Africa.

The Ford Foundation, founded in 1936 by Henry Ford, has provided grants for: international-studies programs at Harvard University, Columbia University, Duke University, Northwestern University, Notre Dame University, University of Denver, and other institutions; the retraining of faculty members in world affairs in more than a hundred colleges;

[7] For a more detailed account of the international activities of various professional associations, see H. Kenneth Barker, "International Education and the Professional Associations," *Phi Delta Kappan*, vol. 51, pp. 244-246, January, 1970.

the support of the Center for Applied Linguistics, which has become a major force in language teaching; the Salzburg Seminar in American Studies; the strengthening of American studies through the American Council of Learned Societies; libraries in countries abroad; scholarships for foreign study for Americans as well as persons from abroad; the construction of the United Nations International School; and many other enterprises in intercultural education.

Numerous other foundations, such as Kellogg, Guggenheim, Kettering, and Pearl S. Buck, have contributed financial support to various programs in international education.

Other Private Organizations. Volumes might be required to record fully the good works of all private organizations in the United States which contribute to the fulfillment of America's philanthropy for educational development abroad. We can consider here only a few which are illustrative.

The Franklin Books Program, composed of public-spirited American educators, businessmen, librarians, and publishers, strengthens book-publishing capacity, book-distribution systems, and libraries in the developing nations of Asia, Africa, and South America. Foster Parents Plan channels financial support and gifts from individual Americans to needy families abroad and permits many children to remain in school who would otherwise have to go to work to help support their families. The English-speaking Union, upon learning that the inability to buy school books prevented 77 percent of the primary school pupils in Pakistan from continuing their education, provided thousands of basic secondary school textbooks for Pakistan and subsequently other countries.

Many local civic organizations, such as Kiwanis, Rotary, and Lions, have sent educational materials abroad and have sponsored a great many of the thousands of people who participate annually in the Experiment in International Living. This enterprise was begun in 1932 by a small group who sought to bring people from many countries together in each other's communities and homes as a means of strengthening intercultural understanding. This paraeducational organization arranges home stays for approximately 4,500 people annually from more than forty-five countries on six continents.

These examples are only a few of American society's far-flung efforts to quicken the interaction

of our people with their fellow men from other lands and thereby to improve the human condition at home and abroad.

Schools and Colleges

International Schools and Colleges. As we have seen, man's dream of a truly international college dates back at least to the time of Comenius. Although multicultural schools and colleges have existed for some time in many places, the truly prototypical international college did not emerge until the last decade. After a successful experimental summer program in 1963, with a student body drawn from twenty-two United Nations countries, the Friends World College was inaugurated at Huntington, New York, in 1965. The Friends World College was conceived and pioneered largely through the efforts of its first president, Harold Taylor. The college is designed to have seven campuses in seven countries. Each student begins his studies at his home campus and spends a semester on each of the other campuses, returning to his home campus to consolidate and evaluate in a thesis his experiences of the four years. The curriculum of the Friends World College emerges from the creative talent of students and faculty from around the world. It is international in the sense that it uses the ideas and points of view of every nation represented to come to grips with the problems of world society.

A four-year international liberal arts college named for Dag Hammarskjold, the late Secretary-General of the United Nations, recently opened its doors to students and faculty from many countries of the world on its campus at Columbia, Maryland. The president and chief organizer of this polycultural college, Robert L. McCan, emphasizes that the college is guided by three simple but fundamental principles: we live in a global village; reason requires that we learn to deal more effectively with rapid cultural changes; and higher education can be made more relevant to our world situation. Most of the students of the college spend their middle two years traveling and engaging in practical work experience in preparation for a vocation.

The Foreign Study League, founded in 1964, is a private educational institution which helps young American students attend summer schools abroad.

Most of its clientele are young people between the ages of 15 and 19. It commonly enrolls approximately seven thousand students annually.

Other international colleges outside the United States include Tagore's Santiniketan, Moscow's Friendship University, and the Experimental College at Copenhagen.

Many people believe that the dream of a world university in the true sense has not yet been realized. Many scholars are still seeking such an ideal. In 1969 two hundred representatives of fifty-one countries met at the University of Vienna for a conference on the university's role in the quest for peace. The urgency facing man in his drive for survival and his hope for future generations was expressed. The proposal receiving the most support was the plan for a world university. The world-university idea was endorsed by U Thant in his 1969 report to the United Nations, and he asked that UNESCO study the feasibility of such a university.

International Programs in American Higher Education. Volumes have been written describing the wide range of college and university effort in international education.[8] We shall describe them briefly here and cite a few varied examples.

Virtually every major American university and many colleges offer programs in comparative education, conduct research on various cultures of the globe, establish special programs for students from other lands as well as programs of study abroad for their own students, and conduct service projects abroad. Stanford University, for example, offers several area-studies programs—East Asia, Latin America, Africa, and Western Europe—through which the cultures of these areas of the world are researched intensively and taught to graduate and undergraduate students interested in majoring in these fields. The University of Wisconsin's Office of International Studies and Programs regards its campus as the world, hardly an idle boast on a campus that houses Ibero-American, Brazilian, Latin-American, African, Russian, Indian, East Asian, Scandinavian, Hebrew, Arabic, and other area studies programs. Michigan State University engages in an ambitious program of service, teaching, and

[8]See, for example, Education and World Affairs, *The University Looks Abroad*, Walker and Company, New York, 1965.

research around the world. The East-West Center at the University of Hawaii capitalizes upon the fiftieth state's strategic position, bridging Oriental and Occidental cultures both ethnically and geographically, to deepen the interaction and understanding of peoples from the Eastern and Western worlds.

One of the most interesting and novel enterprises in international education was inaugurated by Chapman College. Its "World Campus Afloat," housed on the *S. S. Ryndam*, has been embarking for years with five hundred American college students and a staff of fifty for a 111-day voyage to ports in Europe, Africa, and South America. The ship is converted each school season to accommodate a library, student union, theater, classrooms, and other school facilities. Regular courses in the humanities, natural sciences, and social studies are conducted on board, combining book learning with firsthand experience in observing foreign cultures at its many ports of call.

This international thrust by our colleges and universities is not entirely new, but since World War II it has greatly expanded in volume and broadened in purpose. Higher education has long been interested in studying other people but until recently only as a matter of academic curiosity. Now the land-grant college concept of providing teaching, research, and service to the local or state community has been expanded to include the world community. In the entire educational enterprise, few sectors have expanded as significantly as the international dimension of our colleges and universities.[9]

Overseas Schools. The United States maintains approximately 130 overseas schools in eighty countries abroad. Approximately half of their enrollment consists of children of American military and civilian families living abroad; the other half consists of native students from the host countries and their neighbors. Administered through the Office of Overseas Schools in the Department of State, these schools are staffed by both American and foreign educators. Local citizens serve with Americans on more than half of the schools' governing boards. Most of the schools offer courses of study in local language and culture. These schools are visited

[9]For a discussion of the problems of the international enterprise of higher education, see Edward W. Weidner, "U.S. Institutional Programs in International Education," *Phi Delta Kappan*, vol. 51, pp. 239–243, January, 1970.

frequently by native educators as demonstration centers for American educational practice.

Two interesting examples of overseas schools are located in the Lebanese capital city of Beirut. The century-old American University of Beirut is a mecca for students from the Middle East and other countries who are interested in the American model of higher education. Its sister institution, International College, founded in 1881, expanded in 1971 with the creation of a new $4 million community college on a site commanding a magnificent view of the Mediterranean. The new community college was conceived and funded through ten years of campaigning by International College's American president, Thomas Schuller. It serves many Lebanese students who are more interested in practical studies related to the everyday problems of Lebanese life than in the narrow, classical curriculums of the French models, which prevail in other colleges of Lebanon.

One United States ambassador observed that "the United States is doing more good, generating more goodwill, for less money, through the programs of these schools than through any other program I know of." These overseas schools offer a splendid but largely untapped resource for extending the international education for larger numbers of American teachers. A plan for achieving this goal has been developed by the Office of Overseas Schools, the Kettering Foundation, and the State University of New York.

American church boards help to staff and finance, for missionary children and others, many schools such as the Woodstock School in India and Robert College in Turkey. The United States cooperates in establishing American schools in such international centers as Brussels, Copenhagen, Geneva, Rome, and Vienna. These schools provide education for children of many nationalities. Through associations such as the International Schools Service, the administrators, teachers, and parents share ideas and techniques for increasing the effectiveness of this instrument of international education. A syndicate has been formed by the International Schools of Geneva, Switzerland, and the International Schools Association, which represents schools on four continents and which has official status with UNESCO. As more Americans travel and live abroad, these overseas schools attended by American children and others will increase their cooperative efforts, their numbers, and their prestige.

Curriculums in American Schools. The role of American education in today's world is determined, in large measure, by the curriculums of its institutions. The curriculum of the American school is discussed at length in Chapter 14. The discussion here will be confined to a few major aspects of the curriculum most closely related to international education.

Although nearly all the academic disciplines provide latent opportunity for deepening the student's understanding of other people, social studies, the humanities, and foreign languages can be most rewarding if they are well taught and addressed particularly to the goal of cross-cultural understanding. This international emphasis should pervade the learning experiences of students from pre-elementary education through the graduate school. Ralph Bunche, American Undersecretary for the United Nations, grandson of a slave and holder of the Nobel Peace Prize, has stated:

We are today in an international age in which understanding and cooperation among states are the only roads to survival. . . . Our education, I think, should be geared much more to the world, to the future, than it is and with much broader perspective than it now knows.

As Harold Taylor points out in *The World and the American Teacher,* American schools suffer severely from an ethnocentric curriculum largely because the teachers themselves are not well educated in the international realm. Until recently at least, relatively little instructional material has been drawn from other cultures with the exceptions of history, geography, foreign languages, literature, art, and music. Even in these fields the emphasis has been upon Western civilization almost to the exclusion of other cultures. The study of social, economic, and political geography merits at least as much attention as physical geography, which has predominated in the schools. More attention should be devoted to cultural anthropology, social psychology, and intergroup relations, particularly at the secondary and collegiate levels. Instruction in history and other social science courses should develop an appreciation for the great values inherent in the heritage of the democratic way of life and should also face forthrightly the tragic shortcomings of the nation in extending its goals to all the people. The narrow focus of social studies upon Western cultures is being redressed in high schools and colleges with the introduction of African studies. Offerings in Asian and African languages are being increased. Schools are belatedly helping students realize that not all great literature, lovely art, splendid music, or scholarly thought has been produced by Western cultures.

The secondary school curriculums are offering more subjects prefaced by the word and concept of "world"—world history, world geography, world economics, world affairs, world religions, world "isms," world cultures, and world literature.

The colleges, too, are being challenged by worldwide concerns. Many institutions of higher learning have broadened their curriculums to strengthen the student's understanding of the world scene through courses in communication, foreign languages, anthropology, and international relations and through comparative courses in fields such as law, political systems, cultures, and education. Many provide opportunities for overseas study and service.

The study of education in other countries is generally called "comparative education." Educators around the world have long been interested in comparing their own national system of education with those of other countries. Comparative education, long one of the lacunae in teacher education in the United States, has leaped to prominence in recent years. A group of educators organized the Comparative Education Society in 1956 in order to focus attention on this important facet of international understanding. Many universities now offer courses in this field; some have overseas travel seminars that permit administrators, teachers, and students to observe at first hand the educational programs of other lands, and to study these programs directly.

U Thant, Secretary-General of the United Nations and a former teacher and headmaster, has stressed the importance of teachers in strengthening international cooperation:

Better understanding, which is the business of teachers, may not automatically solve world problems, but it will certainly help with many of them. . . . One of the most important tasks of the teacher, as I understand it, is to bring to clear consciousness the common ideals for which men should live. These common ideals have a force that unites. They may prove more lasting than current conflicts; they may prove the agent for resolving or outgrowing some of these conflicts.

In the minds of many thoughtful citizens, the major challenge confronting all education is this problem of building world peace. The task is compelling, and the stakes involve the very existence of human civilization. Perhaps we can take heart from Edmund Muskie's assurance: "I think people like to be summoned to greatness."

Individual Enterprise

Notwithstanding the many organized programs in the realm of international education, the scope and importance of individual initiative in extending cross-cultural education should not be overlooked. Perhaps the most important manifestation of individual enterprise is found in the exchange of students and teachers. Over 100,000 foreign students study in the United States each year. One-fourth of the world's students studying outside their own countries are enrolled in the United States. (Perhaps this indicates that American education is not as bad as some of its critics contend.) Approximately half of these students come to American schools and colleges on their own resources without benefit of fellowships or other grants. More than twenty thousand American students are in full-time study programs abroad each year. Figure 17-3 shows the percentages of foreign students enrolled in the main fields of study here and the percentage of American students studying in the same fields abroad. These figures include only individuals who are engaged in regular academic work at institutions of higher learning. They do not include thousands of teachers and students who go abroad each year to attend summer programs or study tours.

This two-way educational traffic between the United States and many countries of the world is a phenomenon that has arisen largely since World War II. This interchange is prompted by several forces: the desire of individual students and teachers to enrich their understanding of other civilizations; the need of developing countries to look to other countries to train their teachers, businessmen, physicians, engineers, scientists, lawyers, and other professionals; and the need of both American and foreign institutions to seek intellectual breadth and cultural enrichment for their own benefit.

The Junior Year Abroad (JYA) has become a tradition at a number of American universities. Yale has initiated a program in which juniors spend a year abroad, not for academic study but to live and work in unfamiliar cultures in African, Asian, or Latin-

American countries. Stanford has established its own campuses in France, Italy, Germany, Japan, and Taiwan for its students' use abroad.[10]

High school students too are increasingly engaged in study abroad. The first and largest program of exchange of high school students is sponsored by the American Field Service, which arranges for nearly three thousand high school student exchanges annually.

There is good reason to believe that exchanges have a salubrious effect not only upon the exchange student but also upon the host school.

[10] Readers interested in gaining further information about enrolling in study programs abroad are referred to *Handbook on International Study: For U.S. Nationals*, Institute of International Education, New York, 1972; John A. Garraty, Walter Adams, and Cyril J. H. Taylor, *A New Guide to Study Abroad*, Harper & Row, Publishers, Incorporated, New York, 1969.

In addition to the thousands of students, research scholars, teachers, professors, and lay leaders in education, there are other thousands of Americans who go abroad annually. International travel is good per se, especially for students and teachers, but travel accompanied by serious study is better. However, the best teaching-learning situation is found by those Americans who implement cultural empathy by working directly with their overseas peers to promote the commonwealth of humanity.

Another tangible type of exchange is that involving material. This includes one-way, two-way, and multilateral exchanges of equipment and/or information in its various forms. In addition to the more costly reciprocal exchange of personnel is the less expensive and more voluminous program of

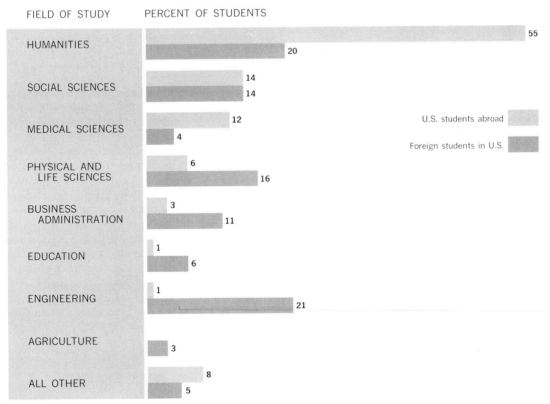

FIGURE 17-3 *What exchange students study. Studies pursued by students abroad reflect the national needs, the priorities, and the social and economic development of their nations. Foreign students in the United States enroll for instruction in education, medicine, and science in larger proportions than American students abroad do. On the other hand, American students abroad in lands with older cultures enroll in far greater proportion for instruction in the humanities and the arts.*

Travel abroad provides rich opportunity for students to deepen their understanding of other people and cultures.

interchanging apparatus, publications, periodicals, letters, postage stamps, and coins.

Books are a common medium of educational exchange. Millions of books have been donated by Americans to overseas schools, colleges, and communities. In some war-devastated countries, the intellectual sustenance of books has replaced CARE packages of food. Orientation kits have often been sent overseas for visitors coming to these shores, and many more packages are needed for those not coming to this country. Students and teachers in the United States need overseas books, especially about art, music, social studies, and languages.

Some of the major issues inherent in educational exchange programs are discussed more fully in Chapter 1.

PROBLEMS

International education, not unlike other forms of education, is beleaguered by many problems. Some of these problems pose serious ideological issues, which are discussed in more detail in Chapter 1.

Conflict between Nationalism and Internationalism

Perhaps the prime ideological deterrent to strong effort in international education is the fierce sense of national pride and loyalty which prompts wariness in some people against any internationalization of public institutions, particularly the schools which deal with young citizens, whom we often over-protect.

Many proponents of international education believe that the conflict between nationalism and internationalism is spurious, that these loyalties to both the nation and the world are additive rather than antagonistic. They hold that the national interest is inextricably related to the world interest and that ethnocentric education is neither in the national interest nor in the world interest. Nevertheless the quarrel rages. It is discussed at greater length in Chapter 1.

Intercultural Differences

International education development is handicapped by great cultural and language differences among nations. Different countries in various stages of development require different priorities in educational development. Different mores require different styles of pedagogy. It is not uncommon to find young students in Africa studying from English or French or Belgian books, which have little relevance and meaning to their own cultures. In some cases, these young nations have inherited colonial school systems based upon an elitist educational system modeled after the former colonial power. Obviously this type of system has little meaning in a country trying to raise itself by its bootstraps. In some countries the first priority should be the extension of basic literacy; in others, fairly sophisticated vocational and technical education attuned to an industrial society should be a more immediate priority. Educational consultants from abroad, Peace Corpsmen, and exchange teachers sometimes have difficulty sorting out the educational aims, values, and traditions which are unworkable in different countries. Many transplanted educational practices which were successful at home have failed abroad because cultural differences have not been considered. Much more research and experience is needed before man can master the task of sharing and modifying his educational know-how effectively in other civilizations.

Inertia in Educational Change

Many scholars have called attention to the slow tempo of change in man's social enterprises, particularly his schools. This reluctance to change educational practice is common to both the new and the old, the rich and the poor nations. Many developing countries are in a great hurry to improve the human condition but must reckon with school systems inherited from former colonial powers. Very often they face a serious disparity between their educational output and their developmental needs. Frequently their colleges produce an abundance of arts graduates and lawyers but a serious undersupply of teachers, scientists, engineers, and other technically trained persons. Many of their curriculums place too much emphasis upon classical education and too little upon the practical needs of everyday life. In some cases great expansion has taken place in primary and higher education, while secondary education has been neglected. A recent UNESCO study concluded that rigid graded organization, unsound promotion practices, poor teaching, and irrelevant curriculum content resulted in excessive wastage in schools. Then, too, the goals of the educational system are often out of phase with the goals of economic and social development.

However, the picture is not entirely bleak. Much more careful educational planning is now taking place in many individual countries, quickened in part by UNESCO and particularly by the International Institute for Educational Planning. Also, the tempo of change is accelerated by the interchange of students and teachers, which is rapidly expanding.

Underfinancing

International education, like all facets of education in most countries, suffers from inadequate financing. Not only are most national school systems underfinanced, but most international education programs also suffer from lack of sufficient funds. A tragic example of this is the United States' inexcusable delay in financing promptly and adequately the International Education Act of 1966. Brilliant and unselfish in concept, this act was never fully implemented with financial resources, and its promise still far outweighs its achievement. This false economy was matched in the early 1970s by Congress's cutback in appropriations even for such well-established international programs as the Fulbright Act and the National Defense Education Act. The benefits of international education are not very evident to the average citizen, and when aroused over domestic problems, he is disposed to retreat into national and academic isolationism.[11] As the International Conference on the World Crisis in

[11] For further discussion of this tragic circumstance, see James M. Davis, "The U.S. Government and International Education: A Doomed Program?" *Phi Delta Kappan*, vol. 51, pp. 235-238, January, 1970.

Education pointed out, there is a real crisis in education's ability to match performance with expectations. The conference noted a worldwide disparity between the hopes of individuals and the needs of society, on the one hand, and the capabilities of the educational systems, on the other. Cruel financial constraints have forced both the developed and the developing countries to turn inward and become preoccupied with internal priorities. Each country of the world has periodically experienced a shortage of buildings, teachers, and instructional materials. Most countries need more money, and, except for the most affluent, an increase in funds will be hard to obtain because education has in many countries already acquired a preemptive share of national income. The only solution for many nations lies in increased financial help from the more prosperous countries.

Shortage of Teachers

One of the most serious handicaps in educational development, both national and international, is the tragic shortage of teachers in many countries. According to conservative estimates by UNESCO, seventy million additional elementary school teachers will be needed throughout the world during the next decade. Present institutions are geared to turn out less than one-third that number in more than three decades. Although modest improvements are being made, it is evident from these statistics that there is no hope of meeting the need adequately; however, the condition may improve. Teachers are the most expensive and the most crucial input in any educational system. Thus the severe imbalance between the demand for and the supply of teachers lies at the heart of the educational crisis.

Educational technology may provide some relief. American Samoa, for example, when faced with a serious teacher shortage, inaugurated a national program of educational television which spread the output of a limited supply of teachers to many more students through the cathode tube. As enrollments in colleges grow, education will be able to claim a larger share of the output for its own needs. But even the most optimistic assessment must conclude that the shortage of teachers will seriously constrain educational development for decades to come in many countries. There is no easy solution to the problem as long as birthrates climb at nearly astronomical rates.

Inadequate Preparation of Teachers

Education for international understanding is further handicapped by the shortage of teachers who are prepared to teach intercultural and international understanding. This is the essential thesis of Harold Taylor's provocative report, *The World and the American Teacher*. Although his work deals with American teachers, his findings would undoubtedly apply to most other countries. Themselves the victims of ethnocentric educational systems, most teachers lack the understanding of other cultures and the personal contact with other peoples to permit effective instruction in intercultural education. Taylor recommends that teacher and student-teacher exchanges be vastly expanded, that the campus for teacher education be thought of as the world, that international study programs on our own campuses be greatly expanded, that components of teacher education be built into existing international educational organizations such as the overseas schools, that more students from other cultures be recruited to teach in American schools, that Peace Corps service be included as a regular component of teacher preparation, and that regional centers be established in various parts of the world for research and study of educational problems. Teachers of all nations need intercultural understanding.

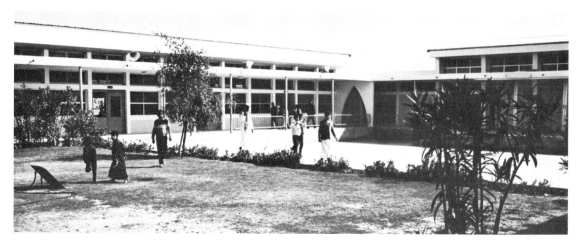

Here is one of many examples of American industry's philanthropy abroad: the Arabian American Oil Company built and turned over to the national school system of Saudi Arabia forty-five schools, such as the one pictured here, for the education of native children and the children of the company's employees, in a country where education is as valuable as oil.

Expectations Too Great

Finally there is the problem of unrealistic expectations of education in relieving the great problems of the world. Without disparaging the tremendous potential of education for improving the human condition, it is nevertheless clear that education alone is not the cure, just as it is not the cause, of many of the great problems of the world. Even if it were, the resources presently available cannot accommodate the greatly accelerated burden of education. As noted earlier, the hopes of the people around the world for a better life, particularly a better life for their children, have been quickened extraordinarily within the past decade. Most people see better education as the prime vehicle in this journey toward a better life. When hopes outrun reality, disillusion and disenchantment may follow. Although man must continue to pin his hopes on the desirable rather than the feasible, the disparity between the two must be accepted with a sense of resignation but not complacency. That so much attention is being directed to education in the midst of world crisis is indicative that better schools may indeed be man's final hope for survival. The historian Arnold Toynbee has spoken of ours as "the first generation since the dawn of history in which man dares to believe it practical to make the benefits of civilization available to the whole human race."

FUTURE

It is apparent that the scope of international education will be broadened and its tempo increased. The volume of exchange of students, faculty, and materials will continue to increase. This increased exchange will include communist-bloc nations and will usually be sustained even during periods of tension in international relations. This increased exchange will be sustained by international organizations such as UNESCO as well as by bilateral agreements between individual nations.

Development education, which is aimed toward the strengthening of the social, political, and economic well-being of nations, will become increasingly widespread, especially among the have-not nations. The yield of this effort will be enhanced through better planning by national and international agencies. Despite this thrust, the need for education will outgrow the capacity of educational systems unless the population explosion can be arrested. The outlook for money and manpower resources to sus-

tain educational development will remain pessimistic for many countries.

Rapid development of educational technology may eventually give mankind a breakthrough in international education. Historians sometimes speak of certain great inventions triggering "quantum jumps" which cause major restructuring of society. In the field of communications, examples would include the invention of speech, writing, the printing press, and—in our time—communications satellites. Consider the miraculous combination of the communications satellite's capability of instantaneous around-the-world telecasting, television's capability of reaching mass audiences, the laser's capability of handling great numbers of long-distance messages simultaneously, programmed instruction's capability of tailoring education to the unique levels and learning styles of any individual, and the computer's capability of managing the interfaces of all these complex telecommunications components. It then becomes possible to conceive of every child in the world having access to a superb educational system in his own home with hardware that could be carried in a suitcase, thanks to miniaturization. This would mean that a child in Timbuktu could have access to any knowledge or instruction that existed anywhere in the world and that his education could equal that of a child in Chicago. This miraculous development could preempt the shortages of classrooms and teachers around the world. Although the technical components of this system already exist in prototypic form, the economic, political, and ethical problems are of course enormous.[12] Wernher Von Braun, deputy associate administrator for planning at NASA, believes that "the world is moving toward a global satellite educational system capable of eradicating illiteracy everywhere."

Eventually man must come to realize that vastly increased expenditures on education are indeed essential to his survival. Much of this increased expenditure must come from the more affluent nations. It must come in a spirit of altruism rather than imperialism. As Philip Coombs warns in the closing sentences of his report *The World Educational Crisis*, "Whatever shape your educational system may be in, if others which must serve the vast

[12] For further discussion of this miraculous possibility, see Isaac Asimov, "Toward the Global Village—The Fourth Revolution," *Saturday Review*, vol. 53, pp. 17–25, 72, Oct. 24, 1970.

majority of this planet's citizens are in a serious state of crisis, then no nation, however rich, can be exempt from the consequences. The educational crisis is everybody's business."

SUMMARY

Dramatic advances in space exploration, military hardware, communications, and transportation are forcing man to hold a cosmic rather than an ethnocentric view of the human condition. Man is slowly learning that international understanding and cooperation are essential to his survival. Increasingly, international education is viewed as the prime vehicle for improving both national welfare and international relations. Although education is not the remedy for all the cares of the world, it is clearly man's best hope. But the hour is late. An educational crisis is upon us because the school population is increasing far faster than school revenues, resulting in a shortage of teachers, classrooms, and materials.

The historical development of international education dates back at least as far as the seventeenth century, with Comenius's proposal of universal schools, books, and language to deepen man's understanding of his globe. In later years other men of vision elaborated these concepts. The latter half of the nineteenth century marked the beginning of many international educational organizations, and many new forms of intercultural educational cooperation, such as educational exchanges, became commonplace in the early twentieth century. World War II and its aftermath precipitated major American programs of educational assistance to less favored countries. Begun at first as a kind of cultural imperialism, this assistance has recently become more altruistic, grounded in the objectives of social progress, freedom, understanding, cooperation, and human dignity. This new emphasis contributes greatly to the cultural enrichment of the United States. Thus international education embraces three major purposes: the survival of man, the improvement of the human condition in disadvantaged nations, and the enrichment of civilization.

The term "international education" commonly includes the study of other people and other lands; the study of world affairs, relations, and problems; and comparative cross-cultural study of academic subjects and professional fields. These substantive categories are commonly pursued through the following activities: programs of international cooperation in educational development and scholarly trade; the exchange of students, teachers, and materials; and technical assistance to the development of education in other countries through foreign aid programs.

Many international educational enterprises are sustained by various public and private international organizations: the United Nations, UNESCO, UNICEF, the World Bank, the International Peace Corps Secretariat, the Institute of International Education, the Alliance for Progress, various international education centers, international professional organizations, and international conferences.

Like most countries, the United States undertakes many international education endeavors through both public and private means. In the public sector, the U.S. Office of Education sponsors educational exchanges, the development of curriculum materials, research, and the preparation of educational specialists in intercultural education. The Peace Corps has sent thousands of volunteers, more than half of them teachers, to help in the development of other nations. The Agency for International Development and many other government organizations have contributed to national development abroad and international understanding at home and abroad. State and local school agencies have also engaged in a variety of educational exchange. Education and World Affairs has been particularly helpful to universities and colleges in improving their capability in international education. Many private United States foundations have invested substantial sums of money to support a wide variety of efforts in cross-cultural education.

Several significant international schools, such as the Friends World College, the Dag Hammarskjold College, and the Foreign Study League, provide partial prototypes of man's long-time dream of an international university, with the world as its campus, the globe's population as its clientele, and the entire realm of knowledge and problems around the world as its curriculum.

Most major American universities and many colleges support various types of centers for regional or international studies, student and faculty exchange programs, and cross-cultural study of academic disciplines and professional fields.

The United States maintains many schools overseas which serve American and often foreign nationals and stand also as showplaces of American educational practice for foreign nationals. American schools both at home and abroad have strengthened their curriculums to broaden their coverage of academic subjects to more global dimensions.

Much educational exchange is prompted by individual initiative in foreign study, work, and travel.

Notwithstanding these substantial accomplishments, many serious problems remain. International interests and cooperation are sometimes constrained by fierce senses of nationalism, although many believe that the international and national interests are more complementary than antagonistic. Intercultural differences in language, custom, values, and prejudices often inhibit free exchange of educational practices. The phenomenon of inertia is particularly manifest in resistance to change backward educational practices in both advanced and undeveloped cultures. Perhaps the severest problem lies in the tragic underfinancing of national educational systems in practically all countries as well as in international programs of cooperation in education. Shortages of teachers and facilities are legion and not likely to improve unless the population explosion is arrested. The teachers and instructional materials that do exist are often not adequate for fine-quality international education.

The outlook for the future of international education is mixed. Although international enterprise in education will continue to expand, it is likely that the need will continue to outweigh the capacity for many years to come. Various forms of educational technology will improve the efficiency of international education but not cure the great shortages for the foreseeable future.

Eventually man must come to realize more fully that more civilized interaction through education is his "last hope for survival" and must finance it accordingly. The educational crisis is ubiquitous. It is everybody's business because the peace and freedom of every man are endangered as long as other men live in poverty, hunger, disease, and ignorance. The very survival of man may be at stake. We urge the reader to engage in this adventure boldly and help shape the educational enterprise so that it may indeed become "man's best enterprise" and his *successful* "hope for survival."

Suggested Activities

1. Read Comenius's essay, "A College of Light" (in Scanlon's book listed in the bibliography which

follows) and analyze his proposals with respect to their contemporary relevance.

2. Select a dozen or more heterogeneous countries from all the continents and compare them with respect to various measures of educational need and accomplishment, such as percentage of total population which is of school age, percentage of school-age population attending school, percentage of population which is illiterate, expenditure per pupil for education, and percentage of national income spent for education. (Various UNESCO publications and The World Crisis in Education *will supply these data.)*

3. Examine an annual report of the Ford Foundation or the Carnegie Corporation and annotate briefly each major effort in international effort which it supports.

4. Sketch the major differences between foreign aid programs for education which are prompted by "cultural imperialism" and those which are prompted by "international cooperation and understanding."

5. Summarize the major undertakings of UNESCO in a recent year.

6. Make an inventory and describe briefly each major undertaking in international education under the aegis of your college or university.

7. Prepare an essay on the theme "Nationalism and Internationalism in Education: Allies or Adversaries?"

8. Evaluate the high school and college curriculums which you have completed in terms of their scope and effectiveness in deepening understanding of other cultures and international relations.

9. Interview a returned educational missionary, exchange student, Peace Corpsman, or teacher in regard to education in another country.

10. Study the educational system of some other country and compare it with that of the United States.

11. Describe a college program that includes a year or a summer abroad.

12. Investigate the requirements for obtaining an overseas assignment in education, such as a Fulbright scholarship, a Peace Corps membership, or a short-term or long-term educational missionary position.

Bibliography

Battle, J. A.: *Culture and Education for the Contemporary World*, Charles E. Merrill Books, Inc., Columbus, Ohio, 1969. A discussion of the interdependent roles of culture and education in contemporary society.

Beck, Carlton E. (ed.): *Perspectives on World Education*, W. C. Brown Company Publishers, Dubuque, Iowa, 1970. A series of articles by a worldwide writing team dealing with the historical development, current practices, and sociocultural factors which may influence the future of education in over forty countries.

Bereday, George Z. F. (ed.): *Essays on World Education: The Crisis of Supply and Demand*, Oxford University Press, New York, 1969. Eighteen essays by a distinguished group of international educators on various aspects of the growing crisis in world education and possible solutions to many problems.

Buxbaum, Edith: *Troubled Children in a Troubled World*, International Universities Press, Inc., New York, 1970. A report of the anxieties and needs of children throughout the world.

Coombs, Philip H.: *The World Educational Crisis: A Systems Analysis*, Oxford University Press, New York, 1968. An overview of the situation in world education, analysis of major problems, and suggestions for priorities and solutions.

Fraser, Stewart E. (ed.): *American Education in Foreign Perspectives: Twentieth Century Essays*, John Wiley & Sons, Inc., New York, 1969. Thirty-nine commentaries by foreign visitors on American life and institutions.

Fraser, Stewart E., and William W. Brickman: *A History of International and Comparative Education: Nineteenth-Century Documents*, Scott, Foresman and Company, Glenview, Ill., 1968. A collection of descriptions of nineteenth-century European education, mostly by American authors, and descriptions of American education in the same century, mostly by European authors.

Melvin, Kenneth: *Education in World Affairs: A Realistic Approach to International Education*, D.C. Heath and Company, Boston, Mass., 1970. A global view of education—its purposes, its dilemmas, and the reorientation necessary for its improvement.

Scanlon, David G., and James J. Shields (eds.): *Problems and Prospects in International Education*, Teachers College Press, Columbia University, New York, 1968. A symposium of statements by leading authorities on the aspirations, progress, and problems inherent in international education.

Shane, Harold (ed.): *The United States and International Education*, Sixty-eighth Yearbook, National Society for the Study of Education, The University of Chicago Press, Chicago, 1969. Part I. A discussion by fifteen outstanding scholars of the scope of American involvement in international education and the relation of foreign experiences to the growth of education in the United States.

Taylor, Harold: *The World and the American Teacher*, American Association of Colleges for Teacher Education, Washington, D.C., 1968. A plea for stronger preparation and experience of American teachers in the international realm with examples of good practices and recommendations for general improvement.

Teaching Positions in Foreign Countries: *Teachers' Guide to Teaching Positions in Foreign Countries*, Ames, Iowa, 1969. Information on nonprofit and governmental agencies seeking teachers for overseas positions, and on how to apply for the positions.

United States National Student Travel Association: *The Student Traveler: Work, Study, Travel Abroad*, New York, 1972. A reference for students on travel opportunities.

Zweig, Michael: in Harold Taylor (ed.), *The Idea of a World University*, Southern Illinois University Press, Carbondale, 1967. The case for an international university—an institutionalized United Nations of the intellect, unimpaired by national limitations.

Glossary[1]
Established Terms Used in Modern Education

Ability grouping: the organization of pupils into homogeneous sections according to intellectual ability for purposes of instruction.

Academic freedom: the opportunity for the teacher to teach, and for the teacher and the student to study, without coercion, censorship, or other restrictive interference.

Academy: an independent secondary school not under public control.

Accelerated program: the more rapid advancement of superior students through school by early completion of advanced work.

Accountability: the responsibility of an educational agency to be held answerable to the public for its performance.

Accreditation: the type of recognition given to an educational institution that has met accepted standards applied to it by a competent agency or official association.

Activity curriculum: a curriculum design in which the interests and purposes of children determine the educative program; selection and planning of activities are undertaken cooperatively by teacher and pupils.

Administrative unit: usually synonymous with *school district.*

Affective learning: the acquisition of feelings, tastes, emotions, will, and other aspects of social and psychological development gained through feeling rather than through intellectualization.

Arbitration: the method of settling employment disputes through recourse to an impartial third party whose decision is usually final and binding. Arbitration may be either voluntary or compulsory.

Articulation: the relationship existing between the different elements of the educational program—the different curricular offerings, the school's program and out-of-school educational activities, and the successive levels of the educational system.

Attendance area: an administrative unit, or subdivision of a unit, consisting of the territory from which children may legally attend a given school building.

Atypical pupil: a loose term used in referring to a pupil who differs in a marked degree from others of a given class or category—physically, mentally, socially, or emotionally.

Audiovisual material: any device by means of which the learning process may be encouraged or carried on through the sense of hearing and/or the sense of sight.

[1] Many of the definitions are taken from or adapted from Carter V. Good (ed.), *Dictionary of Education*, McGraw-Hill Book Company, New York, 1972.

Categorical aid: synonymous with *special-purpose aid.*

Certification: the act, on the part of a state department of education, of granting official authorization to a person to accept employment in keeping with the provisions of the credential.

Cognitive learning: the acquisition by the learner of facts, concepts, and principles through intellectualization.

Collective bargaining: a procedure, usually specified by written agreement, for resolving disagreements on salaries, hours, and conditions of employment between employers and employees through negotiations.

Common learnings: the knowledges, abilities, skills, attitudes, and appreciations that a school regards as essential for all children and youth.

Community school: a school that is intimately connected with the life of the community and that tries to provide for the educational needs of all in the locality. It utilizes neighborhood resources in improving the educational program and sometimes serves as a center for many civic and cultural activities.

Compensatory education: enriched or extended educational experiences or services made available to children of low-income families to compensate for handicaps they suffer as a result of their disadvantaged backgrounds.

Computer-assisted instruction (CAI): direct two-way teaching-learning communication between a student and programmed instructional material stored in a computer.

Consortium: a confederation of persons or agencies joined to undertake an enterprise too large or too complicated to be undertaken efficiently by a single constituent.

Core curriculum: a curriculum design in which one subject or group of subjects becomes a center or core to which all the other subjects are subordinated.

Correlation: the process of bringing together the elements of two or more different subject-matter fields that bear on the same large problem or area of human experience.

Cost-benefit analysis: a means of comparing the costs of a particular undertaking with the benefits it is expected to yield.

Cost-effectiveness analysis: a means of analyzing the extent to which an undertaking accomplishes its objectives in relation to its cost in comparison with alternative undertakings.

Custodial student: a student so limited in mental, social, physical, or emotional development as to require institutional care or constant supervision at home.

Day-care center: a center where young preschool children can be cared for, usually with little or no educational program.

De facto *segregation:* separation of pupils by race for circumstantial reasons, such as housing patterns, rather than for reasons of school policies or practices.

De jure *segregation:* separation of pupils by race on the basis of school policies or practices designed specifically to accomplish such separation.

Development education: education designed specifically to improve the economic, political, and social development of a nation or community.

Developmental task: a task that arises at or about a certain time in an individual's life, the successful achievement of which leads to his happiness and success with later tasks.

Differentiated staffing: educational personnel, selected, educated, and deployed so as to make optimum use of abilities, interests, preparation, and commitments and to give greater opportunity and autonomy in guiding their own professional growth and use.

Dual progress plan: a plan for grouping pupils for instruction in which they are brought together homogeneously during part of the school day for instruction in basic subjects and heterogeneously for the remainder of the day for instruction in other subjects.

Educable child: a child of borderline or moderately severe mental retardation who is capable of achieving only a very limited degree of proficiency in basic learnings and who must usually be instructed in a special class.

Educational park: a large campuslike school plant containing several units with a variety of facilities, often including many grade levels and varied programs, and often surrounded by a variety of cultural resources.

Educational technology: scientific application of the findings of behavioral psychology to instruction that is responsive to the learning needs of individual students; sometimes used in more restricted sense with reference to mechanical and electronic hardware used as media of instruction.

Educational television (ETV): educational programs in the broadest sense—cultural, informative, and instructive—that are telecast usually by stations outside the school system and are received on standard television sets by the general public.

Essentialism: the doctrine that there is an indispensable, common core of culture (knowledge, skills, attitudes, ideals, etc.) that should be taught systematically to all, with rigorous standards of achievement.

Ethics: the science of human conduct; concerned with judgments of obligation and of values.

Exceptional student: used synonymously with *atypical student.*

Existentialism: a philosophic view that holds that the problems of human existence and values are paramount and that an individual's morality is achieved through positive social participation.

Experience curriculum: a curriculum in which the content, activities, and structures of instruction are designed to provide a series of purposeful experiences growing out of the interests, purposes, and needs of the learners.

Flexible scheduling: a technique for organizing time more effectively to meet the needs of instruction by dividing the school day into uniform time modules which can be combined to fit the task.

Group dynamics: a branch of social psychology concerned with the interaction and psychological relationships of members of a group, particularly with relation to the development of common perceptions through the sharing of emotions and experience.

Head Start programs: pre-elementary school programs designed to provide enriched learning opportunity usually for disadvantaged children so that their educational disadvantage in later years is reduced.

Heterogeneous grouping: the classification of pupils by age or grade for the purpose of instruction without regard to similarity in other criteria.

Homogeneous grouping: the classification of pupils for the purpose of forming instructional groups having a relatively high degree of similarity in regard to certain factors that affect learning.

House plan: an arrangement by which attendance units are divided into component "houses" to retain a climate of homogeneity, flexibility, or semi-autonomy within each of the houses.

Humanism: a philosophical view that emphasizes the dignity and interests of human beings and the importance of man in relation to the cosmic world.

Idealism: a doctrine holding that all knowledge is derived from ideas and emphasizing moral and spiritual reality as a preeminent source of explanation.

Independent school: a nonpublic school unaffiliated with any church or other agency.

Individualized instruction: instruction that is particularized to the interests, needs, and achievements of individual learners.

Individually prescribed instruction (IPI): individualized instruction in a systematic, step-by-step program based on carefully selected sequences and detailed listing of behaviorally stated instructional objectives.

In-service education: efforts of administrative and supervisory officials to promote the professional growth and development of educational workers through such means as curriculum study, supervisory assistance, and workshops.

Instructional materials center (IMC): an area where students can withdraw books, newspapers, pamphlets, and magazines and have access to sound tapes, slides, and films; spaces are usually provided for the learner to use these materials.

Instructional television (ITV): lessons telecast specifically for educational institutions and received usually only by special arrangements and on special equipment.

Intelligence quotient (IQ): the most commonly used device for expressing level of mental development in relation to chronological age, obtained by dividing the mental age (as measured by a general intelligence test) by the chronological age and multiplying by 100.

Intercultural education: modifications in attitudes and conduct designed to bring people to accept others for what they are, or can become, and to value the rich and varied contributions of all cultures in the totality of a world community.

Intermediate school: used synonymously with *middle school.*

Intermediate unit: (1) a division of the elementary school comprising grades 4, 5, and 6; (2) a level of school organization between the state and the local district, often but not necessarily coterminous with the county.

Internship: paid service in preparation for a position as teacher or educational specialist, usually under the joint supervision of a university and an experienced teacher or specialist in the field, and correlated with graduate study.

Laboratory school: a school that is under the control of, or closely associated with, a teacher-preparation institution, whose facilities may be used for demonstration, experimentation, and practice teaching.

Liberal arts college: an institution of higher learning with a four-year curriculum emphasizing broad, general education rather than technical or vocational training.

Life-adjustment education: learning designed to equip youths to live democratically with satisfaction to themselves and profit to society as homemakers, workers, and citizens; having special but not exclusive importance for pupils uninterested in academic or college preparatory curriculums.

Mediation: attempt by a third party to help in negotiations or the settlement of an employment dispute through suggestion, advice, or other ways of stimulating agreement, short of dictating its provisions.

Mentally handicapped student: a student whose mental powers lack maturity or are deficient in such measure as to be a hindrance to normal achievement.

Merit rating: an evaluation of the effectiveness of a teacher or other educator based upon a scale of criteria and frequently used for determining salary differentials.

Microteaching: a type of teacher training in which a small group, consisting of teachers, students, and a supervisor, evaluates a brief, discrete teaching task, usually with the help of videotape, to improve teaching method.

Middle school: a type of two- to four-year school organization containing various combinations of the middle grades, commonly grades 5 to 8, and serving as an intermediate unit between the elementary school and the high school.

Minicourse: a short, self-contained instructional sequence.

National assessment: a massive national testing program which helps ascertain the effectiveness of American education and how well it is retained.

Naturalism: a philosophic view that the whole of reality is natural rather than supernatural, emphasizing educational adaptation to the natural developmental stages of the individual.

Nongraded school: a type of school organization in which grade lines are eliminated for a sequence of two or more years.

Ombudsman: a personnel officer who helps students, faculty, and other employees to resolve grievances, cut through red tape, detect patterns of complaints, and recommend desirable changes.

Open education: a learning environment where exploration of and learning about oneself and the world are largely unstructured by schedules, required subjects, buildings, and many other common constraints.

Orthopedic student: a student crippled or otherwise affected by disease or malformation of the bones, joints, or muscles.

Paraprofessional: a lay person who assists the teacher with limited, quasi-professional tasks, such as correcting papers and tutoring; the term is sometimes also used to include teacher aides.

Parochiaid: public funds granted to aid parents of students attending parochial schools.

Performance contract: an agreement between schools and commercial educational agencies which guarantees to produce specified educational results.

Planning-Programming-Budgeting System (PPBS): an application of systems analysis to the allocation of resources to various competing educational purposes and needs through systematic planning, programming, budgeting, and evaluation.

Policy: a judgment, derived from some system of values and some assessment of situational factors, operating as a general plan for guiding decisions.

Pragmatism: a philosophic view according to which the value and truth of ideas are tested by their practical consequences.

Professional education: the total formal preparation that a person completes in a professional school, usually including the aggregate of his professional experience.

Professional negotiations: a procedure, usually less formal than collective bargaining, for resolving differences between professional employees and boards of education in which mediation is accomplished through professional channels.

Professional school: an institution of higher learning or a division of a university that educates persons for the practice of a profession.

Program models: the organization of parts, functions, and processes into a meaningful format for analysis, understanding, and improvements, as for example, models for the preparation of elementary school teachers.

Programmed instruction (also *programmed learning*): subject matter arranged in carefully planned sequences or frames using cues or prompts to elicit responses and providing immediate confirmation of validity or error of the response.

Progressive education: an educational movement emphasizing democracy, the importance of purposeful and creative activity, the real-life needs of students, and closer relationship between school and community.

Psychomotor learning: the acquisition of muscular development directly related to mental processes.

Reconstructionism: a philosophic view which holds that the primary function of education is the reconstruction of civilization through active participation of the school in the improvement of society.

Responsive environment: a learning center, usually well supported by educational technology, which permits the learner to explore freely, to receive immediate feedback in response to his inquiries, and to discover knowledge on his own initiative and at his own pace.

Sanctions: organized refusal by teachers to seek, accept, and in some circumstances continue their employment in school systems during the following school year (usually without violation of existing contracts) until allegedly unsatisfactory conditions are improved.

Segregation academy: a type of private school which functions primarily to educate students whose parents object to desegregation in public schools.

Self-contained classroom: a form of classroom organization in which the same teacher conducts all or nearly all the instruction in all or most subjects in the same classroom for all or most of the school day.

Self-instructional device: a term used to include instructional materials which can be used by the student to induce learning without necessarily requiring additional human instructional assistance;

including teaching machines, programmed textbooks, and other devices.

Shared time: a cooperative arrangement among public and nonpublic schools in which the former offer instruction in non-value-oriented subjects to all pupils and the latter offer instruction in value-oriented subjects to their own pupils.

Simulation: a rather elaborate kind of role playing in which students take part in simulated real-life situations.

Socially handicapped pupil: one whose personality disturbances are severe enough to interfere seriously with his interpersonal relations.

Special education: the instruction of students who deviate so far physically, mentally, emotionally, or socially from so-called "normal students" that the standard curriculum and school environment are not suitable for their needs.

Special-purpose aid: financial aid to local school districts from state or federal agencies for specific, limited purposes only.

Street academies: makeshift educational centers, usually operated by industries or neighborhood agencies, outside of regular school buildings to provide open education for students who reject more formal schooling.

Subject-discipline curriculum: an organization of learning activities and content around the intellectual disciplines of the subjects—their essential themes, principles, structures, concepts, and modes of inquiry.

Subject-field education: that part of the teacher-education program in which the student is provided instruction in the subjects that he plans to teach.

Subject-matter curriculum: a curriculum organization in which learning activities and content are planned around subject fields of knowledge, such as history and science.

Supernaturalism: a doctrine which holds that there is a divine source of truth that transcends nature; when applied to education, this doctrine holds that it is the essential function of the school to teach divinely revealed truth.

Systems analysis: a rational and systematic approach to education, which analyzes objectives, then decides which resources and methods will achieve those objectives most efficiently; each step is carefully measured, tested, and controlled to make sure it moves toward the next objective.

Talking typewriter: a typewriter programmed with sound to teach children the elements of reading and writing.

Teacher aide: a lay person who assists teachers with clerical work, library duties, housekeeping duties, noninstructional supervision, and other nonprofessional tasks.

Teacher Corps: a federally funded program that gives teachers and student teachers opportunities to work with disadvantaged children in their homes and communities while attending courses and seminars on the special problems they encounter.

Teaching machine: a mechanical device which presents programmed instruction one frame or item at a time, requiring overt response by the student, which is recorded by the machine.

Teaching unit: the plan developed with respect to an individual classroom by a teacher to guide the instruction of a unit of work to be carried out by a particular group of learners.

Team teaching: a term applied loosely to a wide variety of collaborative activity in teaching, involving a group of teachers who are jointly responsible for planning, carrying out, and evaluating an educational program for a group of children.

Tenure: a system of school employment in which the educator, having served a probationary period, retains his position indefinitely unless dismissed for legally specified reasons through clearly established procedures.

Terminal education: a level of education not usually followed by a higher one.

Trainable pupil: one who is incapable of achieving significant proficiency in academic skills but who may be trained to attain a limited degree of social acceptance and ability to care for himself, and perhaps even some measure of self-sufficiency.

Ungraded school: synonymous with *nongraded school.*

Unit of learning: a series of organized ideas and activities planned to provide worthwhile experiences for an individual or group and expected to result in a desired outcome.

Voucher plan: a means of financing schooling whereby funds are allocated to students' parents who then purchase education for their children in any public or private school.

Index

LA2TS
.D45
1972

748785

4-WK MAY 2 1974

4-WK SE 107

LA210
.D45
1972

IGHLIGHTS OF *american* **education**

Continued from inside front cover

1920 Federal-state cooperation in vocational rehabilitation education initiated by Smith-Bankhead Act

1925 Oregon decision rendered by the United States Supreme Court, stating that children of compulsory school age cannot be required to attend public schools

1923 World Federation of Education Associations, forerunner of World Confederation of Organizations of the Teaching Profession, organized in San Francisco

1926 Simple, hand-cranked device, prototype of modern teaching machine and programmed learning, invented by Sidney Pressey

1933 Emergency grants for education initiated by Congress during the Depression

1942 Atomic age born on campus of University of Chicago with the first man-made nuclear chain reaction

1944 First GI Bill for veterans' education passed by Congress

1944 United Negro College Fund established

1946 Membership of United States in United Nations Educational, Scientific and Cultural Organization (UNESCO) approved by Congress

1946 Fulbright program for international exchanges approved by Congress

1948 Smith-Mundt Act for global program "in information and educational exchanges" approved by Congress

1948, 1949 McCollum and Zorach decisions of United States Supreme Court rendered on religious instruction in public schools

1950 National Science Foundation created by Congress "for the promotion of basic research and education in the sciences"

1951 Beginning of current curriculum reform in schools initiated by University of Illinois Committee on School Mathematics

1952 Educational television with a national potential born when Federal Communications Commission reserved over 200 channels for noncommercial TV

1953 United States Office of Education made part of Department of Health, Education, and Welfare

1954 Racial discrimination in public schools ruled unconstitutional by United States Supreme Court

1956 Conservative educational philosophy and programs sharpened by establishment of Council for Basic Education

1958 Educational Facilities Laboratory established for research and experimentation in school and college buildings

1958 National Defense Education Act legislated by Congress to strengthen education in science, mathematics, and languages

1960 First volume published on programmed learning

1961 Peace Corps launched by the United States for sending volunteers to work abroad in education and other fields